ENGLISH WORDS
Deriving from the
GREEK LANGUAGE

Surprised??? You are simply Bilingual!!!

By
Matina Psyhogeos

PAGE PUBLISHING, INC.
New York, NY

First originally published by Page Publishing, Inc. 2016

ISBN 978-1-68213-427-6 (pbk)
ISBN 978-1-68213-428-3 (digital)

Printed in the United States of America

DEDICATION

I'm dedicating this lexicon to Mary and Peter Psyhogeos for two reasons: they were late joining my family and had not been mentioned in any of my previous work, and most importantly, however, they both, since the age of two, were using vocabulary far beyond toddler comprehension! Therefore, I believe a book like this is appropriate for Mary and Peter, along with Yiayia's love and fervent wish to always excel. Never stop being intuitive and searching for true knowledge, to continue the altruism and fellowship, which has defined their childhood, throughout their lifetime!

ACKNOWLEDGMENTS

It is with great pleasure that I express my sincerest thanks and gratitude to people who, I suspect, never knew how much they influenced and motivated me to undertake and get involved in such complicated endeavor.

Foremost, my thanks and appreciation to Dr. Thomas C Lelon, who as president of Hellenic College/Holy Cross, asked me to give a lecture in Garrison, New York. I have to admit that I was a little apprehensive because it was my first time giving such a speech (especially in English). He, however, had confidence that it would be fine. The theme was "The Influence and Contributions of the Greek Language to English." Along with all my remarks, the statements and comments of famous people on the subject, I included a list of English words of which the origin was Greek. It was a very small list (approximately 1,000 words). It was, however, evident that the contribution was very extensive and a tremendously important one. That was, even to me, a revelation, and when I realized how important it was to others to find out more on the subject, it became, with the years, an urgent task to do something about it. Seeing the interest of students and people, who loved both languages, to learn as much as possible, I was determined to work on a project like this. Being busy with other endeavors, I neglected it until the end of 2012. In the last ten months, I took it very seriously and completed it! Having completed an e-dictionary of about 14,000 words, and constantly discovering such a wealth of vocabulary to add, I continued the project for another year, or perhaps more, to finish a book. Now an idea that had been implanted years earlier and stayed with me since Dr. Lelon's assignment in the mid-eighties has grown into a reality of a resource showing 30,000 words origins plus other very useful linguistic elements. Therefore, I regard Dr. Lelon the inspiration behind this project, and I am grateful to him for entrusting me with that lecture and recently for his encouragement to continue with this project! Thank you, Dr. Lelon!

My former student and lover of the classics and chiefly of the Greek language, Nicholas F Kourtis, along with many other students of mine who always sought advice, was the reason that I felt the need for this dictionary. Nicholas, a successful attorney now, along with his intellectually dynamic family, seeks constantly to acquire as much information as possible, and that quality is admirable and very important to me!

Nick helped me with my research and even lent me his precious *Law School Dictionary*. When he learned about the project, he advised me and took care in protecting it, in case of an Internet malfunction! I had the confidence on his facility to be objective and thorough. When I asked him near the completion of the lexicon to review some areas, he did not disappoint me! His analytical thought process and eloquence offered invaluable advice! Ευχαριστώ Νίκο, and I hope you, and your family, always keep that thirst for knowledge!

My sincere thanks to Dean Papademetriou, an excellent attorney and publisher, knowledgeable of intellectual property laws, who very kindly helped with the copyrighted page!

My cousin, Nick Merianos, who is the best records keeper and collector of anything that has to do with the Greek language, which he loves so dearly! Any dictionary I needed he had it. I did not have to look elsewhere! Anything written about the language, it was in Nick's file cabinet!

Σ¨ευχαριστώ Νίκο!

My dearest friend, Vasilia Laskaris, who, although, born, raised, and educated in Chicago, learned the Greek language and never stopped reading and e-mailing articles on the language! Bravo, Vasilia, you can see one of those articles toward the end of the dictionary!

I would also like to express my deepest thanks to Tom Rontiris, a superb professional, who did an excellent job designing my Web site for which I have received many compliments, and every time I had a question, he would painstakingly and politely answer it, notwithstanding the elementary level of the question! Thank you, Tom!

My very capable technical adviser, Shache Downs, who saved me many times from a computer calamity! A teacher herself and a whiz in technology who can teach even someone like me who is not technically savvy to be confident and try new procedures! Thank you, Shache! I wish you every possible success in your teaching career and hope you'll enjoy teaching as much as I have enjoyed it!

My friends and colleagues who helped me with any questions I had!

The Rev. Dr. Alkiviadis Calivas, the renowned theologian, who responded to perplexing theological questions (having had contradictory answers among my reliable sources) with just one e-mail—being a walking encyclopedia that he is—took him less than five minutes to reply and solve my problem!

Thank you, Fr. Alkie. You have my undying gratitude for also being such a great liturgist, and from you I understood the divine liturgy and enjoy it thoroughly!

Dr. Penelope Tzougros, one of the best English (or Greek) professors, for that matter, I have ever dealt with! Her superb knowledge of every linguistic element was evident in all the areas of her work! I do suspect, her knowledge of Greek (which I have no claim to—she was proficient before we met) made her aware of the fine points in both languages! I was lucky enough to have crossed her road and had admired her enthusiasm, scholarship, dedication, love of education, and fortitude! I consider her my friend, and did not hesitate to ask her to put her magic touch by reviewing part of this lexicon! Thank you for being so prompt to respond, Penelope!

My medical advisor, Dr. Irene Goranitis, a suberb internist and diagnostician, who, although left Greece as a child, continued to study the language and became an expert in medical terms and their origin; thus, she was in a position to educate me with the corresponding iatric lingo! She even lent me a treasured book by her professor Saschiel K. Gupte in medical school, who loved etymology and root words and published very few tomes of etymologically common hydronyms, toponyms. Although it did not apply to my work, it was greatly appreciated, nonetheless, for entrusting me with such a very personal gift from her respected teacher! Thank you, Irene!

Last but definitely not least, it is my pleasant task to express my sincerest thanks and profound appreciation to the President of Page Publishing, and Mr. Carl Cook, for recognizing, by only a sample of the manuscript, the uniqueness of this project and promptly decided to publish it!

My Publication Coordinator, David Rodax, for his professionalism, cooperation and patience with me! All the editors involved for their excellent work, and finally, all the people who worked so diligently for the successful outcome of this publication!!!

CONTENTS

PREFACE

People who have been involved with the Greek language, professionally, academically, or just out of curiosity to either learn more or write about the language, have known that it is characterized as unique, productive, viable, incomparable to any other language! All those adjectives are not thrown frivolously. These people have discovered that the language was not created carelessly or accidently! It was developed on great elements and infrastructure! That is the reason it has been adapted and used so widely! The etymology (an original Greek word) is so precise and unambiguous, giving insight into the use of those words for a better understanding of a language!

The beginning of all is the Greek alphabet. Every letter is not just a symbol. Most significant quality is the fact that each letter is a number; therefore, in a broader scope, each word is a number.

An enormous amount of knowledge is locked-coded in words due to their mathematical value/worth!

Pythagoras is believed to have been one of the first pioneers on the subject!

Every word (as every letter) has a mathematical infrastructure, and the uniqueness, as it was previously mentioned, lies on the mathematical value each word and each letter possess!

The numbers, the shapes, the harmony, the stars, have something in common. Correlatively, mathematics (numbers), geometry (shapes), harmony (music), astronomy (stars). These four sciences, according to the Pythagorian theory (plus the physical laws which rule them), constitute the four sister sciences!.......

The purpose of this lexicon/dictionary, however, is not to analyze the creation and theory of the development of the Greek language and the Pythagorian equations.

The above reference was included in order to understand why many philosophers, scientists, linguists consider the importance of the Greek language and to demonstrate the eagarness of so many others to include it in their own particular language and dictionaries! As many technology visionaries recognize the need for further research of a language that has not only survived for many centuries but also evolved and had become the most viable language! Paraphrasing the visionary Bill Gates, one of the greatest and best-known technological minds, who in one of his lectures said, if we are to advance further in technology, we will have to tap once again and go deeper into the ancient Greek language and its scientific elements!

I have included, in addition to the aforementioned epithets, another yet adjective: the Greek language is inexhaustible, and indeed it is! By using only the root word and the ten parts of speech, one can create as many words (nouns, adjectives, verbs, adverbs, participles, infinitives—so named due to the fact it is not limited to any case, person, number, or tense). In English, usually the infinitive is the first person singular, as *to read, to form, to create*, etc.; gerunds, a verbal noun, as *the drinking, the reading*, etc. We could go on and on how a language as unique, inexhaustible, and indestructible that has weathered and survived so many eons from the Homeric period (1200–800 BC) to today's Demotic form can help create, shape, mold, and apply new vocabulary to accommodate any changes, conditions, cultures, and situations. It is amazing how such a language can influence new inventions by just borrowing existing vocabulary to define that particular development. Take for example the *Internet*/ Διαδίκτυον(ο). In this case, the English word does not correspond to the Greek word. Nonetheless, by borrowing the compounded words, δια/ διαμέσου + δίκτυον- *inter + net*/ via a *net*, a new word was created by definition only.

Such languages (as ancient Greek and Latin, the classical languages) do not influence and shape by words alone. Other factors contribute as well: grammar, syntax, and many other linguistic principles. It is said that in Homer's time there were approximately six million plus only protogenes words (in other words, using only the first person of a noun or a verb). Imagine using all cases, all tenses, moods, singular and plural, etc. and not even mentioning the mathematical value of those words, what a plethora of words exist, a hidden treasure!

That is an inexhaustible linguistic source, indeed!

Matina Psyhogeos

INTRODUCTION

The love and fascination I felt from a very young age for words—for their definition, origin, formation, and application—along with a specific opportunity I was given mentioned in the acknowledgments, are in part the incentive and motivation to undertake such complicated and time-consuming research to complete this volume.

The objectives of this dictionary/lexicon are (1) to educate people to better understand their own words by understanding their origin (especially illustrating the prefix and suffix and their meanings), (2) to demonstrate the contribution and influence of the Greek language on English by articulating the significant number of English vocabulary originating from the Greek, and (3) to suggest that to whatever extent one is familiar with these English words, one also knows another language: Greek!

This dictionary/lexicon is presented in large part via three main avenues:

The first avenue is a list of the root words (approximately 750 prefixes and suffixes) which are the basis of word formation and consequently much English language creation. Anyone who studies this list (with even many more throughout the lexicon) will also recognize instances where Greek is and/or an indirect contributor through or along with other languages, mainly Latin and in some cases French, in shaping English vocabulary. One example is "television"/- *tele-vision*/τηλεόρασις/η - the Gr. adverb: τήλε/ tele + Lat. vision /όρασις/η – far/ far off + sight/view; "tonsillitis" – Lat. tonsils + Gr. suffix -ίτις/ίτιδα, indicating inflammation.

The second avenue is a corpus of twenty specific disciplines or fields of study whose professional vocabulary is based heavily on the Greek language with a sample of words.

The third avenue is via a broad swath of general English vocabulary itself, consisting approximately of thirty thousand English words deriving directly from the Greek language, for example, "cardiology"/καρδιολογία, *atmosphere*/ατμόσφαιρα, "democracy"/δημοκρατία, etc. In this avenue, the relevant English word is presented, then the original Greek word, and finally the definition in English. If the origin of the English word is apparent, no additional explanation is required; if not, however, an analysis of the word is given. This category also includes some modern fabricated/coinages or "new" Greek (such as οικολογία/ecologia/"ecology," bouzouki, baklava, phyllo/fillo, etc.)

This work should not be understood simply as compilation of existing words.

There are countless instances in which I include numerous clarifications, corrections, notations, and additions had to be included in order to represent the accuracy of the borrowed word or the additional variations and meanings in the Greek language. I do not believe that there exists as extensive a comparable work in this particular area.

The overarching purpose of this dictionary/lexicon is to give a more accurate testimony to the influence and contributions of the Greek language to English. As mentioned before, there are approximately thirty thousand English words whose origin is Greek. It could have been double this number if one includes all the derivative words, or as well many of the words that are part Greek plus part Latin or part French. I decided against that, as the three main avenues alone sufficiently demonstrate how significantly English has been influenced and enhanced by the Greek language. In fact, I believe that one of the reasons English has achieved such worldwide recognition, and has become one of the richest and most adaptable languages, is that it has incorporated within it much of the wealth of the Greek language. To all but students of language, English has incorporated Greek to such an extent that we forget to see the Greek origin. I was amazed with the wealth of both languages and astonished with words taken from the Greek that were not even recognizable!

The study of the development of a language and the etymology of words may seem to nonprofessionals to be intended for someone studying such esoteric specialty! This is not so.

The Greeks developing their language were looking for the ETYMON (thus ETYMOLOGY), the "true sense" of a word. As always they were not engaged in an idle pursuit as they had sensed that special relationship between the word and for what it stands for.

I believe the greatest value of this work, besides articulating the incredible number of Greek vocabulary which has enriched the English dictioanaries, is the wonderful aid it can provide to understanding English by learning and understanding the prefixes and suffixes of the combining forms! This list—really a word toolkit—will benefit anyone, be s/he a word lover, a word puzzle enthusiast, a spelling bee candidate, and most especially, students taking any type of a test, like the SAT, MAT, LSAT, etc., since a substantial part of the test will likely include these compounded words.

Many lexicographers, linguists, and others involved with both languages estimate that between 30–35 percent of English words derive from the Greek language. Through this research and discussion with close to fifteen respectable and reliable sources, my estimate is 40–45 percent, and in some scientific fields using the language as direct and indirect contributor, it is even higher than 50 percent!

The most amazing discovery is how many words exist and how many new words can be formed by using only the prefix or suffix. For example, how many words are there with just the prefix *hyper* /υπέρ – meaning: over, above (as "hyperbole," "hypercritic," hyperemia); the prefix *pneumo* /πνεύμων- lung (as "pneumonia," "pneumonologist," etc.) or with the suffix *–algia* /άλγος – indicating pain (as "hyperalgia"/ excessive pain, "neuralgia"/nerve pain, "otalgia"/earache, etc.) or the suffix -*athon* (indicating some type of race/such as "decathlon"); or -*gnosis* (indicating knowledge, as "stereognosis," "arithmognosis"/ numbers knowledge/ knowledge of numbers); or even *–phobia*, referring to fear, "gefyrophobia"/ fear of bridges, "triskaidekaphobia"/fear of number 13, etc.)

The rewards for someone knowing the origin of words and the compounded words are many! People who have seriously studied Greek or Latin attest to the ways they have benefitted. Their thought process has become organized, grammatical and syntactical skills are mastered, and they have enhanced their ability to understand and teach the English language.

My gratification was indescribable when I realized the significance of this concentrated group of words. Anyone knowing half, or less, of these words in English automatically becomes bilingual! S/he has a fair knowledge of the Greek language as well, and it is not all Greek to them any longer! If reading and pronouncing the Greek correctly is a problem, then by learning the Greek alphabet (at the special course "Greek for Travelers" at the end of this book) in addition to studying the everyday conversation (included in the course), your reward may be fluency!

The same applies to a Greek speaker as well. If he/she knows half of those words in Greek, they can apply them to English and become bilingual.

In tracing the histoy of other languages, one also sees similar development of some modern tongues from a common source; they may not, however, be as well-documented as Greek and Latin or the rest of the Indo-European languages. The Indo-European contains only a small quotient of the world's languages; nonetheless, one-half, if not more, of the world's population has a language of this family.

Among the greatest challenges I had working on this project were the inconsistencies of the various sources that I used, as well as some completely unexplainable (as of yet) changes in word meanings over time. Often I had to dig very deeply to refresh my memory with respect to the correct part of speech or gender or meaning in the reference given to the original ancient Greek. Very helpful here were my thorough studies of the Greek language beginning from Homeric through Attic, to Hellenestic, to modern Greek/ Katharevousa/Puristic, and of course, to today's Demotic.

One such perplexing single word I encountered was "empathy" which, as all English dictionaries, indicate comes form Εμπάθεια/ embatheia (εν + πάθος/inside + passion). "Empathy" is defined in English dictionaries as a synonym of "sympathy" (in other words, one sharing deeply what a person/fellow man feels), and it is the opposite of "antipathy." In Greek, however, the word Εμπάθεια is defined as having "strong antipathy (hatred) for a person thing or situation" (in other words, the wrong definition entirely was given to the word "empathy" and "empathes"/εμπαθής)! An entire paragraph is devoted to this word alone.

One example of the many puzzling areas throughout this process is the case of all the words beginning with the letter *Hh* in English that were derived from the Greek, for example "hero," "history," "hysteria," "Helen," "Homer," etc. These words come from Greek words where the original word began with a vowel and was accented by a rough breathing sign, δασεία/ daseia (ʻ) which had (in ancient Greek) a very soft sound as *h* (like hoi polloi/ οἱ πολλοί), especially in ancient dramas you could distinguish a very soft *h*. That rough sign in the Greek words, was converted into an *Hh* in English. Thus, there are thousands of English words which begin with a consonant *Hh* which in truth derive from Greek words beginning with a vowel with an initial rough breathing sign. The *Hh*, therefore, should have been treated as a vowel! None of the general etymological sources explain why it is a consonant. It was only recently, for the first time, I heard a politician using it as a vowel. He said "Today was an ISTORIC event," using it exactly as it should be used! Now if the *h* was to be used as a consonant (letter with a sound), he should have said "a HISTORIC" and not "an historic," as many people do. In other words, you cannot use the *h* as consonant and as a vowel!

Both breathing (rough/δασεία and smooth/ψιλή) signs and the circumflex/ περισπωμένη accent were eliminated in 1979 in the Greek language, when the monotonic system/single accent system was adopted. Note: Only few words are accented with the breathing sign in this lexicon, just as an example indicating the source. As it was mentioned the breathing signs are no longer in use.

A disappointment with many dictionaries and encyclopedias, was the outright confusion on the origin of a word. Some dictionaries deemed a word to be of Latin origin if it ended in "us," "ous," or "ism." Take for example the word "Hippopotamus," in Greek ιππο-πόταμος, being "ίππος" + "ποταμός" literally meaning horse of a river! Both component words are Greek, but because of the English as ultimately written ends with "-us" rather than "-os," some lexicographers assert its origin as Latin! Other incorrect origins were given to various medical terms. For example, the term "otorinolaryngologist" (in Greek, ωτορινολαρυγκολόγος, oto-rino-laryngo-logos) meaning ear-nose-throat specialist, for some reason, in some sources, has been identified as coming from Latin, even though all the words are Greek. I have to admit that the *Webster Dictionaries* very seldom had such discrepancies and their definitions were the most accurate!

There are too many discrepancies to be mentioned in this introduction and they are explained throughout the text where relevant! Few examples, however, are necessary to support the definition of discrepancies. For example, "aerius"/ of air, airy (in Greek, αέριος which comes from " αήρ-αέρος (gen.) meaning air/ of air), some dictionaries are giving its origin to the Latin " aer" (which, of course, had been adopted from the Greek word "αήρ˘"). Another example is "arterious"/ relating to artery; in Greek the word is "αρτηριακός relating to αρτηρία /artery."

Again the origin is given as Latin :*arteria*! These and other mistaken origins could have been avoided if more reliable sources had been consulted!

Finally, concluding that the study of etymology is not only for people involved in that particular pursuit, I would like to quote William E. Umback (an expert etymologist himself): "The etymologist is engaged in no esoteric pursuit, but one which can help bring to the use of the magnificent complex, which is the English language, an understanding of meanings, distinctions, and implications which are not merely conventional but rooted in the long history through which we have received it." I hope this work can aid in that understanding.

FOREWORD

I am honored by the opportunity to offer a few thoughts as a fore-word to this important work.

It is generally believed that while some portion of English derives from the Greek language, it is limited to a few defined spheres that easily come to mind, and within each such sphere, to a few defined words. Certainly, whether in politics, medicine, sciences and the like, one expects Greek words to be present in the English language to express Greek learning and actions in those subject areas. However, this work demonstrates, through the 30,000+ words it has catalogued for consideration, that the sheer breadth of the foundation that Greek thought and its language established for all of Western civilization is in fact so encompassing, as to become substantially un-discernible to us. It is so elemental an aspect of our existence as to just recede in our minds into part of our human condition. When we actually aggregate all of these defined spheres, for example, democracy, history, philosophy, political science, mathematics, medicine, drama, to name just a few, only then do we understand the enormous sway that Greek civilization has had over all that we consider Western civilization. Once one considers not only the many English words which come directly from the Greek, but also those which have come to English through the subsequent prism of Latin, and from the Romance languages, one should not be surprised that these "Greek words spoken in English" would number in the tens of thousands.

This linguistic heritage is not just mechanical (as there are some words in any language purely mechanical and descriptive), but rather this heritage articulates thoughts about mankind at its deepest level: the trials of humanity, how to strive for a life worth living, how to understand our inter-relationships and our rights and duties with respect to our institutions - such as the state, and how to live honestly and consistently with our nature - in the context of our free will. The more we become cognizant of the Greek roots of the English language, which is increasingly spoken all over the world today, and the concepts embedded in those roots, the more we can access all that civilization wrestled with, and thereby understand more about those questions and our own humanity. By illuminating this heritage, this work also encourages the study of ancient Greek civilization, and thereby in an additional way, can help each of us undertake more meaningful introspection into our own lives.

Nicholas F. Kourtis
Needham, Massachusetts
July 2015

GUIDE TO THIS DICTIONARY
AND KEY TO ABBREVIATIONS

In this dictionary the etymology of the original Greek word is given only if the English definition is not sufficient. The original word, most times, is given in its ancient or puristic form and next to it the modern version follows (ex: polis – πόλις /πόλη, or just the ending η, πόλις/η- theater-θέατρον /θέατρο – or only the ending /o, etc.). If the word is an adjective, due to the fact the Gr. language has three genders, the part of speech is indicated (ex: patriotic, next to the Gr. you will see πατριωτικός, ή, ό [adj.] instead of πατριωτικός, πατριωτική, πατριωτικό [adj.]) (indicating the masculine, feminine, and neuter).

Any other part of speech being a noun, pronoum, verb, adverb, participle, etc., the Gr. word will also correspond to that of the English part of speech: a noun will be a noun, a verb a verb, an adverb will also be an adverb, and so on. Therefore, no explanation is necessary.

For those who cannot read Greek and wish to be able to do so, enough information is given to prepare them. See section "Greek for Travelers."

The study of the list of combining forms is recommended first. That will help enormously in the entire process. Secondly, if one has an interest in one or more of the disciplines listed, see the representative vocabulary and then search the dictionary for additional words. 60

The three columns of the vocabulary represent the English word, Greek origin word analysis (if required), and finally, the definition in English.

Some of the compounded words have been hyphenated deliberately to emphasize and separate the combining forms

Abbreviations

Acc./acc. – accusative/objective (case)
Adj/adj. – adjective
Anat. – anatomy
Anc./anc. – ancient
Archit. – architecture
Adv. – adverb
Biol. – biology
Bot. – botany
Econ. – economy
Eng. – English
Esp./esp. – especially
Ex:/ex: – example
Gen./gen. – genitive

Geo. – geology or geography
Gr. – Greek
Gram./gram. – grammar
Lat. – Latin
Lit. – literature
Med. – medicine
Mod. /mod. – modern
Myth. – mythology
Pl./pl. – plural
Phys. – physics
Specif. – specifically
Theo. – Theology
Zool. – Zoology

You are going to experience some inconsistencies in abbreviations, wording, or even syntax. Those were left unchaged purposely in order to have a reference to the source. For example, you might see "gasses" (in a definition of a word) or "gases" (that indicates that some sources double the *s* in plural of the word "gas" while others do not), or abbreviations some using capital letter (ex: Mod. or mod., Anc. or anc., etc.) or, especially, medical sources not having used commas or periods for very long sentences). If they do not alter the definition of the word, these inconsistencies are not important.

COMBINING FORMS

The following words are all combining forms and are listed by prefix and suffix. By recognizing the root/origin and definition, one is enabled to determine the meaning of unknown words and even create new words.

Prefix

English	Greek Origin	Meaning
Aa-	Αα	without; not (as in atypical; atheist)
Abio-	α + βίος-/ without + life	lifeless (as in abiotic)
Acad-	ακαδημαϊκός, ή, ό (adj.)	academic (pertaining to college/ the university world)
Acanth/acantho	άκανθο-αγκάθι	thorn; thorny (acanthoid)
Achrom-	άχρωμος, η, ο (adj.)	achromatic (without color)
Acro-	άκρο/v (edge)	edge/end/top/at the point (acropolis; acrobat)
Actin- or actino-	ακτίς / ακτίνος (gen.)/ακτίνα	(Mod. Gr.) ray referring to ray(s) (actinography)

Adelfo-	αδελφό (ς) (brother)	referring to sibling(s) (adelfo/ adelphogamy/marriage between siblings)
Aden- adeno-	αδήν/αδένος (gen.)/ αδένας	(Mod. Gr.) gland, pertaining to gland(s) (adenitis; adenoid)
Aer or aero-/air	αήρ/αέρος (gen.) αέρας	(Mod. Gr.) air (aerosol; aeronaut)
Aesth-	αισθησις /η (αισθάνεσθαι – to perceive)	sense(s) (aesthetic; aesthesia)
Aetio- or etio-	αιτία / αίτιον	cause; reason (aetiology/ etiology; etiologic)
Agalma-	άγαλμα	statue (agalmatoid; agalmolatry)
Agora-	αγορά /(αγορείν –to assemble)	meeting/assembling place; market; open/public space (agoraphobia; agoraphobic)
Agr/agri	αγρός/αγροί (pl.) fields	farm(s); field(s) (agriculturist)
Agro-	αγρός	field; farm (agrochemichal, agrotic)
Agri-	αγροί (pl.)	fields; farms (agriculture)
Alg- or algo-	άλγος	pain, suffering (algology/ study of pain)
Allo-	άλλος, η, ο (adj)	other; variation; departure from the normal (as in allergenic; allopathy)
Alpha-	άλφα	first letter of the Gr. alphabet (other meaning: the beginning) (alphabetical; alphabetize)
Ambi-	αμφί	around; able to use both hands with the same ease (ambidextrous)
Amnio -	άμνιον/ ο (αμνός –lamb)	the innermost membrane of the sac enclosing the Embryon. It is filled with a watery fluid (amniotic fluid) (amniocentesis; amnion)
Amphi-	αμφί	around/about/both sides (amphibious/ living in both: land or sea/water; amphitheater - a round or oval building surrounded by rising rows of seats)

Amylo-	άμυλο(ν)	starch (amyloid; amylogen)
An-	αν	without (ex: anorexia: no appetite/ without appetite, an- followed with a vowel, combining form
Ana-	ανά	a.) up/upward (as in anandromous) b.) back/ backward (as in anagram) c.) again (anabolism) d.) throughout (as in analysis) e.) according to / similar to (as in analogy)
Anemo-	άνεμος /άνεμο (obj. case)	wind, combining form (anemometer; anemograph)
Andro-	άνδρός (gen.)/ ανήρ (nomin.) άνδρας	(Mod. Gr.) man, male, masculine (android; Androsphinx - a sphinx with the head of a man and the body of a lion)
Ang- or angio-	αγγείο (ν)	capsule/blood vessel (ex: angina; angiology)
Aniso-	άνισος, η, ο (adj.)	unequal, different (anisometric; anisometropia – an eye condition, having unequal refractive power)
Antho-	ανθό(ς) /άνθος/ ανθείν – to bloom	flower; to sprout (anthology; anthological)
Anthropo-	άνθρωπο(ς)	man; human being (ex: anthropology; anthropomorphic)
Anti-	αντί	against; opposite; before; hostile (antibacterial)
Aph	αφ-/af	away from (aphesis/ letting go)
Apo-	από	away, from, off, cutting off (apocope)
Arch-	αρχή/άρχων	rule, authority/ruler, leader, first (archangel)
Archa-	αρχαϊκός, ή, ό (adj.)	very old; old-fashioned (archaic)
Archeo-	αρχαίος, α, ο (adj.)	ancient (archeology)
Aristo-	άριστος, η, ο (adj.)	excellent; superb (aristocrat; aristocracy)
Arthr- or arthro-	άρθρον	joint (arthritis; arthrology)
Asthen- or astheno	ασθένεια	weak/illness (asthenic; asthenopia/ weakness/fatigue of the eyes, accompanied with pain)

Astro-	άστρο	star (astrology; astrologer)
Atmo-	ατμός	vapor (atmosphere; atmospheric)
Auto-	αυτό /εαυτός /self	for oneself; self (autonomy; autocrat)
Bacterio-	βακτήριο(ν)/ βακτήρια (pl.)	bacterium, tiny creature(s) (bacteriology; bacteriolysis)
Baro-	βάρος	weight (barometer)
Batho-	βάθο(ς	depth/deep (batholiths; bathometer)
Bathy-	βαθύς, βαθειά, βαθύ (adj.)	deep (bathysphere; bathymetry- the scientific study of the oceans; seas, etc.)
Biblio-	βιβλίο	book (bibliophile; bibliography)
Bio-	βίος	life (biology; biomagnetics - a branch of magnetic concerned with how magnetism is related to living organisms)
Blasto-	βλαστός	sprout, embryo (blastogenesis)
Botanic-	βοτανικός, ή, ό (adj.)	pertaining to plants, trees and plant life (botany)
Brach or brachy-	βραχύς, βραχεία, βραχύ (adj.)	short; (brachycranial; brachylogy - conciseness of speech; brevity)
Brady-	βραδύς, βραδεία, βραδύ (adj.) (βραδύ + κινείν)	slow; (bradycardia; bradykinin - to move slowly)
Branchio- branchia (pl.)	βράγχια	gills, windpipe (branchiopods)
Bronch-	βρόγχ(ος)	windpipe (before a vowel) (bronchial; bronchitis)
Broncho-	βρόγχο(ς)	windpipe; bronchial tube (broncoscope; bronchometry)
Bryo-	βρύον	moss; lichen (bryology; bryologic)
Caco-	κακός, ή, ό (adj.)	bad/evil, poor (as in cacophony/bad/poor voice; Cacography - bad writing)
Calli-	καλός / κάλλιστος (superlative)	good; best (calligraphy; calligrafic)
Calo-	καλός, ή, ό (adj.) κάλλος	beauty good, kind (caloyer) cal(l) isthenics - simple gymnastics to develop a slender, beautiful body

Cardio-	κάρδιο/καρδιά	heart (cardiology; cardiac)
Carpo-	καρπός	fruit; harvest combining form (as in carpology; carpophagous /fruit eating)
Cata-	κατά	down, against, according (catalyst) see: kata
Celi- or celio-	κοιλία-κοιλιά	belly; abdomen (celioscopy; celiotomy)
Ceno-	κοινός, ή, ό (adj.)	common (cenobion /κοινός + βίος /communal life)
Ceno-	κενός, ή, ό (adj.)	empty (cenotaph/ κενός + τάφος-empty + tomb)
Cenrto-	κέντρο(ν)	center (centrosphere; centrobaric – having to do with the center of gravity)
Cephalic-	κεφαλικός, ή, ό (adj.)	of the head, skull, or cranium (macrocephalic)
Cephalo-	κεφαλο(ς)-κεφάλι	head (cephalogram; cephalothorax – head and thorax as a single part in some crustaceans and arachnids)
Cerato-	κέρας/ κέρατος (gen.)	horn (ceratoid)
Cero-	κηρο- κηρός	wax (ceroplastic)
Cheil- or cheilo-	χειλ- χειλο- χείλος /χείλη	lip/lips (cheilitis; cheiloplasty)
Cheir- or chiro-	χειρ/χειρός (gen. / χείρα (acc.) /χέρι	(Mod. Gr.) hand (chirography - handwriting/penmanship; chiropractics – scientific study of restoring health, practiced by professionals employing manipulation of the body joints
Chem.- or chemo-	χημ- χημειο (χημεία- chemistry)	combining form (chemotherapy - χημειοθεραπεία; chemotaxonomy - classification of plants and animals using comparative biochemistry)
Chiro/cheiro-	χειρό(ς) (gen. of χειρ)/χέρι (Mod. Gr.)	hand (chiropractor; chiromancy)

Chloro-	χλωρός, ή, ό	(adj.) (chloro- neu. of chloros) fresh/green (chloroform)
Chol- chole- or cholo-	χολ- χολή	bile; gall (cholemia/ cholaemia; cholorrhea)
Chondr- or chondo-	χόνδρ- χοόνδρο- χόνδρος	carlilage (chondritis; chondroid)
Chrom- or chromate-	χρώμα	color (chromosphere)
Chron- or chrono-	χρονο- χρόνος	time (chronic; chronology)
Chryso-	χρυσός, ή, ό (adj.)	gold (chrysalis)
Citri-	κίτρον/ο	citrus; (citric) pertaining to citrus fruit/ citrus family
Clepto- or klepto-	κλέπτειν – to steal	relating to stealing (cleptomania/ kleptomania)
Clima- or climato-	κλίμα/κλίματος (gen.)	climate; weather conditions (climatology)
Clino-	κλίνω/κλίνειν (to slope)	recline, to recline; slope (clinometer; clinometrical)
Clitorid- clitorido-	κλειτο- κλειτωρι- κλειτωρίς / κλειτωρίδος (gen.) /κλειτορίδα	Mod. Gr. clitoris (clitorid-ectomy; clitoridis)
Cosmo-	κόσμο- κόσμος	world; people; universe; world order (cosmopolitan; cosmonaut; cosmology)
Cranio-	κρανίο (v)	skull; cranium (craniometry; craniology)
Cryo-	κρύος, α, ο (adj.)	cold, frost (cryology; cryogenics – scientific study concerned with the production of very low temperatures and their effect on the properties of matter)
Crypto-	κρυπτό – (κρύπτειν-to hide)	something done in secret; hidden (cryptography; cryptogram – something written in code or cipher)
Crystal – or crystallo-	κρύσταλλο- κρύσταλλος	crystal (crystallography; crystallize)

Cyan- or cyano-	κυαν- κυανο- κυανούς	blue (cyanide; cyanogenetic; cyanosis – a bluish coloration of the skin, caused by lack of oxygen or abnormal hemoglobin in the blood)
Cycl- or cyclo-	κύκλο- κύκλος	cycle/circle (cyclic; cyclone)
Cyst- or cysto-	κύστις/η (bladder)	pertaining to bladder (cystolith; cystectomy – the surgical removal of a cyst)
Cyt- cyto-	κύτ-κύτταρο- κύτταρον/ο	cell (cytology; cytolysis – Biol. the disintegration or dissolution of cells)
Dacry- or dacryo-	δάκρυ- δάκρυο- δάκτρυον/δάκρυ (Mod. Gr.)	pertaining to tear(s) (dacryology; dacryocystitis – inflammation of a lacrimal sac)
Dactyl- dactyl-	δακτυλ- δάκυλο- δάκτυλος / δάκτυλο	finger; toe; digit (dactylology/ finger spelling; sign language; dactylography – the study of fingerprints for identification)
Deca-	δέκα	ten (as in decathlon; triskaideca/ δεκατρία/thirteen;
Delta-	Δέλτα - δέλτα	pertaining to the shape of the fourth letter of the Greek alphabet ῀Δ῀ (as in deltoid)
Demo- Demon- or demono-	δήμος	people (democracy; democrat) combining form (demonic) (demonolatry)
Derm- or dermo-	δέρμα	pertaining to skin (ex: dermatitis/ skin inflammation) combining form before a vowel
Dermo-	δέρμα/δέρματος (gen.)	skin, combining form (dermatology)
Di-	δις /(δύο Mod. Gr.)	twice, double, twofold (as in dichroma/having two colors)
Dia-	δια	through; throughout (diachronic)
Dicho-	δίχο/διχοτομείν	asunder/apart/ cut in two (dichotomy)
Dino-	δεινός, ή, ό (adj.)	terrible, fearful, dreadful (as dinosaur)
Dipl- or diplo-	διπλό- διπλούς/ διπλός, ή, ό (adj.)	double; twofold (diplococcus)

Dodeca-	δώδεκα	twelve (dodecagon) also before a vowel dodec- (Dodecanese/ twelve islands)
Dox-	δόξ-δόξα	glory (doxology)
Dromo-	δρόμο(ς)	road, street, roadrace, track (motodrome, etc.)
Dynam- or dynamo-	δύναμις/η	power; strength; force (dynamics) (dynamometer)
Dys-	δυσ- (prefix indicating an adverse situation)	difficult; bad; unlucky; abnormal (dysfunction; dysentery)
Eco-	οικ-οίκος	habitat; home; environment (ecological)
Econ-	οικον-οικονομία	pertaining to the financial world, the economy (economist)
Ecto-	εκτός	outside; external (ectoderm/outer skin)
Ego-	εγώ/ I	pertaining to oneself; conceit (egotist); personal pronoun I
Electro-	ηλέκτρο- (ηλεκτρισμός)	electric, electricity prefix (electrocardiogram)
Embryo-	έμβρυον/ο	fetus; thing newly born; (embryogenic)
Encephalo-	εγκέφαλος	referring to brain (encephalitis)
Enter- or entero-	έντερο- έντερον	intestine (enteritis) intestinal (enterohepatic)
Ento- or endo-	εντο-εντός	inside, within (entoderm)
Entomo-	έντομο	insect, bug (entomology)
Eph-	εφ & ημέρα	lasting only one day (as in ephemeron / short-lived, for the day)
Epic-	έπικ/έπος	something heroic, a speech, song, poem (as the Iliad, Odyssey, etc.)
Epi-	επί	on, upon, to (epicardium; epineurium – the layer of connective tissue surrounding a peripheral nerve)
Epiderm- or epidermo-	επιδερμ(ο) επιδερμίς/ επιδερμίδα (Mod. Gr.)	epidermis (epidermitis - inflammation of the epidermis)

Erg- or ergo-	έργο(ν) /εργασία	work (ergograph; ergometer)
Eros- or eroto-	έρως/έρωτας	love (erotic love) (eroticism; erotogenic)
Erythr- or erythro-	ερυθρό(ν)	red combining form (as in erythroderm/red skin; erythroblast)
Ethno-	έθνο(ς)	group of people/descent; nation (ethnic; ethnicity) combining form
Eu-	ευ/εφ – ev/ef	good; well, favorable (eulogy; euphoria)
Eury-	ευρύς, εία, ύ (adj.)	wide; broad (as in eurypterid/ having broad wings)
Exo- or ex-	έξω	out; outside; outer (exocrinology/ the study of external secretions; exodontia / the branch of dentistry dealing with the extraction of teeth
Galact- or galacto-	γάλα/γάλακτος (gen.)	(of) milk (galactic/ milky- galactocele)
Gamo-	γάμος	marriage (gamogenesis)
Gastr-	γαστήρ (anc.) γαστέρος (gen.)- κοιλιά	stomach; abdomen combining form used before a vowel (as in gastric; gastritis)
Gastro	γαστρίο(ν) / γαστήρ	stomach, belly, anything relating to the stomach (gastroenterologist)
Geo-	γαία/γη	earth, soil (geographic; geology)
Gen- or geno-	γέν- γένο- γένος (γίγνεσθαι- to be born)	race; born; (geneology; genetic)
Gephyro-	γέφυρο-γέφυρα	bridge (gephyrophobia)
Geriatric-	γηριατρικός, ή, ό (adj.)	pertaining to old age (geriatrics)
Giga-	γίγας /γίγαντας	giant combining form (as in gigantic; gigantism – abnormal growth of a body, due to excessive production of growth hormone)
Gloss- or glosso-	γλωσσο- γλώσσα	1 tongue (glossitis) 2 language (glossomathia/ language learning
Glotto-	γλοττίς/γλοττίδος (gen.)/ γλώττα Attic var. of γλώσσα	language; tongue (glottis/ the opening between the vocal chords in the larynx)

Glyc- or glycol-	γλυκύς, εία, ύ, / γλυκός, ιά, ό (Mod. Gr. adj.)	sweet, sugar (glycogen; glycine)
Glyph-	γλυφή (γλύφειν- to carve)	carving; (glyphic; glyphography)
Glypt-	γλυπτικός, ή, ό (adj.)	(γλύπτειν –to engrave, carve; sculpt; chisel (glyptics/ the art of sculpting, carving, or engraving designs
Gono-	γόνος/ απόγονος	offspring, procreation, seed combining form (as in gonophore)
Graph-	γραφ- γραφή/ γράφειν – to write	writing, drawing (graphics)
Grapho-	γράφειν/ γράφω /γραφή	to write/ writing (graphology – the study of handwriting)
Gyne-	γυνή/γυναικός (gen.) γυναίκα (Mod. Gr.)	woman (gynecology; gynaeceum/ or gynoecium – γυναικείο(ν) – of women; feminine)
Gyneco- or gynaeco-	γυνή/γυναικός/ (gen.) /γυναίκα (Mod. Gr.)	woman/women (gynecocracy)
Gyno-	γυνο- γυνή	woman (gynophore – a stalk bearing the gynoecium/ γυναικείον above the petals and stamens) also (as in anc. Greece and Rome women's housing)
Gyro-	γύρος	circle, round (gyroscope)
Haplo-	απλούς (anc.) / απλός, ή ό (adj.) (mod. Gr.)	simple (haploid; haploscope/ a simple stereoscope that is used in the study of depth perception)
Hapt- or hapto-	(άπτειν- αφή / to touch-touch	relating to the sense of touch (haptics)
Hecto-	εκατόν/ό	a hundred; (hecaton; 100; hectokilo – a hundred kilos)
Helico-	έλιξ/ έλικος (gen.)	spiral; spiral-shaped; (helicopter)
Hem- haem- or hema	αίμα/ αίματος (gen.)	blood (hemic; hematoma)
Hemi-	ημι/ήμισυ	half (hemisphere)
Hepat- or hepato ¨	ηπαρ /ήπατος (gen.)	liver combining form (hepatic; hepatitis)

Heter- or hetero-	έτερος/ έτερο (neu.)	other/different (heterosexual)
Hex/hexa-	έξ/έξι/εξάς	six (hexagon; hexaemeron – in six days: Bible an account of the six-day Creation)
Hidr- or hidro-	ιδρώς /ιδρώτος (gen.) ιδρώτας (Mid. Gr.)	sweat combining form (hidradenitis – an inflammatory disease of the apocrine sweat glands; hidrosis; perspiration, excessive sweating)
Hier-	ιερ/ιερός	sacred, prefix used before a vowel (hierarch)
Hippo-	ίππο(ς)	horse (hippodrome; hippopotamus – horse of a river)
Histo-	ιστός	tissue (as in histology)
Holo-	όλος, όλη, όλο (adj.)	whole; all combining form (holoendemic)
Homo-	όμο- όμοιο(ς)	same, equal, alike, similar (homochromatic)
Hydr- or hydro-	ύδωρ/ύδατος (gen.)	water combining form (hydraulics; hydraemia)
Hyelo-	ύελο(ς)	glass (hyeloid/resembling glass)
Hymen- or hymeno-	υμήν / υμένος(gen.) υμένας (Mod. Gr.)	membrane (hymenectomy)
Hyp-	ύπ/υπό	under prefix before a vowel (hypothesis)
Hyper	υπέρ	above/over/more than normal (hypercritical/ too critical)
hypn- or hypno-	ύπνο- ύπνος	sleep (hypnosis; hypnotism; hypnology)
Hypo-	υπό	under, less than, below (hypodermic)
Hyps/hypso	ύψ- /ύψος	height, high (hypsometer)
Hystero-	ύστερο- / ύστερον	uterus, womb (hysterotomy)

FF (Note: that all English words beginning with an *h* and derived from the Gr. language took the *Hh* from the Greek words starting with a vowel and accented with the breathing sign daseia)

Iatro-	ιατρο- ιατρός / γιατρός	doctor, physician (iatrogenic)
Ichno-	ίχνος	trace; footprint; tracing (ichnography)
Ichthy or ichthyo-	ιχθύς /ιχθύος (gen.)	fish (ichthyosis)
Icono-	εικών/εικόνος (gen.)	image (iconography; iconic)
Icosi-	είκοσι	twenty (icosahedrons/a solid figure with twenty plane surfaces
Icter- or ictero-	ίκτερο- ίκτερος	jaundice combining form (icteric; icterus)
Ideo	ιδέα	idea (ideology)
Idio-	ίδιος, α, ο (adj.)	same; identical, one's own (idiomorphic)
Ile- or ileo-	ειλεό- ειλεός	ileum, small intestine (ileocolitis)
Irid- or irido-	ίρις /ίριδος (gen.) ίριιδα (Mod. Gr.)	iris combining form (iridectomy; iridology)
Ischem- or ischaem-	ισχαιμία (ίσχω/ ίσχειν- to stop)	deficient supply of blood to the brain or heart ischaemia or ischemia; ischemic)
Is- or iso-	ίσος, η, ο (adj.)	equal; homogenuous; uniform (isometer)
Kaino-	καινό(ς)	new (kainophobia/extreme fear for new things)
Kali-	κάλιο-	potassium combining form (kaliuresis/kaluresis, excessive excretion of potassium in the urine)
Kary- or karyo- or caryo	κάρυον/ο	nut, kernel, combining form (karyolymph/ Biol. the nucleus of of a cell'; karyokinesis/ metosis)
Kata- /cata-	κατά	down, according, away, downward (katavasis,) against (catastrophe) etc.
Kerato-	κέρατο- (κέρας / κέρατος (gen.)	horn; cornea (keratoid/ horn like) (keratotomy/ insision of the cornea)
Kilo--	κιλο- κιλό	a thousand, combining form one thousand (kilogram)

Kinet- ot kineto-	κινητός, ή, ό (adj.)	moving, motion combining form (kinetics; kinetoplast)
Klept- or kl;epto-	κλέπτ-κλοπή (κλέπτειν – to steal)	stealing, theft kleptomania – a persistent neurotic impulse to steal; kleptolagnia - sexual arousal and gratification produced by committing an act of theft
Kolp-	κόλπ/κόλπος	vagina (kolpitis/inflammation of the vagina)
Kym- kymo-	κυμ- κύμα	wave combining form (kymogram/ a chart produced by a kymograph

Note: Combining forms spelled with a *K* in Greek have changed to a *C* in English, see the letter *C* in the prefix and suffix sections (ex: κακό- caco- (bad); καλό- calo/ good, etc.)

Laryng- or laryngo-	λάρυγγο/λάρυνξ/ λάρυγγος (gen.) λάρυγγας	throat; the passageway connecting the pharynx and trachea/windpipe (laryngitis; laryngology)
Leio- or lio	λείος, α, ο (adj.)	smooth (leiomyoma) A benign tumor as a fibroid; leiomyosarcoma/ a sarcoma composed in part of smooth muscle cells
Lept- or lepto-	λεπτός, ή, ό (adj.)	thin/skinny (leptodactylous/ having thin fingers/toes)
Leuk- or leuko- or leuco-	λευκός, ή, ό (adj.)	white; weakly colored/ colorless (leaukemia) leuco - as in leucoplast
Lexi-	λέξις/λέξη	word (lexicon/dictionary; lexicology)
Lip- or lipo-	λίπος	fat; fatty (lipid; lipoma)
Lith- or litho-	λίθος	stone (lithiasis/formation of stones in the body/gallstones; lithogenic)
Log- or logo-	λόγος	speech, word, reason (logorrhea; logography)
Lymph- or lympho-	λέμφος	special functioning fluid; lymph gland (lymphadenitis/ inflammation of the lymph nodes))

Macr-or macro-	μάκρο(ς)/μακρύς	length, long, large (macrobiotics/ study of prolonging life; macroadenoma/ an adenoma of the pituitary gland that is greater than ten millimeters in diameter)
Magi-	μάγι/μάγος/ μάγοι (πλ.pl.)	wise/fantastic, magician (magical)
Malac- or malaco-	μαλακός, ή, ό (adj.)	soft (malacoplakia/ inflammation of the mucous membrane of a hollow organ) (as the urinary bladder)
mast- or masto-	μαστο - μαστός	breast; nipple; mammary gland (mastitis; mastectomy; mastocytoma)
Mega-	μέγα(ς)	great/powerful, large (megaton; megadose)
Megalo-	μεγάλος, η, ο (adj.)	big, great, grand (megalomania)
Mel-	μέλ/μέλι	honey; esp., the pure, clarified form used in pharmacies
Melan- melano-	μέλαν/ μέλας	black; dark (melanin; melanoma)
Membrane- or membrani- or membrano-	μεμβράνη	a soft, pliable sheet or layer of animal or plant origin (membranous; plasma membrane)
Mening- or meningo-	μήνινγξ/μήνιγγος (gen.) μήνιγγας/ μηνίγγι (Mod. Gr.)	meninges (pl.) (meningitis)
Mes- or mesoo-	μέσος, η, ο (adj.)	mid, middle (as in mesocarp; mesoderm)
Meta-	μετά	after; along with; among (metabolic; metaplasia)
Mete-	μετά	behind, at the back (metencephalon)
Mono-	μόνος, η, ο (adj.)	only, alone, one, single (monoceros/unicorn)
Morph- or morpho-	μορφή	form; shape; structure; type (morphology)
My- or myo	μυς/μυός (gen.)	muscle combining form (myalgia/ pain in one or more muscles; myasthenia/muscular debility)

myc- or myco-	μύκης/μύκητος (gen.) μύκητας (Mod. Gr.)	fungus combining form (mycology; mycosis)
myel- or myelo-	μυελό- μυελός	marrow; bone marrow (myelitis; myelocytoma)
Myriad-	μυριάς / μυριάδος (gen.)	many, thousand, countless, innumerable (myriapod/ having many legs as a millipede and cidipede)
myx- or myxo-	μύκσα (anc.) (μύσσομαι- to blow (nose) / μύξα (Mod. Gr.)	mucus (myxoma-a soft tumor of gelatinous connective tissue similar to the one found in the umbilical cord; mixoid)
Nan- or nano-	νάνο- νάνος	dwarf combining form (nanocephalic/having an abnormally small head; nanism/dwarfism)
Narc- or narco-	νάρκο- νάρκη	temporary loss of senses (narcolepsy; narcissistic)
Necr- or necro-	νεκρός, ή, ό (adj.)	pertaining to death or dead; corpse (necrology; necrobiosis)
Neo-	νέο- νέος, α, ο (adj.)	new; young; recent; latest (Neolithic; neophobia/ extreme fear or aversion to novelty)
Nephr- or nephro-	νεφρο- νεφρός	referring to kidney(s) (nephrology´nephroma)
Neur- or neuro-	νεύρο (v)	nerve (neurotic; neurasthenia; neurology)
Nomo-	νόμος	law (nomography/drafting laws)
Noso-	νόσος	illness/disease (nosology/ the study of diseases)
Nycto-	νυκτός (gen.) νυξ(anc.) νύκτα (Mod. Gr.)	night (nyctolatry/ love for the dark/night)
Nymph- or nympho-	νύμφ- νύμφη/ νύφη	bride; young wife; spring goddess (nymphomaniac)
Nyx-	νυξ/νυκτός (gen.)/ νύκτα (Mod. Gr.)	night (nyctophobia/extreme fear of the dark/night)
Octo-	οκτώ	eight (octagon)

Odont-	οδοντ/ οδους/¨οδόντος (gen.)	pertaining to tooth/ teeth (odontology)
Olig- or oligo-	ολίγος, η, ο (adj.)	small/little/scant (oligophagous/ oligophagos; eating very little; oligaemia/ very little blood)
Onto-	ον/όντος (gen.)	being; existence (ontology)
Omo-	ωμός, ή, ό (adj.)	raw (as in foods) combining form (as in omophagos/ eating raw food)
Omphalo-	ομφαλός	navel, umbilicus combining form (as in omphalitis/ inflammation of the navel)
Oncho- or onco	όγκος	tumor (oncology), blk: mass (oncosphere)
Onych- or onycho-	όωυξ/ όνυχος (gen) / όνυχας(νύχι- Mod. Gr.)	nail (of finger or toe) onychia (pl.) (onycholysis)
Oo-	ωό(v)	egg combining form (as in ootheca; oocyst)
Ophi-	όφι- όφις / όφεως (gen.)/ φίδι (Mod. Gr.)	pertaining to snake(s) (ophiolatry; ophiophobia)
Ophthalm- or ophthalmo-	οφθαλμό- οφθαλμός	dealing with the eye(s) (ophthalmic; ophtalmology)
Orchi-	όρχι- όρχις/ όρχεως (gen.)	pertaining to testicle(s) (orchiectomy)
Orchido-	ορχιδο-	testicle (as in orchidotomy; orchitis/ inflammation of of a testis or of both testes)
Organ- or organo-	όργανο – όργανον	body organ: as heart; kidney, etc. (organomegaly / visceromegaly) (also musical instrument)
Ornitho-	όρνιθο/όρνιθα	dealing with chickens; birds; poultry (ornithology)
Oro-	όρος	mountain (orology, the study of mountains)
Orphan-	ορ/ φαν- ορφανός	a child having no parents (orphanage/ a home for orphans)

Ortho-	ορθός, ή, ό (adj.)	correct; straight; true orthography/ correct writing/spelling; orthopedics/ the branch of medicine dealing with the correction of deformities or prevention of such deformity or injury of the skeleton or tendons and ligaments
Osmo-	οσμή (όζειν- to smell) / όσφρησις /η	smell; the sense of smell (osmosis)
Osteo-	οστεο-όστούν/ οστέα/οστά	pertaining to bone(s) (osteopathy; osteology)
Ot-	ους/ ωτός (gen.) / ώτα(anc. sing. + pl.) αυτί /αυτιά (Mod. Gr.)	ear, ears (otology; otitis)
Oxy-	οξύς, οξεία, οξύ (adj.)	1 sharp: pointed: acute (oxycephaly) 2 quick (oxytocic/ hastening parturition 3 acid (oxyntic/ secreting acid)
Pachy-	παχύς, (ε) ιά, ύ (adj.)	thick; fat (pachyderm/ thick-skinned; pachyonychia/ thickening of the nails)
Paed- or paedo- or ped-	παις/παιδός (gen.) παιδί (Mod. Gr.)	pertaining to child or children (paediadtrics or pediatrics/ medical science dealing with childhood diseases
Pago-	πάγο- πάγος	ice combining form (pagophagia/ eating ice; (pagophobia/fear of ice)
Palaeo- or paleo-	παλαιός, ά, ό (adj.)	ancient; very old (Paleolithic)
Pan-	pas (masc.) παν (neu.)/ παντός (gen.)	every, universal, all (panchromatic/all the colors; pandemic/prevalent over an entire region, country, etc.)
Pancreat- or pancreato-	πάγκρεας/ παγκρέατος (gen.)	a complex gland found behind the stomach pancreatectomy; pancreatic)
Para-	παρά	beside, alongside, beyond (paranormal; par(a)esthesia; paraaortic/close to the aorta)

Path- or patho-	πάθος /παθείν –to suffer	suffering, disease, feeling (pathology; pathogenesis) before a vowel (pathology; pathetic)
Pedi/paedi-	παιδί	child (pediatrician)
Pedo-	παις/παιδός (gen.)	child (pedology; pediatrics)
Pente-	πέντε	five (pentagon)
Peri-	περί	around; about; surrounding; enclosing (periarthritis; Pericarditis /inflammation of the pericardium)
Petr-	πέτρα	rock, stone (petrology; petroid)
Pharmaco-	φάρμακο	drug; medicine (pharmacist; pharmacology)
Pharyngo-	φάρυνξ-φάρυγγος (gen.)	the tube extending from the oral cavity to the first part of the esophagus (pharyngology; pharyngeal)
Phil-	φίλ-/φίλος	friend (Philhellene; Philadelphia)
Phlebo-	φλεψ/ φλεβός (gen.)/ φλέβα (Mod. Gr.)	vein combining form (phlebotomy; phlebology)
Phono-	φωνή	voice (ex: phonograph, also, phon - before a vowel (phonetics)
Photo-	φωτο-	light, picture (phot - before a vowel; photic of, relating to, or involving light) (photography)
Phren-or phreno--	φρένο	mind; mental capacity (phrenic; phrenology)
Phyle-	φυλή	race; tribe (phyletic)
Phyllo-	φύλλο (v)	leaflike; a flat leaf stalk (phylloid)
Phyto-	φυτό(v)	plant; flora combining form (phytogenesis)
Plasm- or plasmo-	πλάσμα/ πλάσματος (gen.)	the fluid part of blood, lymph, etc. (plasmapheresis; plasmacytosis) also, πλάσμα/ plasma in Gr. is creation of someone (ex: God's creation/ Θεού πλάσμα)

Pleio- or pleo-	πλέον/πλείστον (superlative)	more/most (pleiotropy/having multiple phenotypic expressions; pleocytosis/ an abnormal increase in the number of cells, in the cerebrospinal fluid)
Pleur- or pleuro-	πλευρό- πλευρό(ν) πλευρά	side, rib, pleura (pleurisy/ inflammation of the pleura)
Pluto-	πλούτος	wealth, affluence (plutocracy; plutocrat)
Phyto-	φυτό(ν)	plant; flora combining form (phytogenesis)
Pneum- or pneumato-	πνεύμα/ πνεύματος (gen.)	spirit; the presence of air (as in pneumatology)
Pneumon-	πνεύμων/ πνεύμονος (gen.) πνεύμονας (Mod. Gr.)	lung (as in pneumonology)
Politic- or politico-	πολιτικός, ή, ό (adj.)	government, politics (politician; politicize)
Poly-	πολύ/ πολλά (pl.)	a lot; much; many (polyphagia/gluttony/eating too much; polyanthous/ having many flowers)
Porno-	πορνο-	pertaining to prostitution (pornography)
Poso-	πόσο	how much; indicating quantity
Pro-	προ	prior; before (prologue; protoplasm)
Procto-	πρωκτός	referring to the rectum and anus (as in in proctology; proctitis/inflammation of the anus and rectum)
proto-	πρώτος, η, ο (adj.)	the first; original, first in importance (protoplasm; protopathic)
Pseudo- or pseudo	ψεύδο- ψεύδος	false; spurious, lie; not genuine (pseudoarthritis; pseudonym/not real name)
Psych- or psycho- or psyche	ψυχ- ψυχή	soul, spirit (psychopath; psychic)

Psychro-	ψυχρό- ψυχρός, ή, ό (adj.)	cold, icy (psychrophobia; psychrometer)
Ptero-	πτερό(ν)/φτερό	wing; feather (pteroid; pteropod)
Pykno-	πυκνός, ή, ό (adj.)	thick, dense (pycnometer, a vessel of a precise volume used to measure the density of liquids and solids; pycnosis)
Pyo-	πύον	pus combining form (as in pyoderma/inflammation of the skin marked with pus-filled lesions)
Pyr-/pyra-	πυρ/πυρά	fire, heat (pyrotechnics; pyrogeniac); pyromania/ the persistent compulsion to start destructive fires
Rachi-	ράχις/η	spine (as in rachialgia/ pain in the spine)
Radi- or radio-	ράδιο- ράδιον	1 radian energy: radiation (radioactive) 2 radium: x-rays (radiotherapy)
Rheo-	ρέο- (ρέειν / ρέω- to flow)	current; flow; stream (rheology; rheostat)
Rhino-	ρις/ρινός (gen.)	the nose (rhinology; rhinorhea/ excessive mucous; rhinoceros) secretion from the nose
Rhizo-	ρίζο-/ρίζα	root (rhizocarpous; rhizotomy/ surgical procedure of cutting the anterior or posterior spinal nerve roots)
Rhod- or rhodo-	ρόδο- ρόδον	rose; rose-red combining form (rhodopsin- rod + opsis/ rose + sight/ a purplish protein pigment, contained in the rods of the retina, helping the vision in dim light
Rhomb- or rhombo-	ρόμβος / ρέμβειν – to turn	rhombus, a thing that can be turned (rhombic; orthorhombic)
Rhythm-	ρυθμό(ς)	flow, movement (rhythmic; rythmicity, regularity in tempo; rhythmic quality)
sacchar- or acchari-	ζάχαρο- ζάχαρις	sugar (saccharine; saccharometer/ an instrument in measuring the amount of sugar)

Schism-	σχίσμα/σχισμή/ σχίζειν	–to cut/separate the act of causing a split or division in a group or society, esp., in religion (schismatic)
Schizo-	σκίζω/σχίζω	to cleave; to cut (schizophrenia; schizophrenic)
Scler- or sclera-	σκληρός, ή, ό (adj.)	hard; tough (sclerosis; scleroderma)
scope	σκοπός	goal, target; a mark, watcher, spy. Also, combining word forming nouns (as microscope)
Seismo-	σεισμό- σεισμός	earthquake (seismology; seismometer)
Seleno-	σεληνο-/σελήνη	the moon (as in selenography; selenosis/ poisoning due to excessive intake of selenium)
spasm-	σπασμός	involuntary contraction of a muscle (as spasmodic}
spastic-	σπαστικός, ή, ό (adj.)	characterized by smasm(s) (spasticity/ a spastic state or condition)
sperm- spermi- or spermo-	σπέρμα	semen; seed (spermatic; spermatozoon)
sphen- or spheno-	σφην/ σφηνός (gen.) /σφήνα (Mod. Gr.)	a wedge, resembling or shaped like a wedge (the sphenoid bone; sphenogram)
spher- or sphero-	σφαίρα	any round body (spherical; spherocyte/ a more or less globular red blood cell characteristic of some hemolytic anemias; spherocytosis/ the presence of spherocytes in the blood)
Sphygmo-	σφυγμό- σφυγμός	pulse (sphygmograph/ an instrument measuring graphically the movements of the pulse)
splanch- or splancho-	σπλάγχνον/ σπλάγχνα (pl.)	the viscera: the internal organs (splanclnic/visceral; splanchnology)
spleen- spleno-	σπλήν/ σπληνός / σπλήνα	spleen: 1 a large, vascular, lymphatic organ in the upper left of the abdominal cavity, near the stomach; 2 malice or spite, bad temper (spleenic; speenful)

Spondyl- or spondylo-	σπόνδυλος	vertebra (spondylitis/ inflammation of the vertebrae)
Stereo-	στερεός, α, ό (adj.)	1 hard; solid; firm (stereotomy) 2 three-dimensional images (stereoscopic)
Sterno-	στέρνο- στέρνον	sternum: a thin, flat structure of bone and cartilage: Breastbone (sternotomy/surgical incision through the sternum)
Steth- or stetho	στήθος	chest; breast (stethalgia/ pain in the breast; stethoscope)
Stoma- or stomato	στόμα/ στόματος (gen.)	mouth, of the mouth (stomatitis; stomatology/ the branch of medicine dealing with diseases of the mouth)
Strepto-	στρεπτό- στρεπτός, ή, ό (adj.)	twisted (satreptococcus/ any of the genus (streptococcus) bacteria
Stronglyl or strong;ylo-	στρογγυλός, η, ό (adj.)	(round) types of parasites as (strongyloides; strongylus; strongylosis/ infestation with strongyles)
styl- stylo-	στύλο- στύλος	pillar; a slender pointed shape (stylo pharengeus; styloid process/ any of several long, slender, pointed, bony processes (as a sharp spine)
Sym-	συμ-	syn, the n, before a b, m, or p, becomes m (sym): as symbolic/ συμβολικός, symmachy/συμμαχία/ συν+ μάχη- together+in battle)
sympath- sympatho-	συν + παθητικός, η, ό (adj.)	syn + pathetic (the n before p becomes m (mp) (sympathetic nerve; sympathize; symptomatic
Syn-	συν	with, together (as in syndrome; synanthropic)
Syring- or syringe-	σύρινξ-σύριγγος (gen.) σύριγγα (Mod. Gr.)	pipe; tube (syringe; syringomyelia/ a chronic, progressive disease of the spinal cord)
Tachy-	ταχύς, ταχεία, ταχύ (adj.)	fast; quick; swift (tachymeter; taxycardia)

Taen or taeni or tenia	ταινία	tapeworm (taeniasis / infestation by tapeworms)
Tars- or tarso-	ταρσός	the part of the foot between the metatarsus and the leg (tarsus; tarsometatarsus)
Tech(ne)-	τέχνη	art; science, skill (technical)
Techno-	τεχνο-	science, skill, art (technology, etc.)
Tele-	τηλε	far, far off (τηλε-tele/far :ancient Gr. adverb) (telephone/ voice from afar; telegram, etc.)
Telo-	τέλος	the end (ex: telophase/ final stage of mitosis)
Terat- or terato-	τέρας /τερατος (gen.)	monster; developmental malformation (teratogenic; teratology; teratoma/ a type of tumor)
Tetra-	τετράς- τετράδος (gen.) / τετράδα /(Mod. Gr.)	four; any group of four (as in tetragon; tetralogy)
Tetarto-	τέταρτος, η, ο (adj.)	fourth (as tetartocone) combining form
Thanat- or thanato-	θάνατος	death (thanatology/ the study of the phenomena of death and the psychological mechanism for coping with it; thanatophobia/ excessive fear of death)
Theo-	Θεός	God (Theology; theological)
Therm- or thermo-	θέρμη (θερμαίνειν- to heat)	heat (thermometer; thermogenesis)
Thorac- or thoraco-	θώραξ/θώρακος (gen.)	chest, thorax (thoracic aorta; thoracentesis/ aspiration of fluid from the chest
Thromb-	θρόμβος	a clot, blood clot (as in thrombosis)
Thym- or thymo-	θύμος	thymus: a grandular structure o lymphoid tissue thymoma/a tumor coming from the tissue elements of the thymus
thyr- or thyro-	θυρεο- θυρεοειδής	thyroid (thyroditis /inflammation of the thyroid gland)

Topo-	τόπος	place of origin, geographical area (toponym/ name of a place/area)
Toxi- or toxo-	τοξικός, ή, ό (adj.)	poison (toxigenic; toxoplasma)
Tri-	τρις / τρία	the number three (trilogy)
Tribo-	τρίβειν	to rub friction prefix forming nouns (triboelectricity)
Trich- or tricho-	τριξ/τριχός(gen.)/ τρίχα (Mod. Gr.)	hair: filament (trichoptosis/ loss of hair; trichiasis)
Tropho-	τροφή (τρέφειν – to nurture/feed)	nutrition (trophoblast; trophic)
Trop- or tropo-	τρόπος	special way of behavior; manner of response (as in tropism; tropical medicine/ the branch dealing with tropical diseases)
trypan- or trypano-	τρύπανο-τρύπανον	– a borer combining form (trypanosoma/ a genus of parasites that infest the blood; trypanocidal/ destroying trypanosomes)
Typho-	τύφος	an acute infection (typhoid, typhus, typhogenic)
Typhlo-	τυφλός, ή, ό (adj.)	blind, dealing with the eyesight (typhlosis/blindness)
Typo-	τύπος	type, kind (typographer; typographical; typical)
Ulcer- ulcero-	έλκος	abcess; a break in skin (alcerogenic; ulcerous/ having one or more ulcers)
uric-	ούρον- ουρικός, η, ό (adj.)	urine; uric (uric acid; urinary infections/ infection in the urinary tract
Xanth-	ξανθός, ή/ ειά, ό (adj.)	yellow, goldish (xanthoma; xanthomatosis/ presence of multiple xanthomas; xanthochromia/ goldish coloring)
Xen- or xeno-	ξένος, η, o (adj.)	foreign, foreigner, stranger (xenophobia; xenotransplant) xen- before a vowel, as xenic (adj.)
Xer- or xero-	ξερός, ή, ό (adj.)	dry, also, before a vowel: xer-as in (xeric) xero- (xerosis/ abnormal dryness of a body part or tissue)

Xylo-	ξύλο	wood (xylograph, xylophone.)
Zoe	ζωή (ζειν- to live/exist)	life, the name Zoe/ Ζωή
Zo-	ζω- ζώον/ζώο	zoo combining word before a vowel as in (zoanthropy; zooid, etc.)
Zoo-	ζώο	animal (zoology, etc.)
Zool-	ζωολογικός, ή, ό (adj.)	zoological, pertaining to animals
Zygo-	ζυγός	yoke, combining form (as in zygomatic)
Zymo-	ζύμη/ζυμώ/ to mix/ ζυμώνω (Mod. Gr.)	to knead a leaven; to mix, fermentation, enzyme (zymosis – mixing - fermentation)

SUFFIX

English	Greek	Meaning
acusis	ακοή	hearing, combining form (diplacusis/double hearing; hyperacusis)
- aemia, emia or haemia	αίμα	blood, suffix forming nouns (anemia or anaemia)
- aguogue	αγωγός/άγειν	leading; to lead; promotes expalsion (as in galactagogue; emmenaguogue)
-aholic	-ολικός, ή, ό (adj.)	having dependence on, as (alcoholic; workaholic) suffix forming adjectives
-algia	-αλγία	pain suffix (as in neuralgia/ nerve pain; otalgia/ earache)
-androus/andros	-ανδρος (ανήρ/ ανδρός (gen.)	man, husband combining word forming *adjectives* (monandrous/ having only one husband)
-anthous	άνθος	flower combining form used to form adjectives (monanthous; polyanthous, etc.)

-athon	-αθών-αθώνειος	as in Marathon/Μαραθώνειος (indicating some type of race)
-blast	βλαστός	sprout combining form (epiblast)
-biosis	βίωσις/η	indicating a specific way of living combining form (symbiosis/ living together) forming nouns
-biotic	βιωτικός, ή, ό (adj.)	forming adjectives indicating a specified way of living (photobiotic/living in light)
-carp	καρπός	fruit, suffix forming nouns (as in endocarp)
-carpic	καρπερός, ή, ό (adj.)	fruitful, harvest, suffix forming adjectives (as in polycarpic)
-carpous	καρπός	fruit; harvest suffix forming adjectives (apocarpous/ having separate carpels)
-centric	κεντρικός, η, ό (adj.)	in the center (centrist)
-cele	κήλη	hernia, tumor, cyst or swelling (cystocele/ a hernia of the urinary bladder into the vagina)
-chalko	χαλκός	copper, brass combining form (chalcography)
-coele	κοιλία	abdomen; body cavity suffix forming nouns (blastkoele a cavity of the blastoula)
-colpos	κόλπος	vagina, suffix indicating a vaginal disorder (hematocolpos)
-cracy/cratia	- κρατία	as in democracy/δημοκρατία
-cyte	-κύτος	cell (as in lymphocyte)
-derm	δέρμα	skin, combining for before a vowel, skin covering (entoderm)
-derma	δέρμα	skin, suffix indicating a specified type (as in scleroderma)
-dermia	-δερμία	suffix forming nouns indicating specific condition as in (xerodermia/dry skin)
-esis	-δέσις /η / δέσιμο (Mod. Gr.)	binding; or fixation suffix forming nouns as in (bibliodesis/book binding; arthrodesis/the surgical immobilization of a joint)

-dermis	-δερμις/-δερμίδα (Mod. Gr.)	layer of skin or tissue as in (epidermis)
-ectomy	-εκτομή	cutting, cut (as in hysterectomy)/
-emia	-αιμία	blood, suffix forming nouns indicating a condition as in (leukemia; or having specifically something in the blood as in uremia)
-encephalus	-εγκέφαλος	brain, suffix forming nouns indicating 1 fetus having (such) a brain (inience[phallus]) 2 condition of having such a brain (hydrencephalus)
-gamogenesis	γάμος & γέννησις/ γένεσις	sexual reproduction
-gamous	-γάμος	combining form referring to marriage (as in polygamous/ πολύγαμος/ more than one marriages)
-gamy	-γαμία	suffix forming nouns as in (polygamy; monogamy)
-genic	γενε-τικός, ή, ό (adj.)	combining word forming adjectives indicating production or generation (as in photogenic)
-genesis	-γένεσις	origin, creation, formation, combining word forming nouns (as in psychogenesis/ ψυχογένεσις)
-geny	γενεά/γενιά	origin; production suffix forming nouns (as phylogeny)
- glossia	γλώσσα	tongue; refer to as having such tongue (mictoglossia/ small tongue)
-gnomy	γνώμη	the study of judging or determining combining form (as in physiognomy/φυσιογνωμία)
-gnosis	γνώσις/η	knowledge, recognition
-gon	-γωνο(ν)γωνία	angle, combining form, a figure having (a specified number of) angles (as pentagon)
-gram	-γράμμα	suffix forming nouns as in (telegram; radiogram)

-graph	-γραφ(ία)	combining form forming nouns (as in photograph, φωτογραφία, etc.)
-grapher	-γράφος	as in photographer/ φωτογράφος, etc.
-graphic	-γραφικός, ή, ό (adj.)	method or process for recording or describing (as telegraphic)
-holic	-ολικός, ή, ό (adj.)	one who exhibits an obsessive need/interested in something (as in alcoholic, αλκοολικός, etc.)
-iasis	ίασις /η	cure (suffix forming nouns) or a disease indicating a specific kind (as in amoebiasis/amebiasis-infestation with amebas)
-ic	-ικος, -ικη,-ικο (adj, endings)	suffix forming adjectives as (electric/ηλεκτρικός, iatric/ ιατρική; acoustic/ακουστικό, etc.)
-ics	-ικα (pl. neu.) or –ική (fem.)	ending of in Gr. ika, in various siences as in mathematics/μαθηματικά; iatrics/ ιατρική-ιατρικά
-ideo	ιδέα	idea, notion, concept combining form followed by a consonant (ideology)
-ism	- ισμός	as in altruism/ αλτρουϊσμός combining word forming nouns indicating a doctrine, theory, system, etc. esp., such ending in ism/ισμός (communism/κομ(μ)ουνισμός)
-isos	ίσος, η, ο (adj.)	equal; similar; alike (isomorph; isobaths/ισόβαθος)
-lithic	λιθικός, ή, ό (adj.)	referring to stone/ rock (paleolithic)
-itis	- ίτις –ίτιδα	combining word forming nouns (as in arthritis)
-ize	-ίζειν/ -ίζω	to make something or to be, combining word forming verbs (as in Americanize; agonize)
-kinesia	-κινησία	movement, motion as in (akinesia/ witout movement; hyper-kinesia/excessive movement)

-kinesis	-κίνησις/ η	motion; movement (telekinesis/ karyokinesis/cell motion)
-lalia	λαλιά	suffix forming nouns indicating type of specified speech disorders (echolalia/the pathological repetition of what is said by other people, as if echoing them
-lepsy	ληψία	an attack suffix forming nouns (as in epilepsy)
-lexia	λεξις /η- λεξία	suffix forming nouns (dyslexia/ δυσλεξία)
-logy	-λογία	combining word forming nouns (as in anthology/ανθολογία; epilepsy/ επιληψία)
- lyses	λύσις –λύσεις (pl.)	solutions; suffix forming the plural of breaking down of diseased tissues (neurolyses)
-lysis	λύσις	solution, dissolution, dissolving (as in analysis, katalysis)
-lyte	-λύτης	combining form referring to a process of decomposition (as in electrolyte)
-lithic -lytic	-λυτικός, ή, ό (adj.)	combining word forming adjectives (as in analytic/ αναλυτικός)
-lyze	-(λ)ύω/ύειν	combing word forming verbs (as in analyze/αναλύω)
-mastia	μαστός	breast, condition of having such or many breasts or mammary glands (gynecomastia)
-mata	μύωμα/ μυώματα (pl.)	myoma/myomata or myomas; tumors indicating a number of tumors consisting of muscle tissue
-megaly	μεγάλος, η, ο (adj.)	large, enlarged; abnormal enlargement of a body part as (hepatomegaly/ enlargement of the liver)
-melia	μέλος –μέλη (pl.)	part/parts, limb /limbs (microlimelia/ abdormally small and developed extermities)

-metrium	μήτρα – μήτριον	part or a layer of the uterus (endometrium/ενδομήτριον)
-metry	-μετρία/μέτρον	the science of measuring (as in bathymetry, geometry/γεωμετρία)
-morphic	μορφικός, ή, ό (adj.)	having a speiific form or shape (endomorphic)
-morphism	μορφισμός	the quality or state of having a type of shape or form (polymorphism/ having many shapes/forms)
-morphous	μορφή/ - μορφος	shape; form suffix forming adjectives (polymorphous / πολύμορφος / having many forms/ mesomorphous/ having a husky, muscular form/body build)
- morphy	μορφή	indicating what kind of shape or (mesomorphy)
-myces	μύκης/ μύκητες (pl.)	fungus/fungi and certain bacteria as (streptomyces/ στρεπτομύκητες)
- mycete	μύκητας	fungus indicating what kind of fungus (actinomycete/ Ακτινομύκητας)
- nephros	νεφρός	kidney suffix indicating specific part of the kidney (pronephros)
-nomics	-νομική /-νομικά	suffix forming nouns indicating fields of study (as astronomics; economics, etc.)
-nomy	-νομια	suffix forming nouns (as economy/οικονομία; astronomy-αστρονομία)
-odontia	οδούς/ οδόντος (gen. anc. οδόντιον/ δόντι/ δόντια (mod. Gr.)	referring to teeth suffix defining conition or treatment of teeth (orthodontia)
-odynia/odyne	οδύνη	pain, combining form (as in pleurodynia)
-oid	ωειδής/oeides (adj.)	termination of preceding element, suffix forming adjectives (as in crystalloid; android)

-oma	-ωμα	suffix forming nouns indicating a growth -/, tumor, as (lipoma/ λίπωμα; hematoma/ αιμάτωμα)
-onym	ώνυμον	as in (synonym, συνώνυμο(ν)
-onychia	-ονύχια	nails, condition of fingernails or toenails (leukonychia/ white nails)
- onychium	-ονύχιον	a region of the fingernail or toenail (eponychium / the horny part of the epidermis/ cuticle)
-ophthalmia	οφθαλμός	referring to the condition of eyes or sight (microphthalmia/abnormal smallness of the eye(s), usually due to a congenital anomaly
-opia	οπία/ωπία	relating to eyes or sight (as in myopia; hyperopia)
-opsis	όψις/η	sight, view (as oceanopsis/ view of the ocean)
-orama	όραμα	exhibiting greater than the usual volume as in (panorama)
-orchidism	όρχις /όρχεις (pl.)	a condition or form affecting the testes (cryptorchididm)
-orexia	-ορεξία (όρεξις/η)	appetie suffix forming nouns (as anorexia)
-orexic	-ορεξικός, ή, ό (adj.)	suffix forming adjectives (as anorexic)
-osis	-όσις/ωσις /η	indicating abnormal or diseased condition as (psychosis/ ψύχωσις neurosis/νεύρωσις/η)
-ostomy-	-οστομή	indicating surgical procedure as in (colostomy; ileostomy)
-otic	ωτικό(ς)	as in neurotic; combining form
-pathes	-παθής/παθές (adj.)	suffering of (as in cardiopathes/ καρδιοπαθής)
-pathic	παθητός (anc.) παθητικός, ή, ό (adj.)	passive; 1 feeling or affected in a specified way (telepathic) 2 affected by disease of a specific part (myopathic)
-pathy	-πάθεια	as in sympathy/συμπάθεια
-pepsia	πέψις/η –πέψια	digestion suffix forming nouns as (dyspepsia/ δυσπεψία)

-phagous/os	φάγειν/φάγος	as in polyphagous/eating a lot
-phobia	φοβία (φόβος fear)	as in (acro(phobia; thermophobia/ extreme fear of excessive heat)
-phobic	φόβος	fear, as in homophobic; xenophobic/ fear of strangers
-phone	φωνή	voice combining form (as in telephone/τηλέφωνο/ voice from far off)
-phonic	-φωνικός, ή, ό (adj.)	as in telephonic/ telegraphic)
-phony	(συμ) -φωνία	harmony of sounds (as in symphony)
-phoria	-φορία (φέρειν-to bring)	bearing; tendency as in (euphoria) forming nouns
-phoric	-φόρος, α, ο (adj.) φορεύς/ φορέας –bearer)	suffix forming adjectives, having such bearing (thanotophoric/ bearing death)
phyte	φυτό(ν)	plant growing in a specific way, suffix forming nouns (as mikrophyte)
-plasm or plasma	πλάσμα	any of the components of protoplasm suffix forming nouns (endoplasm)
-plast	πλαστός, ή, ό (adj.) (πλάσσειν – to form)	unit of protoplasm (chromoplast)
-plastic	πλαστικός, ή, ό (adj.)	forming, developing suffix forming adjectives (homoplastic)
-plegia	πληγία	as in paraplegia
-pleura	πλευρό/πλευρά	rib, side (as in pleuricy/ πλευρίτιδα)
-pterous	πτέρις /πτέριδος / φτέρα (Mod. Gr.)	fern; featherlike plant, suffix forming adjectives (as in homopterous)
-rhagia/rrhagia	-(ρ)ραγία	bleeding; to burst, suffix forming nouns (as menorrhagia)
-rhagy	ραγή	superficial crack
--scopy	σκοπιά/σκοπείν	examining, suffix forming nouns (as arthroscopy)
-sophy	σοφία	wisdom; skill (as in philosophy)

-sperm	σπέρμα	seed, suffix forming nouns (gymnosperm)
-stasis	στάσις/η	as in metastasis
-stome	στόμα	mouth, combining word forming nouns (as in stomatitis/ στοματίτις /στοματίτιδα)
-stomia	στόμα/στόματος (gen.)	exhibiting a condition of the mouth (as xerostomia/ dry mouth)
-stomy	στόμιο/στόμα	opening, mouth, indicating a surgical opening into a specified part or an organ (as in colostomy)

DISCIPLINES— FIELDS OF STUDY

A sample of words of various areas of study and scientific fields.
The influence and contribution of Greek and elements of the Greek language are evident almost in all areas and disciplines: from art to science, theater and entertainment, literature, politics, theology, to technology, and many more.
The most prevalent areas and vocabulary you are going to encounter in this and other dictionaries are presented in a nutshell in this section of the book:

1 ANATOMY

Anatomy	ανατομία	the science of the morphology or structure of animals or plants 2 the structure of an organism or body 3 a detailed analysis 3 a skeleton
anthropo(s)	άνθρωπος	man; human; human being
aner andro-	ανήρ/ ανδρός(gen.)/ άνδρας (Mod. Gr.)	man; male

gyne: gyneco-	γυνή/γυναικός (γεν.) γυναίκα	woman; female
paedo: paed or pedi	παις/παιδός (gen.)/παιδί	child
ancon	αγκών/ αγκώνος(gen.)/ αγκώνας	elbow
artery	αρτηρία	artery
cardio-	καρδία/καρδιά	heart combining form (cardiology)
carpus	καρπός	wrist
celiac	κοιλία-κοιλιά/ κοιλιακός, ή, ό (adj.)	abdomen; belly
cephalo-	κεφαλή/κεφάλι	head, combining form (cephalopod)
chole	χολή	bile; gall
craniology	κρανιολογία	the science concerned with the variations in size, shape, and proportions of skulls among human races
cranium	κρανίον	skull
dactyl	δάκτυλος/ δάκτυλο	finger or toe
derm: derma-	δέρμα	skin
disk	δίσκος	disk
encephalon	εγκέφαλος	brain
endocardium	ενδοκάρδιον/ο	the thin endothelial membrane lining the cavites of the heart
hepar	ήπαρ/ήπατος (gen.)/σηκώτι (Mod. Gr.)	
nephron	νεφρός/νεφρό	kidney
odondo-	οδούς/ οδόντος/(gen.) δόντι(Mod. Gr.)	tooth
ophthalmo-	οφθαλμός	eye (ophthalmology)
pancreas	πάνκρεας	a large elongated gland situated behind the stomach, secreting the pancreatic juice

pod or podus	πους/ποδός(gen.)/ πόδι	foot (podiatrist)
stomato-	στόμα/στόματος (gen.)	mouth
tarsus	ταρσός	the flat of the foot
trachea	τραχεία	windpipe; the breathing tube

2 ARCHITECTURE

Acroplolis	Ακρόπολις/ Ακρόπολη	the fortified upper part of an ancient city, as the Acropolis in Athens
agora	αγορά	marketplace; (anc.) where people assembled; assembly place
amphitheater	αμφιθέατρον/ο	a round or oval building with an open space(arena) surrounded by rising rows of seats
architect	αρχιτέκτων/ αρχιτέκτονας	a specialist in designing and drawing up plans for buildings, bridges, etc.
asymmetry	ασυμμετρία	lack of symmetry
basis	βάσις /η	base; foundation; the chief supporting factor of anything
Basilica	βασιλική	orig., a royal palace; a Christian church; the ancient Basillica in Rome used as a courtroom
Byzantine	Βυζαντινή/ Βυζάντιον	Byzantium or the Byzantine empire, its culture, etc.; pertaining to the Eastern Orthdox Church
Corinthian style	Κορινθιακός ρυθμός	In the style of Corinth: gracefully elaborate
decastyle	δεκάστυλος	having ten poles, columns or pillars
diastyle	διάστυλος	having two poles, columns or pillars
Doric style	Δωρικός ρυθμός	designating or of a classical order of architecture, distinguished by simplicity of style and form
entasis	έντασις/η	a slight, convex swelling in the shaft of a column

epistyle	επιστύλιον/ο	upon: a style, column, pillar or pole
exedra	εξέδρα	seating area; in ancient Greece, a room, building, or an outdoor area with seats, where discussions were held
helix	έλιξ/έλικος	any spiral; cylinder; an ornamental spiral in arhitecture
heptastyle	επτάστυλος	having seven styles, columns or poles or pillars
hexastyle	εξάστυλος	having six styles, columns, pillars or poles
hippodrome	ιππόδρομος	an arena for equestrian events; in ancient Greece and Rome a course of horse and chariot races surrounded by tiers of seats
hypostyle	υπόστυλος	hypo: under; having roof supported by rows of pillars or columns
Ionic style	Ιωνικός ρυθμός	designating or of a classical order of architecture, represented by ornamental scrolls; Gr. or Rom. Prosody
Mausoleum	μαυσωλείον /ο	1 the tomb of Mausolus, king of Caria, and one of the seven wonders of the ancient world 2 a large imposing tomb
museum	μουσείον /ο	(literally, a place for the Muses or for study); an institution, building or room, in order to preserve and exhibit artistic, historical, or scientific objects
metope	μετώπη	an opening; any of the square areas, plain or decorated between triglyphs in a Doric frieze
mosaic	μωσαϊκός	the process of making picures or designs by inlaying tiny pieces of colorful stone 2 any picture or design made that way
narthex	νάρθηξ / νάρθηκας	the area before the main sanctuary of a church

necropolis	νεκρόπολις /η	a cemetery esp., belonging to an ancient city (the city of the dead)
obelisk	οβελίσκος	a tall, slender, four-sided stone pillar tapering toward its pyramidal top; a dagger
peristyle	περιστύλιον	(peri/around and style); a row of columns forming an enclosure or supporting a roof
plinth	πλίνθος	the square block at the base of a column; pedestal
propylaeum	προπύλαιον	an entrance, vestibule, or portico before a building or group of buildings; before the gate
prostyle	πρόστυλος	pro/before + style); having a portico whose columns, usually four in number, extend in a line across the front only
stoa	στοά	a portico, as in ancient Greece, having a wall on one side and pillars on the other
stylobate	στυλοβάτης	a continuous base or coping for a row of columns
symmetry	συμμετρία	similarity of form or arrangement on either side of a dividing line or plane; proportion
triglyph	τρίγλυφος	in a Doric frieze, a slightly projecting, rectangular block occurring at intervals

3 BIOLOGY

Anamorphosis	αναμόρφωσις /η	Biol. a gradual change of form by evolution
bio-	βίος	life; living things, combining form
Bioastronautics	βιοαστροναυτική	the science dealing with the physical responses of living things to the environment of space and space travel

biocatalyst	βιοκαταλυτής	a substance, as an enzyme or hormone, that activates or speeds up a biochemical reactio
biocenosis	βιοκοινωνία	a community of biologically integrated and interdependent plants and animals
biochemistry	βιοχημεία	a science concerned with the chemistry of life processes in plants and animals
bioenergetics	βιοενεργητική/ βιοενέργεια	a branch of energetics dealing with the nanner a living organism converts food, sunlight, etc. into useful energy
bioecology	βιο-οικολογία	the science dealing with the interrelations of communities of animals and plants with their environment
bioelectric	βιοηλεκτρικός, ή, ό (adj.)	having to do with electrical energy in living tissues
bioethics	βιοηθική	the study of the ethical problems arising from scientific advances, esp., in biology and medicine
biogenesis	βιογένεσις/η	the principle that living organisms originate only from other living organisms closely similar to themselves
biogeography	βιογεωγραφία	the branch of biology that deals with the geographical distribution of plants and animals
biological	βιολογικός, ή, ό (adj.)	of, or connected with biology
biology	βιολογία	the science dealing with the origin, history, physical characteristics, life processes, habits, etc. (it includes botany and zoology)
biometrics	βιομετρική	the branch of biology concerned with its data statistically and by mathematical analysis

biophysics	βιοφυσική	the study of biological phenomena using the principles and techniques of physics
bioplasm	βιόπλασμα	living matter; protoplasm
biopsy	βιοψία	Med. the removal of living tissue from the body for diagnostic examination
biorhythm	βιορυθμός	any biological cycle that involves periodic changes in blood pressure, body temperature, etc.
bioscopy	βιοσκόπηση	Med. an examination to determine whether life is present in the body
-biosis	βίωσις	way of life; way of living, combining form (anabiosis/ bring to life/rejuvenate)
biosphere	βιόσφαιρα	1 the zone of planet earth where naturally occurs, extending from the deep crust to the lower atmosphere 2 the living organisms of the earth
biosynthesis	βιοσύνθεσις /η	the formation of chemical compounds by the enzyme action of living organisms, as in protein
biotechnology	βιοτεχνολογία	the use of the data and techniques of engineering and technology for the study and solution of problems concerning living organisms
biotherapy	βιοθεραπεία	the treatment of disease by means of substances, as serums, vaccines, penicillin, etc., secreted by or derived from living organisms
biotic	βιωτικός / βιωματικός, ή, ό (adj.)	of or relating to life
biotope	βιότοπος	a small area with a uniform environment occupied by a community of organisms

4 BOTANY

Achene	αχαίνιον	any small, dry, indehiscent fruit with one seed which is attached to the ovary wall only at one point, as the strawberry
acrocarpous	ακρόκαρπος	bearing form at the end of the stalk, as some mosses
agrimony	αγριμονία	any plant of a genus (Agrimonia) in the rose family
ananthous	άνανθος	not bearing flower
anemophilous	ανεμόφιλος	pollinated by the wind
angiosperm	αγγειόσπερμα	any of division (Magnoliophyta) of flowering plants having seeds produced within a closed pod or ovary
arum	άρον	any plant of the arum family (esp., genus Arum) characterized by small flowers on a thick spike, within a hoodlike leaf
ascidium	ασκίδιον/ο	Bot. a pitcherlike leaf or structure, as the pitcher plant or bladderwort
chrysanthemum	χρυσάνθεμον/ο	marigold; any of the genus (Chrysanthemum)
crinum	κρίνον/ο	lily; any of a large(Crinum) of tropical bulbous plants of the lily family
endosperm	ενδοσπέρμιον/ο	a tissue which surrounds the developing embryo of a seed and provides food for its growth
epicalyx	επικάλυξ/ επικάλυκας	a ring of small bracts at the base of certain flowers, resembling an extra outer calyx, as in the mallows
epicarp	επικάρπιον/ο	a variation of exocarp
esparto	σπάρτο	either of two kinds of long, coarse grass

euonymus	ευώνυμος	the spindle tree; lit. of good name; lucky; any of a genus (Euonymus) of deciduous or evergreen shrubs and woody vines of the staff-tree family
exocarp	εξώκαρπος	the outer layer of a ripened ovary or fruit, as the skin of the plum; epicarp
geophytes	γεώφυτο	a plant that grows in earth; esp., a perennial whose buds live underground throughout the winter
geranium	γεράνιον/ο	any of a large genus (Geranium) of [plants of the geranium family, having pink or purple flowers]
gymnosperm	γυμνόσπερμα (γυμνό + σπέρμα – naked + sperm)	any of a large division (Pinophyta) of seed plants having the ovules borne on open scales, usually lacking true vessels in the woody tissue
helianthus	ηλίανθος (ήλιοος + άνθος – sun + flower)	sunflower
heliotrope	ηλιοτρόπιον/ο	a sunflower or any other plant whose flowers turn to face the sun
heterophyllous	ετερόφυλλος	growing leaves of different forms
homosporous	ομόσπορος	producing only one kind of spore; isosporous
hydrophilus	υδρόφιλος	needing the presence of water for fertilization
hydrophyte	υδρόφυτος	any plant growing only in water or very wet earth
hypogeal	υπόγειος	growing or maturing underground, as peanuts
lithophytes	λιθόφυτον/ο	any plant that grows on rock surfaces
marguerite	μαργαρίτα	daisy; any of several cultivated chrysanthemums (esp., *Chrysanthemum frutescens*) with a single flower

mesophyte	μεσόφυτον/ο	any plant adapted to grow under medium conditions of moisture
monadelphous	μονάδελφος	having the stamens united by their filamens into one set or bundle, as some legumes
monandrous	μόνανδρος	having only one stamen, as some flowers (having one husband/one man)
monocarp	μονόκαρπος	bearing fruit only once and then dying; said of annuals, biannials and some long-lived plants, as the bamboos and century plants
narcissus	νάρκισσος	any of a genus *(Narcissus)* of bulbous plants of the lily family with smooth, linear leaves and six-parted flowers (such as daffodils and jonquils); a plant with narcotic properties
odontoglossum	οδοντόγλωσσον/ο (οδόντος(gen) + γλώσσα – tooth + tongue)	any of a genus *(Odontoglossum)* of tropical American, epiphytic orchids with clustered flowers of various colors
orchid	ορχιδέα	a perennial plant of the orchid family that grows in the ground or as an epiphyte and is characterized by waxy pollen masses
parthenocarpy	παρθενοκαρπία	the development of a ripe fruit without fertilization of the ovules, as in the banana and pineapple
periblem	περίβλημα	Bot. the meristem that produces the cortex
philodendron	φιλόδενδρον/ο (φίλος + δένδρον/ friend/ lover + tree)	1 any of the genus (Phillodedrum) of tropical American vines of the arum family 2 any similar plant

5 CHEMISTRY

Arsenic	αρσενικόν/ό	a silvery-white, brittle, very poisonous chemical element
azote	άζωτον/ο (α+ ζωή- without + life)	the gas does not support life
barium	βάριον (βαρύς – heavy)	a silver-white, slightly malleable, metallic chemical element, symbol: Ba
biochemical	βιοχημικός	the amount of dissolved oxygen needed to decompose the organic matter in waste water
chemist	χημικός	a specialist in chemistry
chemistry	χημεία	the science dealing with the composition and properties of substances, and with the reactions by which substances are produced from or converted into other substances
chemosynthesis	χημειοσύνθεσις/η	the synthesis by certain bacteria of organic compounds from carbon dioxide and water by the use of energy obtained by the oxidation of certain chemicals
chemotherapy	χημειοθεραπεία	the prevention or treatment of disease by administering chemicals or drugs
chemotropism	χημειοτροπισμός	the tendency of some plants or other organisms to turn or bend under the influence of chemical substances
chloric	χλώριον/ο	of or containing pentavalent chlorine
chlorine	χλωρίνη	a greenish-yellow, poisonous, gaseous chemical element with a disagreeable odor
chrome	χρώμιον/ο	chromium or chromium alloy, esp., as used for plating; a chromium pigment

crystal	κρύσταλλον/ο	a clear, transparent quartz or a very clear, brilliant glass; a piece of this cut in the form of an ornament
crystallize	κρυσταλλοποιείν/ κρυσταλλοποιώ	to cause or to form crystals or give it a definite structure, as a crystalline structure
dialysis	διάλυσις/η	the separation of dissolved substances, as crystalloids, etc.
electrochemistry	ηλεκτροχημεία	the science concerned with electrical energy to bring abouta chemical reaction or with the generation of electrical energy by means of chemical reaction
hydrogen	υδρογονούχος	a flammable, colorless, odorless, gaseous chemical element, the lightest of all known substances: symbol, H
hydrolysis	υδρόλυσις/η	a chemical reaction in which a substance reacts with water so as to be changed into one or more other substances, as starch into glucose, etc.
lithium	λίθιον	a soft, silver-white, metallic chemical element, the lightest known metal
neon	νέον	a rare, colorless, and inert gaseous chemical element, found in small quantities in the earth's atmosphere
photolysis	φωτόλυσις /η	chemical decomposition due to the action of light
plutonium	πλουτώνιον	a radioactive, metallic chemical element of the actinide series similar to uranium and neptunium
synthesis	σύνθεσις/η	the putting together of parts or elements so as to form a whole
thermolysis	θερμόλυσις /η	dissociation of a compound by heat

uranium	ουράνιον	a very hard, heavy, silvery, moderately malleable, radioactive metallic chemical element

6 ECONOMY

Antieconomy	αντί- οικονομία	opposing economy
economia	οικονομία	management of resources of income and expeditures of a state, city, or household
economic	οικονομικός, ή, ό (adj.)	of or having to do with the management of income or expeditures, etc.
economical	οικονόμος, α, ο (adj.)	an economical person; frugal
economic anaemia/ anemia	οικονομική αναιμία	economic weakness
economic geography	οικονομική γεωγραφία	the branch of geography dealing with the relation of economic conditions to physical geography and natural resources
economic system	οικονομικό σύστημα	a set of principles and rules regarding the economy
economic synergy	οικονομική συνεργία (συν + έργον- together + work/συνεργείν to work together)	cooperative action of various forces of the economy
economics	οικονομικά	1 the science concerned with the production, distribution, and consumption of wealth, and the various related problems of labor, finance, taxation, etc.2 economic factors
economist	οικονομολόγος	a specialist in economics
economize	οικονομώ	to manage thriftly, and avoid waste

economy	οικονομία	the management of the income, expences, etc., of a household, community, business, or government
nomisma	νόμισμα	coin or medal; token; paper money; currency
nusmimatic	νομισματικός, ή, ό (adj.)	of coins or medals; or having to do with currency
numismatic plethora	νομισματική πληθώρα	excessive currency; plethora of coins, etc.
numismatic politics	νομισματική πολιτική	the politics governing currencies
numismatics	νομισματική	the scientific study or collection of coins, medals, tokens; paper money, or currencies in general

7 EPIC POETRY and TRAGEDY

Achilles	Αχιλλεύς / Αχιλλέας	Gr. myth. hero and one of the leaders of the Trojan War
Adonis	Άδωνις	Gr. myth. a very handsome young man who was loved by Aphrodite; any handsome man
Aeschylus	Αισχύλος	Gr. tragedian, one of the three best tragedy writers: the other two being Euripides and Sophocles
Agamemnon	Αγαμέμνων / Αγαμέμνονας	Gr. myth. king of Mycenae and commander in chief of the Gr. army in the Trojan War, he was killed, upon his return, by his wife and her lover
Amazons	Αμαζών/Αμαζώνες	Gr. myth. any of a race of female warriors supposed to have lived in Scythia, near the Black Sea
Antigone	Αντιγόνη	Gr. myth. the daughter of Oedipus and Jocasta: she defies her uncle, king Creon, by performing funeral rites for her brother, Polynices

Bacchus	Βάκχος	Gr. and Rom. myth. god of wine and revelry: identified with the Greek Dionysus
Centaur	Κένταυρος	any of a race of monsters with a man's head, trunk, and arms, with a horse's body and legs
Cerberus	Κέρβερος	Gr. and Rom. myth. the three-headed dog guarding the gate of Hades
Circe	Κίρκη	in Homer's Odyssey, an enchantress who turns men into swine
Clytemnystra	Κλυτεμνύστρα	Gr. myth. the wife of Agamemnon, with the aid of her lover, Aegisthus, murdered her husband and was killed by her son, Orestes, in revenge of his father's murder
Creon	Κρέων /Κρέοντας	Gr. legend a king of Thebes who has his niece Antigone entombed alive because she defied him: see Antigone
Cyclops	Κύκλωψ / Κύκλωπες (pl.)	any of a race of giants who have only one eye, in the middle of their forehead
Electra	Ηλέκτρα	shining one; Gr. myth. a daughter of Agamemnon and Klytemnystra who encouraged her brother, Orestes, to kill her mother and her lover who together had murdered their father, Agamemnon
Euripides	Ευριπίδης	one of the three best tragedians of antiquity; writer of trgedies
Helen of Troy	Ελένη της Τροίας	Gr. legent, the beautiful wife of the king of Sparta, Menelaus, her abduction by Paris (prince of Troy) was the cause of the Trojan War
Homer	Ομηρος	Gr. epic poet, Homer lived in the eighth cen. BC: the Iliad and Odyssey are attributed to him

Iphigenia	Ιφιγένεια	Gr. myth. a daughter of Agamemnon, offered by him to Artemis, as a sacrifice to appease her, but according to one of many versions the goddess saved her
Jocasta	Ιοκάστη	Gr. myth. the queen, who unwittingly, marries her own son, Oedipus, and kills herself when she finds out
Laertes	Λαέρτης	1 Gr. myth. the father of Odysseus 2 in Shakespeare's Hamlet, the brother of Ophelia
Medea	Μήδεια	Gr. myth. a sorceress, who helps Jason get the Golden Fleece and later, when was deserted by him, kills their children
Menelaus	Μενέλαος	Gr. myth. the king of Sparta and husband of Helen, who was abducted by Paris, resulting in a ten-year war (the Trojan War)
Nausica	Ναυσικά	Gr. myth. the daughter of the king of Pheaces, Alkinoos, who saw the shipwrecked Odysseus and brought him to her father's palace
Odesseus	Οδυσσεύς/ Οδυσσέας	the hero of the Odyssey, a king of Ithaca, and one of the leaders of the Trojan War
Odyssey	Οδύσσεια	an ancient epic poem, ascribed to Homer, dealing with the wanderings of Odysseus during the ten years following the end of the Trojan War; any adventurous journey

Oedipus	Οιδίπους / Οιδίποδας	Gr. myth. the son of Laius and Jocasta, king and queen of Thebes, who, to avoid the realization of an oracle's prediction that their son will kill his father and marry his mother sent him with a servant to a forest and left him there to die. The baby was found by people of the king of Corinth, who took him and treated his swollen feet (thus his name: οίδημα+πους – swollen + foot). He was raised by the king of Corinth, later solved the riddle of the Sphinx, unwittingly fought and killed his real father and married his mother. When he discovered what he had done, he blinded himself.
Orestes	Ορέστης	Gr. myth. son of Agamemnon and Klytemnystra, who aided by his sister, Electra, avenges the murder of his father, by killing his mother and her lover, Aegisthus
Paris	Πάρις	Gr. Legent, a son of Priam, king of Troy, who abducted Helen and caused the Trojan War
Phedra	Φαίδρα	Gr. myth. the daughter of Minos and wife of Thesseus; she kills herself after her stepson rejects her advances
Scylla and Charybdis	Σκύλλα και Χάρυβδις	Scylla, a dangerous rock on the Italian side of the Straits of Messina, opposite the whirlpool Charybdis: in classical mythology both Scylla and Charybdis were personified as female monsters, between two perils or evils, neither of which evaded without risking the other

Siren	Σειρήν /Σειρήνα	Gr. and Rom. myth. any of several sea nymphs, represented as part bird and part woman, who lure sailors to their death on rocky coasts by seductive singing 2 a woman wo uses her sexual attractiveness to entice or allure men
Sophocles	Σοφοκλῆς	Gr. writer of tragic dramas: lived, c. 496–406 B. C. and is regarded as one of the best three tragedians: the other two Aeschylus and Euripidis
Sphinx	Σφινξ /Σφίγγα	lit. the strangler; 1 Gr. myth. a winged monster with a lion's body and the head and breasts of a woman 2 a person who is difficult to know or understand
Tiresias	Τειρεσίας	Gr. myth. a blind soothsayer of Thebes
Trojan Horse	Δούρειος Ἱππος	Gr. Legent a huge, hollow wooden horse with Greek soldiers hidden inside that is left at the gates of Troy; when the horse was brought in the city, the hidden soldiers creep out, open the gates to the rest of the Greek army, which destroys the city
Trojan War	Τρωϊκός Πόλεμος	Gr. Legent the ten-year war waged against Troy by the Greeks in order to get back king Menalaus wife, Helen, who had been (supposedly) abducted by Paris
Troy	Τροία	ancient city of in Troas, NW Asia Minor: scene of the Trojan War

8 GEOLOGY

Gaea	γαία-/ γη	earth; Myth. the goddess of earth, the mother of the Titans
gaeeology/geology	γεωλογία	the science concerned with the physical nature and history of the earth
geography	γεωγραφία	the descriptive science that deals with the surface of the earth, its division into continents and lands/ countries, the climate, plants, animals, natural resources, populations, and industries of the various divisions
geologic	γεωλογικός, ή, ο (adj.)	of or according to geology
geologist	γεωλόγος	an expert in geology
geomagnetic	γεωμαγνητικός, ή, ό (adj.)	referring to the magnetic properties of the earth
geometric	γεωμετρικός, ή, ό (adj.)	characterized by straight lines, triangles, circles, or other geometric patterns
geometrician	γεωμέτρης	an expert in geometry
geometry	γεωμετρία	the branch of mathematics concerned with points, lines, planes, figures, etc., and examines their properties, measurements, and their natural relation to space
geomorphic	γεωμορφικός, ή, ό (adj.)	1 according to geography 2 with reference to the geography of a particular region
geomorphology	γεω-μορφολογία	the science concerned with the nature and origin of the earth's topographic features
geophysics	γεωφυσική	the science dealing with the physics of the earth, including weather, winds, tides, earthquakes, volcanoes, etc., and their effect on the earth

geopolitics	γεωπολιτική	1 the interrelationship of politics and geography, or the study of this 2 any policy on this, mainly the Nazi doctrine of aggressive geographical and political expansion which aimed to lead to German domination of the world
geoponic	γεωπονικός, ή, ό (adj.) (γαία + πονείν- earth + to toil/labor)	referring to agriculture
georgic	γεωργικός, ή, ό (adj.)	having to do with working the fields; dealing with agriculture 2 Lat. Virgil's georgicum (Carmen) georgic (song) a poem dealing with farming and rural life
geotaxis	γεώταξις/η	the positive or negative, response of a freely moving organism to, or against gravity
geotectonic	γεωτεκτονικός, ή, ό (adj.)	dealing with the structure, distribution, shape, etc., of rock bodies, and with the structural disturbances and alterations of the earth's crust that produced them
geotectonics	γεωτεκτονική	the scientific study dealing with those structural disturbances
geothermic	γεωθερμικός, ή, ό (adj.)	having to do with the heat of the earth's interior
geotropism	γεωτροπισμός	any positive, or negative movement or growth of a plant or sessile animal in response to, or against, the force of gravity

9 LITERATURE

Aesthetics	αισθητική	the study or theory of beauty and the psychological responses to it; specif. the branch of philosophy dealing with art, the creative sources, its forms, and its effects
allegory	αλληγορία	a story in which people, things, and happenings have a hidden or symbolic meaning: allegories are used for teaching or explaining ideas, moral principles, etc.
amphibology	αμφιβολογία	double or doubtful meaning; ambiguity, esp. from uncertain grammatical construction; ambigious phrase, proposition, etc.
anthology	ανθολογία / ανθολόγιον/ο	a garland; collection of short poems or stories; (ανθολόγος /anthologist – one gathering flowers)
antithesis	αντίθεσις /η	1 a contrast or opposition of thoughts, usually in two phrases, clauses, or sentences (ex: you are going; I am staying) 2 the second part of such expression 3 the exact opposite [happy is the antithesis to sad]
aphorism	αφορισμός (αφορίζειν –to divide; mark off)	1 Gr. a distinction, determination 2 a short, concise statement of a principle 3 a short, pointed sentence expressing a wise or clever observation or a general truth; maxim; adage 4 in church, the most serious ecclesiastical punishment
apology	απολογία	speaking in defense; 1 a formal spoken or written defense of an idea, religion, philosophy, policy, etc.2 acknowledgment of an error, injury, insult, etc., along with an expression of regret and a plea for forgiveness

apophthegm	απόφθεγμα	a terse, pointed saying (ex: "Brevity is the soul of wit") also; *apothegm*
archaism	αρχαϊσμός	the use or imitation of archaic words, technique, style, etc.
autobiography	αυτοβιογραφία	the art or practice of writing one's own life/ biography
Bible	Βιβλος	the Scriptures; the sacred book of Christianity; Old Testament and New Testament
biblio-	βιβλίον/ο	book, combining form
bibliography	βιβλιογραφία	the study of the editions, dates, authorship, etc., of books and other writings 2 a list of sources of information on a given subject, period, etc., or of the literary works of a given author, publisher, etc.
biography	βιογραφία	1 the history of individual lives, considered as a branch of literature 2 an account of someone's life written by another; life story
catachresis	κατάχρησις /η	1 incorrect use of a word or words, as misapplication of terminology or by strained or mixed metaphor 2 abuse; misuse; breach of trust
catastrophe	καταστροφή	1 the culminating event of a drama, esp., of a tragedy, by which the plot is resolved; denoument 2 a disastrous end, bringing overthrow or ruin 3 a great and sudden calamity, disaster, or misfortune
critic	κριτικός	1 a) a person who forms and expresses judgments of people or things according to certain standards or values b) such a person whose profession is to write, broadcast or review books, plays, music, paintings, motion pictures, etc.

critique	κριτική	a critical evaluation or analysis of a subject, situation, literary work, art, etc.
dialogue	διάλογος	1 talking to one another; interchange and discussion of ideas, esp., when open and sincere, as in seeking mutual understanding or harmony 2 a conversation (on a book, a story, or a play) also: on a literary work on a single topic
didactic	διδακτικός (διδάσκειν – to teach)	1 used or intended for teaching or instruction 2 morally instructive 3 too much to teach others; boringly pedantic or moralistic
elegiac	ελεγειακός	1 Gr. and Latin Prosody of or composed in dactylic-hexameter couplets, the second line (sometimes called a pentameter) having only an accented syllable in the third and sixth feet: the form was used for elegies and other lyric poems
elegy	ελεγεία	1 any poem in elegiac form 2 a poem or song of lament and praise for the dead, as in Shelley's "Adonais"; a mournful poem
epic	επικός /έπος	a long narrative poem in a dignified style about the deeds of a traditional or historical hero or heroes (poems: as in the Iliad and Odyssey,) with formal characteristics (called classical epic); or a literary epic like Milton's *Paradise Lost*, etc.

epigram	επίγραμμα	1 a short poem with a witty or satirical point 2 any terse witty, pointed statement often with a clever twist in thought (ex: "Experience is the name everyone gives to his mistakes") Syn. saying
epilogue	επίλογος	a closing section added to a novel, play, etc., providing further comment, interpretation, or information
epistle	επιστολή	a letter; message; 1 a letter esp. a long, formal instructive one 2 a) any of the Epistles of the New Testament written by an Apostle b) a selection, usually from these Epistles read in various Christian churches
epithet	επίθετον /o	an adjective, noun, or phrase, often spec. a disparaging one, used to characterize some person or thing (ex: smart aleck, characterizing a self-assertive; cocky person, or "egghead: for an intellectual, etc.) 2 a descriptive name or title (ex: Alexander the Great or America the Beautiful, etc.)
epos	έπος	1 an epic poem; epic poetry 2 a collection of poems of a primitive epic nature, handed over orally 3 series of epic events
euphoria	ευφορία	a feeling of vigor, of well-being, or high spirits
exegesis	εξήγησις	explanation, critical analysis, or interpretation of a word, literary passage, etc. esp. in the Bible
hero	ήρως /ήρωας	to watch over, to protect; 1 Myth. Legend a man of great strength and courage, favored by the gods

heroism	ηρωϊσμός	the qualities and actions o a hero or heroine; bravery, valor, nobility, sacrifice, etc.
idiom	ιδίωμα	1 language or dialect of a people, region, class, etc. 2 the usual way in which the words of a particular language are joined together to express a thought 3 the style of expression characteristic of an individual [the idiom of Carlyle]
idyll	ειδύλλιον /o	1 short poem or prose, describing a simple, peaceful scene of rural or pastoral life 2 Gr. the word ειδύλιο, also means romance; friendly relationship among people or nations
idyllic	ειδυλλιακός	1 of, or having the nature of, an idyll 2 pleasing and simple; pastoral or picturesque
irony	ειρωνεία	1 a method of humorous or subtly sarcastic expression in which the intended meaning of the words is the direct opposite of their usual sense [the irony of calling a stupid excuse: clever] 2 the feigning of ignorance in argument, also called *Socratic irony* (as Socrates often used in Plato's Dialogues)
metaphor	μεταφορά	to carry over; a figure of speech containing an implied comparison, in which a word or phrase ordinarily and primarily used of one thing is applied to another (ex: the curtain of night); cf. Simile; Mixed Metaphor

monologue	μονόλογος	speaking alone; 1 a long speech by one speaker, esp., one monopolizing the conversation 2 a passage or composition, in verse or prose, presenting the words or thoughts of a lone character
mythos	μύθος	a word, speech, story, legend 1 a traditional story of unknown authorship, ostensibly with a historical basis, but serving usually to explain some phenomena of nature, the origin of man,or the customs, institutions, religious rites, etc. 2 any fictitious story, or scientific account, theory, belief, etc.
mythology	μυθολογία	all myths, or such stories collectively
neologism	νεολογισμός	1 a new word or a new meaning for an established word 2 the use of, or the practice of creating, new words or new meanings for established words
oxymoron	οξύμωρον /o	acutely silly; a figure of speech in which opposite or contradictory ideas or terms are combined (ex: bitter sweet; loud silence, etc.)
paradox	παράδοξον /o	1 [Archaic] a statement contrary to common belief 2 a statement that seems contradictory, unbelievable, or absurd but that might be true in fact
parody	παρωδία	1 a literary or musical work imitating the characteristic style of some other work or of a writer or composer in a satirical or humorous way, usually by applying it to an inappropriate subject 2 a poor or weak imitation

pathos	πάθος	suffering; the quality in something experienced or observed which arouses feelings of pity, sorrow, sympathy, or compassion
periphrasis	περίφρασις /η	the use of many words where one or a few would do; roundabout way of speaking or writing circumlocution
philology	φιλολογία	1 orig., the love of learning and literature; study; scholarship 2 old term for linguistics; 3 in Gr. the term still applies
pleonasm	πλεονασμός	the use of more words that are necessary expressing an idea; redundancy
poem	ποίημα	an arrangement of words written or spoken: traditionally a rhythmical composition, sometimes rhymed, expressing experiences, ideas, or emotions in a style more concentrated, imaginative and powerful than that of ordinary speech or prose
prologue	πρόλογος	an introduction to a poem, play, book, etc.; esp., introductory lines spoken by a member of the cast before a dramatic performance
psalm	ψαλμός	a sacred song or poem; a hymn 2 any of the sacred songs in praise to God constituting the Book of Psalms in the Bible (consisting of 150 psalms)
rhetoric	ρητορικός	1 the art of using words effectively in speaking or writing; the art of composition 2 artificial eloquence; showy and elaborate language, but largely empty of specific ideas or sincere emotions

rhyme	ρίμα	a piece of verse, or poem, in which there is a regular recurrence of corresponding sounds, esp., at the ends of lines
sarcasm	σαρκασμός	a taunting, sneering, cutting, or caustic remark; gibe or jeer. Generally ironic 2 the making such remarks 3 their characteristic quality
stichomythia	στιχομυθία	dialogue in brief, alternate lines, as in ancient Greek drama Also: stichomathy
strophe	στροφή	turn; 1 in the ancient Greek theater a) the movement of the chorus in turning from right to left of the stage (cf. *Antistrophe*) b) the part of the choric song performed during this 2 in the Pindaric ode, the stanza responded by the antiphone, in the same metrical pattern
symbol	σύμβολον /o	1 something that stands for, represents, or suggests another thing, esp., an object used to represent something abstract; emblem [the dove a symbol of peace] 2 a written or printed mark, letter, abbreviation, etc.
synonym	συνώνυμον /o	1 a word having the same or nearly the same meaning in one or more senses as another in the same language: opposed: to *Antonym* 2 Biol. an incorrect taxonomic name
synopsis	σύνοψις /η	summary; a statement giving a brief, general review or condensation
tautology	ταυτολογία	needless repetition of an idea in a different word, phrase, or sentence, redundancy; pleonasm

tetralogy	τετραλογία	1 a series of four dramas, three tragic and one satiric, performed together at the ancient Athenian festival of Dionysus 2 any of four related plays, novels, etc.
tetrastich	τετράστιχος	a poem or stanza of four lines
theme	θέμα	1 a) a topic or subject, as of a lecture, sermon, essay, etc. b) a recurring, unifying subject or idea; motif, often one used decoratively 2 a short essay esp. one written as an assignment in a school course Syn: *Subject*
thesis	θέσις /η	a placing; position; 1 a) in a classical Greek poetry the long syllable of a foot b) in later poetry, the short or unaccented syllable or syllables of a foot 2 a proposition maintained or defended in argument
tragedy	τραγωδία	1 a serious play or drama typically dealing with the problems of a central character, leading to an unhappy or disastrous ending brought on, as in ancient drama, by fate and tragic flaw in this character, or, in modern drama, usually by moral weakness, psychological maladjustment, or social pressures 2 a novel or other literary work with similar characteristics
trilogy	τριλογία	a set of three related plays, novels, novels, etc., which together form an extended, unified work, though each has its own unity
tristich	τρίστιχος	a group or stanza of threelines or verse; triplet

10 MEDICINE

Achromatopsia	αχρωματοψία	a visual defect that is marked by total color blindness in which, the colors of the spectrum are seen as tones of white, gray, and black, by poor visual acuity and by extreme sensitivity to light
acromegaly	ακρομεγαλία	chronic hyperpituitarism that is characterized by gradual and permanent enlargement of the flat bones (as the lower jaw) and of the hands and feet, abdominal organs, nose, lips, and tongue which develops after ossification is complete—compare *Gigantism*
adenectomy	αδενεκτομή	surgical removal of one or more glands
adenitis	αδενίτις / αδενίτιδα	inflammation of a gland
adenocarcinoma	αδενοκαρκίνωμα	a malignant tumor originating in glandular epithelium
agoraphobia	αγοραφοβία	abnormal fear of open and public places, resulting in anxiety and panic
allergy	αλλεργία	1 hypersensitivity to a specific substance (such as food, pollen, dust, etc.) or condition (as heat or cold) which in similar amounts is harmless to most people: it is manifested in a physiological disorder 2 a strong aversion

allopathy	αλλοπάθεια	1 a system of medical practice which aims to combat disease by using remedies (as drugs or surgery) that produce effects different from or incompatible with those produced by the disease treated—compare **Homeopathy** 2 a system of medical practice making use of all measures that have been proven to be of value in treatment of disease
alopecia	αλωπεκεία	baldness; loss of hair, wool or feathers
amblyopia	αμβλυωπία	dimness of eyesight, esp. in one eye without apparent change in the eye structure
amnesia	αμνησία	partial or total loss of memory, sometimes including personal identity due to brain injury, shock, fatigue, repression, or illness, sometimes induced by anesthesia
amniocentesis	αμνιοκέντησις /η	the surgical insertion of a hollow needle through the abdominal wall and into the uterus of a pregnant female to obtain amniotic fluid esp. to examine the fetal chromosomes for anabnormality and the determination of the sex
anaemia or anemia	αναιμία	a condition in which the blood is deficient in red blood cells, in hemoglobin, or in total volume
anaesthesiology	αναισθησιολογία	a branch of medical science dealing with anaesthesia and anaesthetics, also **anesthesiology**
analeptic	αναληπτικός, ή, ό (adj.)	a restorative agent; esp., a drug that acts as a stimulant on the central nervous system

analgesia	αναλγησία	insensibility to pain without loss of consciousness
anaphylaxis	αναφύλαξις /η	1 hypersensitivity (as foreign protein or drugs) resulting from sensitization following prior contact with the causative agent 2 *Anaphylactic Shock*
anaplacy	αναπλασία	reversion of cells to a more primitive or undifferentiated form
anatomy	ανατομία	1 a branch of morphology dealing with the structure of organisms—compare *Psysiology* 2 the art of separating the parts of an organism in order to ascertain their position, relations, structure, and functions: *Dissection* 3 the structure of an organism or body 4 a treatise on anatomic science or art
ancylose	αγκύλωσις /η	see Ankylosis
angioma	αγγείωμα	a tumor (as a hemangioma) composed chiefly of blood vessels or lymphatic vessels
ankylosis	αγκύλωσις /η	a stiffening of a joint, caused by the pathological joining of bones or fibrous parts, by injury, or by surgical procedure
anodyne	ανώδυνος (αν + οδύνη – without + pain)	relieving or lessening pain; soothing; anything that soothes pain
anorexia	ανορεξία (αν + όρεξη- without + appetite)	lack of appetite for food: see *Anorexia Nervosa*
anosmia	ανοσμία (αν + οσμή – without + smell)	partial or total loss of the sense of smell

antibiotic	αντιβιωτικός, ή, ό (adj.)	of antibiosis; destroying or inhibiting the growth of bacteria and other microorganisms 2 any of chemical substances produced by microorganisms, specif. bacteria, fungi, and actinomycetes and, having the capacity in dilute solutions, to inhibit the growth of or destroy all those
aorta	αόρτα	the large arterial trunk that carries blood from the heart to be distributed by branch arteries through the body
aphasia	αφασία	loss or impairment of the power to use or comprehend words, usually resulting from brain damage
artery	αρτηρία	any of the tubular branching muscular- and elastic-walled vessels that carry blood from the heart through the body
arthritis	αρθρίτις / αρθρίτιδα	inflammation of joints due to infectious, metabolic, or constitutional causes; also, a specific arthritic condition (as gouty arthritis or psoriatic arthritis)
asphyxia	ασφυξία	lack of oxygen or excess of carbon dioxide in the body that is usually caused by interruption of breathing and that causes unconsciousness
asthma	άσθμα	a chronic lung disorder that is marked by recurrent episodes of airway obstruction (as from bronchospasm) manifested by labored breathing, accompanied by wheezing and coughing and by a sense of constriction in the chest, that is triggered by hyperreactivity to various stimuli (as allergens or a rapid change in air temperature)

atheroma	αθήρωμα	1 fatty degeneration of the inner coat of the arteries 2 an abnormal fatty deposit in an artery
atheroschlerosis	αθηροσκλήρωσις /η	an arteriosclerosis characterized by atheromatous deposits in and fibrosis of the inner layer of the arteries
bacteria	βακτήρια/ βακτήριον/ο (pl. of bacterium)	tiny creatures making up a division (bacteria) of microorganisms which are typically one-celled, have no chlorophyll, multiply by simple division, and can be seen only by a microscope: there are three forms, spherical (cocci), rod-shaped (bacilli), and spiral (spirilla); some cause diseases such as pneumonis and anthrax, and other bacreria are necessary for fermentation, nitrogen fixation, etc.
biopsy	βιοψία	the removal of living tissue from the body for diagnostic examination
blepharitis	βλεφαρίτις / βλεφαρίτιδα (βλέφαρον/ο – eyelid)	inflammation of the eyelids
bronchitis	βρογχίτις / βρογχίτιδα	acute or chronic inflammation of the bronchial tubes
bulimia	βουλιμία	1 an abnormal and constant craving for food 2 a serious eating disorder, it occurs chiefly in females, and is characterized by overeating, usually followed by self-induced vomiting or luxetive or diuretic abuse; it is often accompanied by guilt and depression

carcinoma	καρκίνωμα	a malignant tumor of epithelial origin—compare ***Sarcoma-carcinosarcoma***
cardiology	καρδιολογία	the study of the heart, its function and diseases
cardiopathy	καρδιοπάθεια	any disease of the heart
cataract	καταράκτης	a clouding of the lens of the eye or its surrounding transparent membrane that obstructs the passage of light
catharsis	κάθαρσις /η	purification; 1 purgation, esp., of the bowels 2 the purifying of the emotions or relieving of emotional tensions, etc., by art; concept applied originally by Aristotle to the effect of tragic drama on the audience 3 psychiatry the alleviation of fear, problems, and complexes by bringing them to consciousness or giving them expression
chemotherapy	χημειοθεραπεία	the treatment or prevention of disease (as cancer) or mental disorders by the use of chemical agents
cholera	χολέρα	any of several diseases of humans or animals, usually marked by severe gastrointenstinal symptoms as, an acute diarrheal disease caused by a comma-shaped gram-negative bacillus of bthe genus Vibrio (V.Cholerae, syn. V. comma) check; ***Asiatic Cholera***

chronic	χρόνιος	1 a) a marked by long duration, frequent recurrence over a long time, and often by slowly progressing seriousness: not acute [chronic digestion] b) having a disease for a long time [a chronic patient] 2 continuing indefinitely; perpetual; constant [a chronic worry] 3 by habit, custom, etc., habitual; inveterate [chronic complainer]
cirrhosis	κίρρωσις	a degenerative disease in an organ of the body, esp., the liver, marked by excess formation of connective tissue and, usually, subsequent painful swelling
colon	κόλον	the part of the large intestine that extends from the cecum to the rectum
coma	κώμα	a state of profound unconsciousness caused by disease, injury, or poison
cystitis	κυστίτις/ κυστίτιδα	inflammation of the urinary bladder
diabetes	διαβήτης	any of various abnormal conditions characterized by the secretion and excretion of excessive amounts of urine; esp. :*Diabetes Mellitus*
diagnosis	διάγνωσις/η	1 the act or process of deciding the nature of a diseased condition by examining the symptoms 2 a careful examination and analysis of the facts in an attempt to understand or explain something (ex: the diagnosis of a war; of the economy; etc.)

diphtheria	διφθερίτις / διφθερίτιδα	an acute infectious disease caused by a bacterium (Corynebacterium diptheriae) characterized by weakness, high fever, the formation in the air passages of a tough, membranelike obstruction to breathing, and the production of a poten neurotoxin
diphtheria		
dysentery	δυσεντερία	any of various intestinal inflammations characterized by abdominal pain, along with frequent and intense diarrhea with bloody, mucous feces
dyspepsia	δυσπεψία (δυσ + πέπτειν – hard/difficult+ to soften)	impaired digestion; indigestion; also: *dyspepsy* cf. *Eypepsia*
eczema	έκζεμα	a noncontagious skin disorder of unknown cause, characterized by inflammation, itching, and the formation of scales
electrocardiogram	ηλεκτροκαρδιογράφημα	a graphic tracing showing the variations in electric force which trigger the contractions of the heart: it is used in the diagnosis of heart disease
electrotherapy	ηλεκτροθεραπεία	the treatment of disease by means of electricity
embryo	έμβρυον/ο	an animal in the first stages of growth and differentiation that are characterized by cleavage, the laying down of fundamental tissues, and the formation of primitive organs and organ systems; esp., the developing human individual from the time of implantation to the end of the eighth week after conception—compare *Fetus*
encephalogram	εγκεφαλογράφημα	an x-ray picture of the brain made by encephalography

endocarditis	ενδοκαρδίτις / ενδοκαρδίτιδα	inflammation of the endocardium
epidemic	επιδημικός (επι + δήμος – upon + people)	1 an epidemic disease 2 the rapid spreading of such disease 3 a rapid, widespread occurrence or growth
epilepsy	επιληψία	a seizure; a recurrent disorder of the nervous system, characterized by seizures of excessive brain activity which cause mental and physical dysfunction, as convulsions, unconsciousness, etc.
exophthalmia	εξωφθαλμία	abnormal protrusion of the eyeball, caused by various disorders
gastritis	γαστρίτις / γαστρίτιδα	inflammation of the stomach, esp., the stomach lining
genetic	γενετικός	of the genesis or origin, of someone or something 2 of or having to do with genetics
geriatrics	γηριατρική (γήρας – old age)	the branch of medicine dealing with diseases and problems of old age also, *Gerontology*
glaucoma	γλαύκωμα	any of a group of related eye disorders characterized by increased pressure within the eye, which impairs the vision and may slowly cause eye damage and total loss of vision
gynaecology	γυναικολογία (γυνή/ γυναικός (gen.) + λογία- woman + logy)	the branch of medicine dealing with the study and treatment of the female reproductive system, including the breasts
haematocrit	αιματοκρίτης	1 an instrument for determining usually by configuration the relative amounts of plasma and corpuscles in blood 2 the percent of the volume of whole blood that is composed of bred blood cells as determined by separation of red blood from the plasma also: H*ematocrit*

haemorrhage	αιμορραγία	the escape of large quantities of blood from a blood vessel; heavy bleeding also: **Hemorrhage**
hepatitis	ηπατίτις / ηπατίτιδα (ήπαρ/ ήπατος (gen.)- liver)	inflammation of the liver
herpes	έρπης/έρπητας	any of several inflammatory diseases of the skin caused by herpes virus and characterized by clusters of vesicles, esp., **Herpes Simplex**
herpes keratitis	έρπης κερατίτις	keratitis caused by any of the herpes viruses that produce herpes simplex or shingles
hormone	ορμόνη	a product of living cells that circulates in body fluids and produces a specific often stimulatory effect on the activity of cells usually remote from its point of origin
hormone therapy	ορμονική θεραπεία	the therapeutic effect of hormones: as a) the administration of hormones esp., to increase diminished levels in the body; esp., **Hormone Replacement Therapy** b) a hormone (as estrogen or testosterone) [*hormone therapy* to treat prostate or breast cancer]
hydrophobia	υδροφοβία	1 an abnormal fear of water 2 [from a symptomatic inability to swallow water
hypermnesia	υπερμνησία (υπέρ + μνήμη –hyper + memory)	abnormally sharp memory or vivid recall, seen in certain mental disorders
hyperthermia	υπερθέρμια	1 elevated temperature of the body (as that occurring in heatstroke) –2 the artificial heating of all or part of the body (as in diathermy) for therapeutic purposes (as to treat cancer)

hypertrophy	υπερτροφία	a considerable increase in the size of an organ or tissue, caused by enlargement of its cellular components
hypomania	υπομανία	a mild form of mania, specif. of the manic-depressive psychosis
hypothermia	υποθερμία	subnormal body temperature
hysteria	υστερία	a psychiatric condition variously characterized by emotional excitability, excessive anxiety, sensory and motor disturbances, or the unconscious simulation of organic disorders, such as blindness, deafness, etc. 2 any outbreak of wild, uncontrolled excitement or feeling, such as fits of laughing and crying *Syn. Mania*
iatrogen	ιατρογενής/ ιατρογενές	caused by the doctor or medical treatment: said esp., of symptoms, ailments, or disorders induced by drugs or surgery
-iatry	ιατρεία/ γιατρειά	healing; medical treatment combining form (phychiatry; podiatry)
ileus	ειλεός	colic; an abnormal condition caused by paralysis or obstruction of the intestines and resulting in the failure of intestinal contents to pass through properly
iritis	ιρίτις/ιρίτιδα	inflammation of the iris of the eye
kyphosis	κύφωσις/η	a hump; abnormal curvature of the spine resulting in a hump
laryngitis	λαρυγγίτις/ λαρυγγίτιδα	an inflammation of the larynx, often characterized by a temporary loss of voice

leukemia	λευκαιμία	an acute or chronic disease characterized by an abnormal increase of white blood cells in bodily tissues with or without a corresponding increase of those in the circulating blood
lipoma	λίπωμα	a benign tumor made up of fat tissue
mania	μανία	1 wild or violent mental disorder, specif., the manic-phase of manic depressive psychosis (biopolar), characterized generally by abnormal excitability, exaggerated feelings of well-being, flight of ideas, excessive activity, etc. 2 an excessive, persistent enthusiasm, liking, craving, or interest; obsession; craze [*mania for dancing*]
mastitis	μαστίτις/ μαστίτιδα (μαστός- a breast)	inflammation of the breast or udder; inflammation of the mammary gland usually caused by infection
meningitis	μηνιγγίτις/ μηνιγγίτιδα (μήνιγγες- meninges)	inflammation of the meninges, esp., as result of an infection by bacteria or viruses; see *meninx/meninges*
metastasis	μετάστασις /η	1 a) change of position, state, or form b) the spread of a disease-producing agency (as cancer cells or bacteria) from the initial or primary site of disease to another part of the body; also: the process by which such spreading occurs 2 a secondary malignant tumor resulting from metastasis

migraine	ημικρανία	1 a condition that is marked by recurrent usually unilateral severe headache, often accompanied by nausea and vomiting and followed by sleep, that tends to occur in more than one member of the family, and it is of uncertain origin though attacks appear to be precipitated by dilatation of intracranial blood vessels 2 an episode or attack of migraine [suffers from migraines]
myelitis	μυελίτις / μυελίτιδα	inflammation of the spinal cord or of the bone marrow
myopia	μυωπία	a condition in which the visual images come to a focus in front of the retina of the eye because of defects in the refractive media of the eye, or of abnormal length of the eyeball resulting esp., in defective vision of distant objects; also called nearsightedness; compare *Astigmatism*
narcosis	νάρκωσις /η	a state of stupor, unconsciousness, or arrested activity produced by the influence of narcotics or other chemicals or physical agents
nausea	ναυτία	a stomach distress with distaste for food and an urge to vomit
nephritis	νεφρίτις / νεφρίτιδα	acute or chronic inflammation of the kidney affecting the structure (as of the glomerulus or parenchyma) and caused by infection, a degenerative process, or vascular disease—compare *Nephrosclerosis, Nephrosis*

neuritis	νευρίτις / νευρίτιδα	an inflammatory or degenerative lesion of a nerve marked esp. by pain, sensory disturbances, and impaired or lost reflexes—compare *Neuralgia*
neurosis	νεύρωσις /η	a mental and emotional disorder that affects only part of the personality, is accompanied by a less distorted perception of reality than in a psychosis, does not result in disturbance of the use of language, and is accompanied by various physical, psychological, and mental disturbaces (as visceral symptoms, anxieties, or phobias)
nosology	νοσολογία	1 a classification or a list of diseases 2 a branch of medical science dealing with listing and classifying the various diseases
ophthalmia	οφθαλμία	inflammation of the conjunctiva or the eyeball
ophthalmic nerve	οφθαλμικό νεύρο	the one of the three major branches or divisions of the trigeminal nerve that supply sensory fibers to the lacrimal gland, eyelids, ciliary muscle, nose, forehead, and adjoining parts; ophthalmic division
ophthalmology	οφθαλμολογία	a branch of medical science dealing with the structure, functions, and diseases of the eyes
organism	οργανισμός	an individual constituted to carry on the activities of life by means of organs separate in function but mutually dependent: a living being

osteoarthritis	οστεοαρθρίτις / οστεοαρθρίτιδα	arthritis typically with onset during middle age old age that is characterized by degenerative and sometimes hypertrophic changes in the bone and cartilage of one or more joints and a progressive wearing down of apposing joint surfaces with consequent distortion of joint position and is marked symptomatically, esp., by pain, swelling, and stiffness—-abbr. **OA**
osteopathy	οστεοπάθεια	a bone disease; 2 a system of medical practice based on a theory that diseases are due chiefly to loss of structural integrity which can be restored by manipulation of the parts supplemented by thearapeutic measures (as by the use of medicine or surgery)
otitis	ωτίτις/ωτίτιδα (ους/ ωτός (gen.) – of the ear)	inflammation of the ear
pandemic	πανδημικός	occurring over a wide geographic area and affecting an exceptionally high proportion of the population
paroxysm	παροξυσμός	a sudden attack or a spasm (as of disease) 2 a sudden recurrence of symptoms or an intensification of existing symptoms
peritonitis	περιτονίτις / περιτονίτιδα	inflammation of the peritonium
phlebitis	φλεβίτις / φλεβίτιδα	inflammation of a vein or veins

plasma	πλάσμα	the fluid part of the blood, lymph, or intra-muscular liquid; esp., the fluid part of blood distinguished from the corpuscles, used for transfusions; protoplasm
pleuricy	πλευρίτις/ πλευρίτιδα	inflammation of the pleura characterized by difficult, painful breathing and often accompanied by the exudation of liquid into the chest cavity
pneumonia	πνευμονία (πνεύμων/ πνεύμονος (gen.) – lung/ of the lung)	inflammation or infection of the alveoli of the lungs of varying degrees of severity and caused by bacteria, viruses, etc.
presbyopia	πρεσβυωπία	a form of farsightedness occurring after middle age, caused by a diminished elasticity of the crystalline lens
prognosis	πρόγνωσις /η	a forecast or forecasting; esp., a prediction of the probable course of a disease in an individual and the chances of recovery
prophylaxis	προφύλαξις/η	1 the prevention of or protection from disease; prophylactic treatment 2 Dentistry a mechanical cleaning of teeth to remove plaque or tartar
prosthesis	πρόσθεσις /η	a) the replacement of a missing part of the body, as a limb, eye, or tooth, by an artificial substitute b) such a substitute
psoriasis	ψωρίασις /η	a chronic skin disease characterized by scaly, reddish patches

psychology	ψυχολογία	1 a) the science concerned with the mind, mental, and emotional processes b) the science of human and animal behavior 2 the sum of the actions, traits, attitudes, thoughts, mental states, etc., of a person or group [the psychology of the adolescent]
rachitis	ραχίτις /ραχίτιδα	inflammation of the spine
rheumatism	ρευματισμός	any of various conditions characterized by inflammation and pain in muscles, joints, or fibrous tissue {muscular rheumatism} 2 *Rheumatoid Arthritis*
sarcoma	σάρκωμα	a malignant tumor arising in tissue of mesodermal origin, that spreads by extension into neighboring tissue or by way of the bloodstream— compare *Carcinoma*
schizophrenia	σχιζοφρένεια	a psychotic disorder characterized by loss of contact with the environment, by noticeable deterioration in the level of functioning in everyday life, and by disintegration of personality expressed as disorder of feeling, thought (as in delusions), perception (as in hallucinations) behavior; also called*dementia praecox*
sciatic	ισχιακός	iscium; 1 of, relating to, or situated near the hip 2 of, relating to, or caused by sciatica
sepsic	σηπτικός	of, relating to, or causing putrefaction 2 relating to, involving, caused by or affected with sepsis [septic arthritis] {septic patients}

spasm	σπασμός	I an involuntary and abnormal contraction of muscle or muscle fibers or of a hollow organ (as the esophagus) that consists largely of involuntary muscle fibers 2 the state or condition of a muscle or organ affected by spasms
splenectomy	σπληνεκτομή	the surgical removal of the spleen
stomatitis	στοματίτις / στοματίτιδα	inflammation of the mouth
tachycardia	ταχυκαρδία	elatively rapid heart action whether psychological (as after exercise) or pathological
thalassaemia	θαλασαιμία	any of a group of inherited hypochromic anemias and esp., Cooley's anemia controlled by a series of allelic genes that cause reduction in or failure of synthesis one of the globin chains making up hemoglobin and that tend to occur esp., in individuals of Mediterranean, African, or southeastern Asian ancestry, also called *Mediterranean anemia*
therapeutics	θεραπευτική	a branch of medicine dealing with the application of remedies to diseases (cancer therapeutics) also known as *Therapeusis*
therapy	θεραπεία	the treatment of disease or of any physical or mental disorder by medical or physical means, usually excluding surgery: sometimes used in compounds [hydrotherapy]

toxaemia	τοξαιμία	a condition in which poisonous substances are spread throughout the body by the bloodstream, esp., toxins produced by pathogenic bacteria or by cells of the body: also *Taxemia*
trauma	τραύμα	1 a bodily injury, wound, or shock 2 Psychiatry a painful emotional experience, or shock, often producing a lasting psychic effect and, sometimes neurosis
tympanitis	τυμπανίτις/ τυμπανίτιδα	inflammation of the ear, also called; *Tympanitis*
typhus	τύφος	an acute, infectious disease caused by various rickettsiae esp. Rickettsia prowazekii
uraemia	ουραιμία	a toxic condition caused by the presence in the blood of waste products that are not being eliminated in the urine because of a failure of the kidneys to secrete urine, also: **uremia**
urolith	ουρόλιθος	presence of calculi in the urinary tract
urology	ουρολογία	the branch of medicine concerned with the urogenital and the urinary system and the diseases
xanthopsia	ξανθοψία	a visual disturbance in which objects appear yellow
xenobiotic	βιωτικός	designating or of a chemical substance that is foreign, and usually harmful, to living organisms
xenodiagnosis	ξενοδιάγνωσις	the detection of a parasite (as of humans) by feeding supposedly infected material (as blood) to a suitable intermediate host (as an insect) and later examining the intermediate host for the paraite

| xerophthalmia | ξενοφθαλμία | a dry thickened lusterless condition of the eyeball resulting esp., from a severe deficiency of vitamin A— compare **Keratomalacia** |

11 MUSIC

Acoustics	ακουστική	1 the qualities of a room, theater, etc., that have to do with how clearly sounds can be heard or transmitted in it 2 (sing.) the branch of physics dealing with sound, esp., with its transmission
antiphony	αντιφωνία	1 the opposition of sounds 2 harmony produced by this 3 antiphon 4 antiphonal chanting or singing 5 any response or echo
aria	άρια	an air or melody in an opera, cantata, or oratorio, esp., the solo with instrumental accompaniment
atonal	άτονος	without a tonal center or key
baritone	βαρύτονος	1 the range of a male voice between tenor and bass a) a voice or singer with such range b) an instrument with similar range within its family, as a baritone saxophone c) a part of such a voice or instrument 3 a valved brass instrument of the saxhorn family, also: *barytone*
chord	χορδή	1 the string of the musical instrument 2 a feeling or emotion thought of as being played on like a string of a harp [to strike a sympathetic chord]

diapason	διαπασών	1 a) the entire range of a musical instrument or voice b) the entire range of some activity, emotion, etc. 2 one of the principal stops of an organ, covering the instrument's complete range and producing its characteristic tone quality 3 a swelling burst of harmony 4 a standard of musical pitch
harmony	αρμονία	1 a combination of parts into a pleasing or orderly whole; congruity 2 agreement in feeling, action, ideas, interests, etc.; 3 agreeable sounds in music 4 a) the simultaneous sounding of two or more tones, esp., when satisfying to the ear b) structure in terms of the arrangement, the study of structure *Syn.* **Symmetry**
homophone	ομόοφωνος (ομο + φωνή – same + sound/voice)	any of two or more letters or groups of letters representing the same speech sound (ex: c in civil and s in song)
hymn	ύμνος	a song in praise or honor of God 2 any song in praise or glorification
lyric	λυρικός	suitable for singing as of the accompaniment of a lyre, songlike; specif. designating poetry or a poem mainly expressing the poet's emotions and feelings: sonnets, elegies, odes, hymns, etc.

melody	μελωδία	1 a) pleasing sounds or arrangement of sounds in sequence b) musical quality, as in the arrangement of words 2 a) a sequence of single tones, usually in the same key or mode, to produce a rhythmic whole; often a tune, air, or song b) the element of form having to do with the arrangement of single tones in sequence (distinguished from *Harmony*)
monophony	μονοφωνία	having a single melody without accompaniment or harmonizing parts, as in plainsong
monotone	μονότονος	1 uninterrupted repetition of the same tone; utterance or successive syllables or words, without change of pitch or key 2 a single, unchanged musical tone
music	μουσική	the art and science of combining vocal or instrumental sounds or tones in varying melody, harmony, rhythm, and timbre, esp., so as to form structurally complete and emotionally expressive compositions
orchestra	ορχήστρα	1 in ancient Greek theaters the semicircular space in front of the stage, used by the chorus 2 in modern theaters, the area in front of the stage and below the stage, where the mucisians sit: in full orchestra pit

organ	όργανον /o	a church organ; 1 a) a large wind instrument consisting of various sets of pipes which, as they are opened by corresponding keys on one or more keyboards, allow passage to a column of compressed air that causes sound by vibration b) any of several musical instruments producing similar or somewhat similar sounds
polyphony	πολυφωνία	1 multiplicity of sounds, as in an echo 2 a combining of a number of independent but harmonizing melodies, as in a fugue or canon; counterpoint
rhapsody	ραψωδία	in music: an instrumental composition of free, irregular form, suggesting improvisation
symphony	σύμφωνία	1 harmony of sounds, esp., instruments 2 a) in music: an extended composition for full orchestra, usually having several movements b) an instrumental passage in a composition that is largely vocal or choral c) short for *Symphony Orchestra*
symphony	συμφωνική ορχήστρα	Symphony orchestra
tone	τόνος	in music: a) a vocal or musical sound b) its quality
tritone	τρίτονος	an interval of three whole tones
xylophone	ξυλόφωνον/o	a musical percussion instrument consisting of a series of wooden bars graduated in length so as to sound the notes of the scale when struck with mallets

| zither | κιθάρα | lute; any of a family of musical instruments with strings stretched across a flat soundboard and plucked, bowed, struck with mallets, etc. as the dulcimer, koto, psaltery, etc. 2 a folk instrument of this type of Austria and S Germany |

12 MYTHOLOGY

Acheron	Αχέρων	Gr. and Rom. myth. a river in Hades: often identified as the river across which Charon ferries the dead
Adonis	Άδωνις	a handsome young man loved by Aphrodite, who was killed by a wild boar
Aegeus	Αιγεύς/ Αιγέας	a king of Athens who jumped in the sea and drowned, when he thought his son, Theseus, had been killed by the Minotaur, it is said: the Aegean Sea was named after him
Aegistus	Αίγιστος	the son of Thyestes and lover of Clytemnystra
Aelolus	Αίολος	1 god of the winds 2 a king of Thessaly and the legendary forefather of the Aeolians
Agamemnon	Αγαμέμνων/ Αγαμέμνονας	king of Mycenae and commander-in-chief of the Greek army in the Trojan War, was killed by wife Clytemnystra and her lover
Aglaia	Αγλαϊα	brightness; Brilliance, one of the three Graces
Alcestis	Άλκηστις	the wife of Admetus, king of Thessaly, who sacrificed herself to save her husband's life
Ambrosia	αμβροσία	the food of the gods

Amphitryon	Αμφιτρύων	a king of Thebes and the husband of Alcmene
Andromache	Ανδρομάχη	the wife of Hector
Aphrodite	Αφροδίτη	the goddess of love and beauty
Apollo	Απόλλων	the god of music, poetry, prophecy, and medicine, represented as exemplifying manly youth and beauty
Ares	Άρης	the god of war; son of Zeus and Hera
Argonauts	Αργοναύτες	any of the men who sailed with Jason to search for the Golden Fleece
Ariadne	Αριάδνη	King Minos's daughter, who helped Thesseus, by giving him the thread, to find his way out of the Labyrinth
Artemis	Άρτεμις	the goddess of the moon, wild animals, and hunting, twin sister of Apollo
Aschlepius	Ασκληπιός	the god of healing and medicine
Athena	Αθηνά	the goddess of wisdom, skills, and warfare, also Athene
Atlas	Άτλας	a Titan compelled to support the heavens on his shoulders
Calliope	Καλλιόπη	the beautiful-voiced, the muse of eloquence and epic poetry
Calypso	Καλυψώ	a sea nymph who keeps Odysseus on her island for seven years, according to Homer's *Odyssey*
Cassandra	Κασσάνδρα	the daughter of Priam and Hecuba: in order to win her love, Apollo gives her prophetic power, when thwarted, however, decrees that no one should believe her prophesies
Castor	Κάστωρ/Καστορας	Gr. and Rom. myth. Dioscuri: Castor the mortal twin of Pollux/ Polydeuces /Πολυδεύκης

Cecrops	Κέκρωψ / Κέκροπας	the first king of Attica and founder of Athens, represented as half man and half dragon
Centaur	Κένταυρος	any of a race of monsters with a man's head, trunk, and arms, and a horse's body and legs
chaos	χάος	the disorder of formless matter and infinite space, supposedly to have existed before the ordered universe
Charites (Euphrosyne, Aghlaia, Thalia)	Χάριτες (Ευφροσύνη, Αγλαΐα, Θάλεια):	also known as the three Graces
Charon	Χάρων/Χάροντας	the boatman who ferries souls of the dead across the river Styx to Hades
Daedalus	Δαίδαλος	lit. the artful craftsman; the skillful artist who built the Labyrinth in Crete, and since he was forbidden to leave the island, he, by means of wings he had made, and his son Icarus escaped: see Icarus
Daphne	Δάφνη	a nymph who is changed into a laurel tree to escape Apollo's advances
Demeter	Δήμητρα	the goddess of agriculture and fertility
Deucalion	Δευκαλίων/ Δευκαλίονας	a son of Prometheus: he and his wife Pyrrha were the only survivors of a great flood sent by Zeus
Dionysus/Dionysos	Διόνυσος	the god of wine and revelry
Dioscuri (Castor & Polydeuces/ Pollux Διόκουροι)	Κάστωρ & Πολυδεύκης lit. sons of Zeus (Διός (gen.) of Ζεύς + κουροι/ sons)	twins sons of Zeus and Leda
Dryads	Δρυάδες (pl.)/ Δρυς (sing.)	any of the nymphs in trees; a wood nymph (drys-oak tree)

Echo	Ηχώ	a nymph who, because Narcissus does not return her love, pines away until only her voice remains
Eos	Ηώ /ηούς (gen,)	the goddess of dawn
Erechtheus	Ερεχθεύς / Ερέχθειος	a king of Athens supposedly entombed at the Erechtheum, the temple on the Acropolis
Erinyes	Ερινύες	the Furies
Eris	Έρις /Έριδα	the goddess of strife and discord
Eros	Έρως /έρωτας	the god of love, son of Aphrodite
Eumenides	Ευμηνίδης ευ + μένος eu + mind/temper)	lit. the gracious ones; gracious the mind, temper: the propitiatory euphemism { FURIES}
Europa	Ευρώπη	a Phoenician princess, who was loved by Zeus: he disguised as a white bull, carries her off across the sea to Crete
Eurydice	Ευρυδίκη	the wife of Orpheus
Gaia	Γαία /γη	a goddess who is the personification of the earth, the mother of the Titans
Galatea	Γαλάτεια	a statue of a maiden who was given life by Aphrodite after its sculptor, Pygmalion, falls in love with it
Gorgon	Γοργών /γοργόνα	any of three sisters with snakes for hair, so horrible that the beholder turned to stone
Harnonia	Αρμονία	the daughter of Aphrodite and Ares and wife of Cadmus; personification of harmony and order
Harpies	Άρπυΐες	any of several hideous, filthy, rapacious winged monsters with the head and trunk of a woman and the tail, legs, and talons of a bird

Hebe	Ήβη	the goddess of youth, daughter of Zeus and Hera: she is the cupbearer to the gods
Hephestus	Ήφαιστος	the god of fire and forge, son of Zeus and Hera
Hercules	Ηρακλής	the son of Zeus and Alcmene, renowned for his strength and courage, esp., as shown in his performance of twelve labors imposed on him
Hesperides	Εσπερίδες	the nymphs who guard the golden apples, given as a wedding gift, to Hera by Gaea
Hygeia	Υγεία	the goddess of health
Hypnos	Ύπνος	the god of sleep
Icarus	Ίκαρος	the sun of Daedalus, flying from Crete, with wings that his father had made, went too close to the sun, the wax, which fastened them, melts and he falls to his death (it is believed that the Icarian Sea was named after him)
Irene	Ειρήνη	the goddess of peace, daughter of Zeus and Themis
Iris´	Ίρις /ίριδα	the goddess of the rainbow; in the Iliad she is the messenger of the gods
Jason	Ιάσων/Ιάσονας	a healer; the prince who led the Argonauts, and, with Medea's help, gets the Golden Fleece
Leto	Λητώ	the mother of Apollo and Artemis
Medousa	Μέδουσα	one of the Gorgon monsters, a woman's body with snakes for hair, whoever looked at her turned to stone
Mentor	Μέντωρ/μέντορας	lit. an adviser; the loyal friend of Odysseus, and teacher of his son, Telemachus

Minotaur	Μινώταυρος	a monster with the body of a man and the head of a bull (in some versions it's the other way around: body of a bull and head of a man), confined by King Minos in the Labyrinth, built by Daedalus
Morpheus	Μορφεύς/Μορφέας	the god of dreams, the son of Hypnos/sleep
Muses (9)	Μούσες	Muses, the nine goddesses who preside over literature, the arts and sciences:
Clio, Euterpe, Thalia, Melpomene, Terpsichore, Erato, Polymnia, Urania, Calliope	Κλειώ. Ευτέρπη, Θάλεια, Μελπομένη, Τερψιχόρη, Ερατώ, Πολύμνια, Ουρανία, Καλλιόπη	
Nike	Νίκη	the winged goddess of victory
Nymphs	νύμφες	any of minor nature goddesses, represented as young beautiful and living in rivers, mountains, or trees; nymph/νύμφη/νύφη: a beautiful young woman; a bride
Nyx	Νυξ /νυκτός (gen.)/ νύκτα (Mod. Gr.)	night; the goddess of night
Olympus	Όλυμπος	the home of the gods; Mt. Olympus
Orpheus	Ορφεύς/Ορφέας	a poet-musician with magic musical powers, who descends to the underworld to lead his wife, Eurydice, back to the living, but failed because he broke the injuction not to look at her until they reach the upper world

Pandora	Πανδώρα	the first mortal woman: she let her curiosity take over and opened a box and released all the ills of the world (another version has it that all human blessings escaped and were lost, except: hope)
Phoebe	Φοίβη	Artemis as goddess of the moon; the moon personified
Phoebus	Φοίβος	Apollo as god of the sun; the sun personified
Pluto	Πλούτων	the god ruling over Hades
Prometheus	Προμηθεύς / Προμηθέας	the Titan who stole the secret of the fire from the gods to benefit mankind: Zeus punished him by chaining him to a rock where a vulture was eating his liver during the day which grew back each night and his torture never ended
Pygmalion	Πυγμαλίων	a king of Cyprus and sculptor: see Galatea
satyr	σάτυρ/σάτυρος	any of a class of minor woodland deities, attendant at the festivities of Dionysos or Bachus, usually represented as having pointed ears, short horns, the head and body of a man, and the legs of a goat, and as being fond of riotous merriment and lechery; a lusful or lecherous man
Uranos	Ουρανός	a god who is the personification of the heavens, the son and husband of Gaea and father of the Titans, Furies, and Cyclopes: he was overthrown by his son, Cronus/ Saturn
Zephyrus	Ζέφυρος	a god as the personification of the west wind

Zeus	Ζευς	the father of the twelve main gods, the chief deity; son of Cronus and Rhea, and husband of Hera

13 NUMBERS

1	hen/one	εις /εν (pur. Gr.)/ ένας / ένα (mod. Gr.)	(henotheistic - one believing in one God or god) or (hendia-dys meaning: one of two; a figure of speech in which two nouns joined by "and" are used instead of a noun and a modifier (ex: deceit and words for deceitful words)
	monad	μονάς / μοννάδος (gen.)	one unit
2	dyo- or dio- (prefix)/ two	δύο	(diarchy or diarchy/ rule by 2 people or parties)
	dyad	δυάς/ δυάδος / δυάδα	two units, regarded as one; pair
3	tri- (prefix) /three	τρεις /τρία	(trilogy; triangle)
	triad	τριάς (τριάδα)	a group of three people; things; ideas, etc.
4	tettares – or tesseres – (prefix /four)	τέσσερα	tetra- combining form [tetrachord]
	tetrad	(τετράς 'τετράδος (gen) τετράς / τετράδα	a group or set of four [tetravalent / having four valences/ capacities]
5	pent- penta- (prefix) / five	πέντε	combining form [Pentecost; pentagon]
	pentad	(πεντάς /πεντάδα	a group or set of five; a five-year period [pentathlon]
6	hex-hexa (prefix) –six	έξι	[hexagon] a plane figure with six angles
	hexad	εξάς / εξάδα	a series, group or set of six [Hexapla]

7	hept- hepta/ seven	επτά	combining form [heptagon]
	heptad	επτάς /επτάδα	a series, group or set of seven [heptamerous - having seven parts]
8	octo- eight	οκτώ	[octameter: a line of verse containing eight metrical feet or measures]
	octad	οκτάς /οκτάδα	a series or group of eight [octachord: any eight-stringed musical instrument]
9	ennea-nine	εννέα	combining form [enneamerous: having nine parts]
	ennead	εννεάς(εννεάδος / εννιάδα)	a series or group of nine [books; gods,etc.]
10	deca- ten	δέκα	combining form (Decalogue / Ten Commandments]
	Decad-	δεκα /δεκάδα	series or group of ten [Decameron: Boccaccio's collection of a hundred days, relating the stories of being away for ten days, during a plague]
11	hendeca/ eleven	ένδεκα	combining form eleven [hendecasyllabic: having eleven syllables]
	hendeca-	ενδεκάς /ενδεκάδα	a series or group of eleven [hendecagon/a plane figure with eleven angles and eleven sides]
12	dodec- twelve	δώδεκα	combining form [dodecaphonic: twelve voices]
	dodeca-	δοδεκάς / δωδεκάδα	a series or group of twelve [Dodecanese: twelve islands]
20	icosi /twenty	είκοσι	combining form twenty [icosahedrons: a solid figure with twenty plane surfaces]
100	hecto- / hundred	εκατόν /ό	combining form one hundred [hectoliter/a hundred liters]
	hect-		**combining form a hundred before a vowel [hecatomb:** any great sacrifice to the gods; hecaton + bous /ox]

| 1000 | chilia /
thousand | χίλια | combining form chilia- thousand
[chiliarch: anc. Gr. military
commaner of a tousand men] |
| | chiliad | χιλιάς /χιλιάδα | a thousand years [chiliasm /
χιλιασμός: the belief in the
coming of the millennium] |

14 PHYSICS

Aerodynamics	αεροδυναμική	the branch of aeromechanics concerned with the forces (resistance, preesure, etc.) exerted by air or other gases in motion
aeromechanics	αερομηχανική	the branch of mechanics dealing with air or other gases in motion or equilibrium: it includes aerodynamics and aerostatics
antineutron	αντινετρόνιον/ο	the antiparticle of the neutron, but with a positive magnetic moment (the neutron has a negative magnetic moment)
aperiodic	απεριοδικός	without periodic vibrations; irregular occurrence
astatic	αστατικός	unstable; unsteady; in Physics: not taking a definite position or direction [as an astatic needle]
astrophysics	αστροφυσική	the main branch of astronomy concerned primarily with the physical properties of the universe, including luminocity, density, temperatures and chemical composition

atom	άτομον/ο	uncut; any of the smallest particles of an element which combined with similar particles of other elements to produce compounds: atoms combine to form molecules, and consist of a complex arrangement of electrons revolving about a positively charged nucleus containing (except of hydrogen) protons, neutrons, and other particles
atomic energy	ατομική ενέργεια	nuclear energy
ballistics	βαλλιστική (βάλλειν- to throw)	the science concerned with the motion and impact of projectiles, such as bullets, rockets, bombs, etc.
barometer	βαρόμετρον	an instrument for measuring atmospheric pressure, esp., an aneroid barometer or an evacuated and graduated glass tube *(mercury barometer)*
deuteron	δεύτερον/ο	the nucleus of an atom of deuterium containing one proton and one neutron
diathermancy	διαθέρμανσις /η	the property of transmitting infrared or heat rays
electrode	ηλεκτρόδιον/ο	any terminal that conducts an electric current into or away from various conducting substances in a circuit, as the anode or cathode in a battery, or the carbons in an arc lamp, or that emits, collects, or controls the flow of electrons in an electron tube, as the cathode, plate or grid
electrodynamics	ηλεκτροδυναμική	the branch of physics concerned with the phenomena of electric currents and associated magnetic forces

electromagnetism	ηλεκτρομαγνητισμός	1 the magnetism produced by an electric current 2 the branch of physics dealing with electricity and magnetism
electrolysis	ηλεκτρόλυσις /η	the decomposition of an electrolyte by the action of an electric current passing through
electron	ηλεκτρόνιον/ο	an elementary particle of a charge of negative electricity *(chek the number,...)*
electronics	ηλεκτρονική	the science dealing with the behavior and control of of electrons in vacuums and gases, and with the use of electron tubes, photoelectric cells, transmitors, etc.
energy	ενέργεια	1 in physics: the capacity of doing work; 2 strength of power efficiently exerted 3 the resources, as petroleum, coal, gas, wind, nuclear fuel, and sunlight, from which energy in the form of electricity, heat, etc., could be produced
gyroscope	γυροσκόπιον/ο	a wheel mounted in a set of rings so that its axis of rotation is free to turn in any direction: when the wheel is spun rapidly, it will keep the original direction of its rotation axis no matter which way the ring is turned (used in gyrocompass and to keep moving ships, airplanes, etc.)
hydroelectric	υδροηλεκτρικός	producing, or having to do with the production of, electricity by water power
hydrokinesis	υδροκινητική	the branch of physics having to do with fluids in motion
hydromechanics	υδρο-μηχανολογία	the branch of physics dealing with the laws governing the motion and equilibrium of fluids

hygrometer	υγρόμετρον/o	any of various devices of measuring the absolute or relative amount of humidity of the atmosphere
hydrology	υδρολογία	the science concerned with the qualities of the earth's waters, the distribution on the surface and underground, and the cycle involving evaporation, precipitation, flow to the seas, etc.
kinetic energy	κινητική ενέργεια	the energy of a body resulting from its motion
kymograph	κυμογράφος (κύμα / wave)	an apparatus consisting of a rotating drum for recording wavelike motions, variations, or modulations, such as contractions
magnet	μαγνήτης	any piece of certain kind of material: as iron, that has the property of attracting like material: this property might be permanent or temporary induced
magnetic	μαγνητικός	1 having the properties of a magnet 2 of the earth's magnetism [the magnetic poles]
magnetometer	μαγνητόμετρον/o	1 an instrument for measuring magnetic forces, esp., the earth's magnetic fields 2 an instrument for detecting the presence of magnetic materials by their influence upon the local magnetic field
mass	μάζα	the quantity of matter in a body, as measured by its inertia; the ratio of force: experimentally it is found that the gravitational force on an object is proportional to its mass; of, Matter

mechanics	μηχανική	the branch of physics concerned with the motion of material bodies and the phenomena of the action of forces on bodies,: cf. **Statics; Dynamics; Kinematics**
metal	μέταλλον /o	1 a) any of a class of chemicals elements, as iron, gold, or aluminum, generally characterized by ductility, malleability, luster, and conductivity of heat and electricity
photoelectricity	φωτοηλεκτρισμός	the property shown by certain transparent solids, esp., glass and plastics, of producing double refraction when put under tension or compression, thus permitting stress analysis of models of parts
photon	φωτόνιον/o	a quantum of electromagnetic energy having both particle and wave properties: it has no charge or mass, but possesses momentum and energy
physics	φυσική	1 a natural philosophy 2 a) the science dealing with the properties, changes, interactions, etc., of matter and energy in which energy is considered to be continuous (*classical physics*), including electricity, heat, optics, mechanics, etc., now also is concerned with the atomic scale of nature in which, in this case, is considered to be discrete (*quantum physics*), including such branches as atomic, nuclear, and solid-state physics b) a specific system of physics

proton	πρωτόνιον (πρώτον (neu.) of πρώτος – first)	an elementary particle found in nucleus of all atoms and comprises the atomic nucleus of protium isotope of hydrogen
static	στατικός	causing to stand; 1 of bodies, masses, or forces at rest or equilibrium: opposed to **Dynamic** 2 not moving or progressing, at rest; inactive; stationary
thermodynamics	θερμοδυναμική	the branch of physics concerned with the transformation of heat to and from other forms of energy, and with the laws governing such conversions of energy

15 POLITICS

anarchy	αναρχία	the complete absence of government; political disorder and violence; lawlessness
antidemocracy	αντιδημοκρατία (αντί + δημοκρατία- against + democracy)	opposed to a democratic form of government
apolitical	απολιτικός	totally unconcerned with politics or political issues
aristocracy	αριστοκρατία	government by a priviliged minority or upper class, usually of inherited wealth and social position; a country with such government; oligarchy
autocracy	αυτοκρατία	a government in which one person has absolute authority and power; despotism; dictatorship
democracy	δημοκρατία	majority rule; government elected by the people

democrat	δημοκράτης	an advocate of government by the people
democratization	δημοκρατικοποίησις/η	the introduction and establishing of a democratic form of government
despotic	δεσποτικός, ή, ό (adj.)	autocratic; tyrannical; an absolute ruler
diplomacy	διπλωματία	the skill of conducting official business among nations; diplomatic relations
diplomat	διπλωμάτης	a representative of a government conducting official business with representatives of other governments or nations; one who practices or uses diplomacy
dyarchia	δυαρχία	government shared by two people or two parties
economy	οικονομία	management of a household or state/country; public revenue
enthrone	ενθρονίζειν/ ενθρονίζω	to make a king or a bishop; to put someone on a throne
ethnicity	εθνικότητα	ethnic classification or affiliation; nationality
gerontocracy	γεροντοκρατία	government by elders; governing body of old men
hegemony	ηγεμονία	leadership or dominance, esp., that of one nation or state over others
heptarchy	επταρχία	government by seven people; seven rulers
hierocracy	ιεροκρατία	government by the clergy; priests; ministers, etc. ; a hierarchy
ideology	ιδεολογία	1 the study of ideas, their nature and source 2 the doctrines, opinions, or way of thinking of an individual, a group, a party, a class, etc.; specif. the body of ideas on which a certain political, economic, religious, or social system is based

isocracy	ισοκρατία	a system of government in which all persons involved have equal power
monarch	μονάρχης	1 the one and only ruler of a state or country 2 a hereditary (usually constitutional) head of state; king, queen, etc.
monarchy	μοναρχία	1 rule by only one person (very rare now) 2 a government or state headed by a monarch: called absolute when there are no limitations on the monarch's power, and constitutional when there are limitations
ochlocracy	οχλοκρατία (όχλος – a mob; populace)	government by a mob; ruled by a mob
oligarchy	ολιγαρχία	government by few people; ruled by few
political asylum	πολιτικο(ν) άσυλο(ν)	the protection given to refugees from another country
political system	πολιτικό(ν) σύστημα	a set of facts, principles, rules, organization, and, a methodical planning of procedures, governing politics or government
politics	πολιτική	the science and art of political government; political science
plutocracy	πλουτοκρατία (πλούτος - wealth)	a government by the wealthy; ruled by few affluent people
technocracy	τεχνοκρατία	government by technicians; specif., the theory or doctrine of a proposed system of government in which all economic resources, and by inference the entire social system, would be controlled by scientists and engineers
theocracy	θεοκρατία	lit. the rule of a state by a God or god; government by a person or persons claiming that they rule with divine authority

| Theology | Θεολογία | the study of religious doctrines and matters of divinity; specif. the study of God and the relation between God, mankind and the universe |
| theomachy | θεομαχία (θεός + μάχη – god + battle) | 1 battle against the gods 2 battle among the gods |

16 SCIENCE / SCIENTIFIC RESEARCH AND OTHER STUDIES

Aerodynamics	αεροδυναμική	the branch of aeromechanics dealing with the forces (resistance, pressure, etc.) exerted by air or other gases in motion
aerology	αερολογία	the branch of meteorology concerned with the study of air, esp., in the upper atmosphere
aetiology/ etiology	αιτιολογία	1 the science of causes or origins 2 a) the science of origin of a disease or a specific disease
agrology	αγρολογία	the science of agricultural production
agronomics	αγρονομική/ αγρονομία	the science and economics of crop production; management of farmland
amphibiology	αμφιβιολογία	a branch of zoology concerned with amphibians: those that live in both land or water
anatomy	ανατομία	1 the science of the morphology or structure, of animals or plants 2 the structure of an organism or body 3 a detailed analysis
anemology	ανεμολογία (άνεμος – wind)	the study of winds

anthropology	ανθρωπολογία	the study of humans, esp., of the variety, physical and cultural characteristics, distribution, customs, social relationships, etc., of humanity
anthropometry	ανθρωπομετρία	a branch of anthropology concerned with the measurement of the human body to determine differences in individuals, groups, etc, it is used in medicine, space programs, archaeology, etc.
archaeology	αρχαιλογία	the scientific study of the life and culture of past, esp., ancient, peoples, as of excavation of ancient cities, artifacts, etc.
arithmetic	αριθμητική	the science or art of computing by positive, real numbers, specif. by adding, subtracting, multiplying, and dividing
astrology	αστρολογία	primitive astronomy; the pseudoscience based on the notion that the positions of the moon, sun, and stars affect human lives, that one can forsee the future by studying the stars, etc.
astronautics	αστρονομική	the science concerned with spacecraft and with travel in outer space, esp., to the moon and other planets
astronomy	αστρονομία	the science of the universe in which the stars, planets, etc., are studied, including their origins, evolution, composition, motions, relative positions, sizes, etc.
athleticism	αθλητισμός	an athletic quality; the entirety of physical activities, and the organization of the system of physical exercise

bacteriology	βακτηριολογία	the study of bacteria, either as a branch of medicine or as a science, important in food processing, agriculture, industry, etc.
biology	βιολογία	the science concened with the origin, history, physical characteristics, life processes, habits, etc. of plants and animals; it includes botany and zoology
biophysics	βιοφυσική	the study of biological phenomena using the principles and techniques of physics
botany	βοτανική	the branch of biology dealing with plants, their life structure, growth, classification, etc.
chemistry	χημεία	the science dealing with the composition, structure, and properties of substances and of the transformations they undergo
climatology	κλιματολογία	the science concerned with the climate and climatic or weather phenomena
chronometry	χρονομετρία	the scientific measurement of time
cosmology	κοσμολογία	1 the scientific study of the form, content, organization, and evolution of the universe 2 the branch of metaphysics concerned with the origin and structure of the universe
craniology	κρανιολογία	the scientific study of skulls, esp., human skulls, and their characteristics, as the difference in size, shape, etc.
cryogenics	κρυογονική	the branch of physics concerned with the production of very low temperatures and their effect on the properties of matter

cytology	κυτταρολογία	the branch of biology concerned with the structure, function, multiplication, pathology, and life history of cells
deontology	δεοντολογία	the ethical doctrine which consists of rules that regulate the manner, and esp., the behavior and proper methods of professional duties (doctors, lawyers, journalists, etc.)
dermatology	δερματολογία	the branch of medicine which deals with the skin and its diseases
dietetics	διαιτητική	the science or art of applying the principles of nutrition and studying the type and quantities of food needed for good health
dynamics	δυναμική	a branch of mechanics dealing with forces and their relation, mainly to the motion, sometimes also, to the equilibrium of bodies
ecclesiology	εκκλησιολογία	the study of church architecture; art, iconography, sacred items necessary for the services and sacraments, etc.
ecology	οικολογία	the branch of biology concerned with the relation between living organisms and their environment
electrochemistry	ηλεκτροχημεία	the chemistry dealing with the use of electrical energy in order to bring a chemical reaction, or with the generation of electrical energy through a chemical action

epistemology	επιστημολογία	1 the scientific study of science itself: the object of research and study is the exact definition of the research centers or fields and of the methodological tools 2 the study or the theory of nature, sources, and the limits of knowledge
ethics	ηθική / ήθος	1 the study of standards of conduct and moral judgment; moral and ethical philosophy 2 the system or code of moral behavior of an individual, group, religion, or profession, etc.
ethnology	εθνολογία	the scientific study that researches the structure, evolution, cultural of various nations, esp. of small primitive groups 2 in Biol. the study of the characteristic behavior patterns of animals
gastronomy	γαστρονομία	the art or science of good eating; the careful selection of ingredients and preparation of meals aiming to be tasty and appetizing
geography	γεωγραφία	the science dealing with the surface of the earth, its continents and countries, in addition, examining the climate, plants, animals, inhabitants, natural resources, industries, etc.
geology	γεωλογία	the science concerned with the physical nature and history of the earth, including the structure and development of the crust, the composition of its interior, the various forms of life (as fossils) etc.

geometry	γεωμετρία	the branch of mathematics concerned with points, lines, planes, and figures, also examining their properties, measurements, and mutual relation in space
grammar	γραμματική	lit. something written; 1 the part of the study of language dealing with the forms and structure of words (morphology), their usual arrangement in phrases and sentences (syntax), also in recent years with language sounds (phonology) and word meanings (semantics)
graphology	γραφολογία	the study of handwriting, esp., an indication to character, aptitudes, etc.
glossology	γλωσσολογία	the study of a language; the term "glossology," or "glossotology," was used until the nineteenth cen. after that, the term "linguistics" prevailed
hermeneutics	ερμηνευτική	the art or science of the interpretation of literature
herpetology	ερπετολογία	the branch of zoology concerned with the study of reptiles and amphibians
histology	ιστολογία	the branch of biology dealing with the microscopic study of the structure of tissues
homeopathy	ομοιοπαθητική	a system of medical treatment based in the theory that certain diseases can be treated and cured by treating the patient with small doses of drugs which in healthy persons could produce the same or similar symptoms of those of the disease; cf. *Allopathy*

hymnology	υμνολογία	1 the study of hymns: their origin, history, use, etc. 2 the writing and composition of hymns
hypnotherapy	υπνοθεραπεία	a treatment of a disease by hypnotism
lexicography	λεξικογραφία	the act, art, work, or process of researching, writing, or compiling a dictionary
lexicology	λεξικολογία	the study, origin and meaning of words
limnology	λιμνολογία (λίμνη- lake)	the scientific study dealing with the physical, chemical, biological properties and features of fresh waters, esp., lakes and ponds
logic	λογική	the science of reasoning; science describing relationships among propositions in terms of implication, contradiction, contrariety, conversion, etc.
mathematics	μαθηματικά	a group of sciences (including arithmetic. geometry, algebra, calculus, etc., concerned with quantities, magnitudes, forms, and ther relationship, attributes, etc. by the use of numbers, shapes, and symbols
metallurgy	μεταλλουργία	the science of metals, esp., the one dealing with separating the metals from their ores and preparing them for use, by smelting, forming, refining, etc.

metaphysics	μεταφυσική	the branch of philosophy concerned with the principles and is looking to define the nature of being or reality (ontology) and of the origin and structure of the universe (cosmology): it is closely associated with the scientific study of the nature of knowledge (epistemology)
metapsychology	μεταψυχολογία	speculation about the origin, structure, function, etc., of the mind and the relation among the mental and the physical, regarded as supplemental to psychology
meteorology	μετερεολογία	the science of the atmosphere and atmospheric phenomena; study of the weather, incuding its forecasting
methodology	μεθοδολογία	the science of method, the orderly arrangement; specif. the branch of logic which deals with the application of the principles of reasoning to scientific and philosophical probe and inquiries
oceanography	ωκεανογραφία	the scientific study of the environment in oceans, including the depths of the waters, beds, animals, plants, etc.
oenology/enology	οινολογία	the scientific study of wine and winemaking
oology	ωολογία	the branch of zoology dealing with the study of eggs, esp., the eggs of birds
ophiology	οφιολογία	the branch of zoology concerned with snakes
optics	οπτική	the branch of physics which deals with the nature and properties of light and vision

optometry	οπτικομετρία/ οπτικομέτρησις-η	the measurement of the range and power of vision
palaeontology	παλαιοντολογία	the branch of geology dealing with life forms from the past, esp., prehistoric
pedagogics	παιδαγωγική	the function or profession of an educator; teaching 2 the art or science of teaching
photochemistry	φωτοχημεία	the branch of chemistry concerned with the effect of light or other radiant energy, in producing chemical action, as in photography
physiography	φυσιογραφία	a description of the features and phenomena of nature
psephology	ψηφολογία (ψήφος – vote)	the statistical evaluation of election returns or of political polls
pteridology	πτεριδολογία (πτέρις /πτέριδος (gen.) – fern/ featherlike)	the branch of botany which deals with ferns
rhetoric	ρητορική/ρητορία	1 the art of using words effectively in speaking or writing; the art of prose composition 2 artificial eloquence; showy and flowery language but lacking substance and clear ideas
rhythmics	ρυθμική	science or system of rhythm and rhythmical forms; rhythmic quality
seismology	σεισμολογία (σεισμός- earthquake)	a geophysical science concentrating on earthquakes and related phenomena
selenography	σεληνογραφία (σελήνη – moon)	the study of the surface and physical features of the moon, esp., the mapping of the latitude and longitude
sitology	σιτολογία	the study of foods, their value, nutrition, and the proper diet; dietetics

soteriology	σωτηριολογία (σωτηρία – salvation; Σωτήρ (ας) –Savior)	the scientific study of theology of the divine salvation of humanity, specif. in Christian theology, study of this as effected through Jesus Christ
speleology	σπηλαιολογία	the scientific study and exploration of caves
stoichiometry	στοιχειομετρία (στοιχείον/ο – element, a first principle)	the branch of chemistry concerned with the relationship of elements entering into and resulting from combination, esp. quantitative relationship
strategy	στρατηγική	the science of planning and directing large-scale military operations
teratology	τερατολογία	the branch of biology studying the biological monstrosities and malformations
topography	τοπογραφία	the science or art of drawing on maps and charts or otherwise representing the surface features of a region, including its relief also rivers, lakes, etc.
zoology	ζωολογία	the branch of biology concerned with the life, structure, classification, etc., of animals; the animal life of an area; fauna

17 THEATER

| Amphitheater | αμφιθέατρον/ ο | a round or oval building with an open space (arena) surrounded by rising rows of seats |
| catharsis | κάθαρσις /η | the purifying of the emotions or relieving of emotional tensions, esp., by art; concept applied originally by Aristotle to the effect of tragic drama on the audience |

character	χαρακτήρ/ χαρακτήρος (gen.)/ χαρακτήρας (Mod. Gr.)	a distinctive trait; a person in a play, story, book, etc.
choreography	χορογραφία	the arrangement or the written notation of movements of a dance, esp., a ballet
chorus	χορός	1 in ancient Greek drama, and similar drama, a group of performers whose singing, dancing, and narration provide explanation and elaboration of the main performance 2 in Elizabethan drama, a person who recites the prologue and epilogue
comedian	κωμωδός	an actor who plays comic parts 2 an entertainer who tells jokes, sings comic songs, etc.
comedy	κωμωδία	orig. a drama or narrative with a happy ending or nostalgic theme [Dante's Divine Comedy] 2 any of various types of a play or motion pictures with a humorous theme and funny characters along with a happy ending
cothurnus	κόθωρν/κόθωρνος /κόθορνος	a high, thick-soled boot or buskin worn by actors in ancient Greek and Poman tragedies
cyclorama	κυκλόραμα	a series of large pictures, as of a landscape, put on the wall of a circular room so as to appear in natural perspective to a spectator standing in the center
dialogue	διάλογος	1 talking together; conversation 2 interchange and exchange of ideas, esp., aiming to achieve mutual understanding and harmony

drama	δράμα	a literary composition that tells a story, usually of human conflict, incorporating dialogue and action, performed by actors
hamartia	αμαρτία (αμαρτάνειν – to err)	a sin; in religion the transgression of the divine and ethical laws is regarded as sin and tragic flaw
hubris/hybris	υβρις /η	insolence or arrogance, the result of extreme pride or passion
heroic drama	ηρωϊκό δράμα	a noble, powerful deed as the theme of a play
lyric drama	λυρικό δράμα	a songlike poem made into a play
melisma	μέλισμα (μελίζειν – to sing/ modulate)	sng; a succession of different notes sung upon as single, as orig. in plainsong or, today's especially, in the embellishing phrases of Near Eastern or Asian music; also melismatic
melodrama	μελοδράμα	1 orig. a sensational or romantic stage play with interspersed songs and an orchestral accompaniment 2 now, a drama, as a play or movie, dealing with exaggerated conflicts and emotions, stereotypical characters, etc.
mime	μίμος	an ancient Greek or Roman farce, in which people were mimicked and burlesqued 2 the representation of an action, character, mood, etc., by means of gestures and actions rather than words 3 an actor who performs in mimes; a mimic or pantomimist
monodrama	μονόδραμα	a drama specially written to be performed by a single actor

monologue	μονόλογος	a long speech by one speaker, esp., one monopolizing the conversation
Muse /muses (pl.)	Μούσα/μούσες	the nine goddesses who presided over literature, the arts, and the sciences: Calliope /Καλλιόπη, Clio /Κλειώ, Euterpe /Ευτέρπη, Melpomene / Μαλπομένη, Terpsichore / Τερψιχόρη, Erato/ Ερατώ, Polymnia / Πολύμνια, Urania /Ουρανία, Thalia/ Θάλεια
musical comedy	μουσικο-κωμωδία	a humorous story or satire set to music
orchestra	ορχήστρα	1 in ancient Greek theaters, the semicircular space in front of the stage used by the chorus 2 in modern theaters, in front of and below the stage, where the musicians sit: in full orchestra pit
pantomime	παντομίμα	1 in ancient times, an actor who played his part by gestures and action without speaking 2 action or gestures without words as a means of expression
proscenium	προσκήνιον /o	1 the stage of an ancient Greek or Roman theater 2 a) the apron of a stage b) the plane separating the stage proper from the audience and including the arch *(proscenium arch)* and the curtain within it *(prosciutto)*
protagonist	πρωταγωνιστής	1 the main character in a play, drama, story, or book around whom the action is centered 2 a person who plays a leading or active part

scene	σκηνή	a theater stage in ancient Greece and Rome 2 the place in which any event, real or imagined, takes place [*the scene of the crime*] 3 the setting or locale of the action of a play, opera, concert, etc.
theater or theatre	θέατρον /o	a place where plays, operas, films, etc. are presented
Thespis	Θέσπις	sixth c. BC; Gr. poet the originator of Greek tragedy (thus the term thespian - performer/ator)
tragedy	τραγωδία	a very serious play or drama, dealing with the fate and problems of the protagonist 2 the writing, performing, or theoretical principles of this type of drama

18 THEOLOGY

Agnostic	αγνωστικιστής / αγνωστικίστρια (fem.)	a person who believes that the human mind cannot possibly know if there is a God or an ultimate cause, or anything beyond human phenomena
Agnosticism	αγνωστικισμός	the doctrine of agnostics: distinguished from *Atheism*
Anabaptism	αναβαπτισμός	the doctrine of the radical sect (sixteenth cent.) of the Reformation originating in Switzerland, often persecuted because they opposed the taking of oaths, infant baptism, military service, and the holding of public office

Anathema	ανάθεμα	1 a thing or person accursed or damned or detested; 2 a) a solemn ecclesiastical condemnation of a teaching judged to be gravely opposed to accepted church doctrine or of the originators of such teachings b) the excommunication often accompanying or following such condemnation
angel	άγγελος	1 Theol. a) a messenger of God b) a super-natural being, either good or bad, to whom, greater than human power, intelligence, etc., are attributed
antichrist	αντίχριστος	1 a nonbeliever or opposed to Christ 2 Bible the great antagonist of Christ, expected to spread universal evil before the end of the world, but finally to be conquered at Chist's second coming
anticleric	αντικληρικός	opposed to clergy and to church hierarchy esp., to its influence in public affairs
aphorism	αφορισμός	1 a brief, laconic statement of a principle 2 a short, pithy sentence expressing a wise, or artful observation; a, adage; maxim 3 ecclesiatical: the most severe punishment or condemnation for someone judged as being opposed to the teachings of the religion
aphorize	αφορίζειν / αφορίζω	1 to speak in aphorisms 2 to have someone expelled from church and all the sacraments

Apocalypse	Αποκάλυψις /η	1 any of various Jewish and Christian pseudonymous writings (c. 200 BC–c. AD 300) depicting symbolically the ultimate destruction of evil and the triumph of good 2 a disclosure regarded as prophetic; revelation — [A-] the last book of the New Testament; *Book of Revelation*
Apologetics	Απολογητική	the branch of theology concerned with the defence and proof of Christianity
Apostle(s)	Απόστολος / Απόστολοι(pl.)	1 a person sent out on a special mission 2 any of the twelve disciples of Christ, sent out by him to teach the gospel 3 any of a group of early Christians
archangel	αρχάγγελος	the chief angel; an angel of high rank
archbishop	αρχιεπίσκοπος	a bishop of the highest rank
atheism	αθεϊσμός	1 the belief that there is no God, or denial that God or gods exist
atheist	αθεϊστής (α + θεός- without + god)	one who rejects all religious beliefs and denies the existence of God
baptism	βάπτισμα/ βάπτισις /η	1 a sacrament of admitting one to Christianity; one of the seven Sacraments in the Eastern Orthodox Church
Baptist	Βαπτιστής	John the Bapist; one who baptizes
baptistery	βαπτιστήριον/ο	a place, esp., of church where the Christening or baptism takes place 2 a baptismal font or tank (**κολυμβήθρα- kolymbethra**))
baptize	βαπτίζειν /βαπτίζω	to immerse an individual in water (or sprinkle one with water) as a symbol of admission nto Christianity or to a specific Christian church

Bible	Βίβλος	1 the sacred book of Christianity; Old Testament and New Testament: some Roman Catholic versions include all or part of the Apocrypha 2 the Holy Scriptures of Judaism, identical to the New Testament of Christianity
blaspheme	βλάσφημος (βλασφημείν – to speak evil of)	characterized by blasphemy
blasphemy	βλασφημία	1 contemptuous or profane language: speech, writing, or action concerning God, or anyone or anything held as sacred 2 any remark or action that is irreverent or disrespectful
catechesis	κατήχησις /η (κατηχείν – to instruct)	religious instruction; oral instruction
catholic	καθολικός	1 of general scope or value; universal; all-inclusive 2 broad in sympathy, tastes, or understanding 3 of any of the orthodox Christian churches (e,.g., the Roman, Greek Orthodox, Anglo-Saxon, etc.), as distinguished from the Reformed or Protestant churches; 3 a member of the Catholic church
Catholicism	Καθολικισμός	the doctrine, faith, practice, and organization of a Catholic church esp., of the Roman Catholic Church
chiliasm	χιλιασμός (χίλια – a thousand)	belief in the coming of the millenium
chrism	χρίσμα	1 consecrated oil used in baptisms and other sacraments 2 a sacramental anointing wih the consecrated oil

Christ	Χριστός	1 the Messiah whose coming is prophesied in the Old Testament 2 Jesus of Nazareth, regarded by Christians as the realization of the Messianic prophecy: orig. titled *(Jesus the Christ)*, later used as part of the name *(Jesus Christ)*
Christianity	Χριστιανισμός / Χριστιανοσύνη	1 the Christian religion, based on the New Testament 2 the Christians collectively; 3 a particular Christian religious system; the Christian world
church /ecclesia	κυριακή (Κυρίου οικία- Lord's house) /εκκλησία	a building set apart or consecrated for public worship, esp., one for Christian worship
cleric	κληρικός	person ordained for religious service; priest, minister, rabbi, etc.
clergy	κληρικοί	relating to clerics collectively
demon or daemon	δαίμων/ δαίμονος (gen.)/δαίμονας (Mod. Gr.)	1 a devil; evil spirit 2 a person or thing regarded as evil, cruel, etc. *[the demon of jealoucy]* 3 a person of great skill or aptitude [a demon in math], etc.
Deuteronomy	Δευτερονόμιον	the fifth book of the Pentateuch in the Bible, in which the law of Moses is set down in full for the second time: abbrev: Deut, De, or Dt
devil	διάβολος	the chief evil spirit, a supernatural being subordinate to, and foe of, God and the tempter of human beings; Satan; any evil spirit; demon
dogma	δόγμα	1 Theol. a doctrine or body of doctrines formally and authoritatively affirmed 2 a doctrine, tenet; belief, all three collectively 3 a positive, arrogant assertion of opinion

ecclesia	εκκλησία	assembly; 1 Ecclec. a) members of a church; a church building
ecclesiology	εκκλησιολογία	the study of church architecture, art, etc.
Epiphany	Επιφάνεια	an appearance or manifestation of God or other supernatural being 2 in many Christian churches, including the Greek Orthodox Church, an annual celebration held January 6, commemorating both the revealing of Jesus as the Christ to Gentiles in the persons of the Magi and the baptism of Jesus; also called the *Twelfth Day*
Epistle	Επιστολή	1 a) any of the letters in the New Testament written by an Apostle b) a selection, usually from these Epistles, read in various churches
Eucarist	Ευχαριστία (thanks, gratitude)	1 Holy Communion; the consecrated bread and wine (representing the body and blood of Christ), used in the Holy Communion
eulogia	ευλογία	blessing; 1 orig. the Eucarist 2 bread blessed but not consecrated and given to the congregation at the end of services,
eulogy	ευλογία (ευλογείν- to speak well of, to bless)	1 speech or writing in praise of a person, event, or thing, esp. a formal speech praising a person who has died 2 high praise; commendation

evangelism	ευαγγελισμός	1 a zealous effort to spread the gospel, as in revival gatherings or by televised services; preaching the gospel 2 any relentless effort in propagandizing for a cause; also (E) Ευαγγελισμός της Θεοτόκου –Annunciation of the Mother o God: Ecclec. the angel Gabriel's announcement to Mary that she was chosen togive birth to Jesus (Luke 1:26–38) commemorated on the twenty-fifth of March
Genesis	Γένεσις	the first book of the Bible, presenting an account of the Creation: abbrev. G en, Gn, or Ge
Gnosticism	Γνωστικισμός	an occult salvational system, heterodox and syncretistic, stressing gnosis as essential, viewing matter as evil, and variously combining ideas derived esp., from mythology, ancient Greek philosophy, ancient religions, and eventually, from Christianity
Hagiographa	Αγιόγραφα (άγιο + γράπτειν- sacred / holy + to wtite)	lit. writings; the third and final part of the Jewish Scriptures, those books are not in the Law nor theProphets
hagiography	αγιογραφία	1 a book or writings, or and assemblage of writings about the lives of saints, also: *Hagiology /Αγιολογία*
hegumen	ηγούμενος	the chief monk; the highest rank in monastic life
Heptateuch	Εξάπτευχος	the first seven books of the Bible

herecy	αίρεσις /η	any teaching or doctrine of a certain religion that differs from the official dogma of that religion; having beliefs that are opposed to church dogma
Hexapla	Εξαπλά	an addition having six versions arranged in parallel columns
hierarchy	ιεραρχία	1 a system of the church government by priests or other clergy in graded ranks 2 a group of persons or things arranged in order of rank, grade, class, etc.
hierocracy	ιεροκρατία	government by priests or other clergy
homoiousian	ομοιούσιος ("ομοιος + ουσία – same (like) + essence)	Theol. of or holding the teaching: of God the Father and God the Son are of a similar essence, not the same essence, this was the belief of the heretics; see **Homousian/homousios**
Homousian/ homousios	ομοούσιος, α, ο (adj.)	Theol. the word **homoousios** was introduced and used by the Fathers of the First Ecummenical Synod to express the relations of the Father and the Son within the Godhead. The Father and the Son are of the **same essence** (homousios/ ομοούσιος) and NOT of **similar essence** (homoeousios/ ομοιούσιος) as the heretics taught! It is used in the Symbol of Faith or the Creed: And in one Lord Jesus Christ… begotten, not created, of one essence with the Father, through whom all things were made
hymn	ύμνος	1 a song in praise or honor of God, or gods 2 a song expressing praise or glorification

hymnology	υμνολογία	1 the study of hymns, their origin, history, use, etc. 2 the writing or composition of hymns
icon	εικών /εικόνα	1 an image; figure; representation; 2 Eastern Orthodox Church an image of Christ, Mary, saints, etc., venerated as sacred
iconoclasm	εικονοκλασία	opposing the religious use of images and or avocating the destruction of those images
iconostasis	εικόνοστάσιον /ο	Eastern Orthodox Church a partition or screen, decorated with icons
idolater	ειδωλολάτρης	1 a person who worships an idol or idols 2 a devoted admirer
Judaism	Ιουδαϊσμός	1 the Jewish religion, a monotheistic religion based on the laws and teachings of the Holy Scriptures and the Talmud 2 the Jewish way of life; observance of Jewish morality, traditions, celebrations, etc. 3 Judaism collectively
kerygma	κήρυγμα (a herald-κηρύσσεν – to preach, proclaim)	Christian Theol. 1 preaching of the Gospel, emphasizing the essence and the spirit of the Gospel 2 as in preaching the word of God; catechesis
kyrie eleison	Κύριε ελέησον	Lord have mercy (on us)
latria	λατρεία (λατρεύειν-to worship// serve / latris – hired servant)	a worship saved only for God alone; distinguished from *Dulia or Hyperdulia*
liturgy	λειτουργία (Θεία Λειτουργία – Divine Liturgy)	1 the Eucharist service, esp., (Divine Liturgy) in the Eastern Orthodox Church

Methodism	Μεθοδισμός	1 belief and practices of Methodists, with emphasis on personal and social responsibility and John Wesley's ideal of Christian perfection: influenced by Arminianism 2 excessive adherence to systematic adherence (from method / μεθοδος – a system; orderly process)
monastery	μονή/ μοναστήρι	a building or residence for monks, nuns, or others who have withdrawn from the world for religious reasons
monasticism	μοναχισμός	the monastic system or way of life, the way of life of monks and nuns; austere, ascetic, etc.
Monotheism	Μμονοθεϊσμός	the belief or doctrine that there is only one God
Monothelete	Μονοθελήτης	a devotee of Monothelitism, the Christian teaching, considered as heretical and was codemned by the Sixth Ecumenical Synod/ Council (680–681), according to which Jesus, although had two natures, the divine and human, had only one will (monothelism) and only one energy (monoenergism), and not two wills and two energies
Octateuch	Οκτάτευχος	the first eight books of the Old Testament
Orthodoxy	Ορθοδοξία	1 an orthodox belief, a doctrine, custom, etc. 2 the quality or fact of being orthodox: comforming to the Christian faith as formulated in the early ecumenical creeds and confessions, characteristic of any of the churches embodying the Eastern Orthodox Church

Pantheism	Πάνθεον (παν + θεος – all +god)	1 a temple for all the gods 2 a structure where famous dead persons of a nation are entombed or commemorated
patriarch	πατριάρχης	1 the highest rank in the Eastern Orthodox Church 2 the oldest person in a family or tribe
Pentateuch	Πεντάτευχος	the first five books of the Bible
Pentecost	Πεντηκοστή	1 a Christian celebration on the seventh Sunday and fifty days after the Resurrection/ Easter 2 commemorating the descent of the Holy Spirit upon the Apostles
polytheism	πολυθεϊσμός	the belief in many gods or more than one God: opposed to *Monotheism*
presbyter	πρεσβύτερος	an elder; in the Gr. Orthodoc Church is also a higher rank for a priest, and pesbytera / πρεσβυτέρα is the title for the wife of a priest
prophecy	προφητεία	1 to declare or predict (something) 2 prediction of the future under the influence of divine guidance; act or practice of a prophet 3 a book of prophecies
prophet	προφήτης	a person who speaks for God; speaking under the influence of the Holy Spirit; a religious teacher
psalm	ψαλμός	1 a sacred song or poem; hymn 2 any of the hymns praising God constituting the book of Psalms in the Bible
schism	σχίσμα	1 a split or division in an organized group or society, esp., a church 2 the act of causing or trying to cause a split or a division in a church

synaguogue	συναγωγή	1 an assembly for Jews for worship and study 2 the Jewish religion as organized in such local congregations
synod	σύνοδος	1 a) an ecclesiastical council; specif. Roman Catholic Ch a regional or international meeting of bishops b) Eastern Orthodox Ch Holy Synod 2 a high governing body in certain Christian churches.
theocracy	θεοκρατία	lit. the rule of a state by God or a god 2 government by a person or persons claiming to rule with divine authority
theologian	θεολόγος	a specialist in theology
theology	θεολογία	1 the study of religious doctrines and matters of divinity; specif. the study of God and the relations between God, mankind and the universe 2 a specific formulation or systemization of religious doctrine or belief as set forth by a given religion or denomination or by one or more individuals
Theophany	Θεοφάνεια	the celebration of Christ's baptism; a manifestation of God
theosophy	θεοσοφία	a religious or semireligious set of occult beliefs rejecting Judeo- Christian revelation and theology, often incorporating elements of Buddhism and Brahmanism, and held to be based on a special mystical insight or on superior speculation

19 UNITS OF MEASUREMENT

Cubic	κυβικός, ή, ό (adj.)	having three dimensions, or having. the volume of a cube whose length, width, and depth (or height) each measure the given unit [a cubic foot /κυβικό μέτρο]
decagram	δεκάγραμμον /o	ten grams; gram/(γράμμα/ letter/γραμμάριον/ gram – γράφειν/ [to write] lit. what is written; a small weight; the basic unit of mass in the metric system by 10 (decagram)
decaliter	δεκάλιτρον /o	ten liters
decameter	δεκάμετρον /o	ten meters
erg-	έργον /o (work)	Physics the unit of work or energy in the cgs (metric) system, being the work done by one dyne acting through a distance of one centimeter
hectogram	εκατόγραμμον /o	one hundred grams
hectoliter	εκατόλιτρον /o	one hundred liters
hectometer	εκατόμετρον /o	one hundred meters
gram	γραμμαριον /o	small weight; the basic unit of mass in the metric system, equal to about (.0022046 pound or 15.43 grains)
kilo	κιλόν /ό (χίλια/ chilia- a thousand)	kilogram; a thousand grams
kilogram	κιλόγραμμον /o	1,000 grams
kilometer	χιλιόμετρον /o	a thousand meters
liter	λίτρον /o	the basic metric unit of capacity equal to 1 cubic decimeter or 61.025 cubic inches (1.0667 liquid quarts or .908 dry quart)
mega-	μέγας / μέγα	great; mighty; combining form
megacycle	μεγάκυκλος	one million hertz; megahertz

metre /meter	μέτρον /o	the basic metric unit of linear measure, equal to c. 39.37 inches: now officially equal to the distance light travels in a vacuum in 1/299,792,458 of a second: abbrev: m
micro-	μικρός, ή, ό (adj.)	small, minute (microcosm) combining form
micron	μικρόν (neu of μικρός -mikros	a unit of linear measure equal to one millionth of a meter, or a thousandth of a millimeter

20 ZOOLOGY

Acanthopterygian	ακανθοπτερύγιον	any pteroid fish, as bass, perch, etc.
Acephalus	ακέφαλος	without head; Zool. having no part of the body differentiated as the head
actinia	ακτίνια (ακτίς - a ray)	any of the genus (Actinia) of the sea anemones
amphibios/ amphibious	αμφίβιος	surviving in both, land and water; any of a class (amphibian) of coldblooded, scaleless vertebrates, consisting of frogs, toads, newts, salamanders, and caecilians, that usually begin life in the water as tadpoles with gills and later develop lungs
amphipoda	αμφίποδα	any of an order (Amphipoda) of malacostracan crustaceans with a vertically thin body and one set of legs for jumping or walking and another set for swimming as the sand hopper
amphioxus	αμφίοξος (αμφί + οξύς – both + sharp)	of a subphylum (Chephalo-chordate) of small, fishlike chordates that have a permanent notochord, extending from the anterior to the posterior end; cephalochordate

anuran	άνουρα (αν + ουρά – without + tail)	any of an order (Anoura) of tailless, jumping amphibians with a broad body and well-developed hind legs, consisting of frogs and toads
apterous	άπτερος (α + πτερόν + without + wing/feather)	any having no wings or feathers
arhthropod	αρθρόποδον /ο	any of the phylum of (Arthropoda) of invertebrate animals with jointed legs, a segmented body, and an exoskeleton, including insects, crustaceans, arachnids, and myriapods
artiodactylous	αρτιοδάκτυλος	any of an order (Artiodactyla) of hoofed mammals having even number of toes, including swine, hippopotamuses, and all ruminants
autonomous	αυτόνομος, η, ο (adj.)	a) existing, functioning, or developing independently of other parts or forms b) autotrophic c) resulting from internal causes; autonomic
brachiopods	βραχιόποδα	a member of a phylum (Brachiopoda) of marine animals with hinged upper and lower shells enclosing two armlike parts with tentacles, used for guiding minute food particles to the mouth
brachypterous	βραχύπτερος (βραχύς + πτερόν – short +wing)	having incompletely developed or very short wings, as certain insects
cephalothorax	κεφαλοθώραξ / κεφαλοθώρακας	the head and the thorax united as a single part, in certain crustaceans and arachnids

chiropter	χειρόπετρα (χειρ + πτερόν- hand + wing)	any mammal in the phylum (Chiroptera) consisting of bats that have the ability to fly due to the membrane that connects the large hands
chrysalis	χρυσαλλίς / χρυσαλλίδα (χρυσός – gold)	the pupa of a butterfly, the form of the insect when between the larval and adult stages and in a case or coccoon
coenosarc	κοινοσάρκιον / ο	the fleshy portion of the stalks and stolons of hydroids that secretes the perisarc
coenurus	κοίνουρος (κοινός + ουρά – common + tail)	the compound larva of any of certain tapeworms causing any of various diseases, as the staggers; esp., the larva causing gid (coenurosis)
crocodile	κροκόδειλος	any of a subfamily (Crocodylinae) of large, flesh-eating lizardlike crocodilian reptiles living in or around tropical streams and having thick, horny skincomposed of scales and plates, a long tail, and a long, narrow, triangular head with massive jaws
decapods	δεκάποδον / ο	any of the order of (Decapoda) of crustaceans having ten legs, as a lobster, shrimp, or crab; also a squid
dolphin	δελφίς / δελφίνος (gen.) / δελφίνι (Mod. Gr.)	any of two widespread families (Platanistidae and Delphinidae) of toothed whales having high level of intelligence and usually a beaklike snout
echinoderm	εχινόδερμον / ο	any of a phylum (Echinodermata) of marine animals with a water-vascular system and usually with a hard, spiny skeleton and radial body, including the starfish and the urchin

elephant	ελέφας / ελέφαντας	any of an order (Provoskidea) of huge, thick-skinned, almost hairless mammals, the largest of extant four-footed animals, with a long snout (the trunk) and two ivory tusks; there are two existing species the Asian or Indian (Elephant maximus), which is usually domesticated, and the African elephant (Lexodonta Africana) which has a flatter head and larger ears
gastropod	γαστερόποδον / ο	any of a large class (Gastropoda) of mollusks having one piece, straight or spiral shells, as snails limpets, etc., or having no shells, as certain slugs
halcyon	αλκυών/ αλκυόνος (gen)	1 a legendary bird, identified with the kingfisher, which supposedly has a peaceful, calming influence on the sea at the time of the winter solstice 2 any of a genus (Halkyon) of kingfishers of S Asia and Australia
hemipteran	ημίπτερα (ημί + πτερόν- half + wing)	a true bug; any of the order of (Hemiptera) of insects with sucking mouth parts and forewings thickened toward the base, as water bug or squash bug; also called true bug
hydrozoan	υδρόζωα	of a class (Hydrozoa) of cnidarians having a saclike body consisting of two layers of cells, and a mouth that opens directly into the body cavity

leopard	λεόπαρδις /η	any of various large, ferocious cats, including the jaguar and snow leopard; esp., a species (Panthera pardus) of Africa and S Asia usually having a tawny coat spotted with black
lion	λέων / λέοντας / λιοντάρι	a large, powerful cat (Panthera leo), found in Africa and SW Asia, with a tawny coat, a tufted tail, and in the adult male a shaggy mane: in folklore the lion is considered as the king of beasts
lynx	λυγξ/ λυγκός (gen./ λύγκας (Mod. Gr.)	any of a genus (Lynx) of wildcats found throughout the Northern Hemisphere and characterized by a ruff on each side of the face, relative long legs, a short tail, long, usually tuffed ears and keen vision, as the bobcat or the Canada lynx of North America
macrouran	μάκρουρος (μακρύς + ουρά – long + tail)	any of various decapoda with large abdomen, including the lobster and shrimp
myriapod	μυριάποδον / ο	having many legs: said of the millipede and centipede
nautilus	ναυτίλος	kind of shellfish, it is believed that it sails in its shell as in a ship; the first larval stage in the development of certain crustaceans
odontophore	οδοντοφόρος	a muscular structure of most mollusks, usually protrusile, supporting the radula
oyster	όστρεον/ο	1 any of various bivalve mollusks with an irregularly shaped, unequal shell, living attached to rocks, other shells, etc., and widely used as food

pachyderm	παχύδερμον / ο (παχύ + δέρμα – thick + skin)	any of certain large, thick-skinned, hoofed animals, as the elephant, rhinoceros, and hippopotamus, formerly classified together.
panther	πάνθηρ / πάνθηρος /πάνθηρας	1 a leopard; specif., a) a black leopard b) a large or fierce leopard 2 *Cougar*
pelican	πελεκάν / πελεκάνος	any of the genus (Pelecanus, family Pelecanidae) of pelecaniform birds with a distensible pouch hanging from the lower bill: used to scoop up or store fish
pheasant	φασιανός	any of a number of large gallinaceous birds (family Phasianidae), usually with a long, sweeping tail and brilliant feathers: cf. *Partridge*
phyllophagous	φυλλοφάγος	feeding on leaves
python	πύθων / πύθωνος / πύθωνας	any of the genus (Python, family Boide) of very large, nonpoisonous snakes of Asia, Africa, and Australia that crush their prey to death
squirrel	σκίουρος	any of a family (Sciuridae) of small rodents living in trees, on the ground, or in a burrows and usually having a long bushy tail, including flying squirrels, chipmunks, and marmots
taenia	ταινία	a tapeworm (esp., of the genus (Taenia)
teredo	τερηδών /τερηδόνος (gen.) / τερηδόνα	any of a genus (Teredo) of long shipworms which feed on wood
xylophagous	ξυλοφάγος	eating, boring into, or destroying wood, as certain mollusks or the larvae of certain insects
zygodactyl	ζυγοδάκτυλος	having the toes arranged in two opposed pairs, two in the front and two in the rear

ENGLISH WORDS DERIVING FROM THE GREEK LANGUAGE

English	Greek	Definition
	A	
Aa	Ἄλφα (Α, α)/**Alpha**	first letter of the Greek Alphabet; also, the beginning
abacus	αμπάκος	counting board; arithmetic book
abiogenesis	α-βίος + γένεσις (α + βίος + γένεσις / **without + life + genesis**)	lifeless; spontaneous generation
abiogenist	α-βιος / γενετιστής (αβιογενετιστής)	one believing in abiogenesis
abiogenesis	αβιογένεσις/η	spontaneous generation
abiotic	αβιοτικό, ή, ό (adj.)	of nonliving substances or environmental factors
abulia	αβουλία (α + βουλή/ βουλησία- **without + will/determination**)	indecision; Psychol. loss of the ability to exercise willpower and make decisions
abulic	άβουλος, η, ο (adj.)	an indecisive person; one without willpower of his own

abranchiate/ abranchial	α-βράγχια	animal without gills
abyss	άβυσσος	a big fissure in the earth; chasm; anything too deep for measurement; the ocean depths; 2 Theol. the primeval void or chaos before the Creation
abyssal	αβυσσαλέος, α, ο (adj.)	bottomless; chaotic
abyssal zone	αβυσσαλέα ζώνη	ecological zone along the deep ocean floor between the bathyal and hadal zones
acacia	ακακία	shittah tree; any of several trees, shrubs or other plants of the mimosa family.
acacus	άκακος, η, ο (adj.)	without evil, good person
academe	ακαδημαϊκότητα	belonging to academia
academia	ακαδημία	the academic world
academics	ακαδημαϊκά	scholastics, scholarly, pertaining to colleges and universities
academician	ακαδημαϊκός	a member of the Academy: scholar, writer, poet, artist, etc., who follows certain academic rules or conventions
academy	ακαδημία	1 a school offering special training in a field; 2 an association of scholars, writers, artists, etc. 3 The Academy, the public park in Athens, where Plato taught and founded a school for the study of philosophy 4 the Academic world
acaleph or acalephe	ακαλήφη	a nettle; any of several invertebrate animals as jellyfish, that swim or float about in the open sea; coelenterate or ctenophore
acanthine	ακάνθινος, η, ο (adj.)	of or resembling an acanthus or its leaves

acantho-	άκανθo- άκανθος / αγκάθι (Mod. Gr.)	thorn combining form
acanthoid	(ο, η) ακανθώδης (το) ακανθώδες (adj.)	spiny; spine-shaped
acantho-pterygian	άκανθος + πρερύγιον/ πτερόν (ακανθοπτερύγιον/ο)	thorn + fin; wing any percoid fish, as the bass or perch
acanthus/acanthos	άκανθος	thorn plant; any plant of the Acanthus family, often with lobed, spiny leaves
acarpous	άκαρπος, η, ο (adj.)	not bearing fruit; sterile
acatalyctic	ακατάληκτος, η, ο (adj.) (α + καταλήγειν- without + having an end)	incessant, endless
acedia	ακηδία (α + κήδος – not + care)	1 the lack of care and interest 2 an onset of distaste for and boredom with all religious practices 3 spiritual sloth or apathy, esp., that resulting from such an onset
acedic	(ο, η) ακηδής (το) ακηδές (adj.)	1 one who lacks care and interest 2 having spiritual sloth or apathy
Aceldama	Ακέλδαμα	field of blood; Bible the field near Jerusalem bought with the money given to Judas for betraying Jesus: Acts 1:19; Matt: 27:8; a place of bloodshed
acephalous	ακέφαλος, η, ο (adj.) (α/without- κεφάλι/ head)	headless
Achaea/Achaia	Αχαϊα	ancient and present region in N. Peloponnesus
Achaeans	Αχαιοί	people of Achaea
Achates	Αχάτης	in Virgil's Aeneid a loyal companion of Aeneas, Also, achates/αχάτης is a colorful precious gem

Achilles/Achilleus	Αχιλλεύς /Αχιλλέας	Gr. myth warrior, one of the leaders of the Trojan War and Homer's hero, who killed Hector and he himself, was killed by Paris by hitting his only vulnerable spot, his heel
Achilles' heel	αχίλλειος πτέρνα	one's vulnerable or susceptible spot
Achilles' tendon	αχίλλειος τένων/ τένοντας	the tendon connecting the back of the knee to the muscles of the calf of the leg
achondro-plasia	α + χόνδρο + πλάσις /η –without + tissue + formation	a congenital disorder of bone formation that results in deformities and dwarfing of the skeleton; a generic disorder disturbing normal growth of cartilage
achromatism	αχρωματισμός	the condition or the quality of being achromatic; lack of color
achromatopsia	αχρωματοψία (α/ without –χρώματ/ color-οψία/vision	a visual defect that is marked by total color blindness in which the colors of the spectrum are seen as tones of white, gray, and black, by poor visual acuity, and by extreme sensitivity to bright light
achromia	αχρωμία	absence of normal pigmentation, esp., in red blood cells and skin
achromus/acromous	άχρωμος, η, ο (adj.)	colorless; without color
achlohydria	αχλω-υδρία (α χλωρ + ύδωρ- without – water + chloric)	a stomach disorder in which the stomach fails to secrete hydrochloric acid
aclinic	(ο, η) ακλινής (το) ακλινές (adj.)	without inclination; unswerving
acme	ακμή (from¨ακμάζειν" / to peak)	summit, peak, highest point, age of maturity, point of culmination
acolyte	ακόλουθος, η, ο (adj.)	follower; a person officially appointed or delegated to serve thus; also an altar boy; an attendant, a follower, helper

acoustic	ακουστικός, ή, ό (adj.) (ακούειν- to listen, hear)	dealing with hearing
acoustical	ακουστικός, ή, ό (adj.)	having to do with the control of sound
acoustically	ακουστικώς/ ακουστικά (adv.)	with reference to acoustics; from the standpoint of acoustics
acoustician	ακουστικός	an expert in acoustics
acoustics	ακουστική	the quality of a room, theater, church, school, etc., that has to do with how clearly sound can be heard or transmitted; the branch of physics dealing with sound, esp. its transmission
acousto-optics	ακουστικο- οπτικά	the branch of physics concerned with the relationship between acoustics and light
acre	αγρός	field, lit. place in which cattle are driven 1a unit of land measure equal to 160 square rods or 43,560 square feet(.405 hectare) 2 (pl.) a large quantity
acritical	α + κριτικός, ή, ό/ without + judging- critiquing	1 not critical; having no tendency to criticism or critical judgment 2 Med. showing no signs of a crisis
acro -	άκρο(ν)	at the point; top; end; height; combining form (acrophobe)
acrobat	ακροβάτης (ακρο/ point - βαίνω/walk)	walking on tiptoe/performer of tricks in tumbling or on trapeze
acrocarpous	ακρο + καρπός / end + fruit	bearing fruit at the end of the stalk
acrogen	ακρογενές	a plant, such as a fern or moss, having a perennial stem with the growing point at the tip
acrolith	ακρόλιθος	in early Greek sculpture, a statue with stone head, hands, and feet, and wooden trunk

acromegaly	ακρομεγαλία (άκρο + μεγάλο- end + big)	a disease in which there is enlargement of the head, hands, and feet, resulting from an overproduction of growth hormone that is caused, usually, by a tumor in the pituitary
acromion	ακρώμιον/ο	the outer end of the spine of the scapula that protects the glenoid cavity, forms the outer angle of the shoulder, and articulates with the clavicle; also called acromial process
acronical or acronycal	ακρόνυκτος (άκρο + νυξ/νυκτός (gen.) −end + night)	
acronym	ακρώνυμον/ο	a word formed from the first (or few) letters of many words (ex: NASA, IRA, etc.)
acropetal	ακροπέταλον/ο	developing or moving from the base of stem toward the apex. It used to describe the development of tissues or movement of hormones in plants
acrophobia	ακροφοβία (άκρο(ν)/edge, top- φόβος/fear)	abnormal fear of being in high places or heights
acrophobe	ακρο /φόβος/ top/ high + fear	someone with excessive fear of heights
acropolis / Acropolis	ακρόπολις/η / Ακρόπολις/η	I fortified highest part of the city 2 the Acropolis of Athens where the Parthenon was built
acrostic	ακρόστιχος (άκρο /στίχος + end + line/verse)	a verse or arrangement of words in which certain letters in each line, such as the first or last, when taken in order to spell out a word, motto, etc.
actin- or actino- prefix	ακτίς /ακτίνος (gen.)/ακτίνα (Mod. Gr.)	ray combining form

actinia	ακτίνια	any of a genus (Actinia) of sea anemones
actinic	ακτινικός, ή, ό (adj.)	having to do with actinism
actinism	ακτινισμός	the property of ultraviolet light, x-rays, or other radiation by which chemical changes are produced
actinium	ακτίνιον/ο	a white metallic radioactive chemical element found with uranium and radium in pitchblende and other minerals, or, formed in reactors by the neutron irradiation of radium: symbol: Ac
actinograph	ακτινογράφος	a recording actinometer
actino-graphy	ακτινο-γραφία	the recording of rays, x-ray
actinoid	(ο, η) ακτινοειδής (το) ακτινοειδές (adj.)	having a radial form, as a sea anemone
actinometer	ακτινόμετρον/ο	1 Physics an instrument for measuring the intensity of the sun's rays, or the actinic effect of light rays 2 Photog. exposure meter
actino-morphic	ακτινο-μορφικός, ή, ό (adj.)	Biol. having radial symmetry, as a flower or a starship Also, actinomorphous
actinology	ακτινολογία	science of light rays and their chemical effects
actinometer	ακτινόμετρον/ο	Physics: an instrument for measuring the intensity of the sun's rays or the actinic effect of light rays
actino-mycosis	ακτινο-μυκήτωσις/η	an infection caused by certain actinomycetes that may result in bony degeneration of the jaws, and abscesses in the lungs, intestines, etc., of humans and other mammals

action-mycete	ακτινο-μύκητας	any of various bacteria (order Actinomycetales) with a branching, filamentous structure; esp., any of a family (Actinomycetaceae) of Gram-positive bacteria that are pathogenic to humans and animals
actinotherapy	ακτινοθεραπεία	application for therapeutic purposes of the chemically active rays of the electromagnetic spectrum (as ultraviolet light or x-rays)
-acy	-ατεία or -ατία	indicating governing; rule suffix forming nouns as (supremacy; democracy, etc.)
acyclic	ακρυλικός, ή, ό (adj.)	of or pertaining to acrylic acid or products made of it
adamant	αδάμας/διαμάντι (Mod. Gr.)	diamond, unconquerarble; unbreakable 1 not giving in or relenting, unyielding
adamantine	αδαμαντίνη (αδαμάντινος,/ αδαμαντένιος, αδαμαντένια, αδαμαντένιο) (adj.)	of or like adamant; hard as steel, very hard, as dental enamel; unbreakable; unyielding; firm
adelpho-	αδελφό- αδελφός	brother, combining form (adelphogamy)
adelpho-gamy	αδελφός + γάμος - αδελφογαμία (sibling/brother + marriage)	marriage between siblings
adelphopoiesis	αδελφοποίησις /η; αδελφότης/ αδελφότητα	the joining of individuals or groups in a bond of brotherhood
aden/adeno	αδήν-αδένας (Mod. Gr.)	combining form gland
adenalgia	αδεναλγία	pain in a gland
adenitis	αδενίτις/αδενίτιδα	glandural inflammation
adeno-carcinoma	αδενο-καρκίνωμα	malignant tumor in the gland(s)
adenoids	αδενοειδή (pl.)	growths of lymphoid tissue

adenoid- ectomy	αδενοειδή-εκτομή	surgically removed adenoids
adenoma	αδένωμα	benign growth of a gland
adenopathy	αδενοπάθεια	any glandural disease
adenosis	αδενίτις/αδενίτιδα	any disease of glands
adiabatic	αδιάβατος (α-διαβατός)	not passable
adiaphorous	αδιάφορος, η, ο (adj.)	morally neutral; indifferent
Adonis	Άδωνις	1 a handsome young man loved by Aphrodite; who was killed by a wild boar 2 any very handsome young man
adrenalin	αδρεναλίνη-επινεφρίνη/ επινεφριδίνη	Biol. one of the main hormones of the epinephrine glands (endocrine organs above the kidneys)
adrenergic	αδρεν-εργητικός, ή, ό (adj.)	1 releasing epinephrine or a similar substance [the adrenergic nerves of the sympathetic nervous system] 2 like epinephrine in chemical activity [an adrenergic drug]
adynamia	αδυναμία/ α / δύναμη-without/ power, strength	weakness; without strength/ power, lack of vital force
adytum	άδυτος, η, ο (adj.)	not to be entered; a sanctum; a shrine
aedes	(ο, η) αηδής/ (το) αηδές (adj.)	distasteful; unpleasant; disgusting
Aegean	Αιγαίον/ο	1 in or of the Aegean Sea 2 designating or of the culture of the Bronze Age people who lived in the Aegean Islands and nearby regions
Aegean Islands	Νήσοι του Αιγαίου/ Νησιά του Αιγαίου	the islands in the Aegean Sea; specif. Lesvos/Lesbos, Chios, the Cyclades, and the Dodecanese
Aegean Sea	Αιγαίον Πέλαγος	arm of the Mediterranean between Greece and Turkey

Aegeus	Αιγεύς/Αιγέας	Gr. myth. king of Athens who drowned when he thought that his son, Theseus, who had gone to Crete to kill the Minautur, had been killed (the Aegean Sea was named after him)
aegis	αιγίς/αιγίδα	shield that protected Zeus; goatskin; protection
Aeneas	Αινείας	Gr. and Rom. myth. a Trojan, son of Anchises and Venus/Aphrodite, and hero of Virgil's epic Aeneid: escaping from ruined Troy, Aeneas wanders for years (as Odysseus) before coming to Latium: he is considered the forefather of the Romans
Aeolian	αιολός, ή, ό (adj.)	of Aeolis or its people; of the wind 2 any of the Greek tribes that settled in ancient Thessaly
aeolian harp	αιολική άρπα	a box with an opening in it across, when the gut strings are stretched, is tuned in unison and when air blows over the strings, varying harmonies are produced
Aeolic	αιολικός, ή, ό (adj.)	a dialect or a group of dialects of ancient Greek spoken chiefly in Aiolis, Boeotia, and Thessaly
Aolis	Αιολίς	ancient region on the NW coast of Minor Asia consisting of a group of cities settled by the Aiolians
Aeolus	Αίολος	Gr. myth 1 the god of the winds 2 the king of Thessaly, the legendary forefather of the Aiolians
aeon- or aeono-	αιών/αιώνος (gen.) /αιώνες (pl.)	a hundred years; an eternity; a very long time; century/ centuries combining form Also Eon

aeonium/aeonian	αιώνιος, α, ο (adj.)/ αιών-αιώνας (n.,)/century	lasting for ages; immortal
aeonobios	αιωνόβιος, α, ο (adj.)	lasting for ever; a very long time; for eons/αιώνες
aer- or aero-	αήρ/αέρος (gen.)	air, combining form used before a vowel (aerial)
aero/air prefix	αερο-/ αέρος (gen.)/ αέρας (Mod. Gr.)	air combining form
aerial	αέριος/αέρινος, η, ο (adj.)	light as air/not substantial; aetherial; delicate
aerobe	αέρο – βίος / air& life	microorganism that can live only where oxygen exists
aerobic	αεροβικός/ή/ό (ajd.)	able to live, grow or take place only where there is free oxygen present; designating or involving exercise
aerobiology	αεροβιολογία	the study of microbes, pollutants, etc. that travel through the air
aeorodrome	αεροδρόμιον/ο	an airport, smaller size airport
aerodynamic	αεροδυναμικός, ή, ό (adj.: masc. fem. neu.)	exerted force by air
aerodynamics	αεροδυναμική	the branch of aeromechanics that deals with the forces (resistance, pressure, etc.) exerted by air
aerography	αερογραφία	branch of metereology concerned with the study of air in the upper atmosphere
aerologic	αερολογικός, η, ό (adj.)	pertaining to aerology
aerology	αερολογία	the branch of meteorology concerned with the study of air, esp. in the upper atmosphere/ Also, in Greek, the word means pointless/aimless chat (used in pl. αερολογίες/aerologhies)

aeromechanics	αερο-μηχανική/ μηχανολογία	the branch of mechanics dealing with air or other gases in motion or equilibrium: it includes aerodynamics and aerostatics
aero-meteorograph	αερο-μετεωρο-γραφία	metereograph used in an aircraft or balloon
aerometer	αερόμετρον/ο	an instrument for measuring the weight and density of air or other gasses
aeroneurosis	αερονεύρωσις/η	a nervous disorder of airplane pilots supposedly caused by the tension/ stress of excessive flying
aeronaut	αεροναύτης (αέρας / air & ναύτης/sailor)	pilot of a balloon or airship
aeronautics	αεροναυτική	science, art, or work of designing, making and operating aircraft
aerophagia	αεροφαγία	an abnormal spasmodic swallowing of air: often a symptom of hysteria
aerophobia	αεροφοβία (αέρας & φοβία/air & fear)	extreme fear of air and wind/drafts
aerophore	αεροφόρος	1 a device for supplying air to the lungs, in case of oxygen shortage 2 an apparatus that cleans air to be breathed again, used as by firefighters
aerosphere	αερόσφαιρα	the atmosphere surrounding the earth
aerostat	αερόστατον/ο	an airship, balloon, or other aircraft that is filled and sustained by means of one or two containers filled with a gas lighter air
aerostatics	αεροστατική	the branch of aeromechanics that deals with the equilibrium of air or other gasses, and with the equilibrium of solid bodies, such as aerostats, floating in air or other gasses

aerotheraputics	αεροθεραπευτική	the process of treating disease by the use of air, esp. by exposing patients to change in atmospheric treatment
aerotherapy	αεροθεραπεία	treatment with the use of clean air
aero-therapeutics	αερο-θεραπευτική	the treatment of disease by the use of air, esp., by exposing patients to changes in atmospheric pressure
aero-thermo-dynamics	αερο-θερμο-δυναμική	the study of the relationship of heat and mechanical energy in gasses, esp. air
aery	αέριος, α, ο (adj.)	airy; unsubstantial; visionary
Aescylus/Aescylos	Αισχύλος	c. 525–456 BC one of the three best tragedians, known as the Father of tragedy/drama; the other two greatest tragedians of antiquity being, Euripides and Sophocles
Aesculapian	Ασκληπιείον/ο	1 of Aesculapius/Asclepeus; the sacred place of Asclepius 2 medical
Aesculapius/Asclepius	Ασκληπιός/Ασχλαπιός	Gr. and Rom. myth. the god of medicine and of healing, son of Apollo
Aesopic	αισωπικός, ή, ό (adj.)	anything relating to Aesop
Aesop	Αίσωπος	real or legendary Gr. author of fables supposed to have lived around the sixth cen. BC
Aesopian	αισώπειος, α, ο (adj.)	of Aesop or characteristic of his fables 2 concealing real purposes or intentions; always having a social and educational message; dissembling (known as the Aesopean language)
aestherial/ethereal	αιθέριος, α, ο (adj.)	1 of or like the ether, or upper regions of space very light, airy, delicate 3 not earthly; heavenly; celestial 4 Chem. of, like,or containing ether, esp., if mixed with an essential oil

aesthesis	αίσθησις/η	sense; perception; feeling
aesthete	αισθητής	1 a person highly sensitive to art and beauty 2 a person artificially cultivates artistic sensitivity or makes a cult of art and beauty 3 the word aesthete often is used derogatorily to connote effeteness or decadence
aesthetic	αισθητικός, ή, ό (adj.)αισθάνομαι(v.)	to perceive; feel; sensitive to art and beauty; indicating good, artistic taste
aesthetician	αισθητικός (n.)	expert in aesthetics
aestheticism	αισθητισμός	doctrine that aesthetic principles underline all human values
aesthetics	αισθητική	the study or theory of beauty and of the psychological responses to it; sensitivity to art and beauty and specif. the branch of philosophy dealing with the creative sources, its forms, and its effects
aetiological	αιτιολογικός, ή, ό (adj.)	pertaining to aetiology
aetiology	αιτιολογία	1 the assignment of a cause or the cause assigned [the aetiology of the folkway] 2 the science of causes or origins 3 a) the science of the causes or origin of diseases b) the origin of a specific disease. Also etiology
agalma-	άγαλμα	statue, combining form (agalmatoid/ (statuelike)
aether or ether	αιθήρ/αιθέρας	1 a light volatile, flammable liquid, esp. formerly used as an anesthetic 2 any of various organic compounds characterized by an oxygen atom attached to two carbon atoms

agalmatine	αγαλματένιος, α, ο (adj.)	someone resembling a statue in beauty
agalmato-philia	άγαλμα /φιλία/ αγαλματοφιλία	excessive desire for statues
agalmato-phobia	αγαλματο-φοβία (αγάλματος (gen. case of agalma)	extreme fear of statues
Agamemnon	Αγαμέμνων/ Αγαμέμνονας	Gr. myth. king of Mycenae and commander-in-chief of the Greek army in the Trojan War. Upon his return from Troy he was killed by his wife Clytemnestra and her lover.
agamete	αγαμέτης (α + γαμέτης –without + gamete / reproduction cell)	any asexual reproductive cell that develops directly into an adult without fertilization, as in certain protozoans
agamic	άγαμος, η, ο (adj.)	not married; asexual; not having a sexual union
agamo-genesis	άγαμος / γένεσις-γέννησις/η	Biol. asexual reproduction as by fission, budding, parthenogenesis, etc.
agamous/agamos	άγαμος, η, ο (adj.)	not married; unmarried
agape	αγάπη	love; fraternal love; affection
Agatha	Αγαθή (αγαθός, ή, ό, adj.)	good; guileless; ingenuous, innocent; feminine name
Agesilaus/Agesilaos	Αγησίλαος	442–360 BC king of Sparta, during the decline of its supremacy in ancient Greece
Aglaia	Αγλαΐα	lit. brightness, one of the three Graces (the other two: Eufrosyne and Thaleia); a feminine name
ageusia	α + γεύση/ αγευσία(n.)/ άγευστος, η, ο (adj.)	without taste; tasteless
Agnes	Αγνή (αγνός, ή, ό, adj.)	pure; chaste; feminine name
agnathia	α + γνάθος	–without one or both jaws the congenital complete or partial absence of one or both jaws

agnogenic	αγνογενής/αγνογενές (άγνοια + γένος – ignorance + origin)	of unknown cause
agnosia	αγνωσία (α & γνώσις/γνώση- without & knowledge)	lack of knowledge; ignorance, or inability to recognize familiar sounds or objects, etc., due to brain damage
agnostic	αγνωστικιστικός, ή, ό ((adj.)	follower of agnosticism
agnosticism	αγνωστικισμός	the doctrine of agnostics; distinguished from Atheism
-agogue	- αγωγός (άγειν- to lead)	substance that promotes the secretion or expulsion of, combining form (as in: emenagogue; galactagogue). Also, -agog
agon	αγών/αγώνας/ αγώνες (pl.)	contest; completion; assembly; any type of competition: athletic, literary, etc. Also, struggle
agonist	αγωνιστής/ αγωνίστρια (fem.)	one who participates in struggles; fighter; warrior
agonistes	αγωνιστές (pl.)	people fighting for a cause, warriors, fighters
agonistic	αγωνιστικός, ή, ό (adj.)	fit for a contest; 1 of ancient Gr. athletic contests/games 2 combative 3 strained for effect
agonize	αγωνίζεσθαι/ αγωνίζομαι/αγωνιώ	1 to contend for a prize 2 to make convulsive efforts; struggle 3 to be in agony, or great pain; feel anguish
agony	αγωνία	great mental struggle and pain; anguish
agora	αγορά	marketplace and place for assemblies (as in ancient Greece)
agora-nomos	αγορά / νόμος (market /law)	the law/rules set for assemblies
agoraphobia	αγορά - φοβία/ αγοραφοβία	abnormal fear of being in open spaces

agoraphobic	αγοραφοβικός,ή, ο (adj.)	one who is excessively afraid being in open spaces
agrapha	άγραφος, η, ο / άγραφα (pl.) (adj. from: α/ not-γράφω/write)	not written; unwritten
agraphia	α + γράφειν / without + to write	the partial or total loss of the ability to write
agri-	αγρός/ αγροί (pl.)	combining word, agriculture esp., in relation to technology or businesses associated with farming
agrimony	αγριμονία	1 any plant of a genus (Agrimonia) in the rose family, typically having little yellow flowers on spiky stalks and bearing burlike fruit 2 Hemp Agrimony
agriology	αγριολογία (άγριος, α, ο, adj.)	wild, the study of the customs of nonliterate people whose culture is marked by a simple technology
agro-	prefix αγρός	farm; field, soil combining form
agrobiology	αγρο-βιολογία (αγρός + βιολογία -field + biology)	the science of plant growth and nutrition as applied to the improvement of crops and control of soil
agrobiologic	αγρο-βιολογικός, ή, ό (adj.)	pertaining to agriobiology
agrochemichal	αγρο-χημικά	chemichals used to improve the quality and quantity of farm products
agrology	αγρολογία	science of agricultural production
agronomics	αγρονομία- αγρονομική	science and economics of crop production; management of farmland
agronomist	αγρονόμος	a specialist in agronomy; overseer of the lands

agronomy	αγρονομία	the science and economics of crop production; management of farmland
agrostology	αγροστολογία (αγροστίς- a type of grass)	the branch of botany dealing with grasses
ahistoric	αχιστόριστος, η, ο (adj.) (α ιστορία – not related + history)	not related to or concerned with documented history; not knowing history; ignorant of history
-aholic	-αολικός, ή, ό (adj.)	suffix forming adjectives indicating excessive need for something like alcohol; work, etc. (workaholic)
ailourophile	αιλουρόφιλος	a person who is attracted or devoted to cats or to the cat family
ailourophobia	αίλουρος + φοβία/ αιλουροφοβία	fear of the feline group; fear of cats
air	αήρ/ αέρας	the elastic, invisible mixture of gases (mainly nitrogen and oxygen, as well as hydrogen, carbon dioxide, argon, neon, helium, etc.) that surrounds the earth; atmosphere
airplane	αεροπλάνο- αεροσκάφος (from αερο/air/aero)	heavier than air fixed-wing aircraft
airy	αέριος, α, ο (adj.)	1 in the air; high up 2 of air 3 open to the air; breezy 4 unsubstantial as air; visionary 5 light as air; delicate; graceful 6 lighthearted; vivacious 7 affectedly nonchalant; grand
Aitolia	Αιτωλία	region of ancient Greece, on the Gulf of Corinth
Aitolians	Αιτωλείς	the inhabitants of Aitolia
alabaster	αλάβαστρος	a variety of calcite found esp., in slalactites and stalagmites, sometimes streaked like marble

Alcestis	Αλκηστις/η	Gr. myth. wife of the king of Thessally, Admetus: she offered her life to save her husband's, but was saved from Hades by Hercules
alchemist	αλχημιστής	a practitioner of alchemy
alchemy	αλχημεία	1 an old name for chemistry, with philosophic and magical associations, studied in the Middle Ages: its main aims were to change base metals into gold and to discover the elixir of perpetual youth 2 a power or process of changing one thing to another; esp., a seemingly miraculous power or process of changing one thing into something better
alcohol	αλκοόλ	distilled spirit, colorless volatile; pungent liquid
alcoholic	αλκοολικό, ή, ό (adj.)	1 of or containing alcohol 2 causing it by alcohol or liquor containing it 3 suffering from consumption of alcohol or alcoholism
Alcoholic Anonymous	Ανώνυμοι Αλκοολικοί (pl.)	an organization of alcoholics and recovering alcoholics who seek, through mutual counseling, to avoid lapses into drinking
alcoholism	αλκοολισμός	habitual consumption of alcohol
alcoholometer	αλκοόμετρον/ο	an instrument. Usually an hydrometer, for determining the percentage of alcohol in a liquid
alethiology	αληθειολογία (αλήθεια + λόγος- truth and word)	religion of truth
alevrone	άλευρον/αλεύρι	wheat flour; flour

Alexander	Αλέξανδρος (αλέξειν + ανδρός / to defend + man (gen. of ανήρ/aner)	Lit. defender of man; masculine name
Alexander the Great	Μέγας Αλέξανδρος	c. 356–323 BC; king of Macedonia; and one of the greatest military generals of all times who helped spread the Greek culture and language, from Asia Minor and Egypt to India, that era known as the Hellenistic Period
Alexandra	Αλεξάνδρα	(fem. of Alexander) a feminine name
Alexandria	Αλεξάνδρεια	a seaport in Egypt, on the Mediterranean at the W end of the Nile delta, founded by Alexander the Great, and, later a center of Hellenistic culture
Alexandroupolis	Αλεξανδρούπολις /η	seaport in NE Greece, on the Aegean, near the border of Turkey
alexia	αλεξία (α + λέξη –without + word/speech)	without word or speech; the loss of the ability to read, caused by lesions of the brain; word blindness
alexi-pharmac	αλεξι-φάρμακον/ο (αλέξειν + φάρμακον – to avert + drug/poison)	an antidote
-algia	suffix -αλγία (άλγος/ αλγειν- pain/ to feel pain)	combining word forming nouns (as in neuralgia, etc.)
algo-	to άλγος	pain, combining form (algophobia)
algolagnia	αλγολαγνεία (άλγος+ λαγνεία - pain + lust)	abnormal sexual pleasure by inflicting pain and suffering (as masochism or sadism); a perversion

algology	αλγολογία	the branch of botany dealing with algae; psychology
algometer	αλγόμετρον/ο	a device for measuring the intensity of pain caused by pressure
algometry	αλγομετρία	the theory or process of measuring of pain
algophobia	αλγοφοβία	an abnormal or excessive fear of pain
algorithm	αλγόριθμος	1 Math. a) any systematic method of solving a certain kind of problem b) the repetitive calculations used in finding the greatest common divisor of two numbers (called in full Euclidean algorithm) 2 Comput. a predetermined set of instructions for solving a specific problem in a limited number of steps
aliphatic	άλειμμα (αλείφειν-to rub/spread/anoint) αλειφατικός, ή, ό (adj.)	1 pertaining to fat or oil 2 of or relating to a large group of compounds, structured in open chains, including alcanes (paraffins) alcenes (olefins), and alkynes (acetylenes)
allantoid	(ο, η) αλλαντοειδής (το) αλλαντοειδές (adj.)	sausage shaped; of or like allantoids
allegorical	αλληγορικός, ή, ό (adj.)	1 of or characteristic of allegory 2 that is or contains an allegory
allegorist	αλλήγορος	a writer of allegories
allegorize	αλληγορείν/ αλληγορώ	1 to make into or treat as an allegory 2 to interpret in an allegorical sense; to make or use allegories

allegory	αλληγορία	1 story in which people, things, or happenings have a symbolic or hidden meaning: allegories used for teaching or explaining ideas, moral principles, etc. 2 the presenting of ideas by means of such stories 3 any symbol or emblem 4 description of one thing under the image of another
allel- or allelo-	αλλήλων/ αλλήλοις	of one another combining form (allelopath)
allele	αλλήλων	1 either of a pair of genes located at the same position on both members of a pair of chromosomes and conveying characters that are inherited in accordance with Mendelian law 2 any of the alternative forms of a gene that may occur at a given locus
allelopathy	αλληλοπάθεια	the repression or destruction of plants from the effect of certain toxic chemical substances produced and released by other, nearby plants
alleluia / Hallelujah	Αλληλούϊα/ αλληλούϊα	an exclamation, hymn, or song of praise to God
allergen	αλλεργενής/ αλλεργενές	a substance that induces allergy
allergenic	αλλεργενικός, ή, ό (adj.)	having the capacity to induce an allergy
allergic	αλλεργικός, ή, ό (adj.)	1 of, relating to, or characterized by allergy 2 affected by an allergy: subject to an allergic reaction
allergist	αλλεργιολόγος	an expert in allergies
allergic encephalo-myelitis	αλλεργική εγκεφαλο-μυελίτις	a condition that is produced by an allergic response following the introduction of an antigenic substance into the body

allergic rhinitis	αλλεργική ρινίτις/ ρινίτιδα	rhinitis caused by exposure to an allergen; esp. hay fever
allergy	αλλεργία	1 altered bodily reactivity (as hypersensitivity) to an anigen in response to a first exposure 2 exaggerated or pathological reaction (as by sneezing, coughing, difficult breathing, itching, or skin rashes)
allo-	άλλος, η, ο (adj.)/ άλλο- neu. of άλλος	other, departure from the normal; different; reversal; renewal, combining form (allonym; allomorph, etc.)
allochthonous	αλλοχθόνιος, α, ο (adj.)	originating elsewhere; not native to a place
allo-gamy	αλλογαμία	the process of cross-fertilizing; cross-fertilization
allo-genic	(ο, η) αλλογενής (το) αλλογενές (adj.)	of or having to do with genes from different genotypes, esp., in regard to allografts
allograft	αλλο + γράπτειν – different + sketching	a graft of tissue or an organ taken from an individual of the sme species as the recipient but with different hereditary factors; homograft
allograph	αλλογράφημα	Linguis. 1 any of the ways a unit of a writing system, as the letter of an alphabet, is formed or shaped 2 any of the units or combinations of units that can represent a single phoneme, morpheme, syllable, etc.
allomerism	αλλομερισμός (άλλο + μέρος – other + part)	variation in chemical composition without change in crystalline form
allometry	αλλομετρία/ αλλομέτρησις/η	the study and measurement of the relative growth of a part of an organism in comparison with the whole

allomorph	αλλόμορφος, η, ο (adj.)	1 Minerology a) any of the crystalline forms of a substance existing in more than one such form b) paramorph 2 Linguis. Any of the variant forms of a morpheme as conditioned by position or adjoining sounds
allopathist or allpopath	αλλοπαθητικός	a person who practices allopathy
allopathy	αλλοπάθεια	treatment of diseases by remedies that produce effects different from or opposite to those produced by the disease: loosely applied to the general practice of medicine today, but in strict usage opposed to Homeopathy
allopatric	αλλοπάτριος, α, ο (adj.)	Biol. of or pertaining to species of organisms occurring in different but often adjacent areas
allophane	(ο, η) αλλοφανής (το) αλλοφανές (adj.)	changing appearance; a transclucent, hydrated silicate of aluminum of varying composition and color, typically occurring in the form of stalactites or as incrustations on chalk or sandstone
allophone	αλλόφωνον/ο	Linguis. any of the variant forms of a phoneme as conditioned by position or adjoining sounds [the relative short (a) of mat, and the relatively long (a) of mad, are allophones
alloplasm	αλλόπλασμα	1 the first of protoplasm from which cilia, flagella, etc., develop 2 Metaplasm

allotropy	αλλοτροπία/ αλλότροπος	of or in another manner; the property that certain chemical elements and compounds have of existing in two or more different forms, as carbon in the form of charcoal, diamond, lampblack, etc. Also alotropism
almond	αμύγδαλον/ο (αμυγδαλή- αμυγδαλιά – the tree)	1 a) the edible, nutlike kernel of the small dry peachlike fruit of a tree (Prunus amygdalus) of the rose family growing in warm regions b) the tree itself 2 anything shaped like an almond, oval and pointed on one or both ends 3) the light- tan color of the almond shell
aloe	αλόη	any of a large genus (Aloe) of plants of the lily family, native to Africa, with fleshy leaves that are spiny along the edge and with drooping clusters of tubular, red or yellow flowers 2 a bitter laxative drug, made from the juice of certain aloe leaves
alopecia	αλώπηξ-αλεπού- αλωπηκία	fox; baldness; loss of hair
Alpha	Άλφα	1 name of the first letter of the Greek alphabet 2 the Beginning of anything 3 Astron. the name assigned to the brightest star in each constellation: followed by the name of the constellation in the genitive: as Alpha Centauri Chem. designating the first of two or more positions in which the substituting atom or radical appears relative to some particular carbon atom in an organic compound: usually written α-: the other positions in order are beta/ βήτα (β-), gamma/γάμμα (γ-), delta/ δέλτα (δ-), etc.

Alpha and Omega	Άλφα και Ωμέγα	the first and last letters of the Gr. alphabet 2 beginning and the end: cf: the Rev. 1:8
alphabet	αλφάβητο	the letters of an alphabet (starting with the first two letters of the Gr. alphabet, arranged in a traditional order alpha/ άλφα, beta/ βήτα) 1 the letters of a language, arranged in a traditional order 2 a system of characters, signs, or symbols used to indicate letters or speech sounds 3 the first elements or principles, as of a branch of knowledge
alphabetical	αλφαβητικός/ ή/ό (adj.)	1 pertaining to the use of an alphabet 2 arranged in the regular order of an alphabet
alphabetize	αλφαβητίζω	to arrange in alphabetical order of the alphabet
alpha-numeric	αλφα-αριθμητικός, ή, ο (adj.)/-νουμερικός	having or using both alphabetical and numerical symbols
Alpheus	Αλφειός	Gr. myth. a river god who pursues Arethusa until she is changed into a stream by Artemis
alphosis	αλφισμός (αλφός –white)	dull-white leprosy, leukoderma
altruistic	αλτρουϊστικός, ή, ό (adj.)	of or motivated by altruism; unselfish, Syn. Philanthropic
artruistically	αλτρουϊστικώς/ αλτρουϊστικά (adv.)	acting in an altruistic manner
altruism	αλτρουϊσμός	1 unselfish concern of the welfare of others/selflessness 2 Ethics the doctrine that the general welfare of society is the proper goal of an individual's actions: opposed to Egoism
altruist	αλτρουϊστής/ αλτρουϊστρια (fem.)	a person who cares for the welfare of others

alyssum	άλυσσος, η, ο (adj.) άλυσσον (neu.)(α/ without + λύσσα/ madness/rage)	cured madness, rage 1 any of a genus (Alyssum) of crucifers with white or yellow flowers and grayish leaves 2 Sweet Alyssum
amaranth	αμάρανθος/ αμάραντος	unfading flower 1 any of the genus (Amaranthus) of plants of the amaranth family 2 (Old Poet.) and imaginary flower that never fades or dies 3 dark purplish red
amaranthine	αμαρανθίνη/ αμαραντίνη	1 of or like the amaranth 2 unfading or undying 3 dark purplish red
amaryllis	αμαρυλλίς / αμαρυλλίδα	a shepherdess's name [in poems by Virgil and Theocritus] any of several plants (esp., genus Hippeastrum) of the lily family bearing several white, purple, pink, or redflowers on a leafless stem, including the belladona lily
amavrosis	αμαύρωσις/η	blackening/partial or total blindness
Amazon	αμαζών/αμαζόνα	female warrior; river in South America 1 Gr. myth. any of a race of female warriors supposed to have lived in Scythia nerar the Black Sea 2 a) a tall, strong, aggressive woman 3 a small, greenish parrot (genus Amazona) of Central and South America, often kept as a pet 4 any of genus (Polyergus) of ants that makes slaves of other ants, also known as Amazon ant
Amazonian	αμαζόνειος, α, ο (adj.)	1 of or charactersistic of an Amazon (tall, strong aggressive woman, etc.) 2 of the Amazon River or the country around it

ambi-	αμφί-	both combining form (ambidextrous/double-dealing)
ambly-	αμβλύς, αμβλεία, αμβλύ (adj.)	dull; not sharp
amblygonite	αμβλυγώνιος, αμβλυγωνία/ αμβλυγώνιον/ο (adj.)	obtuse-angled; 1 a pale-green or white crystalline mineral, Li (AIF)PO: it is an ore of lithium and occurs in pegmatitic rocks
amblyopia	αμβλυωπία	a loss in sharpness of vision, esp. when not traceable to any intrinsic eye disease
amblyopic	αμβλυωπικός, ή, ο (adj.)	one suffering from amblyopia
amplyoscope	αμβλυοσκόπιον/ο	an instrument for training amblyopic eyes to function properly
ambo or ambon	άμβων/ άμβωνος (gen. / άμβωνας(mod. Gr.)	pulpit or raised reading stand, esp. in early Christian church
ambrosia	αμβροσία (αν + βροτος – not + mortal)	immortal 1 Gr and Rom. myth. the food of the gods 2 anything that tastes and smells delicious 3 ragweed
ambrosial	αμβρόσιος, ια, ο (adj.)	1 of or fit for the gods; devine 2 like ambrosia; delicious; fragrant
ambrotype	αμβρότυπος	an early kind of photograph, consisting of a glass negative backed by a dark surface as to appear positive
amenorrhea	αμηνόρροια (α + μηνόρροια – without +menstruation)	abnormal absence or suppression of menstruation
amethyst	αμέθυστος, η, ο (adj.)/not drunken	1 a purple or violet variety of quartz, used in jewelry 2 popularly, a purple variety of corundum, used in jewelry 3 purple or violet
amianthus	αμίαντος	without spot; undefiled

amnesia	αμνησία (α + μνήμη –without + memory)	forgetfulness; loss of memory; partial or total loss of memory caused as of brain injury or by shock
amnesty	αμνηστία/αμνηστεία	pardon; forgiving 1 pardon esp., for political offenses against a government 2 (Archaic) a deliberate overlooking as of an offense
amnestic	αμνηστευτικός, ή, ό (adj.)	one who has received amnesty
amniocentesis	αμνιοκέντησις / κέντηση (αμνός + κέντηση- amnio sac + puncture)	the surgical procedure of inserting a hollow needle through the abdominal wall into the uterus of a pregnant woman and extracting amniotic fluid, which may be analyzed to determine the sex of the developing fetus or the presence of disease, genetic defects, etc.
amnion	αμνός	lamb; 1 the innermost membrane of the sac enclosing the embryo of a mammal, reptile, or bird: it is filled with a watery fluid [amnionic fluid] 2 a similar membrane of certain invertabrates, esp. insects
amoeba or ameba	αμοιβάς/αμοιβάδος (gen.) /αμοιβάδα (Mod. Gr.)	1 a one-called, microscopic organism belonging to any of several families of rhizopods that move and feed using pseudopodia and reproduce by fission; esp. any of a genus (Amoeba) found in soil or water or a parasitic genus (Entamoeba) found in higher animals and humans 2 something indefinite in shape or perpetually changing, like an amoeba

amoebiasis/ amebiasis	αμοιβάδωσις /η	infestation with amoebas, esp. with protozoan (Entamoeba histolytica) parasitic in the intestines or liver
amoebic/ameboid	(ο, η) αμοιβαειδής/ (το) αμοβαειδές (adj.)	of or characterizing amoeba; amoeba-like; resembling or related to an amoeba (the spelling 'ameba' is now standard in scientific usage, however, the spelling "amoeba" is still clearly preferred in general usage
amoebic dysentery	αμοιβαειδής δυσεντερία	a form of dysentery caused by an amoeba (Entamoeba histolytica)
amorphous	άμορφος (α + μορφή –without-shape/ form)	shapeless; without definite form
ampelopsis	άμπελος-αμπέλι/ vineyard + ύψος/hight	a climbing vine or shrub
amphi- prefix	αμφί	around or about; both side/ends
amphi-arthosis	αμφι-άρθωσις/η	Anat. a slightly movable articulation (as a symphysis or a syndesmosis); a form of jointing in which cartilage connects the bones and allows only a slight motion
amphibian or amphibious	αμφίβιος (αμφί/ both + βίος/life)	1 that could live in both on land and in water; living a double life 2 that can operate or travel on both land or water 3 designating, of, or a military peration involving the landing of assault troops on a shore from seaborne transports 4 having two natures or qualities; of a mixed nature
amphibiology	αμφιβιολογία	branch of science examining life of amphibians
amphiboly	αμφιβολία	ambiguity; doubt

amphibolic	αμφίβολος, η, ο (adj.)	having an uncertain or irregular outcome: used of stages of fevers or the critical period of disease, when prognosis is uncertain
amphi-bology	αμφιβολογία/ αμφιβολία	ambiguity; 1 double or doubtful meaning; ambiguity, esp., from uncertain grammatical construction 2 an ambiguous phrase, proposition, etc. also amphiboly
amphibrach	αμφι-βραχύς	short; a metrical foot consisting in Greek and Latin verse
amphi-chroic	αμφί-χρωϊκός, ή, ό (adj.) (αμφί + χρώμα – both + color)	Chem. exhibiting either of two colors under varying conditions, as litmus
amphicoelus	αμφίκοιλος, η, ο (adj.) (αμφί + κοίλος- both + cave/hollow)	concave on both sides, as the vertebrae of certain fishes
amphi/ctyon	αμφικτύων/ αμφικτύονες	those who dwelt around amphiktyonies (pl.)
amphictyony	αμφικτυονία / αμφικτιονία	in Ancient Greece, a confederation of states was established around a religious center, as at Delphi
amphimixis	ανάμειξις /ανάμιξη (αμφί + μίξις- uniting together)	1 Biol. the uniting of male and female germ cells from two individuals in reproduction 2 crossbreeding
amphioxus	αμφίοξος / αμfί + οξύς – both + sharp)	lancelet; cephalochordate
amphipod/ amphipoda	αμφίποδα	any of an order (Amphipoda) of malacostracan crustaceans with a vertically thin body and one set of legs for jumping and walking and another set for swimming
amphi-pro-style	αμφι-πρόστυλος	Archit. having columns at the front and back but none along the sides

amphistylar	αμφίστυλος (αμφί + στύλος – both + pillar)	Archit. having columns at both front and back or on both sides
amphi-theater	αμφιθέατρον/o	1 a round or oval building with an open space (arena) surrounded by rising rows of seats 2 a scene of conflict, competition, etc.; arena 3 a sloping gallery in a theater 4 a lecture hall with a sloping gallery, esp., one for observing medical procedures in a medical school or hospital 5 a level place surrounded by rising ground
amphi-theatrical	αμφι-θεατρικός, ή, ό (adj.)	relating to the amphitheater
amphithecium	αμφί + θήκη (both +case)	Bot. the outer layer of cells in the spore case of a bryophyte
amphora	αμφορεύς/ αμφορέως (gen.) / αμφορέας (Mod. Gr.) (αμφί + φορεύς- both/ around +bearer)	a tall jar with a narrow neck and base and two handles, used by the ancient Greeks and Romans
amphoteric	αμφότερος/ αμφότεροι (pl.)	Chem. having both acid and basic properties
anyglale /amyglalae	αμυγδαλή/ αμυγδαλαί (puristic Gr.pl.) αμυγδαλές (Mod. Gr. pl.)	1 tonsil(s) 2 the one of the four basic ganglia in each cerebral hemisphere that is part of the limbic systemand consists of an almond- shaped mass of gray matter in the roof of the lateral vertical (also called amygdaloid body or nucleus)
amygdale	αμύγδαλον/o αμύγδαλα (pl.)	almond(s);
amygdal-ectomy	αμυγδαλο-εκτομή	the surgical reoval of the amyglalae
amygdalo-	αμύγδαλο (v)	almond (combining form)

amygdaloid	(ο, η) αμυγδαλοειδής (το) αμυγδαλοειδές) (adj.)	resembling an almond
amylo- prefix	άμυλον	starch not ground in the mill
amylogen	αμυλογενές	the water-soluble part of the starch granule: also called amylose
amyloid	(ο, η) αμυλώδης (το) αμυλώδες (adj.)	starchy food
amylolysis	αμυλόλυσις/η	changing from starch into soluble substances by the action of enzymes or by hydrolysis with dilute acids
amylum	άμυλον (α + μύλος – not + mill)	starch (alevron) (meal); not ground at a mill Chem. technical name for starch
ana-	prefix ανά	1 up, upward (as in: anadromous) 2 back, backward (as in: anagram) 3 again (as in:anabaptism) 4 throughout (as in: analysis) (plus all compound words) 5 according to, similar to (as in: analogy)
Anabaptism	αναβαπτισμός/ αναβάπτιση	second baptism
Anabaptist	αναβαπτιστής	any member of a radical sixteenth cent. Sect of the Reformation originating in Switzerland, often persecuted because they opposed the taking of oaths, infant baptism, military service, and the holding of public office
Anabasis	Ανάβασις /ανάβαση	the unsuccessful military expedition of Cyrus the Younger to overthrow Artaxerxes II/ a book on the subject by Xenophon / Ξενοφών /Ξενοφώντας

anabatic	αναβατικός, ή, ό (adj.)	moving upward
anabiosis	αναβίωσις/ αναβίωση	to come to life again; revival
anabole	αναβολή	a rising up; delaying; putting off
anabolic	αναβολικός, ή, ό (adj.)	pertaining to anabolism
anabolism	αναβολισμός	a process in a plant or animal by which food is changed into living tissue
anachronism	αναχρονισμός	referring to the wrong time/ anything that seems to be out of its proper time in history
anachronistic	αναχρονιστικός, ή, ό (adj.)	anything /anyone that is or seems to be out ot its proper time in history; living in the past
anaclastic	ανακλαστικός, ή, ό (adj.)	causing refraction
anaclisis	ανάκλισις/η	leaning back
anaclitic	ανάκλιτος, η, ο(adj.)	to lean upon; reclining
anacoluthon	ανακόλουθον	1 inconsequent 2 a change from one grammatical construction to another within the same sentence, sometimes as a rhetorical device 3 not following
anacrusis	ανάκρουσις/η	push back; beginning of a tune
anadem	ανάδημα	a head wreath/garland
anadiplosis	αναδίπλωσις/η	repetition of the last word(s) of a clause or line of a verse at the beginning of the next; redoubling
anadromous	ανάδρομος- ανήφορος	running up; ascend; aclivity
anaemia or anemia	αναιμία (αν/ without-αίμα/blood)	condition in which there is a reduction of a number of red blood corpuscles and symptoms of exhaustion

anaerobe	αναερόβιος	a microorganism that can live and grow where there is no air or free oxygen: it may not be able to grow if any oxygen is present
anaerobic	αναεροβικός, ή, ό (adj.)	1 of or produced by anaerobes 2 able to live and grow where there is no air or free oxygen, as certain bacteria
anaesthesia or anesthesia	αναισθησία (αν + αίσθησις - without + feeling/sense)	1 a partial loss of the sense of pain, temperature, touch, etc., produced by disease 2 a loss of sensation induced by an anaesthetic, hypnosis, or acupuncture and limited to a specific area see: anesthesia; anesthetic, etc.
anaglyph	ανάγλυφον- ανάγλυφο	1 an ornament, as a cameo, carved in low relief; 2 a photograph made up of two slightly different views, in complementary colors, of the same subject: when looked at through a pair of corresponding color filters, the picture appears three-dimensional
anaglyptic	αναγλυπτικός, η, ό (adj.)	pertaining to anaglyphs
anagoge/anagogy	αναγωγή	reference to a principal; spiritual uplifting
anagogic	αναγωγικός, ή, o (adj.)	one practicing anagogy
anagram	ανάγραμμα	1 writing the letters of a name (word) backward 2 a word or phrase made from another by rearranging the letters (ex: dear-read; now-won, etc.) 3 (in p.) a game whose object is to make words by arranging letters from a common pool or by forming anagrams from other words

ana-grammatism	ανα-γραμματισμός	the skill or art of doing anagrams
ana-grammatize	αναγραμματίζω	the ability to form; create or play angrams
analemma	ανάλημμα	support; substructure
analeptic	αναληπτικός, ή, ό (adj.) {ανά/up-λήψις (λαμβάνειν) to receive }	restorative esp. stimulating the nervous system and counteracting drowsiness or the effects of sedatives
analgesia	αναλγησία	painlessness; in a fully conscious state in which a person does not feel painful stimuli
analogous	ανάλογος, η, ο (adj.)	similar or comparable in certain respects
analogy	αναλογία	proportion; similarity in some respects between things otherwise unlike; partial resemblance
analphabetic	αναλφάβητος η, ο (adj.)	uneducated, not knowing the ABCs
analysis	ανάλυσις/η	1 dissolving; a statement of a process; detailed explanation and description 2 a separating or breaking up of any whole into its parts, esp. with an examination of these parts to find out their nature, proportion, function, interrelationship, etc. 3 Linguis the use of word order and uninflected function words instead of inflected, in order to express syntactic relationships 4 Math. a branch of mathematics, including calculus, dealing with functions and limits and their generalizations 5 Systems Analysis, in the last (or final) analysis after all factors have been considered

analyst	αναλυτής	a person who analyzes, being a news analyst; a psychoanalyst; a systems analyst, etc.
analytic	αναλυτικός, ή, ό (adj.)	1 of analysis or analytics 2 that separates into constituent parts 3 skilled in or uses analysis [an analytic mind] 4 Linguis. expressing syntactic relationships by the use of uninflected function words instead of inflections (ex: in English, more often instead than in this instance oftener) 5 Logic necessarily true by virtue of the meaning of its component terms alone, without reference to the external fact and with its denial resulting in self-contradiction; tautologous [an analytic proposition]: opposed to **Synthetic**
analytical	αναλυτικός, ή, ό (adj.)	pertaining to analysis, the opposite of synthetic-συνθετικός, ή, ό (adj.)
analytical chemistry	αναλυτική χημεία	a branch of chemistry dealing with the identification of compounds and mixtures (qualitative analysis) or the determination of the proportions of the constituents (quantitative analysis): techniques commonly used are titration, precipitation, spectroscopy, chromatography, etc.
analytical geometry	αναλυτική γεωμετρία	the branch of geometry in which a coordinate graphic system makes visible, using points, lines, and curves, the numerical relationships of algebraic equations. Also called **coordinate geometry or Cartesian geometry**

analytical philosophy	αναλυτική φιλοσοφία	a twentieth cent. philosophic movement characterized by its method of analyzing concepts and statements in the light of common experience and ordinary language, in order to eliminate confusion of thought and resolve many traditional philosophical problems
analytical psychology	αναλυτική ψυχολογία	the system of psychology developed by C. G. Jung as a variant of psychoanalysis
analytics	αναλυτική	the part of logic having to do with analyzing
analyze	αναλύειν //αναλύω	separating (a word, idea, thing, etc.) into its parts in order to find out their nature, proportion, function, etc.
anamnesis	ανάμνησις/η	reminiscence, recollection, recollecting past events
anamnestic	αναμνηστικός, ή, ό (adj.)	pertaining to anamnesis; an anamnestic picture, letter; something to remember, etc.
anamorphosis	αναμόρφωσις /η	1 reformation; renewal; renovation; restoration 2 a technique of perspective to produce a distorted image a distorted image that will look normal when viewed from a particular angle or with a special mirror 3 Biol. a gradual change of form by evolution
anamyotrophic/ amyotrophic	ανα-μυοτροφικός, ή, ό (adj.)	amyotrophic lateral schlerosis (ALS) a disease that breaks down tissues in the nervous system
anandrous	άνανδρος (αν + ανδρός – gen. of ανήρ (anc./ Gr. άνδρας (Mod. Gr.) – not + man)	(lit. not fit to be a man) timid; cowardly; dastard; recreant; lacking courage
ananthous	άνανθος	without flowers

anapaest or anapest	ανάπαιστος (ανα + παίειν- back + to strike	(so called for reversing the dactyl) 1 a metrical foot consisting, in Greek and Latin verse, of two short syllables followed by a long one, or, as in English, of two unaccented syllables followed by an accented one
anapaestic	αναπαιστικός, ή, ό (adj.)	pertaining to anapaest
anaphase	ανάφασις/η	Biol. the stagein mitosis, after the metaphase and before the telophase, in which the divided chromosomes move apart toward the poles of the spindle
anaphora	αναφορά (ανα + φέρειν – back + to bear/bring)	repetition of a word or phrase at the beginning of successive clauses, lines, of verse, etc., anaphora/αναφορά in Greek also means report, petition, dispatch (military)
anaphrodisia	αναφροδισία	lack of sexual desire
anaphrodisiac	αναφροδισιακός, ή, ό (adj.)	of, relating to, or causing absence or impairment of sexual desire; a drug, etc., that lessens sexual desire
anaphylactic	αναφυλακτικός, ή, ό (adj.)	of, relating to, or affected by or causing anaphylaxis
anaphylaxis	αναφύλαξις /η (ανα/ back – φύλαξις – a guarding; φυλάσσειν/to guard)	a condition of hypersensitivity to proteins or other substances, requiring previous exposure to the allergenic substance and resulting in shock or other physical reactions
anaplasis or anaplasia	ανάπλασις /η / αναπλασία	reversion of cells to more primitive or undifferentiated form
anaplastic	αναπλαστικός, η, ό (adj.)	Med. characterized by a reversion to a more primitive, imperftectly developed form: said of cells, esp., when cancerous

anaplasty	ανάπλαστος, η, ο (adj.)	imperfectly developed form
anaplerotic	αναπληρωτικός, ή. ό (adj.)	substitute; alternate; surrogate
anapodeictic	αναπόδεικτος, η, ο (αν + απόδειξη)	not proven
anaptyxis	ανάπτυξις/η	expansion; explanation; augmentation
anarchic	αναρχικός, ή, ό (adj.)	a person who promotes anarchy
anarchist	άναρχος/ αναρχικός	disregarding the rules/laws
anarchism	αναρχισμός	the theory that all forms of government interfere unjustly with the liberties of individuals
anarchy	αναρχία	complete absence of government; political disorder and violence
anarthria	ανάρθρωσις-η (α + άρθρωσις - without + arthron/ articulation)	inability to produce or articulate speech or words
anarthrous	άναρθρος, η, ο (adj.) (αν + άρθρωσις/η-without + good diction)	inarticulate; complete inability to produce articulate speech
anasarka	ανάσαρκα (ανα - σάρκωμα)	generalized edema with accumulation of serum in the connective tissue
Anastasia	Αναστασία	a girl's name deriving from Anastasis: meaning Resurrection
anastigmatic	αναστιγματικός, ή, ό (adj.)	free from, or corrected for, astigmatism; specif., designating a compound lens made up of one converging and one diverging lens so the astigmatism of one, is neutralized by the equal and opposite astigmatism of the other

anastomosis	αναστόμωσις/ η (ανα/back * στόμα/mouth)	to provide opening through the mouth (as in surgical procedures)
anastrophe	αναστροφή (ανα + στροφή/ back + turn)	reversal of the usual order of the parts of a sentence (ex: "Came the dawn"); inversion; turning back
anatase	ανάταση	stretching; prolongation (to lengthen or extend)
anathema	ανάθεμα	a thing or person accursed or damned; a solemn ecclesiastical condemnation
anathematize	αναθεματίζειν/ αναθεματίζω	to utter an anathema against someone or something; curse
anatomical	ανατομικός, ή, ό (adj.)	pertaining to anatomy; skilled in anatomy
anatomize	ανατέμνειν/ ανατέμνω	to dissect (an animal or plant) in order to examine the structure 2 to analyze in great detail
anatomy	ανατομία (ανα + τέμνειν- up + to cut)	1 the structure of an organism or body 2 the dissecting of an animal or plant in order to determine the position, structure, etc.., of its parts 3 the science of the morphology or structure of animals or plants 4 a detailed analysis 5 (Archaic) a skeleton
Anaxagoras	Αναξαγόρας	c.500–428 BC; Gr. philosopher from Ionia who taught in Athens
Anaximanter	Αναξίμανδρος	Gr. philosopher; astronomer; mathematecian
anchor	άγκυρα	any device that holds something else secure, anchor of a boat; a person who anchors a team, a newcast, etc.
ancon	αγκών/αγκώνας	elbow; Archit. a bracketlike projection supporting a cornice; console

anchylosis	αγκύλωσις /η	curved; crooked
ancylostomiasis	αγκυλοστομίασις/η	crooked mouth; 1 infestation or disease caused by hookworms: esp., a lethargic anemic state due to blood loss through the feeding of hookworms in the small intestine 2 technical term for hookworm disease
andro-	ανήρ/ανδρός (gen.)/ άνδρας (Mod. Gr.)	pertaining to males, man
androgen	αδρογενές	any substance or hormone causing masculine characteristics
androgenous	(ο, η) ανδρογενής/ (το) ανδρογενές (adj.)	producing only male offspring
androgynous	ανδρόγυνος	both male and female in one; hermaphroditic
android	(ο, η) ανδροειδής(το) ανδροειδές (adj.)	
Andromache	Ανδρομάχη	Gr. myth. wife of Hector; feminine name meaning: battle of man
androphobia	ανδροφοβία	extreme fear of men
andro-sphinx	άνδρο-σφίνξ-σφίγγα	creature with the head of a man and body of a lion
anectodal	ανεκδοτολογικός, ή, ό (adj.)	of or like an anectode; interesting but not of great importance or substance
anectode	ανέκδοτος, η, ο (adj.)	something that has not been published; (ανέκδοτο(ν) (a joke; humorous story)
anemia/anaemia	αναιμία (αν/without +αίμα/blood)	condition in which the normal amount of red blood cells is reduced
anemic	αναιμικός, ή, ό (adj.)	pertaining to anemia; one having loss of energy, vitality
anemo-	άνεμος	wind, combining word (anemometer)

anemograph	ανεμογράφος	instrument for recording the velocity, of the wind
anemographic	ανεμογραφικός, ή, ο (adj.)	pertaining to the velocity and duration of the wind
anemology	ανεμολογία	the study of winds; velocity, duration, etc.
anemometer	ανεμόμετρον/ο	a gauge for determining the force or speed of the wind and sometimes its direction
anemometry	ανεμομετρία/ ανεμομέτρηση	the process of determining the speed and direction of the wind with an anemometer
anemone	ανεμώνη	Bot. any of a number related plants of the genus (Anemone) of the buttercup family with cup-shaped flowers
anemophilous	ανεμόφιλος, η, ο (adj.)	pollinated by the wind
anemoscope	ανεμοσκόπιον/ο	instrument for showing or recording the direction of the wind
anencephaly	αν + εγκέφαλος – without + brain	congenital malformation of the skull with the absence of all or part of the brain
anergy	ανεργία (ανευ without + εργο/ εργασία /work)	unemployment; no work
aneroid	α + νερό –without water (ο, η) ανεροειδής (το) ανεροειδές (adj.)	without fluid, liquid; not using liquid/fluid
anesthesia	αναισθησία	total or partial loss of the sense of pain, temperature, touch, etc.; loss of sensation induced by an anesthetic, hypnosis, trauma, etc.
anesthesiologist	αναισθησιολόγος	physician specializing in anesthesiology
anesthetic	αναισθητικό	producing anesthesia; a drug, gas, etc., used to produce anaesthesia before surgery

aneurism/aneurysm	ανεύρισμα	sac formed by enlargement of a weakened wall of an artery, a vein, or the heart caused by disease or injury
angaria/angary	αγγαρεία	impressments for public service
angariate	αγγαρεύειν/ αγγαρεύω	imposing compulsory work; public service
angel	άγγελος	messenger; Theol. a messenger of God b. a supernatural being, either good or bad
angelic	αγγελικός, ή, ό (adj.)	spititual, heavenly, lovely, innocent as an angel etc.
angelo-latry	αγγελο-λατρεία	excessive worship to angels
angelology	αγγελολογία	the branch of theology dealing with angels
angina	άγχος (αγχώδης κατάσταση)	1 any inflammatory disease of the throat; localized spasm of pain or any condition marked with such spasms 2 a condition marked by recurrent pain, usually in the chest and left arm, caused by a sudden decrease of the blood supply to the heart (angina pectoris)
angio-	αγγείο(ν)	case, capsule, container, blood vessel, combining form (angiology)
angio-cardiography	αγγειο - καρδιογραφία	making x-ray pictures of the heart
angiogram	αγγειόγραμμα	pertaining to angiography
angiography	αγγειογραφία	process of making x-ray pictures of blood vessels after first injecting a radiopaque substance
angiology	αγγειολογία	the study of blood vessels and lymph vessels
angioma	αγγείωμα (αγγείο + όγκος- vessel + tumor)	tumor made up mainly of blood vessels

angioplasty	αγγειοπλαστική	any of various techniques for repaining/replacing damaged blood vessels by surgery, lasers or tiny inflatable balloons
angiosarcoma	αγγείο + σάρκωμα	a sarcoma (malignant tumor) containing many vessel-like structures
angiosperm	αγγειόσπερμα	any of a division (Magnoliophyta) of flowering plants having seeds produced within a closed pod or ovary, including monocodyledons and dicodyledons
angle	αγκύλη	crooked curve or bend
anhydrite	ανυδρία (αν + ύδωρ/ νερό (Mod. Gr.) without + water	anhydrous calcium sulfate; a granular, white or light-colored mineral resembling marble, often found together with rock salt
anhydrous	άνυδρος, η, ο (adj.)	1 arid; waterless; 2 Chem. having no water of crystallization; not hydrated
anise	άνισον	a plant of the ambel family, with small white or yellow flowers
aniso-	άνισος, η, ο (adj.)	unequal; uneven
anisomerous	(ο, η) ανισο-μερής, (το) ανισομερές (adj.)	Bot. of or describing a flower having an unequal number of petals, stamens, or other floral parts; characterized of having unequal parts
anisometric	ανισομετρικός, ή, ό (άνισος -μέτρον /unequal/ uneven-meter)	having assymetrical parts
anisometropia	ανισομετροπία	a condition of both eyes in which they have unequal refractive power

anisotropic	ανισοτροπικός, ή, o (adj.)	1 Bot. assuming a new position in response to external stimuli 2 Physics: having properties, such as conductivity or speed of transmission of light, etc., that vary according to the direction they are measured
ankylosis	αγκύλωσις/ αγκύλωση	stiffening of the joints, caused by the pathological joining of bones or fibrous parts, by injury, or surgical procedure
anode	άνοδος (ανά + οδός- up + way)	way up; a way going upward; 1 in an electrolytic cell,the positively charged electrode, toward which current flows 2 in an electron tube, the principal electrode for collecting electrons operated at a positive potential with respect to cathode 3 in a battery that is a source of electric current, the negative electrode
anodyne	αν + οδύνη- without + pain (ανώδυνος, η, o (adj./ painless)	relieving or lessening pain
anomalous	ανώμαλος, η, o (adj.)	deviating from the normal
anomaly	ανωμαλία	deviation from the normal 1 departure from the regular arrangement, general rule, or usual method, abnormality 2 Astron. a measurement used for any orbiting body, as a planet's angular distance around its orbit from its perihelion, taken as viewed from the sun
anomy or anomie	ανομία	lawlessness; lack of purpose, identity, or ethical values in a person or in a society; rootlessness
anonym	ανώνυμον/o	without a name

anonymity	ανωνυμία	a condition or fact of not being known; being anonymous
anonymous	ανώνυμος/η/ο (adj.) (αν/without/ όνομα/name)	with no name; known or acknowledged; not easily distinguished from others
anopheles	(ο, η) ανωφελής, (το) ανωφελές (adj.)	without benefit; any of a genus of mosquitos that can transmit diseases, esp. malaria
anorexia	ανορεξία (αν όρεξις/η –without + appetite)	without appetite; lack of desire for food
anorexia nervosa	νευρική ανορεξία (νευρικός, ή, ό, adj./ nervous)	an eating disorder, chiefly in young women, characterized by aversion to food and obsession with weight loss
anorexic	ανόρεχτος, η, ο (adj.)	suffering from anorexia, suppressing appetite for food
anoxemia	αν + οξυγόνο + αίμα (without +oxygen+ blood)	a reduction of the normal amount of oxygen in the blood, as in high altitudes
anoxia	αν + οξυγόνον/ο – without + oxygen)	Med. total deprivation of oxygen, hypoxia
anosmia	ανοσμία (αν + οσμή – without + smell)	total or partial loss of the sense of smell
Antaeus	Ανταίος	Gr. myth. a giant wresler who is invincible as long as he is touching his mother, the earth
antagonism	ανταγωνισμός	rivalry; competition; opposition
antagonist	ανταγωνιστής/ ανταγωνίστρια (fem.)	1 a person who competes or opposes another; adversary; opponent; rival 2 a muscle; drug, etc., that acts in opposition to or counteracts another
antagonistic	ανταγωνιστικός, ή, ό (adj.)	competitive; opposing; showing antagonism, rivalry
antagonize	ανταγωνίζομαι	to struggle against; to oppose or counteract
antarctic	ανταρκτικός, ή, ό (adj.)	of or near the South Pole or the region around it

Antarctica	Ανταρκτική	land area about the South Pole or the region around it, completely covered by an ice shelf (many times considered a continent)
antelope	αντιλόπη	deer; a fabulous horned animal; any of a group of swift, bovid ruminants usually living in wild herds on the plains of Africa and Asia
anthelion	ανθήλιον αντί/ against + ήλιος /sun	a rarely seen, hazy white spot at the same altitude as the sun, but opposite in the sky, caused by a reflection from the atmosphere, snow or ice
anthem	it derives from: αντίφωνος, η, ο (adj.) (αντί/ opposite/ against-φωνή/voice	1 religious song sung antiphonally ; 2 a religious choral song usually based on words from the Bible 3 song of praise or devotion to a nation, college, etc.
anther	ανθήρ/ ανθηρός, ή, ό (adj.)	blooming, a sprout, stalk
anthesis	άνθησις /η (ανθείν / to bloom,)	the state of full bloom in a flower
antho-	άνθος	flower, combining word
anthocarpous	ανθόκαρπος	designating of or a false fruit, as the pineapple or strawberry, formed from the separate ovaries of one or several blossoms
anthologist	ανθολόγος	one who anthologizes, makes an anthology
anthologize	ανθολογώ	to make anthologies
anthology	ανθολογία/ ανθολόγιο(ν)	a garland collection of short poems, stories, poems, excerpts, etc.
anthophore	ανθοφόρος	an elongated stalk, between the sepals and the petals of some flowers, that supports the flowering parts

-anthous	-ανθος	suffix forming adjective referring to flowers (of a specified kind or number (as in monanthous/having one flower)
anthracite	ανθρακίτις/ ανθρακίτιδα	hard coal which gives much heat but little flame and smoke
anthracoid	(ο, η) ανθρακοειδής, (το) ανθρακοειδές (adj.)	resembling anthrax, like anthrax; coal
anthracosis	ανθράκωσις/η	black lung disease; a benign deposition of coal dust within the lungs from inhalation of sooty air
anthrax	άνθραξ/άνθρακας	(burning) coal; an infectious hemorrhagic disease
anthrop – or anthropo-	ανθρωπος	man; human being, combining form (anthropology)
anthropocene	(άνθρωπος| + καινός – human + new/young/ fresh + cene)	denoting a geological period
anthropo-centric	ανθρωπο-κεντρικός, ή, ό (adj.)	considers man the center of the universe
anthropo-centrism	ανθρωπο-κεντρισμός	the theory that man is the center and purpose of creation
anthropo-genesis	ανθρωπο-γένεσις/η	the study of man's origin and development
anthropo-genic	(ο, η) ανθρωπο-γενής, (το) ανθρωπογενές (adj.)	caused by man, as pollution etc.
anthropo-graphy	ανθρωπογραφία	the branch of anthropology dealing with the distribution of humans according to their physical characteristics, language, etc.
anthropoid	(ο, η) ανθρωποειδής, (το) ανθρωποειδές (adj.)	resembling a human
anthropo-latry	ανθρωπολατρεία	idolizing man; men in general
anthropologist	ανθρωπολόγος	a person who specializes in anthropology

anthropology	ανθρωπολογία	science of human nature
anthropo-metry	ανθρωπο-μέτρησις /η	a branch of anthropology dealing with measurement of the human body to determine differences in individuals, groups, etc,. It is used in medicine, space programs, anthropology, etc.
anthropo-morphic	ανθρωπομορφικός (άνθρωπος/man + μορφή –man +shape/form)	characterized or, resulting from anthropomorphism
anthropo-morphism	ανθρωπο-μορφισμός (άνθρωπος + μορφή/ man +shape/form)	the attributing of human shape or characteristics to a god
/anthropo-phagy	ανθρωποφαγία (άνθρωπος + φάγειν - to eat man/sarc)	cannibalism
anthroposophy	ανθρωπο –σοφία	a religion or a mystical system or movement similar to theosophy, founded by Rudolf Steiner in 1912
anti- prefix	αντί	1 against; opposite; before; instead of; hostile to; opposed to [antilabor] 2 that counteracts, that operates against [antiaircraft] 3 prevents, cures or neutralizes [antitoxin] 4 opposite, reverse [antiperistalsis] 5 rivaling [antipope] 6 having the superficial aspect, but not the usual characteristics of [antihero]
antibacterial	αντι-βακτηριακός	it checks the growth or effect of bacteria
antiballistic	αντιβαλλιστικός, ή, ό (adj.)(αντί + βάλλειν- against + to hit)	intended to intercept and destroy a ballistic missile in flight

antibiosis	αντιβίωσις/ αντιβίωση	association between organisms that is harmful to one of them, as a fungus producing an antibiotic that inhibits neighboring vacteria
antibiotic	αντιβιωτικός, ή, ό (adj.)	destroying or inhibiting the growth of bacteria and other organisms; any of certain chemical substances produced by various microorganisms, specif. bacteria, fungi, actinomycetes; the antibiotics, including penicillin, etc. and used in the treatment of various infectious diseases
anti-catalyst	αντί-καταλύτης	a substance that slows down a chemical reaction
anti-Christ	αντίχριστος (αντί –Χριστός)	nonbeliever in Christ; against Christ; opposing Christ
anti-cline	αντί + κλίνειν	decline in opposite direction; a sharply arched fold of stratified rock from whose central axis, the strata slope, going down in opposite directions
anti-cyclone	αντί + κυκλών/ κυκλώνος (gen.) – opposite + cycle	Metereol., a motion of rotating winds over a vast area spinning out from a high pressure center (clockwise in the Northern Hemisphere) and generally causing fair weather
antidoron	αντίδωρον/ο (αντι + δώρον – back + gift)	reciprocal offering/gift; Eastern Orthodox Church: the blessed piece of bread which, people receiving Holy Communion **take**, and at the end of the Divine Litugy the priest gives to the congregation
antidote	αντίδοτο(ν)	given as a remedy to counteract a poison
antidromic	αντί + δρόμος / αντιδρομικός, ή, ό (adj.)	Physiol. conveying nerve impulses in a direction opposite to the normal

antigen	αντιγενές	a protein, toxin, or other substance of high molecular weight, to which the body reacts by producing antibodies
Antigone	Αντιγόνη	daughter of Oedipus and Jocaste, who defied the order of the king and buried her brother Polynices
Antigonus	Αντίγονος	382–301 BC Macedonian general under Alexander the Great, nicknamed the Cyclops
anti-hero	αντι - ήρωας- hero	someone lacking hero qualities; the opposite of hero
anti-lithic	αντι-λιθικός, ή, ό (adj	preventing the formation or development of calculi, as of the urinary tract; against-stone; an antilithic substance
anti-logarithm	αντί-λογάριθμος	the number that results when the base is raised to a power by a logarithm [103 = 1,000. is expressed by: the antilogarithm of 3 to the base 10 is 1,000, or antilog 3 = 1,000, or log 1,000 =3]
antilogism	αντιλογισμός	the theory or practice of contradictory ideas, statements, or terms
antilogy	αντιλογία (αντί + λογία/against + word/speech)	a contradiction or disagreement in ideas, statements, or terms
anti-monarchical	αντι-μοναρχικός, ή, ό (adj.)	one being against or opposed to the monarchy
antinomy	αντινομία	1 being againt a law, regulation,etc., to another 2 contradiction or inconsistency between to apparently reasonable principles or laws

anti-parallel	αντι-παράλληλος, η, ο (adj.)	1 designating lines or planes that intersect with other lines or planes to form pairs of equal angles that are the reverse of the equal angles formed by the intersection of the same lines or planes with parallel lines 2 designating vectors that are parallel but opposite in direction
antipathetic	αντιπαθητικός, ή, ό (adj.)	attracting antipathy; not likeable; opposed or antagonistic character, tendency, etc.
antipathy	αντιπάθεια (αντί/ – πάθος)	opposite/negative feeling (the opposite/ antonym of sympathy)
anti-periodic	αντι-περιοδικός, ή, ό (adj.)	preventing the periodic return of attacks of disease, as of certain fevers, esp. malaria; an antiperiodic substance or drug
anti-phlogistic	αντι-φλογιστικός, ή, ό (adj.)	counteracting inflammation and fever; an antiphlogistic substance
antiphon	αντίφωνο/ν	hymn/psalm chanted or sung in responsive, alternating parts
antiphony	αντιφωνία	opposition of sounds (the opposite of symphony)
antiphasis	αντίφασις /η	contradiction; discrepancy; inconsistency
antiphatic	αντιφατικός, ή, ό (adj.)	contradictory, conflicting, inconsistent
antiphrasis	αντίφρασις αντί-φράσις/η	use of words or phrases in a sense opposite to the usual one, as for ironic effect
antipode	αντίποδας	anything dramatically opposite; exact opposite
antipodes pl.	αντίποδες (πλ.)	opposite feet/ diametrically opposed
antipsychotic	αντιψυχωτικός, ή, ό (adj.)	tranquilizing; neuroleptic

antipyretic	αντι-πυρετικός, ή, ό (αντί-πυρετός)	against fever; reducing fever
antiseptic	αντισηπτικός, ή, ό (adj.)	preventing infection
anti-spasmodic	αντι-σπασμωδικός, ή, ό (adj.)	relieving or preventing spasms, esp., of smooth muscle; an antispastic drug
antistatic	αντιστατικός, ή, ό (adj.)	reducing static electric charges, as on textiles, waxes, polishes, etc., by retaining enough moisture to provide electrical conduction
antistrophe	αντιστροφή (αντι + στρέφειν – against, opposite + to turn)	turning about; 1 in the ancient Greek theater, a) the return movement, from left to right of the stage, made by the chorus answering the previous strophe b) the part of the choric song performed during this 2 in poems with contrasting or parallel stanza systems, a stanza of the second system
antistrophic	αντιστροφικός, ή, ό (adj.)	pertaining to antistrophe
antithesis	αντίθεσις/αντίθεση	1 a contrast or opposition of thoughts, usually in two phrases, clauses, or sentences (ex: you are going; I am staying) 2 the second part of such an expression 3 a contrast or opposition 4 exact opposite [good is the antithesis of evil]
antithetical	αντιθετικός, ή, ό (adj.)	1 of or containing antithesis 2 exactly the opposite
antitype	αντίτυπος	1 the person or thing represented or foreshadowed by an earlier type or symbol 2 an opposite type
antonym	αντώνυμον/ο αντωνυμία	opposite in meaning; antonymia: pronoun

antrum/antron	άντρον/ο	cave; a cavity, esp. one within a bone, as either of a pair of sinuses in the upper jaw
anuria	ανουρία	partial or total fairure of the kidneys to produce urine
aorist	αόριστος/αόριστη περίοδος	past tense; indefinite period
aort- or aorto-	αόρτα	combining form (aortic; aortography)
aorta	αόρτα	the main artery of the body carrying blood from the left ventricle of the heart to all main arteries
aortic	αορτικός, ή, ό (adj.)	of, relating to, or affecting an aorta
aortic stenosis	αορτική στένωσις/η	a condition usually the result of disease in which the aorta and, esp., its orifice is abnormally narrow
aortitis	αορτίτις/αορτίτιδα	inflammation of the aorta
aortgraph	αορτογράφημα	an x-ray picture of the aorta made by arteriography
aortography	αορτογραφία	arteriography of the aorta
aortographic	αορτογραφικός, ή, ό (adj.)	pertaining to arteriography
apatetic	απάτη (n.) απατητικός, ή, ό (adj.)	deceit; deceiving; serving to deceive potential attackers
apathes	(ο, η) απαθής/ (το) απαθές (adj.)	feeling little or no emotion; unmoved
apathetic	απαθητικός, ή, ό (adj.)	1 having little or no emotion; unmoved 2 not in-interested; indifferent; listless
apathy	απάθεια	lack of passion/emotion total or partial loss of power to use or understand words
aperiodic	α –περιοδικός, ή, ό (adj.)	1 occurring irregularly; 2 Phys. without periodic vibrations
apetalous	απέταλος, η, ο (adj.)	Bot. without petals

aph- (prefix)	αφ/από /apo	off, from, away from, combining form
aphagia	αφαγία (α + φαγειν- not + to eat)	difficulty to swallow
aphakia	αφακία (α + φακός- without/not + lens)	absence of the crystalline lens of the eye; resulting in anomalous state of refraction
aphakic	άφακος (α + φακός- without + lens)	one who had the lens of an eye removed
aphanite/aphanes	(ο, η) αφανής,(το) αφανές (adj.) (α + φαίνειν – not + to appear)	invisible; not seen without an anaided eye; also in Gr. it means someone that has not achieved well-deserved fame or recognition, as aphanes hero or aphanes politician, etc.
aphasia	αφασία	total or partial loss of ability to use or understand words caused most of the time by brain injury or disease
aphasic or aphasiac	αφασικός, ή, ό (adj.)	of, relating to, or affected by aphasia
aphasiologist	αφασιολόγος	an expert in aphasiology
aphasiology	αφασιολογία	the study of aphasia
aphelion	από – αφ + ήλιος (αφ/af it is followed by a vowel)	from sun; the point farthest from the sun in the orbit of a planet or comet, or of a man-made satellite in orbit around the sun: opposed to perithelion
apheresis/aphaeresis	αφαίρεσις-η (αφαιρείν) (to deduct/take away)	deduction
aphesis	άφεσις	letting go; absolution; forgiveness
aphonia	αφωνία (φωνή/ voice + α/without)	loss of voice/sound; without sound/voice
aphonic	άφωονος, η, ο (adj.)	voiceless/ without a voice
aphorism	αφορισμός/ αφορίζειν	statement of a principle; to divide; mark off; maxim, adage
aphoristic	αφοριστικός, ή, ό (adj.)	of or like an aphorism

aphorize	αφορίζειν/αφορίζω	to speak or write in aphorisms
aphosphorosis	αφωσφορωσις/η	a deficiency disease, esp., in cattle caused by inadequate intake of dietary phosphorus
aphotic	άφωτος, η, ο (adj.)	without light, esp. in areas without sunlight
aphrodisiac	αφροδισιακός, ή, ό (adj.)	arousing or increasing sexual desire; any drug or other agent
Aphrodite	Αφροδίτη	Gr. myth. the goddess of love and beauty, Rom. Venus; also, a girl's name
aphtha/aphthae (pl.)	άφθα	(in English occurring in plural) eruption; thrush a small, white spot or pustule, caused by either viral or fungal infections, that appears in the mouth, on the lips or in the gastrointestinal tract in certain diseases, as thrush
aphthoid	(ο, η) αφθοειδής (το)αφθοειδές(adj.)	resembling aphtha; thrush (-ulcer)
aphthous stomatitis	αφθο-στοματίτις/ στοματίτιδα a	very common disorder of the oral mucosa, characterized by the formation of canker sores and it has a multiple etiology or origin
aphyllous	άφυλλος, η, ο (adj.)	without leaves; leafless
aplanatic	απλάνευτος, η, ο (adj.)	unerring; Optics corrected for spherical aberration and coma: said of lens
aplastic anemia	απλασία/ incomplete development + αναιμία	a form of anemia resulting from a failure of the bone marrow to produce adequate quantities of the essential blood components, including leucocytes and platelets
apnea or apnoia	άπνοια	without breath; temporary stopping of breathing; asphyxia

apneusis	άπνευσις/η	sustained tonic contraction of the respiratory muscles resulting in prolonged inspiration
apo- prefix	από	from, away from; off
apocalypse	αποκάλυψις/η	1 any ofvarious Jewish and Christian pseudonymous writings (c. 200 BC–c. AD 300) depicting symbolically the ultimate destruction of evil and triumph of good 2 a disclosure regarded as prophetic; revelation; the last book of the New Testament; book of Revelation
apocalyptic	αποκαλυπτικός, ή, ό (adj.)	revealing; manifest pertaining to apocalypse;
apocatastasis	αποκατάστασις /η	restoration; resettlement
apocope	αποκοπή (απο +κόπτειν – from + to cut off)	1 cut off; cutting or dropping off 2 droping off the last sound or sounds of a word (ex: mos' for most)
apocrypha	απόκρυφα (από + αποκρύπτειν/ κρυφά)	hidden; any writing doubtful of its authenticity or authorship
apodictic or apodeictic	αποδεικτικός, ή, ό (adj.)/ αποδεικνύειν	to show by argument; that can clearly be shown or proved; absolutely certain or necessarily true
apodosis	απόδοσις/η	giving back; the clause that expresses the conclusion/ result in a conditional sentence; opposed to protasis
apogee	απόγειο/απόγαιο (από-γαία/ far + earth)	the point farthest from the earth in the orbit of the moon or of a man-made satellite
apogeotropism	από + γεω-τροποπισμός	Biol. a tendency to grow or move away from the earth or from the pull of gravity

apolitical	απολιτικός, ή, ό/ απολίτικος, η, ο (adj.)	not connected nor concerned with politics
Apollo	Απόλλων/ Απόλλωνας	Gr. and Rom. myth. the god of music, poetry and prophecy, and medicine, represented as exemplifying manly youth and beauty: later identified with Helios; any handsome young man
Apollonian	απολλώνιος, α, ο (adj.)	1 of, like, or having to do with Apollo 2 well-ordered, rational and serene: distinguished from Dionysian
apologetic	απολογητικός, ή, ό (adj.)	defending in writing or speech/showing realization of and regret for a fault, wrong, error, insult, etc.
apologetics	Απολογητική	the branch of theology having to do with the defense and proofs of Chrisianity
apologist	απολογητής/ απολογιστής	a person who writes or speaks in defense or justification of a doctrine, faith, action, etc.
apologize	απολογούμαι	expressing regret for something said or done
apology/apologia	απολογία	expression of regret; also speaking in defence; a formal spoken or written defense of an idea, religion, philosophy, etc.
apomict	από + μικτός, ή, ό (adj.)	a plant that reproduces by apomixis, or has been produced by apomixis
apomixis	απόμειξις/ απόμιξις/η	asexual reproduction
apomorphine	απο-μορφίνη	a crystalline alkaloid, produced by synthesis from morphine: used as an emetic and expectorant

aponeurosis	απονεύρωσις/η (από + νεύρον)	fibrous membrane that covers certain muscles or connects them to their origins or insertions
aponeurotic	απονευρωτικός, ή, ό (adj.)	pertaining to aponeurosis
apophasis	αποφαίνομαι-απόφασις/η	final judgment; decision
apophthegm/ apothegm	απόφθεγμα	terse, pointed saying; a short pithy saying
apophthegmatic	αποφθεγματικός, ή, ό (adj.)	one that contains terse sayings; saying a lot in brief statements
apophyge	αποφυγή (από + φεύγειν-off/ from + to flee)	1 Archit. the concave curve where the end of a column spreads into its base or capital 2 fleeing away from something; escape from someone or something
apophysis	απόφυσις /η (από + φύειν)	any natural outgrowth or process, esp. on the verterba or other bone
apoplectic	αποπληκτικός, ή, ό (adj.)/απόπληκτος	having apoplexy
apoplexy/apoplexia	αποπληξία	crippled by a stroke
aporia	απορία	doubt; perplexity
apoprotein	απο-πρωτεϊνη	a protein that combines with a prosthetic group to form a conjugated protein
apoptosis	απόπτωσις/η	a genetically directed process of cell self-destruction that is marked by the fragmentation of nuclear DNA and is a normal physiological process eliminating DNA-damaged, superfluous, or unwanted cells; also called **_programmed cell death_**
aposiopesis	αποσιώπησις/η	to be silent; a sudden breaking off of a thought in the middle of a sentence
apostacy	αποστασία	defection; turning away from duty or party

apostate	αποστάτης	defector; deserter; one who forsakes one allegiance in favor of another
apostasize	αποστατώ	to become a deserter
Apostle	Απόστολος/ από- στέλλειν/ from- to send	each of Christ's twelve Apostles; person sent forth
apostolic	αποστολικός, ή, ό (adj.)	pertaining to the Apostles
Apostolic Fathers	Αποστολικοί Πατέρες	a group of early religious writers, followers of the apostles
apostrophe(1)	αποστροφή	turning towards one person in the audience
apostrophe(2)	απόστροφος/ απόστροφο(ν), (αποστρέφω/ to turn)	mark placed; turn away; punctuation mark
apothecary	αποθήκη	storehouse; warehouse; a drugstore
apothecarist	αποθηκάριος	one working at a storehouse, warehouse (Archaic) druggist or pharmacist (formerly apothecaries prescribed and sold drugs, medicine)
apothegm	απόφθεγμα	a terse, pointed saying; to utter a short, pithy aphorism also apophthegm
apothem	απόθεμα	1 Math. the perpendicular from the center of a regular polygon to any one of its sides 2 (Geolog.) lodgment; 3 an accumulation of deposited material in Gr, the word απόθεμα, has also the meaning: deposit, saving; stock reserve
apotheosis	αποθέωσις/η	deification; glorification of a person or thing; extreme enthusiasm
apotheosize	αποθεώνω	1 to make a god of; deify 2 idolize; glorify

apotropaic	αποτρόπαιος, α, ο (adj.)	someone/something that provokes horror; revolting; hideous (ex: apotropaic murder)
apple of discord	μήλο της έριδος	Gr. myth. a golden apple marked "For the most beautiful," claimed by Athena, Hera and Aphrodite, which was awarded by Paris to Aphrodite: in return she helped him kidnap the beautiful Helen of Sparta, thus starting the Trojan War; anything causing trouble, discord or jealoucy
apraxia	απραξία (α + πράξις-η/ not + action)	1 inaction 2 complete or partial loss of the ability to perform complex muscular movements, resulting from damage to certain areas of the brain without any paralysis or damage to normal functions
apsis	αψίς/αψίδα	arch; curvature; curve
apterous	άπτερος, η, ο (adj.) (α- πτερόν + without +wing)	1 wingless; flightless bird of New Zealand 2 Biol. having no wings or winglike parts
apteryx	απτέρυξ – (άπτερος, η,ο (adj.)	without wings; kiwi: any of the tailless New Zealand birds, with underdeveloped wings hairlike feathers, and a long slender bill, it feeds mainly on insctes and worms
apyretic	απύρετος, η, ο (adj.)	Med. without fever; no temperature
arachnid	αραχνίς/αράχνη	spider; any of the large class of (Arachnida) of arthropods, usually with four pairs of legs, either lungs or trachea, liquid diet, no antennae, simple eyes, terrestrial environment, sensory pedipalps, and a body divided into cephalothorax and abdomen, including spiders, scorpion, mites, and tics

arachno-dactyly	αραχνο-δακτύλιος	a hereditary condition characterized esp., by excessive length of the fingers and toes
arachnoid	(ο, η) αραχνοειδής (το) αραχνοειδές	1 Anat. designating the middle of three membranes of the brain and spinal cord and lies between the dura mater and the pia mater [the arachnoid membrane] 2 Bot. covered with or consisting of soft fine hairs or fibers 3 Zool. of or like a arachnid
arachnoiditis	αραχνοιδίτις / αραχνοιδίτιδα	inflammation of the arachnoid membrane
arachno-phobia	αραχνο-φοβία	pathological fear or loathing of spiders
Arcadia	Αρκαδία	1 ancient a relatively isolated region of Greece in central Peloponnesus 2 region of modern Greece occupying the same general area, retaining in illusion the rural simplicity of the ancient region
Arcadian	Αρκάς-Αρκάδος (gen.) /αρκαδικός, ή, ό (adj.)	1 a native, resident of Arkadia; 2 rustic, peaceful, romantic and simple 3 a person of simple habits and tastes
arch – arche- or archi-	αρχή	beginning; first, primitive, primary, combining form
archae-bacteria	αρχαιο-βακτηρία	any of the class of primitive bacteria having unusual cell walls, lipids, etc.
arch-enteron	αρχέντερον/ο	the cavity of the gastrula of an embryo forming a primitive gut

archetype	αρχέτυπος (αρχή + τύπος – first/ primitive + type)	1 the original pattern, or model, from which all other things of the same kind are made; prototype 2 a perfect example of a type or group 3 in the Jungian psychology, any of several innate ideas or patterns in the psyche, expressed in dreams, art, etc., as certain basic symbols and images. Syn. model
archetypical	αρχετυπικός, ή, ό (adj.)	pertaining to archetype
archon	άρχων/άρχοντας	ruler/first/chief, combining form
arch- or archi-	αρχ- αρχή-άρχων	combining form beginning, first, ruler
archaeo- or archeo-	αρχαίος, α, ο (adj.)	combining form ancient/ original archaeo-astronomy/ archeoastronomy αρχαίο-αστρονομία scientific study of the practice of astronomy, esp., prehistoric people, through examining excavations of astronoamical sites
archaeology/ archeology	αρχαιολογία	the scientific study of the life and culture of ancient people by excavating ancient cities and articrafts
archae-ornis	αρχαίο + ορνις/ όρνιθος (gen.) ancient + bird	an extinct bird (genus Archaeornis) of the Jurassic period that resembled the archaeopteryx
archaeo-pteryx	αρχαιο-πτέρυγα (αρχαίο-πτέρυξ/ ancient-wing)	an extinct reptilian bird of the Jurassic Period
archaic	αρχαίος-αρχαϊκός, ή, ό (adj.)	old; ancient; belonging to another time
archaism	αρχαϊσμός	the use or imitation of archaic words; technique, etc.
archaize	αρχαϊζειν/αρχαϊζω	make ancient; use archaisms

archangel	Αρχάγγελος	chief angel; an angel of high rank
archbishop	αρχιεπίσκοπος	bishop of the highest rank
archdeacon	αρχιδιάκονος	church official, ranking just below a bishop
archdiocese	αρχιεπισκοπή	the diocese of an archbishop
archean	αρχαίος, α, ο (adj.)	ancient; Geol. designating or occurring in the earlier part of the Precabrian Era; esp. designating the highly crystalline igneous and metamorphic rocks formed at that time
archeological	αρχαιολογικός, ή, ό (adj.)	pertaining to ancient times
archeologist	αρχαιολόγος	expert in archeology
archeology/ arcaeology	αρχαιολογία	the scientific study of the past: life and culture of ancient peoples through excavations of cities, artcrafts, etc.
archimandrite	αρχιμανδρίτης	Eastern Orthodox Church; a celibate priest; the head of a monastery or a number of monasteries
Archimedes	Αρχιμήδης	c. 287–212 BC; famous Gr. mathematician and inventor
archipelago	αρχιπέλαγος	a sea with many islands, originally was referred to: the Aegean Sea
architect	αρχιτέκτων/ αρχιτέκτονας	a specialist in designing and drawing plans for buildings, bridges, etc.
architecture	αρχιτεκτονική	ancient architecture has contributed greatly to the world: the three most celebrated column styles being: the Doric; Ionic and Corinthian (see: the three, each listed alphabetically)
archon	άρχων/άρχοντας	chief; ruler; chief magistrate

archy	αρχή (αρχειν; - to rule)	government; authority
arctic	αρκτικός,ή, ό (adj.)/ - άρκτος	bear; northern constellation
Areopagite	Αρεοπαγίτης	any member of Areopagus (Supreme Court) in ancient Athens (the title still applies in Modern Greece, since Areopagus/ Άρειος Πάγος, is the highest court of the land)
Areopagus	Άρειος Πάγος	a rocky hill northwest of the Acropolis, Athens 1 the high court of justice that met there in ancient Athens. 2 any supreme court, and the highest court of Greece today.
Arethusa	Αρεθούσα	1 Gr. myth. a woodland nymph, changed to a stream by Artemis so might escape her pursuer, Alpheus 2. North American orchid (Arethusa Bulbosa) with one pink flower and one long leaf that grows only with the fruit
Ares	Άρης	Gr. myth. the god of war, son of Zeus and Hera : identified with the Roman Mars
Argo	Αργώ	Gr. myth. the ship that Jason sailed to find the Golden Fleece
argon	αργόν (neu. of αργός, (adj.) – slow, inert, idle)	a colorless, odorless chemical element of the noble gasses constituting 1% of the atmosphere it is used in incandencent lightbulbs, radio tubes, etc.
Argolis	Αργολίς/ Αργολίδος (gen.)/ Αργολίδα	region on the NE coast of Peloponnesus, which was dominated in ancient Greece by the city-state of Argos
argonaut	αργοναύτης	any of the men who sailed on the Argo

Argos	Ἀργος	ancient city-state in the NE Peloponnesus; it dominated Peloponnesus from the seventh cent. BC until the rise of Sparta; city at the same region today
argyr- or argyro-	άργυρος	silver
argyria	αργυρία	permanent discoloration of skin caused by medicinal silver preparations
argyrophilic	αργυρο-φιλικός, ή, ό (adj.)	having an affinity for silver
argyrophile	αργυρόφιλος	one who loves silver
aria	άρια	a song or melody in an opera, cantata, or oratorio, esp. for solo voice with instrumental accompaniment
Ariadne	Αριάδνη	Gr. myth. King Minos's daughter who gives Thesseus the thread which helped him to find his way out of the labyrinth after he killed the Minotaur
Aristides	Αριστείδης	c. 530–c. 468 B. C.; Athenian general and statesman known for his honesty, he was called the Just
aristocracy	αριστοκρατία	nobility, high birth; peerage, blue blood
aristocrat	αριστοκράτης	nobleman
aristocratic	αριστοκρατικός, ή, ό (adj.)	one belonging to the noble class
Aristophanes	Αριστοφάνης	c. 450–c. 388 BC Greek writer of satirical dramas
Aristotelian	αριστοτέλειος, α, ο (adj.)	characteristics of Aristotle or his philosophy
Aristotelian ethics	αριστοτέλεια ηθική	the subject is concerned with the human aim to achieve αρετή(areti)/virtue of character (ήθος/ ethos). Excellent character leads to good living, ευδαιμονία/eudaimonia

Aristotelian logic	αριστοτέλεια λογική (συλλογισμός)	Aristotle's method of deductive logic, characterized by the syllogism
Aristotle	Αριστοτέλης	ancient Greek philosopher (student of Plato /Πλάτων/ Πλάτωνας) considered to be, by many historians, the best and the most diverse of all other philosophers, noted for his work on logic, metaphysics, ethics, politics, and more
arithmetic	αριθμητική	science/art of computing by positive real numbers (specifically by adding, subtracting, multiplying, deviding)
arithmetical	αριθμητικός, ή, ό (adj.)	
arithmetician	αριθμητικός/ αριθμητιστής/ αριθμομνήμων	person skilled in arithmetic; one expressing himself in numbers or solving difficult mathematical problems
arithmomania	αριθμομανία	a morbid compulsion to count objects
arithmophobia	αριθμοφοβία	excessive fear of numbers
Armageddon	Αρμαγγεδών	1 Bible, the place where the last, decisive battle between the forces of good and evil is to be fought before Judgment Day: Rev, 16:16 2 any great, decisive battle
aroma	άρωμα	fragrance; pleasant smell; perfume
aromatherapy	άρωμα + θεραπεία	treatment with aromatic oils from herbs and flowers, etc., for their supposed therapeutic effects applied to the skin, as in massage, or when the scent is inhaled
aromatic	αρωματικός, ή, ό (adj.)	fragrant; sweet smelling; odoriferous

aromatize	αρωματίζω	1 to make aromatic 2 Chem. to make into an aromatic compound
arrheno-blastoma	αρρενο-βλάστωμα (άρρεν(neu. of άρρην)/άρρενος (gen.) + βλαστός – male + sprout)	sometimes malignat tumor of the ovary that by the secretion of male hormone induces development of secondary characteristics
arrhythmia	αρρυθμία	any abnormality/irregularity in the heart's beating
arrhythmic	αρρυθμικός, ή, ό (adj.)	1 lacking rhythm or regularity 2 of, relating to, characterized by, or resulting from arrhythmia
arsenic	αρσενικό (αρσενικός, ή, ό) adj.	1 strong, muscular 2. a silvery-white, brittle, very poisonous chemical element, compounds of which are used in making insecticides, glass, medicines, etc.
arseno-	άρσενο-	combining form having arsenic as a constituent (as arsenopyrite)
arsenopyrite	αρσενο-πυρίτις/ πυρίτιδα	a hard, brittle, monoclinic, silvery-white mineral, FeAsS, an important ore of arsenic
arsis	άρσις /η (αίρειν- to lift up, raise up)	a lifting up; omission; 1 in classical Greek poetry the short syllable or syllables of a foot 2 in later poetry, the long or accented syllable of a foot 3 Music the unaccented part of a measure; upbeat
Artemis	Άρτεμις	Gr. myth. the goddess of the moon, wild animals, and hunting; twin sister of Apollo, Roman Diana
arterio- or arteri-	αρτηρία	artery, combining form (arteriosclerosis)
arteria	αρτηρία	artery

arterial	αρτηριακός, ή, ό (adj.)	1 of or like an artery or arteries 2 designating or of the blood in the arteries, which has been oxygenated in the lungs or gills and is brighter red than that in the veins 3 of or being a main road or channel with many branches
arteriogram	αρτηριογραφία/ αρτηριογράφημα	an x-ray obtained by arteriography
arteriography	αρτεριογράφησις/η	x-ray examination of arteries after injection of radiopaque dyes
arteriole	αρτηρίδιον/ο	any of the smaller blood vessels intermediate in size and position between arteries and capillaries
arteriolitis	αρτηριολίτις/ αρτηριολίτιδα	inflammation of the arterioles
arteriopathy	αρτηριοπάθεια	any disease of the arteries
arteriorrhaphy	αρτηριοραφή	a surgical procedure of suturing an artery
arterio-sclerosis	αρτηριο-σκλήρωσις /η	an abnormal thickening, and loss of elasticity, of the walls of the arteries, often present in old age
arterio-sclerotic	αρτηριο-σκληρωτικός, ή ό (adj.)	of, relating to, or affected by arteriosclerosis
arteritis	αρτηρίτις/ αρτηρίτιδα	an inflammatory disorder of the arteries
artery	αρτηρία	1 anyone of the system of thick-walled blood vessels that carry blood away from the heart: cf. vein, capillary 2 a main road or channel
arthr- or arthro-	άρθρον/ο	a joint combining form (arthralgia, arthroscopy)
arthralgia	αρθραλγία (αρθρο + αλγία- joint + pain)	pain in the joint(s)
arthrectomy	αρθρεκτομή	surgical excision of a joint

arthritic	αρθριτικός, ή, ό (adj.)	of, or relating to arthritis; suffering from arthritis
arthritis	αρθρίτις/αρθρίτιδα	inflammation of joint(s) due to infectious, metabolic, or constitutional causes; also: a specific arhthretic condition (as gouty arthritis, or psoriatic arthritis)
arthro-	άρθρο -	joint combining form (arthroscopy)
arthro-centesis	άρθρο-κέντησις /η	the surgical puncture of a joint
arthrodesis	αρθρόδεσις /η	the surgical immobilization of a joint so the bones grow solidly together: artificial ankylosis
arthro-dysplasia	αρθρο-δυσπλασία	abnormal development of a joint
arthrogram	αρθρόγραμμο	radiograph of a joint made by arthrography
arthrography	αρθρογραφία/ αρθρογράφιση	the radiographic visualization of a joint after an injection of a radiopaque substance
arthro-gryposis	αρθρο-γρύπωσις/ (γρυψ/γρυπός (gen.)	bend /curved 1 congenital fixation of a joint in an extended or flexed position 2 any of a group of congenital conditions characterized by reduced mobility of multiple joints due to contractures causing fixation of the joints in extension or flexion
arthrologist	αρθρολόγος	a specialist in arthrology
arthrology	αρθρολογία	the branch of medicine dealing with the study of joints
arthron	άρθρον/ άρθρωσις /η	joint (in Greek, arthron/ άρθρον/ο, has also the meaning article)
arthropathy	αρθρο-πάθεια	any joint disease
arthroplasty	αρθρο-πλαστική	plastic surgery of a joint: the operative formation or restoration of a joint

arthropod	αρθρόποδον/ο	any of a phylum (Arthropoda) of invertebrate animals (as insects, arachnids, and crustaceans) that have a segmented body and jointed appendages, and usually a shell of chitin molted at intervals
arthroscope	αρθροσκόπιον/ο	a fiber-optic endoscope used inside a joint for diagnostic or surgical procedures
arthroscopy	αρθροσκόπησις/η	an examination of a joint with an arthroscope, also: a surgical procedure of a joint, using an arthroscope
arthrosis	άρθρωσις	1 an articulation or line of juncture between bones 2 a degenerative disease of a joint 3 Linguis. in Gr. Also, correct speech pattern
arthrotomy	αρθροτομή	incision into a joint
artiodactyl	αρτιοδακτύλιος, α, ο (adj.) even + finger/toe;	1 any of an order of (Artiodactyla) of hoofed mammals having an even number of toes, including swine, hippopotamus, and all ruminants (antilope, buffalo, cattle, camel, etc.) (artiodactylous)
arum	άρον	the cockoopint; any plant of the arum family (esp. genus Arum) which is characterized by small flowers on a thick spike, within a woodlike leaf
aryepiglottic	αρυεπιγλωττίς/ επιγλωττίδα	relating to, or linking the arytenoid cartilage and the epiglottis

arytenoid	(ο, η) αρυτενοειδής (το) αρυτενοειδές (adj.)	1 relating to, or being either of two small cartilages to which the vocal chords are attached and which are situated at the upper back part of the larynx 2 relating to, or being either of a pair of two muscles or an unpaired muscle of a larynx
arytenoids-ectomy	αρυ-τενοειδής –εκτομή	a surgical procedure for the excision of an arytenoid cartilage
asbestos	άσβεστος/ασβέστης/ ασβέστιο	any of several grayish amphiboles or similar minerals that separate into long, threadlike fibers: because certain varieties do not burn, do not conduct heat, or electricity, and are often resistant to chemicals, they are used for making fire-proof materials, electrical insulation, roofing, filters, etc.
asbestoid	(ο, η) ασβεστώδης (το) ασβεστώδες (adj.)	resembling asbestos or containing asbestos
asbestosis	ασβέστωσις/η	a form of pmeumoconiosis caused by inhaling asbestos particles
ascariasis	ασκαρίασις /η	infestation ascarids or disease caused by this, esp., infestation of the intestines by a particular roundworm (Ascaris Lambricoides)
ascarid	ασκαρίς/ασκαρίδος (gen.) /ασψαρίδα (Mod. Gr.)	intestinal worm; any of genus (Ascaris) of parasitic roundworms
ascetic	ασκητικός, ή, ό (adj.)	a person who lives a life of austerity, in order to purify himself/herself
ascetical/asketes	ασκητής	a monk; hermit; cenobite; member of a Christian religious order

asceticism	ασκητισμός	the practice of self-abnegation, extreme self-discipline through discipline of the flesh, will, and mind as a hermit, monk, or nun
ascidian or ascidium	ασκίδιον-ο	Bot. a pitcherlike leaf or structure, as of the pitcher plant or bladderwort
Asclepius	Ασκληπιός	Gr. myth. the god of healing and medicine, identified with the Roman Aesculapius
asco- prefix	ασκός	wineskin; bladder; bag
ascocarp	ασκός + καρπός	Bot. a structure shaped like a globe, cup or disk containing spore sacs; sac fruit of an ascomycetous fungus
Ascension Day	Ημέρα Αναλήψεως/ της Αναλήψεως	Bible the bodily ascent of Jesus on the fortieth day after the Resurrection: Acts 1: 9
ascus	ασκός	sac 1 the membranous oval or tubular spore case of ascomycete 2 in ascomycetous fungi, a sac in which spores (usually eight) are produced and meiosis occurs
asepsis	σηψαιμία/σήψις/η	1 the condition of being aseptic 2 the methods of producing or maintaining an aseptic condition; aseptic treatment or technique
aseptic	ασηπτικός, ή, ό (adj.)	1 preventing infection (aseptic techniques 2 free or freed from pathogenic microorganisms (an aseptic operating room)
asexual	ασεξουαλικός, ή, ό (adj.)	1 having no sex or sexual organs; sexless; 2 designating or of production without the union of male and female germ cells: budding and fission are types of asexual reproduction 3 reproduction: without union of individual, or gametes

Asia	Ασία	Mythological daughter of Iapetos; the continent of Asia
Asiatic	ασιατικός, ή, ό (adj.)	of Asia, its people, their languages and cultures; native or inhabitant of Asia: now generally the preferred term
Asiatic cholera	ασιατική χολέρα	an acute, severe, infectious disease caused by bacteria (Vibrio cholera): characterized by profuse diarrhea, intestinal pain, and dyhydration
-asis	-ασις	combining word forming nouns indicating a condition [as elephantiasis; psoriasis, etc.]
asp	ασπίς/ασπίδα	shield; any of the small poisonous snakes of Africa, Arabia, or Europe
asparagus	ασπάραγος) anc.) / σπαράγγι /σφαράγγι (mod. Gr.)	to spring up, sprout; any of a genus (Asparagus)
Aspasia	Ασπασία	fifth cen. BC an Athenian woman celebrated for her beauty and intelligence; wife or for some mistress of Pericles
aspermia	ασπερμία (α + σπέρμα –without + sperm)	1 inability to produce or ejaculate semen 2 having no seed
asphalt	άσφαλτος, η, ο (adj.)	brown or black substance/ a mixture used for cementing, paving, roofing, etc.
asphygmia	ασφυγμία (α + σφυγμός- without + pulse)	the lack of a normal number of pulse
asphyxia	ασφυξία (α + σφυγμός - w/ out, no + pulse)	loss of consciousness as a result of too little oxygen and too much carbon dioxide in the blood; stopping of the pulse
aspyxiant	ασφυξιαντικός/ ασφυκτικός, ή, ό (adj.)	causing or tending to cause asphyxia; an asphyxiant substance or condition

asphyxiate	ασφυξιώ	1 to cause asphyxia in 2 to suffocate; to undergo asphyxia 2 to kill or make unconscious by inadequate oxygen, presence of other noxious agents, or other obstruction to normal breathing
astasia	αστασία	muscular incordination in standing; unsteadiness
astatic	αστατικός, ή, ό (adj.)	1 unstable; unsteady 2 Physics not taking a definite position or direction (an astatic needle in a galvanometer is not affected by the earth's magnetism)
aster	αστήρ/αστέρας	star, any of the genus (Aster) of the composite family
aster-	αστήρ	combining form, forming nouns: star or starlike structure
astereo-gnosis	αστερεόγνωσις / αστερεογνωσία	loss of the ability to recognize the shapes of objects by handling them
asterisk	αστερίσκος	used in printing; notes to indicate footnote, references, omissions, corrections, etc.
asterism	αστερισμός	group; cluster of stars that may (or may not) form a canstellation
asterixis	αστήριξις /η (α + στηρίζειν – not + hold steady)	a motor disorder characterized by jerking movements (as the outstretched hands) and associated with various encephalopathies due, esp., to faulty metabolism
asteroid	(ο, η) αστεροειδής/ (το) αστεροειδές (adj.)	any of the small planets ranging from 1,000 km (621 mi.) to less than 1 km. (0.62 mi.) in diameter
asthen- or astheno-	ασθεν- ασθένεια	weak combining form (asthenopia)
asthenia	ασθένεια (α + σθένος- without + strength)	bodily weakness; illness; lack or loss of strength: Debility

asthenic	ασθενικός, ή, ό (adj.)	1 pertaining to asthenia; one being ill; early term for ectomorphic 2 debilitated 3 characterized by slender build and slight muscular development
asthenopia	ασθενωπία	a strained condition of the eye
asthenopic	ασθενοπικός, ή, ό (adj.)	pertaining to asthenopia
asthma	άσθμα	a generally chronic disorder characterized by wheezing, coughing, difficulty in breathing, and a suffocating feeling, caused by an allergy to inhaled substances, stress, or other factors
asthmatic	ασθματικός, ή, ό (adj.)	suffering from asthma
asthmogenic	(ο, η) ασθμαγενής (το) ασθμαγενές (adj.)	causing asthmatic attacks
astigmatic	αστιγματικός, ή, ό (adj.)	1 pertaining to astigmatism 2 correcting astigmatism 3 having or resulting from a distorted vision, view, or judgment
astigmatism	αστιγματισμός α/without + στιγματισμός/ stigma)	an irregularity in the curvature of a lens including the lens of the eye, resulting in an indistinct or distorted image; distorted view or judgment, as due to bias
astomatous	αστόματος, η, ο (adj.) (α + στόμα/ without + mouth)	mouthless
astragal	αστράγαλος	anklebone in humans
astragal-ectomy	αστραγαλεκτομή/ αστράγαλο-εκτομή	
astragalus	αστράγαλος	Anat. old term of the talus
astr- or astro-	άστρο (ν)	star, combining form

astrobiology	αστροβιολογία	the branch of biology that investigates the existence of organisms on planets other than earth
astrodome	αστροδόμιο(ν)/ αστροδομή	domelike transparent structure for housing astronomical or navigational instruments
astrodynamics	αστροδυναμική	branch of dynamics dealing with the motion and gravitation of natural and artificial objects in space
astrolabe	αστράλαβον (άστρο + λαμβάνειν- star + to receive/take)	an instrument originally used to find the altitude of a star, etc., and later was replaced by the sextant
astrologer	αστρολόγος	expert in astrology
astrological	αστρολογικός, ή, ό (adj.)	pertaining to astrology; anything that has to do with the stars
astrology	αστρολογία	a pseudoscience based on the notion that the positions of the moon, sun, and stars affect human affairs, and one can predict the future by studying the stars; the primitive astronomy
astrometry	αστρονομία	the branch of astronomy dealing with /the measurement of the position, motion and distance of the planets and stars
astronaut	αστροναύτης (άστρο +ναύτης / star + sailor	a person trained to travel to outer space; make rocket flights; sailor of the stars
astronautical	αστροναυτικός, ή, ό (adj.)	1 of or having to do with astronomy 2 extremely large, as the numbers or quantities used in astronomy
astronautics	αστροναυτική	the science dealing with spacecraft and with travel in outer space, esp. to the moon and other planets

astronomer	αστρονόμος	expert in astronomy
astronomical	αστρονομικός, ή, ό (adj.)	having to do with the astronomy; extremely large, as the numbers or quantities used in astronomy
astronomy	αστρονομία	the science of the universe in which the stars, planets, etc., are studied including their origin, evolution, composition, motions, relative positions, sizes, etc.
astro-photography	άστρο-φωτογραφία/ φωτογράφησις /η	photography of both visible and invisible celestial objects
astrophysics	άστροφυσική	the branch of astronomy dealing primarily with the physical properties of the universe.
astro-sphere	άστρο-σφαίρα/ αστρόσφαιρα	Biol. 1 centrosphere 2 all of an aster except the centrosome
asyllabic	ασυλλαβικός, ή, ό΄/ ασυλλάβιστος, η, ο (adj.) α + συλλαβή- without + syllable)	not syllabic; incapable of forming a syllable or the nucleus of a syllable
astylar	α + στύλος /without + pillar (support)	Archit. having no columns or pilasters
asylum	άσυλον/ο	1 a sanctuary (as a temple, church); where criminals, debtors, etc., were safe from arrest; 2 the protection given by a sanctuary or refuge or by one country to refugees from another country; 3 an institution for the mentally ill 4 inviolable; shelter
asymbolia	ασυμβολία (α + σύμβολα – not recognizing + symbols)	loss of the ability in recognizing symbols
asymmetrical	ασυμμετρικός, ή, ό/ασύμμετρος, η, ο (adj.)	not symmetrical

asymmetry	α-συμμετρία	1 lack of symmetry 2 Chem. the symmetrical structure of a molecule, esp., of srereoisomers containing carbon atoms
asymptomatic	ασυμπτωματικός, ή, ό (adj.) (α+σύμπτωμα-συμπτώματα-no+ symptom/symptoms)	without symptoms; presenting no signs of disease
asymptote	ασύμπτωτος (α + συν + πίπτειν – not + together + to fall)	Math. a straight line always approaching but never meeting a curve; tangent to a curve at infinity
asymptotic	ασυμπτωτικός, ή, ό (adj.)	pertaining to asymptote
asynapsis	ασύναψις /η	failure of pairing of homologous chromosomes in meiosis
asynclitism	ασυγκλιτισμός	presentation of the fetal head during childbirth with the axis oriented obliquely to the axial planes of the pelvis
asynchronism	α-συγχρονισμός	lack of synchronism/failure to occur at the same time
asynchronous	ασύγχρονος, η, ο (adj.) (α + συν + χρόνος – not + together + time)	not synchronized; not occurring at the same time
asyndetic	ασυνδετικός, η, ο/ ασύνδετος, η, ο (adj.) (α + συνδέειν – not + to bind together- connect)	not connecting; not binding together
asyndeton	α-σύνδετος, η, ο (adj.)/ ασύνδετον – neuter of ασύνδετος α + σύνδεσμος/c without + connection/union)	not united; not bound together

asynergia or asynergy	ασυνεργία	lack of coordination (as of muscles); not working together
asystole	ασυστολή	a condition of weakening or sensation of the systole; weakening heartbeats
Atalanta	Αταλάντη	Gr. myth. a beautiful swift-footed maiden who offers to marry any man able to defeat her in a race: Hippomenes wins by dropping three golden apples, which she stops to pick up, along the way
ataractic	ατάρακτος, η, ο (adj.)	calm; undisturbed
ataraxia	αταραξία	tranquility/calmness of mind and emotions
ataxia	αταξία (α + τάξις – not + order/ arrangement)	disorder; inability to coordinate voluntary bodily movement, as in walking; lack of order
ataxic	αταξικός, ή, ό/ άτακτος, η, ο (adj.)	unable to keep order; incapable of being orderly
atelectasis	ατελέκτασις/η (ατελής + έκτασις-incomplete + stretching)	1 ectasis; stretching out; 2 the collapse of all or part of a lung; also defective expansion of the pulmonary alveoli at birth
ateliosis	ατελείωσις /η	incomplete development; esp. dwarfism associated with anterior pituitaty deficiencies and marked by essentially normal intelligence and proportions
ateliotic	ατελείωτος, η, ο (as an adj.)	of, relating to, or affected by ateliosis
ateliotic (as a noun, but in Gr. as an adj)	(ο, η) ατελής (το) ατελές	not complete; unfinished; one affected by ateliosis
atheism	αθεϊσμός α-θεός/ without-God	not believing in God
atheist	αθεϊστής/άθεος	without God; doubting the existence of God
Athena/Athina	Αθήνα	modern name of Athinai / Athens the capital of Greece

Athena	Αθηνά (with the accent on the –ά)	the goddess of wisdom; a girl's name
Atheneum	Αθήναιον	temple dedicated to Athena
Athenian	Αθηναίος/Αθηναία	the resident of Athens
Athens	Αθήναι/Αθήνα	capital of Greece
atherectomy	αθηρεκτομή	removal of atheromatous plaque from within a blood vessel by utilizing a catheter, usually fitted with a cutting blade or griding burr
athermancy	αθέρμανσις/ αθέρμανση (α + θέρμανση – without heat/ θερμαίνειν- to heat)	property not transmitting infrared or heat rays
athermanous	αθερμαντικός, ή, ό (adj.)	not being heated; of, or related to athermancy
athero-	αθήρωμα	a tumor, combining form (atherogenesis)
atherogenesis	αθηρογένεσις /η	the formation of atheroma
athrogen or atherogenic	(ο, η) αθηρογενής (το) αθηρογενές (adj.)	relating to or causing atherogenesis (atherogenic diets)
atheroma	αθήρωμα	1 tumor filled with grainy matter or deposits of small fatty nodules on the inner coat of the arteries, often accompanied by degeneration of the affected areas; also, such an nodule or arterial plaque 2 an abnormal fatty deposit in the arteries
atheromatosis	αθηρομάτωσις/η	a disease characterized by atheromatous degeneration of the arteries
atherosclerosis	αθηροσκλήρωσις/η	form of arteriosclerosis associated with the formation of atheromas 2 an arteriosclerosis characterized by atheromatous deposits in and fibrosis of the inner layer of the arteries

Athinae or Athina	Αθήναι/ Αθήνα (Mod. Gr.)	Athens
athlete	αθλητής/ αθλήτρια (fem.)	contestant in a game, competing for a prize or money; trained in physical strength, skill, stamina, and speed
athletic	αθλητικός, ή, ό (adj.)	physically strong; strong and well balanced; agile and graceful; nimble
athleticism	αθλητισμός	an athletic quality; all the athletic activities combined, various endeavors and the entire organization of the system
athletics	αθλητικά	sports, games, exercises, etc., requiring strength, skill, stamina, speed, and above all, character and ethos, etc.
-athon	suffix as in Marathon/ walkathon, telethon, etc. –αθών/θώνας	as in: Μαραθών/Μαραθώνας /Μαραθώνειος indicating length or endurance; an athletic achievement
Athos	Άθος/ Άγιον Όρος	Mount Athos known as the Holy Mountain: autonomous monastic district in NE Greece (Chalkidiki peninsula): 130 sq. mi.(336 sq. km)
Atlantean	ατλανταίος, α, ο (adj.)	like an Atlas; strong; gigantic
atlantes	άτλαντες (πλ. pl.)	plural of atlas; in architecture supporting columns
Atlantic	Ατλαντικός Ωκεανός	Atlantic Ocean
Atlas	Άτλας	Gr. myth. name of a Titan compelled to hold the heaven on his shoulders/ also a book of maps
atmo-	ατμό-/ ατμός	steam, vapor, combining form (atmosphere)

atmosphere	ατμόσφαιρα (ατμός & σφαίρα/ vapor & sphere)	1 the gaseous envelope(air) surrounding the earth to the height of c. 1,000 km (c. 651 mi.): it is c. 21% oxygen, 78% nitrogen, and 1% other gases, and rotates with the earth, because of gravity 2 the gaseous mass surrounding any star, planet, etc. 3 the air in any given place 4 a pervading or surrounding influence or spirit; general mood or social environment 5 the general tone of a work of art; music or play (with a fateful atmosphere), etc. 6 physics a unit of pressure equal to 101, 325 newtons per sq. in. (1,469 lbs per in.)
atmospheric	ατμοσφαιρικός, ή, ό (adj.)	1 of or in the atmosphere [atmospheric lightning] 2 caused or produced by the atmosphere [atmospheric pressure] 3 having or giving an atmosphere [atmospheric music]
atmospherics	ατμοσφαρικά	disturbances in reception, produced by natural electric discharges, as in a storm, static; the phenomena producing these disturbances
atom	άτομον-ο (neuter of άτομος, η, ο (adj.) /τέμνειν – uncut/ to cut	1 uncut; indivisible; any of the indivisible particles 2 the smallest particle of an element that can exist either alone or in combination postulated by philosophers as the basic component of all matter

atomic	ατομικός, ή, ό (adj.)	1 of an atom or atoms 2 of, using, or powered by nuclear energy [an atomic submarine] 3 involving the use of nuclear wapons [atomic warefare] 4 having its atoms in an uncombined form [atomic oxygen] 5 very small; minute
atomic energy	ατομική ενέργεια	nuclear energy; the enery released from an atom in nuclear reactions or by radioactive decay: esp., the energy released in nuclear fission or nuclear fusion
atomic theory	ατομική θεωρία	the theory that all material objects and substances are composed of atoms, and that various phenomena are explained by the properties and interactions of these atoms
atomicity	ατομικότης/ ατομικότητα	the special characteristics of each individual, or the sef-sufficiency as a person 2 Philos. the quality or all qualities or properties of a human entity, that distinguish it from others
atomics	ατομική	science dealing with atomic structure and esp., with atomic energy
atomism	ατομισμός	philosophical theory that the universe is made up of tiny, simple, indivisible particles that cannot be destroyed
atomist	ατομιστής	existing as a single entity; distinguished by others as a particular indvidual; self-engrossed
atomos	ά-τομος, η, ο (adj.) (α/un & τομή/cut)	uncut; unable to separate
atonic	ά-τόνος/άτονος, η, ο (adj.)	caused by atony; also unaccented

atony	ατονία	lack of bodily or muscle tone
atopic dermatitis	άτοπη δερματίτις /δερματίτιδα	a chronic eczematous skin condition esp. of children, characterized by intense itching, inflammation, and xerosis and occurring chiefly in those with a personal or familial history of atopy
atopy	ατοπία	a genetic disposition to develop an allergic reaction [as allergic rhinitis, asthma, or atopic dermatitis] and produce elevated lavels of IgE upon exposure to an environmental antigen and esp. one inhaled or ingested
atrichia	ατριχία	congenital or acquired baldness
atropa or Atropa	άτροπα	a genus of Eurasian and African herbs (as belladonna) of the nightshade family (Solanaceae) that are a source of medicinal alkaloids (as atropine)
atrophic	ατροφικός, ή, ό (adj.)	relating to or characterized by atrophy
atrophic rrhinitis	ατροφική ρινίτις /ρινίτιδα	1 a disease of swine that is characterized by purulent inflammation of the nasal mucosa, atrophy of the nasal concae, and abnormal swelling of the face 2 Ozena
atrophy	ατροφία	1 decrease in size or wasting away of a body part or tissue: also: arrested development, or loss of a part or organ incidental to the normal development, or life of an animal or plant 2 to undergo or cause to undergo atrophy

atropine	ατροπίνη	a racemic mixture of hyoscyamine usually, obtained of belladonna and related plants (family Solanaceae), and used esp. in the form of its hydrate sulfate: it is known for its anticholinergic effects (pupil dilation or relief of smooth muscle spasms)
atropinism	ατροπινισμός	by atropine
Attic	Αττικός ή, ό (adj.)	of Attica; of or characteristic of Athens or its people, their language or culture; Athenian 2 classical; simple; restrained, etc., said of a style 3 the Attica dialect became the literary language that great works were written in ancient Greece
Attica	Αττική	1 state of ancient Greece, occupying a peninsula in the SE part and after the fifth cen. BC, a region dominated by Athens 2 region of modern Greece, in the general area
Atticism	Αττικισμός	1 an Attic idiom, style or custom, etc. 2 a graceful, restrained phrase or expression
atypical	ατυπικός, ή, ό (adj.)	not typical; not characteristic
Augean	Αυγείας	1 Gr. Legent of Augeas, king of Elis, or his stable, which held 3,000 oxen and had not been cleaned for thirty years, until Hercules cleaned it in one day by diverting one or two rivers through it thus, accomplishing one of his twelve labors 2 filthy or corrupt
augite	αυγίτης (from αυγή/ sunlight/dawn)	brightness, a precious stone
aura	αύρα	an invisible emanation (as the aroma of a flower)

austere	αυστηρός, ή, ό (adj.)	having a harsh, severe; stern look/manner
austerity	αυστηρότητα	the quality/condition of being austere, used also in case of tightened economy; in Gr. the word λιτότητα /frugality is used instead of austerity regarding the economy
aut-	αυτ(ο)	combining form (used before a vowel)
autarchy	αυταρχία	1 absolute rule or sovereignty; autocracy 2 a country under such rule
autarchic	αυταρχικός, ή, ό (adj.)	one behaving as an autocrat, very rigid, extremely strict
autarcky	αυτάρκεια	self-sufficiency; independence 2 economic self-sufficieny, esp. on a national basis; on a national policy of getting along without imports
aut-ecology	αυτό + οικολογία	the ecological study of a single organism or of a single species of organisms; cf. senecology
authentic	αυθεντικός, ή, ό (adj.)	original; pure; genuine
authenticity	αυθεντικότητα	reliability; genuineness; serious intent
autism	αυτισμός	1 a developmental disorder that appears by age three and that is variable in expression but is recognized and diagnosed by impairement of the ability to form normal social relationships, by the impairement to communicate with others, and by stereotyped behavior patterns 2 Psychol. a state of mind characterized by daydreaming, hallucinations, and disregard of external reality
autistic	αυτιστικός, ή, ό (adj.)	one affected by autism

auto-	εαυτός /αυτός	self, combining form (autograph)
auto-analyzer	αυτό-αναλυτής	any of various automatic devices that test and analyze chemicals, blood, etc.
autobiography	αυτοβιογραφία	one writing about his/her life
autocephalous	(εαυτός/ self + κέφαλος/ cephalos)	self-governing; independent
autochthon	αυτόχθων/ αυτόχθονας	aborigine/sprung from the land itself
autocracy	αυτοκρατία	a government having absolute power; dictatorship; despotism
autocrat	αυτοκράτης	absolute ruler; anyone having unlimited power over others
autodidact	αυτοδίδακτος, η, ο (adj.) (διδάσκειν – to teach)	teaching oneself; self-taught; a person who is self-educated
auto-eroticism or erotism (adj.)	αυτο-ερωτισμός;	1 pleasurable sensations or tensions arising in the erogenous body zones without external stimulation 2 self-initiated activity aimed in reducing sexual excitations, as in masturbation
autogenic	(ο, η) αυτογενής (το) αυτογενές (adj.)	of or relating to any of several relaxation tenchiques that actively involve the patient (as by medication or biofeedback) in attempts to control physiological variables (as blood pressure)
autogenous	αυτόγενος/ αυτογενής	1 produced independently of external influence or aid: entogenous 2 originating or derived from sources within the same individual (an autogenous graft) (an autogenous vaccine)
autograft	αυτό + γράφειν – auto + to write/ sketch/draw	a tissue or organ that is transplanted from one part to another part of the same body

autograph	αυτόγραφον/ο	1 written with one's own hand; signature/esp., of a famous person, which is valued as a memento 2 a thing written in one's handwriting; original manuscript; holograph
auto-hemolysis	αυτο-αιμόλυσις/η	hemolysis of red blood cells by factors in the serum of the person from whom the blood is taken
auto-hemotherapy	αυτο-αιμοθεραπεία	treatment of disease by modification (as by irridation)
auto-hypnosis	αυτο-ύπνωσις/η	the act of hypnotizing oneself
autokinesis	αυτοκίνησις/η	spontaneous or voluntary movement
autologous	αυτόλογος, η, ο (adj.)	1 derived from the same individual 2 derived from the same organism or from one of its parts (an analogous graft)
autolysis	αυτόλυσις/η	the destruction of cells or tissues by their own enzymes
automatic	αυτόματος, η, ο (adj.)	self moving; involuntary motion
automatism	αυτοματισμός	1 the quality or condition of being automatic 2 automatic action 3 Philos. the theory that the human or animal body is a machine governed by physical laws and that consciousness does not control but only accompanies its actions 4 Physiol. a) action independent of outside stimulus, as sleepwalking b) action not controlled by the will, as the heartbeat c) the power of such action 5 Psychol. an automatic or unconscious action, as a tic 6 free expression of the unconscious mind by releasing it from control of the conscious: a surrealist concept

autonomic	αυτονομικός, ή, ό (adj.)	1 occurring involuntarily; automatic 2 of or controlled by the autonomic nervous system 2 Biol. resulting from internal causes, as through a mutation
autonomic nervous system	αυτονομικό νευρικό σύστημα	the part of the nervous system responsible for control and regulation of the involuntary bodily functions, including those of the heart, blood vessels, visceral smooth muscles, and glands
autonomous	αυτόνομος, η, ο (adj.)	of or having to do with autonomy; independent
autonomy	αυτονομία	self-government; independence; the fact or condition of being autonomous, independent; any state governing itself
autophobia	αυτοφοβία	extreme fear of being alone or in solitude
autoplasty	αυτο-πλαστική	repairing injuries by grafting in tissue from another part of the patient's body
autopsy	αυτοψία	seeing with one's own eyes; examination and dissection of a dead body
auto-radio-graph	αυτο- ραδιο-γράφημα	an x-ray photograph by bringing an object containg radioactive material into close contact with an emulsion on a film or plate: it shows the action of radio activity in the object. Also radiogram
autotelic	(ο, η) αυτοτελής-(το) αυτοτελές (adj.)	complete in by himself/herself/itself; having an end in itself (ex: autotelic story)
auto-therapy	αυτοθεραπεία	self-treament
auto-top-agnosia	αυτο-τόπος – a-γνώση – auto-area-not- knowing	loss of the ability to recognize or orient a bodily part due to a brain lesion[1]

autotroph	αυτότροφος, η, ο (adj.)	1 an autotrophic organism 2 needing only carbon dioxide carbonates as a source of carbon and a simple inorganic nitrogen compound for metabolic synthesis
autotrophic	αυτο-τροφικός, ή, ό (adj.)	making its own food by photosynthesis, as a green plant ot by chemosynthesis, as any of certain bacteria
auxesis	αύξησις/η	growth/increase in size
avitaminosis	α-βιταμίνωσις/η	without vitamins; disease resulting from a vitamin deficiency
axenic	αξενικός, ή, ό (adj.) (adj.)/ άξενος, η, ο (adj.)	free from other foreign organisms
axiology	αξιολογία/ (from άξιος- worthy)	branch of philosophy dealing with the nature of value and the types of value, as in morals, aesthetics, religion, and metaphysics
axiom	αξίωμα	authority, as that of a president or a high position; statement universally accepted as true; maxim
axiomatic	αξιωματικός, ή, ό (adj.)	of or like an axiom; self-evident or aphoristic (in Gr. the word αξιωματικός/captain, is also a rank in the arm forces or the police force, etc.)
axis	άξων/άξονας	a real or imaginary straight line on which an object rotates or it is regarded as rotating (the axis of the planet)
axoplasm	αξόπλασμα	the protoplasm of an axon
axosomatic	αξοσωματικός, ή, ό (adj.)	relating to or of being a nerve synapse between the cell body of one neuron and an axon of another
azine		

az- or azo-	άζωτον/ο	N=N combining form
azo	άζωτον/ο	relating to, containing, or being the group N=N united at both ends to carbon
azoic	άζωος, η, ο / αζωϊκός (adj.) (α + ζωή/ without life)	without life; lifeless
azotemia	άζωτο αίμα – azoton + blood	the accumulation of nitrogenous substances in the blood, resulting from failure of the kidneys to remove them
azygo-	άζυγο- (ά+ ζυγός – not + yoke)	unmatched; azygos: anatomical part not being one of a pair
azygo-graphy	αζυγο-γραφία	radiographic visualization of the azygos system of veins after injection of a radiopaque medium
azygos or azygous	άζυγος, η, ο (adj.)	unmatched; having no mate

B

Babylonia/Babylon	Βαβυλών/ Βαβυλωνία	ancient empire in SW Asia
bacteria	βακτήριον/ βακτηρία	tiny creatures making up a division of microorganisms which are typically one-celled
bacterio-	βακτήριο- βακτήρια	tiny creatures making a division (bacteria), combining form
bacteriology	βακτηριολογία	the study of bacteria, either a branch of medicine or as a science (important in food processing, agriculture, industry, etc.)
bacteriolysis	βακτηριόλυσις/η	dissolution or destruction of bacteria
bacteriophage	βακτηριοφαγία	any virus that infects bacteria
bacteriostasis	βακτήριο-στάσις/η	arresting of the growth or multiplication of bacteria
bacterium	βακτήριον	(sing.) of bacteria

bacteroid	(ο, η) βακτηροειδής/ (το) βακτηροειδές	resembling bacteria
baklava	μπακλαβάς	sweet made with phyllo dough (very thin pastry sheets) 1 with nuts, sugar, cinnamon and syrup; a Greek and Middle Eastern rich, tasty desert
baptisia	βαπτίσια/βαφτίσια	baptism; a sacrament or a ceremony of admitting a person to Christianity
baptism	βάπτισμα/ βάπτισις/η	baptizing or being baptized; sacrament of admitting a person to Christianity
Baptist/baptist	Βαπτιστής	John the Baptist; a person who baptizes; a member of the Protestant denomination
baptistery	βαπτιστήριον/ο	a place in church for baptizing
baptize	βαπτίζειν/βαπτίζω/ βαφτίζω	to immerse in water or pour/ sprinkle water in performing the sacrament of baptism
barbarian	βάρβαρος	an alien or foreigner; in ancient times anyone non-Greek; non-Roman; anyone without civilization was regarded as primitive/savage
barbaric	βαρβαρικός, ή, ό (adj.)	uncivilized; primitive; wild; crude
barbarism	βαρβαρισμός	the use of words and expressions not standard in a language; the state of being primitive without civilization
bar-	βάρος, βαρύ	weight; heavy
barbarity	βαρβαρότητα	cruel or brutal behavior; inhumanity
baritone	βαρύτονος	deep-toned; the range of a male between tenor and bass
barium	βαρύ (neu. of βαρύς)	heavy; silver-white, slightly malleable, metallic chemical element used in alloys
baro- prefix	βάρος/ βαρύς, βαρειά, βαρύ (adj.)	weight, heavy

barograph	βαρογράφος	a barometer that records changes in atmospheric pressure on a revolving cylinder
barology	βαρολογία	the branch of meteorology dealing with the atmospheric pressure and gravitation
barometer	βαρόμετρο(ν)	an instrument measuring atmospheric pressure
barometric	βαρομετρικός, ή, ό (adj.)	pertaining to barometry; anything having to do with the atmospheric pressure
basic	βασικός, ή, ό (adj.)	of, at, or forming a base, fundamental, essential
basil	βασιλικός	royal plant, any of a genus (Ocimun) of fragrant plants of the mint family
basilica (stoa)	βασιλική στοά	royal portico
basis/base	βάσις/η	base, foundation or chief supporting factor of anything; fundamental principle or theory, as of a system of knowledge
batho-	βάθος/βαθύς	depth; deep; combining form (bathometer)
batholith	βαθόλιθος	a large deep-seated rock intrusion, usually granite
bathometer	βαθόμετρον/ο	instrument measuring the depths of large bodies of water
bathos	βάθος	depth
bathy-	βαθύς, βαθειά, βαθύ (adj.)	deep, plunge into; sink
bathymetry	βαθυμέτρησις/η	the science for measuring the depth of oceans, seas, etc., 2 the topographic maps of the sea resulting from those measurements
batracho-	βάτραχος /βάτραχο (αιτ/obj.)	frog, combining form
batrachoid	(ο, η) βατραχοειδής, (το) βατραχοειδές (adj.)	resembling a frog

B (beta)	Ββ (Βήτα)	the second letter of the Gr. alphabet; (pronounced vita); the second of a group or series; Beta particle; Beta wave
benthos	βυθός	1 the depth of the sea/ocean; the bottom of a body of water 2 all the plants and animals living on or closely associated with the bottom of a body of water, esp. the ocean
bex	βηξ/ βηχός (gen.) / βήχας (Mod. Gr.).	cough, coughing
biathlon	δυ - άθλος /άθλημα– two + game/contest	a winter sports event combining cross-country skiing and and rifle marksmanship
Bible	Βίβλος	1 the sacred book of Christianity; Old Testament and New Testament: some versions also include all or part of the Apocrypha 2 collection of writings and Scriptures 3 the Holy Scripture of Judaism, identical to the Old Testament of Christianity 4 writings sacred to a religion
biblio-	βιβλίο/book	combining form, anything pertaining to book
biblical	βιβλικός, ή, ό (adj.)	according to the Bible; pertaining to the Bible
biblicist	βιβλιστής	one who studies and translates the Bible; an expert on the Bible; a specialist in biblical literature
bibliographer	βιβλιογράφος (from βιβλίο + γράφω/ γράφειν – to write)	writer of books
bibliography	βιβλιογραφία (βιβλίο/book + γράφω/write)	the study of the editions, dates, authorship, etc., of books and other writings
bibliolatry	βιβλιολατρεία	1 excessive veneration of books 2 excessive adherence to a literal interpretation of the Bible

bibliomania	βιβλιομανία	extreme love for books; esp. having mania in collecting rare books
bibliophile	βιβλιόφιλος, η, ο (adj.)	a friend/lover/ admirer of books; one who collects books
bibliopole	βιβλιοπώλης (βιβλίο |πωλείν- book + to sell)	one who sells books; bookseller
bibliotheca	βιβλιοθήκη	library; bookcase; a book collection; a bookseller's catalogue
bibliotheca	βιβλιοθήκη	library; bookcase; a book collection; a bookseller's catalogue
bibliotherapy	βιβλιο – θεραπεία – book + therapy	the use of selected reading materials as therapeutic adjuvants in medicine and psychiatry; also: guidance in the solution of personal problems through directed reading
bio-	βίος	life; of living things, combining form (biology)
biology	βιολογία (from βίος /life- λογία- study/ logy/word)	1 science that deals with the origin, history, physical characteristics, life processes, habits, etc.
biopsy	βιοψία	the removal of living tissue from the body for diagnostic examination
biorhythm	βίος + ρυθμός- life + rhythm	any biological cycle that brings periodic changes in blood pressure, body temperature, etc.
bios	βίος	life; of living thing
bioscopy	βιοσκόπισις/η	Med. an examination to determine whether life is present in the body
-biosis	βίωσις /η	way of life, combining word forming nouns indicating a specified way of living (ex: symbiosis)

biosphere	βίος + σφαίρα – life + sphere	1 the zone of planet earth where naturally occurs, extending from the deep crust to the lower atmosphere 2 the living organisms of the earth
bio-synthesis	βιοσύνθεσις /η	the formation of chemicals compounds by the enzyme action of living organisms, as in protein syntesis
bio-technology	βιο-τεχνολογία	the use of the data of techniques of engineering and technology for the study and solution of problems concerning living organisms
bio-telemetry	βιο+τηλε + μέτρηση –life + far + measuring	the use of telemeters to monitor the physical condition or responses of human beings, animals, etc.
biotherapy	βιοθεραπεία	the treatment of disease by means of substances, as serums, vaccines, antibiotics, etc., secreted by or derived from living organisms
biotic	βιοτικός, ή, ό (adj.)	of life or living things, or caused by living organisms
-biotic	-βιοτικό	of life combining form forming adjectives of or having a specified way of living (as: photobiotic)
blaspheme	βλασφημείν/ βλασφημώ	to curse; revile; to speak irreverently or profanely of God or sacred things
blasphemous	βλάσφημος, ή, ο (adj.)	speaking of God in an irreverent manner; profane; foulmouthed
blasphemy	βλασφημία	profane or contemptuous speech, writing, or action concerning God or anything held as divine; any remark or action held to be irreverent or disrespectful

-blast	βλαστός	sprout; embryo, germ combining form (epiblast)
blastema	βλάστησις/η – βλαστάνειν (to bud, sprout)	the undifferentiated embryonic tissue from which cells, tissues, and organs are developed
blasto- prefix	βλαστός	germinating embryo (blastogenesis)
blastoderm	βλαστός + δέρμα	the part of a fertilized ovum that gives rise to the germinal disk from which the embryo develops
blastogenesis	βλαστο-γένεσις/η	1 reproduction by asexual means, as by budding in corals; 2 the theory that the germ plasm transmits hereditary characteristics: opposed to pangenesis
blastoid	(ο, η) βλαστώδης (το) βλαστώδες (adj.)	sprout/germ; sproutlike
blastula/blastocyst	βλαστο-κύστις (sprout + cyst)	an embryo at the state of development in which it consists of usually one layer of cells around a central cavity, forming a hollow sphere
blenna	βλέννα	mucus; a sticky, thick, semi-diaphanous mucus flowing off some glands (as rhino-mucus, mucus of the nose)
blenoid	(ο, η) βλεννώδης (το) βλεννώδες (adj.)	resembling mucus
botanical	βοτανικός, ή, ό (adj.)	1 pertaining to plants and plant life 2 of or connected to the science of botany 3 of or belonging to a botanical species
botanist	βοτανολόγος	a student or a specialist in botany
botanize	βοτανίζειν/βοτανίζω	1 to gather plants for botanical study 2 to study plants, esp. in their natural environment; to investigate the plant life of a region

botany	βοτανική	1 the branch of biology that studies plants, their life, structure, growth, classification, etc. 2 the plant life of an area 3 the characteristics or properties of a plant or plant group
botryoidal	(ο η) βοτρυοειδής (το) βοτρυοειδές	a bunch of grapes; resembling a bunch of grapes
botrytis	βοτρύτις/βοτρύτιδα:	a plant disease that blackens flower buds
brachy-cephalic	βραχύς + κεφάλι (short + head)	having a short/broad head
brady-	βραδύς, εία, ύ (adj.)	slow, combining form
bradycardia	βραδυκαρδία	abnormally slow heartbeat; below sixty beats per minute for an adult
brome	βρώμη	oats; any of large genus of grasses of the temperate zone; a few are crop plants, but others are weeds
bromine	βρώμα	stench; a chemical element, usually in the form of a reddish brown, corrosive liquid that volatilizes to form a vapor that has an unpleasant odor and is very irritating to mucous membranes: used in making dyes, in photography, etc.
bronchial tubes	βρόγχος/οι (pl.)	the large tubes (bronchi) that lead from the windpipe carrying the air that has been breathed in through the mouth and nose
bronch- prefix (used before a vowel)	βρόγχος	as in bronchitis
bronchi	βρόγχοι	pl. of bronchus/bronchos
bronchial	βρογχικός, ή, ό (adj.)	of or pertaining to bronchi
bronchiectasis	βρογχο-έκτασις/ η	stretching out; an irreversible, chronic enlargement of certain bronchial tubes

bronchitis	βρογχίτις-βρογχίτιδα	inflammation of the mucous lining of the bronchial tubes
broncho-	βρόγχος	windpipe combining form (bronchorragia)
broncho-pneumonia	βρόγχο-πνευμονία	inflammation of the bronchi accompanied by inflamed patches in the nearby lobules of the lungs
bronchorragia	βρόγχο-αιμορραγία	hemorrhaging in the bronchial tubes
bronchoscope	βρογχοσκόπιον/ο	a slender, tubular with a small electric light for examining or treating the windpipe or the bronchi
brontology	βροντολογία (βροντή + λογία – thunder +logy/word)	branch of zoology dealing with the genus of Brontosaurus
brontosaur	βροντόσαυρος	thunder, any of the genus of sauropod dinosaurs of the Jurassic and Cretaceous periods
Byron	Βύρων/Βύρωνος (gen.)/Βύρωνας (Mod. Gr.)	George Gordon Byron, an English nobleman known as Lord Byron. A great poet and fervent Philhellene, with his writings, idealism, and love of freedom, energized and invigorated the enslaved (for four hundred years) Greek nation, to successfully defeat and free itself from the Ottoman Empire
Byronism	βυρωνισμός	the artistic and ideological wave that resulted by the influence of the work and paradigm of Lord Byron's life that became a subject and example for others to emulate

Byzantine	βυζαντινός, ή, ό (adj.)	a native or inhabitant of Byzantium 1 of or Byzantium or the Byzantine Empire, its culture, language, etc. 2 of or pertaining to the Eastern Orthodox Church 3 resembling the government or politics of the Byz. Empire, in structure, spirit, etc., specif. characterized by complexity, deviousness, intrigue, etc. 4 Archit. designating of or a style developed in Byzantium and Eastern Europe, between the fourth and fifteenth cent. characterized by domes over square areas, round arches, elaborate mosaics, etc. 5 Art. designating of or the decorative style of the mosaic frescoes of the Byzantine Empire
Byzantine Empire (AD 395–1453)	Βυζαντινή Αυτοκρατορία	in SE Europe and SW Asia, cap. Constantinople (AD 330)
Byzantium	Βυζάντιον	ancient city (founded c. 600 BC) on the site of modern Instabul (changed from Constantinople)

C

Cachectic/cachexic	καχεκτικός, ή, ό (adj.)	one suffering from cachexia
cachexia	καχεξία (κακός/ bad + έξις/habit)	a weakened, emaciated condition of the body, esp. as associated with a chronic illness
caco -	κακός, ή, ό (adj.)	bad; evil, combining word caco-demon/caco-daemon κακος + δαίμων-κακοδαίμονας evil spirit; devil

cacoethes	(ο, η) κακοήθης/ (το) κακοήθες (adj.) (κακός/evil + ήθος/ character/ethos; (ethical qualities)	bad, evil; someone with wicked idiosyncracy
cacography	κακογραφία	bad handwriting; incorrect spelling
cacomelia	κακο/bad – μέλος / body part	deformity of a limb/ cacomelia is congenital
cacophony	κακοφωνία	harsh jarring sound; dissonance/inharmonious sound
Caiaphas	Καϊάφας	Bible, the high priest who presided at the τrial that led to the condemnation of Jesus: Matt. 26:57–66
cainotophobia	καινός/new-φοβία/ fear?	extreme fear of anything new
calathus	κάλαθος/καλάθι	a basket for fruit or vegetables (used a lot in ancient times; in art,) it symbolizes abundance and fruitfulness
calo-	καλός, ή, ό (adj.)	good, combining form
calotype	καλός-τύπος- καλότυπος, η, ο (adj.)	good type
caloyer	καλόγερος	monk (in the Eastern Orthodox Church), also, good old age/ καλό γήρας /καλά γηρατειά
calligraphic	καλλιγραφικός, ή, ό (adj.)	pertaining to beautiful handwriting
calligraphy	καλλιγραφία (κάλλος/beauty and γράφω/ γράφειν/to write)	beautiful handwriting, esp. as an art
calligraphist	καλλιγράφος	specializing in calligraphy
Calliope	Καλλιόπη	Gr. myth. the muse of eloquence and epic music; a keyboard instrument like the organ, having a series of steam whistles; also, a feminine name

calliopsis	κάλλος +όψις / όψη (beauty and looks, appearance)	beautiful appearance
Calypso	Καλυψώ	in Homer's *Odyssey*, a sea nymph who keeps Odysseus on her island for seven years; an orchid (Calypso bulbosa)
calyptra	καλύπτρα-κάλυπτρο/ καλύπτειν	covering for the head, veil to conceal; cover
calyx	κάλυξ/κάλυκας	outer covering, pod; the outer whorl of protective leaves (sepals) of a flower, usually green
camel	κάμηλος/καμήλα (Mod. Gr.)	either of two species of large domesticated ruminants (genus Camelus) with a hamped back, long neck, and large, cushioned feet
camera	κάμαρα	a vaulted chamber; a device for taking photographs
campus	κάμπος/καμπύλη/ καμπή	bend, curve; corner; 1 the grounds, sometimes including the buildings of a school, college or university, a hospital, an industrial or commercial firm, a hospital, etc.
campylo-tropous	καμπυλο – τρόπος (bend + way)	curved; having a flower ovule with a structure that is partially inverted, with the stalk attachment at the bottom and the opening near the bottom
canal	κανάλι	pipe or tube; 1 an artificial waterway for transportation or irrigation 2 a river artificially improved by locks, levees, etc., to permit navigation 3 any of the narrow lines, visible from earth, on the planet Mars, once thought by some to be canals, but now known to be optical illusions 4 any television station or channel

canasta/canister	κάνιστρον/ο	basket; a card game, a variation of rummy
cancer	καρκίνος	crab; malignant tumor
cancerphobia or / cancerophobia	καρκινοφοβία	1 excessive fear of getting cancer 2 false impression that one has cancer
canceroid/ cancroids (ο, η)	καρκινοειδής (το) καρκινοειές (adj.)	resembling cancer; cancerlike
cane	κάννα/καλάμι (Mod. Gr.)	pipe, tube; 1 the slender, joined usually flexible stem of any of certain plants, as bamboo or rattan 2 any plant with such a stem, as sugar cane or sorghum
cannabis	κάνναβις / η	marijuana or any other substance derived from the flowering tops of the hemp
canon	Κανών/κανόνος (γεν. gen.) /κανόνας (Mod. Gr.)	the officially recognized books of the Bible, a rule, law of the church; sacred writings admitted to the catalog according to the rule; a body of rules principles, criteria, etc.
canthus	κάνθος	either corner of the eye, where the eyelids meet
carat	κεράτιον/κέρας/ κέρατος (gen.), καράτι (Mod. Gr.)	little horn; 1 a unit of weight of precious stones and pearls, equal to 200 milligrams; 2 karat
carcinogen	(ο, η) καρκινογόνος (το) καρκινογόνο	any substance that produces cancer
carcinogenesis	καρκινογένεσις /η	the possible combination of various procedures and mechanisms that might cause cancer
carcinoma	καρκίνωμα	any of several kinds of cancerous growths deriving from epithelial cells (see: sarcoma)
carcinomatosis	καρκινο-μάτωσις/η	a condition in which a carcinoma has spread extensively throughout the body

carcinophilia	καρκινοφιλία	Med. the property or characteristic of certain organs and tissues to develop cancer or metastasis from carcinomas that exist in the body
carcinophobia	καρκινοφοβία	extreme fear of cancer or getting cancer
cardi- prefix	καρδία/καρδιά	heart combining form used before a vowel (cardiac)
cardiac	καρδιακός, ή, ό (adj.)	1 of, near or affecting the heart 2 relating to the part of the stomach connected with the esophagus 2 a person with a heart disorder
cardio - prefix	κάρδιο- καρδία/ καρδιά	heart
cardiogram	καρδιογράφημα	electro-cardiogram; a graphic tracing showing the variations in electric force which trigger the contractions of the heart: it is used for diagnostic purposes of the heart
cardioid	(ο, η) καρδιοειδής (το) καρδιοειδές (adj.)	heart-shaped; Math. A curve more or less in the shape of a heart, traced by a point on the circumference of a circle that rolls around the circumference of another circle
cardiologist	καρδιολόγος	specialist for the heart; heart specialist
cardiology	καρδιολογία	the branch of medicine dealing with the heart, its functions and its diseases
cardio-myopathy	καρδιο-μυοπάθεια	any of various diseases of the heart muscle
carditis	καρδίτις/καρδίτιδα	inflammation of the heart
carotid	καρωτίς/ καρωτίδος (gen.)/ καρωτίδα(Mod. Gr.) καρωτίδες (pl.)	the two great arteries of the neck; designating, of, or near either of the two principle arteries, one on each side of the neck, which convey the blood from the aorta to the head

-carp	καρπός	fruit, combining form comprising nouns (endocarp)
carpel	καρπός	fruit, 1 a simple pristil, regarded as a single ovule-bearing leaf or modified leaflike structure 2 any of the segments of a compound pistil, usually having a single stigma
carpo-	καρπός	fruit; harvest; seeds, combining form (carpology), also, carp- before a vowel
-carpous	-κάρπος /καρπός	combining form forming adjectives, fruited; having a certain number of fruits, or a certain kind of fruit (apocarpous)
carpus	καρπός	wrist; Anat. the wrist or the wrist bones
carrot	καρότον/ο	a biennial plant ((Daucus carota) of the umbel family, with ferlike leaves 2 the fleshy orange-red root of the cultivated strain of this plant (var. sativa), eaten as a vegetable
cassiterite	κασσίτερος	tin, native tin dioxide, the chief ore of tin: it is brown or black and very hard and heavy
cata/kata	κατά	1 down (as in catabolism,) 2 away, completely (as in catalysis,) 3 against (catapult) 4 throughout (cataphoresis) 5 backward (cataplacia,) also cat- before a vowel, combining form
catabolism	καταβολισμός (βολή/βάλλειν	a throw/ to throw; the process in a plant or animal by which living tissue is changed into energy and waste products of a simpler chemical composition; destructive metambolism

catachresis	κατάχρησις/η (κατά + χρήσθαι- against + use)	misuse of a word; incorrect use of a word or words, as by misapplication of terminology or by strained or mixed metaphor; any exaggerated use of the normal, as in catachresis of alcohol, etc.
cataclysm	κατακλυσμός	a great flood; any great upheaval that causes sudden and violent changes
catacomb	κατακόμβη	any of the series of vaults or galleries in an underground burial place, usually in plural (catacombs/κατακόμβες)
catalectic	καταληκτικός, ή, ό (adj.)	pertaining to the end; conclusion; conclusive
catalepsy	κατάληψις/η κατά- down + λαμβάνειν/ to take/seize	a seizing, grasping, to seize
catalogue/catalog	κατάλογος	a complete/extensive list; an alphabetical card file
catalysis	κατάλυσις/η	dissolution; the speeding up or, sometimes, slowing down of the rate of a chemical reaction caused by the addition of some substance that does not go to a permanent chemical change; overthrow (esp. a government or political system); dissolution
catalyst	καταλύτης	any person or substance acting as an agent / stimulus in bringing about a hastening result
catalyze	καταλύω	to change or to bring about a catalyst
cataplasia	κατά + πλασία/ πλάθειν	Biol. a change in cells or tissues, characterized by reversion to an earlier stage
cataplasm	κατάπλασμα	a poultice, most of the time medicated

catapult	καταπέλτης (κατά + πάλλειν – against + to toss /hurl)	to move quickly; to be hurled; (an ancient military contrivance for throwing or shooting spears, stones, etc.)
cataract	καταρράκτης	1 a large waterfall 2 any strong flood or rush of water 3 an eye disease in which the crystalline lense or its capsule becomes opaque, causing partial or total blindness
cataractoid	(ο, η) καταρραψτώδης (το) καταρρακτώδες (adj.)	resembling a cataract; cataractlike
catarrh	καταρρέειν/ καταρρέω/ καταρροή	to flow down; flowing down; inflammation of a mucous membrane, esp., of the nose or throat
catarrhine	(κατά + ριν/ ρινός(gen.) ρίνα/ μύτη (Mod. Gr.)	having a nose with the nostrils placed close together and opening to the front; a catarrhine animal, as a human, gorilla, or chimpanzee
catastasis	κατάστασις-η (καθίσταναι- κατά + ιστάναι-to set up, cause to stand)	condition, situation; the heightened part of the action in ancient drama, leading directly to the catastrophe
catastrophe	καταστροφή	destruction, disaster, calamity; any sudden misfortune; Geol. a sudden, violent change as an earthquake
catastrophic	καταστροφικός, ή, ό (adj.)	destructive; devastating; ruinous
catastrophism	καταστροφισμός	1 the former theory that geologic changes are caused in general by sudden upheavals rather than gradually 2 an outlook envisioning imminent catastrophe
catastrophist	καταστροφεύς / καταστροφέας	one who causes great damage; someone destroying and brings great destruction; unleashing devastation

catatonia	κατατονία (κατά / + τόνος/tension/stress	Psychiatry. a syndrome esp. of schizophrenia marked by stupor or catalepsy, often alternating with phases of excitement
catechism	κατηχισμός/ κατηχίζειν	the teaching of the Christian faith; a handbook of questions and answers for teaching the principles of a religion, or similar handbook for teaching the fundamentals of any subject
catechesis	κατήχησις/η	instruction; esp. religious instruction
catechist	κατηχητής- κατηχήτρια(fem.)	a teacher of the Christian doctrine
catechize	κατηχίζειν/κατηχίζω	to teach, esp., in the principles of religion, or other subjects, by the method of questions and answers
catechumen	κατηχούμενος, η, ο (adj.)	a person instructed in the fundamentals of Christianity, or receiving instruction in any other subject
categorical	κατηγορικός- κατηγορηματικός, ή, ό (adj.)	absolute; positive; direct; explicit, without qualifications or conditions
categorize	κατηγορείν/ κατηγορώ	to accuse; predicate. Also, in Eng. to classify; to place in a category, group
category	κατηγορία (κατά + αγορεύειν (against + to declaim; address an assembly/agora)	accusation; assertion; 1 a class or division in a scheme of classification 2 Logic. any of the various basic concepts into which all knowledge can be classified
catharsis	κάθαρσις /η	cleansing/purification of body or soul; venting of emotional tension; abreaction, release
cathartic	καθαρτικός, ή, ό (adj.)	purgative; laxative; effecting catharsis; a medicine for stimulating evacuation of the bowels

catheter	καθετήρ/καθετήρος (gen.)/καθετήρας (Mod. Gr.)	a slender, hollow tube, as of metal ot rubber inserted into a body passage, vessel, or cavity for passing fluids, making examinations, etc., esp. one draining urine from the bladder
catheterize	καθετηριάζω	to insert the catheter into a body passage
cathode	κάθοδος	decent; going down (coined by Michael Faraday) 1 in an electrolytic cell, the negative electrode, from which current flows 2 in a vacuum tube, the negatively charged electron emitter 3 the positive terminal of a battery
catholic	καθολικός, ή, ό (adj.)	all-inclusive; universal; 1 of general scope or value; broad in sympathies, tastes, or understanding; liberal 2 of the Christian church as a whole; of any of the orthodox Christian churches, including the Roman, Greek Orthodox, Anglo-Catholic, etc., as distinguished from the Reformed or Protestant churches 3 a member of any of the Catholic churches, esp., the Roman Catholic
Catholicism	Καθολικισμός	the doctrine, faith, practice, and organization of the Roman Catholic Church
catholicity	καθολικότης/ καθολικότητα	the quality or state of being catholic; universal, as in taste, sympathy, or understanding; liberality, as in ideas
catholicize	καθολικίζω	to make or become catholic; to convert or be converted to Catholicism
catholicon	καθολικόν (neut. of καθολικός)	[Archaic] a supposed medicine to cure all diseases; panacea

catoptrics	κατοπτρική (κατοπτρικός, ή, ό (adj.)/κάτοπτρον/o – mirror/ mirrorlike)	the branch of optics dealing with reflection of light of mirrors or mirrorlike surfaces
caustic	καυστικός, ή, ό (adj.)	irritating; burning; 1 that can burn, eat away, or destroy tissue by chemical action; corrosive 2 cutting or sarcastic in utterance; biting; sarcastic
Cecrops	Κέκρωψ/Κέκροπας	Gr. myth. the first king of Attica and the founder of Athens, represented as half man, half dragon
-cele	κήλη	hernia; tumor; swelling, combining form (blastocele)
celiac	κοιλιακός, ή, ό (adj.)/ κοιλία	—abdomen; relating to the abdominal cavity (see coele)
cemetery	κοιμητήριον/ κοιμάμαι/to sleep/ rest	resting place; sleeping area
-cene/ceno-	καινός, ή, ό (ad.) / καινούριος, α, ο (adj. Mod. Gr.)	new, latest, recent, combining form esp., designating a specified epoch in the Cenozoic Era/ Καινοζωϊκή Εποχή, (Miocene)
ceno -	κοινό (neut. of κοινός, common)	combining form (cenospecies)
ceno -	κενός, ή, ό (adj.)	empty combining form (cenotaph/empty tomb))
cenobite	κοινόβιον/κοινό + βίος/common + living	communal life
ceno- /cene	καινός, ή, ό (adj.)	new, recent combining form
cenogenesis	καινό+ γένεσις /η - recent/new+ birth/breeding	the development of structures in the embryonic or larval stage of an organism that are adaptive and do not appear in the evolutionary history of its group: Paligenesis

cenospecies	κοινό + είδος/ γένος / common |kind/genus	separate species of organisms that are related through their capability of interbreeding, as dogs and wolves for example
cenotaph	κενός / τάφος/ κενοτάφιον/ο	empty tomb; a monument or empty tomb honoring a person or persons whose remains are elsewhere
cenozoic	καινοζωίκός, ή, ό (adj.) (καινός + ζωίκός/cene + zoic)	designating or of the geologic era following the Mesozoic and including the present; it began approximately 65 million years ago and is characterized by the development of many varieties of mammals (the Cenozoic Era/ Καινοζωίκή Εποχή) (see the list of combining forms for the discrepant definitions of the combining form ceno + cene--)
Centaur/Ceunturus	Κένταυρος	Gr. myth. monster with a man's head, trunk, and arms, and a horse's body and legs. Also the teacher of Achilles; Centaurus α S canstellation between Hydra and Crux, containing Alpha Centauri
centaury	κενταύρειον	the centaur Chiron was said to have discovered medicinal properties of the plant, any of the genus (Centaurium) of small plants of the gentian family, with flat clustersof red or rose flowers
center	κέντρον/ο	1 a point equally distant from all points of the circumference of a circle or the surface of a sphere 2 the point around which anything revolves
central	κεντρικός, ή, ό (adj.)	in, at, or near the center; equally distant or accessible from various points

centralize	συν-κεντρώνω/ συγκεντρώνω	to organize under one control; to make central; to concentrate the power or authority of, in a cental organization
centri-	κέντρο-	center, combining form, centro
centric	κεντρικός, ή, ό (adj.)	in, at, or near the center; central; or of having a center
-centric	κεντρικό	combining form 1 having a center or centers (of a specified kind or number) [concentric) 2 having a specified thing as its center (geocentric)
centro-	κέντρον/ο	combining form center (centrospheres)
centro-baric	κέντρο βάρους (center + of weight)	having to do with the center of gravity
cendroid	(ο, η) κεντρώος, α, ο (adj.)	in the center of an area or space (center of Boston)
centrosome	κέντρο+ σώμα	a very small body near the nucleus in most animal cells, consisting of a centriole surrounded by a centrospheres: in mitosis it divides, and the two parts move to opposite poles of the dividing cell
centrosphere	κέντρο-σφαίρα	1 Biol. the portion of the centrosome surrounding the centriole; center of an aster 2 Geol. the central part of the earth
centrum	κέντρον	1 a center 2 Anat. the part of the vertebra supporting the disks in a spinal column
cephal-	κεφαλή /κεφάλι	head, combining form used before a vowel (cephalic)
cephalalgia	κεφάλι + άλγος αλγία (head + pain)/κεφαλόπονος (Mod. Gr.)	headache
cephalic	κεφαλικός, ή, ό (adj.)	pertaining to the head 1 of the head, skull, or cranium 2 in, on, or near the head

cephalo	κέφαλος/κεφάλι	head (combining form) any word dealing with the head, skull, or brain
cepha-lom-eter	κέφαλο-μέτρον/ κεφαλόμετρο	an instrument measuring the head or skull; skull measure
Cerberus	Κέρβερος	(Myth.) three-headed dog that guarded the gate of Hades
cero-	κηρός /κερί (Mod. Gr.)	wax, combining word (ceroplast)
ceroplastic	κηροπλαστικός, ή, ό (adj.) (κηρός + πλάσσειν – wax + to mold)	modeled in wax; having to do with wax modeling, molding
ceroplastics	κηροπλαστική	the art in modeling in wax or the art of molding with wax
cetology	κητολογία	the branch of zoology dealing with whales
cetos	κήτος -	sea monster
chalaza	χαλάζι	hail
chaeta	χαίτη	hair; mane, a bristlelike projection, or seta, esp. on an annelid worm
chaeto- prefix	χαίτη	mane, shock of hair or bristles
chaetopod	χαίτη + πους/ ποδός(gen.) - hair + foot	Zool. Any of a former class (Chaetopoda) of annelids; including the earthworms and leeches
Chalcedon	Χαλκηδών	ancient Greek city in Bosborus, opposite Byzantium: site of the fourth ecumenical council, AD 451
Chalcidice	Χαλκιδική	peninsula in NE Greece, extending into the Aegean and terminating into three prongs
Chalkis	Χαλκίς/Χαλκίδα	seaport in E Greece and the capitol of the prefecture of Evvoia /Evboea.
chalko-	χαλκός	copper; brass combining form (chalkocite)
chalcography	χαλκογραφία	the art of engraving on copper or brass

chalcoid	(ο, η) χαλκοειδής (το χαλκοειδές) (adj.)	resembling copper or brass; copperlike
chamaeleon/ chameleon	χαμαιλέων/ χαμαιλέοντος (gen.) χαμαιλέοντας (Mod. Gr.)	on the ground; 1 any of various of the ancient lizards (Chamaeleontidae) with an angular head, prehensile tail, eyes that move independently of each other, the ability to change skin color rapidly and a long, agile tongue for catching prey 2 other types of lizards, as the American chameleon 3 a changeable or fickle person
chamomile	χαμόμηλον/ χαμομήλι (Mod. Gr.)	earth apple; any plant of two genera (Anthemis and Marticaria) of the composite family, with strong-smelling foliage, esp., a plant (Anobilis) whose dried, daisylike flower heads are used as a medicine and making tea
chaos	χάος	abyss; 1 the disorder of formless matter and infinite space supposed to have existed before the ordered universe; 2 extreme confusion and upheaval
chaotic	(ο, η) χαώδης (το χαώδες (adj.)	in a state of chaos; total confusion; in a completely confused or disordered condition
character	χαρακτήρ/ χαρακτήρας	moral constitution of an individual or group; moral strength; fortitude; good reputation 2 from χαράσσειν/ charassein/ to engrave: an instrument, any letter, symbol or figure, etc.3 style of printing and or handwriting 4 a statement about the behavior, qualities; qualafications, etc. esp. by a former employer; reference 5 a person in a play, a story, a book, etc. an odd, eccentric, or noteworthy person

characteristic	χαρακτηριστικός, ή, ό (adj.)	of or constituting a special distinctive trait, feature, quality, or peculiarity of someone or something (ex: his beautiful voice; her great attitude; the warm climate of the state, etc.)
characterization	χαρακτηρισμός	delineation of character or creation of characters in a play/story, etc., the art of characterizing
characterize	χαρακτηρίζω	describe; depict; identify; to describe or portray the particular qualities, features or traits of; to define the special trait(s), of a person or thing (as, his witty remarks are legendary; her unique voice; etc.)
charisma	χάρισμα	a special quality/charm; God's gift; grace; favor
charismatic	χαρισματικός, ή, ό (adj.)	having or resulting from charisma; charming,; captivatin
Charybdis	Χάρυβδις/η	Gr. myth. a sea monster which was destroying any ship going nearby; an old name also of a whirlpool off the NE coast of Sicily (now called Galofalo)
chasm	χάσμα	a deep crack in the earth's surface; abyss
cheilitis	χειλίτις/χειλίτιδα	inflammation of the lips
chemical	χημικός, ή, ό (adj.)	element with a disagreeable odor
chemist	χημικός	an expert; specialist in chemistry

chemistry	χημεία	1 the science dealing with the composition and properties of substances, and with the reactions by which substances are producedfrom or converted into other substances 2 any process of synthesis/analysis similar to the one used in chemistry (chemistry of wit) 3 interaction between people, esp. with respect to emotional or intellectual qualities; rapport [mutual sexual attraction]
chemo-prophylaxis	χημειο-προφύλαξις/η	the prevention of disease by the use of chemical drugs
chemosphere	χημεία + σφαίρα (chemistry + sphere)	an atmospheric zone approximately 19 to 80 km (11.8 to 49.7 mi.) above the earth's surface, in which photochemical reactions take place
chemosynthesis	χημειοσύνθεσις/η	the synthesis by certain bacteria of organic compounds from carbon dioxide and water by the use of energy obtained by the oxidation of certain chemicals as hydrogen sulfide or ammonia: see also, **Photosynthesis**
chemotaxonomy	χημειο-ταξινομία –ταξινόμηση	the biological classification of plants and animals using comparative biochemistry, esp. by studying cartain proteins
chemotherapy	χημειοθεραπεία	treatment by chemicals or drugs
chemotropism	χημεία + τρόπος/ chemistry + way, manner	the tendency of certain plants or other organisms to turn or bend under the influence of chemical substances
cherry	κεράσιον/κεράσι	a small, fleshy fruit (derived by the ancients from Cerasus, city on the Black Sea)

chiasm	χίασμα	to mark with X; 1 a crossing or intersection of the optic nerves in the hypothalamus of the brain 2 a point of contact between chromosomes during meiosis where two chromatids interchange corresponding segments 3 any crosswise function 4 a deep crack in the earth's surface; abyss
chiasmus	χιασμός	rhetoric inversion of two parallel phrases, clauses, etc. (ex: she went to London; to New York went he)
chiastic	χιαστός, ή, ό (adj.)	placing a X crosswise
chiliad	χιλιάς/χιλιάδος (gen.) /χιλιάδα (Mod. Gr.)	a thousand; a group of 1,000
chiliarch	χιλιάρχης	leader of a thousand; in Ancient Greece the military commander of a thousand men
chiliasm	χιλιασμός	belief in the coming of the millennium
Chimera	χιμαιρών /χίμαιρα	Gr. myth. a fire-breathing monster, usually represented as having a lion's head, a goat's body, and a serpent's tail 1 any similar fabulous monster 2 an impossible or foolish fancy 3 Biol. an organism having two or more genetically distinct types of cells due to mutation, grafting, etc.
chimerical	χιμαιρικός, ή, ό (adj.)	1 imaginary; fantastic; unreal 2 absurd; impossible; indulging in unrealistic fancies; visionary
chimerism	χιμαιρισμός	the occurrence of genetically distinct cell types in a single organism
chiro - prefix	χείρ/χείρα/χέρι	arm; hand

chirographa	χειρόγραφα	handwritten documents by an official/clerk
chirographer	χειρογράφος	skilled in chirography
chirography	χειρογραφία	handwriting; penmanship
chirology	χείρα-λόγος-λέγειν	using sign language with hands to communicate with deaf-mute peole
chiromancy	χειρομαντεία	palmistry: an art supposedly telling a person's character, or fortune by the lines and marks of that person's hand
Chiron	Χείρων/Χείρονας	the wisest of all the centaurs, famous for his medical knowledge: he was also the teacher of Asclepius, Achilles and Hercules
chiro-podist	χειρο-ποδικός, (χέρι/ hand + πόδι/foot)	one who specializes in trating both hands and feet
chiropractor	χειροπρακτικός	a specialist in bone manipulation
chiton	χιτών/χιτώνας	1 loose garment of varying length, similar to a tunic, worn by men and women in ancient Greece 2 any of a class of (Polyplacophora) of mostly small, ovoid marine molluskus, having a dorsal shell consisting of eight articulating calcareous plates and ventral foot
chlamys	χλαμύς/χλαμύδα	a short mantle clasped at the shoulder worn by men in ancient Greece
Chloe	Χλόη	blooming, verdant; feminine name
chlor-	χλωρό-	fresh, combining form before a vowel (clor-acne)
chloacne	χλωρό + ακνας/ facial eruption	an acnelike skin disorder caused by exposure to chlorinated hydrocarbons
chlorine	χλωρίνη	a greenish-yellow, poisonous, gaseous chemical element

chlorite	χλωρίτης	bright-green, complex silicate mineral, similar in structure to the micas
chloro- prefix	χλωρό (χλωρός, ή, ό, (anj,)	pale green; fresh, green
chloroform	χλωροφόρμιον/ο	a toxic carcinogenic, colorless, volatile liquid; to kill with chloroform
chloroplast	χλωροπλάστης	a green, oval plastid containing chlorophyll and carotenoids found in the cytoplasm of many plant cells
chlorosis	χλόρωσις /η	a form of iron-deficiency anemia, sometimes affecting girls at puberty turning the skin to a greenish color, in Bot. plants affected by lack of chlorophyll and or light, lose their green color
chlorophyl	χλωροφύλλη	the green pigment found in the chloroplasts of plant cells
choir/chorus	χορός/χορωδία	a group of singers trained to sing together (in ancient tragedies the chorus played a very important role)
cholecystis	χολοκύστις/η (χολοκυστίτιδα)	gallbladder; inflamed gallbladder
cholecystectomy	χολή-κύστις -εκτομή	removal of the gallbladder
cholelith	χολή-λίθος/ χολόλιθος	gallstone
cholera	χολέρα	tropical intestinal disease
choleric	χολερικός, ή, ό (adj.)	1 having choler as the predominant humor, hence of bilious temperament; 2 having or demonstating a quick temper; petulant
cholesterol	χοληστερίνη (χολή/ στερεός)	substance found in fats and oils
chole-	χολή	bile, gall
cholic	χολικός, ή, ό (adj.)	having to do with bile, gall

chondrite	χόντριον (deriving from: chondros)	the type of stony meteorite that contains chondrules: a rounded mass of various minerals, the size of a pea or smaller
chondro	χόνδρος	cartilage; grain, combining form (chondroma/ a cartilaginous benign tumor)
choragus	χορηγός (χορός + άγειν/ dance +to lead	1 the leader of a chorus in an ancient play 2 any leader of a play or band 3 the sponsor of a dance or play
chord	χορδή	1 string of an instrument 2 a feeling or emotion thought of being played on like the string of a harp 3 Aeron. a) an imaginary straight line extending directly through an airfoil from the leading to the trailing edge b) the length of such a line 4 Engineering a principal horizontal member in a rigid framework, as of a bridge 5 Geom. a straight line segment joining any two points on an arc, curve, or circumference
chorde/chorda	χορδή	string; tendon
chorea	χορεία (χορός/ dance)	1 choral dance 2 a disorder of the nervous system characterized by irregular, jerking movements caused by involuntary muscular contractions
choreograph	χορογράφημα/ χορογραφή	design or plan of movements of a dance
choreographer	χορογράφος	one who designs the dance movements, sequence, etc.
choreography	χορογραφία	the arrangement or notation of the movements of a dance

choreography	χωρογραφία (χώρος/area/- γράφειν/to write)	the art of mapping or describing a region / district or a particular area, district, or country
chorion	χόριον/ο	fetal membrane 1 the outermost of the two membranes that completely envelop a fetus 2 the outer membrane or shell of the eggs of insects and other invertebrates
chorography	χωρογραφή/ χωρογραφία (χώρος/ open space/area)	Geography: the art of mapping or describing a region or district; a map or description of a particular region or district
choroid	(ο, η) χοροειδής (το) χοροειδές (adj.)	designating or of the chorion or certain other vascular membranes; the dark, vascular membrane that forms the middle coat of the eye, between the sclera and retina
chorus	χορός	dance, a band of dancers or singers; in ancient Greek drama/tragedy, a company of performers provided explanation and elaboration of the theme and action by singing, dancing, and narrating
chrestomathy	χρηστομάθεια (χρηστός + μανθάνειν/ useful +to learn)	learning useful information; acquiring well-suited/ appropriate knowledge
chrism	χρίσμα/ευχέλαιον	anointing; unction oil
Christ	Χριστός	the anointed; the Messiah whose appearance was prophesied in the Old Testament, Jesus of Nazareth
Christian	Χριστιανός	Christ's follower
Christianity	Χριστιανοσύνη	the Christian religion; Christians collectively; the state of being a Christian

Christology	Χριστολογία	the theological study of Christ and the relation of the divine and the human within Him
Christopher	Χριστόφορος	bearer of Christ; a masculine name
chroma	χρώμα	color, combining form (chromatography)
chromatelopsia/ achromatopsia	αχρωματοψία	color blindness
chromatic	χρωματικός, ή, ό (adj.)	highly colored
chromatism	χρωματισμός	coloring something; painting; to give a hue, color, to a subject or theme
chromatosis	χρωμάτωσις/η	pigmentation
chromato-	χρώμα/χρώματος (Gen. case of χρώμα/chroma)	color; of chroma
chromatogram	χρωματόγραμμα	the arrangement of zones or bands resulting from a chromatographic separation
chromatograph	χρωματογράφημα	display or record of the result of the above separation
chromatography	χρωματογραφία	the process of separating various constituents of a mixture in order to determine, through analysis, their quantity and quality
chromatosis	χρωμάτωσις/ χρωμάτωση	pigmatosis
chromatics	χρωματική	the study of colors with reference to hue and saturation
chromio	χρώμιο	chemical element; white metal
chromo -	χρώμο/χρώμα	color, combining word
chromo-dynamics	χρωμο-δυναμική	a theory that describes how gluons and their forces bind quarks together to form protons, neutrons, etc.

chromogen	χρωμογόνος	1 any substance that can become a pigment or coloring matter, as substance in organic fluids that forms colored compounds when oxidized, or a compound, not itself a dye 2 any of certain bacteria that produce a pigment
chromo-lithograph	χρώμο+ λίθο + γράφειν- color +stone +graph	a colored picture printed by the lithographic process from a series of stone or metal plates, the impression from each plate being in different color
chromonema	χρώμα + νήμα/ color + thread	coiled twisted, threadlike filament contained in a chromatid at all stages of mitosis
chromoprotein	χρώμο- πρωτεϊνη	a conjugated protein containing a pigment
chromosome	χρωματό-σωμα/ χρωματο- σώματα (pl.)	one of several small rod-shaped bodies in the nucleus of a cell
chromosphere	χρωμοσφαίρα	the pinkish, glowing region around a star, esp., the sun between the hot, dense photosphere and the much hotter, tenuous corona
chronic	χρόνιος,α, ο (adj.)	lasting a long time or recurring often said of a disease and distinguished from acute; of long duration
chronicle	χρονικά	historical record or register of facts or events arranged in the order they occurred
chrono-	χρόνος	time, combining form (chronology)
chronobiology	χρονοβιολογία	the study of biological activity in relation to time, as various cycles and rhythms

chronodiagram	χρονοδιάγραμμα	the board where all programmed preset deadlines, for a project, are registered; a schedule
chronogram	χρονόγραμμα	1 an inscription in which certain letters, made more prominent, express a date in Roman numerals (as in **MCMXLV=1945**) 2 a record kept by a chronograph
chronograph	χρονογράφος	any of various instruments (as a stopwatch) for measuring and recording brief, precisely spaced intervals of time
chronological	χρονολόγηση	arranged in the order of occurrence; of chronology
chronological	χρονολογικός, ή, ό (adj.)	according to time sequence 1 arranged in the order of occurrence 2 of chronology, esp. containing or relating to an account of events in the order of their occurrence
chronology	χρονολογία	science of measuring time in fixed periods and of dating events: arrangement of events, dates etc., in the order of chronological occurrence
chronometer	χρονόμετρον/ο	a scientific instrument for measuring time pricisely
chronometry	χρονομετρία	the scientific measurement of time
chronoscope	χρονοσκόπιον/ο	an instrument for measuring very small intervals of time
-chroous	χρώος	akin to color/chroma combining form forming adjectives (isochroous/having the same color in all parts)
chrysalis	χρυσαλίς/χρυσαλίδα	the pupa of a butterfly, the form of an insect
chrysanthemum	χρυσάνθεμον/ο	marigold; golden flower between the larval and adult stages, and in the case of a coccoon

chryselephantine	χρυσελεφάντινος, η, ο (adj.)	made of, or overlaid with, gold and ivoty, as some of the ancient Greek statues
chryso-	χρυσός, ή, ό (adj.)	gold; golden; yellow combining form
chrysoderma	χρυσόδερμα	pigmentation of the skin resulting from deposits of gold
chrysoprase	χρυσό + πράσο –gold + leek	so called from the color; a light-green variety of chalcedony, sometimes used as a semiprecious stone
Chrysostom	Χρυσόστομος	(St. John the Chrysostom,) it was said that his speech was golden/words coming off his mouth were like gold; eloquent speaker, church Father in the Greek Orthodox faith (c. AD 347–407)
chrysotile	χρυσό + τίλλειν – gold + to pluck out; uneave, topaz;	1 a yellowish-green gem derived chiefly from varieties of olivine 2 a yellowish-green, reddish, or brownish variety of olivine
chthonian	χθόνιος, α, ο (adj.)	one coming/originating from the earth; designating or of the underworld of the dead and its gods or spirits; dark, primitive, and mysterious; also chthonic
chyle	χυλός (from χύειν/ to pour)	juice; humor; chyle; a milky fluid composed of lymph and emulsified fats; it is formed from chime in the small intestine, is absorbed by the lacteals, and is passed into the blood through the thoracic duct; "also, in Gr. the definition of chyle/χυλός: a liquid paste; a puree of flour, or other starch, and water, any other liquid, or chyme

chyme	χυμός (χύειν – to pour)	the thick, semifluid mass resulting from the gastric digestion of food: it passes from the stomach into the small intestine, where the chyle is formed from it; also in Gr., the fluid contained in fruit; the fluid from nutritional plants, etc.
cinema	κίνημα/κίνησις/η/ κινηματογράφος/ σινεμά	motion; movement (short for cinematography)
cinematographer	κινηματογραφιστής	the leading camera operator of a moviemaking crew
cinematography	κινηματογραφία	the art, science, and work of photograph in making films of the cinema
cinnamon	κιννάμωμον/ κανέλα (Mod. Gr.)	1 the yellowish-brown spice made from the inner dried bark of several trees or shrubs (genus Cinnamomun) of the laurel family, native to the East Indies and SE Asia 2 made or flavored cinnamon
Circe	Κίρκη	in Homer's *Odyssey*, an enchantress who turned men to swine and kept Odysseus for many years under her spell
cirrhosis	κίρρωσις/η	a degenerative disease in an organ of the body, esp., the liver, marked by excess formation of connective tissue, followed, usually, by painful swelling
cirsoid	(ο, η) κιρσοειδής (το) κιρσοειδές (adj.)	enlargement of a vein, like a varix or enlarged blood vessel; varicose
cissoid	(ο, η) κισσοειδής (το) κισσοειδές (adj.) κισσός + είδος/ivy + kind/type	ivylike Math. a curve converging into a pointed tip; designating the angle formed by the concave sides of two intersecting curves: opposed to sistroid

citri-	κίτρο	citrus fruit, combining form (citric) (citr- before a vowel)
citrus	κίτρο-	citrus; lemon, lime, orange, any type of yellowish-greenish fruit of trees or shrubs of the genus (Citrus)
citrus	κίτρον	lemons, limes, oranges, grapefruits, and any other fruit of the (Citrus family)
cladoceran	κλάδος + κέρας – branch + horn	a hornlike branch, shoot
cladophyll	κλάδος + φύλλο/ branch + leaf	a green, flattened branch arising from the axil of a leaf, with the shape and function of a foliage leaf
classical	κλασικός, ή, ό (adj.)	of the art, literature, and culture of the ancient Greeks and Romans, their writers and artists; a classical scholar: a person well versed in or devoted to Greek and Roman literature and culture
classics	κλασικά	a student or a specialist of classics
classicism	κλασικισμός	the aesthetic principles or qualities regarded as characteristic of ancient Greece and Rome; objectivity, formality, balance, simplicity, restraint, etc., generally contrasted with Romanticism; knowledge of the literature and art of ancient Greece and Rome; classical scholarship
classicist	κλασικιστής	an advocate of the principles of classicism; a student or specialist in ancient Greek and Roman literature
cleisto-	κλειστός, ή, ό (adj.)	closed, combining form (cleistogamous)

cleistogamous	κλειστός + γάμος	closed + marriage; mating Bot. having small, unopened, self-pollinating flowers, usually in addition to the more elaborate flowers
cleistogamy	κλειστό - γάμος / closed + union	Bot. self-pollination of certain unopened flowers
clematis	κληματίς/ κληματίδα/ κληματόβεργα	κλήμα/vine any of a genus (Clematis) of perennial plants and woody vines of the buttercup family, with bright-colored flowers of varying size and form
clergy	κληρικός/κλήρος	collectively; people ordained for religious services: as priests, ministers, rabbis, etc.
Cleomenes	Κλεομένης	name of three Spartan kings of the sixth to the third cen. BC, including **Cleomenes III** (ruled c.235–c. to 220 BC) who sought to institute sweeping social reforms
clepsydra	κλέπτειν + ύδωρ/ to steal + water	water clock (see: Kleptomania)
clepto-	κλέπτω/κλοπή	to steal; theft, combining form
cleptomania	κλεπτομανία	see Kleptomania
climacteric	κλιμακτερικός, ή, ό (adj.)/κλιμακτήριος	1 a period in the life of a person when an important physiological change occurs; specif., the period of menopause 2 any crucial period 2 any crucial period
climactic	κλιματικός, ή, ό (adj.)	of, constituting, or in the order of a climax
climate	κλίμα	the prevailing or average weather conditions of a place, as determined by the temperature and meteorological changes over a period of years
climatology	κλιματολογία	the science dealing with climate and climatic phenomena

climax	κλίμαξ/κλίμακα	ladder; 1 a rhetorical series of ideas, images, etc., arranged progressively so that the most forceful is last 2 the final, culminating element or event in a series
clinic	κλινική/κλίνη/bed	bedside; center where patients are treated
clinical	κλινικός, ή, ό (adj.)	pertaining to bedside treatment; having to do with the direct treatment and observation of patients; purely scientific; practice
clino-	κλίνω-/κλίνειν	to recline, combining form
clinometer	κλινόμετρον/ο	instrument for measuring angles of slope or inclination
Clio	Κλειώ	Gr. myth. the muse of history; any of the awards in advertising (Clios); female name
clitoris	κλιτωρίς/ κλιτωρίδα/ κλιτωρίδες (pl.)	a small, sensitive, erectile organ at the upper end of the vulva
clone	κλων-κλώνος- κλωνάρι	branch, twig; an individual produced by cloning; a person or thing very much like another
clonism	κλωνισμός/ κλωνοποίησις/η	the technical process to genetically reproduce identical organisms from an original, animal or plant
Clotho	Κλώθω-κλώθειν	to spin; Gr. and Rom. myth. that one of the three Fates who spins the thread of human life
Clytemnestra/ Clytaemnestra	Κλυταιμνήστρα	Gr. myth. wife of Agamemnon, with the aid of her lover Aegisthus murders her husband, and to avenge the father's death, Orestes kills his mother

coccus/cocci (pl.)	κόκκος/κόκκοι (pl.)	kernel; seed; berry; 1 a bacterium of a spherical shape any of the carpels, containing one seed, into which compound fruits split when ripe
coccoid	(o, η) κοκκώδης (το) κοκκώδες (adj.)	kernellike; one consisting of seeds or having proportional composition; one containing cocci
-coccus	κόκκος	suffix forming nouns coccus: used in names of various bacteria [gonococcus]
coccyx	κόκυχ/κόκυγος (γεν.)/κόκυγας (Mod. Gr.)	so called because it is shaped as a cuckoo's beak; a small triangular bone at the lower end of vertebral column, formed by the fusion of four rudimentary vertebrae and articulating with the sacrum
cochlea	κοχλίας/ κοχλιός	snail, snail shell; shellfish; the spiral-shaped part of the inner ear, containing the auditory nerve endings
cockle	κοχύλιον/κοχύλι	shell, shellfish; konchylion, shellfish 1 any of a family (Cardiidae) of marine bivalve mollusks wit two heart-shaped, radially ridged shells 2 a cockleshell 3 a wrinkle; pucker
coelacanth	κοίλος + άκανθος / hollow + thorn	any of an order (Coelacanthiformes) of bony fishes, now extinct except of the latimeria
-coele	κοιλία/κοιλιά	belly; body cavity; chamber of the body or of an organ (blastocoele)
coelenteron	κοίλο + έντερον/ο /	hollow + intestine the internal body cavity of coelenterates, flatworms, etc.
coeliac	κοιλιακός, ή, ό (adj.) κοιλία/belly	cavity; chamber of the body or of an organ; pertaining to the abdominal area

coelom	κοίλωμα	the main body cavity of most higher multicellular animals, in which the visceral organs are suspended
coenesthesia	κοινός αίσθησις/η – common + feeling/emotion	Psychol. the mass of undifferentiated sensations that make one aware of the body and its condition, as in the feeling of well-being or illness. Also, cenesthesis or cenesthesia
coeno- or -ceno	κοινός, ή, ό (adj.)	common, combining form (coenogenesis/ cenogenesis)
coenosarc	κοινό |σαρξ/ σαρκός(gen.)/ σάρκα (Mod. Gr.) – common + flesh	the fleshy portion of the stalks and stolons of hydroids that secretes the perisarc
coen-zyme	κοινό – ζύμη	an organic substance of low molecular weight that is not protein and can unite with a given protein, apoenzyme, to form an active enzyme complex
colectomy	κολεκτομή	removal of part of the large intestine extending from the cecum (blind intestine) to the rectum
coleus	κολεός	a sheath: so named because of the way in which the stamens are joined; any of a genus (Coleus) of plants of the mint family, native to Africa and the East Indies, grown for their bright-colored leaves
colic	κωλικός	severe abdominal pain caused by spasm of one of the internal organs, usually the intestines; a condition of infants characterized by frequent crying due to discomfort
colitis	κολίτις/κολίτιδα	inflammation of the large intestine

collage	κόλλα/κολάζ	sticky substance; glue; 1 an art form in which bits of objects, as newspapers, cloth, pressed flowers, etc., are pasted together on a surface in incongruous relationship for their or suggestive effect
collagen	κολλαγόνον/ο	a fibrous protein found in connective tissue, bone, and cartilage
collagenous	(ο, η) κολλαγενής, (το) κολλαγενές (adj.)	pertaining to collagen; collagenlike
collenchyma	κόλλα + ένχυμα- glue + a steeping, infusion	plant tissue consisting of elongated shells thickened at the corners, often found between the epidermis and the cortex of young stems
colloid	(ο, η) κολλώδης (το) κολλώδες pertaining to glue/ kola/κόλλα	1 a) a solid, liquid, or gaseous substance made up of very small, insoluble, nondiffusible particles (as single large molecules or masses of smaller molecules) that remain in suspension, in a surrounding solid, liquid, or gaseous medium of different medium b) all living matter contains colloidal material, and a colloid has only a negligible effect on the freezing point, or vapor pressure of the surrounding medium 2 the iodine-containing, gelatinous proteinstored in the thyroid
collotype	κόλλα + τύπος / glue + kind/type	a photo-mechanical process by which inked reproductions are transferred to paper directly from an image formed of a sheet of hardened gelatin; the printed reproduction
collyrium	κολλύριον/ο	an eye losion; eyewash

colobus	κολοβός	maimed; curtailed; any of the genus (Colobus) of thumbless, long-haired, black-and-white African monkeys
colocynth	κολοκύνθις/η	a perennial vine of the gourd family, whose small, dried fruits are used in making a strong cathartic 2 a vine type plant producing any type of the gourd family: squash, pumpkin, etc.
colon	κόλον	Anat. the part of the large intestine that extends from the cecum to the rectum
colophon	κολοφών/ κολοφώνος (gen.) /κολοφώνας (Mod. Gr.)	summit; top; end 1 a notation often placed in a book, at the end, giving facts about its production 2 the distinctive emblem of the publisher, as on the title page or the cover of a book
colossal	κολοσσιαίος, α, ο (adj.)	huge; gigantic; like a colossus in size; astonishing, great; extraordinary
colossus	κολοσσός,	1 gigantic statue; /person of great status/influence 2 any great/huge person or thing 3 the Colossos of Rhodes, the gigantic statue of Apollo at the entrance of Rhodes, one of the seven wonders of the world (c. 280 BC) (not surviving today)
colostomy	κόλον + στόμιο	the surgical operation of forming an artificial anal opening in the body from the colon
colpitis	κολπίτις/κολπίτιδα	inflammation of the vagina; vaginitis
coma	κώμα/κώματος (gen.)	fatigue, effort; deep, prolonged unconsciousness caused by injury or disease; a condition of stupor or lethargy

comatose	(ο, η) κωματώδης/ (το) κωματώδες (adj.)	of, like, or being in a stupor, coma, or lethargy; torpid; sluggish in functioning
comedic	κωμκιός, ή, ό (adj.)	pertaining to comedy
comedian/comic	κωμωδός/κωμικός	an actor who plays comic parts; an entertainer who tells jokes, sings funny songs
comedy	κωμωδία	orig. a drama or play with a happy ending; a novel, play or narrative having a comic, humorous theme, tone, etc., the comic element in a literary work; an amusing or comic event or sequence of events
comic	κωμικός, ή, ό (adj.)	intended amusing; humorous, funny 1 the humorous element in art or life 2 a comic strip or a comic book
comma	κόμμα (κόπτειν – to cut off, split)	clause in a sentence, that which is cut off; 1 mark of punctuation (,) used to indicate a slight separation of sentence elements, as in setting off nonrestrictive or parenthetical elements, items in a series, etc., a slight pause
comodiographer	κομωδιογράφος	a comedy writer
Comus	Κώμος	Gr. and Lat. myth. a young semi-god of festivity and revelry
conch	κογχύλι	mussel; shell 1 a) the large, spiral, univalve shell of any of various marine mollusks b) such a mollusk often edible
concha	κόγχη	1 Anat. any of several structures resembling shell in form as a thin, bony projection inside the nasal cavity, the hollow of the external ear, or the whole external ear 2 Archit. the half dome covering, an apse

conchoid	(o, η) κογχοειδής (το) κογχοειδές (adj.)	a curve traced by an end point of a segment of constant length located on a straight line that rotates about a fixed point, while the other end point of this segment moves along a straight line that does not go through the fixed point
conchologist	κογχυολόγος	an expert in conchology
conchology	κογχυολογία	the branch of natural history dealing with the shells of mollusks
condyle	κόνδυλος	knuckle; orig., hard lumb or knob, 1 a rounded process at the end of a bone, forming a ball-and-socket joint with the hollow part of another bone 2 an articular prominence of a bone
condyloid	(o, η) κονδυλοειδής (το) κονδυλοειδές	condylelike; bulged; swollen; having the shape of a condyle
condyloma	κονδύλωμα	a wartlike inflammatory growth on the skin, usually occurring near the anus or genital organs
cone	κώνος	a wedge, peak, 1 a flat-based, single-pointed solid formed by a rotating straight line that traces out a closed-curved base from a fixed vertex point that it is not in the same plane as the base; 2 any object or mass shaped like a cone
conic/conical	κωνικός, ή, ό (adj.)	resembling or shaped as a cone; conelike
conium	κώνιον/ο	hemlock; any of a small genus (conium) of poisonous biennial herbs of the umbel family, with carrotlike leaves and rounded fruits, as the poison hemlock (the poison given to Socrates, after his trial)

conoid	(ο, η) κωνοειδής (το) κωνοειδές (adj.)	conelike; shaped like a cone; resembling a cone
copepod	κουπί + πους/ ποδός(gen.)/ πόδι (Mod. Gr.) oar + foot	any of a class (Copepoda) of small, sometimes parasitic, crustaceans living in either salt or fresh water
copro-	κόπρος	dung; feces; excrement, combining form (coprology)
coprology	κοπρολογία	the treatment of scatological or pornographic subjects in art and literature
coprophagous	κοπροφάγος	feeding on excrements, as some beetles
coprophagy	κοπροφαγία	eating dung; feces
coprophilia	κοπροφιλία	Psychol. an abnormal interest in feces
coprophobia	κοπροφοβία	extreme fear or disdain of excrements
Cora	κόρη	maiden; a feminine name
coracii	κοράκι (κόραξ/ κόρακας – raven	of or belonging to an order (coriceformes) of birds with a strong, sharp bill, fused strong toes, and usually bright coloration (known also as coraciiform)
coracoid	(ο, η) κορακοειδής (το) κορακοειδές (adj.)	like a raven; designating or of a rudimentary bony process on the shoulder blade in mammals, or a bone in monotremes and certain fossil reptiles that extends from the shoulder blade to the breastbone; this bony process or bone process
cord	κορδόνι	1 a thick string or a thin rope 2 any force acting as a force or a bond 3 from use of a cord in measuring 4 cloth with a ribbed surface; corduroy

coriander	κορίαντρον/ο / κορίαννον/ο	1 a European annual herb (Coriandrum sativum) of the umbel family 2 its strong-smelling, seedlike fruit used in flavoring food and liqueur, and, formally, in medicines
Corinthian	Κορινθιακός ρυθμός	Corinthian-style column is the most ornamental of the three (the other two being Doric and Ionic)
cornice	κορωνίς/κορωνίδα	curved object; 1 a horizontal molding projecting along the top of a wall, building, etc. 2 a projecting, decorative strip above a window, designed to keep a curtain rod from showing
cosmetic	κοσμητικός, ή, ό (adj.)	beautifying or desighned to improve the complexion, hair, etc.; improving the appearance without major changes
cosmetician	κοσμητολόγος/ αισθητικός	a person who is in the beauty business, working or selling cosmetics
cosmetology	κοσμητολογία / αισθητική	the art or skill of treating with or applying cosmetics, as in beauty shops and, in general, being involved in the beauty culture
cosmic	κοσμικός, ή, ό (adj.)	pertaining to the universe, the world; wordly
cosmo-	κόσμο/κόσμος	people; world; universe
cosmogony	κοσμογονία	universe; world order; the study of the origin of the universe, the creation
cosmographer	κοσμογράφος	an expert in cosmography

cosmography	κοσμογραφία	1 a general description of the world 2 the science dealing with the structure of the universe as a whole and of the related parts: geology, geography, and astronomy, which are branches of cosmography
cosmology	κοσμολογία	science studying the origin and evolution of the universe
cosmonaut	κοσμοναύτης	sailor of the world or of the universe
cosmopolitan	κόσμος/world/ people + πολίτης/ citizen	citizen of the world; not bound by local or national habits or prejudices; at home in all the countries of the world
cosmopolis	κοσμόπολις/η	a large city inhabited by people from many different nations
cosmopolite	κοσμοπολίτης	a cosmopolitan person; a citizen of the world
cosmos	κόσμος	universe, world, people, harmony 1 the universe considered as a harmonious and orderly system 2 any of the genus (Cosmos) of tropical American plants of the composite family; with featherlike leaves and heads of white, pink, or purple flowers
cothurnus/cothurn	κόθωρν/κόθορνος	a high, thick-soled boot worn by actors in ancient Greek and Roman tragedies playing heroic roles
cranio-	κρανίον/ο	cranium; skull combining form (craniology)
craniology	κρανιολογία	the scientific study of the skull, esp., human skulls and their characteristics; including differences in size, shape, etc.
craniometer	κρανιόμετρον/ο	an instrument for measuring skulls

craniometry	κρανιο-μέτρησις-η	the science meausuring skulls; cranial measurement
craniotomy	κρανιοτομή	the surgical operation of opening the skull, as for brain operations or in childbirth
cranium	κρανίον	cranium; the bones forming the enclosure of the brain; brainpan; the skull, including the lower jaw
crater	κρατήρ/κρατήρος (gen.) κρατήρας (Mod. Gr.)	1 in ancient Greece or Rome, a kind of large bowl or jar shaped as an amphora 2 a bowl-shaped cavity, as at the mouth of a volcano or on the surface of the moon 3 a pit resembling this, as one made by an exploding bomb or fallen meteor
Creon	Κρέων/Κρέοντας (Mod. Gr.)	Gr. legend, a king of Thebes who had his niece Antigone entombed alive because she had defied him and buried her brother. See Antigone
Crete	Κρήτη	1 Greek island in the E Mediterranean: 3,218 sq. mi. (8, 334 sq. km.) 2 Sea of S section of the Aegean Sea, between Crete and the Cyclades
Creusa	Κρέουσα	Gr. and Rom. myth. 1 the bride of Jason, killed by the sorcery of the jealous Medea 2 the wife of Aeneas and daughter of Priam, lost in the flight from captured Troy
crico-	κρίκος	ring-shaped, combining form (circoid cartilage; circopharyngeal)
cricoid	(ο, η) κρικοειδής (το) κρικοειδές (adj.) (κρίκος-ring)	1 ring-shaped; designating or of the ring-shaped cartilage forming the lower part of the larymx

cricoid cartilage	κρικοειδής χόνδρος	a cartilage of the larynx which articulates with the lower part of the thyroid cartilage and with which the arytenoids cartilages articulate
crico-pharyngeal	κρίκο + φάρυγγικός	of or relating to the cricoids cartilage and the pharynx
cricothyroid	κρικοθυρεοειδής	a triangular muscle of the larynx that is attached to the cricoids and thyroid cartilages, and it is the principal tensor of the vocal chords, also called cricothyroid muscle
crinoid	(ο, η) κρινοειδής (το) κρινοειδές (adj.)	1 lily-shaped 2 designating or of a class (Crinoidea) of enchinoderms, some of which are flowerlike in form and are anchored by a stalk, others of which are free-swimming 3 an animal of this class, as a sea lily or feather star
crisis	κρίσις/η	judgment; the turning point of the disease; a time of great danger or trouble; often one that threatens to result in unpleasant consequences [an economic crisis]
criterion	κριτήριον/ο	means of judging; a standard rule, rule, or test by which something can be judged; measure of value
critic	κριτικός, ή, ό (adj.) (κρίνειν - to discern)	1 one who grasps the meaning, perceives; expresses judgments of people or things according to certain standards or values; such a person whose profession to write or broadcast such judgments of books, movies, music, articles, plays, paintings, television, sports events, etc.

criticism	κριτικισμός	1 the act of making judgments; analysis of qualities and evaluation of comparative worth, esp., in literary or artistic works; censure; disapproval 2 Phil. Philosophical system which is based on the work of the German philosopher Immanuel Kant (1724–1804)
criticize	κριτικάρω	to find fault; disapprove; judge severely
critique	κριτική	1 critical analysis or evaluation of a subject, situation, literary work, etc., 2 the art or act of criticizing; criticism
crocodile	κροκόδειλος	lizard; 1 any of a subfamily (Crocodilinae) of large flesh-eating, lizardlike crocodilian reptiles living in or around tropical streams and having thick, horny skin, composed of scales and plates, a long tail, and a long, narrow, triangular head with massive jaws 2 leather made from a crocodile's hide
crocodile tears	κροκοδείλια δάκρυα	insincere tears or a hypocritical show of grief (from an old belief that crocodiles shed tears while eating their prey)
crocodilian	κροκοδείλιος, α, ο (adj.)	of or like a crocodile; of reptiles including the crocodile, alligator, caiman, and gravial
cryo-	κρύος, α, ο (adj.) κρύο-	cold, freezing, frost, combining form (cryophobia)
cryo-biologist	κρύο- βιολόγος	expert in cryo-biology
cryo-biology	κρυο-βιολογία	branch of biology studying organisms, esp., warmblooded animals, at low temperatures
cryo-phobe	κρύο + φόβος	one having extreme fear of the cold

cryophobia	κρυοφοβία	excessive fear of cold
cryo-therapy	κρύο-θεραπεία	treatment with cold or ice
crypt	κρύπτη/κρύπτειν/ κρύβω	to hide, underground chamber or vault
cryptic	κρυπτικός,ή, ό (adj.)	having a hidden or ambiguous meaning
cryptogram	κρυπτό + γράφειν - hidden + to write	something written in code or cipher
crystal	κρύσταλλο	a clear, transparent quartz; a very clear, brilliant glass
crystallogist	κρυσταλουργός/ κρυσταλλοκαλλιτέχνης	1 an expert in crystalorgy 2 an artist working with crystals
crystalorgy	κρυσταλουργία/κρυσταλλοτεχνία	1 the science dealing with crystals 2 the art dealing with the cultivation and process of physical crystals
crystalloid	(ο, η) κρυσταλλοειδής, (το) κρυσταλλοειδές (adj.)	resembling a crystal
cteno-	κτένα/κτενίζω – comb/to comb	combining form
ctenoid	(ο, η κτενώδης (το) κτενώδες (adj.)	resembling a comb; having an edge with projections like the teeth of a comb, as the posterior margin of the scales of certain fish
cube	κύβος	a solid with six equal, square sides; anything having this shape; the product obtained by multiplying a given number or quantity by its square
cubic	κυβικός, ή, ό (adj.)	having the shape of a cube
cuboic	(ο, η) κυβοειδής, (το) κυβοειδές (adj.)	resembling a cube
cubism	κυβισμός	a movement in art, esp., in the early twentieth cent. characterized by the separation of the subjects into cubes and other geometric forms in abstract arrangements

cyano-	κυανούς/ κυανός, ή, ό (adj.)	having greenish blue or dark blue color combining form
cyano-bacteria	κυανο-βακτηρία	blue-green algae
cyanosis	κυάνωσις/κυάνωση	the blueness of the skin; a bluish coloration of the skin or mucous membranes, caused by lack of oxygen or abnormal hemoglobin in the blood
cybernetics	κυβερνητική (κυβερνήτης-helmsman/ governor)	the science dealing with the comparative study of human control systems, as the brain and nervous system, and complex electronic systems
Cyclades	Κυκλάδες	group of islands of Greece on the S Aegean 925 sq. m. (2,758 sq. km.); pop. 88, 000
Cycladic	κυκλαδικός, ή, ό (adj.)	pertaining to the Cyclades islands; anything having to do with the Cyclades islands
cyclamen	κυκλάμενον/ο	any of a genus (Cyc lamen) of plants of the primrose family, having heart-shaped leaves and white, pink, or red flowers with reflexed petals
cycle	κύκλος	circle; 1 a recurring period of a definite number of years, used as a measure of time 2 a period of time within which a round of regularly recurring events or phenomena is completed [the business cycle] 3 a very long period of time; an age [the Golden Age of Athens]
cyclical	κυκλικός, ή, ό (adj.)	Geom. circular
cyclist	μοτο-συκλετιστής	one riding a bicycle, motorcycle, etc.
cyclo- prefix	κύκλο- κύκλος	circle, wheel combining form (cyclometer)
cycloid	(ο, η) κυκλοειδής/ (το) κυκλοειδές (adj.)	circular (Geom.) a curve traced by any point on the radius; resembling a circle

cyclometer	κυκλόμετρον/o	an instrument in measuring the arcs of circles
cyclone	κυκλών/κυκλώνας	moving in a circle; windstorm with a violent, whirling movement; atmospheric disturbance
Cyclopean	κυκλώπειος, α, ο (adj.)	huge, gigantic, enormous
cyclopedia/ cyclopaedia	(εγ)	early word for encyclopedia
cycloplegia	κυκλο-πληγία	paralysis of the muscles of the eye responsible for visual accommodation
Cyclops	Κύκλωψ/κύκλωπας	any of the race of giants who have only one eye
cyclorama	κυκλόραμα	a series of large pictures as of a landscape, put on the wall of a circular room appearing to the spectator, standing in the center, in a natural perspective
cyclosis	κύκλωσις/η	a regular cyclic movement of protoplasm within a cell; surrounding; enveloping
cyclothymia	κυκλωθυμία	an emotional condition characterized by alternate periods of elation and depression; in its more severe form called bipolar
cyesis	κύησις/κύηση	pregnancy
cygnet	κύκνος	swan (from Gygnus, Gr. myth., a king of the Lingurians who was changed into a swan)
cylinder	κύλινδρος	1. Geom. a) a solid figure described by a line which always has a point in common with a given closed curb, b) anything having the shape of a cylinder, whether hollow or solid

cymbal	κύμβαλον	a circular, slightly concave brass plate used as a percussion instrument producing a variety of metallic sounds
cymene	κίμινον/ο	cumin; a colorless hydrocarbon, occurring in three isomeric forms, the most common is found in the oil of certain plants, as cumin and thyme
cyma	κύμα	wave; something swollen; a billow
cymatic	κυματιστός, ή, ό (adj.)	making waves
cymatoid	(ο, η) κυματώδης (το) κυματώδες (adj.)	resembling waves
cymatophilia	κυματοφιλία	extreme love for riding the waves (as the surfers)
cymatophobia	κυματοφοβία	extreme fear of waves
cynic	κυνικός, ή, ό (adj.)	a member of a school of ancient philosophers who stressed independence from wordly needs and pleasures, they became critical of the rest of society and the material interests (Diogenes was the most famous of the Cynics)
cynical	κυνικός, ή, ό (adj.)	having contemptuous disbelief in human goodness; sneering; sarcastic, etc.
cynicism	κυνισμός	1 the philosophy of the Cynics (the best-known Cynic being Diogenes) who held virtue to be the only good and stressed independence from wordly needs and pleasure; they became critical of the rest of society and its materialism
Cypriot	Κύπριος, Κύπρια () κυπραΐκος, η, ο (adj.)	an inhabitant of Cyprus; anything relating to Cyprus

Cyprus	Κύπρος	a Mediterranean island, south of Turkey: colonized by the Phoenicians and the ancient Greeks; it was ruled, at various periods, by many empires, became British territory (1914), gained independence and a member of the Commonwealth (1960). the north part of the island, from 1974, is under the occupation of Turkey, in 1984 auto-declared that section "Turkish Republic of N. Cyprus"
cypsela	κυψέλη	a hollow vessel: akin to cube (κύβος) an achene derived from an inferior ovary, as in plants of the composite family
cyst-	κύστις/η	any sac in the body filled with liquid or semi-liquid substance, also combining form before a vowel (cystolith)
-cyst	κύστις /η	suffix forming nouns (blastocyst)
cystectomy	κύστ-εκτομή	1 the surgical removal of a cyst 2 surgical removal of the gallbladder or of part of the urinary bladder
cystic	κυστικός, ή, ό (adj.)	1 of or like a cyst 2 having or containing a cyst or cysts 3 enclosed in a cyst 4 Anat. of the gallbladder or the urinary bladder
cystitis	κυστίτις/κυστίτιδα	inflammation of the bladder
cysto-	κύστις/η	bladder; sac, combining form
cystocarp	κύστο + καρπός (sac + fruit)	a fruitlike structure (sporocarp) developed after fertilization in the red algae
cystocele	κύστοκήλη	a hernia of the urinary bladder into the vagina
cystoid	(ο, η) κυστοειδής (το) κυστοειδές (adj.)	resembling a cyst; a cystlike formation

cystolith	κυστόλιθος (cyst + stone)	Bot. a crystalline deposit of calcium of carbonate occurring as a knob on the end of a stalk within a plant cell
cystoscope	κυστοσκόπιον/ο	an instrument for visually examining the interior of the urinary bladder
cystoscopy	κυστο-σκοπιά/ σκόπηση	examination of the urinary badder or tract with the aid of a cystoscope
cystotomy	κυστο-τομή	the surgical operation making an incision into the urinary bladder or gallbladder
-cyte	κύτος	cavity; a hollow, empty combining form (lymphocyte)
Cythera	Κύθηρα	Greek island just south of Peloponnesus
cyto-	κύτος	a hollow; cell or cells combining form (cytology; cytoplasm)
cyto-genetics	κύτος + γενετική	the science correlating cytology and genetics as they relate to the behavior of chromosomes and genes in cells with regard to heredity and variations
cyto-kinesis	κυτο-κίνησις/η (motion/movement)	cytoplasmic changes occurring in a cell during mitosis, meiosis, and fertilization
cyto-kinin	κυτο-κινείν (to move)	of a group of organic compounds which behave like hormones in plants, promoting cell division and cell differentiation into roots and shoots, inhibiting aging, etc.
cytologist	κυτολόγος	an expert in cytology; a student of the life history of cells
cytology	κυτολογία	the branch of biology dealing with the structure, function, pathology, and life history of cells
cytolysin	κύτο – λύειν	a substance or antibody that produces cytolysis

cytolysis	κύτο + λύσις/η (cell + solution)	Biol. the disintegration or dissolution of cells
cytoplasm	κύτο + πλάσμα	the protoplasm of a cell, outside of a nucleus
cyto-taxonomy	κύτο ταξονομία (cell + stracture/order)	the branch of taxonomy that uses cytologic structures, esp., the chromosomes, as an aid in classifying organisms
cyto-tropho-blast	κύτο-τροφή-βλαστός (cell + food +blast)	the thickened, inner part of the mammalian placenta nearest to the fetus, covering the chorion during early pregnancy

D

Dacryo-	δάκρυο(ν)	tear combining word (dacryology)
dacryo-cystitis	δάκρυο-κυστίτις/κυστίτιδα	inflammation of the lacrimal gland, which secretes the salty fluid (tears) to lubricate the eyeball
dacryon	δάκρυον/δάκρυ	tear
dacryology	δακρυολογία	the study of the gland(s) producing tears
dacryorrea	δακρύρροια (δάκρυ & ροή-tear & flow)	excessive flow of tears
dactyl	δάκτυλος /δάκτυλο	finger; toe
dactylic	δακτυλικός, ή, ό (adj.)	a dactylic line of poetry
dactylo – prefix	δάκτυλο	finger; toe; digit
dactylogram	δακτυλογράφημα	a fingerprint
dactylography	δακτυλογραφία/δακτυρογράφηση	1 the study of fingerprints as a means of identification 2 writing in a typewriter
dactylology	δακτυλολογία	communication with the fingers; sign language
-dactylous/-dactylia suffix	δάκτυλος/δάκτυλο/δάκτυλα (Mod. Gr.pl.)	finger, fingers combining form
dactylitis	δακτυλίτις/δακτυλίτιδα	an infection of a finger or a toe

daedalian	(ο, η) δαιδαλώδης (το) δαιδαλώδες (adj.)	something or someone that is complicated; difficult to get through
Daedalus	Δαίδαλος	Gr. myth. the skillful artist and builder of the Labyrinth in Crete, from which, he, along with his son Icarus, attemped to escape by making wings to fly
daemon/demon	δαίμων/δαίμονας	evil spirit; Satan
daemonic	δαιμόνιος, α, ο (adj.)	relating to daemon; also, one having exceptional ability, ingenious; dynamic
dasyure	δασύουρος (δασύς + ουρά- thick + tail)	hairy; any of a family (Dasiuridae) of small, mostly Australian marsupials that feed on flesh or insects
deacon	διάκων/διάκονος	a cleric ranking just below the priest
deca	δέκα	pertaining to number ten combining form
decad	δεκάς/δεκάδα	a group of ten; a period of ten years;
decade	δεκάδα/δεκάδες (pl.)	any group of ten; a period of ten years, esp., in the Gregorian calendar
decagon	δεκάγωνον/ο	a polygon having ten sides and ten angles
decagonal	δεκάγωνος, η, ο (adj.)	having ten angles
decagram	δεκάγραμμον/ο	having ten lines
decalitre	δεκάλιτρον/ο	containing ten litres
Decalogue	Δεκάλογος	Ten Commandments
decameron	δεκαήμερον (δέκα & ημέρα/ημέρες (pl.)	– ten + days
decameter	δεκάμετρον/ο	ten meters
decapod	δεκάπους/ δεκάποδας	ten-legged; any of an order (adecapoda) of crustaceans having ten legs, as a lobster, shrimp, or crab

Decapolis	Δεκάπολις/η	an ancient region of NE Palestine, mostly north of the Jordan, occupied by a confederation (formed c. 65 BC) of ten Greek cities
decasyllable	δεκασύλλαβος	a word or a line of a verse having ten syllables
decathlete	δεκαθλητής	participating in a decathlon
decathlon	δέκαθλον/ο	an athletic contest in which each contestant competes in ten events (100-meter dash, long jump, 16-pound shot-put, high jump, 110-meter hurdles, discus throw, pole vault, javelin throw, and 1,500-meter run): the winner must receive the highest total points
decathlete	δεκαθλητής	participating in a decathlon
deictic	δεικτικός, ή, ό (adj.)	1 directly pointing out or proving 2 Linguis. having the function of pointing out or specifying, and having its reference determined by its context [as the words **this**, **there**, **you**, etc. are deictic] also, in Gr. are defined as: δεικτικές αντωνυμίες – deictic pronouns
deleterious	δηλητήριος, α, ο (adj.) / δηλητηριώδης	poisonous; harmful to health or to well -being; injurious
Delos	Δήλος	a small Cycladic island in the Aegean; legendary birthplace of Artemis and Apollo; W of Myconos, from where many tourists take day trips to admire that beautiful place and enjoy the antiquities
Delphi	Δελφοί	on the slope of Mount Parnassus, town of ancient Phocis, is the famous seat of the ancient oracle of Apollo

Delphic	δελφικός, ή, ό (adj.)	1 of Delphi 2 designating or of the Delphic oracle of Apollo at Delphi 3 obscure in meaning; ambigious; oracular
delphinium	δελφίνιον/δελφίνι	dolphin, for some resemblance of the nectar of a dolphin, any of the genus of (Delphinium) of plants of the butter-cup family, bearing spikes of spurred, irregular flowers, usually blue, on tall stalks: several species are poisenous
Delta	Δ, δ (δέλτα)	fourth letter of the Greek alphabet
deltiology	δελτιολογία	collection and study of postcards, usually as a hobby
deltoid	(ο, η) δελτοειδή, (το) δελτοειδές (adj.)	1 shaped as a delta, triangular 2 designating or of a large, triangular muscle which covers the shoulder and raises the arm away from the side; the deltoid muscle
demagogic	δημαγωγικός, ή, ό (adj.)	of, like, or characteristic of a demagogue or demagogy
demagogue	δημαγωγός (δήμος + αγωγός/ άγειν – people + leader/to lead)	1 orig. the leader of the common people 2 the person who tries to stir up the people by appeals to emotion, prejudice, etc.
demagogy	δημαγωγία	control of the people, the methods or practices of a demagogue
Demeter	Δήμητρα	Gr. myth. the goddess of agriculture and fertility: identified with the Rom. Ceres; a feminine name
democracy	δημοκρατία (from: demos/people +κρατείν/to rule)	rule by the people

democrat	δημοκράτης	one who practices democracy (voting for the people who govern, obeying the laws set by the government, etc.)
democratic	δημοκρατικός, ή/ό (adj.)	of, belonging to, or upholding democracy; treating people of all classes in the same way; not snobbish; being popular by most people
demos	δήμος	the people; the masses; common people
demotic	δημοτική	popular or common as in language
demographer	δημογράφος	an expert in demography
demographics	δημογραφικά	the demographic characteristics of a population, esp. as classified by age, sex, income, etc., for market research, sociological analysis, etc.
demography	δημογραφία	the statistical science dealing with the distribution density, vital statistics, etc., of human populations
demon/daemon	δαίμων/δαίμονος (gen,) δαίμονας (Mod. Gr.)	a devil; evil spirit; 1 a person or thing regarded as evil, cruel, etc. [the demon of jealousy] 3 a) a person who has great energy or skill [a demon at golf] b) an enthusiast or devotee [a speed demon]
demoniac	δαιμονιακός, ή, ό (adj.)	1 possessed or influenced by a demon; 2 of a demon or demons; 3 like or characteristic of a demon; fiendish; frenzied, also demoniacal: a person supposedly possessed by a demon
demonism	δαιμονισμός	1 belief in the existence of powers of demons
demonisist	δαιμονιστής	one who believes and practices demonism

demonize	δαιμονίζειν/ δαιμονίζω	1 to make into or as if into a demon 2 to bring under the influence of deamon(s)
demono-	δαίμων/δαίμονος (gen,)/ of demon	combining form (demonolatry)
demonolater	δαιμονολάτρης	one who believes in the powers of demons
demonolatry	δαμονολατρία	the worship of demons
deontology	δεοντολογία	medical, journalistic; law, etc., ethics; the ethical behavior for various fields
derm-	δέρμ-	skin, combining form before a vowel (dermis)
derma	δέρμα	skin, epidermis
dermatitis	δερματίτις/ δερματίτιδα	inflammation of the skin/eczema
dermatologist	δερματολόγος	skin specialist
dermatology	δερματολογία	study relating to the skin
dermatosis	δερμάτωσις/η	any skin disease
dermis	δερμίς/δερμίδα	the real/true skin
di-	δις-δύο	two. twice, twofold combining form
dia	διά	through; between, combining form
diabetes	διαβήτης	a disease in which the body has the inability to handle glucose
diabolic	διαβολικός, ή, ό (adj.)	very wicked and cruel; of the devil
diabolism	διαβολισμός	dealing with the devil or devils, as by sorcery or witchcraft; belief or worship of the devil/devils
diagnosis	διάγνωσις /η	the determination of a disease
diagnostic	διάγνωστικός, ή, ό (adj.)	of or constituting a diagnosis
diagnostician	διαγνωστικός/ διαγνωστής	one skilled in determining the nature of a disease
diagonal	διαγώνιος, α, ο (adj.)	extending slantingly between two corners

diagram	διάγραμμα/ διαγράφειν	to mark out by lines; 1 a geometric figure used to illustrate a mathematical statement, proof, etc. 2 a sketch, drawing, or plan that explains a thing by outlining its parts and their relationships, workings, etc. 3 a chart or graft explaining or illustrating ideas, statistics, etc.
dialect	διάλεκτος	1 a form of language peculiar to a locality or group and differing from the standard language in grammar, syntax, etc. 2 discourse; discussion 3 Idio lect, the sum total of an individual's speech 4 any form of speech considered as deviating from a real or imaginary standard speech
dialectic	διαλεκτικός, ή, ό (adj.)	the art or practice of exchanging opinions or ideas logically, often by the method of asking questions and answers, so as to determine their validity
dialectician	διαλεκτιστής	a logician; an expert in dialect
dialectology	διαλεκτολογία	the scientific study of dialects
dialogical	διαλογικός, ή, ό (adj.)	of or marked by dialogue
dialogist	διαλογιστής	1 a writer of dialogues 2 one who participates in a dialogue
dialogue	διάλογος/ διαλέγομαι	talking together; conversation
dialysis	διάλυσις/η	method of separating substances in solution form
dialytic	διαλυτικός, ή, ό (adj.)	something that can enter a substance and separate it; pertaining to dialysis
dialyze	διαλύω/διαλύειν	to apply dialysis or separate by dialysis

diameter	διάμετρος (δια + μέτρο-through + measure)	a line segment passing through the center of a circle, sphere, etc., from one side to another
diametric	διαμετρικός, ή, ό (adj.)	1 of or along a diameter 2 designating an opposite, a contrary, a difference, etc., that is wholly so; complete
diametrically	διαμετρικώς (anc./ διαμετρικά (mod. Gr.)(adverb)	entirely opposite (good and evil are dramatically opposites)
diamond	αδάμας/ διαμάντι	a mineral consisting of nearly pure carbon in crystalline form, usually colorless, the hardest natural substance known
dianoesis	διανόησις /η	intellect; intelligence; thought
dianoetic	διανοητικός, ή, ό (adj.)	anything having to do with the intellect
dianthus	δίανθος	a flower; any of the genus (Dianthus) of plants of the pink family that includes the carnation and sweet william
diapason	διαπασών	the entire range of a musical instrument or voice; a swelling burst of harmony
diapauses	διάπαυσις/η	a period of delayed development or growth accompanied by reduced metabolism and inactivity; a pause
diaphanous	(ο, η) διαφανής, (το)διαφανές (adj.)	transparent
diaphoresis	(δια + φέρειν – through + bear)	a carrying away; profuse perspiration
diaphoretic	διαφορετικός, ή, ό (adj.)	1 producing or increasing perspiration 2 diaporetic medicine, treatment, etc. 3 different
diaphragm	διάφραγμα	large muscle separating the inside of the chest from the inside of the abdomen; contraceptive device

diaphysis	διάφυσις/η	shaft of a long bone, as distinguished from the growing ends
diapophysis	διαπόφυσις/η	the transverse process of a vertebra
diarchy	διαρχία (δύο + αρχή-two + rule)	government shared by two rulers, powers, etc.
diarrhea	διάρροια	loose bowel movement
diarthrosis	διάρθρωσις /η (δια + άρθρωσις – through +joint)	to connect by a joint; Anat. any articulation, as of the hip, permitting free movement in any direction
diaspora	διασπορά	dispersed community of a given people; any scattering with a common origin, background, religion, etc.
diastema	διάστημα	a natural space in the body, spec. the gap between two teeth, esp. of the upper jaw; space, also. In Gr. to διάστημα (neut.) means: the space/outer space
diastrophism	διαστροφή- δια + στρέφειν/ aside + to turn	distortion; 1 the process by which the earth's surface is reshaped through rock movements and displacements 2 formation so made
diatessaron	διατεσσάρων- δια + τεσσάρων / gen. of τέσσαρες –through + four	the four Gospels combined into a single account
diathermic	διαθερμικός, ή, ό (adj.)	relating to diathermy; letting heat rays pass freely
diathermy	διαθερμία	1 treatment of an injury or disease by electrotherapy/ heat 2 medical treatment in which heat is produced beneath the skin by a high-frequency electric current, radiation, etc., to warm or destroy tissue

diathesis	διάθεσις/η	disposition; constitution that makes one prone to a disease
diatom	διάτομον/ο / δια + τέμνειν/ τομή- through + to cut/cutting	any of a class of microscopic algae; one-celled or in colonies, whose cell walls consist of interlocking parts and valves and contain silica: diatoms are a source of food for all kinds of marine life
diatomic	διατομικός, ή, ό (adj.)	1 having two atoms in the molecule 2 having two replaceable atoms or radicals in the molecule
diatonic	διατονικός, ή, ό (adj.) δια + τείνειν- through+ to stretch/tend	stretched through (the notes) music designating, of, or using a scale of eight tones that it's either a major scale or a Minor scale diatonically/ διατονικώς/ά (adverb)
diatribe	διατριβή	1 learned discussion; thesis; dissertation 2 a bitter, abusive criticism or denunciation
dibasic	διβασικός, ή, ό (adj.)	1 denoting or of an acid with two hydrogen atoms, either or both of which maybe replaced by basic radicals or atoms to form a salt 2 having two atoms of a monovalent metal
dicho -suffix	δίχο- (διχοτομώ-1 cut in two)	asunder; apart/in two combining form (dichotomy/ cut in two) and dich- before a vowel (dic linous/ two - bed)
dichotomize	διχοτομώ/ διχοτομίζω	to perform or undergo dichotomy; to separate in two
dichotomous	διχότομος, η, ο (adj.)	pertaining to dichotomy
dichotomy	διχοτομή/διχοτομία/ διχοτομώ/cut in two	division in two parts
dichromatic	διχρωματικός, ή, ό (adj.)	1 having two colors 2 or of characterized by dichromatic/ two colors

dichromatism	διχρωματισμός	1 the quality or condition of being dichromatic/ having two colors 2 color blindness in which a person can see only two of the three primary colors (red, green, and blue) (dichroism)
dichroscope	διχρωσκόπιον/ο	an instrument for studying dichroism
diclinous	δίκλινος, η, ο (adj.) (δις + κλίνη/ two + bed)	Bot. having the stamens and pistils in separate flowers
dicrotic	δίκροτος, η, ο (adj.) (δις+ κρότος/ two + pulse, beat, noise)	double-beating; of or having a double pulse beat with each heartbeat [a decrotic artery]
dicrotism	δικροτισμός	the quality or condition of being dicrotic or having two pulse beats
dictator	δικτάτωρ/ δικτάτορας	a ruler with absolute power and authority, esp., one who exercises it tyrannically
dictatorship	δικτατορία	the position or office of a dictator; a state ruled by a dictator
didache	διδαχή	the teaching (of the twelve apostles)
didactic	διδακτικός, ή, ό (adj.)	used or intented for teaching or instruction
didactics	διδακτική	the branch of pedagogics that deals with the methodology and problems of teaching; the art or science of teaching, esp. instruction in teaching methods
didymous	δίδυμος, η, ο (adj.)	twin, double; Biol. growing in pairs
diegesis	διήγησις/η	narration, narrative
dieresis	διαίρεσις/η /διαιρείν	division; to divide

diet	δίαιτα	1 what a person or animal usually eats and drinks; daily food allowance 2 a special or limited selection of food or drink, chosen or prescribed to promote health or to gain or lose weight
dietetic	διαιτητικός, ή, ό (adj.)	of, relating to, or designed for a particular diet of food and drink
dietetics	διαιτητική	the study of the kinds and quantities of food needed for health
dietician	διαιτολόγος	an expert in dietetics; specialist in planning of meals or diets
digamma	δίγαμμα δι – two + γάμμα	resembling 2 gamma (Γ) in form
digamous	δίγαμος, η, ο (adj.)	married twice after death or divorce of the first spouse (or married to two spouses at the same time, not legally of course)
digamy	διγαμία	being married twice during the same period
dilemma	δίλημμα	an argument necessitating a choice between equally unfavorable or disagreeable alternatives; a predicament; any situation when one has to choose between unpleasant alternatives
dilemmatic	διλημματικός, ή, ό (adj.)	pertaining to a perplexed/ confused situation
dimerous	δίμερος, η, ο (adj.)/ διμερής -διμερές (δις + μερος/ two + part)	having two parts; spec., a) having two members in each whorl (as in flowers) b) having two-jointed tarsi (said of insects)
dimeter	δίμετρος, η, ο (adj.)	1 a line of verse containing two metrical feet 2 verse consisting of dimeters; having two metrical feet

dimorphic	διμορφικός, ή, ό (adj)	having two forms or shapes
dimorphism	διμορφισμός	1 Bot. the state of having two different kinds of leaves, flowers, stamens, etc., on the same plant or in the same species 2 mineralogy: the property of crystallizing in two forms 3 Zool: the occurrence of two types of individuals in the same species, distinct in coloring, shape, size, etc.
dimorphous	δίμορφος, η, ο (adj.)	pertaining to dimorphic; having two forms or shapes
dino-	δεινός, ή, ό (adj.)	terrible, dreadful, combining form (dinosaur)
dinosaur	δεινόσαυρος	1 any of two orders **{Ornithischia or Shaurischia}** of extinct, mostly land-dwelling, four-limbed of the Mesozoic Era 2 someone or something thought of as being old-fashioned, outmoded, resistant to change (dinosaurian)
diocese	διοίκησις/η	management; administrative activity; administration
diode	δίοδος	1 a) an electron tube of the high-vacuum type with a cold anode and a heated cathode, used as a rectifier of alternating current, a demodulator,etc. b) a low-pressure, gas-filled electron tube used as a rectifier 2 a semiconductor device used in a similar manner
Diogenes	Διογένης	c. 412–c. 323 BC; Gr. Cynic philosopher; well-known for his ascheticism
Diomedes	Διομήδης	Gr. legend. a Greek warrior at the siege of Troy, who helps Odysseus steal the statue of Athena

Dionysia	Διονύσια (pl.)	any of the various ancient festivals in honor of Dionysus, esp. those at Athens where the Greek dramas originated
Dionysian	διονυσιακός, ή, ό (adj.)	1 Dionysiac 2 of the orgiastic nature of the Dionysia; wild; frenzied, and sensuous: distinguished from the Apollonian 2 of any of several historical figures named Dionysus
Dionysus /Dionysos	Διόνυσος	Gr. myth. the god of wine and revelry: identified with the Rom. Bacchus
dioptre/ diopter	δίοπτρον (δια + όψις- through + sight)	a unit of measure of the power of a lens, equal to the power of a lens with a focal length of one meter; spyglass
dioprtic	διοπτρικός, ή, ό (adj.)	relating to dioptrer; 1 of optical lenses or the method of numbering them according to their refractive powers; dioptral 2 of dioptrics; refractive 3 helping the sight by refractive correction
dioptrics	διοπτρική	[Archaic] the branch of optics dealing with the refraction of light through lenses
diorama	διόραμα	1 a picture painted on a set of transparent cloth curtains and looked at through a small opening 2 a miniature scene, wholly or partially three-dimensional, depicting figures in a naturalistic setting 3 a museum display of a preserved or reconstructed specimen, as of a wildlife in a simulation of its habitat
diphtheria	διφθηρία	disease causing the development of membrane in nose and throat

diphasic	διφασικός, ή, ό (adj.)	having two phases
diplo-	διπλούς/ διπλός	double; twofold, combining form
diploid	διπλούς/ διπλός, ή, ό (adj.)	1 double or twofold 2 Biol. having twice the number of chromosomes normally occurring in a mature germ cell: most somatic cells are diploid
diploma	δίπλωμα	a certificate of honors; a degree on graduation
diplomacy	διπλωματία	the conducting of relations between nations; skill in dealing with people
diplomat	διπλωμάτης	a representative of a government who conducts relations with other governments; specialist in diplomacy
diplomatic	διπλωματικός, ή, ό (adj.)	of or connected with diplomacy
diplont	διπλ + ov/ όντος(gen.)/ double + a cell; organism	an animal or plant whose somatic nuclei are diploid/twofold
diplopia	δπλωπία	a vision disorder in which a single object appears double; double vision
dipso-	διψώ/δίψα	to thirst; thirst, combining form
dipsomania	διψομανία	excessive desire for fluids/ water; extreme thirst; an insatiable craving for alcoholic drink
dipsomaniac	διψα +μανιακός, ή, ό (adj.) thirst + maniac	someone with excessive desire for drinking; pertaining to dipsomana
disks	δίσκος-δίσκοι (pl.)	pads located between each of the vertebrae
diuresis	διουρία/συχνοουρία	frequent urination; an increased or excessive excretion of urination

diuretic	διουρητικός, ή, ό(adj.)	medication increasing the flow of urine
dolma/dolmades	ντολμάς/ ντολμάδες (pl.)	Greek and Mid. Eastern dish consisting of ground meat, rice, chopped onion, spices, etc., wrapped in grape leaves or cabbage leaves
doolie	δούλος	slave; a freshman at the US Air Force Academy
Doric	Δωρικός, ή, ό (adj.)	the Doric column is the oldest and the simplest of three main columns of architecture which adorned many famous buildings of antiquity and they are found all over the world today (the other two being, the Ionic and Corinthian)
Dorothea	Δωροθέα (δώρο+ Θεός/ gift + God)	gift of God; feminine name, variation Dora, Doris; Dorothy
domatophobia	δωματοφοβία	exteme fear for being in a room or house
dose	δόσις/η (from δίνω/ δούναι- to give)	1 amount of medication required each time 1 amount of of punishment or other unpleasant experience undergone at one time 2 the amount of radiation delivered to a particular area or to a given part of the body
dox- suffix	δοξ-δόξα	glory; praise; combining form
doxology	δοξολογία	a hymn of praise to God, starting with the phrase "Glory to the Father, to the Son, and the Holy Spirit"
doxography	δοξογραφία	the writings of the dogmas and theories of the philosophical schools
dracaena	δράκαινα (feminine of dracon)	any of the genus (Dracaena) of tropical shrubs and trees of the agave family, including the dragon tree

drachma	δραχμή (lit. a handful from δράσσεσθαι; to grasp a handful)	1 an ancient GR. silver coin 2 an ancient Gr. unit of weight approximately equal to the weight of the silver coin 3 the basic monetary unit of modern Greece till it was replaced by the Euro
Draco/Dracon	Δράκων	1 seventh cent. BC; Athenian statesman and lawgiver 2 Astron. a large N constellation containing the north pole of the ecliptic
Draconian	δρακόντειος, α, ό (adj.)	extremely strict; the phrase "Draconian Laws/δρακόντειοι νόμοι" is credited to the Athenian lawmaker Dracon, whose laws were so cruel that a phrase was later written stating "by blood, not ink Dracon wrote his laws"
dragon	δράκων/δράκοντας	serpent; 1 a mythical monster, usually represented as a large reptile with wings and claws breathing out fire and smoke 2 a fierce person; esp., a fiercely watchful female guardian or chaperone 3 a large serpent or snake 4 Bible a word used to translate several Hebrew words now having the meaning: serpent, jackal, Old Serpent (Satan), etc. 5 the constellation Draco
drama	δράμα	a literary composition that tells a story, usually of human conflict
dramatic	δραματικός, ή, ό (adj.)	having the characteristics of drama, esp., the conflict
dramatics	δραματική	the art of performing or producing dramatic plays
dramatist	δραματουργός	a playwright, one who writes dramatic plays

dramatisize	δραματοποιώ	to make into a drama, for a performance on stage, or a movie, etc.; over dramatizing a situation, etc.
drastic	δραστικός, ή, ό (adj.)	acting with force; having a strong or violent effect; severe; harsh; extreme
dromo- prefix	δρόμο-δρόμος	road; roadrace; street
-dromous	δρόμος	road, race; running, moving, combining form (catadromous)
dromomania	δρομομανία	excessive desire for roadraces, or the road
dromophobia	δρομοφοβία	extreme fear of the road or road races
drosera	δροσερός, ά (ή), ό (adj.) (δρόσος/ δροσιά (n.)/ dew)	dewy, dew, cool, any of the genus [Drosera] of small plants of the sundew family, having leaves covered with adhesive hairs that trap insects, which are digested by the plant
drosophila	δροσόφιλα	loving dew; any of the genus (Drosophila, family Drosophilidae) of tiny fruit flies used in laboratory experiments, and great reproductive capacity
dryad	δρυς/δρυός (gen.)	oak tree; Gr. and Rom. myth. any of the nymphs living in trees, wood nymph
dulia	δουλεία and δουλειά	(the first, with the accent on the ί, means slavery, with the accent on the (ά) means work, service
dynamia	δύναμις/η	energy; strength, power
dynamic	δυναμικός, ή, ό (adj.)	having power; strength; force
dynamism	δυναμισμός	the theory that force or energy, rather than mass and motion, is the basic principle for all the phenomena
dynamo-	δύναμις/η	power; force combining form (dynamometer)

dynamometer	δυναμόμετρον/ο	an apparatus for measuring mechanical power, as of an engine
dynast	δυναστής (δύνασται- to be strong)	a ruler, esp. a hereditary ruler
dynasty	δυναστεία	a succession of rulers who are members of the same family; the period during which a certain family reigns
dys- prefix	δυσ-/κακός/σκληρός	bad, hard, difficult
dysarthria	δυσάρθρεια	stammering; difficulty in articulating words due to disease of the central nervous system
dysarthrosis	δυσάρθρωσις/η	1 dislocation; deformity of a joint 2 a condition of reduced joint motion due to deformity, dislocation, or disease
dysbasis	δύσβασις/η (δys + βαίνειν – difficult/ hard + to walk)	difficulty in walking
dyscrasia	δυς + κράσις (δυσκρασία/ bad temperament	an abnormal imbalance in some part of the body, esp., in the blood
dysemesia	δυσ-έμετος	painful vomiting
dysentery	δυσεντερία	1 group of disorders produced by irritation of the bowels 2 a disease characterized by severe diarrhea with passage of mucus and blood and usually caused by infection; diarrhea
dysesthesia	δυσαισθησία (δυς + αίσθησις/η - bad + feeling/sense)	impairment in sensitivity esp. to the touch
dysgenic

of a stock | (ο, η) δυσγενής (το) δυσγενές (adj.) | causing deterioration of heredity qualities |
| dysgraphia | δυσγράφια | inability to write, as a result of brain dysfunction |
| dyskinesia | δυσκινησία | inability to make any physical movement/motion |

dyslexia	δυσλεξία	1 impairement of the ability to read, often as the result of genetic defect or brain injury 2 a variable often familial, learning disability involving difficulty in acquiring and processing language that is typically manifested by a lack of proficiency in reading, spelling, and writing
dyslexic/ dyslectic	δυσλεκτικός, ή, ό (adj.)	pertaining to dyslexia; one affected by dyslexia
dysmenorrhea	δυσμενόρροια	painful or difficult menstruation
dyspepsia	δυσπεψία	indigestion; dysfunction of the digestive system and the difficulty that follows during digestion
dyspeptic	δύσπεπτος, η, ο (adj.)	1 suffering from dyspepsia 2 morose; grouchy 2 one affected by dyspepsia
dysphagia	δυσφαγεία (δυς + φάγειν/ hard + to eat)	Med. difficulty in swallowing;
dysphasia	δυσφασία	impairement of the ability to speak or, oftentimes, to understand language, due to brain injury, brain tumor, etc.
d ysphonia	δυσφωνία (δυς + φωνή/ difficult + voice)	impairement of the ability to produce speech, sounds, because of hoarseness
dysphoria	δυσφορία	Psychol. a generalized feeling of ill-being; esp., an abnormal feeling of anxiety
dysplasia	δυσπλασία	a disordered growth or faulty development of various tissues or body parts
dyspneia	δύσπνοια	labored or difficult breathing
dysrhythmia	δυσρυθμία	lack of rhythm, as of the brain waves or in speech patterns

dysthymia	δυσθυμία	a mood disorder characterized by chronic depressed or irritable mood often accompanied by other symptoms (as eating and sleeping disturbances, and poor self-esteem)
dysthymic	δυσθυμικός, ή, ό (adj.)	one affected with dysthymia
dystithia	δυσ-στήθια-στήθος/ breast	difficulty in breastfeeding
dystocia	δυσ-τοκετός / δύσκολος-τοκετός	difficult childbirth
dystonia	δυστονία	lack of normal muscle tone due to disease or infection
dystopia	δυστοπία	1 a hypothetical place, society, or situation in which conditions and the quality of life are dreadful 2 a novel or other work depicting a dystopian society or place (opposed to Utopia)
dystrophic	δυστροφικός, ή, ό (adj.)	poorly developed; caused by dystrophy
dystrophy	δυστροφία	weakening of muscle due to abnormal development
dysuria	δυσουρία	difficult or painful urination
dystropy	δυστροπία	bad behavior, terrible manners

E

Ebonite	εμπονίτης	early term for hard rubber
ebony	έμπενος	the hard, heavy, durable wood of any of various trees, esp. of a group of persimmons native to tropical Africa, Asia, and Sri Lanka: it is used for furniture and decorative woodwork
ecbolic	εκβολικός, ή, ό (adj.) (εκβολή – a throwing out)	speeding up childbirth or produces abortion

eccentric	εκκεντρικός, ή, ό (adj.)	1 peripheral, peculiar in ideas 2 not having the same center, as two circles one inside the other: opposed to concentric 3 not having the axis exactly in the center; 4 deviating from the norm, as in conduct; out of the ordinary; odd; unconventional
eccentric hypetrophy	εκκεντρική υπερτροφία	hypertrophy of the wall of a hollow organ and esp. the heart with dilation of its cavity
eccentricity	εκκεντρικότητα	1 deviation from what is ordinary or customary, as in conduct and manner; oddity; unconventionality; peculiarity 2 the state, quality, or amount of being eccentric 3 Math. the ratio of the distances from any point of a conic section to the focus and to the dietrix: the value of this ratio determines the tyoe of conic section 4 Mech. the distance between of a shaft and the center of its eccentric wheel: sometimes, erroneously, called a throw—Syn: Idiosyncracy
ecchymosis	εκχύμωσις/η (εκ- χύειν - to pour off/ out)	Med. the flow of blood to the tissues due to the rupture of the vessels: it appears with a darkening of the skin (hematoma)
ecclesia	εκκλησία	a Christian assembly; church
ecclesiastic	εκκλησιαστικός, ή, ό (adj.)	pertaining to the church; of the church, the organization of the church
ecclesiology	εκκλησιολογία	the study of the history, architecture, art, etc., of the church
ecdysis	έκδυσις/η/ εκδύειν (to strip off)	getting out; Zool. the shedding of an outer layer of skin or integument, as by snakes or insects

ecesis	οίκησις/η (οίκος/ οικία- home/ residence)	the successful establishment of a plant or animal in a new locality
echidna	έχιδνα	any of a family (Tachyglossidae) of small, toothless, Australassian monotremes with a long, tapering snout and a sticky, extensible tongue; anteater
echino -	εχίνος /αχινός	sea urchin; combining form (echinoderm)
echiinococcus	εχινόκοκκος	any of a genus (Echinococcus) of tapeworms that cause disease in mammals
echinoderm	εχινόδερμον/ο	any of the phylum (Echinodermata) of marines, animals
echinoid	(ο, η) εχινώδης (το) εχινώδες	of or like a sea urchin; any of a class (Echinoidea) of echinoderms, including the sea urchins and sand dollars
echinus	εχίνος/αχινός	sea urchin; Archit. a) molding under the abacus of the capital of a Doric column b) any of several similar moldings
echo	ηχώ	reverberating sound; repetition or imitation of words; style; ideas, etc.
echolalia	ηχώ + λαλιά – echo + sound, speech defect /λαλείν – to talk, prattle	the automatic repetition by someone of words spoken in his or her presence, esp., as a symptom of mental disorder
eclampsia	εκλαμψία	an attact of convulsions; specif., a disorder that may occur late in pregnancy, characterized by convulsions, edema, and elevated blood pressure
eclectic	εκλεκτικός, ή, ό (adj.)	intellectually inclusive; to select; pick; selective

eclecticism	εκλεκτισμός	an eclectic system or method of thought; the using or upholding of such system
eclipse	έκλειψις/η	partial or total obscuring of one celestial body by 1 another; a dimming or extinction, as of fame or glory; to leave out, fail
ecliptic	εκλειπτικός, ή, ό (adj.)	the great circle on the celestial sphere
eclogue	εκλογή	selection, election, choice
eco- prefix	οίκος /οικία	habitat; environment
ecol-	οικος + λόγος	pertaining to home, surroundings
ecological	οικολογικός, ή, ό (adj.)	relating to the environment
ecologist	οικολόγος	an expert in ecology
ecology	οικολογία	the study of the branch of biology dealing with living organisms and their environment
econ-	οικον- οικονομία	refers to finances and the economy
econometrics	οικονομετρία	the use of mathematical and statistical methods in the field of economics to verify and develop economic theories
economic	οικονομκός, ή, ό (adj.)	of or having to do with the management of the income, expenditures, etc., of a household, business, or government
economical	οικονόμος/ οικονόμα (fem.)	prudent with finances; not wasting money, fuel, food, etc., economic factors
economic geography	οικονομική γεωγραφία	the branch of geography dealing with the relation of economic conditions to physical geography and natural resources

economics	οικονομικά	the science dealing with the production, distribution, and consumption of wealth and with the various related problems of labor, finance, taxation, etc.
economist	οικονομολόγος	a specialist in economics
economy	οικονομία	1 the management of the income, expeditures, etc., of a household, business, community, or government 2 a) careful management of wealth, resources, etc., avoidance of waste by careful planning, thrift, or thrifty use b) restrained or efficient use of one's materials, technique, etc., esp. by an artist 3 a) a system of producing, distributing, and consuming wealth b) the condition of such a system [a healthy economy]
ecosphere	οικόσφαιρα (οίκος + σφαίρα)	the zone of the earth, a planet, a star, etc., which contains or is capable of containing living organisms; specif., the biosphere
ecosystem	οικο-σύστημα	a system made up of a community of animals, plants, and bacteria interrelated together with its physical and chemical environment
ecstasy	έκστασις/η	exaltation; a state of being overpowered by emotion, as by joy, grief, or passion
ecstatic	εκστατικός, ή, ό (adj.)	having the nature of, or characterized by ecstacy
ecthyma	έκθυμα	inflammation of the skin, characterized by large pimples that rupture and become crusted
ecthyreosis	εκ –θυρεοειδής	absence or loss of function of the thyroid gland

ecto-	εκτός-έξω	out, outside
ectocardia	εκτός – καρδία/ά	displacement of the heart
ectoderm	εκτός -δέρμα	outmost layer of cells of an animal embryo; the layer or layers of cells composing the skin, nervous system, etc., in all animals except protozoans and sponges
ectodermic	εκτοδερμικός, ή, ó (adj.)	pertaining to the outer layer of skin
ectogenesis	εκτός-γένεσις/η	the growth process of an embryonic tissue in an artificial environment, as a test tube
ectogenous	(ο, η) εκτογενής (το) εκτογενές (adj.)	that can develop outside the host: said of certain parasitic bacteria
ectomorphic	εκτομορφικός, ή, ó (adj.)	designating or of the slender type, developed from the ectodermal layer of the embryo, as skin, nerves, brain, and sense organs
-ectomy (suffix)	εκ-τομή	excision
ectopia	έκτοπος	away from a place, an abnormal position of a body part or an organ, esp., at birth
ectoplasm	εκτο-πλάσμα	1 the outer layer of the cytoplasm of a cell: distinguished from entoplasm 2 the vaporous, luminous substance believed by spiritualists to emanate from a medium in a trance, or from an object undergoing telekinesis
ectosarc	εκτοσάρξ/ εκτοσάρκα	the ectoplasm of one-celled animals
ectype	έκτυπο(ν)	engraved in relief; a reproduction of an original work; a copy
ecumenical	οικουμενικός, ή, ó (adj.) (οικουμένη/ universe	of the whole world; general or universal; esp. concerning the Christian church as a whole

Ecumanism / ecumenicism	Οικουμενισμός	1 the ecumenical movement among the Christian churches; 2 the principles or practice of promoting cooperation or better understanding among differing religious faiths
eczema	έκζεμα	itching disease of the skin
edaphic	εδαφικός, ή, ό (adj.) (έδαφος/ soil, ground)	Ecol. pertaining to the chemical and physical characteristics of the soil, without reference to the climate
edema	οίδημα	excessive accumulation of tissue fluid; a swelling tumor; a similar swelling in plant cells and tissues
egis/aegis	αιγίς /αιγίδα	1 the shield of Zeus; goatskin; [a short goatskin cloak of Zeus] 2 a protection; sponsorship; auspices
ego	εγώ	εγώ/ I, self; individual/part of the mind that possesses reality and attempts to bring harmony between instincts and reality
egocentric	εγωκεντρικός, ή, ό (adj.)	self-centered; one viewing everything in relation to oneself
egoism	εγωϊσμός	conceit; the tendency to be self-centered or to consider only one's own interests; selfishness
egoist	εγωϊστής	a person who is self-centered or selfish
egoistic	εγωϊστικός, ή, ό (adj.)	egotistical; arrogant
egolatry	εγωλατρεία	extreme love for oneself
egomania	εγώ-μανία/εγωμανία	morbid self-esteem
egomaniac	εγωμανής (εγώ + μανία/excessive liking + self)	someone demonstrating extreme love for himself or herself
ego-psychology	εγώ + ψυχολογία	the study of the adaptive and mediating functions of the ego and their role in personality development and emotional disorder

egotism	εγωΐσμός	exaggerated evaluation of oneself
eidetic	ειδητικός, ή, ό (adj.)	constituting a figure; designating or of mental images that are unusually vivid and almost photographically exact
eidolon	είδωλον/ο	1 an image without real existence; phantom; apparition 2 an ideal person or thing
elastic	ελαστικός, ή, ό (adj.)	to set in motion; able to spring back to its original size, 1 shape or position after being stretched, squeezed, flexed expanded, etc.; flexible; springy
elasticity	ελαστικότητα	the quality or condition of being elastic; springiness; flexibility; resilience
elastin	ελαστίνη	a yellow, fibrous protein that is the basic constituent of elastic connective tissue, as in a lung or an artery
elater	ελατήριον/ο	1 an elastic filament that scatters the ripes spores, found in certain spores found in certain plants, as in the capsule of liverwort 2 an elastic component of machinery that sets in motion the mechanism
elaterium	ελατήριος, α, ο (adj.) ελατήριον (neu.)/ ελαύνειν	to drive 1 a cathartic obtained from dried of the squirting cucumber of the gourd family; in Gr. ελατήριον/ elaterium is an elastic component, of machines or apparatus; a spiral component
Electra	Ηλέκτρα (lit. the snining one)	Gr. myth. the daughter of Agamemnon and Clytemnestra: who encourages her brother, Orestes, to kill their mother and her lover, who together had murdered their father Agamemnon

Electra complex	σύμπλεγμα της Ηλέκτρας	Psychoanalysis the unconscious tendency of a daughter to be attached to her father and be hostile towards her mother: cf. Oedipus Complex
electric	ηλεκτρικός, ή, ό (adj.)	electron/akin to shining
electricity	ηλεκτρισμός	energy having magnetic or chemical and thermal effect
electrify	ηλεκτρίζω	to charge with electricity; to give a shock of excitement; an electric current
electro-	ηλεκτικόν/ό	electric, combining form
electro-acoustics	ηλεκτρο-ακουστικά/ ακουστική	the branch of acoustics dealing with the conversion of sound into electricity and vice versa, as in a microphone or speaker
electro-analysis	ηλεκτρο-ανάλυσις/η	analysis of a substances by means of electrolysis
electro-cardiogram	ηλεκτρο-καρδιογράφημα	a graphic tracing showing the variations in electric force which trigger the contractions of the heart: used to make a diagnosis of a heart disease
electro-cardiography	ηλεκτρο-καρδιογραφία	machine recording the electrical activity of the heart muscles
electrode	ηλεκτρόδιον/ο	any terminal that conducts an electric current into or away from various conducting substances in a circuit, as the anode or cathode in a battery or the carbons in an arc lamb, or that emits, collects, or controls the flow of electrons in an electron tube, as the cathode, plate, or grid
electro-dynamics	ηλεκτροδυναμική	the branch of physics dealing with the phenomena of electric currents and associated magnetic forces

electro-encephalo-gram	ηλεκτρο-εγκεφαλο-γράφημα	a graphic tracing of the variations in electric force in the brain
electrograph	ηλεκτρογράφος	1 an electrical device for etching or engraving plates 2 a telegraphic instrument for transmitting photographs, drawings, etc.
electro-hydraulics	ηλεκτρο-υδραυλική	designating or of a process for converting electrical energy to high-pressure, mechanical shock waves by the discharge of a high-voltage arc under the surface of a liquid medium: used in metal shaping, breaking up rock, etc.
electrokinetics	ηλεκτροκινητική	the branch of electrodynamics dealing with electricity in motion, or electric currents
electrolysis	ηλεκτρόλυσις/η	a decomposition of an electrolyte by the action of an electric current passing through it; the removal of unwanted hair with an electrified needle
electrolyte	ηλεκτρολύτης	any substance which in solution or in a liquid form is capable of conducting an electric current by the movement of its dissociated positive and negative ions to the electrodes
electrolyze	ηλεκτρολύεν/ ηλεκτρολύω	to subject to, or decompose by electrolysis
electromagnet	ηλεκτρο-μαγνήτης	a soft iron core surrounded by a coil of wire, that temporarily becomes a magnet when an electric current flows through the wire
electromagnetic	ηλεκτρο-μαγνητικός, ή, ό (adj.)	of, produced by, or having to do with electromagnetism or an electromagnet

electro-magnetism	ηλεκτρο-μαγνητισμός	I magnetism produced by an electic current 2 the branch of physics that deals with electricity and magnetism
electro-mechanical	ηλεκτρομηχανικός	designating or of a mechanical device or operation that is activated or regulated by electriity
electro-metallurgy	ηλεκτρο-μεταλλουργία	the branch of metallurgy having to do with the use of electricity, as for producing heat in smelting, refining, etc., or refining, plating, or depositing metals by electrolysis
electrometer	ηλεκτρόμετρον/ο	a device for detecting or measuring differences of potential by means of electrostatic forces
electron	ηλεκτρόνιον/ο	a stable elementary particle that forms a part of all atoms
electronic	ηλεκτρονικός, ή, ό (adj.)	of electrons; characterized by the prevalence of electronic equipment, etc
electronics.	ηλεκτρονική	I the science that deals with the behavior and control of electrons in vacuums and gases and with the use of electron tubes, protoelectric cells, transistors, etc. 2 electronic equipment, systems, etc.
electrophorus	ηλεκτροφόρος (φόρος / φέρειν-bearing/ to bear)	an apparatus consisting of an insulated resin disk and a metal plate, used in generating static electricity by induction
electrophysiology	ηλεκτροφυσιολογία	I the study of the electrical properties of living cells 2 the study of the production of electric currents by living organisms

electroscope	ηλεκτροσκόπιον/o	an instrument for detecting very small charges of electricity, electric fields, or radiation: it can indicate whether they are positive or negative, as by the divergence of electrically charged strips of gold leaf (**electroscopic, adj.**)
electrostatic	ηλεκτροστατικός, ή, ο (adj.)	1 of or to do with electrostatics 2 designating of or a speaker in which electric force is applied to metal plates causing a diaphragm suspended between them to vibrate
electrostatics	ήλεκτροστατική	the branch of electromagnetic theory dealing with electric charges at rest, or static electricity: cf. **Electrokinetics.**
electrotherapist	ηλεκτροθεραπευτής	a specialist in electrotherapy
electrotherapy	ηλεκτροθεραπεία	the treatment of disease by means of electricity
electrotype	ηλεκτροτυπία	printing; 1 a plate made by electroplating a wax or plastic impression of the original page of type, etc. 2 a print made of such plate
electrum	ηλεκτρόνιον/o	a stable elementary particle that forms a part of all atoms and has a negative charge and moves in orbits around the nucleus of the atom: the number of the electrons is equal to the number of protons of the nucleus
elegiac	ελεγειακός, ή, ό (adj.)	prosody of or composed in dactylic-hexameter couples, the second line (sometimes called a pentameter) having only one accented syllable in the third and sixth feet: the form was used in elegies and other lyric poems

elegist	ελεγειογράφος	a writer of elegies
elegy	ελεγεία	1 any poem written in elegiac verse 2 a poem or song of lament and praise for the dead, as plative tone
elephant	ελέφας/ελέφαντας	any of the order (Proboskidea) of huge, thick-skinned almost hairless mammals
elephantiasis	ελεφαντίασις/η	a chronic disease characterized by the enlargement of certain parts of the body, esp., the legs and the genitals
elephantine	ελεφάντινος, η, ο (adj.)	of an elephant or elephants
ellipse	έλλειψη (ελείπειν – to fall short)	falling short of a perfect circle; Geom. the path that a point moves so that the sum of its distances from two fixed points, the foci, is constant
ellipsis	έλλειψις/η	1 Gram. the omission of a word or words necessary for complete grammatical construction but understood in the context (ex: "if possible" for " if it is possible")
ellipsoid	(ο, η) ελλειψοειδής (το) ελλειψοειδές (adj.)	Geom. 1 a solid formed by rotating an ellipse around either axis: its plane sections are all ellipses or circles; shaped as an ellipsoid
elliptic/elliptical	ελλειπτικός, ή, ό (adj.)	not being complete, having defects; 2 of or characterized by ellipsis; with a word or words omitted with obscure, incomplete constructions, etc.
elytron	έλυτρον/ο	a covering; sheath; Zool. the thickened and textured wings of some insects, esp. beetles, which act as protective covering of the rear wings

emblem	έμβλημα	1 [historical] a picture with a motto or verses, allegorically suggesting some moral truth, etc. 2 a visible symbol of an idea; thing, class of people, etc. (ex: the cross is a symbol of Christianity, etc.)
emblematic	εμβληματικός, ή, ό (adj.)	symbolic; or of serving as an emblem
emboli/emboly	εμβολή	insertion; putting in; 1 *embryology* the process by which cells move inward during gastrulation to form the archenteron 2 the obstruction of a blood vessel by an embolus
embolism	εμβολισμός/ εμβολιασμός	Med. the obstruction of a blood vessel by an embolus too large to pass through it
embolus	έμβολος/έμβολο	anything put in, wedge; any foreign matter, as a blood clot or air bubble, carried in the bloodstream and capable of causing emboly/emboli; (in Gr. also: εμβολιον/ο-embolion means vaccine/shot)
embryo-	έμβρυο-	combining form (embryology)
embryo	έμβρυον/ο	1 earliest stage of development of a young human organism in the uterus, from conception to about the eighth week (fetus) 2 an early or underdeveloped stage of something
embryogenesis	εμβρυογένεσις/η	the formation and development of the embryo
embryogenic	(ο, η) εμβρυογενής (το) εμβρυογενές (adj.)	something developing parallel to the embryo or because of it (like a growth/tumor)
embryograph	εμβρυογραφία	an imaging/ photograph of the embryo; ultrasound
embryologist	εμβρυολόγος	a specialist in embryology

embryology	εμβρυολογία	the study of the development of the embryo
embryonic	εμβρυονικός, ή, ό (adj.)	like an embryo but in the early underdeveloped stage
emesis	έμετος	vomiting
emetic	εμετικός, ή, ό (adj.)	drug causing vomiting
Emmanouel	Εμμανουήλ	(Lit. God with us) masc. name
emmena	έμμηνα (εν + μήνα – each + month)	menstruation; occurring every month
emmenology	εμμηνολογία	the study of menstruation
emmeno-agogue	εμμηνο-αγωγός	anything used to stimulate the menstrual flow
emmetropia	εμμετροπία (έμμετρος/ εν + μέτρον- in +measure)	the condition of normal refraction of light in the eye, in which vision is perfect
empathy	εμπάθεια/εν & πάθος (inside/deep and passion)	(see the following) I have to make a parenthesis here and emphasize the misunderstanding that exists concerning the meaning of the word, "empathy." According to English dictionaries the word "empathy" (taken from the Gr εμπάθεια/empathia) means passion, affection for others, and it's synonym to "sympathy." That is wrong, as far as the words εμπάθεια / εμπαθής/ empathetic, imply, they are diametrically the opposite: The Gr. definition for Εμπάθεια/empathια: having ill feelings, unhealthy passion, animosity toward others, and it's the opposite of "sympathy." Εμπαθής/empathes: someone having hatred; hostile passion
emphasis	έμφασις -έμφαση	force of expression, thought, feeling, action, etc. /special stress given as to a syllable, a word, or phrase in speaking

emphatic	εμφατικός, ή, ό (adj.)	expressed, felt, or done with emphasis
emphysema	εμφύσημα	lung disease characterized by the thinning and loss of elasticity of lung tissue
empiric	εμπειρικός, ή, ό/ έμπειρος/η, ο (adj.)	experienced; 1 a person who relies solely on practical experience rather than scientific principles 2 [Archaic) a charlatan; quack. In Gr. empiros /έμπειρος /
empirognomon	εμπειρογνώμων	one who has experience or is a specialist in a given field
empiricism	εμπειρικισμός	1 experimental method; search for knowledge by 1 observation and experiment 2 a) a disregarding of scientific methods and relying solely on experience b) [Archaic] quackery 3 Philos. the theory that sense experience is the only source of knowledge
empiricist	εμπειριστής	one specializing in the method and theory of empiricism
emporium	εμπόριον/ο	trading place; mart; pertaining to trade and commerce; marketplace
enarthrosis	ενάρθρωσις/η (έναρθρος, η, ο (adj.)	jointed; articulate
encaenia	εγκαίνια	celebration commemorating the founding of a city, church, university, etc.
encaustic	εγκαυστικός, ή, ό (adj.)	done with a process of burning in or applying heat; a method of painting in which colors in wax are fused to a surface with hot irons
encaustics	εγκαυστική	a study of the encaustic process
encephalic	εγκεφαλικός, ή, ό (adj.)	pertaining to the brain

encephalitis	εγκεφαλίτις/ εγκεφαλίτιδα	inflammation of the brain
encephalogram	εγκεφαλογράφημα	x-ray of the brain
encephalo-myelitis	εγκεφαλο-μυελίτις/ μυελίτιδα	inflammation of the brain and spinal cord; specif., a virus disease of horses and other animals, sometimes communicable to people
encephalon	εγκέφαλος	the brain
encephalopathy	εγκεφαλοπάθεια	any disease of the brain
enchiridion	εγχειρίδιον/ο (εν + χειρ/χέρι – in + hand)	a handbook; manual
enchondroma	εγχόνδρωμα (εν + χόνδρος – in + cartilage)	a benign cartilaginous tumor
enchorial	εγχώριος, α, ο (adj.)	native; of or used in a particular country; popular, esp., demotic
enclitic	εγκλιτικός, ή, ό (adj.) (εν + κλίνειν – in + to lean)	to lean toward 1 pertaining to grammatical declension of nouns and conjugation of verbs 2 dependent on the preceding word for its stress
encomium	εγκώμιον/ο	praise; hymn to a victor; a formal expression of high praise; eulology; tribute; panegyric
encyclical	εγκυκλικός, ή, ό(adj.)	in a circle/for general circulation and words associated with en or in-kyklos/circle
encyclopedia/ encaclopaedia	εγκυκλοπαίδεια	a book or set of books giving information on all or many branches of knowedge
encyclopedic	εγκυκλοπαιδικός, ή, ό (adj.)	of or like an encyclopedia; esp., giving many comprehensive in scope subjects
encyclopedism	εγκυκλοπαιδισμός	encyclopedic knowledge or learning; the organized and systematic gathering of knowledge of a certain scientific field or branch

encyclopedist	εγκυκλοπαιδιστής	1 someone who compiles an encyclopaed ia 2 the **Encyclopedists**, the great writers of the French encyclopedia (1751–1772) which contained the advanced ideas, thoughts, and notions of that period
endeictic	ενδεικτκός, ή, ό (adj.)	symptomatic; indicative
endemic	ενδημικός, ή, ό (adj.)	indicating an inside-the-area disease
endermic	ενδερμικός, ή, ό (adj.)	administered through the skin
endo-	ενδο- ΄εσω- εντός (inside/inner)	combining form indicating within; inner; interior
endoblast	ενδο-βλαστός	the inner layer of cells of the embryo
endocardial	ενδοκαρδιακός, ή, ό (adj.	pertaining to the interior of the heart
endocarditis	ενδοκαρδίτις-ενδοκαρδίτιδα	inflammation of the inner lining of the heart (especially the heart valves)
endocarp	ενδο-καρπός	the inner layer of the pericarp of a ripened ovary or fruit, as the pit surrounding the seed of a drupe
endoceliac	ενδοκοιλιακός, ή, ό (adj.) κοιλία-abdomen	pertaining to the inner abdominal area
endocranium	ενδοκρανίον/ο	1 dura mater (the outermost, toughest, and most fibrous of the three membranes covering the brain and the spinal cord 2 the processes supporting the brain in the head of an insect
endocrine	ενδο + κρίνειν – **inside + to separate**	1 designating or of any gland producing one or more hormones 2 any such a hormone, as the thyroid or its thyroxine

endocrinal	(ο, η) ενδοκρινής (το) ενδοκρινές (adj.)	pertaining to the inner excretions (of the glands)
endocrinology	ενδοκρινολογία	the branch of medicine dealing with the endocrine glands and their hormones
endocrinologist	ενδοκρινολόγος	a specialist in endocrinology
endoderm	ενδοδέρμα	inner layer of cells of an embryo (from which the lining of the digestive track is formed)
endo-dontitis	ενδο-δοντίτις/ δοντίτιδα	inflammation of the dental pulp
endogenous	(ο, η) ενδογενής (το) ενδογενές (adj.)	originating internally; developing from within
endogeny	ενδογένεσις/η / ενδογονία	Biol. Growth from within; endogenous formation of cells
endometrial	ενδομήτριος, α, ο (adj.)	developing within the uterus
endometrium	ενδομήτριον/ο	the inner lining of the uterus
endo-metritis	ενδομητρίωσις/η	inflammation of the lining of the womb
endometrium	ενδομητρίτις/ ενδομητρίτιδα	tissue lining the interior of the womb
endomorph	ενδόμορφος, η, ο	1 a person of the endomorphic physical type 2 a mineral esp., a crystal enclosed within another
endomorphic	ενδομορφικός, ή, ό (adj.)	1 of an endomorph 2 designating or of the round, fat physical type characterized by predominance of the structures developed from the endodermal layer of the embryo, as the internal organ 2 having a heavy rounded body build often with a marked tendency to become overweight—compare *Ectomorphic, Mesomorphic*
endomorphism	ενδομορφισμός	structural change caused in an intrusive igneous rock by the action of the surrounding rock

endophyte	ενδόφυτον/ο	any plant that grows within another plant, as certain parasitic fungi or algae
endoplasm	ενδόπλασμα	the inner part of the cytoplasm of a cell: distinguished from **Ectoplasm**
endoscope	ενδοσκόπιον/ο	an instrument for examining visually the inside of a hollow organ of the body, as the bladder or rectum
endoscopy	ενδοσκόπησις/η	a method of examining a body cavity or an organ
endothermic	ενδοθερμικός, ή, ό (adj.)	designating of, or produced by a chemical change in which there is absorption of heat
energetic	ενεργητικός, ή, ό (adj.)	vigorous; forceful
energize	ενεργοποιώ/ (ενεργοποιείν)	invigorate; empower; activate
energy	ενέργεια	inherent power; capacity for vigorous action
engram	έγγραμμα	1 Biol. a hypothetical permanent change produced by a stimulus in the protoplasm of a tissue 2 Psychol. a permanent effect produced in the psyche by stimulation, assumed in explaining persistence of memory
enharmonic	εναρμόνιος, α, ο	in equal temperament, designating or of tones, as C# and Db, that are identical in pith but are written differently according to the key in which each occurs: enharmonic tones are especially important in instruments of fixed pitch, as the piano
enigma	αίνιγμα	a perplexing usually ambiguous statement; riddle

enigmatic	αινιγματικός, ή, ό (adj.)	of, or like an enigma; perplexing; baffling
enomania	οίνος + μανία/ οινομανία (wine + mania)	extreme desire for alcoholic drink
enology/oenology	οινολογία	the science or study of wines and winemaking
entasis	έντασις/η	a stretching; increased of emotional pressure; Archit. a slight convex swelling in the shaft of a column; it prevents the illusion of concavity produced by a perfectly straight shaft
enstrophe	ενστροφή	turning inward
enteralgia	εντεραλγία	pain in the intestines
enteric	εντερικός, ή, ό (adj.)	pertaining to the intestines
enteritis	εντερίτις /εντερίτιδα	inflammation of the intestinal tract by infection or irritated by food
enteron	έντερον/ο	intestine gut
enthalpy	ενθαλπία (εν εν + θάλπειν- in + warm in) θαλπωρή/ warmth	a measure of the energy content of a system per unit mass
enthrone	ενθρονίζω (εν + θρόνος / throne)	1 to place on a throne; make a king or bishop 2 to accord the highest place; to exalt
enthronement	ενθρόνισις/η/ ενθρονισμός	the event or ceremony of enthroning
ento- prefix	εντός	inside, within, inner
entoblast	εντός + βλαστός – within + sprout)	inner embryo
entoderm	εντός + δέρμα	inner skin
entomo-	έντομο(v)	insect/insects combining form (entomology)
entomological	εντομολογικός, ή, ό (adj.)	pertaining to insects
entomologist	εντομολόγος	expert in entomology

entomology	εντομολογία	the branch of zoology dealing with insects
entomophagous	εντομοφάγος	feeding manly on insects
entopic	εντοπικός, ή, ό (adj.)	located in the proper place
enuresis	ενούρησις	bed-wetting
enzootic	εν-ζωοτικός, ή, ό (adj.) /ζωϊκός	affecting animals in a certain area, climate, or season: said of diseases (an enzootic disease)
enzymatic	εν-ζυμωτικός, ή, ό (adj.)	one contributing to enzymic formation
enzymon	ένζυμον/ένζυμα (pl.)	substance produced by living cells
enzymology	εν-ζυμολογία	the science dealing with the structure and properties of enzymes and the chemical reactions they catalyze
eon/aeon	αιών/αιώνας	an age; a lifetime, eternity; a century; Geol. a) a period of time greater than an era, as the Phanerozoic Eon b) an indefinite period of time
Eos	Ηώς	dawn; Gr. myth. the goddess of dawn, identified with the Roman goddess Aurora
eparchy	επαρχία	1 a) in th Byzantine Empire, an administrative district b) in modern Greece, a political subdivision of a province 2 Eastern Orthodox Church a diocese
epeirogeny	ηπειρογένεσις/η	movements to uplift or depression affecting large areas of the earth's crust and producing continents, ocean basins, etc.
ependyma	επένδυμα (επί + ένδυμα – over + garment)	1 an upper garment 2 the membrane lining the central cavities of the brain and the spinal cord

epenthesis	επένθεσις /η (επί + θέσις – upon + placing)	1 Phonet. a change which involves the insertion of an unhistoric sound or letter in a word, as the b in mumble or an extra syllable 2 the inserted sound or letter
ephebe/ephebus	έφηβος/ έφηβη (fem.)	a young man; a young woman; (esp. in ancient Athens)
ephebic	εφηβικός, ή, ό (adj.)	pertaining to puberty; early manhood/ womanhood
ephemeral	εφήμερος, η, ο (adj.)	short-lived, something lasting a day
ephemeris	εφημερίς/ εφημερίδος/ εφημερίδα (Mod. Gr.)	a diary,; a calendar; a table giving the computed positions of a celestial body for every day of a given period; in mod. Gr. the word ephemeris/εφημερίδα is translated: newspaper
epicardium	επικάρδιον (επί + καρδία-on/ over + heart)	layer of the heart, also called visceral pericardium
epi-	επί	at, on, to, upon, over, besides, combining form
epic	επικός, ή, ό (adj.)	a long narrative poem in a dignified style about the deeds of a traditional or historical hero or heroes
epicedium	επικήδειος (επί + κηδεία- on, at + funeral)	eulogy at funeral
epicenter	επίκεντρον/ο (επί + κέντρον – upon + center or pivot point)	1 place of the origin/focus of an earthquake 2 the center or focal point of an unpleasant activity or event
epicranium	επικράνιον/ο	επί/on, upon the structure covering the cranium/skull
epicrisis	επίκρισις/η	judgment; critique
epicritic	επικριτικός, ή, ό (adj.)	judging, criticizing; being critical

epi-cycloid	επί-κυκλωειδής/ κυκλωειδές	the curve traced by a point of the circumference of a circle that rolls around the outside of a fixed circle
Epidaurus	Επίδαυρος	an ancient city in Argolid, famous even today for the theater with its superb acoustics (built around the middle of the fourth c. BC)
epidemic	επιδημικός, ή, ό (adj.)	disease affecting a great number of people in an area, at the same time
epidemiology	επιδημιολογία	study of the occurrence and symptom s of epidemics
epidermis	επιδερμίς/ επιδερμίδα	1 outermost layer of the skin in vertebrates, having no blood vessels and consisting of several layers of cells, covering the dermis/skin, illus 2 any of various other integuments
epidermoid/ epidermic	επιδερμικός, ή, ο (adj.)	having the nature of, relating to the epidermis
epididymis/ epididymes (pl.)	επιδίδυμοι (επί + δίδυμοι – upon + twins)	testicles; a long oval-shaped structure attached to the rear upper surface of each testicle, consisting mainly of the sperm ducts of the testicles
epigastric	επί-γαστρικός, ή, ό (adj.)	1 of or located within the epigastrium 2 of or pertaining to the front walls of the abdomen
epigastrium	επιγάστριον/ο (neut) of επιγάστριος, α, ο (adj.)	the stomach; Anat. the upper middle portion of the abdomen, including the area over and in front of the stomach
epigeal + epigeous	επίγειος, α, ο (adj.)	on the earth 1 Bot. a) growing on or close to the ground b) emerging from the ground after germination (said of cotyledons)

epigene	επίγονος	descendant; born late; an inferior descendant; follower or imitator (apogone- απόγονος / descendant) 2 Geol. produced or formed on or near the earth's surface [epigene rocks]
epigenesis	επιγένεσις/η	1 the theory that the embryo, influenced by its internal and external environmen, develops progressively by stages, forming structures that were not originally present in the egg: cf: Preformation Med. the appearing of secondary symptoms
epigenetic	επιγενετικός, ή, ό (ad.)	1 of, or having the nature of epigenesist 2 Geol. a) produced on or near the surface of the earth b) formed or deposited later than the enclosing rocks: said of the deposits, structures, etc.
epiglottis	επιγλωττίς/ επιγλωττίδα	lid covering the opening of the windpipe and prevents food from getting into the voice box or the lungs
epigram	επίγραμμα	any terse witty, pointed statement, often with a clever twist in thought; inscription
epigrammatic	επιγραμματικός, ή, ό (adj.)	1 of the epigram or full of epigrams 2 having the nature of an epigram; terse, witty, etc.
epigrammatism	επιγραμματισμός	the use of epigrams or a style characterized by epigram
epigraph	επιγραφή/ επιγράφειν	1 an inscription on a building, monument, etc. 2 a brief quotation placed at the beginning of a book, chapter, etc.
epigraphist	επιγραφολόγος	a specialist in epigraphy also, archeologist /αρχαιολόγος

epigraphy	επιγραφική	1 the study dealing with deciphering, interpreting, and classifying inscription, esp., ancient inscriptions; 2 inscriptions collectively
epilepsy	επιληψία	symptom of some disorder of the brain
epileptoid/epileptic	επιληπτικός, ή, ό (adj.)	resembling epilepsy; epilepsy-like symptoms
epilimnion	επιλίμνιον (επί + λίμνη – on/ upon + lake)	marshy lake; a not frozen, warm upper layer of oxygen-rich water that is above the thermocline
epilogue	επίλογος	a closing section of a book, play, etc., providing further comment, interpretation, or information
epimysium	επί + μυς/μυός (gen.) –upon +muscle	the sheath of connective tissue surrounding a muscle
epinephrine	επινεφρίνη/ επινεφρίδη	a hormone secreted by the medulla of the adrenal gland, that stimulates the heart, increases blood sugar, muscular strength, endurance, etc.; adrenalin: it is extracted from animal adrenals or prepared synthetically
epineurium	επίνευρον (επί + νεύρον/ο – upon + nerve)	the layer of connective tissue surrounding a peripheral nerve
Epiphany	Επιφάνεια	appearance; revelation; 1 most Christian churches celebrating the baptism of Jesus 2 a) an appearance or manifestation of a supernatural being, b) a moment of sudden intuitive understanding; a flash of insight; an experience (Αποκάλυψις/Apocalypse)

epiphenomenon	επιφαινόμενον	1 a phenomenon that occurs with and it seems to result from another but has no reciprocal effect or subsequent influence 2 Med. a secondary or additional occurrence in a course of a disease, usually unrelated to the disease
epiphysis	επίφυσις/η (επιφύειν – to grow upon)	a growth upon, excrescence; 1 the end part of a long bone which is at first separated from the main part by cartilage, but later fuses with it by ossification 2 the pineal body: in full, **epiphysis cer-e-bri**
epiphyte	επίφυτον/ο	a plant that grows on another plant, but it is not a parasite and produces its own food by photosynthesis, as certain orchids, mosses, and lichens; air plant 2 a plant parasitic on the external surface of an animal body
epiphytology	επιφυτολογία	the study of epidemic plant diseases
Epirus	Ήπειρος	1 ancient kingdom of the E coast of the Ionian Sea, in what is now S Albania and NW Greece 2 region of modern Greece, in the general area
episcia	επίσκιος, α, ο (adj.) επί + σκιά- on + shade/shadow	shaded; any of the genus (Episcia) of tropical American of the gesneria family with elliptical, hairy leaves and white to red flowers
episcopacy	επισκοπή	the system of church government by bishops
episiotomy	επισιοτομή-επίσιον / pubic region	an incision of the perineum, often performed childbirth to prevent injury to the vagina

episode	επεισόδιον/ο	in a novel, a play, poem, etc., any part of the story, or a narrative digression, that is complete in itself; an incident
episodic	επεισοδιακός, ή, ό (adj.)	1 having the nature of an episode; incidental 2 divided into episodes, often not closely related or well intergrated
epistasis	επί + στάσις / a stopping – εφίσταμαι- to place upon	Genetics the suppression of gene expression by one or more genes
epistaxis	επίσταξις/η (επι + στάζειν /επι + στάζειν– upon + bleed; to bleed at the nose)	Med. nosebleed; to fall in drops Med. nose bleeding
episteme	επιστήμη	good knowledge; science
epistemic	επιστημικός, ή, ό (adj.)	of or having to do with knowledge or the ways of knowing
epistemologist	επιστημολόγος	specialist in epistemology
epistemology	επιστημολογία	the study or theory of the nature, source and limits of knowledge
epistemonic	επιστημονικός, ή, ό (adj.)	scientific, having to do with science
epistle	επιστολή	a letter, message; any of the letters in the New Testament written (Epistole(s)) by an Apostle
epistler	επιστολεύς/ επιστολέας	1 a letter writer 2 the person reading the epistle in church
epistyle	επιστύλιον/ο επί + στύλος – upon + column	stylite; a building upon a column

epitaph	επιτάφιος	a eulogy; 1 an inscription on a tomb or gravestone in memory of the person buried there 2 a short composition in prose or verse, written as a tribute to a dead peron; the Epitaphios of Christ, on Good Friday, in the Eastern Orthodox Church
epitasis	επίτασις/η (επί + τείνειν – upon + to stretch)	stretching; intensity; the part of the play, esp., in classical drama, between the protasis, or exposition, and the catastrophe and denouncement
epitaxy	επίταξις /επιταξία (επί + τάξις - upon + arranging)	the overgrowth in layers of a crystalline substance, deposited in a definite orientation on a base or substratum composed of different crystals
epithalamium	επιθαλάμιον (επί + θάλαμος – upon/at + bridal chamber)	an arch, hollow; a song or poem in honor of a bride or bridegroom or for both, nuptial song
epithelial	επιθηλιακός, ή, ό (adj.)	relating to epithelium; like an epithelium
epithelioma	επιθηλίωμα (επί + θηλή – upon + nipple)	any tumor composed mostly of epithelial cells; a former term for the malignant tumor of the skin
epithelium	επιθήλιον/ο (επί + θηλή- upon + nipple)	cellular tissue covering external body surfaces, as the epidermis, or lining internal surfaces, as hollow organs, vessels, etc.; it consists of one or more layers of cells with little intercellular material
epithet	επίθετον/ο	an adjective, noun, or phrase; in Gr. epitheton is an adjective describing a noun and also, the last name of a person; surname

epitome	επιτομή (επί + τέμωειν – upon + to cut)	abridgment; 1 a short statement of the main points of a book, report, incident, etc.; abstract, summary 2 a person or thing that shows all the typical qualities of something (ex: he is the epitome of knowledge)
epoch	εποχή	the beginning of a new and important period in the history of a big event; in Gr. the word epoch/ εποχή, also means: season
epode	επωδός – (άδω-ωδή/to sing-song)	1 a form of lyric poem, as of Horace, in which a short line follows a longer one 2 the stanza that follows the strophe and antistrophe in a Pindaric or ancient Greek ode
eponym	επώνυμον/ο	last name/also, used to designate a disease/syndrome/ organ of a person who first discovered it; a real or mythical person from whose the name of a nation, institution, etc. is derived
eponymous	επώνυμος, ή, ό (adj.)	1 one who is regarded trustworthy to sign a document that guarantees the accuracy 2 a well-known, famous person that his/her name is recognized immediately
eponymy	επωνυμία	the name derivation of a people, nation,etc., from the name of a real or mythical person
epopee	εποποιία	the making of epics; an epic poem or poetry (as Homer's work)
epos	έπος	a collection of poems of a primitive epic nature, handed down orally: epic poem/poetry

epsilon	έψιλον	the fifth letter of the Gr. alphabet, to distinguish it from **ai/αι** alpha yiota
Erato	Ερατώ	beloved, Gr. myth. the muse of erotic lyric poetry; also, a girl's name
Erectheium	Ερέχθειον/o	the famous Ionic architecture temple on the Acropolis, built during the Golden Age of Athens (fifth c. BC)
eremite	ερημίτης	hermit; a religiou recluse
eremophobia	ερημοφοβία (έρημος + φόβος- **deserted, alone + fear**)	extreme fear of being alone
erethism	ερεθισμός	irritation; physiol. an abmormal extreme irritability of an organ, tissue, etc.
erg/ ergo-	έργον	work, the unit of work or energy in the cgs (metric) system, being the work done by one dyne acting through a distance of one centimeter, combining form
ergograph	εργογράφημα/ εργογράφος	an instrument measuring and recording the amount of work that a muscle is capable of doing
ergometer	έργον + μέτρον/ εργόμετρον/o – **work + meter**	an instrument in measuring the work done by a muscle or muscles over a period of time
ergonomics	εργονομικά	the study of the people adjusting to their environment; esp., the science that seeks to adapt to work or working conditions to suit the worker
ergophilia	εργοφιλία	excessive love for work
ergophilos	εργασία/έργο + φίλος – **work + lover/friend**	workaholic; one having excessive love for work
ergophobia	εργοφοβία (έργο, εργασία/ + φόβος/ **work + fear**)	extreme fear of work

Erinyes	Ηρινύς/ Ηρινύδες (pl.)	Gr. myth. Furies
Eris	῎Ερις/ἔριδος (gen.)	Gr. myth. the goddess of strife and discord
eristic	εριστικός, ή, ό(adj.)- ερίζειν /έρις - to dispute, to strife	dispute; strife; of, or provoking controversy or given to sophistical argument and spacious reasoning; a person who engages in dispute or argument
erogenous	(ο, η) ερωγενής/ (το) ερωγενές	producing sexual excitement; designating or, of those areas of the body that are particularly sensitive to sexual stimulation
Eros	έρως/έρωτας	love; Gr. myth. the god of love, son of Aphrodite; sexual love or desire
erotic	ερωτικός, ή, ό (adj.)	pertaining to sexual l desire
eroticism	ερωτισμός	erotic quality or character; sexual desire, behavior or instincts; preoccupation with sex
eroticize	ερωτοτροπώ	arousing sexual desire
erotogenic/ erogenous	(ο, η) ερωτογενής (το) ερωτογενές (adj.)	an area of the body that is easily sexually stimulated
erotomania	ερωτομανία	abnormally strong sexual desire
erotophobia	ερωτοφοβία	extreme fear of sexual love
erythema	ερύθημα	an abnormal redness of the skin caused by various agents, as sunlight, drugs, etc., that irritate and congest the capillaries
erythrism	ερυθρίασις/η	unusual redness, esp. of the hair of mammals or the feathers of birds
erythro-	ερυθρός, ά, ό (adj.)	red, combining form
erythroblast	ερυθροβλάστη	a small nucleated cell, found normally in the marrow of bones from which an erythrocyte develops

erythrocyte	ερυθροκύταρον/ο	a mature red blood cell that normally does not have a nucleus: it is a very small circular disk with both faces concave and contains hemoglobin, which carries oxygen to the body tissues
erythroderma	ερυθρόδερμα	skin disturbance with extreme redness
erythroid	(ο, η) ερυθροειδής/ (το) ερυθροειδές	reddish in color
erythron	neuter of: ερυθρός, ά, ό(ν)(adj.)	the red blood cell system as an organic unit, comprising the erythrocytes, their sources of production, destruction, etc.
eschatological	εσχατολογικός, ή, ό (adj.)	of or pertaining to the last things or end of time
eschatology	εσχατολογία (έσχατος + λογία/ furthest + logy)	the branch of theology, or doctrines, dealing with death, resurrection, judgment, immortality, etc.
esophagus	οισοφάγος	the tube connecting the stomach to the throat
esoteric	εσωτερικός, ή, ό (adj.)	inner, within 1 a) intended for or understood by only a chosen few, as an inner group of disciples or initiates (said of ideas, literature, philosophy, etc.) b) beyond the understanding or knowledge of most people; abstruse 2 confidential; private, opposed to: Exoteric
esthetic/ aesthetic	αισθητικός, ή, ό (adj)	of esthesia/aesthesia; having to do with sensation
estrogen	οιστρογόνον/ο	any of several female sex hormones or synthetic compounds that cause estrus
estrogenic	οιστρογόνος, η, ο (adj.)	of estrogen; or producing estrus

estrus/oestrus	οίστρος	gadfly, sting, frenzy 1 the periodic sexual excitement of most female placental mammals, corresponding to rut in males; heat 2 the period of this when the female will accept mating with the male, characterized by changes in the sex organs
etecian	αιτήσιος, α, ο (adj.)	annual, happening every year
ether	αιθήρ/αιθέρας	organic liquid used as anesthetic
ethereal	αιθέριος, α, ο (adj.)	1 very light, airy, delicate; 2. not earthly, heavenly, celestial 3 Chem. of, like, or containing ether
ethic	ηθική	1 a system of moral standards or values (the humanist ethic) 2 a particular moral standard or value (the success ethic)
ethical	ηθικός, ή, ό(adj.)	having to do with ethics or morality of or conforming to moral standards 2 conforming to the standards of conduct of a given profession, or group
ethics	ηθικολογία	the study of stardards of conduct and moral judgment; moral philosophy
ethicist	ηθικιστής	person versed in ethics/ devoted to ethical ideals
ethics	ηθική	the study of standards of conduct and moral judgment
ethnarch	εθνάρχης	the leader of a nation
ethnic	εθνικός, ή, ό(adj.)	pertaining to races of mankind
ethnicity	εθνικότης/ εθνικότητα	ethnic classification or affiliation
ethno-	έθνο- (έθνος)	nation; ethnic group or division
ethno-botany	εθνο-βοτανική	the study of how plants are used in a particular culture

ethnocentrism	εθνοκεντρισμός	1 the emotional attitude that one's ethnic group, nation, or culture is superior 2 an excessive or inappropriate concern for racial matters
ethnographer	εθνογράφος	specialist in ethnography
ethnography	εθνογραφία	the branch of anthropology that deals descriptively with specific cultures, esp., those of nonliterate peoples or groups
ethnologic	εθνολογικός, ή, ό (adj.)	pertaining to ethnology, of or ethnology
ethnologist	εθνολόγος	a specialist in ethnology
ethnology	εθνολογία	the branch of anthropology that studies comparatively the cultures of contemporary, or recent societies or language groups
ethnomusicology	εθνο-μουσικολογία	the study of the music of a particular region and its sociocultural implications, esp. of music outside the European art tradition 2 the comparative study of the music of different cultural groups
ethnos	έθνος	nation; motherland; country
ethology	ηθολογία	character portrayal; Biol. the scientific study of the characteristic behavior and patterns of animals
ethos	ήθος	character, disposition; the characteristic of and distinguishing attitudes, habits, beliefs, etc, of an individual or of a group
etiology/aetiology	αιτιολογία	study of the causes of a disease
etymological	ετυμολογικός, ή, ό(adj.)	of or according to the etymology, or to the principles of etymology
etymologically	ετυμολογικά (adv.)	abiding by the principles of etymology

etymologist	ετυμολόγος/ ετυμόλογος	an expert in etymology, one skilled in etymology
etymology	ετυμολογία	1 the origin and development of a word, affix, phrase, etc.; the tracing of a word or other form back as far as possible in its own language and to its source in contemporary or earlier languages; 2 the branch of linguistics dealing with word origin and development
eu	prefix ευ/εφ (καλός) /ev/ef	good, favorable
eucalyptus	ευκάλυπτος	the oil (of the eucalyptus tree) used for nasal solution or mouthwash; a tree
Eucarist	Ευχαριστία	the Christian sacrament of Holy Communion; giving thanks
Euclid	Ευκλίδης	Gr. mathematician (300 BC): author of a basic work in geometry
Euclidian geometry	Ευκλίδειος γεωμετρία	pertaining to Euclid's principles
eudemonia/ eudaemon	ευδαιμονία/ ευδαίμων (blessed with good fortune)	happiness or well-being; specif., in Aristotle's philosophy, happiness or well-being, the main universal goal, distinct from pleasure and derived from a life of activity governed by reason
eudemonism/ evdaemonism	ευδαιμονισμός	the ethical doctrine that personal happiness is the chief good and the proper aim of action, esp., when such happiness conceived of in terms of well-being based on virtuous and rational self-realization
Eugenia	Ευγενία (ευ/good + γένος/γενιά/origin/	well-born, noble, girl's name
Eugene	Ευγένιος	male's name, meaning: well-born

eugenics	ευγενική/ευγονική	the movement devoted in improving the human species through the control of hereditary factors in mating
eulogia	ευλογία	blessing, eulogy
eulogize	εγκωμιάζω/ (ευλογείν)	to praise highly; extol; to compose eulogy, to eulogize
eulogy	ευλογία /εγκώμιο)	speaking favorably
eupatrid	ευπατρίδης	1 one who has noble and aristocratic heritage 2 in ancient Athens and Rome a member of the highest/ noblest society
eupepsia	ευπεψία	normal digestion; digestibility, opposed to dispepsia
eupeptic	εύπεπτος, η, ο (adj.)	1 having normal digestion 2 healthy and happy; cheerful
euphemism	ευφημισμός (εύφημος – of good sound or omen)	1 the use of a word or phrase that is less expressive or direct but considered less distasteful, less offensive, etc., than another 2 a word or phrase so substituted (ex: remains instead of corpse)
euphemistic	ευφημιστικός, ή, ό (adj.)	one who talks euphemistically; complimentarily
euphonic	ευφωνικός, ή, ό (adj.)	one having a good voice, sound, harmonious
euphony	ευφωνία (καλή φωνή, καλλιφωνία)	normal, clear condition of the voice
euphoria	ευφορία	exaggerated sense of well-being
eupnea	εύπνοια	good/normal respiration
euphoric	ευφορικός, ή, ό (adj.)	having high spirits, well-being
eury-	ευρύς, ευρεία, ευρύ	wide, broad combining form
eurybath	ευρύς + βάθος / wide/broad + depth	Biol. an organism that can live in a wide range of water depths; opposed to Stenobath (narrow bath (os / narrow depth)
Eurydice	Ευρυδίκη	Gr. myth. the wife of Orpheus; a feminine name

euryhygric	ευρύς + υγρός/ wide + humid	Biol. able to withstand a wide range of humidity
euryphagous	ευρύ φάγος/φάγειν- wide + eater/to eat	eating a wide variety of foods
eurytherm	ευρύς + θερμο/ θερμοκρασία – wide + temperature	an organism that can live in a wide range of temperatures; opposed to Stenotherm - narrow range temperatures
eurythmic	εύρυθμος, η, ο (adj.)	characterized by perfect proportions and harmony
eurythmy	ευρυθμία	1 rhythmic movement 2 harmonious proportion 3 a method of teaching dancing or rhythmic movement, esp., to the recitation of verse or prose
eurytopic	ευρύς + τόπος- wide + place, area	widely distributed; Biol. able to withstand a wide range of environmental conditions; opposed to Stenotopic - narrow range enviromental conditions
eusitia	ευσιτία	normal, good appetite
eureka	εύρηκα (βρήκα)	found, discovered; "I have found (it) / Εύρηκα": excamation supposedly uttered by Archimedes when he discovered a way to determine the purity of gold by applying the principle of specific gravity
Europe	Ευρώπη	continent between Asia and the Atlantic Ocean
Euterpe	Ευτέρπη (εφ + τέρπειν- good/well + to delight/ charm	charming; Myth. the muse of music and lyric poetry ; feminine name
euthanasia	ευθανασία	mercy killing; happy death; put to death as painlessly as possible;
euthanize	ευθανατώνω	to put to death by euthanasia
eutheroid	ευ-εφ&θηρωειδής	good thyroid
Evangel/evangelio	ευαγγέλιον/ο	"Good News" or Gospel

evangelical	ευαγγελικός, ή, ό (adj.)	1 in, of, or according to the gospels or teachings of the New Testament 2 of those Protestant churches, as the Methodist and the Baptist, that emphasize salvation by faith and reject the efficacy of the sacraments and good deeds alone
Evangeline	Ευαγγελία	bearer of good news; a feminine name
evangelion	ευαγγέλιον/ο	gospel
evangelist	ευαγγελιστής	bearer of good news
exanthema/ exanthema		
exarch	έξαρχος	provincial governor
exarchate	εξαρχάτο	Byzantine political term, an area governed by a provincial governor
exedra	εξέδρα	in ancient Greece, a room, building, or outdoor area, where conversations, meetings, and philosophical discussions were held
exegesis	εξήγησις/η	explanation; critical analysis, or interpretation of a word literary passage, etc., esp. in the Bible
exegete	εξηγητής	an expert in exegesis
exegetics	εξηγητική	the science, study, or practice of exegesis
exo-	έξω	outside; outer; outer part, combining form
exobiology	εξωβιολογία	the branch of biology investigating the possibility of extraterrestrial life and the effects of extraterrestrial environments on living organisms from the earth
exocardia	εξωκαρδία	abnormal position of the heart

exocentric	εξωκεντρικός, ή, ό (adj.)	Linguis. Designating or of a construction whose syntactic function differs from that of any of its constituents (opposed to Endocentric)
exocrine	(ο, η) εξωκρινής (το) εξωκρινές (adj.)	[as in the endocrine] designating or of any gland secreting externally, either directly or through a duct
exocytosis	εξωκύτωσις /η	a process in which a cell releases a large molecule, particle, etc.: opposed to **Endocytosis**
exodondia	εξω –δόντια/ εξαγωγή-	tooth extraction
exodondics	έξω + οδοντιατρική	the branch of dentistry dealing with teeth extraction
exodus	έξοδος	a going out or forth 1 the departure of the Israelites from Egypt 2 the second book of the Pentateuch in the Bible, which describes this and gives the law of Moses; also in Greek, exodos means exit
exogamy	εξωγαμία	1 the custom, often inviolable, of marrying only outside one's own clan, tribe, or ethnicity
exogamous	εξώγαμος, η, ό (adj.)	child whose parents are not married
exogenous,	(ο, η) εξωγενής (το) εξωγενές	1 developing from without; originating externally 2 Biol. of or relating to external factors, as food or light, that have an effect upon an organism
exophthalmia	εξωφθαλμία/ εξοφθαλμία	abnormal bulging of the eyeballs
exophthalmos	εξω-οφθαλμός/ εξοφθαλμός	having bulging eye(s) usually caused by overactivity of the thyroid gland

exorcise/exorcize	εξορκίζω/εξορκίζειν	to swear a person; to banish an evil spirit 1 to drive [any evil spirit or spirits] out or away by ritual prayers, incantations, etc. 2 to free from such spirits through rituals or incantations
exorcism	εξορκισμός	1 the act of exorcising; 2 a verbal formula or ritual used during exorcism
exorcist	εξορκιστής	1 a person who exorcises 2 Roman Catholic Church a member of the second highest of the four minor orders
exosphere	εξώσφαιρα	the outermost portion of a planet's, esp. the earth's, atmosphere, consisting of a hot layer of light atoms often moving at escape velocity
exoteric	εξωτερικός, ή, ό (adj.)	external; 1 of the outside world; 2 limited to a select few or an inner group of disciples; suitable for uninitiated ; opposed to esoteric
exothermic	εξωθερμικός, ή, ό (adj.)	designating or of a chemical change in which there is a liberation of heat, as in combustion
exotic	εξωτικός, ή, ό (adj.)	1 foreign; not native 2 strange or different in a way that is triking or fascinating; strangely beautiful, enticing, etc.; exotic flowers; exotic beauty, etc.

F

Fantasia	φαντασία	a medley of familiar tunes; musical compositions with a structure determined by the composer's fancy

fantastic	φανταστικός, ή, ό (adj.)	existing in the imagination; imaginary; unreal; also, fantastic implies something extraordinary as fantastic weather, fantastic view, etc.
fantasy	φαντασία	imagination; wild, visionary fancy; illusion; phantasm
fleboscrerosis	φλεβοσκλήρωσις/η	hardening of the vein
flebotomy	φλεβοτομή	incision of the vein
fronesis/phronesis	φρόνησις/η	wisdom, intelligence, intellectual virtue, practical wisdom
frenetic	φρενικός, ή, ό (adj.) (φρήν/φρενός (gen.) phren – mind)	pertaining to anything connected to the brain/mind, its function, disease, etc.
frenzy	φρενίτις/φρενίτιδα	madness; inflammation of the brain; wild or frantic outburst of feeling or action; specif. brief delirium that is near insanity

(Note: The majority of Greek words starting with the letter Φ/F, in English, correspond to Ph.)

G

Gaia/gaea	γαία-γη	earth; Gr. myth. a goddess who is the personification of the earth, the mother of the Titans
gala- prefix	γάλα	milk, combining form (galactoid)
galactic	γαλακτικός, ή, ό (adj.)	pertaining to milk; milky
galactoid	(ο, η) γαλακτώδης (το) γαλακτώδες	resembling milk; milklike; full of milk
galactorrhea	γαλακτόρροια	abnormally excessive milk flow
galaxy	γαλαξίας	Milky Way; a large independent system of stars, typically containing millions to hundreds of billions of stars

gamete	γαμέτης	a reproductive cell that is haploid and can unite with another gamete to form the cell (zygote) that develops into a new individual
gamic	γαμικός, ή, ό (adj.)	Biol. that can develop only after fertilization: said of such an ovum
gamma	Γάμμα	1 the third letter of the Gr. Alphabet 2 the third of a group or series; 3 a number indicating the degree of contrast between the darkest and lightest parts of a photographic image 4 a microgram
gamo-	γάμος	marriage; union; sexually united combining form
gamogenesis	γάμος + γέννησις/ γένεσις- marriage + genesis	sexual reproduction; reproduction by the uniting of gametes
gamophobia	γαμοφοβία	extreme fear of marriage
gamos	γάμος	marriage; wedding; the legal union
gangrene	γάγγραινα	decay of tissue in a part of the body when the blood 1 supply is obstructed by injury, disease, etc.
gangrenous	(o, η) γαγγραινώδης (το) γαγγραινώδες(adj.)	relating to gangrene
gastr- prefix	γάστρ- (γάστρον/ο)	pertaining to the abdominal area, combining form used before a vowel
gastric	γαστρικός, ή, ό (adj.)	pertaining to the stomach
gastritis	γαστρίτις/ γαστρίτιδα	inflammation of the stomach and esp. the stomach lining
gastro- prefix	γάστρο/γαστήρ	stomach
gastroectomy	γαστροεκτομή	surgical removal of all or esp. part of the stomach
gastro-enteritis	γαστρο-εντερίτις- γαστρ-εντερίτιδα	inflammation of the stomach and the intestines

gastro-enterologist	γαστρο-εντερολόγος	expert of the digestive system
gastro-enterology	γαστρο-εντερολογία	the medical specialty dealing with disorders of the digestive system
gastro-intestinal	γαστρο-εντερικός, ή, ό (adj.)	of the stomach and intestines
gastrology	γαστρολογία	medical specialty dealing with disorders of the digestive system
gastronomic	γαστρονομικός, ή, ό (adj.)	pertaining to one who enjoys and has discriminating taste for foods, and given to the pleasures of dining; gastronome; epicure; gourmet
gastronomist	γαστρονόμος	a specialist in gastronomy and gourmet cooking
gastronomy	γαστρονομία	the art or science of good eating
gastrorrhagia	γαστρορραγία	extreme stomach hemorrhage
gastroscope	γαστροσκόπιον/ο	a fiber-optic endoscope inserted through the mouth for visually inspecting the inside of the stomach
gato-	γάτος/γάτα (fem.)	cat; feline (gatophilia)
gatophilia	γατοφιλία	extreme love for cats
gatophobia	γατοφοβία	extreme fear of cats
genealogical	γενεαλογικός	tracing the line of descent
genealogist	γενεαλόγος	expert in tracing the descent from an ancestor
genealogy	γενεαλογία	charting the history of descent of a person or family
genesis	γένεσις/η	origin; development; creation from the beginning
genetic	γενετικός,ή, ό (adj.)	of the genesis, or origin, of someone or something
genetics	γενετική	the branch of biology dealing with heredity and variation in similar or related animals and plants
geneticist	γενετιστής-γενετίστρια (fem.)	specialist in generics

geo-	γαία/γη	the earth, combining form
geobotany	γαιο-βοτανική	the science dealing with the relationship between specific plant species and the substrata from which they receive their nourishment
geocentric	γαιο-κεντρικός, ή, ό (adj.)	measured or viewed as from the center of the earth
geo-chemistry	γαιο-χημεία	the branch of chemistry dealing with the chemical composition of the earth's crust and the chemical changes that occur there
geochemist	γαιο-χημικός	expert in geochemistry
geochronology	γαιο-χρονολογία	the branch of geology concerned with the age of the earth and its minerals, the dating of evolutionary stages in plant and animal development, etc.
geo-chronometry	γαιο-χρονομετρία	the measurement of geologic time, as from the decay of radioactive elements
geodecy	γη + διαιρείν- earth + divide	the branch of applied mathematics concerned with measuring, or determining the shape of, the earth or a large part of its surface or with locating exactly points on its surface
geodynamic	γαιοδυναμικός, ή, ό (adj.)	pertaining to the activity and forces inside the earth
geodynamics	γαιοδυναμική	the study of the activity and forces inside the earth
geognosy	γαιογνωσία/earth + knowledge	the branch of geology dealing with the composition of the earth and the distribution of its various strata and mineral deposits
geographer	γεωγράφος	specialist in geography

geographical	γεωγραφικός, ή, ό (adj.)	pertaining to the geography of a particular region
geography	γεωγραφία	science dealing with the surface of the earth, its divisions into continents and countries,; the climate, inhabitants, industries of various divisions, also, animals and plants
geoid	(ο, η) γεωειδής (το) γεωειδές (adj.)	the earth viewed as a hypothetical ellipsoid with the surface represented as a mean sea level
geologic	γεωλογικός, ή, ό (adj.)	or of according to geology
geologist	γεωλόγος	expert in geology
geology	γεωλογία	the science dealing with the physical nature and history of the earth; the structure of the earth's crust in a given region, area, or place
geomagnetic	γεωμαγνητικός, ή, ό (adj.)	of, or pertaining to the magnetic properties of the earth
geometric	γεωμετρικός, ή, ό (adj.)	of, or according to geometry
geometrician	γεωμετριστής	specialist in geometry
geometrize	γεωμετρώ/ γεωμετρείν	to use geometric principles; to work out geometrically
geometry	γεωμετρία	to measure the earth; 1 the branch of mathematics dealing with points, lines, planes, and figures and examines their properties, measurement, and mutual relations in space
geomorphic	γεωμορφικός, ή, ό (adj.)	or, of pertaining to the shape of the earth or its topography
geomorphology	γεωμορφολογία	the science dealing with the nature and origin of the earth's topographic features
geophagy	γαιοφαγία -χωματοφαγία	soil, earth eating (esp. in famine areas due to lack of food)

geophone	γαιόφωνον/ο	an electronic receiver designed to pick up vibrations transmitted through rock, ice, etc.
geophysicist	γαιοφυσικός	expert in geophysics
geophysics	γαιο-φυσική	the science dealing with the physics of the earth, including weather, winds, tides, earthquakes, volcanoes, etc., and their effect on the earth
geopolitics	γεωπολιτική	the interrelationship of politics and geography, or the study of this
geoponic	γέωπονικός, ή, ό (adj.) (γη + πονείν- earth/soil +toil)	to till the ground, relating to agriculture
geostrophic	γεωστροφικός, ή, ό (adj.) (γεω + στροφή/στρέφειν- earth +twist/turning)	designating or of a a force producing deflection as a result of the earth's rotation
geothermic	γεωθερμικός, ή, ό (adj.)	having to do with the heat of the earth's interior designating or of a force producing deflection as a result of the earth's rotation
gephyro-	γέφυρα	bridge, combining form
gephyrophobia	γεφυροφοβία	extreme fear of bridges
geriatric	γηριατρικός, ή, ό (adj.)	pertaining to old age
geriatrics	γηριατρική	the branch of medicine dealing with symptoms and diseases of old age; medical study of old age
geriatrophobia	γηρατοφοβία (γήρας/ γήρατος(gen.) + φόβος-old age + fear)	extreme fear of old age
giga-	γίγα(ς)/γίγαντας	giant, combining form
gigantic	γιγαντιαίος, α, ο (adj.)	like a giant, enormous, colossal, immense

gigantism	γιγαντισμός	abnormally great growth of the body, due to an excessive production of growth hormone by the anterior lobe of the pituitary gland
gigatomachy	γιγαντομαχία (γίγας + μάχη – giant + battle)	1 Gr. myth. the war between the giants and the gods 2 the war between giant powers
glaucoma	γλαύκωμα	eye disease when the pressure of the fluid increases
glioma	γλοιός/ γλοίωμα	gluey/ tumor of the nerve cells
glossa	γλώσσα	tongue
glottis	γλωττίς/ γλωττίδος (gen.)	the space between the vocal chords
glucose	γλυκύς, γλυκεια, γλυκύ/γλυκός (adj.)- γλυκόζη	sweet; sweetness; a crystalline monosaccharide occurring naturally in fruits, honey, and blood; the commercial form, also containing dextrin and maltose, is prepared as a sweet syrup or, upon destination as a white solid
gluteus	γλουτός	buttock
gnome	γνώμη/γνωμικόν/ό	1 opinion, thought, perception, intelligence 2 a wise, pithy saying; maxim; aphorism; apothegm; motto
gnomic	γνωμικός, ή, ό (adj.)	1 wise and pithy; full of aphorisms 2 designating of or a writer of aphorisms
gnomon	γνώμων- εμπειρογνώμων	inspector/indicator, specialist in a field
gnomy-	γνώμη/γνωμάτευση	science of judging or determining
-gnosis	γνώσις/η	gnosis; knowledge; recognition
gnostic	γνωστικός	a person belonging to any of a number of groups (many of which claimed to be Christians) that flourished in the second and third centuries, and that taught a doctrine of salvation through spiritual knowledge

Gnosticism	γνωστικισμός	a salvational system, heterodox and syncretistic, stressing knowledge/gnosis as essential, matter as evil and variously combining ideas, derived esp. from mythology, ancient Gr. philosophy, ancient religions, and eventually, from Christianity
-gon	- γωνον (γωνία)	an angle, combining form a figure having a number of angles, as trigon, pentagon, exagon, etc.
gram	γραμμάριον/ο	small weight; the basic unit of mass in the metric system, equal to about (.0022046 pound or 15.43 grains): officially equal to the weight of one cubic centimeter of distilled water: abbrev. g or gm
grammar	γραμματική	1 study of correct writing and speaking 2 the part of the study of language which deals with the forms and structure of words (morphology), with their customary arrangement in phrases and sentences (syntax) and now often with language sounds (phonology) and words meanings (semetics) 3 a) the elementary principles of a field of knowledge b) treatise on these
grammarian	γραμματικός	an expert in grammar
grammatical	γραμματικός, ή, ό (adj.)	confirming to rules of grammar
grammatology	γραμματολογία	the scientific study or science concerned with the historical base of written records of a nation in their entirety

gramophone	γραμόφωνον/ο (γράφειν + φωνή – writing + voice)	phonograph
graph-	γραφ-ή/γράφειν	combining form (could act as a prefix: graphic or graphemics or as a suffix: photographer, stenographer, etc.)
graphemics	γραφική/γραφιμική	the branch of language study dealing with the relationship between speech sounds and the writing system of a language
-grapher	-γράφος	combining form, an agent of a specified process/method for recording or describing (telegrapher, stenographer, etc.)
graphic	γραφίστας	one who is able to write, paint, design
-graphic	- γραφικός, ή, ό (adj.)	combining form forming adjectives of or relating to a (specified) method or process for recording or describing (as, telegraphic, stenographic, etc.)
grapho-	γραφή/γράφειν	combining form, writing; to write
graphologist	γραφολόγος	expert in handwriting
graphology	γραφολογία	a study of handwriting, esp. as a clue to the character, aptitude, etc.
-graphy	-γραφία	combining from forming nouns (photography/φωτογραφία; geography/γεωγραφία, etc.)
Greco- Greco-Roman	γκραικός/γκρεκός Ελληνο-Ρωμαϊκή	combining form, Greek influenced by both (Greco-Roman art, Greco-Roman resling, etc.)
Greece	Ελλάς/Ελλαδα	country in the S Balkan Peninsula, including many islands in the Aegean, Ionian and Mediterranean seas
Greek	Έλληνας/ Ελληνίδα (fem.)	an inhabitant of Greece or of Greek descent

Greek	ελληνικός, η, ό (adj.) ελληνικά (pl.)	anything Greek and plural the Greek language which constitutes a separate branch of the Indo-European language family
Greek Orthodox Church	Ελληνική Ορθόδοξος Εκκλησία	the established church of Greece and the Greek Orthodox people on other lands as well. An autonomous part of the Eastern Orthodox Church
gymnasium	γυμνάσιον/ο/ γυμναστήριον/ο	a place for excercising, also in some European countries, including Greece (γυμνάσιο/ gymnasium), a secondary school (high school)
gymnast	γυμναστής/ γυμνάστρια (fem.)	expert/trainer of gymnastics
gymnastic	γυμωαστικός, ή, ό (adj.)	of or having to do with gymnastics
gymnastics	γυμναστική	physical exercise; physical training and activity
gymnophobia	γυμνοφοβία (γυμνός, ή, ό + φόβος/ naked + fear)	extreme fear of the naked body
gymnosophist	γυμνός + σοφιστής – naked/nude + sophist	a member of an ancient Hindu sect of ascetics who wore little or no clothing at all
gyneco/gynaeco-	γυνή-γυναίκα/ woman	pertaining to women, combining form
gynecoid	(ο, η) γυναικοειδής/ (το) γυναικοειδές (adj.)	like a woman; resembling a woman
gynecocracy	γυναικοκρατία	government by women
gynecologist	γυναικολόγος	specialist in gynecology
gynecology	γυναικολογία	science dealing with the female body and the reproductive organs including the breasts
gynecomastia	γυναικομαστεία	enlargement of male breasts
gynophobia	γυναικοφοβία	abnormal fear of women
gyro-	γύρος	combining word a circle; a circular or spiral motion

gyroscope	γυροσκόπιον/ο	a wheel mounted on a set of rings so that its axis of rotation is free to turn in any direction

The words that follow, among many others, that begin with an *h* come from the Greek language. The *h* represents the rough breathing sign (') δασεία/thaseia, which used to be placed on vowels (before the monotonic system prevailed in modern Greek, and the breathing signs were eliminated). Some words (just as a reminder and examples) are written with the (') in this dictionary. The majority of the Greek words, however, are not accented. (According to the demotic/ popular language of today, the breathing signs and the circumflex/περισπωμένη (-) are not used.) It should be taken for granted all English words here, starting with an *Hh*, and, many that are not included in this work, are originating from the Greek words, starting with a vowel and were accented with the rough breathing sign daseia (') which in English is replaced with the letter *Hh*. (The original breathing sign, on ancient Gr. words, had a soft *h* sound, ex: hoi.)

H

Hades	Ἅδη ς	1 Gr. myth. a) the home of the dead, beneath the earth b) the god of the underworld 2 Bible the state or resting place of the dead: name appears in some modern translations of the New Testament
haemal	αιμάτινος, η, ο (adj.)	having to do with blood: see **hemal**
haematic	αιματικός, ή, ό (adj.	see **hematic**
haematocele	αιματοκήλη	see **hematocele**
haematocrit	αιματοκρίτης	see **hematocrit**
haematologic	αιματολογικός, ή, ό (adj.)	see **hematological**
haematologist	αιματολόγος	see **hematologist**
haematology	αιματολογία	see **hematology**
haemo-	αίμα	see **hemo-**
hagio	άγιος, α, ο (adj.)	saint; saintly; holy; sacred, combining form

Hagiographa	Αγιόγραφα	writings; the third and final part of the Jewish Scriptures, those books not in the Law of the Prophets
hagiographer	αγιογράφος	1 any of the authors of the Hagiograph 2 biographer of a saint or saints
hagiography	αγιογραφία	1 a book or writing, or an assemblage of these, about the lives of saints 2 such books or writings as a field of study
hagiolatry	αγιολατρεία	worshiping saints or anything sacred; holy
hagiology	αγιολογία	the study of hagiography
halcyon	αλκυών/αλκυόνος (gen.)/αλκυόνα (Mod. Gr.)	1 legendary bird, identified with the kingfisher, which is supposed to have a peaceful, calming influence on the sea at the time of the winter solstice 2 Zool. any of the genus [Halcyon] of kingfishers of S Asia and Australia; tranquil, happy, idyllic, etc., esp., **halcyon days,** in Gr. αλκυονίδες ημέρες: the sunny, lovely days that interrupt the bad winter weather
halieutic	αλιευτικός, ή, ό (adj.) (αλιεύειν – to fish)	pertaining to fishing and fishery
halieutics	αλιευτική	the study of the art of fishing
Hallelujah/ Halleluiah	Αλληλούϊα	praise the Lord! exclamation hymn
Hapax	άπαξ/απαξ	once, a word or phrase occurring only once
haplo-	απλός, ή, ό (adj.)	simple, combining form
haplology	απλολογία	the dropping of one of two similar or identical successive syllables or sounds in a word (ex: interpretive for interpretative)

haploscope	απλοσκόπιον /o	a simple stereoscope which is used in the study of depth perception
hapto	(άπτειν – αφή / to touch- touch)	contact, touch, combining form (haptics)
haptic	απτός, ή, ό – απτικός, η, ό (adj,)	1 relating to, or based on the sense of touch 2 characterized by a predilection for the sense of touch
haptics	απτική	the science dealing with the sense of touch
Harmonia	Αρμονία	1 Gr. myth. the daughter of Aphrodite and Ares and wife of Cadmus; 2 personification of harmony and order; harmony
harmonic	αρμονικός, ή, ό (adj.)	peaceful, harmonious in feeling or effect; agreeable
harmonically	αρμονικά (adv.)	harmoniously
harmony	αρμονία	congruity; agreement in feeling, action, ideas, interests, etc., in music: the simultaneous sounding of two or more tones, esp. when satisfying in the ear
Harpy/harpies (pl.)	Αρπυα/¨Αρπυαι (pl.)/ Άρπυες (Mod. Gr.)	lit. snatchers; 1 Gr. myth. any of several hideous, filthy, rapacious winged monsters with the head and trunk of a woman and the tail, legs, and talons of a bird 2 (h-) a relentless, greedy, or grasping person 3 (h-) a shrewish woman
hebdomad	εβδομάς/εβδομάδα (έβδομος, η, ο/επτά – seventh/seven)	seven days; a week
hebdomadal	εβδομαδιαίος, α, ο (adj.)	weekly; something occurring every week (ex: weekly magazine, newspaper; meeting, etc.)

Hebe	Ἥβη	youth; Gr. myth. the daughter of Hera and Zeus and goddess of youth, also the cupbearer to the gods
hebeephrenia	ήβη + φρένα/ φρενίτιδα- youth +mind	a form of schizophrenia characterized by childish or silly behavior, disorganized thinking, delusions and hallucinations, usually beginning in adolesence
hebephrenic	ήβη φρενικός, ή. ό (adj.)	pertaining to one suffering from the affliction of hebephrenia
Hebraic	εβραϊκός, ή, ό (adj.)	characterististic of the Hebrew language, culture, ethical system, etc.
Hebrew	Εβραίος/Εβραία	Jewish
Hecatomb	εκατόμβη/ εκατομβών (εκατόν + βους – hundred +ox(en)	any large-scale of slaughter or sacrifice; in ancient Greece, any great sacrifice to the gods; specif., the slaughter of 100 cattle at one time
hecto-	εκατό-	a hundred, combining form
hectogram	εκατόγραμμον/ο	a metric measure of weight equal to 100 grams (3.527 ounches)
hectoliter	εκατόλιτρον/ο	a metric measure of weight equal to 100 liters (26.418 gallons)
hectometer/ hectometer	εκατόμετρον/ο	a metric measure of linear measure equal to 100 meters (109.36 yards)
Hector	Ἕκτωρ/ Ἕκτορας	the greatest Trojan hero in Homer's *Iliad*, killed by Achilleus to avenge the death of Patroclus: Priam's oldest son; a masculine name
Hecuba	Εκάβη	in Homer's *Iliad*: wife of Priam and mother of Hector, Troilus, Paris, and Cassandra
hedonic	ηδονικός, ή, ό (adj.)	having to do with pleasure
hedonism	ηδονισμός	devotion to pleasure

hegemonic	ηγεμονικός, ή, ό (adj.)	one characterized by being connected to hegemony or to power; royal; princely, imperial, etc.
hegemonism	ηγεμονισμός	the policy or practice of a nation in aggressively expanding its influence over other countries
hegemony	ηγεμονία	leadership; to lead; leadership or dominance, esp. that of one state or country over others
hegumen	ηγούμενος	the arch-monk at a monastery, the leader
helcoid	(ο, η) ελκώδης/ (το) ελκώδες	resembling an ulcer; ulcerlike symptoms
helcosis	έλκωσις/η	formation of an ulcer
Helen	Ελένη/ used to be: 'Ελένη (the harsh breathing)	sign (') became an h) a girl's name and the name of Helen of Troy
helico-	έλιξ/έλικος (gen.)	combining form, spiral, spiral shaped, also, before a vowel helic-
helicoid	(ο, η) ελικοειδής (το) ελικοειδές (adj.)	shaped like, or coiled in the form of a spiral, as in the shell of a snail
Helicon	Ελικών/ ελικώνος (gen.)/Ελικώνας (mod. Gr.)	1 mountain group in SC Greece, on the Gulf of Corinth 2 in Gr. mythology the home of the Muses; the highest peak, 5,735 f. (1,750 m)
helicopter	ελικόπτερον(ν)	a kind of vertical-lift aircraft
helio-	ήλιο-ήλιος	combining form, sun, sunlight
helios	ήλιος	sun; Helios, Gr. myth. the god of sun
heliophobia	ηλιοφοβία	extreme fear of sunlight
heliosis	ηλίωσις	sunstroke
heliotherapy	ηλιοθεραπεία	type of treatment by the rays of the sun or using an ultraviolet lamp

helix	ἑλιξ/ἑλικας (ελίσσειν – to turn around)	1 any spiral; to turn or moving around 2 Anat. the folded rim of cartilage around the outer ear 3 Arch. an ornamental spiral as a volute on a Corinthian or Ionic (style) capital
Hellas	Ελλάς/Ελλάδα (previouslywith the rough breating sign: 'Ελλάς/ 'Ελλάδος (gen.))	Greece
Hellenic	ελληνικός, ή, ό (adj.) (Ελληνικός, ή, ό (adj.)	Greek, of the history, culture, language, etc.
Hellenism	Ελληνισμός ('Ελληνισμός)	the character; culture, thought or ethical system of ancient Greece
Hellenist	Ελληνιστής (' Ελληνιστής)	Philhellene; friend or supporter of the Greek people
Hellenistic	Ελληνιστικός, ή, ό (adj.) ('ελληνιστικός)	characteristic of Hellenism
Hellenize	Ελληνίζειν	(became popular in 323 BC, when Hellenism (Greek language, history, and culture) was expanded throughout the lands Alexander the Great had conquered)
Hellespont	Ελλήσποντος	**the sea of Helle/ Ελλη;** the Derdanelless
helot	είλωτας/είλωτες (pl.)	slaves in ancient Sparta
helotism	ειλωτισμός	1 the condition of a helot; serfdom or slavery 2 Biol. a form of symbiosis, as among some ants, in which one species dominates and uses workers of another species
hema-/haema (prefix)/	αίμα	blood
hematic	αιματικός, ή, ό (adj.)	pertaining to blood

hematoid	(ο, η) αιματώδης, (το) αιματώδες (adj.)	resembling blood; bloodlike substance
hematologist	αιματολόγος	specialist in the study of blood and its diseases
hematology	αιματολογία	the branch of medicine studying the blood and blood diseases
hematoma	αιμάτωμα	swelling containing clotted blood
hematocrit	αιματοκρίτης (αίμα + κριτής- blood + judge)	the proportion of red blood cells to a volume of blood measured by a hematocrit; hematocrit reading calibrated tube
hemato-metaghysis	αιματο-μετάγγισις/η	blood transfusion
hemi-	ημί-ήμισυ	half
hemic	αιματικός, ή, ό (adj.)	pertaining to blood
hemicrania	ημικρανία (ημί & κρανίο(ν)- half & skull)	headache on one side of the head only/migraine
hemicycle	ημικύκλιον/ο	1 a half circle 2 a semicircular room, wall, etc.
hemi-hydrate	ημί & υδρεύειν/ ύδωρ (half & hydrate/water)	hydrate with two-to-one ratio of molecules of substance to molecules of water
hemi-parasite	ημί-παράσιτος	an organism that may be either free-living or parasitic
hemiplegia	ημιπληγία	paralysis on one side of the body, caused by damage to the opposite side of the brain
hemiptera	ημίπτερος, η, ο (adj.)	half-winged; a true bug
hemisphere	ημισφαίριον/ο (ημί &σφαίρα- half & spere)	globe, half of a sphere
hemispheric	ημισφαιρικός, ή, ό (adj.)	pertaining to hemisphere
hemispheroid	(ο, η) ημισφαιροειδής (το) ημισφαιριοειδές (adj.)	a half of a spheroid

hemodynamics	αιμοδυναμική	study of the flow of blood and the forces involved
hemoid	(ο, η) αιμοειδής, (το) αιμοειδές (adj.)	resembling blood; bloodlike fluid
hemolysis	αιμόλυσις/η	destruction of elements of the blood
hemopathy	αιμοπάθεια	blood disease
hemo-pericardium	αίμο-περικάρδιον/ο	blood in the heart sac
hemopexis	αιμοπηξία	blood coagulation
hemophilia	αιμοφιλία	defective coagulation of the blood with strong tendency to bleed
hemophiliac	αιμοφιλιακός, ή, ό (adj.)	one afflicted by hemophilia
hemophobia	αιμοφοβία	aversion to blood
hemoptysis	αιμόπτυσις/η	spitting up of blood
hemorrhage	αιμορραγία	extreme loss of blood from a blood vessel
hemorrhoids	αιμορρωίδες (πλ.pl.)	enlarged, dilated veins inside or just outside the rectum/ also known as piles
hemostasis	αιμόστασις/η	stopping hemorrhaging
hendeca	ένδεκα/ εν(α) + δέκα –one +ten)	one and ten, eleven
hendecagon	ενδεκά-γωνον/ο	a solid figure with eleven plane surfaces
hepar	ήπαρ/ήπατος (gen.) (Mod. Gr. σηκώτι)	liver
heparin	ηπαρίνη	substance which prevents blood clotting
hepatitis	ηπατίτις/ηπατίτιδα	swelling and soreness of the liver
hepatogenic	(ο, η)ηπατογενής, (το) ηπατογενές (adj.)	produced in the liver
hepatoma	ηπάτωμα	tumor, originating in the liver
hepatomegaly	ήπατο-μεγάλο/ liver-large	enlargement of the liver
hepatopathy	ηπατατοπάθεια	liver disease

Hephaestus	Ἥφαιστος	
hypostasis	υπόστασις/η	Greek term meaning "substance" that came, in Christian Theology, to designate a Person of the Trinity (Father, Son, and the Holy Spirit)
hepta-	επτά	seven, combining form
heptad	επτάς/επτάδα	a series or a group of seven
heptagon	επτάγωνον/ο	seven-cornered; a plane figure with seven angles and seven sides
heptahedron	επτάεδρον/ο	a solid figure with seven plane surfaces
heptameter	επτάμετρον/ο	a line of verse containing seven metrical feet or measures
heptarchy	επταρχία	government by seven rulers; a term used by historians
heptasyllabic	επτασυλλαβικός, ή, ό (adj.)	having seven syllables
Heptateuch	Επτάτευχος (επτά + τεύχος – seven + book/volume)	the first seven books of the Bible
Hera	Ἥρα	wife of Zeus
Herculean	ηράκλειος, α, ο (adj.)	of Hercules; 1 a) having the great size, strength, or courage of Hercules, very powerful and courageous b) something very difficult to accomplish [a herculean task]
Hercules	Ηρακλής	Myth. the son of Zeus and Alcmene, renowed for his great strength and courage, indicated by the twelve labors that were imposed on him to perform; any very large powerful man

heresy	αίρεσις/η	a school of thought; a sect; a religious belief opposed to the orthodox doctrines of the church, esp., such a belief specifically is denounced by the church
heretic	αιρετικός, ή, ό (adj.)	a person who abides by a heresy
hermaphrodite	ερμαφρόδιτος, η, ο (adj.)	altered; 1 a person or animal with the sexual organs of both the male and the female 2 a plant having stamens and pistils in the same flower
hermaphroditism	ερμαφροδιτισμός	1 the condition of being both male and female 2 androgynous culture 3 of or marked by male and female characteristics
Hermaphriditus	Ερμαφρόδιτος	Gr. myth. the son of Hermes and Aphrodite: while bathing, he becomes united in a single body with a nymph
hermeneutic	ερμηνευτικός, ή, ό (adj.) ερμηνεύειν - to interpret	interpretive
hermeneutics	ερμηνευτική	the art or science of the interpretation of literature
Hermes	Ερμής	Gr. myth the god who served as herald and messenger of the other gods, generally pictured wearing winged shoes and hat, carrying a caduceus: he was also the god of science, commerce; eloquence, and cunning, and guide of departed souls to Hades: identified with the Roman Mercury
hermit	ερημίτης (έρημος - desert)	1 a person who lives alone in a lonely and secluded spot, often out of religious beliefs; recluse 2 a brown spiced cookie made of nuts and raisins

hermetic	ερμητικός, ή, ό (adj.)	1 of or derived from Hermes Trismegistus/ the thrice greatest, and his lore 2 a) magical; alchemic b) hard to understand; obscure 3 [from use in alchemy] completely sealed by fusion, soldering, etc., so as to keep air or gas from getting in or out; airtight
Hermeticism Esoteric Philosophy	Ερμητισισμός Εσωτερική Φιλοσοφία	often incorporating elements of alchemy, magic, and occult wisdom
hero	ήρως/ήρωας	1 a person admired for courage, nobility, or exploits, esp. in war; 2 any person, esp. a man, admired for qualities or achievements and regarded as an ideal or role model; 3 the central figure of a novel, play, poem, etc., with whom the reader/audience is supposed to sympathize with
Herod	Ηρώδης	c. 73–4 BC; Idumean king of Judea, called Herod the Great
Herodotus	Ηρόδοτος	c.484–c 425 B. C.; Gr. historian, known as the Father of History
heroic	ηρωϊκός, ή, ό (adj.)	like or characteristic of a hero; of or a hero and his deeds; a heroic poem
heroin	ηρωίνη	morphine chemically altered to make it three times stronger
heroine	ηρωίς/ ηρωϊδα	the feminine of hero (see above) the same qualities of courage, nobility, etc., apply to a girl or woman heroine
heroism	ηρωϊσμός	the qualities and actions of a hero or heropine; bravery, sacrifice; valor, nobility, etc.
herpes	έρπης/έρπητας	skin disease characterized by clusters of small blisters

herpetologist	ερπητολόγος	a specialist in herpetology
herpetology	ερπητολογία	the branch of zoology, having to do with the study of reptiles and amphibians
Hesperia	Εσπερία	the name of Italy (in ancient times) and the Roman name for Spain; Western Land
Hesperian	εσπερινός	western evening; Hesperos, the evening star
Hesperides	Εσπερίδες	the nymphs guarding the golden apples given as a wedding gift by Gaea to Hera
hetaera	'εταίρα	in Ancient Greece a courtesan; concubine; companion (usually well-learned women keeping company with philosophers, writers, scientists, etc,)
hetaerism	εταιρισμός	pertaining to hetaera; a communal marriage (among some early people)
hetero-	έτερο- έτερος, ετέρα, έτερο (adj.)	meaning :other, different, combining form
hetero-chromatic	(')έτερο- χρώμα	consisting of different or contrasting colors
heterodox	ετερόδοξος, η, ο (adj.)	departing or opposed to the usual beliefs or established doctrines, esp. in religion; inclining toward heresy; unorthodox
heterodoxy	ετεροδοξία	the quality or fact of being opposed to the established doctrines; a heterodox belief or doctrine
hetero-geneous	(ο, η)'ετερογενής (το) ετερογενές (adj.)	differing in structure/quality, dissimilar; of unlike nature
heterogenesis	ετερογένεσις/η (έτερο-γενεά)	alternation of generations
heteronomous	έτερο –νόμος (differing/other and law)	subject to another's law or rule

heteronym	ετερώνυμον	words with the same spelling but different meaning
heterophony	ετεροφωνία	the playing of a passage of music with simultaneous variations in melody or rhythm by two or more performers
heterophyllous	ετερόφυλλος, ή, ο (adj.)	growing leaves of different forms on the same stem or plant
heterophylophilos	ετεροφυλόφιλος, η, ο (adj.)	heterosexual
heterophylophilia/ heterophilia	ετεροφυλοφιλία (έτερο + φυλο + φιλία – other+gender+love or attraction)	heterosexuality, sexual desire for one of the opposite sex
heuristic	ευρίσκω-εύρηκα/ ευρίσκειν	inventor; discoverer; to invent, discover
heuristics	ευριστική/ ευρηματική	heuristic method/procedures
hex	έξ/εξι	six
hexa-	έξ	combining form followed with either a consonant or vowel
hexachord	εξάχορδον/ο	having six musical strings
hexad	εξάς/εξάδα	a group or a series of six
hexaemeron	εξαήμερον	1 Bible an account of the six-day period of the Creation, esp. that in the Genesis
hexagon	εξάγωνος, η, ο(v) (adj.)	a plane figure with six angles and six sides
hexagonal	εξαγωνικός, ή, ό (adj.)	pertaining to exagon/εξάγωνον ('έξι/six & γωνία/) (the ' [daseia] became an h)
hexagram	εξάγραμμο	a six-pointed star formed by extending the sides of a regular hexagon or by placing one equilateral triangle over another (as in the Star of David)
hexahedron	εξάεδρο(v)	a solid figure having six planes

hexamerous	εξαήμερος, η, ο (έξι/ six & ημέρα/day)	six-day period; six days
hexameter	εξάμετρον/o	six meters
hexangular	εξαγωνιακός, ή, ό (adj.)	having six angles
hexastich	εξάστιχο	a poem or stanza of six lines
hexateuch	εξάτευχος	book; the first six books of the Bible
hidrosis	ίδρωσις /η/ ιδρώνω	sweating to sweat
hier-	ιερό – sacred	combining word used before a vowel
hierarch	ιεράρχης	presiding priest over sacred rites, chief priest
hierarchical	ιεραρχικός, ή, ό (adj.)	of a hierarch or hierarchy
hierarchism	ιεραρχισμός	the principles, practices, or authority of hierarchy
hierarchy	ιεραρχία	power or rule by a hieracrh; 1 a system of church government by priests or other clergy in graded ranks 2 the group of officials, esp. the highest officials, in such a group
hiero	ιερός, ή, ό /ιερόν/ sacred, holy (adj,)	also in the Orthodox Church: Ιερόν/ό (neut.) means: Altar
hierocracy	ιεροκρατία	government/rule by priests or other clergy
hieroglyph	ιερόγλυφον/o	a carving; symbol; sign; hard to understand
hieroglyphic	ιερόγλυφικός, ή, ό (adj.)	pertaining to hieroglyphics; difficult to understand; a method of writing using symbols, pictures, etc.
hierology	ιερολογία	the religious lore and literature of a people
hierophant	ιεροφάντης	in ancient Greece a priest of a mystery cult
hilarious	ιλαρός, ή, ό (adj.)	cheerful; noisily merry
hilarity	ιλαρότης/ιλαρότητα	the state of being hilarious; noisy merriment; boisterous gaity

Hippocrates	Ιπποκράτης	Greek physician; the father of medicine
Hippocratic Oath	Ιπποκράτειος Όρκος	every physician, upon graduation, takes the oath which establishes the ethics of his/her profession
hippo- prefix	ίππος	horse
hippodrome	ιππόδρομος/ ιπποδρόμιο(ν)	an arena for equestrian events; in ancient Greece and Rome a course of horse and chariot races
hippopotamus	ιπποπόταμος	river horse, horse of the river
histo-	ιστός	tissue, combining form
histoblast	ιστοβλαστός	tissue blast
histology	ιστολογία	science dealing with /the microscopic structure of tissues
historian	ιστορικός (n).	an authority of history; a writer of history
historic	ιστορικός, ή, ό (adj.)	famous through history
historiographer	ιστοριογράφος	a historian, esp. one assigned to write the history of an institution, country, etc.; an expert in historiography
history	'ιστορία/ ιστορία	1 an account of what has or might have happened in the life or narrative, play, story, etc. 2 in chronological order recorded happenings of a country, institution, family etc., 3 all recorded events of the past
hoi polloi	οι πολλοί	the general population/masses
holocaust	ολοκαύτωμα	genocide, slaughter of a group of people or ethnicity
homeo/homoeo	όμοιο- / ¨ομοιος, α, ό (adj.)	same, identical, combining form
homeo-path	ομοιο-παθητικός, ή, ό (adj.)	one who accepts the principles of homeopathy
homeopathy	ομοιοπαθητική	method of treating diseases that involves giving medication causing symptoms similar to the ones being present

Homer	Όμηρος	Gr. epic poet of c. eighth cen. BC, both epic poems: the *Iliad* and *Odyssey* are attributed to him; a masculine name, also the Gr. word: όμηρος means hostage
Homeric	Ομηρικός, ή, ό (adj.)	pertaining to Homer; Homer's work
homo-	όμοιος, α, o (adj.)	same; equal; identical
homogeneous/ homogenous	(o, η) ομογενής (το) ομογενές (adj.)	1 of the same nationality/race or kind of the same structure
homologous	ομόλογος, η, o (adj.)	agreeing; corresponding 1 corresponding in structure, position, character, etc.: opposed to **Heterologous** 2 Biol. corresponding in basic type of structure and deriving from a common primitive origin 3 Immunology a) of a serum given to and derived from the same species b) of a serum given to another species but fighting the same bacterium
homonym	ομώνυμον/o	having the same name (a word having the same pronunciation differing in meaning/origin)
homonymous	ομόνυμος, η, o (adj.)	1 having the same name 2 of, or having the nature of, a homonym
homousian/ homousios	ομοούσιος, α, o (adj.) Ecc. Theol.	used by the Fathers of the First Ecumenical Synod to express the relation of the Father and the Son within the Godhead. The Father and the Son are of the *same essence* and not homoiousios/ ομοιούσιος – of the similar essence as the heretics believed
homophile	ομοφυλόφιλος/ ομόφιλος	homosexual; friend/ lover of the same sex
homophilia	ομοφιλία	homosexuality

homophobia	ομοφοβία	extreme fear of homosexuality
homophobe	ομοφοβικός, ή, ό (adj.)	one who fears homosexuals
homosexual	ομοφυλόφιλος, η, ο (ομο/same- φύλο/ sex-φίλος/friend)	desire for a partner of the same sex
horizon	ορίζων/ορίζοντας	limit, the extent of one's outlook; a circular imaginary line where it seems the sky touching land or sea
horizontal	οριζόντιος, α, ο (adj.)	parallel to the plane of the horizon; not vertical; flat and even
hormonal	ορμονικός, ή, ό (adj.)	pertaining to hormones
hormone	ορμόνη	substance found in organs of the body (as the adrenal glands, the pituitary, etc.)
horologe	ωρολόγιον/ ωρολόγι/ρολόϊ	timepiece; clock; hourglass
horologist	ωρολόγος	expert in horology/ maker of timepieces
horology	ωρολογία	art of measuring time/ making timepieces
horoscope	ωροσκόπιον/ο	observer of the hour of birth; 1 the position of the planets and the stars with relation to one another at a given time, esp. at the time of a person's birth regarded in astrology as determining one's destiny
hubris	ὕβρις	wanton insolence, or arrogance resulting from excessive pride or from passion
hyacinth	υάκινθος	bluebell, blue larkspur, hence a blue gem; a bluish purple flower,
hyaline	υαλίνη/υάλινος, η, ο (adj.)/glassy	glassy substance
hyelo-	ύελος /γυαλί	glass

hyalogen	(ο, η) υαλογενής/ (το) υαλογενές (adj.)	any of the various insulable substances found in animal tissue and producing hyalins
hyaloid	(ο, η) υαλοειδής(το) υαλοειδές (adj.)	having the appearance of glass; glassy
hyaloid membrane	υαλοειδής μεμβράνη	a delicate membrane containing the vitreous humor of the eye
hyaloplasm	ύαλο-πλάσμα	the basic substance of the protoplasm of the cell
hydatic	υδατικός, ή, ό (adj.)	a cyst containing watery fluid and the larvae of certain tapeworms, found in the body tissue esp. the liver of many animals
hydrarthrosis	ύδωρ + άρθρωσις/ water + joint	accumulation of fluid in all the joints
hydraulic	υδραυλικός, ή, ό (adj.)	of a water organ; of hydraulics; operated by the force and movement of liquid
hydraulics	υδραυλική	science of liquids in motion; the branch of physics having to do with the mechanical properties of water and other liquids in motion and with the application of these properties in engineering
hydro-	ύδωρ-ύδατος (γεν.gen.)	water, combining form
hydrocephalus	υδροκέφαλος	a condition characterized by abnormal amount of fluid in the cranium
hydrocyst	υδροκύστις-η	cyst containing water
hydroelectric	υδροϋλεκτρικός, ή, ό (adj.)	producing electricity by water power
hydrogen	υδρογόνο(ν)	a flammable, colorless, odorless, gaseous, chemical, the lightest of all substances (symbol, H)

hydrography	υδρογραφία	the study, description, and mapping of oceans, lakes, and rivers, esp. with reference to their navigational and commercial uses
hydroid	(ο, η) υδροειδής (το) υδροειδές (adj.)	like a hydra or polyp; of or related to an order [Haydroida] of hydrozoans, including the hydras and many colonial marine species
Hydrokinetic	ύδωρ + κίνησις /η – water + movement (υδροκινητικός, ή, ό (adj.)	of the motions of fluids of the forces producing or influencing such motions
hydrokinetics	υδροκινητικ	the branch of physics dealing with fluids in motion
hydrology	υδρολογία	the science dealing with the waters of the earth, their distribution on the surface and underground, and the cycle involving evaporation, precipitation, flow to the seas, etc.
hydromancy	υδρομαντεία	divination by the observation of water; looking at the water predicting what is going to happen
hydromechanics	υδρομηχανική	the branch of physics having to do with the laws governing the motion and equilibrium of fluids
hydrometallurgy	υδρομεταλλουργία	the recovery of metals by a liquid process
hydropathy	υδροπαθητική	a method of treatment attempting to cure all illnesess by the use of water, including consumption of mineral water and hydrotherapy
hydrophilia	υδροφιλία	excessive love of the water
hydrophobia	υδροφοβία	extreme fear of water

hydrophone	υδρόφωνον/ο	an instrument used in detecting, and registering the distance and direction of sound transmitted through water
hydroplane	υδροπλάνον/ο	a small, light motorboat with hydrofoils or with a flat bottom rising in steps to the stern so that it can skim along the water's surface at high speeds; a seaplane
hydrosalpinx	υδρο-σάλπινξ/ σάλπιγγα/ σάλπιγγες (pl.)	abnormal distension of one or both fallopian tubes with fluid usually due to inflammation
hydroscope	υδροσκόπιον/ο	a device resembling a periscope, for viewing objects at some distance below the surface of water
hydrosphere	υδροσφαίρα	all the water on the surface of the earth, including oceans, lakes, rivers, glaciers, etc.: water vapor, clouds, etc., may be considered part of the atmosphere or hydrosphere
hydrotherapeutics	υδροθεραπευτική	the study of treating diseases by means of water (hydrotherapy)
hydrotherapy	υδροθεραπεία	treatment of disease by means of water
hyena/hyaena	ύαινα	any of various wolflike carnivores (family, Hyaenidae) of Africa and Asia with powerful jaws; mean, thought as cowardly though
Hygeia	Υγεία	Gr. myth. the goddess of health; health
hygiene	υγιεινή	1 science dealing with health and prevention of disease 2 sanitary practices; cleanliness (personal hygiene)
hygienic	υγιειϊνός, ή, ό (adj.)	pertaining to health and observance of the rules; promoting health; healthful; sanitary

hygienist	υγιειονολόγος	an expert in hygiene
hygro-	υγρό-	wet, moist, combining form
hygric	υγρός, ή, ό (adj.)	wet; moist
hygrograph	υγρογράφος	an instrument which continuously records atmospheric humidity
hygrometer	υγρόμετρον/ο	any of various instruments of measuring the absolute or relative amount of moisture in the air
hygrometry	υγρομετρία	the branch of meteorology dealing with measuring the atmospheric humidity
hygroscope	υγροσκόπιον/ο	an instrument that indicates without actually measuring, changes in atmospheric humidity, as by swelling or color change
hygrophilous	υγρόφιλος	1 pertaining to absorbing fluids, esp., water. 2 in plants or organisms the ones that thrive in very moist areas
hygrothermgraph	υγρο-θερμογράφος	an instrument that measures and records atmospheric humidity and temperature on the same graph
hylozoism	ύλη + ζωή- matter + life /υλοζωϊσμός	the doctrine that all matter has life, or that life is inseparable from matter
hymen	υμήν	membrane fold located at the entrance of the female sex organ
hymenectomy	υμήν/υμένος (gen.)	a surgical procedure of the hymen
hymn	ύμνος	a song in praise or honor of God, or a god(s); a festive song
hymnode	υμνωδός	a writer or composer of hymns
hymnody	υμνωδία	the singing of hymns; hymns collectively

hymnology	υμνολογία	1 the study of hymns, their history; use, etc. 2 the writing and composition of hymns
hypacusia	υπό & ακοή/ under & hearing	faulty hearing
hyperaemia	υπεραιμία	an excessive blood flow or congestion of blood in an organ, tissue, etc.
hyperaemic	υπεραιμικός, ή, ό (adj.)	having an increased blood flow in an organ, tissue, etc.
hyp - prefix	υπ- (υπό)	combining form used before a vowel meaning under
hypalgesia	υπό & άλγος/ υποαλγησία	less sensitivity to pain
hypabyssal	υπό-αβυσσώδες	Geol. designating of or igneous rocks solidified at moderate depths
hypaethral	υπαίθριος, α, ο (adj.)	open to the sky; roofless
hyper prefix	υπέρ	over, above, more than normal, excessive also, compining form
hyperacusia	υπέρ –ακοή/ hearing -ακούω / to hear	acute hearing
hyperalgesia	υπερ-αλγεσία	increased sensitivity to pain; enhanced intensity of pain
hyperbole	υπερβολή	exaggeration for effect and not meant to be taken literally
hyperbolic	υπερβολικός, ή, ό (adj.)	exaggerated or exaggerating
hyperbolism	υπερβολισμός	a hyperbolic statement; exaggerated assertion
hyperbolize	υπερβάλλω	express with or use hyperbole
hyper-catalyctic	υπερ-καταλυκτικός, ή, ό (adj.)	having one or more extra syllables
hyperchromia	υπερ-χρωμία	1 excessive pigmentation of the skin 2 a state of the red cells marked by the increase in the hemoglobin content
hypercritic	υπερ-κριτικός, ή, ό (adj.)	to critique too severely, hard to please
hyperdulia	υπερδουλεία	excessive willfulness

hyperemia	υπεραιμία	an increased blood flow or congestion of blood in an organ, tissue, etc.
hyper-emesis	υπέρ-εμετικός, ή, ό (adj.)	abnormal amount of vomiting
hyper-esthesia	υπερ-αισθησία/ above normal-sensitivity	an abnormal sensitivity of the skin or other organ
hypergamy	υπέρ-γάμος / above-marriage	marriage with a person of higher social class or position
hyper-glycemia	υπέρ-γλυκαιμία/ excessive-sugar	an abnormally high concentration of sugar in the blood
hyper-hidrosis	υπέρ-ίδρωσις/η	excessive sweating
hyperopia	υπερωπία	abnormal vision
hyperosmia	υπεροσμία (υπέρ + οσμή- excessive+ sens of smell)	excessive increase of the sense of smell
hyperpnea	υπέρ-πνοή	abnormally rapid breathing; panting
hyperpyrexia	υπέρ-πυρετός	extremely high fever
hyper-sideremia	υπέρ + σίδερο + αίμα- excessive/ over +iron + blood	the presence of abnormally excessive concentration of iron in the blood
hyper-trichosis	υπερ-τρίχωσις/η	excessive hairiness
hyper-thermia	υπερθέρμια-υπέρ- θέρμανσις/η	abnormal high temperature
hyperthyroid	υπερ-θυρεοειδής	of, relating to, or affected to excessive activity of of the thyroid land
hyper-trophy	υπερτροφία	enlargement of a tissue or organ
hypnagogic	υπνογωγικός, ή, ό (adj.)	causing sleep
hypno-	ύπνος	sleep, combining form (hypnotism)
hypnoanalysis	υπνοανάλυσις/η	the use of hypnosis or hypnotic drugs in combination with psychoanalytic technics
hypnosis	ύπνωσις/η	trance induced through verbal suggestion or concentration upon on a subject

hypnotherapy	υπνοθεραπεία/ ύπνος-θεραπεία/ sleep-treatment	treatment through sleep
hypnotic	υπνωτικός, ή, ό (adj.)	any drug inducing sleep
hypnotism	υπνωτισμός	the study/science of hypnosis
hypnotist	υπνωτιστής	a person who induces hypnosis
hypnotize	υπνωτίζω	to put into a state of hypnosis; spellbind
hypo -	υπό	under; below; beneath (hypodermic)
hypochondria	υποχονδρία	undue concern about one's health/suffering from imaginary illnesses
hypochondriac	υποκχονδριακός, ή, ό (adj.)	one who suffers from hypochondria, always imagining illnesses
hypocoristic	υποκοριστικός, ή, ό (adj.)	calling by endearing names, pet name
hypocrisy	υποκρισία	a pretending to be what one is not; or to feel what one does not feel, esp., a pretense of virtue, piety, philanthropic, etc.
hypocrite	υποκριτής m.)/ υποκρίτρια (f.)	a person who pretends to be someone that is not; a person who pretends to be better than he or she is; mimicry, playing a part
hypoderm/ hypoderma	υπόδερμα	the layer under the skin [hypodermis]
hypodermic	υποδερμικός, ή, ό (adj.)	of the parts under the skin
hypodontia	υπό + δόντια- less/ under – teeth	a congenital condition marked by a less than normal number of teeth: *partial anodontia*
hypodynamic	υπό + δυναμις / δυναμικός, ή, ό (adj.) – under + power/strength)	characterized by or exhibiting a decrease in strength or power [the hupodynamic heart)
hypogastrium	υπογκάστριον	abdominal region

hypogeal	υπόγειος, α, ο (adj.)	underground; 1 of, or occurring in, the region below the the surface of the earth 2 Bot. growing or maturing underground, as peanuts or truffles (esp. cotyledons) 3 burrowing, living, or developing beneath the ground, as certain insect lavrae
hypogeum	υπόγειον/ο	an underground callar; vault; tomb, etc.
hypoglossal	υπογλώσσιον/ο	under the tongue
hypoglycemia	υπογλυκαιμία	condition when the level of the blood sugar is abnormally low or significantly reduced
hypohidrosis	υποίδρωσις /η	abnormally diminished sweating opposed to **Hyper-hidrosis**
hypokinesis	υποκίνησις /η (υπό κίνησις – under + motion)	a condition of abnormally diminished muscular movement; also, hypokinesia
hypolimnion	υπολίμνιον/ο υπό + λίμνη – under + lake/ a pool of standing water	an unfrozen lake's cold, lowermost, stagnant layer of oxygen-poor water that is below the thermocline: opposed to **Epilimnion**
hypomania	υπομανία	a mild form of mania, spec. of themanic phase of manic-depressive psychosis
hypomastia	υπομαστεία	unusually small breasts
hypomenorrhea	υπομηνόρροια	deficient menstruation
hyponoia	υπονόηση/ νοημοσύνη	mental sluggishness
hypophrenia	υποφρένεια/ φρενίτιδα	feeblemindedness
hypophysis	υπόφυσις/η υπό φύειν	undergrowth; underdeveloped
hypopraxia	υποπραξία	deficient activity

hypostasis	υπόστασις/η	supporting foundation; Christian Theo. a) the unique nature of the one God b) any of the three in the Trinity, Father, Son and the Holy Spirit, having the divine nature fully and equally
hypopyon	υπό + πύον- under + pus	a kind of ulcer; an accumulation of pus in the cavity the cornea and the lens of the eye
hypostyle	υπόστυλος (υπο- στύλη-στύλος / under-pillar)	having a roof supported by rows of pillars or columns
hypotaxis	υπόταξις/η	submission; syntactic subordination of one clause or a construction to another
hypotension	υπότασις /η	very low blood pressure
hypotenuse	υποτείνουσα υπό + τείνειν- to subtend/ under +to stretch	the longest side of a right triangle, located opposite the right angle
hypothalamus	υποθάλαμος	the part of the diencephalon (the posterior end of the forebrain) that forms the floor of the third ventricle and regulates many basic body functions, as temperature
hypotheque/ hypothec	υποθήκη	pledge; security or right given to a creditor over a debtor's property without transfer of possession or title
hypothesis	υπόθεσις/η	supposition; an unproven theory
hypothetical	υποθετικός, ή, ό (adj.)	based on, involving, or having the nature of a hypothesis; logic conditional
hypothyroid	υποθυροειδής	deficient thyroid gland
hypotonia	υποτονία/ατονία	very low strength; weakness
hypotonic	υποτονικός, ή, ό (adj.)	having abnormally low tension or tone, esp. of the muscles

hypoxia	υπο-οξίδωση	an abnormal condition due to the decrease in the oxygen supplied to or utilized by body tissue
hypso-	ύψος	height, high, combining word also hyps- before a vowel
hypsography	υψογραφία/ υψογράφιση	the science of measuring the configuration of land or underwater surfaces with respect of to a datum plane, as sea level
hypsometer	υψόμετρον/ο	a device for determining height above sea level by measuring atmospheric pressure; an instrument for measuring the height of trees by triangulation
hypsometry	υψομετρία	the branch of of science dealing with measurement of surface elevations above any level reference plane, esp., sea level
hysterectomy	υστερεκτομή	surgical removal of whole or part of the womb
hysteresis	υστέρησις/η/ υστερείν	deficiency; to be behind, come short
hysteria	υστερία	psychological state; neurosis resulting from failure to face reality
hysterical/hysteric	υστερικός. ή, ό (adj.)	one being in a state of hysteria
hystero-	ύστερο (v)	uterus, womb
hysterogenic	(ο, η) υστερογενής (το) υστερογενές	causing hysteria
hysteroid	(ο, η) υστεροειδής (το) υστεροειδές	resembling hysteria
hysteron proteron	ύστερον πρώτερον (latter/earlier)	a figure of speech in which the logical order of ideas is reversed (ex: I die, I faint, I fail)
hysterotomy	υστεροτομή	incision of the uterus as in a Caesarean section

(All the above, starting with the letter *Hh*, have one thing in common, in ancient and puristic Greek all began with a vowel and were accented with the harsh breathing sign δασεία/thaseia/daseia ('), which in English became *H*, due to the fact the thaseia (') had a soft "h" sound, as in "hoi/οι'."

I

Iamb	ίαμβος	a metrical foot consisting, in Greek and Latin verse, of one short syllable followed by a long one, or, as in English verse, of an unaccented syllable followed by one accented
iambic	ιαμβικός, ή, ό (adj.)	or of made up of iambs; an iambic line of poetry
-iasis	-ίασις	1 process or condition 2 pathological or morbid condition [hypochondriasis] combining form
iatric	ιατρικ/ιατρικός, ιατρική, ιατρικό (adj.)/ ίασθαι- to cure/ heal	medical; medicine, combining form [iatrogenig]
iatrics	ιατρική	the science of medicine
-iatrics	-ιατρική	the treatment of disease; specialty of medicine (as in pediatrics/παιδιατρική) combining form
iatro-	ιατρός/γιατρός	medical doctor; physician, combining form
iatrogenic	(ο, η) ιατρογενής (το) ιατρογενές (adj.)	term meaning "caused by the doctor"
iatrology	ιατρολογία	the study of medicine
-iatry	-ιατρεία (γιατρειά- healing)	medical treatment combining form [psychiatry; podiatry]
Icaria	Ικαρία	Greek island in the Aegean Sea, southwest of Samos
Icarian	Ικαριώτης/ Ικαριώτισσα (masc. + fem)	the inhabitant of Icaria

Icarus	Ἴκαρος	Myth. the son of Daedalus; escaping from Crete by flying with wings made by his father. Icarus flew too close to the sun. The heat melted the wax that kept the wings fastened and he fell to his death in the sea, thus the name: the Icarian Sea
ichneumon	ιχνεύμων (ιχνεύειν/ ίχνος – to track out, to hunt after/ footprint; track)	lit. tracker
ichno-	ίχνος	trace, footprint, track, combining form [ichnology]
ichnogram	ιχνογράφημα	footprint; tracing
ichnography	ιχνογραφία	tracing out; 1 a scale drawing of a ground plan of a building; floor plan 2 the art of planning such plans
ichnology	ιχνολογία	the scientific study of fossil footprints
ichthy-	ιχθύς	fish, combining form
ichthyophobia	ιχθυοφοβία	extreme fear of fish
ichthyosis	ιχθύωσις/η	condition of very dry and scaly skin in babies
icon	εικών/εικόνα	an image, figure, representation; Eastern Orthodox Church; an image of Christ, Mary, a saint, etc., venerated as sacred
iconic	εικονικός, ή, ό (adj.	of, or having the nature of, an icon
icono-	εικών-εικόνος (gen.)	image, figure
iconoclasm	εικονοκλασία	the actions or beliefs of an iconoclast
iconoclast	εικονοκλάστης	one opposed to the religious use of images or avocating the destruction of those images
iconography	εικονογραφία	the art of representing or illustrating pictures, figures, or images, etc.

iconolatry	εικονολατρεία	the worship of icons
iconology	εικονολογία	the study of the meaning of works of visual art through the analysis of subject matter, symbolism, and imagery style and historical context
iconostasis	εικονόστασις/ εικονοστάσιο(v)	Eastern Orthodox Church: a partition or screen adorned with icons, separating the sanctuary from the rest of the church
icosahedron	εικοσάεδρον/ο	a solid figure with twenty plane surfaces
icosi-	είκοσι	twenty, combining form
-ics	-ικος, η, ο (adj.) (-ικα neuter pl.)	combining form (physics/ φυσική –athletics/ αθλητικά, etc.)
icteropatitis	ικτεροπατίτις/ υπατίτιδα	jaundice; inflammation of the liver
icterus/icteros	ίκτερος	jauntice
idea	ιδέα	concept, plan, project; a thought, mental conception or image
ideal	(ο, η) ιδεώδης (το) ιδεώδες	concept of perfection
idealism	ιδεαλισμός	behavior or thought based on a conception of things as they should be or as one would wish them to be; idealization
idealist	ιδεαλιστής (masc.)/ ιδεαλίστρια (fem.)	a person whose behavior or thought is based on ideals; visionary or dreamer
idealistic	ιδεαλιστικός, ή, ό (adj.)	of or characteristic of an idealist
ideo	ιδέα	combining form (ideology)
ideological	ιδεολογικός, ή, ό (adj.)	pertaining to an ideology
ideologue	ιδεολόγος	1 a zealous exponent or advocate of a specified ideology 2 a student or specialist in ideology

ideology	ιδεολογία	1 the study of ideas, their nature and source 2 thinking or theorizing of an idealistic, abstract, or impractical nature; fanciful speculation 3 the doctrines, opinions, or way of thinking of an individual, class, etc., specif. the body of ideas on which a particular political, economic, or social system is based
idio-	ίδιος / ίδια/ίδιο	same, identical; personal; own; [idiotype] combining form
idiosyncrasy	ιδιοσυγκρασία/ ιδιοτροπία/ ιδιορρυθμία	peculiarity, the temperament or mental constitution, any personal peculiarity or mannerism to a person or group, any personal peculiarity, mannerisms, etc.
idiocy	ιδιωτεία	complete slow mental development; the state of being an idiot
idiom	ιδίωμα	form of expression; local dialect
idiopathy	ιδιοπάθεια	disease or condition of which the cause is unknown
idiosyncracy	ιδιοσυγκρασία	mode of behavior; peculiar characteristics
idiot	ιδιώτης	1 common, layman 2 ignorant; having slow mental development
idol	είδωλον-ο	an image of a god, used as an object or instrument of worship
idolater	ειδωλολάτρης	a person who worships an idol or idols
idolatry	ειδωλο-λατρεία	excessive devotion to or reverence for some person or thing; worship of idols
idolize	ειδωλοποιείν/ ειδωλοποιώ	to make an idol; to love or admire excessively; adore

idrosis	ίδρωσις/ιδρώτας/ ιδρώνω	sweating; to sweat
ileitis	ειλεΐτις/ειλεΐτιδα	inflammation of the ilium
ileo-	ειλεο- (ειλεός)	combining form, ileum (ileostomy)
ileocolitis	ειλεοκωλίτις/ ειλεοκωλίτιδα	inflammation of ileum
ileostomy	ειλεοτομή	surgical operation making an opening in the ileum
ileum/ileus	ειλεός	I the lowest part of the small intestine, opening into the large intestine 2 an abnormal condition caused by paralysis or obstruction of the intestine and resulting in the failure of intestinal contents to pass properly
Iliad	Ιλιάς/Ιλιάδα	a long Greek epic poem, attributed to Homer, dealing with events during toward the end of the Trojan War
Ilium	Ίλιον	Latin name for Troy
iodic	(ο, η) ιωδιούχος, το ιωδιούχο(ν) (adj.)	containing iodine
iodine	ιώδιον/ιώδιο	nonmetallic chemical element
iodize	ιώδιο + -ιζειν-ίζω/ iodine + -izo the ending of verbs,)	treating with iodine
iodometry	ιωδιο-μετρία/μέτρο- iodine & measure	measuring amounts of iodine
iodous	(ο, η) ιώδης (το) ιώδες	something containing poison
Ionian (Islands)	Ιόνια νησιά	group of islands in the W. coast of Greece, on the Ionian Sea /Ιωνικό(ν) Πέλαγος
Ionic (style)	Ιωνικός Ρυθμός	this column style is most famous for its scrolls (see: architecture, or, the other two styles, Corinthian and Doric)
iophobia	ιοφοβία	extreme fear of poison, infection

iota (eota)	Ι,ι (ιώτα/γιώτα)	the ninth letter of the Gr. alphabet
iotacism	ιωτακισμός	1 excessive use of the Greek leter iota 2 a change, esp. in Greek, of other vowel sounds to the sound e (ι, iota), represented by this letter
Iphigenia	Ιφιγένεια	Gr. myth. daughter of Agamemnon, offered by him as a sacrifice to Artemis, and in another version, she was saved by the goddess who made her a priestess
Irene	Ειρήνη	peace 1 a feminine name 2 Gr. myth. the goddess of peace, daughter of Zeus and Themis: identified with the Roman Pax
irenic	ειρηνικός, ή, ό (adj.)	promoting peace; pacific; peaceful: Ειρηνικός Ωκεανός-Pacific Ocean
iridectomy	ιριδεκτομή (ιρις/ ιριδα + εκτομή- iris + removal)	surgical removal of the colored part of the eye
iridic	ιριδικός, ή, ό (adj.)	1 or of containing iridium 2 designating or of a chemical compound containing tetravalent iridium 3 of the iris of the eye
irido-	ιρις/ίριδος (gen.)	rainbow; the colored part of the eye combining form
iridotomy	ιριδοτομία	the simple procedure and incision of the iris of the eye
iris	ίρις/ίριδα	1 a rainbow 2 a rainbow like show or play of colors 3 the round, pigmented membrane surrounding the pupil of the eye, having muscles that adjust the size of the pupil to regulate the amount of light entering the eye 4 any of the large genus (Iris) of perennial plants

iritis	ιρίτις/ιρίτιδα	inflammation of the iris
ironic	ειρωνικός, ή, ό (adj.)	meaning the contrary of what is expressed
ironist	είρων	a writer or speaker noted for the frequent use of irony
irony	ειρωνεία	a method of humorous or subtly sarcastic expression in which the intended meaning of the words is the direct opposite of their usual sense (the irony of calling a stupid plan clever)
isagoge	εισαγωγή (εισάγειν – to lead in/ introduce)	an introduction, as to a branch of study
isagogics	εισαγωγική	the study of the literary history of the Bible, considered as introductory to the study of Bible interpretation
ischaemia	ισχαιμία (ισχειν + αίμα- to hold + blood	a lack of blood supply in an organ or tissue
ischium	ισχίον	hip, hip joint; the lowermost of the three sections of the innominate bone; bone on which the body rests when sitting
iseiconia	ίσο + εικόνα (equal +image)	a condition in which the size of the image is the same in both eyes: opposed to Aniseiconia (the size of the image not the same in both eyes)
iso-	ίσος, η, ο (adj.)	equal, identical, combining form
isobar	(ο, η) ισοβαρής) (το) ισοβαρές (adj.) (ίσος + βάρος – equal + weight)	a line on a map connecting points having equal barometric pressure at a given reference altitude, commonly sea level over a given period or a given time 2 any atom that has the same atomic weight (or mass number) as another atom but a different atomic number, as carbon -14 and nitrogen -14

isocracy	ισοκρατία	a system of government in which all persons have equal political power
isochronism	ισοχρονισμ ός	something happening in equal chronical intervals; synchronism
isochronous	ισόχρονος, η, ο (adj.)	one that has the same duration (with another) synchronized 2 something that takes place in consistent intervals (as pulses, vibrations, etc.); regular: opposed to irregular; inconsistent
Isoctates	Ισοκράτης	Athenian orator and rhetorician (436–338 BC)
isocyclic	ισοκυκλικός, ή, ό (adj.)	consisting of or being a ring of atoms of the same element
isodiametric	ισοδιαμετρικός, ή, ό (adj.)	having equal diameters or axes, as certain cells
isodynamic	ισοδυναμικός, ή, ό (adj.)	1 of or having equal force 2 connecting or showing points on the earth's surface having equal magnetic intensity [isodynamic lines on a map]
isoelectronic	ισοηλεκτρονικός, ή, ό (adj.)	designating or of any of two or more atoms which have the same number of electrons around the nucleus and similar spectral and physical properties
isogeothermic	ισογεωθερμικός, ή, ό (adj.)	an imaginary line or curved plane connecting points beneath the earth's surface that have the same average temperature
isogonic	ισογωνικός, ή, ό (adj.)	1 of or having equal angles 2 connecting or showing points on the earth's surface that they have the same average temperature

isomer	(ο, η) ισομερής (το) ισομερές (adj.)	1 Chem. any of two or more chemical compounds having the same constituent elements in the same proportion by weight but differing in the structure of their molecules 2 Physics any of two or more nuclei possessing the same number of neutrons and protons, but existing in different energy states, and thus having different radioactive properties
isomerism	ισομερισμός	the state or relation of isomers
isometric	ισομετρικός, ή, ό (adj.	1 of, indicating, or having equality of measure 2 [pl.] a method of physical exercise in which one set of muscles is tensed, for a periods of seconds, in opposition to another set of muscles or to an immovable object
isometry	ισομετρία	1 equality of measure 2 Geog. equality of height above sea level
isomorphic	ισομορφικός, ή, ό (adj.)	1 having similar or identical structure or form Biol., Chem. showing isomorphism
isomorphism	ισομορφισμός	1 Biol. a similarity in appearance or structure of organisms belonging to different species or races 2 Chem. an identity or close similarity in the crystalline form of substances usually containing different elements but having similar composition 3 Math. one-to-one correspondence between two mathematical systems, sets, etc., that preserves the basic operations, as the correspondence between binary numbers and decimal numbers, each a set of real numbers

isonomia	ισονομία	equality of laws, rights, or privileges
isosceles	ισοσκελές	Geom. designating a figure with two equal sides, esp., a triangle
isoseismal	ισοσεισμικός, ή, ό (adj.) – ίσος + σεισμός/ equal + earthquake	1 of equal intensity of earthquake shock 2 connecting or showing points of such equal intensity on the earth's surface [isoseismal lines on a map]
isotone	ισότονο	any atom that has the same number of neutrons as another atom but a different atomic number
isotonic	ισοτονικός, ή, ό (adj.)	Chem. solution that presents the same osmotic pressure as another
isthmian	ίσθμιος, α, ο (adj.)	of an isthmus; of the Isthmus of Panama; of the Isthmus of Corinth, or the games held there in ancient times; a native or inhabitant of an isthmus
isthmus	ισθμός	1 a narrow strip of land having water at each side and connecting two larger bodies of land 2 Anat. the narrow part of an organ
ixia	ιξός	1 a parasitic plant 2 birdlime: from the viscid nature of some of the species; any of a genus (Ixia) of South African plants of the iris family, with grasslike leaves and funnel-shaped flowers

J

Jason	Ιάσων/Ιάσονας (lit. healer)	Gr. myth. who leads the Argonauts and with Medea's help gets the Golden Fleece; masculine name

jealous	ζηλότυπος, η, ο (adj.)-ζηλιάρης	envious; possessive; one characterized by jealoucy
jealousy	ζηλοτυπία - ζήλεια	1 the adverse feeling one has toward someone who succeeds in life or who has more than him 2 the condition when a partner believes or suspects that his/her spouse is cheating; envy
Jocasta	Ιοκάστη	Gr. myth. the queen who unwittingly marries her son, Oedipus; when she finds out kills herself
Judaea/Judea	Ιουδαία	ancient region of S Palestine under Persian, Greek, and Roman rule
Judaic	Ιουδαϊκός, ή, ό (adj.)	1 of Judah 2 of the Jews or Judaism; Jewish
Judaism	Ιουδαϊσμός	1 the Jewish religion, a monotheistic religion based on the laws and teachings of the Holy Scriptures and the Talmud 2 the Jewish way of life; observance of Jewish morality, traditions, ceremonies, etc. 3 Jews collectively; Jewry
Judas (Iscariot)	Ιούδας (Ισκαριώτης)	Bible the disciple who betrayed Jesus: Matt: 26:14, 48

K

Kaino-	καινός, ή, ό/ καινούριος, α, ο (Mod. Gr.) (adj.)	new, combining form
kainophobia	καινοφοβία	extreme fear of new things
kakosmia	κακοσμία (κακός + οσμή/ bad + smell)	foul odor
kakotrophy	κακοτροφία (κακός, ή, ό + τροφή / bad + food)	malnutrition

kaleidoscope	καλός –είδος – σκόπιον (good/ beautiful, type/ form, scope)	tubular instrument containing colorful pieces of glass, plastic, etc., forming beautiful images
Kappa	Κκ- κάππα	tenth letter of the Greek alphabet
karyo-	κάρυον	1 kernel, nut 2 Biol. the nucleus of a cell combining form (karyolymph)
karyokinesis	καρυο-κίνησις	mitosis: the indirect and more comm. on method of nuclear division of cells (see **mitosis**)
karyolymph	καρυο – λύμφη/ λέμφος	a colorless, watery liquid found inside of the nucleus cell
karyoplasm	καρυόπλασμα (κάρυο + πλάσμα	neucleoplasm
kata-	κατά	down (see cata- for more definitions)
katabatic	καταβατικός, ή, ό (adj)	moving downward: said of air currents or winds
katabolic	καταβολικός, ή, ό (adj.)	relating to katabolism
katabolism	καταβολισμός	breaking down process in metabolism
katharevousa	καθαρεύουσα	[Mod. Gr. lit. being pure] the form of modern Greek language that conforms to classical Greek usage and it was the official language of Greece till 1976
katharsis/ catharsis	κάθαρσις/η	purification (see catharsis)
kelotomy	κοιλοτομή	relief of hernia strangulation by incision
keno-	κενός, ή, ό (adj.)	empty, vacant
kenophobia	κενοφοβία	extreme fear of empty spaces
kenosis	κένωσις/η (κενός, η, ό – empty)	an emptying; Christian Theol. the voluntary self-abasement of second person of the Trinity in becoming human
kenotic	κενωτικός, ή, ό (adj.)	pertaining to kenosis

keratin	κερατίνη	a tough, fibrous, insoluble protein forming the principle matter of hair, nails, horn, etc.
keratitis	κερατίτις-κερατίτιδα	inflammation of the cornea
kerato-	κέρατο(ν)	horn, combining form
keratoectomy	κερατοεκτομή/ κερατοτομία	surgical removal of part of the cornea
keratogenous	(ο, η)κερατογενής (το) κερατογενές (adj.)	causing the growth of horny tissue
keratoid	(ο, η) κερατοειδής (το) κερατοειδές (adj.)	hornlike, horny
keratoma	κεράτωμα	horny growth
keratoplasty	κερατοπλαστική	surgical procedure of grafting new corneal tissue onto the eye
keratosis	κεράτωσις/η	a horny growth of the skin, as a wart
keratotomy	κερατοτομή	surgical incision of the cornea
kero-	κηρός/κερί	wax, combining form
kerogen	κηρογενές	solid bituminous material in some shales, which yields petroleum when heated
kerosene	κηροζίνη	a thin oil distilled from petroleum or shale oil, used as fuel, solvent, illuminant, etc.; coal oil. Also, esp. in scientific and industrial usage, esp. keroseni
kerygma	κήρυγμα	preaching, sermon, proclamation
kilo-	κιλό-χίλια	a thousand, combining form
kilogram	χιλιόγραμμο	a thousand grams
kilometer	χιλιόμετρο	a thousand meters
kinematics	κινηματική (κίνημα/κινήματος (gen)/ κινείν - / motion/to move	the branch of mechanics dealing with motion in the abstract, without reference to the force or mass
kinescope	κινητοσκόπιον/ο	1 picture tube 2 a film recording of a television program

kinesics	κίνησις-κινείν/ κινούμαι- motion/ to move	the study of facial and bodily movements
kinesiology	κίνησις/η + λόγος/ κινησιολογία	science of human muscular movements (as in physical education)
kinesthesia/ kinaesthesia	κιναισθησία (κινείν + αίσθησις- to move + perception)	the sensation of position, movement, tension, etc., of parts of the body, perceived through nerve-end organs in muscles, tendons and joints. Also, **Kinesthesis**
kinetic	(κίνησις) – κινητικός. ή, ό (adj.) (movement, motion);	energetic, dynamic; of or caused by motion
kinetic energy	κινητική ενέργεια	the energy of a body, that results from its motion
kinetics	κινητική	1 the branch of mechanics dealing with the motions of material bodies under the action of given forces; dynamics
kinetic theory	κινητική θεωρία	the theory that the minute particles of all matter are in constant motion and that the temperature of a substance is dependent on the velocity of this motion, increased motion being accompanied by increased temperature: according to the kinetic theory of gases, the elasticity, diffusion, pressure, and other physical properties of a gas are due to the rapid motion in straight lines of the molecules, to their impacts against each other and the walls of the container, to weak cohesive forces between molecules, etc.
kineto-	κινητός, ή, ό (adj.)	moving, being able to move from one point to another with ease, combining form (kinetoplast)

klepht	κλέφτης	1 thief 2 a member of the brave Greek patriot bands who fought the Ottoman Empire
kleptomania	κλεπτομανία	an abnormal persistent impulse to steal, not prompted by need
kleptomaniac	(ο, η) κλεπτομανής (το) κλεπτομανές (adj.)	one suffering from kleptomania
koine	κοινός, ή, ό (adj.) κοινή (fem) κοινή διάλεκτος/ common dialect	1 the language used throughout the Greek world, from Syria to Gaul, during the Hellenistic and Roman periods: the spoken language consisted of colloquial Attic, enhanced by Ionic words and supplemented by other dialects, the language of that period is also known as Hellenistic Greek in which the New Testament / Καινή Διαθήκη, is written 2 a regional dialect or language that has become the common language of a larger area
kolp-	κόλπ(ος)	pertaining to vagina
kolpitis	κολπίτις-κολπίτιδα	inflammation of the vagina
kopiopia	κόπος- οπια-ωπία (strain/labor and (eye)sight)	eyestrain
Kos	Κως	Greek island in the Dodecanese, off the SW coast of Turkey
krater	κρατήρ/κρατήρας	an ancient Greek jar with broad body, a wide neck, and two handles, used for mixing water and wine
Krete	Κρήτη	see Crete
kreotoxism	κρέας-τοξικός, ή, ό (adj.)	meat poisoning
Kronos	Κρόνος/Χρόνος	Myth. the son of Earth and the Sky/Uranus, father of Zeus and the other gods 2 Astron. a planet

krypton	κρυπτόν/ό	something done in secrecy
kudos	κύδος (Anc. Gr.)	glory, fame, honor; high praise
kurtosis	κύρτωσις/η (κυρτός, ή, ό (adj.)	bending; hump; stooping
kylix	κήλιξ	a lavishly decorated, ancient Greek cup with a stem and a wide, shallow bowl; also cylix
kymo-	κύμα	wave
kymogram	κυμογράφημα	the chart produced by kymograph
kymograph	κυμογράφος	an apparatus consisting of a rotating drum for recording wavelike motions, variations, or modulations, such as muscular contractions
kymoid	(ο, η) κυμοειδής (το) κοιμοειδές (adj.)	resembling wave or wavelike movements
kyogenic	(ο, η) κυογενής/ (το) κυογενές	causing pregnancy
kyphosis	κύφωσις /η	condition in which the spine is abnormally curved in the chest area
kyphotic	κυφωτικός, ή, ό (adj.)	having an abnormal curvature of the spine resulting in a hump
Kyrie Eleison	Κύριε Ελέησον	Lord have Mercy: Ps. 123:3, Matt. 15:22
Kythera/Cythera	Κύθηρα	see: Cythera

Most English words deriving from Greek words starting with a *K*, in English are spelled with a *C*.
(See letter *C*,)

L

Labarum	λάβαρον/ο	a royal cavalry standard carried before enperors or kings, in war, esp. the one carried for the first time by Constantine, being the first emperor who had adopted Christianity

labyrinth	λαβύρινθος	complicated irregular network of passages or paths; maze; the first built by King Minos of Crete to house the Minotaur
Laconia	Λακωνία	now a region of the SE coast of Peloponessus, GR. In ancient Greece it was a separate country (state) dominated by the city-state Sparta
laconic	λακωνικός, ή, ό (adj.) (Λάκων-λάκωνος (gen.)/ Λάκωνας) (mod. Gr.)	of, or Laconia; Laconians known for their frugality of words and expressions, however, words or expressions uttered were profound and meaningful; using very few words
laconism	λακωνισμός (λακωνίζειν - to speak in brief)	1 brevity of speech or expression 2 laconic speech or expression
laic	λαϊκός, ή, ό (adj.) (λαός- the people)	of the laity; secular; layman
lambda	(Λ,λ) λάμδα	eleventh letter of the Greek alphabet
lambdoid	(ο, η) λαμδοειδής (το) λαμδοειδές (adj.)	shaped like the Gr. letter Λ/L
laparoscope	λαπαροσκόπιον/ο	a, usually, rigid endoscope that is inserted through an incision in the abdominal wall and is used to examine visually the interior of the peritoneal cavity, called *peritoneoscope*
laparoscopist	λαπαροσκόπος	a physician or surgeon performing laparoscopies
laparoscopy	λαπαροσκόπησις/η	1 visual examination of the abdomen by means of a laparoscope 2 an operation (as tubal ligation or gallbladder removal) involving laparoscopy
laparotomy	λαπαροτομία/ λαπαροτομή	surgical section of the abdominal wall

laryngeal	λαρυγγικός, ή, ό (adj.)	of, in, or near the larynx; used for treating the larynx
laryngectomy	λάρυγγεκτομή	surgical removal of part or all of the larynx
laryngitis	λαρυγγκίτις/ λαρυγγκίτιδα	temporary loss of voice; inflammation of the larynx
laryngo-	λάρυγγο- (λάρυνξ/ λάρυγγκος (gen.)	larynx, combining form
laryngologist	λαρυγγολόγος	specialist in laryngology
laryngo-logy	λαρυγγολογία	branch of medicine dealing with diseases of the larynx
laryngoscope	λαρυγγοσκόπιον/ο	a special instrument for examining the larynx and adjacent organs
laryngoscopy	λαρυγγοσκόπησις/η	Med. examination of the larynx and the phonetic chords
laryngotomy	λαρυγγοτομή/ λαρυγγοτομία	an incision of the larynx to relieve pain resulting from disease or injury
larynx	λάρυνξ-λάρυγκας (Mod. Gr.)	the passage connecting the pharynx and trachea (windpipe)
latria	λατρεία/λατρεύειν (worship/to worship)	worship which is due to God alone: distinguished from dulia/slavery
-latry	-λατρεία	indicating devotion to; suffix forming nouns (ex: plutolatria/ πλουτολατρεία- excessive devotion to wealth, etc.)
lemniscus	λημνίσκος	a band of sensory fibers and esp. nerve fibers, in the central nervous system, usually terminating in the thalamus; also called fillet; *Medial Lemniscus*
lemo-stenosis	λαιμο-στένωσις/η	stricture of the esophagus
Leonidas	Λεωνίδας	King of Sparta (c. 508–480 BC) who fought bravely, along with his three hundred Spartans, the Persans in Thermopylae, was defeated due to treachery
leper or leprous	λεπρός	one afflicted with leprosy

lepra	λέπρα/λέπρωσις/η	leprosy/an infectious disease caused by the microorganism mycobacterium: leprae
leprologist	λεπρολόγος	a specialist in the study of leprosy and its treatment
leprology	λεπρολογία	study of leprosy
leproma	λέπρωμα	a nodular lesion of leprosy
lepromatous leprocy	λεπρωματική λέπρα	the one of the two major forms of leprosy that is characterized by the formation of lepromas, the presence of numerous Hansen's bacilli in the lesions, and a negative skin reaction to lepromin and that remains infectious to others until treated—compare **Tuberculoid Leprocy**
leprocin	λεπροσίνη	an extract of human leprous tissue used in a skin test for leprocy infection
leprostatic	λεπροστατικός, ή, ό (adj.)	an agent that inhibits the growth of Hansen's bacillius
leprosy	λέπρωσις/λέπρα	a progressive infectious disease caused by infection with an acid-fast bacillus of the genus **Mycobacterium** (M. leprae) and characterized by the formation of nodules on the surface of the body and esp. on the face or by the appearance of tuberculoid macules on the skin that change and spread and are accompanied by loss of sensation, followed later in both types, if not treated, by involvement of nerves with eventual paralysis, wasting of muscle, and production of deformities and mutilations; also called Hansen's disease, lepra; the two types: **Lepromatous Leprosy and Tuberculoid Leprosy**

lepto-	λεπτό- (λεπτός, ή, ό (adj.)	thin, skinny, slender, fine
lepto-dermic	λεπτο-δερμικός, ή, ό (adj.)	thin-skinned
leptophonia	λεπτοφωνή λεπτό + φωνή/ thin + voice	having a feeble voice
lesbian	λεσβεία/λεσβία	a woman homosexual (attributed to the poetess Sappho and her followers in the island of Lesbos)
lesbianism	λεσβιασμός	homosexuality between women
Lesbos	Λέσβος/Μυτιλήνη	a Greek. island of the Aegean Sea
lethargic	ληθαργικός, ή, ό (adj.)	one lacking energy
lethargy	ληθαργία	lack of energy or stupor: a state in which the mind and senses are dulled
Lethe	Λήθη/λήθη	forgetfulness; oblivion, etc. Gr. and Rom. myth. the river of forgetfulness, flowing through Hades, whose water produces loss of memory in those who drink of it.
leukemia	λευκαιμία	any of a group of neoplastic diseases of the blood-forming organs, resulting in an abnormal increase of leucocytes, accompanied often by anemia and enlargement of the lymph nodes, spleen, and liver. Also **leukaemia**
leukemic	λευκαιμικός, ή, ό (adj.)	one affected by leukemia
leukemo-genesis	λευκαιμο-γένεσις	induction or production of leukemia
leukemoid	(ο, η) λευκαιμοειδής (το) λευκαμοειδές	resembling leukemia; leukemialike
leuko-	λευκό-(λευκός, ή, ό (adj.)	white or light-colored; or colorless, combining form

leucocyte	λευκοκύτταρον/ο	white blood cell; any of the small, colorless nucleated cells in the blood, lymph, and tissues, which are important in the body's defenses against infection, including granular types such as neutrophils, eosinophils, and basophils, also, nongranular types such as lymphocytes and monocytes; white blood corpuscle
leukodermia/ leukoderma	λευκοδερμία/ λευκόδερμα	condition in which there is loss of skin pigment in certain parts of the body; white patches of the skin
leuko-dystrophy	λευκο-δυστροφία	any of several inherited diseases characterized by progressive degeneration of myelin in the brain, spinal cord, and peripheral nerves
leuko-encephalopathy	λευκο-εγκεφαλο-πάθεια	any of various diseases affecting the brain's white matter; esp. **Progressive Maltifocal Leukoencephalopathy**
leucoma	λεύκωμα	a dense, white opacity of the cornea, caused by injury or inflammation
leuko-nychia	λευκονυχία (λευκό + νύχια – white + nails)	a white spotting, streaking, or discoloration of the fingernails caused by injury or disease
leukorrhea	λευκόρροια	whitish, yellowish, or greenish discharge from the vagina resulting from inflammation or congestion of the uterine or vaginal mucous membrane
leukosarcoma	λευκοσάρκωμα	lymphosarcoma accompanied by leukemia
leukosis	λεύκωσις/η	abnormal pallor; leukemia; any of various leukemic diseases of paultry

leukotome	λευκοτόμος	a canula through which a wire is inserted and used to cut the white matter in the brain in lobotomy
leucotomy	λευκοτομή	lobotomy; surgical severance of nerve fibers connecting the frontal lobes to the thalamus, for the relief of some mental disorders
lexi- prefix	λέξις/η	word, combining form
lexical	λεξικός, ή, ό (adj.)	a stock of words, organized vocabulary
lexicographer	λεξικογράφος (λεξικόν - dictionary/ γράφειν –to write)	a person who writes or compiles a dictionary
lexicography	λεξικογραφία	the writing or compiling a dictionary/dictionaries
lexicologist	λεξικολόγος	a specialist in dictionaries
lexicology	λεξικολογία	the study of the meaning(s) and origin(s) of words
lexicon	λεξικόν	a dictionary; the special vocabulary of a particular author, a field of study, etc., the full vocabulary of a language (esp. an ancient one); Linguis. The total stock of morphemes in a language
lexicostatistics	λεξικό-στατιστική	a technique used in **glottochronology** ΓΛΩΣΣΟΧΡΟΝΟΛΟΓΙΑ to determine the time when the languages under study separated, based on the statistical comparison of sample word lists from those languages
lexiphile	λέξις- φίλος / φίλος λέξεων	lover of words, someone having extreme love for words
lexis	λέξις /η	word

lichen	λειχήν/λειχήνας	any of various small plants composed of a particular fungus and a particular alga growing in an intimate symbiotic association and forming a dual plant, commonly adhering in colored patches or spongelike branches to rock, wood, soil, etc. 2 any of various skin diseases characterized by papules and enlarged skin markings
lichenology	λειχηνολογία	the study of lichens
licorice	γλυκόριζα (γλυκύς +ρίζα- sweet + root)	1 a European perennial plant (Glycyrrhiza glabra) of the pea family, with spikes of blue flowers and short, flat podes 2 the dried root of this plant or the black extract made from it, used in medicine 3 candy flavored with this extract or in imitation of it
limnetic	λιμναίος, α, ο (adj.) λίμνη/lake	designating of, or living in the open waters of lakes away from shore vegetation
limnology	λιμνολογία	the science dealing with the physical, chemical, and biological properties and features of fresh waters, esp. lakes and ponds
limnophobia	λιμνοφοβία	excessive fear and avoidance of lakes and ponds
lion	λέων/λέοντος (gen.) λιοντάρι (mod. Gr.)	1 a large, powerful cat 2 a person of great courage and strength 3 a prominent person who is in demand socially; celebrity
lip-	λίπος	fat, fatty tissue, combining form before a vowel (lipaemia)
lipaemia/lipemia	λιπαιμία	the presence of an excess of fats or lipids in the blood; specif. *Hypercholesterolemia*

lipectomy	λιπεκτομή	the excision of subcutaneous fatty tissue esp. as a cosmetic surgical procedure
lipo-	λίπος	fat or fatty, combining form
lipoatrophy	λιποατροφία	an allergic reaction to insulin medication that is manifested as a loss of sucuteneous fat
lipo-chondro-dystrophy	λίπο-χοντρο-δυστροφία/ thick fat +dystrophy	mucopolysaccharidosis: any of a group of inherited disorders (as Hunter's syndrome and Hurler's syndrome) of glycosaminoglycan matabolism that are characterized by the accumulation of glykosaminiglycans in the tissues and their excretion in the urine
lipodystrophy	λιποδυστροφία	a disorder of fat metabolism, esp. involving loss of fat from, or deposition of fat in tissue
lipogenesis	λιπογένεσις/η	1 formation of fat in the living body, esp. when excessive or abnormal 2 the formation of fatty acids from acetyl coenzyme A in the living body
lipoid	(ο, η) λιποειδής (το) λιποειδές (adj.)	any of various substances resembling fat
lipolysis	λίπος + λύσις / fat + solution)	the decomposition of fat, as during digestion; the hydrolysis of fat
lipoma	λίπωμα	fatty tumor, usually benign
lipoprotein	λιπο-πρωτεϊνη	a complex of fat and protein molecules
liporous	λιπαρός, ή, ό (adj.)	fat; fatty; greasy
liposarcoma	λιποσάρκωμα	cancerous tumor composed of undeveloped fat cells
litany	λιτανεία	1 series of fixed invocations and responses, used in prayers 2 a repetitive recitation, listing, or specification; a request

liter/litre	λίτρον/ο	a pound; the basic metric unit of capacity equal to 1 cubic decimeter or 61.025 cubic inches (1.0567 liquid quartsor .908 dry quart): it is the volume of a kilogram of distilled water at 4 degrees Celcius)
lithiasis	λιθίασις /η	formation of stone in the body (e.g., gallstones)
lithic	λιθικός, ή, ό (adj.)	1 of stone 2 Chem. of lithium 3 Med. of calculi
litho-	λίθος	stone, rock
lithograph	λιθογράφημα	a print or copy by the process of lithography
lithography	λιθογραφία	the art or process of printing from a flat stone or a metal plate by a method based on the repulsion between grease and water
lithoid	(ο, η) λιθοειδής (το) λιθοειδές (adj.)	having the nature of a stone; stonelike
lithology	λιθολογία	1 the scientific study of rocks, usually with the naked eye or with a little magnification 2 loosely, the structure and composition of a rock formation
lithometeor	λιθομετέωρον/ο	solid material, except ice, suspended in the atmosphere, as dust, smoke or pollen
lithophytes	λιθόφυτον/ο	a plant that grows on rock surfaces
lithosphere	λιθόσφαιρα	the solid, rocky part of the earth; the earth's crust
lithotomy	λιθοτομή	surgical procedure to remove stones from the bladder
liturgical	λειτουργικός, ή, ό (adj.)	of, or constituting a liturgy 2 used or using a liturgy
liturgics	λειτουργική	the study of liturgies, or the forms of public worship

liturgist	λειτουργός	1 a person who advocates the use of a liturgy 2 a priest or a specialist in liturgies
liturgy	λειτουργία	in the Eastern Orthodox Church, called the Divine Liturgy/Θεία Λειτουργία; the Eucharistic Service 2 prescribed forms for public worship in any of various religions or churches
lobe	λοβός	a round projecting part; specif. a) the fleshy lower end of the human ear b) any of the main divisions of an organ separated by fissures, etc. [a lobe of the brain, lung, or liver] c) any of the major divisions of a simple leaf that is not divided completely to the midrib or base d) any of the loops in the radiation pattern of a television antenna
lobectomy	λοβεκτομή	the surgical removal of a lobe, as of a lung
lobotomy	λοβοτομή	an incision to a lobe
lochia	λοχεία	the uterine discharge from the vagina that occurs for several days after childbirth
logarithm	λογάριθμος (λόγος + αριθμός – word +number)	Math. the exponent expressing the power to which a fixed number (the base) must be raised in order to produce a given number (the antilogarithm): logarithms computed to the base 10 are often used for shortening mathematical calculations
logarithmic	λογαριθμικός, ή, ό (adj.)	pertaining to logarithms, equations
logic	λογική	the science of correct reasoning/valid induction or deduction

logical	λογικός, ή, ό (adj.)	pertaining to the principles of logic
logician	λογικιστής	expert in logic
logistic	λογιστικός, ή, ό (adj.)	skilled in calculation
logistics	λογιστική	the branch of military science having to do with procuring, maintaining, and transporting materials (weapons, etc.), personnel, and facilities
logo- prefix	λόγος	speech, discourse, study
logogram	λογόγραμμα	letter/character or symbol used to represent an entire word
logography	λογογραφή	speech writing
logogriph	λογόγριφος (λόγος / γρίφος)	word riddle
logomachy	λογομαχεία	strife, contention in words or argument about words
logophile	λογόφιλος / φίλος λόγου	friend; lover of words or speech
logorrhea	λογόρροια/ λογοδιάρροια	excessive talkativeness, esp. when incoherent and uncontrollable
logos	λόγος	word/reason/thought; it is almost impossible to define fully the Gr. word (LOGOS): it can mean "word" (of course), "discourse," "mind," "scheme," "speech," or many other things
logotype	λογότυπος	single type body or matrix containing a short, often-used letters or words
lordosis	λόρδωσις/η	forward curvature of the spine, producing a hollow in the back
lotus	λωτός	Gr. Legend a) a fruit that was supposed to induce a dreamy languor and forgetfulness b) the plant bearing the fruit, variously supposed to be the date, the jujube, persimmon, etc. 2 any of various waterlilies, esp. the white lotus

loxodromic	λοξοδρομικός, ή, ό (adj.)	one having taken an oblique course
loxodromics	λοξοδρομία/ λοξοδρόμησις/η	swerving; diversion
lycanthrope	λυκάνθρωπος (λύκος + άνθρωπος- wolf + man)	werewolf
lycanthropy	λυκανθρωπία	1 [Archaic] a mental illness in which one imagines of being a wolf 2 *Folklore*, the magical power to transform oneself or another to a wolf
Lyceum	λύκειον/ο	1 so called from the neighboring temple of Apollon Lykeios] 2 the grove at Athens where Aristotle taught 3 in Greece the equivalent of the US high school
lychnis	λυχνίς/λυχνίδος / λυχνίδα (λύχνος – lamp)	light; lamp 1 any of a genus (Lychnis) of plants of the pink family, with red, pink, or white flowers
Lycurgus	Λυκούργος	real or legendary Spartan lawgiver of about the ninth c. BC
lymph	λύμφη/λέμφος	a clear, yellowish fluid resembling blood plasma
lymphadenitis	λυμφοαδενίτις/ λέμφο-αδενίτιδα	inflammation of the lymph nodes
lymphangitis	λυμφαγγίτις/ λεμφαγγίτιδα	inflammation of the lymphatic vessels
lympho-	λέμφος/λύμφη	lymph, combining form (lymphocyte)
lymphocytosis	λεμφοκύτωσις/η	a condition characterized by an increase in the number of lymphocytes in the blood, as in acute or chronic infection
lymphoma	λέμφωμα	any of a group of diseases characterized by progressive enlargement of lymphoid tissue resulting from the proliferation of malignant lymphoid cells

lymphopoeisis	λεμφοποίησις/η	the production of lymphocytes
lynx	λύνξ	any of the genus (Lynx) of wild cats; prob. so named from its shining eyes
lyra/lyre	λύρα	a small stringed instrument of the harp family, used by the ancient Greeks to accompany singers and reciters
lyric	λυρικός, ή, ό (adj.)	suitable for singing as of the accompaniment of the lyre, songlike; specif., designating poetry, expressing the poet's emotions and feelings; sonnets, elegies, hymns, etc., are lyric poems
lyrical	λυρικός, ή, ό (adj.)	lyric: characterized by or expressing rapture or great enthusiasm
lyricism	λυρισμός	1 lyric quality, style or character [Shelley's lyricism] 2 emotional and poetic expression of enthusiasm, etc.
lyricist	λυρικός/ λυριστής	writer of lyrics, esp. lyrics for popular songs
lysi-	λύσι(ς)/η	freeing, dissolving, loosening, prefix forming nouns (lysimeter)
-lysis	λύσις /η	loosening, dissolving, solution; the process of cell destruction through the action of specific lysins; the gradual ending of disease symptoms, combining form (analysis)
-lyte	lytos/lyein anc. Gr	a substance subjected to a process of decomposition (electrolyte), combining form
-lytic	λυτικός, ή, ό (adj.)	1 of, relating to, or causing (a specified kind of) dissolution or decomposition 2 Biochem. undergoing hydrolysis by enzymes, suffix forming adjectives (as in analytic/αναλυτικός)

lytta	λύσσα	[lit. madness] thought to be a worm under a dog's tongue causing rabbies, a band of cartilage lying along the underside of the tongue of dogs and certain other carnivores
-lyze	λύω/λύειν	analyze, electrolyze, etc., suffix forming verbs

M

Macedon	Μακεδών/ Μακεδόνος (gen.)/ Μακεδόνας	Mod. Gr. an inhabitant of Macedonia
Macedonia	Μακεδονία	1 province of Northern Greece with Thessaloniki as its capital 2 ancient kingdom in SE Europe devided among Greece, the country of Macedonia, and Bulgaria 3 country in the Balkan Peninsula: formerly (1946–1991) a constituent republic of Yugoslavia
machine	μηχανή	an engine, a structure consisting of a framework and various fixed and moving parts, for doing some special work
macro-	μακρύς-μάκρος/ long-length	combining form (macrobiotics)
macrobiosis	μακροβίωσις /η	longevity
macrobiotics	μακροβιωτική	the study of prolonging life
macrocephalus	μακροκέφαλος	having an unusually long head
macrocephaly	μακροκεφαλία	a condition in which the head or cranial capacity is abnormally large opposed to Microcephaly /μικροκεφαλία-abnormally small head
macrocosm	μακρόκοσμος	the great world, long world, the universe (opposite:microcosm/ small world)

macrodont	μακρόδοντα (μακρυά/μεγάλα & δόντια)	having large (long) teeth
macroeconomics	μακρό-οικονομικά	the branch of economics dealing with all the forces at work of the or with the interrelationship of large sectors, as in employment or income
macropodia	μακρυα-πόδια	having large (long) feet/legs
macropterous	μακρόπτερος, η, ο (adj.)	having unusually long (large) wings/ fins
macroscopic	μακροσκοπικός, ή, ό (adj.)	being visible to the naked eye, opposed to microscopic: not visible to the naked eye
macrosomia	μακρύ-σωμα	gigantism, long/large-bodied
macruran	μακρά-ουρά	long tail. Any of various macropods with long abdomens, including lobsters and shrimp
maenad	μαινάς/μαινάδος (gen.) μαινάδα (μαίνεσθαι- to rave)	1 a female votary of Dionysus, who took part in the wild, orgiastic rites that characterized his worship 2 a frenzied or raging woman
Magi-	μάγος/μάγοι	member of a priestly caste, the wise men; magician
magic	μάγια /μαγεία	the use of charms, spells, and rituals in seeking or pretending to cause or control events, or govern certain natural or supernatural forces; occultism
magical	μαγικός, ή, ό (adj.)	fantastic; extraordinary results
magician	μάγος	an expert in magic; sorcerer; wizard
magnet	μαγνήτης	any piece of certain kinds of material, iron, that has the property of attracting like material; a person or thing that attracts

magnetic	μαγνητικός, ή, ό (adj.)	having the properties of a magnet (as in magnetic needle; magnetic force, etc.)
magnetic pole	μαγνητικός πόλος	1 either pole of a magnet, where the magnetic lines of force seem to be concentrated 2 either point on the earth's surface toward which the needle of a magnetic compass points: the north and south magnetic poles do not precisely coincide with the geographical poles
magnetics	μαγνητική	the branch of physics dealing with magnets and magnetic phenomena
magnetism	μαγνητισμός	the property, quality, or condition of being magnetic; power to attract
magnetize	μαγνητίζω	1 to make into a magnet; give magnetic to steel, iron, etc.
magneto-	μαγνήτο-	see magnet, combining form (magnetosphere)
magnetometer	μαγνητόμετρον/ο	1 an instrument for measuring magnetic forces esp. the earth's magnetic field 2 an instrument for detecting the presence of magnetic materials by their influence on the local magnetic field: often used to screen for weapons at airports, etc.
magnetosphere	μαγνητόσφαιρα	a region surrounding a planet in which the planet's magnetic field is stronger than the interplanetary field: the solar wind gives it a cometlike shape with the tail extending from the night side of the planet for vast distances

Μαία	Μαία	Gr. Lit. mother (baby talk for meter/metera/μήτηρ/ μητέρα,(Gr. myth. one of the Pleiades. Mother of Hermes by Zeus. Later the month of May was named in her honor)
maia	μαία/μαμμή	midwife
maieutics	μαιευτική	obstetrics; designating or of the Socratic method of helping a person bring forth and become aware of latent ideas or memories. a method Socrates adopted from his mother who was a maia/midwife
malaco-	μαλακός, ή, ό (adj.) μαλακό- neu. of μαλακός	soft combining form (malacology)
malacosarkosis	μαλακο-σάρκωσις/η	softness of muscle tissue
malacosteon	μαλακο-οστά / οστέων/of bones (gen.)	softness of the bones
malacostraca	μαλακόστρακα	of a large class (Malacostraca) of highly evolved crustaceans typically consisting of nineteen segments, including the decapods, krill, and isopods
malactic	μαλακτικός, ή, ό adj.)	having the quality of being soft
mania	μανία	violent passion or desire/ extreme behavior
maniac	μανιακός, ή, ό (adj.)	showing excessive anger; obsessed by violent passion or desire
mantic	μαντικός, ή, ό (adj.)	of or having powers of divination; prophetic; seer
mantis	μάντης	Gr. a prophet, seer, a kind of insect; any of an order (Mantodea) of slender, elongated insects that feed on other insects and grasp their prey with stout, spiny forelegs often held up together as if praying

marasmus	μαρασμός	a wasting away; a condition of progressive emaciation, esp. in infants, as from inability to assimilate food
Marathon	Μαραθών/ Μαραθώνας	ancient Greek village in E Attica or a plain nearby, where the Athenians under Miltiades defeated the Persians under Darius I (490 BC)
Marathon race	Μαραθώνιος αγώνας	1 a footrace of 26 miles, 385 yards, run over an open course, esp. as an event of the Olympic Games or as an annual athletic event in various cities: after the legendary Greek runner (said by some historians to be Phidippides) who ran from the battlefield of Marathon to Athens to announce their victory over the Persians, exhausted, uttered "NENIKIKAMEN/ WE HAVE WON" collapsed and died 2 any long-distance or endurance contest
marble	μάρμαρον/ο	white stone; a hard, crystalline or granular, metamorphic limestone, white or variously colored and sometimes streaked or mottled 2 a) a piece or slab of this stone, used as a monument, inscribed record, etc. b) a piece of sculpture or marble
marmarosis	μαρμάρωσις/η	covering an area with marble
martyr	μάρτυς/μάρτυρας	a person who chooses to suffer or die than giving up his/ her beliefs and principles
martyrdom	μαρτύριον/ο	1 the state of being a martyr 2 the death or suffering of a martyr 3 torture; long, continuous suffering;

martyrology	μαρτυλολόγιον/ο	1 listed names of martyrs 2 a historical account of religious martyrs, esp. Christian martyrs 3 the branch of ecclesiastical history dealing with the lives of martyrs
mass	μάζα	1 a quantity of matter forming a body of indefinite shape and size, usually of relatively large size; lump 2 a large quantity or number [a mass of bruises] 3 bulk; size; magnitude
mastectomy	μαστεκτομή	surgical removal of the breast(s)
mastic	μαστίχα	1 a yellowish resin obtained from a small Mediterranean evergreen tree (Pistacia lentiscus) of the cashew family, used as an astringent and in making varnish, adhesives, etc. 3 any of various pasty substances used as adhesives, sealants, etc.
mastitis	μαστίτις/μαστίτιδα	inflammation of the breasts
mastoid	(ο, η) μαστοειδής (το) μαστοειδές (adj.)	1 shaped like a breast or nipple 2 designating of, or near a projection of the temporal bone behind the ear; mastoid projection
mastology	μαστολογία	study of the breasts
mathematical	μαθηματικός, ή, ό (adj.)(μανθάνειν/ to learn)	[inclined to learn; to pay attention to, be alert] 1 of, having the nature of, or concerned with mathematics 2 rigorously exact, precise, accurate, etc.
mathematical logic	μαθηματική λογική	a modern type of formal logic using special symbols for propositions, quantifiers, and relationships among propositions and concerned with the elucidation of permissible operations upon such symbols; **Symbolic logic/συμβολική λογική**

mathematician	μαθηματικός	an expert or specialist in mathematics
mathematics	μαθηματικά	the group of sciences (including arithmetic, geometry, algebra, calculus, etc.) dealing with quantities, magnitudes, and forms, and their relationships, attributes, etc., by the use of numbers and symbols
Matthew	Ματθαίος	1 Bible one of the four evangelists to whom the first Gospel is ascribed (also Saint Matthew) 2 the first book of the New Testament, telling of Jesus's life 3 a masculine name
mausoleum	μαυσωλείον/ο	[the name was taken from Mausolus, king of Halicarnassus: included among the seven wonders of the ancient world (with cap. M)] 1 a large, imposing tomb 2 a building with vaults for the entombment of a number of bodies
mechanic	μηχανικός	a worker skilled in using tools or in making, operating and repairing machines
mechanical	μηχανολόγος	1 having to do with, or having skill in the use of machinery or tools 2 produced or operated by machinery or a mechanism 3 of, or in accordance of, the science of mechanics (in Greek: μηχανολόγος μηχανικός / mechanical engineer)

mechanics	μηχανική	1 the branch of physics dealing with the motion of material bodies and the phenomena of the action of forces on bodies: cf. statistics, dynamics, kinematics 2 theoretical and practical knowledge of the design, construction, operation, and care of machinery 3 the mechanical aspect; technical part [the mechanics of writing]
mechanism	μηχανισμός	1 the working parts or arrangement of parts of a machine; works; [the mechanism of a clock] 2 a) a system whose parts work together like those of a machine [the mechanism of the universe] etc. 3 the theory or doctrine that all the phenomena of the universe, particularly life, can ultimately be explained in terms of matter moving in accordance with the laws of nature
mechanization	μηχανοποίησις/η	the use of machines and in general of mechanical means in order to assist or replace human work
mechanize	μηχανοποιώ	1 to make mechanical 2 to do or operate by machinery and not by hand 3 to bring about the use of machinery in (an industry, etc.) 4 to equip (an army, etc.) with motor vehicles, tanks, etc., for greater mobility and striking power
mechanotherapy	μηχανοθεραπεία (μηχανή + θεραπεία- machine + therapy)	the treatment of disease, injuries, etc., by using mechanical devices, massage, etc.

Medusa	Μέδουσα	Gr. myth. one of the three Gorgons/γοργόνες, slain by Perseus
mega-	μέγας-μέγα (objective case)	great, mighty, powerful, combining form (megalomania)
mega-cephalic	μέγα- κέφαλος- κεφαλικός, ή, ό (adj.)	having a large head; esp. having a cranial capacity larger than the average
megacephaly	μεγαλοκεφαλία/ μεγακεφαλία	extremely large head, and abnormal condition
megacycle	μεγάκυκλος	very large circle
megadose	μέγα + δόση- large + dosage	abnormally large dose, esp. of a vitamin
mega-gaea	μέγα-γαία/γη	mighty/large earth; one of the three primary zoogeographic areas of the earth including Europe, Africa, Asia, certain islands southeast of Asia, the Polar and temperate areas of North America
megalgia	μεγαλγία	acute pain; painful condition
megalith	μέγα-λίθος/ μεγάλιθος	a huge stone, esp. one used in Neolithic monuments or by ancient peoples
megalithic	μεγαλιθικός, ή, ό (adj.)	having been built with megaliths, huge stones
megalo-	μεγάλος, η, ο (adj.)	big, large, great, powerful, combining form
megalo-cardia	μεγαλοκαρδία	abnormal enlargement of the heart
megalocephalic	μεγαλοκεφαλικός/ μεγακεφαλικός, ή, ό (adj.)	having large head
megalogastria	μεγάλος /γάστριον – big + stomach	enlargement of the stomach
megalohepatia	μεγάλο+ ήπαρ/ ήπατος (gen.) – large + liver	enlargement of the liver
megalomania	μεγαλομανία	disorder characterized by delusions of personal grandeur, power, or wealth

megalomaniac	(ο, η) μεγαλομανής, (το) μεγαλομανές (adj.)	one suffering from megalomania
megalomelia	μεγάλα + μέλη / big + limbs/parts	unusually large limbs or body parts
megalopolis	μεγαλόπολις /η/ μεγαλούπολις/η	great city; an extensive, heavily populated, continuously urban area, including any number of cities
megaphone	μεγάφωνο(ν)	a large funnel-shaped device for increasing the volume of the voice
megapod/ mega-pode	μέγα + πόδια / large + feet	large-footed; big-footed
mega- scopic	μεγασκόπιο(ν)	opposite of microscope
megasphere	μέγα + σφαίρα – large +sphere	a sphere larger than microsphere
mega-therium/ therion	μεγα-θηρίο(ν)	a large beast; any of the extinct genus (Megatherium) of very large, plant-eating, ground-dwelling sloths
megaton	μεγάτονος	the explosive force of a million tons of TNT: a unit for measuring the power of nuclear weapons
melalgia	μελαλγία (μέλος + αλγος- part/ limb + pain)	pain in the extremities
melancholia	μελαγχολία	depression and self-pity
melancholy	μελανο + χολή / black + bile, gall	a tendency to be sad and depressed
melanin	μελανίνη	black or brown pigment
melano-glossia	μελανό-γλωσσα	black tongue
melanoma	μελάνωμα	tumor arising from a pigmented mole
melanopathy	μελανοπάθεια	excessive skin pigmentation
mel-	μέλι	honey, in the purest form, sweet
melodic	μελωδικός, ή, ό (adj.)	of, or having the nature of melody

melodize	μελοποιώ	to set to music; compose melodies; to make melodious
melodrama	μελόδραμα	a sensational or romantic stage play with interspersed songs and an orchestral accompaniment
melodramatic	μελοδραματικός, ή, ό (adj.)	of, or like melodrama; sensational, violent, and extravagantly emotional
melody	μελωδία	pleasing sounds or arrangement of sounds in sequence; a sequence of single tones usually in the same key or mode to produce a rhythmic whole
membrane/ membrane	μεμβράνη	a thin, soft, pliable sheet of layer, especially of animal or vegetable tissue, serving as a covering or lining, as of an organ or part
membranoid	(ο, η) μεμβρανοειδής,(το) μεμβρανοειδές (adj.)	resembling a membrane
menarche	μην/ month + αρχή/ arche, start, beginning	the first menstrual period of a girl in puberty
meninges/mininges	μήνιγγες (πλ. pl.)	the three layered membranes that cover and protect the brain and the spinal cord
meningioma	μηνιγγίωμα	tumor arising from membrane covering the brain
meningitis	μηνιγγίτις/ μηνιγγίτιδα	inflammation of the lining of the brain and the spinal cord
meningo-malacia	μηνιγγο-μαλακεία	softening of a membrane
meninx	μήνιγξ-μήνιγγας/ μηνίγγι	any of the three membranes that envelop the brain and the spinal cord

meniscus	μηνίσκος	1 a crescent or crescent-shaped thing 2 a lens convex on one side and concave on the other 3 fibrous cartilage within a joint, esp., of the knee 4 Physics the curved upper surface of a column of liquid: as a result of capillarity it is concave when the walls of the container strongly attract the liquid, as with water, and it is convex when the liquid is more strongly attracted to itself, as with mercury
menolipsis	μηνόληψις/η	temporary absence of menstruation
menopause	μηνόπαυσις/η	the end of the menstrual period, therefore, the end of childbearing age or change of life
menorrhagia	(έμ) μηνορραγία	excessive bleeding during the menstrual period
menoschesis	μηνόσχισις/η	suppression of menstruation
menology	μηνολόγιον (μην/ μηνός (gen.) +λόγος- of the month + word/account)	1 a calendar of the months, with their events 2 a listing of saints, with brief biologies, arranged in calendar order
menostaxis	μηνόσταξις/η	prolonged menstruation
Mentor	μέντωρ/μέντορας	an advisor; Gr. myth. (with cap. M) the loyal friend and advisor of Odysseus, and teacher of his son, Telemachus; a wise and loyal advisor; a teacher or coach
merotomy	μέρος/ + τομή/ part + cutting	cutting into parts/sections
mesenteric	μεσεντερικός, ή, ό (adj.)	pertaining to mid-intestine

mesentery	μεσέντερον/(μέσος + έντερον- mid + intestine)	a supporting membrane or membranes enfolding some internal organ and attaching it either to the body wall or to another organ; esp., a double thickness of the peritoneum, enfolding most of the small intestine and attaching it to the spinal wall of the abdominal cavity
meso-	μέσος, η, ο/ μεσαίος, α, ο (adj.)	middle, intermediate, combining form mes- before a vowel (mesenteric)
mesocarp	μεσοκάρπιο(ν)	the middle layer of the wall of a ripened ovary or fruit
mesoderm	μέσο-δέρμα/ middle + skin	the middle layer of cells of an embryo, from which the skeletal, reproductive, muscular, vascular, connective, etc., tissues develop
mesogastrium	μέσο-γάστριο(ν)	the region of the abdomen above the region of the navel
Mesolithic	μεσολιθικός, ή, ό (adj.)	designating or of an Old World cultural period (c. 10,000–c. 8,000 BC) between the Paleolithic and the Neolithic, characterized by the earliest exploitation of local and relatively permanent food resources and the use of microliths, the Mesolithic period; Middle Stone Age
mesomorphic	μεσομορφικός, ή, ό (adj.)	of a state intermediate between the liquid and the crystalline; of or like liquid crystal
mesonephros	μέσο-νεφρός/ middle + kidney	the exctretory organ serving as the adult kindney in fish and amphibians and as the embryonic of higher vertebrates

mesosphere	μέσο-σφαίρα	the atmospheric zone or shell located above the stratopause at an altitude of c. 55 to 80 km (c.34 to 50 miles) and characterized by a decrease in temperature with increasing altitude
mesothelioma	μέσο-θηλίωμα	a tumor of the mesothelium, often malignant and thought to be caused, most commonly, by inhaling asbestos particles
mesothelium	μεσοθήλιο(ν)	epithelium or mesodermal origin; specif., the thin mesodermal epithelial lining the pericardial, pleural, peritoneal, and scrotal cavities
mesothorax	μεσοθώραξ/ μεσοθώρακας	the middle one of the three segments of an insect's thorax
Mesozoic	μεσοζωϊκός, ή, ό (adj)	designating or of a geologic era after the Paleozoic and before Cenozoic: it covered a period between c. 225,000,000 and 65,000,000 years ago, and it is characterized by the development and extinction of the dinosaurs, the appearance of flowering plants, grasses, birds, etc. the Mesozoic Era or it rocks
meta-	μετά	along with, after, between, among, combining form
metabolic	μεταβολικός, ή, ό (adj.)	of, involving, characterized by, or resulting from metabolism
metabolism	μεταβολισμός	basal, minimum amount of energy necessary in maintaining life, when the body is in complete rest
metacarpus	μετακάρπιον/ο	five bones in the palm of the hand
metachrosis	μετάχρωσις/η	change of color
metacyesis	μετακύησις	extrauterine pregnancy

metagenesis	μεταγένεσις/η	Biol. reproduction in which there is alternation of an asexual generation, as in many cnidarians
metagysis	μετάγγισις/η	blood transfusion
metal	μέταλλον/ο	1 a) any of a class of chemical elements, as iron, gold, or aluminum, generally characterized by ductility, malleability, luster, and conductivity of heat and electricity: these elements act as cations in chemical reactions, form bases with the hydroxyl radical, and can replace the hydrogen of an acid to form a salt b) any alloy of such elements, as brass and bronze 2 any substance or thing consisting of metal
metallic	μεταλλικός, ή, ό (adj.)	1 of, or having the nature of, metal 2 containing, yielding, or producing metal
metallography	μεταλλογραφία	the study of the structure and physical properties of metals and alloys, esp. by the use of the microscope and x-rays
metalloid	(ο, η) μεταλοειδής (το) μεταλωειδές (adj.)	an element having some but not all, the properties of metal; resembling metal
metallophobia	μεταλλοφοβία	extreme fear of metallic objects
metallurgy	μεταλλουργία	1 to work in metals or mines; 2 the science dealing with the separation of metals from their ores and preparing them for use, by smelting, refining, etc.
metamathematics	μετά + μαθηματικά	the logical study of the nature and validity of mathematical reasoning and proof
metamer	μεταμερής-μεταμερές (μετά + μέρος – along with + part)	Chem. a compound exhibiting metamerism with another or others

metamerism	μεταμερισμός	1 Chem. the type of isomerism in which chemical compounds have identical proportions of the same elements and the same molecular weight, but have radicals differing in type or position, with resulting differences in chemical properties 2 Zool. the condition of being made up of metameres
metamorphic	μεταμορφικός, ή, ό (adj.)	characterized by, causing or formed by substance; transformation
metamorphism	μεταμορφισμός	1 Metamorphosis 2 change in the mineralogical, structural, and textural composition of rocks under pressure, heat, chemical action, etc., which turns limestone into marble, granite into gneiss, etc.
metamorphose	μεταμορφώνω	to give new form; to change radically (as with supernatural energy) someone's shape or form (as Kirke changed Odysseus's companions into swine); to change the shape, form, nature, character, etc., of someone completely
metamorphosis	μεταμόρφωσις/η	1 change of form, shape, structure, or substance; transformation, as, in myths, by magic or sorcery 2 a marked or complete change of character, appearance, condition, etc. 3 Biol. a change in form, structure, or function as a result of development; specif., the physical transformation, more or less sudden, undergone by various animals after the embryonic state 4 Med. a pathological change of form of some tissues 5 Theol. Metamorphosis of Christ

metanefros	μετά + νεφρός – after + kidney	the excretory organ lying behind the mesonefros in an embryo, which in mammals, reptiles, and birds develops into a permanent, or adult kidney
metaphor	μεταφορά (μετά + φέρειν – over + to carry)	1 to carry over something 2 a figure of speech containing an implied comparison, in which a word or phrase ordinarily and primarily used of one thing is applied to another (ex: the curtain of night, instead of the darkness of night or the winter of life, instead of the old age, etc.)
metaphoric	μεταφορικός, ή, ό (adj.)	relating to one transporting people or things; transportation means; one who expresses thoughts and ideas in metaphors
metaphysical	μεταφυσικός, ή, ό (adj.)	1 of, connected with, or having the nature of, metaphysics 2 very abstract, abstruse, or subtle: often a derogatory usage 3 beyond the physical or material; incorporeal, supernatural, or transcendental
metaphysics	μεταφυσική	lit. after the physics (in reference to location after the *Physics* in early collections of Aristotle's works) 1 the branch of philosophy that deals with first principles and seeks to explain the nature of being or reality (*ontology*) and of the origin and structure of the universe (*cosmology*): it is closely associated with the study of the nature of knowledge (*epistemology)* 2 speculative philosophy in general 3 esoteric, often mystical or theosophical lore 4 the theory or principles of some branch of knowledge 5 popularly, any very subtle or difficult reasoning

metaplasia	μεταπλασία	1 abnormal change of one adult tissue to another 2 conversion of one tissue to another, as of cartilage into bone
metaplasm	μετάπλασμα	1 that part of the contents of a cell which consists of lifeless matter, as certain fatty or starch granules 2 an irregularity Gr, metaplasmos/ μεταπλασμός formation of cases of nouns from a missing nom. (meta- over + plassein- to form), a change in a linguistic form made by the addition, omission, or transposition of a sound or sounds or a syllable or syllabes
metapsychology	μεταψυχολογία	speculation about the origin, structure, function, etc., of the mind and about the relation between the mental and the physical, regarded as supplemental to psychology
metasomatism	μετασωματισμός	the process by which minerals of a rock or ore body are replaced by minerals of different chemical composition, usually as a result of action by ascending waters
metasomatosis	μετασωμάτωσις/η	the resulting process of metasomatism
metastasis	μετάστασις/η	to place in another way; Med. the spread of disease from one part of the body to another unrelated to it, as of the cells of a malignant tumor by way of the bloodstream or lymphatics 2 change of form or matter; transformation
metastatic	μεταστατικός, ή, ό (adj.)	that is caused by metastasis
metatarsus	μετατάρσιον/ο	part of the foot between the ankle and the start of the toes

metathesis	μετάθεσις/η	a going over; transposition; to put over; transpose; change over; Chem. the interchange of elements or radicals between compounds, as when, two compounds react with each other to create two new compounds
metathorax	μεταθώραξ/ μεταθώρακας	the hindmost of the three segments of an insect's thorax
metazoan	μετάζωα	in some systems of classification, any of the large subkingdom (Metazoa) made up of all animals whose bodies, originating from a single cell, are composed of many differentiated cells arranged into definite organs
metazoic	μεταζωϊκός, ή, ό (adj.)	having to do with the Metazoa subkingdom
mete-/meta-	μετά	after, beyond, combining form
metempsychosis	μετεμψύχωσις/η (μετά + ψυχή- after + soul)	the supposed passing of the soul at death to another body either human or animal; transmigration
meteor	μετέωρο(ν)/μετέωρα (pl.) μετά + αιωρείν- beyond + hovering in the air/lift up	1 the luminous phenomenon observed when a meteoroid is heated by its entry to the earth's atmosphere; shooting star 2 Meteorol. Any atmospheric phenomenon, as precipitation, lightning, or a rainbow
meteoric	μετεωρικός, ή, ό (adj.)	like a meteor; momentarily dazzling or brilliant, flashing, or swift
meteorite	μετεωρίτης	the part of a relatively meteoroid that survives passage through the atmosphere and falls to the surface of a planet or the moon as a mass of metal or stone

meteorograph	μετεωρογράφος	an apparatus for automatically recording various weather conditions, as moisture, temperature, etc.
meteoroid	(o, η) μετερωειδής (το μετερωειδές (adj.)	any of the small, solid bodies traveling through outer space, which are seen as meteors when they enter the earth's atmposphere
meteorological	μετεωρολογικός, ή, ό (adj.)	of weather or climate; of the atmosphere or atmospheric phenomena
meteorologist	μετεωρολόγος	an expert or specialist in meteorology
meteorology	μετεωρολογία	the science dealing with the atmosphere and atmospheric phenomena; the study of weather including weather forecasting
meter/metre	μέτρον/ο	1 a) rhythm in verse; measured, patterned arrangement of syllables, primarily according to stress or length b) the specific rhythm as determined by the prevailing foot and the number of feet in the line [iambic meter] c) the specific rhythmic pattern of a stanza as determined by the kind and number of lines 2 the basic pattern of beats in successive measures of a piece of music: it is usually indicated in the time signature 3 [meter] the basic metric unit of linear measure, equal to c. 39.37 inches: now officially equal to the distance light travels in a vacuum in 1/299,792,458 of a second (abbrev. m)

method	μέθοδος	pursuit, system; a way of doing anything; mode; procedure; process; esp., a regular, orderly, definite procedure of teaching, researching, etc.
methodic	μεθοδικός, ή, ό (adj.)	orderly; systematic
Methodism	μεθοδισμός	the beliefs and practices of Methodists, emphasizing personal and social responsibily; excessive adherence to systematic procedure
methodology	μεθοντολογία	the science of method, or orderly arrangement; specif., the branch of logic concerned with the application of the principles of reasoning to scientific and philosophical inquiry
metamorphosis	μεταμόρφωσις/η	change of shape and structure
metastasis	μετάστασις/η	movement of bacteria or a disease from one part of the body to another
methyl	μεθύλιον/ο	the monovalent hydrocarbon radical CH3 normally existing only in combination, as in methanol
metonym	μετώνυμον/ο	a word or phrase used in metonymy, as a substitute for another
metonymy	μετωνυμία	a figure of speech in which the name of one thing is used in place of another associated with or suggested by it (ex: "the White House" for "the President" or "the Kremlin" for "Russia,"etc.)
metope	μετώπιον/ο (μετά + οπή – between + an opening	any of the square areas, plain or decorated, between triglyphs in a Doric frieze

metopic	μετωπικός, ή, ό (adj.) (μέτωπον/ο- forhead)	referring to the forehead; of the forehead; frontal
-metra	μήτρα	uterus; womb combining form (hemometra) a specified condition of the uterus
metralgia	μητραλγία	pain in the uterus
metrectacia	μήτρα + έκτασις/η – womb + extend /stretch	dilatation of the uterus
metre	μέτρον/ο	measure, to mark off
metric	μετρικός, ή, ό (adj.)	a) of the meter (unit of linear measure) b) designating or of the system of measurement based on the meter and gram
metric system	μετρικό σύστημα	a decimal system of weights and measures based on the meter and the kilogram; compare CGS, MKS
metritis	μητρίτις/μητρίτιδα	inflammation of the uterus
metro-	μήτρα	uterus; womb, combining form (metrodynia)
metro-carcinoma	μητρο-καρκίνωμα/ καρκίνος μήτρας	cancer of the uterus
metrodynia	μητροδυνία/ μητροδύνη	intense pain in the uterus
metrological	μετρολογικός, ή, ό (adj.)	relating to, or using the metric system
metrology	μετρολογία	the science of weights and measures; a system of weights and measures
metropathy μητροπάθεια	any uterine disorder metropolis	μητρόπολις/η (μήτηρ/μητρός (gen.) + πόλις – mother +city) 1 the main city, often the capital, of a country, state or region 2 any large city or center of population, culture, etc.

metropolitan	μητροπολιτικός, ή, ό (adj.)	1 constituting or of a metropolis 2 designating of or a metropolitan 3 in the Eastern Orthodox Church: Metropolitan: a bishop ranking just below a Patriarch
metrorrhagia	μητρορραγία	bleeding of the vagina not related to menstruation
Mm (mi/me)	Μ,μ (Μι)	the twelfth letter of the Gr. alphabet
miasma	μίασμα (μιαίνειν – to pollute)	pollution; 1 a vapor rising as from marshes or decomposing animal or vegetable matter, formerly supposed to poison and infect the air, causing malaria, etc.
micro-	μικρός, ή, ό (adj.)	small; tiny, combining form (microscopic)
microanalysis	μικροανάλυσις/η	the chemical analysis identification of very small quantities
microbe	μικρόβιον/ο	tiny, living organism seen only through a microscope
microbiologist	μικροβιολόγος	specialist in microbiology
microbiology	μικροβιολογία	science dealing with microscopic organisms
microcardia	μικροκάρδια/ μικροκαρδία	abnormal smallness of the heart
microcephalic	μικροκέφαλος, η, ο (adj.)	having an abnormally small head
microcephaly	μικροκεφαλία	a condition of abnormal smallness of the head, usually associated with mental retardation
microchemistry	μικροχημεία	the chemistry of microscopic or submicroscopic quantities or objects
microcoria	μικροκόρη	smallness of the pupil
microcosm	μικρόκοσμος	a little/small world; miniature universe

microeconomics	μικρο –οικονομικά	a branch of economics dealing with certain specific factors affecting an economy, as the behavior of individual consumers, the marketing of particular products, etc.
microelectronics	μικρο-ηλεκτρονική	the science dealing with the theory, design and application of microcircuits
microglossia	μικρή + γλώσσα	abnormally small tongue
micrograph	μικρογράφος	an apparatus for doing extremely small writing, drawing, or engraving
micrography	μικρογραφία/ μικρογράφησις/η	1 the description, depiction or study of microscopic objects 2 the art or practice in writing in tiny characters
micromastia	μικρό + μαστός/ small and breast	unusually small breasts
micrometer	μικρόμετρον/ο	an instrument for measuring very small distances, angles, diameters, etc., used on a telescope or microscope
micrometeorite	μικρό-μετεωρίτης	a very small meteorite, esp., one that drifts through the earth's atmosphere to the ground without becoming incandescent
micrometereology	μικρο-μετεωρολογία	the branch of meteorology dealing with small-scale processes, physical conditions and interactions of the lowest atmosphere, esp., in the first few hundred feet above the earth's surface
micrometry	μικρομετρία	measuring with micrometers
micron	μικρόν/ό	small, tiny, minute; a unit of linear measure equal to one millionth of a meter or a thousandth of a millimeter

Micronesia	Μικρονησία (μικρό + νήσος- small +island)	country on a group of islands in the W Pacific, official name: **Federated States of Micronesia**
Micronesian	μικρονήσιος, α, ο (adj.)	of Macronesia; the people of Macronesia, an inhabitant of those islands, culture, customs, etc.; any of the Austronesian languages spoken in Micronesia
microorganism	μικρο-οργανισμός	any microscopic or ultramicroscopic animal or vegetable organism; esp., any of the bacteria, protozoan, viruses, etc.
microphone	μικρόφωνο(v)	an instrument containing a transducer that converts the mechanical sound waves into an electric signal, used in telephony, radio, sound amplification, etc.
micropsia	μικρή + όψη- small +sight/view	defective eyesight/seeing things smaller than they are
microscope	μικροσκόπιον/ο	instrument that enlarges an object for better visual examination
microscopic	μικροσκοπικός, ή, ό (adj.)	tiny, able to be observed only under a microscope
microseism	μικροσεισμός	a very slight tremor or quivering of the earth's crust
microtome	μικροτόμος	any of various precision instruments for cutting thin sections, as of organic tissue, for study under a microscope
microtomy	μικροτομή	the skill or work of using a microtome
migraine	ημικρανία (ημι + κρανίον-half +cranium/skull)	a type of intense periodically returning headache, usually limited to one side of the head and often accompanied by nausea, visual disorders, etc.

mime/mimesis	μίμησις /η (μίμος-μίμησις/ imitator - imitation)	1 an ancient Greek or Roman farce, in which people or events were mimicked an burlesqued 2 the representation of an action, character, mood, etc. 3 mime/ mimic: an actor who performs in such acts 4 mimesis: a) Art, literature imitation or representation b) Biol. mimicry
mimicry	μιμητική	1 the practice or art, or a way of mimicking 2 close resemblance in form, color, or behavior, of one organism to another or to some object in its environment, as of some insects to the leaves or twigs of plants: it serves to disguise the organism from predators
mimosa	μιμόζα	any of a the large genus (Mimosa) of trees, shrubs and herbs of the mimosa family, growing in warm regions
Minoan	μινωϊκός, ή, ό (adj.)	designating or of a Bronze Age culture that flourished in Crete from c. 3,000–1100 BC
Minos	Μίνως/Μινωας	Gr. myth. a king of Crete, son of Zeus by Europa, after he dies he becomes one of the three judges of the dead in the lower world 2. many others by the name Minos, succeeded to the throne, thus the Minoan civilization was developed
Minotaur	Μινώταυρος (Μίνως + ταύρος – Minos + bull/taurus)	Gr. myth. a monster with the body of a man and a bull's head (some versions have the body of a bull and head of a man) confined by Minos in a labyrinth built by Daidalus and annually was fed with seven young boys and seven maidens from Athens, till was killed byTheseus

miso-	μίσος (μισείν/μισώ)	hatred of; to hate; despise combining form (misogyny)
misandry	μισανδρεία, μισώ/ανδρεία	hating man, male hater
misanthrope	μισάνθρωπος, (μισώ- άνθρωπος/ hating –man, people)	antisocial; a person suffering from psychopathic personality; sociopath
misanthropy	μισανθρωπιά	hatred of all people
misogamist	μισόγαμος	hating marriage/weddings
misogamy	μισογαμία	hatred of marriage
misogynist	μισογύνης	hater of women
misogyny	μισογυνία	hatred of women
misology	μισολογία (μισώ +λόγος – hate + word	hatred of argument, debate, or reasoning
misoneism	μισονεϊσμός (μισώ + νέος- hate + new)	hating anything new; hatred of innovation and change
mitosis	μίτωσις/η (μίτος/ κλωστή- thread)	Biol. the indirect and more common method of nuclear division cells, consisting typically of prophase, metaphase, anaphase, and telophase: the nuclear chromatin first appears as long threads which shorten and thicken to form the typical number of chromosomes, each of which splits lengthwise to double in number with half of each set, then moving toward opposite poles of the cell to become reorganized into two nuclei with the normal number of chromosomes
mitral	(ο, η) μιτροειδής (το) μιτροειδές	of, relating to, being or adjoining a mitral valve or orifice
mitral cell	μιτροειδές κύτταρον/ο	any of the pyramidal cells of the olfactory bulb about which terminate numerous fibers from the olfactory cells of the nasal mucosa

mitral stenosis	μιτροεϊδής στένωσις /η	a condition usually the result of disease in which the mitral valve is abnormally narrow
mitral valve	μιτροεϊδής βαλβίδα	a valve in the heart consisting of two triangular flaps which allow indirectional blood from the left atrium to the left ventricle;also called biscupid valve, left artioventricular valve
mneme	μνήμη	memory
mnemonic	μνήμη-μνημονικός, ή, ό (adj.)	memory 1 having to do with remembering 2 of mnemonics, or memory; mnemonic device
mnemonics	μνημονική	the technique or system of improving the memory by the use of certain formulas
-mnesia	-μνησία (μνήμη)	memory suffix forming nouns indicating the type or condition of memory (as amnesia, paramnesia, etc.)
mono-	μόνο- μόνος, η, ο (adj.)	1 one; only; alone; single 2 affecting a single part (monoplegia)
monad	μονάς/μονάδα (μόνος-alone)	a unit, unity 1 a unit, something simple and indivisible 2 Biol. a) any simple single-celled organism, specif. a simple type of flagellated protozoan or protist b) any of the nuclei formed at the completion of meiosis 3 Chem. a monovalent atom, element, or radical 4 Philos. an entity or elementary being thought of as microcosm or ultimate unit
monadelphous	μονάδελφος	lit. only brother Bot. having the stamens united by their filaments into one set or bundle, as some legumes

monadic	μοναδικός, ή, ό (adj.)	the one and only; one that has no equal; someone that cannot be compared to another; incomparable; unequalled; unique
monadism	μοναδισμός	the theory that the universe consists of monads
monarch	μονάρχης	the sole ruler of a state or country 2 the hereditary (often constitutional) head of a state, king, queen, etc.
monarchic	μοναρχικός, ή, ό (adj.)	favoring or supporting a monarchy; of, haracteristic of, or like a monarch or monarchy
monarchism	μοναρχισμός	monarchical principles or the advocacy of these
monarchy	μοναρχία	1 rule only by one person 2 a government or state headed by a monarch: called **absolute** when there is no limitation on the monarch's power, **constitutional** when there is such limitation
monastery	μοναστήρι	a convent; a building or residence for monks, nuns or others who have withdrawn from the world for religious reasons
monastic	μοναστικός, ή, ό (adj.)	1 of or characteristic of a monastery 2 of or designating the ascetic and austere life of monks or nuns
monasticism	μοναχισμός	the monastic system or way of life
monatomic	μονατομικός, ή, ό (adj.)	1 a) consisting of one atom (said of a molecule) b) having one atom in the molecule 2 containing one replaceable atom or atomic group

monism	μονισμός (μόνος – single)	Philos. 1 the doctrine there is only one ultimate substance or principle, whether mind (idealism), matter (materialism), or some third thing that is the basis for both 2 the doctrine that reality is an organic whole without independent parts Cf. Dualism, Pluralism
monk	μοναχός	one who lives alone; a male religious ordinarily living in a monastery or hermitage, usually under vows and a common rule: distinguished from Friar
monochromatic	μονοχρωματικός, ή, ό (adj.)	1 of or having one color 2 of or producing electromagnetic radiation of one wavelength, or of a very small range of wavelengths 3 of or having to do with monochromatism
monochrome	μονόχρωμος, η, ο (adj.) μονοχρωμία	having one color; 1 a painting, drawing, design, or photograph in one color or shades of one color 2 the art or process of making these
monocline	μονόκλινος, η, ο (adj.) (κλίνειν –to incline/lean)	single bed, couch; Geol. 1 dipping in one direction: said of strata, or rock layers 2 strata dipping in the same direction
monocracy	μονοκρατία	government by one person; autocracy
monodic	μονωδικός, ή, ό (adj.)	pertaining to one singing alone
monodist	μονωδός	a writer or singer of a monody
monodrama	μονόδραμα	drama acted or written to be performed by one actor/performer

monody	μονωδία	1 ancient Greek literature, an ode sung by one voice, as in a tragedy; lyric solo, generally a lament or a dirge 2 a poem in which the poet mourns someone's death 3 Music a) an early vocal style having a single voice with continuo accompaniment, as in Baroque opera b) a composition in this style 4 monophony
monogamistic	μονογαμικός, ή, ό (adj.)	married to only one person at a time
monogamous	μονόγαμος	one who practices and upholds monogamy
monogamy	μονογαμία	the state or custom of being married to one person at a time, or of having only one mate at a time
mnogastric	μονογαστρικός, ή, ό (adj.) (γάστριον/o-stomach)	having a stomach with only a single compartment (as in humans)
monogenesis	μονογένεσις/η	1 the hypothetical descent of all living organisms from a single original organism or cell 2 asexual reproduction, as by budding or spore formation
monogenic	μονογενικός, ή, ό (adj.)	Biol. designating of or a mode of inheritance in which a character is controlled by one pair of genes 2. Zool. producing offspring of one sex/ γένος only, as females only in some species of aphids (monogeny)
monoglot	μονόγλωσσος, η, ό (adj.)	one knowing only one language in contrast to a polyglot
monogram	μονόγραμμα	a character or figure made up of two or more letters, often inicials of a name, combined in a single design: used on correspondence paper; ornaments, clothing, etc.

monograph	μονογραφία	1 orig., a treatise on a single genus, species, etc., of plant or animal 2 a book or long article, esp., a scholarly one, on a single subject or a limited aspect of a subject
monolith	μονόλιθος	1 only single block or piece of stone, as in architecture or sculpture 2 something made of a single block of stone, as an obelisk 3 something like a monolith in size, unity of structure or purpose, unyielding quality
monologue	μονόλογος	a long speech by one speaker, esp. one monopolizing the conversation; the words or thoughts of one character in a play
monomania	μονομανία	1 excessive interest in or enthusiasm for some one thing; craze 2 Med. mental disorder esp., when limited in expression to one idea or area of thought
monomaniac	μονομανιακός, ή, ό (adj.)	an individual affected by monomania
monomelic	(ο, η) μονομελής (το) μονομελές (adj) (μόνο + μέλος- one +part/limb)	relating to or affecting only one limb
monomer	(ο, η) μονομερής (το) μονομερές (adj.)	a chemical compound that can undergo polymerization
monometallic	μονομεταλλικός, ή, ό (adj.)	1 of or using one metal 2 of or based monometallism
mononeuritis	μονονευρίτις/ μονονευρίτιδα	nerve inflammation affecting only one nerve
mononeuritis multiplex	μονονευρίτιδα πολύπλοκη	neuritis that affects several nerves

monometallism	μονομεταλλισμός	1 the use of only metal usually gold or silver, as the monetary standard 2 the doctrine or policies supporting this
mononeuropathy	μονο-νευρο-πάθεια (only-neuro- pathy/ disease)	a nerve disease affecting only one nerve
monophobia	μονοφοβία	extreme fear of being alone
monophonic	μονοφωνικός, ή, ό (adj.)	1 of, or having the nature of monophony 2 designating or of sound reproduction using a simple channel to carry and reproduce sounds through one or more sound speakers
monophony	μονοφωνία	1 music having a single melody without accompaniment or harmonizing parts, as in plainsong 2 monody
monophthong	μονόφθογγος (μόνο + φθόγγος – only + sound, voice)	a simple vowel sound during the utterance of which the vocal organs remain in a relatively unchanging position, as (a), (oo), or (i)
monophyletic	μονοφυλετικός, ή, ό (adj.)	1 of a single stock 2 developed from a single ancestral type
monoplane	μονοπλάνο	an airoplane or glider with only one main supporting surface, or a pair of wings
monoplegia	μονοπληγία	paralysis affecting a single limb, body part, or a group of muscles
monopode	μονόπους/ μονοπόδαρος μόνος+ πους /ποδός (gen.) πόδι (Mod. Gr.) – only- foot	having only one foot; a monopode creature; specif. a member of a fabled race of monopod men
monopole	μονόπολος	a hypothetical elementary particle of great mass, that has only one pole of magnetic charge: **Magnetic monopole**

monopolist	μονοπώλης	one who monopolizes or has a monopoly
monopolization	μονοπώλησις/η	the state of having a monopoly of a product or service
monopolize	μονοπωλείν/ μονοπωλώ	1 to get, have or to exploit a monopoly of 2 to get full possession or control of: dominate completely [monopolize the discussion] **Smonopoly** μονοπώλιον/ο exclusive control of a commodity or service in a given market
monospermic	μονοσπερμικός, ή, ό (adj.)	relating to monospermy
monosperm	μονόσπερμος, η, ο (adj.)	having only one seed; **monospermy:** the system in which a single sperm cell fertilizes an ovum
monostich	μονόστιχος, η, ο (adj.) (μόνο + στίχος – only + a line/verse)	1 a poem consisting of only one metrical line 2 one line of poetry
monostrophe	μονόστροφος, η, ο (adj.)	a poem in which all the stanzas have the same metrical form: monostrophic
monosyllabic	μονοσυλλαβικός, ή, ό (adj.) (μόνο + συλλαβή –only +syllable)	1 having only one syllable [monosyllabic word] 2 consisting of monosyllables 3 using, or speaking in monosyllables, often so to seem terse or uncomminicative
monosyllable	μονοσύλλαβος, η, ο (adj.)	a word of one syllable
monotheism	μονοθεϊσμός	the belief or doctrine that there is only one God
monotheist	μονοθεϊστής	one believing in one God
Monothelite	Μονοθελήτης	a follower of Monotheletism

Monotheletism	Μονοθελητισμός	a Christian theory or doctrine which stated that Jesus Christ has two natures (the divine and human) but only one will/ thelesis/θέλησις)τηε διωινε= Formulated in 638, enjoyed considerable popularity for a while, even gaining some patriarchal support, before being rejected and denounced as heretical in 680–681 at the Sixth Ecumenical Synod/ Council of Constantinople. The Synod decreed that if Christ has two natures, then he must also have two wills, otherwise the fullness of his humanity would be impaired. Christ is fully and truly God and fully and truly man (Θεάνθρωπος/ Theanthropos – Θεός + άνθρωπος – God + man)
monotone	μονότονος, η, ο (adj.)	1 uninterrupted repetition of the same tone; utterance of successive syllables or words without change of pitch or key 2 monotony or sameness of tone, style, manner, or color, etc. 3 one doing recitation, speaking, signing or chanting in a monotonous style
monotony	μονοτονία	1 sameness of tone or pitch or continuance of the same tone without variation 2 lack of variation or varity 3 tiresome, sameness, or uniformity

monotype	μονότυπος, η, ο (adj.) (μόνο + τύπος – only + type/kind)	1 Biol. the only type of its group, as a single species constituting a genus, a single genus constituting a family, etc. 2 Art a) a unique print from a metal or glass plate on which a picture has been made, as with paint or ink b) the method of making such prints 3 printing type produced by monotype
monotypia	μονοτυπία	the skill of using the monotype method
moron	μωρός, ή, ό (adj.)	1 a very foolish, stupid person 2 Med. a person affected with mild mental retardation
morosis	μόρωσις/ η	feeblemindness; a tropical contagious disease
morphine	μορφίνη	a bitter crystalline addictive narcotic
morphogenesis	μορφογένεσις/η (μορφή + γένεσις – form/shape + genesis/creation)	the formation and differentiation of tissues and organs
morphological	μορφολογικός, ή, ό (adj.)	of, relating to, or concerned with form or structure
morphologist	μορφολόγος	an expert in morphology
morphology	μορφολογία	1 the branch of biology dealing with the form and structure of animals and plants 2 the branch of linguistics tha deals with the internal structure of and forms of words 3 any scientific study of form and structure, as in physical geography 4 form and structure, as of an organism regarded as a whole
morphosis	μόρφωσις/η	1 the mode of developmental formation of an organism or any of its parts 2 in Greek the word morphosis/μόρφωσις also means education

mosaic	μωσαϊκός, ή, ό (adj.)	1 the process of making pictures or designs by inlaying tiny pieces of colored stone, glass, tile, etc., in mortar; anything resembling such a picture or design (as a floor, wall, or any decorative scene) 2 any work made in this process 3 Bot. any of the virus diseases that cause wrinkling or mottling of leaves
moustache	μουστάκι (μύσταξ-μύστακος(gen. Anc. Gr.)	see Mustache
Muse/muse	Μούσα	a patron goddess of the arts
museum	μουσείον/ο	an institution, building or room for preserving and exhibiting artistic, historical or scientific objects
music	μουσική	the art and science of combining vocal or instrumental sounds or tones in varying melody, harmony, rhythm, and timbre, esp., as to form structurally complete and emotionally expressive compositions
musical	μουσικός, ή, ό (adj,)	1 of or for the creation, production or performance of music 2 having the nature of music; melodious or harmonious 3 fond of, sensitive to, or skilled in music 4 a theatrical, or film production often elaborately costumed and staged
musical comedy	μουσική κωμωδία	a funny or satirical theme performed as a musical play
musician	μουσικός	a person skilled in music, esp. as a professional performer, composer, or conductor
musicologist	μουσικολόγος	a specialist in musicology

musicology	μουσικολογία	the systematized study of the science, its history, forms, and methods of music
musk	μόσκος/μόσχος	1 a substance with a strong, penetrating odor, obtained from a small sac [musk bag] under the skin of the abdomen in the male musk deer: used as the basis of numerous perfumes 2 a similar substance secreted by certain other animals, as alligator, musk ox, etc.; any of these substances are created synthetically 3 any of several plants having a musky scent
mustache	μύσταξ/ μύστακος (gen. anc. Gr)/ μουστάκι (mod. Gr.)	1 the hair that a man grows on the upper lip (often used in plural indicating the two halves of the growth) 2 the hair growing on the upper lip
myalgia	μυαλγία	muscle pain
myasthenia	μυασθένεια	muscle weakness; muscular weaknes or fatigue
myatonia	μυατονία	prolonged muscle spasm, often a manifestation of certain diseases of the muscles; muscle limbness
mycelium	μυκήλιον (μύκης/ μύκητος (gen.) μύκητας (Mod. Gr.)- mushroom/ fungus)	1 the thallus or vagitative part, of a fungus, made of a mass or network of threadlike tubes
Mycenae	Μυκήναι/Μυκήνες	ancient city in Argolis, in NE Peloponnesus
Mycenean	μυκηναϊκός, ή, ό (adj.)	1 of Mycenae 2 designating or of a Bronze Age civilization which existed in Greece, Crete, Asia Minor, etc., from c. 1700–c.1100 BC
myceto-	μύκητος (gen. of μύκης/ fungus/ mushroom)	combining form (mycetoma)

mycetoma	μυκήτωμα	a chronic infection of the skin and subcutaneous tissues, esp., of the foot, characterized by a tumorous mass consisting mostly of fungi
-mycin	-μυκίνη	combining form used often as the ending in antibiotics derived from fungus (erythromycin)
myco-	μύκης	fungus, combining form (mycology)
mycobacterium	μυκοβακτήριον/ο	any of the genus (Mycobacterium) of rod-shaped, Gram-positive bacteria, as those causing tuberculosis and leprosy
mycology	μυκητολογία/ μυκολογία	1 the branch of botany dealing with fungi 2 all the fungi of a region
mycosis	μυκητίασις/η	1 the growth of parasitic fungi in any part of the body 2 a disease caused by such fungi
mydriasis	μυδρίασις/η	excessive or prolonged dilation of the pupil of the eye
myectomy	μυεκτομή	surgical excision of part of a muscle
myelin/myeline	μυελίνη (μυελός- marrow)	a soft white substance of lipid and protein that is secreted by oligodendrocytes and Schwann cells forming a sheath about axons
myelin basic protein	μυελίνη βασική πρωτεΐνη	a protein that is a constituent of myelin and is often found in higher than normal amounts in the cerebrospinal fluid of people affected with some demyelinating disease (as multiple scherosis)
myelitis	μυελίτις /μυελίτιδα	inflammation of the spinal cord or of the bone marrow

myelo-	μυελός	marrow; bone marrow (myeloma), spinal cord (myelogram), combining form also, myel- before a vowel
myeloblast	μυελοβλάστης	a large mononuclear mongranular bone marrow cell; esp., one which is a precursor of a myelocyte
myelocytosis	μυελοκύτωσις/η	the presence of excess numbers of myelocytes, esp., in the blood or bone marrow
myelodysplasia	μυελοδυσπλασία	a developmental anomaly of the spinal cord: myelodysplasia syndrome
myelodysplastic	μυελοδυπλαστικός, ή, ό (adj.)	one suffering from myelodysplasia
myelogenic	μυελογενής/ μυελογενές	of, relating to, originating in or produced by the bone marrow
myelogenous leukemia	μυελογενής λευκαιμία	1 leukemia characterized by proliferation of myeloid tissue (as of the bone marrow and spleen) and an abnormal increase in the number of granulocytes, myelocytes, and myeloblasts in the circulating blood 2 leukemia originating or produced by the bone marrow
myelography	μυελογραφία	radiographic visualization of the spinal cord after injection of a contrast medium into the spinal subarachnoid space
myeloid	(o, η) μυελοειδής (το) μυελοειδές (adj.)	of or relating to the spinal cord; resembling bone marrow
myelolipoma	μυελο-λίπωμα	benign tumor, esp., of the adrenal glands that consists of fat and hematopoietic tissue
myeloma	μυέλωμα	a primary tumor of the bone marrow formed of any one of the bone marrow cells (as myelocytes or plasma cells) and usually involving several different bones at the same time

myelon	μυελός	bone marrow; spinal cord
myelomatosis	μυελομάτωσις/η	blood in the bone marrow
myelopathy	μυελοπάθεια	disease of the spinal cord
myeloplegia	μυελοπληγία	spinal paralysis
myelo-phthisic	μυελο-φθισικός, η, ό (adj.) (μυελός + φθίσις – marrow + tuberculosis)	affected by myelophthisis **tuberculosis of the bone marrow**
myelophthisic anemia	μυελοφθισική αναιμία	anemia in which the blood-forming elements of the bone marrow are unable to reproduce normal blood cells, which is commonly caused by specific toxins or by overgrowth of tumor cells
myelo-poiesis	μυελο-ποίησις/η (μυελός + ποιείν- marrow + to make/create)	1 production of marrow or marrow cells in bone marrow; esp. formation of blood granulocytes
myocardiac	μυοκαρδιακός, ή, ό (adj.)	of, relating to, or involving the myocardium
myocarditis	μυοκαρδίτις/ μυοκαρδίτιδα	inflammation of the myocardium (the heart muscle)
myocardium	μυοκάρδιο(ν)	the muscular substance of the heart
myoclonus/ myelospasm	μυελοσπασμός	involuntary twitching or spasm of a muscle or muscles
myoid	(ο, η) μυώδης/ (το) μυώδες (adj.)	resembling a muscle
myogram	μυογράφημα	a graphic representation of the phenomena (as intensity) of muscular contractions
myograph	μυογράφος	an apparatus for producing myograms
myology	μυολογία	the study of muscles
myoma	μύωμα	tumor consisting of muscle tissue
myomectomy	μυωμεκτομή	surgical removal of the myoma
myopathy	μυοπάθεια	any muscle disease
myope	μύωπας	one who is nearsighted

myopia	μυωπία	nearsightedness
myosis	μύωσις/η	contraction of the eye pupil
myositis	μυοσίτις/μυοσίτιδα	muscle inflammation
myospasm	μυοσπασμός	muscle spasm
myotasis	μυότασις/η	stretching of the muscle
myria-	μύρια	combining form, many, thousand, countless
myriad	μυριάς/μυριάδα	thousands; countless; any indefinitely large number; a great number of people or things
myyriapod	μυριόποδας	having many legs; said esp. of millipedes and centipedes
myrmeco-	μύρμηγκο(s) (gen.;)-/ μύρμηξ/μύρμηγκας/ μυρμήγκι	combining form, ant; of ant
myrmecology	μυρμηγκολογία	the branch of entomology dealing with the ant family
myrmecologist	μυρμηγκολόγος	expert in myrmecology
myrmecophagous	μυρμηγκοφάγος	feeding on ants
Myrmidon	μυρμιδών/ μυρμιδόνος (gen,) μυρμιδόνες	Gr. legend. any of the tribe of Thessalians warriors who fought under Achilles in the Trojan War 2 an unquestioning follower or subordinate
Myron	Μύρων	famous Greek sculptor of the fifth cen. BC (his most famous work being the *Discus Thrower*)
myrth	μύρθα	a fragrant bitter-tasting gum resin exuded from several plants, used in making incense, perfume, etc.
myrtle	μυρτιά/μύρτος	any of a genus (Myrtus) of plants of the myrtle family
mystagogic	μυσταγωγικός, ή, ό	one who is initiated into religious mysteries
mystagogue	μυσταγωγός	a person who interprets religious mysteries or initiates others into them

mystagogy	μυσταγωγία	interpreting religious mysteries
mysterious	μυστήριος, α, ο (adj.)	implying or characterized by an aura of mystery or vague/secretive behavior
mystery	μυστήριον	supernatural thing (Mod. Gr. N.T,. divine secret; Mysterion/ ΜυστήριονSacrament ;)
mystic	μυστικιστής;μυστικός (secretive)	belonging to secret rites; having difficulty to explain powers
mysticism	μυστικισμός	doctrines or beliefs of mystics; vague, obscure, or confused thinking or belief
myth	μύθος	1 word, speech, story, legend, fable; traditional or unknown authorship, ostensibly with a historical basis, but serving usually to explain some phenomenon of nature, the origin of man, or the customs/ traditions, religious rites, etc. 2 such stories collectively; mythology 3 any ficticious story or unscientific account, theory, belief, etc., also, myth abbreviation for mythology
mythic	μυθικός, ή, ό (adj.)	of, or having the nature of, a myth or myths, also: mythical, imaginary, ficticious
mythicize	μυθοποιώ	to make into, or explain as, a myth; a tale
mytho-	μύθος- μύθο (objective case)	combining form, myth
mythographer	μυθογράφος	a person who creates, collects, or writes myths/fables: Aesops Fables /Μύθοι του Αισώπου
mythologist	μυθολόγος	an expert in mythology
mythology	μυθολογία	a telling of tales and legends; also, the science/study of myths
mythomania	μυθομανία	habitual lying or exaggeration
mythomaniac	(ο, η) μυθομανής, (το) μυθομανές (adj.)	someone who habitually exaggerates

mythopoeia	μυθοποίησις/η	the making of myths; creating myths
mythopoeic	μυθοποιός	one who creates myths
mythos	μύθος	myth; the complex of attitudes, beliefs, etc.
myxo/myx-	μύξα	mucus, slime
myxoidema/ myxedema	μυξοίδημα	Med. severe hypothyroidism, characterized by firm inelastic edema, dry skin and hair, in addition, loss of mental and physical strength and vigor
myxoma	μύξωμα	tumor of the mucus tissue (usually benign)
myxomatosis	μυξωμάτωσις/η	1 the presence of many myxomas 2 an infectious virus disease in rabbits transmitted by mosquitoes (characterized by tumorous growths, like myxomas)
myxomycete	μυξομύκητας	any of primitive organisms, usually classified as a thallophyte [division Myxomecota] but also as myxatozoan, that are found on decaying vegetation
myxorrhea	μυξόρροια	mucus flow

N

N,n (ne)	N,ν (Νι/)	the thirteenth letter of the Gr. alphabet
Naiad, naiad	Ναϊάς/ναϊάδος (gen.) /ναϊάδα (Mod. Gr.) (ναείν – to flow)	1 Gr. and Rom. myth. any of the nymphs living in and giving life to springs, fountains, rivers, and lakes 2 girl or woman swimmer 3 Bot. any of a family of monocotyledonous, subemerged, freshwater plants with only one genus (Najas), having linear opposite leaves 4 Zool. the aquatic nymph of certain insects, as the dragonfly and mayfly
nanism	νανισμός	the condition of being abnormally or exceptionally small in stature
nano-	νάνος	dwarf; a one billionth part of, combining form
nanocephalic	νανοκεφαλικός, ή, ό (adj.)	having an abnormally small head
nanogram	νανογράφημα	one billionth of a gram
nanometer	νανόμετρο(v)	one billionth of a meter
nanometry	νανομετρία/ νανομέτρηση	unit of length equal to one millionth of a milliometre
nanotechnology	νανο-τεχνολογία	a hypothetical method or process of creating microminiature equipment by manipulating atoms and molecules as if they were parts of a machine
nanus	νάνος	dwarf; height of one being much smaller than the normal
naphtha	νάφθα (νεφέλη- cloud)	1 flammable, volatile, oily liquid produced by the fractional distillation of petroleum

narcissism	ναρκισσισμός	in love with oneself; excessive interest in one's appearance, comfort, importance, abilities, etc.
Narcissus	Νάρκισσος	Gr. myth. when the beautiful youth who, after Echo's death, is to pine away for love of his own reflection in a spring and changes to narcissus/narkissos
narco-	νάρκη	temporary loss of the senses and mobility
narcoanalysis	ναρκοανάλυσις/η	psychotherapy performed under sedation, for the recovery of repressed memories together with the emotion accompanying the experience
narcoleptic	ναρκοληπτικός, ή, ό (adj.)	of, relating to, or affected with necrolepsy
narcolepsic	ναρκοληψικός, ή,ό (adj.)	an individual who is subject to attacks of narcolepsy
narcolepsy	ναρκοληψία	1 disease of unknown origin with periodic episodes of sleep any time day or night 2 a condition characterized by brief attacks of deep sleep, often occurring with cataplexy and hypnagogic hallucinations
narcomania	ναρκομανία	morbid desire for narcotics
narcophobia	ναρκοφοβία	extreme fear of narcotics
narcosis	νάρκωσις /η	1 a state of stupor, unconsciousness, or arrested activity produced by the influence of narcotics or other chemicals, or physical agents—*Nitrogen Narcosis*
narcosynthesis	ναρκοσύνθεσις /η	a method of treating an acute traumatic neurosis by working with a patient while under the influence of a narcotic drug

narcotic	ναρκωτικός, ή, ό (adj.)	producing a state of unconsciousness; any sleep-inducing drug
narcotize	ναρκώνω	1 to treat or subject to a narcotic 2 to put into a state of narcosis
narthex	νάρθηξ/νάρθηκας	the part of the church immediately after the entrance and before the main sanctuary
nauplius	ναύπλιος (ναύς + πλέειν –ship + to sail)	kind of shellfish, said to sail in its shell as in a ship
nausea	ναυτία	seasickness; a feeling of sickness at the stomach, with an impulse to vomit; disgust; loathing
naut-	ναύτ (ης/ναυτιλία / sailor/having to do w/the sea or navigation)	combining form
nautical	ναυτικός, ή, ό (adj.)	seaman; of, or having to do with sailors, ships, or navigation
nautilus	ναυτίλος	one working professionally at sea
necro- prefix	νεκρός, ή, ό (adj.)	corpse, dead body; one that is dead/deceased
necrobiosis	νεκροβίωσις/η	the process of decay and death of body cells
necrologist	νεκρολόγος	a specialist in necrology
necrology	νεκρολογία	1 a list of people who have died within a certain period, as that in a newspaper 2 a death notice; obituary
necromancer	νεκρομάντης	one practicing necromancy
necromancy	νεκρομαντεία	1 practice of claiming to foretell the future by alleged communication with the dead 2 black magic; sorcery
necromania	νεκρομανία	obsession with death

nacrophane	νεκροφάνεια	1 giving the appearance of dead 2 a condition of the human body when vital signs indicate there is no life, in reality they have temporarily ceased to function
necrophile	νεκρόφιλος	one affected with necrophilia
necrophilia	νεκροφιλία	1 an abnormal fascination with death and the dead 2 obsession with and usually erotic interest in or stimulation by corpses
necrophagia	νεκροφαγία	the eating of dead bodies; esp., the practice on carrion
necrophobia	νεκροφοβία	excessive fear of death
necropolis	νεκρόπολις /η	a cemetery, esp., one belonging to an ancient city
necropsy	νεκροψία	autopsy; examination of a dead body
necrosis	νέκρωσις /η	death of part of the body due to absence of blood supply
necrotic	νεκρωτικός, ή, ό (adj.)	affected with, characterized by, or producing necrosis
necrotic enteritis	νεκρωτική εντερίτις / εντερίτιδα (Mod. Gr.)	either of two often fatal infectious diseases, esp. by intestinal inflammation, necrosis, and by diarrhea: a) one affecting young swine, caused by a bacterium of the genus *Salmonella* (S. choleraesuis), also called *necro* b) one affecting paultry and caused by a bacterium of the genus *Clostridium* (C. perfringens)
necrotic rhinitis	νεκρωτική ρινίτιδα	a necrobacillosis arising in facial wounds of swine bullosa
necrotomy	νεκροτομή	1 dissection of corpses 2 surgical removal of dead bone
nectar	νέκταρ	it was regarded as the drink of the myth. gods; the drink of immortality

nemat-	νήμα – νήματος (gen.)	thread; what is spun, combining form, threadlike (nematic)
nematic	νηματικός, ή, ό (adj.)	designating a kind of liquid crystal in which the molecules spontaneously align themselves with their axes parallel
nemato-	νήμα/νήματος (gen.)	what is spun, thread; threadlike
nematocyst	νηματο-κύστις /η	any of the intracellural stinging structures characteristic of all cridarians, as the jellyfish: it contains a threadlike sting
Nemesis	νέμεσις/η /νέμειν	to distribute, deal out, Gr. myth. the goddess of retributive justice, or vengeance; just punishment; retribution
neo-	νέο / νέος, α, ο (adj.)	young, new, recent, combining form
neogala	νέο-γάλα	first milk after childbirth
neogenesis	νέο-γένεσις/η	new formation; regeneration, esp. of tissue
neon	νεον(net. of : νέος, νέα, νέο (v)	new, a rare colorless and gaseous chemical element
neolithic	νεολιθικός, ή, ό (adj.)	designating or of to an Old World cultural period (c. 8000– c. 3500 BC) characterized by polished stone tools, pottery, weaving, agriculture, and sometimes megaliths
neologism	νεολογισμός	1 a new word or a new meaning for an established word 2 the use of, or the practice of creating, new new words or new meanings for already established words 3 a word coined by a psychotic individual, which is meaningless except to the coiner
neopathy	νεοπάθεια	new disease or complication
neophilism	νεοφιλισμός	excessive love for new things
neophobia	νεοφοβία	extreme fear of new things

neophyte	νεοφυτικός, ή, ό (adj.)/νέος +φυτό- new + plant	newly planted
neoplasia	νεοπλασία	1 the growth of new tissue 2 the process of tumor formation 3 a tumorous condition of the body—*Prostatic Intraepithelial Neoplasia*
neoplasm	νεόπλασμα	a new growth of tissue serving no physiological function: *Tumor*
Neoplatonism	Νεο-πλατωνισμός	a school of philosophy developed by Plotinus in Alexandria, based on a modified Platonism, and postulating a single source from which all forms of existence emanate and with which the soul seeks mystical union
nepiod	(ο, η) νηπιώδης (το) νηπιώδες	pertaining to something very young and immature; like an infant
nepiology	νηπιολογία	study of newborns
nephr-	νεφρός (anc.) νεφρό	kidney combining form (nephrectomy) νεφροί (anc. pl. of νεφρός / nephroi)
nephralgia	νεφραλγία	pain in a kidney
nephrectomy	νεφρό-εκτομή/ kidney-incision/cut	surgical removal of one kidney or both kidneys
nephrelcus	νεφρό(ς)-έλκος	renal ulcer
nephric	νεφρικός, ή, ό (adj.)	pertaining to the kidney
nephritic	νεφριτικός, ή, ό (adj.)	renal; of, relating to, or affected with nephritis
nephritis	νεφρίτις /νεφρίτιδα	inflammation of the kidneys
nephro-	νεφρός/ νεφρό(ν)	pertaining to kidney(s)
nephrogenic	νεφρογενικός, ή, ό / νεφρογενής/ νεφρογενές (adj.)	1 originating in the kidney: caused by factors originating in the kidney [—hypertension] 2 developing into or producing kidney tissue
nephrogram	νεφρογράφημα	x-ray of the kidney(s)

nephtography	νεφρογράφος / νεφρογραφία	radiography of the kidney(s)
nephrolithiasis	νεφρολιθίασις/η (νεφρό + λίθος – kidney + stone)	1 formation of kidney stones; 2 a condition marked by the presence of renal calculi
nephrologist	νεφρολόγος	a specialist in nephrology
nephrology	νεφρολογία	study of the kidneys; a medical specialty concerned with the kidneys and esp. with their structure, functions, or diseases
nephroma	νέφρωμα	tumor in the outer portion of the kidney; Med. a malignant tumor of the renal cortex
nephropathy	νεφροπάθεια	an abnormal state of the kidney; esp. one associated with or secondary to some other pathological process
nephroptosis	νεφρόπτωσις /η	abnormal mobility of the kidney: floating kidney
nephrorhaphy	νεφρορραφή	1 the fixation of a floating kidney by suturing it to the posterior abdominal wall 2 the suturing of a kidney wound
-nephros	νεφρός/νεφρό	kidney; suffix forming nouns (pronephros)
nephrosclerosis	νεφροσκλήρωσις /η	hardening of the kidney; specif. a condition that is characterized by sclerosis of the renal arterioles with reduced blood flow and contraction of the kidney, associated usually with hypertension that terminates in renal failure and ueremia; compare *Nephritis*
nephrosis	νέφρωσις/η	1 disintegration of the kidney without signs of inflammation 2 a noninflammatory disease of the kidneys, chiefly affecting function of the nefrons; compare *Nephritis*

nephrostomy	νεφροστόμιον	the surgical of an opening between a renal pelvis and the outside of the body
neur- or neuro-	νεύρ/ νεύρο	nevre, combining form (neural; neurology)
neuralgia	νευραλγία	painful disorder of one or more nerves
neurapraxia	νευραπραξία (νεύρο + απραξία – nerve + no action)	an injury to a nerve that interrupts conduction causing temporary paralysis but not degeneration and that is followed by a complete and rapid recovery
neurasthenia	νευρασθένεια	exhaustion of the nerves
neurasthenic	νευρασθενικός, ή, ό (adj.)	1 relating to, or having neurasthenia 2 a person affected with neurasthenia
neurectomy	νευρεκτομή	surgical removal of a nerve or part of a nerve
neuritis	νευρίτις/νευρίτιδα	disorder of one or more nerves
neuroanatomy	νευρο-ανατομία	the anatomy of nervous tissue and the nervous system
neuro-arthro-pathy	νευρο-αρθρο-πάθεια – nevre- joint-illness)	a joint disease (as Charcot's joint) that is associated with a disorder of the nervous system
neurobiology	νευροβιολογία	science for the study of nerves
neuroblast	νευροβλαστός	any of the embryonic cells from which the nerve cells develop
neuro-blastoma	νευροβλάστωμα	malignant tumor of the nervous system
neuro-cardio-genic syncope	νευρο-καρδιο-γενής συγκοπή	a usually transitory condition that is marked esp. by fainting associated with hypotension, peripheral vasodilation, and bradycardia resulting from increased stimulation of the vegus nerve; also called *Vasovagal syncope*
neuro-chemistry	νευρο-χημεία	the branch of neurology dealing with the chemistry of the nervous system

neuro-cranium	νευρο-κρανίον	the part of the cranium that encloses the brain
neuro-dermatitis	νευρο-δερματίτις / δερματίτιδα	a chronic eczematous dermatitis /inflammation arising from continuous rubbing or scratching, of a real or imagined irritation of the skin
neurogenesis	νευρογένεσις /η	development of nerves, nervous tissue, or the nervous system
neurogenetics	νευρογενετική	a branch of genetics dealing with the nervous system and its development
neurogenic	(ο, η) νευρογενής, (το) νευρογενές (adj.)	indicating any disorder that originates from within the nervous system; stimulated or induced by nervous factors
neuro-histology	νευρο-ιστολογία	a branch of histology dealing with the nervous system and its diseases
neuro-hormonal	νευρο-ορμονικός, ή, ό (adj.)	1 involving both neural and hormonal mechanism 2 of, relating to, or being a neurohormone
neuro-hypophysis	νευρο-υπόφυσις /η	the portion of the pituitary gland that is derived from the embryonic brain, is composed of the infundibulum and neural lobe, and is involved with the secretion of various hormones
neuroid	(ο, η) νευροειδής, (το) νευροειδές (adj.)	resembling the nerve
neurologist	νευρολόγος	expert in neurological diseases
neurology	νευρολογία	science dealing with the nervous system
neurolysis	νευρόλυσις /η	the breaking down of nervous (as from disease or injury)
neuron	νεύρον/ο	nerve
neuronitis	νευρίτις/νευρίτιδα	inflammation of a nerve
neuropath	(ο, η) νευροπαθής (το) νευριπαθές (adj.)	an early term for neurotic

neuro-pharmacologist	νευρο-φαρμακολόγος	a specialist in neuropharmacology
neuro-pharmacology	νευροφαρμακολογία	a branch of medical science dealing with the action of drugs
neuro-psychiatrist	νευρο-ψυχίατρος	a specialist in neuropsychiatry
neuro-psychiatry	νευρο- ψυχιατρία/ ψυχιατρική	a branch of medicine concerned with disorders of both the mind and the nervous system
neuro-psychologist	νευρο-ψυχολόγος	a specialist in neuropsychology
neuropshychology	νευρο-ψυχολογία	1 a science concerned with the integration of psychological observations on behavior, and the mind with neurological observations on the brain and the nervous system 2 the psychology of the nervous system
neurosis	νεύρωσις/η	any of various mental functional disorders, characterized by anxiety, compulsions, phobias, depression, etc.
neurotic	νευρικός, ή, ό (adj.)	characteristic of, or having a neurosis; excitable; edgy
neurotomy	νευροτομή	1 the dissection or cutting of nerves 2 the division of a nerve (as to relieve neuralgia)
neurotrauma	νεύρο + τραύμα – nerve + trauma	injury to a nerve or to the nervous system
nike	νίκη	victory; Nike: Gr. myth. the winged goddess of victory, also, a girl's name
nomisma	νόμισμα	currency, coin
nomismatic	νομισματικός, ή, ό (adj.)	of or having to do with currency
nomismatics	νομισματική	the study or collection of coins, medals, paper money, etc.
nomo- prefix	νόμος	law, combining form

-nomy	- νομία (νόμος –law/order)	to assign; arrange, suffix forming nouns indicating the systematized knowledge of or the system of laws governing, or a sum of knowledge regarding a specified field (taxonomy, astronomy, etc.)
nomocanon	νομο/κανών/κανόνας	a collection of canons and imperial laws relative or comparable thereto
nomographer	νομογράφος	one who writes on the subject of laws
nomography	νομογραφή/ νομογραφία	a treatise or description of laws
nomotheta	νομοθέτης	a lawgiver such as **Solon** and **Lycurgus** among the Greeks and **Ceasar**, **Pompey** and **Sylla** among the Romans
nosema	νόσημα	sickness; disease; illness
noso-	νόσος	illness, combining form (nosology)
nosocomial	νοσοκομιακός, ή, ό (adj.) (νοσοκομείον/ο – hospital)	of or beginning in a hospital or medical facility; esp., of a hospital-acquired disease or infection; (nosocomial disease or infection)
nosologic	νοσολογικός, ή, ό (adj.)	pertaining to nosology
nosologic	νοσολογικός, ή, ό (adj.)	pertaining to nosology
nosologist	νοσολόγος	a specialist in nosology
sologist	νοσολόγος	a specialist in nosology
nosology	νοσολογία	science of diseases classification 2 a branch of medical science dealing with the classification of diseases
nosophilia	νοσοφιλία	extreme desire to be sick
nosophobia	νοσοφοβία	extreme fear of being sick

nostalgia	νοσταλγία	1 a longing to go back to one's home, hometown, or homeland homesickness 2 a longing for something far away or long ago, or for former happy circumstances
nostalgic	νοσταλγικός, ή, ό (adj.)	relating to nostalgia
nostology	νοστολογία (νόστος – a return)	early term *for* **Gerontology**
nostomania	νοστομανία	Psychiatry, excessive or abnormal nostalgia
nyx/nyct- or Nyx	νυξ/νύκτα	night; Gr. myth. the goddess of night
nyctaopia/ nyctalopia	νυκταλωπία	inability to sleep at night or in low light (during the day)
nycterine	νυκτερινός, ή, ό (adj.)	occurring at night
nycto-	νυξ/νυκτός (gen.)	of the night, combining form
nyctophobia	νυκτοφοβία	extreme fear of the night or the dark
nyctotyphlosis	νυκτοτύφλωσις/η	night blindness
nymph	νύμφη	bride; young wife; spring goddess
nympholepsy	νυμφοληψία	seized by nymps
nymphomania	νυμφομανία	uncontrollable desire by a woman for sex
nymphomaniac	νυμφομανής	pertaining to nymphomania
nystagmus	νύστα/νυσταγμός	an involuntary, rapid eye movement of the eyeball
nystagmic	νυσταγμένος, η, ο (adj. partic.)/ νυσταλέος, α, ο (adj.)	pertaining to nystagmus, sleepy

O

ocean	ωκεανός	the outer sea (in contrast to Mediterranean), orig. thought as a great river flowing around the earth

oceanaut	ωκεοναύτης	1 aquanaut; a person trained to live and work in a watertight underwater chamber in and from which he can conduct oceanographic experiments 2 a skin diver
oceanic	ωκεανικός, ή, ό (adj.)	living in, or produced by the ocean
Oceanid	Ωκεανίς/ Ωκεανίδος (gen.)/ Ωκεανίδες (pl.)	Gr. myth. any of three thousand ocean nymphs, daughters of Oceanus and Tethys
oceanography	ωκεανογραφία	study of the environment of the oceans, including the waters, depths, beds, animals, plants, etc.
oceanographer	ωκεανογράφος	scientist studying the oceans
oceanographic	ωκεανογραφικός, ή, ό (adj.)	pertaining to oceanography
oceanology	ωκεανολογία	1 the study of the sea in all its aspects, including oceanology, geophysical phenomena, undersea exploration, economic and military uses, etc. 2 the greater outer stream supposedly encircling the earth
Oceanus	Ωκεανός	Gr. myth. a Titan, father of the Oceanides (3,000 ocean nymphs), and ruler of the sea before Poseidon
ochlo-	όχλος	unruly crowd; mob
ochlocracy	οχλοκρατία	government by a mob (disorderly people)
ochlophobia	οχλοφοβία	extreme fear of crowds
October	Οκτώβριος	the tenth month of the year having thirty-one days
octagon	οκτάγωνο(ν) (οκτώ + γωνία- eight + angle)	a plane figure with eight angles and eight sides
octamerous	οκτάμερος (οκτώ- μέρος–μέρη/ eight-part(s)	having eight parts

octametron	οκτάμετρον/ο	having eight meters
October	Οκτώβριος	the eighth month of the ancient Roman calendar, when the year began in March
octopus	οκτάπους/ οκταπόδι/χταπόδι	1 any of various octopods, having eight sucker-bearing arms around the mouth 2 a soft saclike body, eight sucker-bearing arms around the mouth, etc. 3 anything suggesting an octopus; esp. an organization with branches that reach out in a powerful and influential manner
octosyllabic	οκτώ-συλλαβικός, ή, ό (adj.)	1 containing eight syllables, as a line or verse 2 containg lines of eight syllables
octosyllable	οκτώ-συλλαβή (οκτωσύλλαβη)	a word or a line of verse having eight syllables
octuple	οκτάπλους/ οκταπλούν	eightfold, consisting of eight parts
odotectomy	οδοντοεκτομή	tooth extraction
odont-	οδούς (Anc. Gr.)/ οδών/οδόντος (gen.) όδόντας / δόντι (Mod. Gr.)	tooth
odontalgia	οδόντας / αλγία / οδονταλγία	toothache
-odontia	- δόντια	combining form: forming nouns showing a condition or a mode of treatment of the teeth (orthodontia)
odontitis	οδοντίτις/οδοντίτιδα	tooth inflammation
odontiasis/odontosis	οδοντίασις/η —οδόντωσις/η	teething; the formation of the first teeth of a person
odontic	οδοντικός, ή, ό (adj.)	pertaining to the teeth
odontoclasis	οδοντόκλασις /η	breaking a tooth
odontogenesis	οδοντογένεσις /η	the formation and development of teeth

odontogenic	οδοντογενικός, ή, ό / οδοντογενής **(adj.)**	1 forming or capable of forming teeth (odontogenic tissues) 2 containing or arising from odontogenic tissues (odontogenic tumor)
odontologist	οδοντολόγος	a specialist in odontology
odontology	οδοντολογία	1 a science concerned with the structure, development, and the diseases of teeth 2 forensic odontology
odontoma	οδόντωμα (οδόντας + ογκος – **tooth and tumor.oncos)**	a tumor arising from the same tissue off which teeth are formed and contains dental tissue (as enamel)
odontotomy	οδοντοτομή	incision of the tooth
-odynia	-οδύνια/οδύνη	pain combining form (indicating pain in a specific organ or part) [pleurodynia]
odynophagia	οδυνοφαγεία (οδύνη-φαγείν/ **pain-to eat)**	painful swallowing; difficulty eating
odynophobia	οδυνο-φοβία (οδύνη-φόβος)	extreme fear of pain
odyne/odynia	οδύνη	pain, combining form
Odysseus	Οδυσσεύς/Οδυσσέας	the hero of the Odyssey, Latin name: Ullyses
Odyssey	Οδύσσεια	long journey; dangerous adventure (Homer's *Odyssey*) the long and dangerous Oddysseus return to Ithaka, his homeland, after the Trojan War
Oedipus	Οιδίπους / Οιδίποδας **(lit. swollen feet)**	Gr. myth. the son of Laius and Jocasta, king and queen of Thebes, but was raised by the king of Corinth, when later returned to Thebes unwittingly kills his father and marries his mother

Oedipus Complex	οιδιπόδειον σύμπλεγμα	1 Psychoanalysis the unconscious tendency of a child to be attached to the parent of the opposite sex and hostile or jealous to the other parent: its persistence in adult life results in neurotic disorders: orig. restricted to a son's attachment: cf. *Electra Complex* 2 abnormal love of a child usu. of a boy for his mother
oenology	οινοπωλεία	science or study of wines and winemaking
oenologist	οινολόγος	expert in wines; connoisseur
olig- or oligo-	ολίγος, η, ο (adj.)	little; small; scant; deficiency; few, combining form (oligarchy)
oligaemia or oligemia	ολίγο+ αίμα – little + blood	a condition in which the total volume of the blood is reduced
oligarch	ολιγάρχης	any of the rulers of an oligarchy
oligarchy	ολιγαρχία	form of government in which the ruling power belongs to few people
oligo-daktylism	ολίγα δάκτυλα	the presence of fewer than five digits on a hand or foot
oligophrenia	ολιγο-φρενία (ολίγα + φρένα / deficient + brain)	mental retardation; subaverage intellectual ability equivalent to or less than an IQ of 70 that is accompanied by significant deficits in abilities (as in communication or self-care) necessary for independent daily living, is present from birth or infancy, and is manifested esp. by delayed or abnormal development, by learning difficulties and by problem in social adjustment
oliguria	ολιγοουρία	reduced excretion of urine
oligo- prefix	ολίγος, η, ο (adj.)	small, little, scant
oligophagous	ολιγοφάγος	feeding upon a limited amount of food, eating very little

oligopoly	ολιγοπώλειο(ν)	control of a commodity or service, in a given market, by a small number of companies or suppliers
oligopsony	ολιγο-ψώνια/ small-purchases	control of purchase of food
oligotrophic	ολιγοτροφικός, ή, ό (adj.)	sustained by very little food
Omega	Ω, ω (ωμέγα)	the twenty-fourth letter of the Gr. alphabet, also meaning the end, e,g., from Alpha to Omega: from beginning to end
O (omicron)	O, o (όμικρο(ν)	the fifteenth letter of the Gr. alphabet
omo-	ωμός, ή, ό (adj.)	raw (as in foods)
omophagia	ωμοφαγία	eating raw meat, vegetables, etc.
omophagos	ωμοφάγος	someone eating raw foods
omphalo-	ομφαλός	1 navel, umbilicus 2 a central point 3 a rounded stone in Apollo's temple at Delphi, regarded as the center of the world by the ancients; omphalo- combining form
omphalectomy	ομφαλεκτομή	a surgical procedure of the navel
omphalic	ομφαλικός, ή, ό (adj.)	pertaining to navel
omphalitis	ομφαλίτις/ ομφαλίτιδα	inflammation of the navel
omphalocele	ομφαλοκήλη	protrusion of abdominal contents through an opening at occurring esp. as a congenital defect
omphalo-phlebitis	ομφαλο-φλεβίτις / φλεβίτιδα	a condition (as navel ill) characterized by or resulting from inflammation and infection of the umbilical vein
onco - prefix	όγκος/όγκο (objective case)	bulk, mass, tumor
oncocyte	ογκοκύτταρον/ο	an acidiphilic granular cell esp. of the parotid gland

oncocytoma	ογκοκύτωμα	a tumor (as of the parotid gland) consisting chiefly or entirely of oncocytes
oncogene	(ο, η) ογκογενής (το) ογκογενές (adj.)	any of various genes that when activated, as from radiation or a virus, may cause a normal cell to become cancerous
oncogenesis	ογκογένεσις /η	causing tumors
oncologist	ογκολόγος	a physician specializing in oncology
oncology	ογκολογία	the branch of medicine dealing with neoplasms
oncolysis	ογκόλυσις /η	the destruction of tumor cells
oneiric	ονειρικός, ή, ό (adj.)	having to do with dreams
oneiro	όνειρον/ο	dream, combining word
oneiromancy	ονειρομαντεία	practice foretelling the future by interpreting dreams
onomastic	ονομαστικός, ή, ό (adj.)	to name, having to do with a name or names
onomastics	ονομαστική	the study of origin, form, meaning of names esp., proper names
onomatopoeia	ονοματο-ποιϊα	echoism; the use of words whose sounds reinforce their meaning or tone as in poetry
onto-	ον/όντος (gen.)	being; existence, combining form (ontology)
ontogeny	οντογένεια	the life cycle of an organism; biological development of the individual
ontology	οντολογία	the branch of metaphysics dealing with the nature of being, reality, or ultimate substance
onych- or onycho	όνυξ /όνυχος/ όνυχας/ νύχι	nail of the finger or toe, combining form (onycholysis)
onychectomy	ονυχεκτομή	surgical excision of a fingernail ot toenail
onychia	ονυχίασις /η/ονυχία	inflammation of the matrix of a nail often leading to suppuration and loss of the nail

-onychia	ονύχια/ονυχία	combining form, condition of the nails of the fingers or toes (leukonychia)
onycholysis	ονυχόλυσις /η	a loosening of a nail from its nail bed beginning at the free edge and proceeding to the root
onycho-gryposis	ονυχο-γρύπωσις /η	1 the hypertophic deformity of a toenail which is enlarged and hardened, changes direction and is curved as a horn 2 an abdormal condition of the nails characterized by marked hypertrophy and increased curvature
onycho-madesis	ονυχο-μάδησις /η	loosening and shedding of the nails
onycho-mycosis	ονυχομύκωσις/η	a fungal disease of the nails
-onym suffix	ώνυμον	as in acronym; synonym; pseudonym; etc.
onyx	όνυξ/όνυχος(γεν/ gen.)/όνυχας	its color resembles that of a fingernail; variety of agate with alternate colored layers, used as a semiprecious stone
oo	ωόν/αυγό	egg or ovum, combining form
oocyesis	ωοκύησις /η	extrauterine pregnancy in an ovary
oocyst	ωοκύστις/η	a sporozoan zygote undergoing sporogenous development
oocyte	ωόν + κύτταρο(ν) – egg + cyte/cell	Embryology: an egg that has not yet undergone maturation
oogenesis	ωογένεσις/η	the process by which the ovum is formed in preparation for its development
ootheca	ωοθήκη	an egg case, as of certain mollusks and insects
ophi-	όφις	snake; serpent, combining form
ophiolatry	οφιολατρεία	the worship of serpents
ophiologic	οφιολογικός, ή, ό(adj.)	pertaining to ophiology
ophiologist	οφιολόγος	expert in serpents, snakes

ophiology	οφιολογία	the branch of zoology dealing with snakes/serpents
ophitic	οφιτικός, ή, ό (adj.)	snake stone; designating the texture of the stone/rock
ophthalm-	οφθαλμό- οφθαλμός	eye; (ophthalmology) eyeball (ophthalmo-dynamometry)
-ophthalmia	-οφθαλμια	combining form, a condition of the eyes (as microphthalmia)
ophthalmia	οφθαλμία	severe inflammation of the eyeball or conjunctiva
ophthalmic	οφθαλμικός, ή, ό (adj.)	1 of, relating to, or situated near the eye 2 supplying or draining the eye or structures in the region of the eye
ophthalmic artery	οφθαλμική αρτηρία	a branch of the internal carotid artery following the optic nerve through the optic foramen into the orbit and supplying the eye and the adjacent structures
ophthalmic nerve	οφθαλμικό νεύρο	one of the three major branches or divisions of the trigeminal nerve tha supply sensory fibers to the lacrimal gland, eyelids, ciliary muscle, nose, forehead, and the adjoining parts; also called *ophthalmic division*
ophthalmo-dynamo-metry	οφθαλμο-δυναμο-μετρία/μέτρηση	measurement of the arterial blood pressure in the retina
ophthalmo-	οφθαλμός/μάτι (Mod. Gr.)	eye, combining form
ophthalmologist	οφθαλμολόγος	physician specializing in eyes, eye doctor
ophthalmology	οφθαλμολογία	branch of medicine dealing with the structure, functions, and diseases of the eye
ophthalmo-plegia	οφθαλμο-πληγία	paralysis of some or all the muscles of the eye
ophthalmoscope	οφθαλμοσκόπιον/o	instrument used for viewing the interior of the eye, consisting of a concave mirror with a hole in the center through which the observer examines the eye

ophthalmoscopy	οθαλμοσκόπηση	examination of the eye with an ophthalmoscope
-opia suffix	-ωπία / μυωπία	as in myopia, presvyopia, etc.
orchido-	ορχίδέας (gen.)	of orchid, combining form
orchi-	όρχι/ορχιδέα	pertaining to orchid(s)
orchidology	ορχιδεολογία	the branch of horticulture dealing with orchids
orchidotomy	ορχιδοτομή	surgical incision of a testicle
orchiectomy	ορχιδεκτομή	surgical removal of one or two testicles; castration
orchiodynia	ορχιοδυνία	testicle pain
orchioncus	όρχι-όγκος	tumor of the testes
orchis	όρχις	testicle
orchitis	ορχίτις /ορχίτιδα	inflammation of the testicle(s)
-orexia	-ορεξία (όρεξη- appetite)	suffix forming nouns (anorexia, without appetite)
oreximania	ορεξιμανία	extreme desire for food
organ or organ-	όργανο(ν)	group of tissue with specific function in the body; also a musical instrument, combining form (organize)
organic	οργανικός, ή, ό (adj.)	of or having to do with a bodily organ; some of the simple compounds of carbon, as carbon dioxide
organism	οργανισμός	individual animal or plant
organist	όργανο-παίκτης	an organ player
organization	οργάνωσις/η	1 organizing or being organized; a body of persons organized/consolidated for a specific purpose 2 Biol. the formation of fibrous tissue from a clot or exudates by invasion of connective issue cells and capillaries from adjoining
organize	οργανώνω	providing with an organic structure; to arrange in an orderly way

organizer	οργανωτής	1 one responsible to organize 2 Biol. a region of a developing embryo (as part of the dorsal lip of the blastophore) or a substance produced by such a region that is capable of inducing a specific type of development in undifferentiated tissue; also called *inductor*
orgasm	οργασμός	sexual climax
orgy	όργιο(v)/όργια (pl.	in ancient Greece and Rome feasting and wild celebration in worship of certain gods, esp. Dionysos (the god of wine and revelry); any wild merrymaking in a group, esp. with sexual activity
ornis	όρνις/όρνιθος (gen.)	bird; chicken
ornithic	ορνιθικός, ή ό (adj.)	of or characteristic of birds
ornitho-	όρνις-όρνιθος (gen.)/ όρνιθα (obj.)	bird/birds, combining form (ornithology, also before a vowel, ornith-)
ornithoid	(ο, η) ορνιθοειδής (το) ορνιθοειδές (adj.)	resembling a bird in appearance or structure
ornithologist	ορνιθολόγος	a specialist in ornithology
ornithology	ορνιθολογία	the branch of zoology dealing with birds; paultry
ornithopod	ορνιθόποδας	any of the suborder (Ornithopoda, order Ornithischia) plant-eating dinosaurs that walked upright on digitigrade hind feet
ornithosis	ορνίθωσις/η	a virus disease (such as psittacosis) transmitted by birds
oro-	όρος	mountain
orogeny	ορογένεια	the formation of mountains through structural disturbance of the ear´παθλτρυth's crust, esp. by folding and faulting

orography	ορογραφία	the branch of physical geography dealing with mountains
orology	ορολογία	the study of mountains
orphan	ορφανός, ή, ό (adj.)	a child whose parent or parents have died
orphanage	ορφανοτροφείο(ν)	an institution for orphans
Orpheus	Ορφεύς/Ορφέας	Gr. myth. a poet-musician with magic musical powers, who descends to the underworld to lead his wife, Euridice, back from the dead; he failed though because he breaks the injuction not to look at her till they reach the upper world
Orphic	ορφικός, ή, ό (adj.)	of or characteristic of Orpheus or the mystic doctrines and rites in worship of Dionysos ascribed to him
Orphism	Ορφισμός	the rites and religion ascribed to Orpheus as founder
ortho-	ορθρός, ή, ό (adj.)	correct, straight, true, combining form
orthochromatic	ορθοχρωματικός, ή, ό (adj.)	designating or of photographic film that is sensitive to all colors except red and deep orange
orthodontics	ορθοδοντιατρική	the branch of dentistry concerned with diagnosing, correcting, and preventing irregularities of the teeth and correct occlusion
orthodox	ορθόδοξος, η, o (adj.)	conforming to the usual beliefs or established doctrines, as in religion, politics, etc.; approved or conventional (orthodox ideas)
Orthodox Church	Ορθόδοξος Εκκλησία	Eastern Orthodox Church

Orthodoxy	Ορθοδοξία	1 the quality or fact of being orthodox 2 an orthodox belief, doctrine, custom, etc.
orthoepy	ορθοεπεία ορθός + έπος/right + epos, a word	the study of pronunciation; phonology; the standard pronunciation of a language
orthogenesis	ορθογένεσις	Biol. a now discredited theory which states that the progressive evolution of certain organisms, in a restricted direction throughout successive generations, is independent of outside influences and natural selection
orthognathic	ορθογναθικός, ή, ό (adj.)	correcting deformities of the jaw and the associated malocclusion (orthognathic surgery)
orthognathous	ορθό +γνάθος (correct + jaw)	having the jaws in line with the lower jaw, neither projecting nor receding
orthogonal	ορθογώνιος, α, ο (adj.)	having the right angles; perpendicular; rectangular
orthographic	ορθογραφικός, ή, ό (adj.)	of or characterized by orthography
orthography	ορθογραφία (ορθός + γράφειν correct + write)	correct writing 1 spelling in accord with accepted usage 2 any style or method of spelling 3 spelling as a subject for study
ortho-kerato-logy	ορθο-κέρατο-λογία	the branch of optometry dealing with the problems of the cornea
orthopedics	ορθοπαιδική	branch of medicine dealing with surgery of bones and joints
orthopedist	ορθοπαιδικός	specialist in orthopedics
orthoscope	ορθοσκόπιο (v)	an instrument for examining the interior of the eye
orthoscopic	ορθοσκοπικός, ή, ό (adj.)	giving a true flat image without distortion
orthosis	όρθωσις/η	correction of an infirmity
orthostatic	ορθοστατικός, ή, ό (adj.)	pertaining to standing position

orthopnea	ορθοπνοή	position in which difficult breathing is aided by propping up head and shoulders
orthopsychiatry	ορθοψυχιατρική	branch of psychiatry dealing mainly with adolescents
orthuria	ορθή-ουρία/ ορθ(ο)ουρία	normal frequency of urination
osm- or osmo-	οσμή	smell combining form (osmotic)
osmetic	οσμητικός, ή, ό (adj.)	having acute sense of smell
osmesis	όσμησις /η	smell; the sense of smell
osmosis	όσμωσις/ η-οσμή	the tendency of a solvent to pass through a semipermeable membrane, as the wall of a living cell, into a solution of a higher concentration; (through) osmosis
ophresis	όσφρησις /η	the sense of smell
ostectomy	οστεο-εκτομή	surgical removal of a bone
osteitis or ostitis	οστεϊτις/ οστεϊτιδα	bone inflammation
osteo-	οστεο-	pertaining to bone(s), combining word (osteopathy)
osteoarthritis	οστεοαρθρίτις/ αρθρίτιδα	degenerarive joint disease; arthritis typically with onset during middle age or old age that is characterized by degenerative and sometimes hypotrophic changes in bone and cartilage of one or more joints and a progressive wearing down of opposing joint surfaces with consequent distortion of joint position, and is marked symptomatically, esp., with pain, swelling and stiffness, abbr. *OA;* also called degenerative arthritis, degenerative joint disease, hypertophic arthritis; compare ***Rhumatoid Arthritis***

osteoclasis	οστέο + κλάσις/η– bone + a breaking	1 the breaking down and absorption of bony tissue 2 the breaking of a bone to correct a deformity esp., after a badly healed old fracture
osteo-arthro-pathy	οστεο-αρθρο-πάθεια	a disease of joints or bones; specif., a hypertrophic condition marked esp., by clubbing of the fingers and toes, painful swollen joints and periostitis, and subperiosteal bone formation chiefly affecting the long bones (as the radius or fibula) and that usually occurs secondary to another disease (as bronchiectasis or cirrhosis); also called *acropathy*
osteocarcinoma	οστεο-καρκίνωμα	bone cancer
osteochondritis	οστεο-χονδρίτις/ χονδρίτιδα	inflammation of both bone and cartilage from which bone is formed (οστόν/ χόνδρος-bone&cartilage)
osteoid	(ο, η) οστεοειδής (το) οστεοειδές (adj.)	resembling a bone
osteology	οστεολογία	study of the bones
osteoma	οστέωμα	tumor composed of various parts of bone
osteomalacia	οστεομαλακία	softening of bone(s)
osteomyelitis	οστεομυελίτις/ οστεομυελίτιδα	inflammatory bone disease caused usually by infection/ also it can occur after a bone is fractured
osteo-necrosis	οστεο-νέκρωσις /η	necrosis of bone; esp., *Avascular Necrosis*
osteopath	οστεοπαθητικός	a practitioner of osteopathy
osteo-pathetics	οστεοπαθητική	method of treatment believing that cure is achieved by bone manipulation

osteopathy	οστεοπάθεια	1 any disease affecting the bones 2 a system of medical practice based on a theory that diseases are due chiefly to loss of structural integrity which can be restored by manipulation of the parts supplemented by therapeutic measures (as the use of medicine or surgery)
osteopetrosis	οστεοπέτρωσις/η	a rare hereditary disease characterized by extreme density and hardness and abnormal fragility of the bones with partial or complete obliteration of the narrow cavities; also called *Albers-Shonberg disease*
osteoplasty	οστεοπλασία	1 surgery of or based on replacement of bone by restorative operations 2 a school of medicine and surgery employing various methods of diagnosis and treatment, but placing special emphasis on the interrelationship of the musculoskeletal system to all other body systems
osteoporosis	οστεοπόρωσις/η	a disorder that causes a gradual decrease in both the amount and strength of bone tissue; reduction of bone density accompanied by increasing porocity and brittleness
osteo-radio-necrosis	οστεο-ραδιο-νέκρωσις /η	necrosis of bone following irradiation
osteosarcoma	οστεο-σάρκωμα	a sarcoma derived from bone or containing bone tissue; also called ***osteogenic sarcoma***
osteosclerosis	οστεο-σκλήρωσις /η	abnormal hardening of bone or bone marrow
osteoma	οστέωμα	benign tumor composed of bony tissue

osteosis	οστέωσις/η	formation of bony tissue
osteosynthesis	οστεο-σύνθεσις/η	the operation of uniting the ends of a fractured bone by mechanical means (as a wire)
osteotomy	οστεοτομή	surgical operation of dividing a bone or cutting out a piece of a bone
-ostomy suffix	-όστομη	any surgery connecting a hollow organ to the outside of the body or to another hollow organ (as colostomy)
-ostosis	-όστέωσις /η	ossification of a specified part or a specified degree, combining form (hyperostosis)
ostracism	οστρακισμός	1 in ancient Greece, the temporary banishment of a citizen 2 a rejection or exclusion by general consent, as from a group or from acceptance by society
ostrasize	οστρακίζω/ οστρακίζειν(v.)	to bar, banish, exclude; to exile by votes written on tiles or potsherds/ ostrakon - a shell, potsherd
ostracod/ostracon	όστρακο(v)	any of various classes (esp. Ostracoda) of small, freshwater or marine crustaceans
ot- or oto-	ους/ωτός αυτί	ear, combining form (otitis; otorhinolaryngology)
otalgia	ωταλγία	earache; any pain or ache of the ear
otic	ωτικός, ή, ό (adj.)	pertaining to the ear
otitis	ωτίτις/ωτίτιδα	inflammation of the ear
otologist	ωτολόγος	ear specialist
otology	ωτολογία	the branch of medicine dealing with the ear and its disorders
otopathy	ωτοπάθεια	any ear disease
otolith	ωτόλιθος	a calcareous concretion in the internal ear composed of masses of otoconia; also called *statolith*

otoplasty	ωτοπλασία	plastic surgery of the external ear
otorrhoea or otorrhea	ωτόρροια	a discharge from the external ear
oto-rhino-laryngo-logist	ωτο-ρινο-λαρυγγο-λόγος	ear-nose-larynx/throat specialist
otorhinolaryngology	ωτο-ρινο-λαρυγγο-λογία	branch of medicine dealing with ear, nose, and larynx (throat)
otosclerosis	ωτοσκλήρωσις/η	1 deafness caused by hardening of the tissues and bones of the inner ear 2 growth of spongy bone in the inner ear which gradually obstructs the oval window or round window or both and progressively causes increasing deafness
otoscope	ωτοσκόπιο(ν)	instrument examining the ear
ototoxic	ωτοξικός, ή, ό (adj.)	producing, involving, or being adverse effects on organs or nerves involved in hearing or balance
oxy-	οξύς, οξεία, οξύ (adj.)	sharp; acute, combining form
oxyblepsia	οξυβλεψία	acute vision
oxycinesia	οξυκινησία	acute motion
oxycephaly	οξυκεφαλή	a condition in which the skull has a peaked or a somewhat conical shape
oxygen	οξυγόνο(ν)	acid producing; a colorless, odorless, tasteless, gaseous chemical element that occurs free in the atmosphere
oxygenate	οξυγονώνω	1 to mix, treat, or combine with oxygen 2 to increase or enrich the quantity of oxygen
oxy-hydrogen	οξύ + υδρογόνον	of or using a mixture of oxygen and hydrogen to produce a hot flame used for welding or for cutting metals

oxymoron	οξύμωρο(ν) (neu. of οξύμωρος)	acutely silly, a figure of speech in which opposite or contradictory ideas or terms are combined (ex: run slowly; sour sweet, etc.)
oxytone	οξύς-τόνος	having an acute accent on the last syllable
oxyuriasis	οξυ-ουρίασις /ουρία	infestation with or disease caused by pinworms (as of the genera Enterobiusand Oxyuris)
ozone	όζον/όζοντος (gen.)	an unstable pale-blue gas O3 with a penetrating odor, it is an allotropic form of oxygen

P

Pachy- prefix	παχύς, παχειά, παχύ (adj.)	fat; thick; flabby
pachyblepharon	παχύ-βλέφαρον	thickening of the eyelid
pachychephalous	παχύς-εγκέφαλος	thickening of the brain wall
pachychilla	παχειά-χείλια/χείλη	thick lips; fat lips
pachyderm(a)	παχύδερμα	thick skin
pachyglossa	παχύ-γλώσσα (παχειά/thick, fat-γλώσσα/tongue)	thick tongue
pachyhemia	παχύ-αίμα	thickening of the blood
pachy-meningitis	παχύ μενιγγίτις / μενιγγίτιδα -	inflammation of the dura matter
pachymeter	παχύ-μέτρο (πάχος/ thickness)	instrument measuring thickness
pachynsis	πάχυνσις/η	thickening; fattening
pachyonyhia	παχυνυχία/ παχυά-νύχια	thickening of the nails; thick nails
pago-	πάγος	ice
pagophagia	παγοφαγεία	the compulsive eating of ice, which is a symptom of lack of iron
pagophile	παγόφιλος	someone having extreme attachment to ice

pagophobia	παγοφοβία	abnormal fear of ice or icy conditions
paleo-	παλαιός/ παλαιόν (neu.)	early ancient, old, prehistoric
paleo-anthropology	παλαιό- ανθρωπολογία	the branch of anthropology dealing with early forms of fossil humans, and examines the evolution of the human race
paleo-biology	παλαιο-βιολογία	the branch of biology dealing with the life of people who lived in ancient times writings, collectively 2 the study of describing or deciphering ancient writings
Paleolithic	παλαιολιθικός, ή, ό (adj.)	Paleolithic Period, subdivided into the Lower (to c. 150,000 BC), Middle (to c. 38,000 BC), and Upper stages; Old Stone Age
Paleontology	παλαιοντολογία	the branch of geology concerned with life-forms of the past, esp., prehistoric life-forms, through the study of fossils 2 a treatise on this subject
palaeo-pathologist	παλαιο-παθολόγος	a specialist in paleopathology
palaeo-pathology	παλαιο-παθολογία	a branch of pathology concerned with diseases of former times as determined esp. from fossil or other remains
pan-	παν/παντός /(gen.) πάντα (pl.)	all; everyone, everything
panacea	πανάκεια	Myth. panacea was regarded as a deity personification of therapy that could (with the help of various plants and herbs) cure everything; a medicine that could heal any disease; cure-all
panarthritis	παν-αρθρίτις/ παναρθρίτιδα	inflammation of the entire joint

pancreas	πάνκρεας	a large lobulated gland that in humans is lying in front of the upper lumbar vertebrae and behind the stomach, and is somewhat hammer-shaped and firmly attached anteriorly to the curve of the duodenum with which it communicates through one or more pancreatic ducts and consists of 1 tubular acini secreting digestive enzymes which pass to the intestine and function in the breakdown of proteins, fats, and carbohydrates 2 modified acinar cells that form islets of Langerhans between the tubules and secrete the hormones insulin and glucagon 3 a firm connective tissue capsule that extends supportive stands into the organ
pancreat-	πανκρεατ- (πάνκρεας)	pancreas, combining form (pancreatitis; pancreatectomy)
pancreat-ectomy	πανκρεατ-εκτομή	surgical excision of all or part of the pancreas
pancreatic	πανκρεατικός, ή, ό (adj.)	of, relating to, or produced in the pancreas
pancreatic cholera	πανκρεατική χολέρα	a syndrome characterized esp. by severe watery diarrhea and hypokalemia that often due to an excessive secretion of vasoactive intestinal peptide from a vipoma esp. of the pancreas; also known as: *Verner-Morrison syndrome*
pancreatitis	πανκρεατίτις/ πανκρεα-τίτιδα	inflammation of the pancreas
pandemic	πανδημικός- πανδημική- πανδημικό (adj.)	the spread of an infectious disease in a large area at the same time

panegyric	πανηγυρικός, ή, ό (adj.)	1 festivities in a public space 2 a formal speech or writing praising a person or event 2 high or hyperbolic praise; laudation
pan-encephalitis	παν-εγγεφαλίτις / εγγεφαλίτιδα	inflammation of the brain affecting both white and gray matter
panethnic	παν-εθνικός/ πανεθνικός, ή, ό (adj.)	pertaining to the entire nation
pan-hidrosis	παν-ίδρωσις /η	perspiration over the entire body
pan-hysterectomy	παν-υστερ(ο)εκτομή	complete removal of the womb/uterus
panic	πανικός	extreme anxiety; of sudden fear; 1 a sudden, unreasoning, hysterical fear 2 a widespread fear of the collapse of the financial system, resulting in unreasoned attempts to turn property into cash, withdraw money, etc. 3 to panic and react to a crisis with some frantic often disastrous action
panoply	πανοπλία	a complete suit of armor
panoptic	πανοπτικός, ή, ό (adj.)	including in one view (everything within sight)
panorama	πανόραμα	a picture or series of pictures of a landscape, historical, entertainment, sports event, etc.; an unlimited view in all directions
panoramic	πανοραμικός, ή, ό (adj.)	pertaining to panorama; extremely beautiful view
pan	πας/ παν	all, every, universal
pantheism	πανθεϊσμός	1 the doctrine that God is not a personality, but all laws, forces, manifestations, etc., of the self-existing universe are God 2 the worship or toleration of worship, of all gods or various cults

pantheistic	πανθεϊκός, ή, ό (adj.)	relating to pantheism (as in pantheistic theory)
pantheon	πάνθεον	1 a temple for all the gods 2 all the gods of a people 3 a building in which famous or glorified dead persons of a nation are entombed or commemorated (ex: the Pantheon of Heroes)
panther	πάνθηρ/πάνθηρος (gen.) /πάνθηρας (Mod. Gr.)	1 a leopard; specif. a) a black leopard, b) a large or fierce leopard 2 Cougar
panto-	παντός (gen.) of pan (neu) of πας)	combining form (pantheism)
pantomime	παντομίμα	1 any dramatic presentation played without words using only action and gestures 2 the art of acting without words using only, action and gestures 3 in ancient Greece and Rome dramatic plays where actors perfomed with action and gestures to the accompaniment of music or of words sung by a chorus
pantophobia	πανοφοβία	extreme fear of everything in general
papa	πάππα(ς) /μπαμπάς	baby talk for daddy (father or grandfather) see: *pappus*
paper	πάπυρος	1 a thin, flexible material made usually in sheets from a pulp prepared from rags, wood, or other fibrous material, and used for writing or printing on, for packaging, as structural material, as a fabric substitute, etc. 2 single piece or sheet of paper, written or printed, etc.

pappus or pappous	πάππος /παππούς	old man; grandfather; hense substance resembling gray hairs Bot. a group or tuft of prongs, bristles, scales, simple, or branched hairs, as the achenes of the dandelion, forming the modified calyx of the composite and certain other families and serving in the dispersal of the fruit
papyrus	πάπυρος	1 a tall water plant (Cyperus papyrus) of the sedge family, abundant in the Nile region in Egypt and widely cultivated as an ornament 2 a writing material made from this plant by the ancient Egyptians, Greeks and Romans, by soaking, pressing, and drying thin slices of its pith laid crosswise 3 any ancient document or manuscript on papyrus
papyrology	παπυρολογία	learning the art or skill to produce and treat papyrus
para- or par-	παρά-	beside, alongside of; beyond, aside from, combining form (parathyroid, parabiosis, etc.)
paraaortic	παρ-αορτικός, ή, ό (adj.)	close to the aorta [paraaortic lymph nodes]
parabiosis	παρα-βίωσις /η	the anatomical and physiological union of two organisms either naturally or artificially produced
parable	παραβολή (παραβάλλειν – to throw beside)	an allegorical relation, parable; an analogy 1 a short, simple story, usually of an occurrence of a familiar kind, from which a moral or religious lesson can be drawn 2 the parables Jesus used talking to his apostles or the crowds

parabola	παραβολή	lit. application, comparison Geom. a plane curve which is the path, or locus, of a moving point that remains equally distant from a fixed point (*focus*) and from a fixed straight line (directrix); curve formed by the section of a cone cut by a plane parallel to the side of the cone
parabolic	παραβολικός, ή, ό (adj.)	of, in the form of, or expressed by a parable
paracentesis	παρακέντησις/η	a surgical puncture of a cavity of the body (as with a trocar or aspirator) usually to draw off any effusion
paracholera	παραχολέρα	a disease clinically resembling Asiatic cholera but caused by a different vibrio
parachroma	παράχρωμα	discoloration
paracusia or paracusis	παρακουσία	any hearing defect; disorder in the sense of hearing
paracyesis	παρακύησις/η	pregnancy outside the uterus
paradigm	παράδειγμα	example; 1 a) a pattern, example, or model b) an overall concept accepted by most people in an intellectual community, as those in one of the natural sciences, because of its effectiveness in explaining a complex process, idea, or set of data 2 Gram. an example of a declension or conjugation, giving all the inflectional forms of a word
paradigmatism	παραδειγματισμός	being an example; a role model for others to emulate

paradise	παράδεισος	heaven; abode of the blessed; 1 the garden of Eden 2 the abode of the righteous after death; abode of God and the blessed 3 a place or condition of great or perfect satisfaction, happiness, or delight
paradisiacal	παραδεισιακός, ή, ό (adj.)	of, like, or fit for paradise
paradox	παράδοξος, η, ο (adj.)	1 a statement contrary to common belief 2 a statement that seems contradictory, unbelievable, or absurd but may be true in fact 3 a statement that is self-contradictory and, hence, false 4 a person, situation, act, etc., that seems to have contradictory or inconsistent qualities
paradoxical	παραδοξολόγος	one having the nature of, or expressing a paradox (also, paradoxically/παραδόξως (adv.)
paraeconomy	παρα-οικονομία	illegal money; not following free enterprise rules and regulations; black market
paraesthesia/ paresthesia	παραισθησία	a sensation of pricking, tingling, or creeping of the skin, having no objective cause and usually associated with injury or irritation of a sensory nerve or nerve root
paragoge	παραγωγή (παρά + άγειν - to lead)	the addition to a sound or sounds to the end of the word, either grammatically (as in drowned) or without etymological justification, as in the nonstandard drownded (droun'did) or for ease in pronunciation, as in amidst, etc. In Greek the word paragoge/ παραγωγή means: production and παράγω - I produce

paragraph	παράγραφος (παρά + γράφειν/ beside + to write)	a distinct section or subdivision of a chapter
paragraphia	παραγραφή (παρά + γράφειν- at the side of + to write)	Med. a form of aphasia, usually due to cerebral injury, characterized by the unintentional omission, transposition, or insertion of letters or words in writing 2 παραγραφή also in Greek: loss of the write to claim or dispute an issue due to expiration date
paraleipsis	παράλειψις/η (παρά + λείπειν- beside + to leave)	omission; a rhetorical device in which a point is stressed by suggesting that it is too obvious or well known to mention (ex: not to mention the expense involved"
parallactic	παραλλακτικός, ή, ό (adj.)	pertaining to parallax
parallax	παραλλαγή/ παράλλαξις/η (παραλλάσσειν/ to vary)	decline, wander, change; the apparent change in the position of an object resulting from the change in the direction or position from which it is viewed
parallel	παράλληλος, η, ο (adj.)	extending in the same direction and at the same distance apart at every point, so as never to meet
parallelism	παραλληλισμός	the state of being parallel; In Philos. the doctrine that mind and matter function together, at the same time, but without any casual interaction
parallelogram	παραλληλόγραμμα	a plane figure with four sides, having the opposite sides parallel and equal
paralogism	παραλογισμός	illogical reasoning; reasoning contrary to the rules of logic; faulty argunent
paralysis	παράλυσις/η	1 loss of movement or sensation in one or more parts of the body 2 any condition of helpless inactivity or of inability to act

paralytic	παραλυτικός, ή, ό (adj.)	pertaining to paralysis; a paralyzed person
paralyze	παραλύω/παραλύειν	to cause loss of muscle control and/or feeling
paramenia	παραμηνία	irregular/abnormal menstrual period
paramnesia	παραμνησία	Psychol. 1 distortion of memory with confusion of fact and fantasy
parameter	παράμετρος	1 Math. a quantity or constant whose value varies with the circumstances of its application, as the radius line of a group of concentric circles, which varies with the circle of consideration
parametrical	παραμετρικός, ή, ό (adj.)	designating or of auxiliary medical personnel, such as midwives, medics, laboratory technicians, nurses' aides, etc. also paramedic, a person in paramedical work
parametrium	παραμήτριο(ν)	tissue surrounding and supporting the womb
paramyotonia	παρα-μυοτονία	an abnormal state characterized by tonic muscle spasm
paranoia	παράνοια	chronic psychosis, characterized by fear, suspicion, and imaginary paranoid thoughts; schizophrenic state
paranoid	παρανοϊκός, ή, ό (adj.)	person suffering from paranoia
paranoid schizophrenia	παρανοϊκή σχιζοφρένεια	schizophrenia characterized esp. by percecutory or grandiose delusions or hallucinations
paranymph	παράνυμφος/ παράνυμφη (παρά + νύμφη- beside + nymph/bride)	bridesmaid
paraphasia	παραφασία	aphasia in which the person uses wrong words or uses words or sounds in senseless combinations

paraphilia	παραφιλία	a pattern of reccurring sexually arousing mental imagery or behavior that involves unusual and esp. socially unacceptable sexual practices (as sadism, masochism, fetishism, or pedophilia)
paraphiliac	παραφιλικός, ή, ό (adj.)	1 of, relating to, or characterized by paraphilia; a person who engages in paraphilia
paraphimosis	παραφίμωσις /η	a condition in which the foreskin is retracted behind the glans of the penis and cannot be brought back to its original position
paraphrenia	παραφρενία/ παραφρένια	1 the group of paranoid disorders 2 any of the panoid disorders; also, *Schizophrenia*
paraphobia	παραφοβία	mild phobia
paraphrase (n.)	παράφρασις/η (ουσ.)	rewording of meaning
paraphrase (verb)	παραφράζω	to express in other words a spoken or written statement/work
paraphrastic	παραφραστικός, ή, ό (adj.)	having the nature of, or forming paraphrase; using different words to something spoken or written (paraphrastically/ παραφραστικά, adverb)
paraplegia	παραπληγία	1 loss of motion and sensation in the legs and lower body 2 paralysis of the lower half of the body with involvement of both legs, usually due to disease or injury to the spinal cord
paraplegic	παραπληγικός, ή, ό (adj.)	one affected by paraplegia
parapraxis	παράπραξις/η	a faulty act (as a Freudian slip) of purposeful behavior
paraprotein	παρα-πρωτεϊνη	any of various abnormal serum globulins with unique physical and electrophoretic characteristics

para-protein-emia	παρα-πρωτεΐν-αιμία	the presence of paraprotein in the blood
parapsoriasis	παραψωρίασις /η	a rare skin disease characterized by red scaly patches similar to those of psoriasis but causing no sensation of pain or itch
parapsychology	παραψυχολογία	the branch of psychology that investigates psychic phenomena, as telepathy, extrasensory perception (ESP), or clairvoyance
paraphysis	παράλυσις /η (παραλύειν –to loosen or weaken)	1 partial or complete loss, or temporary interruption of a function, esp., of voluntary motion or of sensation in some part or all of the body 2 any condition of helpless inactivity or of inability to act
parasite	παράσιτο(ν)	1 any animal or plant which lives inside of another animal or plant 2 a person as in ancient Greece, who amused and flattered the host in order to get a free meal, or any person who benefits at the expence of others without any useful contribution; a hanger-on 3 Biol. an organism living in, with, or on another organism in parasitism
parasitemia	παρασιταιμία	condition in which parasites are present in the blood;, used esp. to indicate the presence of parasites without clinical symptoms
parasitic	παρασιτικός, ή, ό (adj.)	1 relating to or having the habit of a parasite: living in another organism 2 caused by or resulting from the effects of parasites
parasitism	παρασιτισμός	1 an intimate association between organisms of two or more kinds; esp. one in which a parasite obtains benefits from a host which it usually harms

parasite- Parasito-	παρασιτ- παράσιτο	parasite, combining form (parasitology)
parasitologist	παρασιτολόγος	an expert in parasitology
parasitology	παρασιτολογία	a branch of biology dealing with parasites and parasitism, esp. among animals
parasitisis	παρασιτίτις / παρασίτωσις /η	the infection or inflammation caused by parasites in an organism
para-sympathetic	παρα-συμπαθετικός, ή, ό (adj.)	of, relating to, being, or acting on the parasympathetic nervous system
para-sympathetic nervous system	παρα-συμπαθετικό- νευρικό- σύστημα	the part of the automatic nervous system that contains chiefly chlorinergic fibers, that tends to induce secretion, to increase the tone and contractility of smooth muscle, and to slow the heart rate, and that consists of a cranial part and a sacral part; also called *Sympathetic Nervous System*
para-sympatho-lytic	παρα- συμπαθο- λυτικός, ή, ό (adj.)	tending to oppose the psychological results of parasympathetic nervous activity or of parasympathomimetic drugs
parasynthesis	παρασύνθεσις /η	Linguis. the process of forming words by compounding and addition of derivational suffixes (ex: big-hearted from big heart + ed, etc.)
parasynthetical	παρασυνθετικός, ή, ό (adj.)	of, relating to, or involving parasynthesis
parasystole	παρασυστολή	an irregularity in cardiac rhythm caused by an ectopic pacemaker

parataxis	παράταξις/η	the placing of related clauses, phrases, etc., in a series without the use of connecting words (ex: "I came, I saw, I conquered"); also, the placing in specific positions according to a given manner/method (ex: the placing of a group/students or soldiers in a parade or any other activity (the word parataxis in Greek has various meanings as well)
parathyroid	(ο, η) παραθυροειδής/ (το)παραθυροειδές (adj.)	designating or of any of four small oval glands on or near the thyrhoid gland: they secrete a hormone important in the control of the calcium-phosphorus balance of the body
para-thyroid-ectome	παρα-θυροειδ-εκτομή	surgical removal of one or all the parathyroid glands
parathyroid hormone	παραθυροειδής ορμόνη	a hormone of the parathyroid gland that regulates the metabolism of calcium and phosphorus in the body; abbr. *PTH*
paratyphoid	(ο, η) παρατυφώδης/ (το) παρατυφώδες (adj.)	designating of, or causing an infectious disease closely resembling typhoid fever, but usually milder and caused by bacteria
parazoan	παράζωα	any of the subkingdom (Parazoa) of animals, consisting only of the phylum of sponges, having two tissue layers only and lacking a nervous system and true digestive cavity
paregoric	παρηγορικό	derivative of opium that helps relieve pain or diarrhea

parenchyma	παρέγχυμα	1 Anat. the essential and distinctive tissue of an organ, or an abnormal growth as distinguished from its connective tissue, blood vessels, etc. 2 Bot. a soft tissue made up of thin-walled, undifferentiated living cells with air spaces with air spaces between them, constituting the main substance of plant leaves and roots, the pulp of fruit, the central portion of stems, etc. Zool. a spongy mass of tissue packing the spaces between the organs of some invertebrates
parenthesis	παρένθεσις /η	1 an additional word, clause, etc., places as an explanation or comment within an already complete sentence: in writing or printing it is usually marked off by curved lines ( ), dashes, or commas 2 either or both of the curved lines ( ), used to mark off parenthetical words, etc., or to enclose mathematical or logical symbols that are to be treated as a single term 3 an episode or incident, often an irrelevant one; interlude
paresthesia	παραισθησία	see paraesthesia
parodist	παρωδός	a writer of parodies
parody/parodia	παρωδία (παρά + ωδή-beside + song)	1 a) a literary or musical work imitating the characteristic style of some other work, or of a writer or composer in a satirical or humorous way, usually by applying it to an inappropriate subject b) the art of writing such works 2 a poor or weak immitation

paronychia	παρωνυχία	infection of the tissues at the base of the nail
paroniria	παρα-όνειρα	frightful dreams
paropsis	παροψίς/παροψίδα	vision disorder
parorexia	παρορεξία	craving for special foods
parosmia	παροσμία	smelling imaginary odors
parotid	παρωτίς/παρωτίδα	located near the ear
parotitis	παρωτίτις/ παρωτίτιδα	inflammation of the parotid gland
paroxysm	παροξυσμός	sudden attack/recurrence of symptoms
paroxysmal dyspnea	παροξυσμική δύσπνοια	cardiac asthma; occurs in paroxysms usually at night and is characterized by difficult wheezing, difficult breathing, respiration, pallor, and anxiety
paroxysmal tachycardia	παροξυσμική ταχυκαρδία	taxycardia that begins and stops abruptly and that is initiated by a premature supraventricular beat originating in the atrium or in the atrioventricular node, or by a premature ventricular beat
parthern- partherno-	παρθένος /παρθένα	virgin; without fertilization, combining form (parthenogenesis)
partheno-genesis	παρθένο- γένεσις /γέννηση	reproduction by development of an unfertilized, usually female gamete that occurs esp. among lower plants and invertebrate animals
parthenos	παρθένος/παρθένα	virgin; an epithet of several of the Greek goddesses esp., Athena
Parthenon	Παρθενών/ Παρθενώνας	the Doric temple of Athena built (in the fifth cent. BC) on the Acropolis in Athens: one of the most famous antiquities for its perfection, its sculpture is attributed to Phidias
paruria	παρουρία	abnormality in excretion of urine

patho -	πάθος	feeling; suffering; adverse feeling, combining form (pathology)
pathobiology	παθο-βιολογία	1 the study of the diseases and esp. of the structural and functional changes produced by them 2 the anatomic and physiological deviations from the normal that constitute disease or characterize a particular disease
pathetic	παθητικός, ή, ό (adj.)	1 expressing arousing, or intended to arouse pity, sorrow, sympathy, or compassion; pitiful 2 pitifully unsuccessful, ineffective, etc. [a pathetic performance]
pathogenic	(ο, η) παθογενής (το) παθογενές (adj.)	pertaining to the abiliy to produce disease
pathogenesis	παθογένεσις/η (adj.)	chain of events leading to the development of disease
pathologic	παθολογικός, ή, ό (adj)	1 of or relating to pathology (pathologic/pathological laboratory) 2 altered or changed by disease (pathologic tissue); also indicative of disease
pathologist	παθολόγος	a specialist in pathology; a physician who interprets and diagnoses the changes caused by disease in tissues and body
pathology	παθολογία	the study of diseases; a treatise on or compilation of abnormalities
pathomania	παθομανία	abnormal desire to commit crime
patho-morphology	παθο- μορφολογία	morphology of abnormal conditions
pathophobia	παθοφοβία	extreme fear of disease

patho-physiology	παθο-φυσιολογία	the physiology of abnormal state/condition, specif. the functional changes that accompany a particular syndrome or disease
pathos	πάθος (παθείν, πάσχειν- to feel, suffer)	feeling, suffering, disease; the ability to experience intense feelings, emotions (of love, hatred, etc.)
-pathy	-πάθεια	suffix forming nouns indicating 1 feeling (apathy) (telepathy) 2 a specified disease of a specified part or type (myopathy) 3 therapy or system of therapy based on a (specified) unitary theory of disease or its treatment (homeopathy)
Patmos	Πάτμος	an island in the Dodecanese, in the SE Aegean: where St. John wrote the Book of Revelation (1:9)
patri-	πατήρ/ πατρί (dative case) / πατέρας (Mod. Gr.)	father
Patras/Patra	Πάτραι /Πάτρα	1 seaport in W Greece, on the Gulf of Patras 2 Gulf of arm of the Ionian Sea, in the NW Peloponnesus
patriarch	πατριάρχης	the father and ruler of a family or tribe; also, the highest-ranked bishop in the Greek Orthodox and Eastern Orthodox Church: Οικουμενικός Πατριάρχης/ Ecumenical Patriarch of Constantinople
Patriarchate	πατριαρχείον	the position, rank, jurisdiction, territory, etc., of a patriarch

patriarchy	πατριαρχία	1 a form of a social organization in which the father or the eldest male is recognized as the head 2 government, rule, or domination by men, as in a family or tribe
patricide	πατρικτόνος / πατροκτόνος (πατρί (dat. of πατήρ) + κτείνειν/κτόνος- to kill/killer)	1 the act of murdering one's father 2 the person responsible for the act
patriot	πατριώτης	fellow countryman; one who loves and with loyally or zealously supports his own country
patriotic	πατριωτικός, ή, ό (adj.)	pertaining to patriotism
patriotism	πατριωτισμός	expressing love, support, and dedication for one's own country
Patroclus	Πάτροκλος	Gr. myth. a Greek warrior and friend of Achilles, killed by Hector in the Trojan War
pause	παύσις /η	1 a short period of inaction; temporary stop, break, or rest as in speaking, reading, exercising, etc. 2 hesitation; interruption; delay [pursuit with pause] 3 any mark of punctuation indicating a break 4 Music a) holding of a tone or rest beyond its written value, at the discretion of the performer
pea	πίσος /μπιζέλι	1 an annual, tendril-climbing plant (Pisum sativus) of the pea family with white or pinkish flowers and green seedpods 2 its small, round, smooth, or wrinkled seed, used as vegetable 3 any of various similar plants, as the cowpea; and the seeds of any of those plants

pectin	πηκτίνη (πηκτός/ πηχτός – thick; coagulated)	a water-soluble carbohydrate, obtained from certain ripe fruits, which yields a gel that is the basis of jellies and jams
pedagogic	παιδαγωγικός, ή, ό (adj.)	characteristic of teachers or of teaching or the pedagogic system
pedagogue	παιδαγωγός	a teacher, often a pedantic, dogmatic teacher
pedagology	παιδαγωλογία/ παιδαγωγική	the art or science of teaching, esp., instruction in teaching methods
pederast	παιδεραστής	a man who practices pederasty, esp., with a boy as a passive partner
pederasty	παιδεραστεία	sexual intercourse through the anus
pedi- suffix	παις /παιδί	child, combining form
pediatrician/ paediatrician	παιδίατρος	specialist in childhood diseases
pediatrics	παιδιατρική	branch of medicine dealing with children's diseases
pedo-	παις/παιδός (gen.)	of child (paidos, genitive case of pais/ Mod. Gr. παιδί), combining form
pedodontics	παιδο-οδοντική/ οδοντιατρική	the branch of dentistry dealing with children's teeth
pedophilia	παιδοφιλία	abnormal fondness for children
pedophobia	παιδοφοβία	extreme fear of children; having extreme fear of having/ giving birth to children
penology	ποινολογία (ποινή + λόγος – punishment - word)	the study of the reformation and rehabilitation of criminals and the management of prisons
pentagon	πεντάγωνον/ο (πέντε + γωνία - five + corner)	five-sided
Pentateuch	πεντάτευχο(ν)	the five first books of the Bible
pentathlete	πενταθλητής	participant in the pentathlon

pentathlon	πένταθλο(ν)	an atlthetic event with five contests, where an athlete competes in all five—long jump, javelin throw, 200-meter dash, discus throw, and1,500-meter run (in the Olympic games the five contests differ)
pentatonic	πεντατονικός, ή, ό (adj.)	designating of or to a musical scale having five tones to the octave
Pentecost	Πεντηκοστή	fifty days after Easter, celebrating the descent of the Holy Spirit on the Apostles; also, fifty days after the Passover
Pendelikon	Πεντελικόν	pertaining to Mt. Penteli in Greece that produced the best marble
peptic	πεπτικός, ή, ό (adj.)	pertaining to the digestive tract
peri-	περί	around, about, surrounding, enclosing, near compining form: 1 near: around (perimenopausal) 2 enclosing: surrounding (periarterial)
perianth	περίανθος	the outer envelope of a flower, including the calyx and corolla
periaortic	περι-αορτικός, ή, ό (adj.)	relating to, occurring in, or being the tissue surrounding the aorta
peri-arterial	περι-αρτηριακός, ή, ό (adj.)	of, relating to, occurring in, or being the tissues surrounding the arteriole
peri-arthritis	περι-αρθρίτις / αρθρίτιδα	inflammation of the structures (as the muscles, tendons, and bursa of the shoulder) around a joint
periapsis	περίαψις/η	the nearest point to the gravitational center in the orbit of any satellite

periblem	περίβλημα περί & βάλλειν- to surround)	robe, to envelop; Bot. the meristem that produces the cortex
peribronchial	περι-βρογχικός, ή, ό (adj.)	of, relating to, occurring in, affecting, or being the tissues surrounding a bronchus [a peribronchial growth]
pericardi-	περικαρδιτ- περικάρδιον/ο	combining form 1 pericardium (pericardiectomy) 2 pericardial (pericardiophrenic artery)
pericardial	περικαρδι(α) κός, ή, ό (adj.)	of, relating to, or affecting the pericardium, also: situated around the heart
pericardiostomy	περικαρδιοστόμιο/ περικαρδιοστομή	surgical formation of an opening of the pericardium
pericardio-tomy	περικαρδιοτομή	surgical incision of the pericardium
pericarditis	περικαρδίτις/ περικαρδίτιδα	inflammation of the sac surrounding the heart (the pericardium)
pericardium	περικάρδιο(ν)	the thin, close membranous sac surrounding the heart and the roots of the great blood vessels of vertebrates and consists of an outer fibrous coat that loosely invests the heart and is prolonged on the outer surface of the great vessels except the inferior vena cava and a double serous coat of which one layer is closely adherent to the heart, while the other lines, the inner surface of the outer coat with the intervining space, being filled with pericardial fluid
pericarp	περικάρπιο(ν)	Bot. the wall of a ripened ovary, sometimes consisting of three distinct layers: endocarp, mesocarp, and exocarp; Anat. the part of the hand that surrounds the carpus

pericentric	περικεντρικός, ή, ό (adj.)	of, relating to, or involving the centromere of a chromosome [pericentric inversion]
perichondritis	περιχοντρίτις / περιχοντρίτιδα	inflammation of the perichonrdium
perichondrium	περιχόντριο(ν)	the membrane of white fibrous connective tissue covering cartilage, except at joints
Periclean	(περίοδος) Περικλέους/ Περικλή (gen.)	referring to the greatest period of Ancient Athens (the Golden Age), fifth cen. BC
Pericles	Περικλής	Athenian statesman and general, during his lifetime Athens achieved her greatest glory
pericolic	περικωλικό(ν)	around the colon
pericoronitis	περικορωνίτις / περικορωνίτιδα	inflammation of the gum around the crown of a partially erupted tooth
perimeter	περίμετρος	1 the outer boundary of a figure/ or area 2 total length of this 3 an optical instrument of testing the scope of vision, and the visual powers of various parts of the retina. Syn. **Circumference**
perimetry	περιμέτρησις/η	the testing of the scope of vision, by means of a perimeter
perimetrium	περιμήτριο(ν)	covering tissue of the womb
perinefric	περινεφρικός, ή, ό (adj.)	situated around the kidneys
perineurium	περινευρικόν/ό (περί + νεύρον – around + nerve)	the sheath of dense connective tissue that envelops a bundle of nerve fibers composing a peripheral nerve

period	περίοδος	1 the interval between recurrent astronomical events, as between two full moons 2 the interval between certain happenings (a ten-year period of peace) 3 a portion of time, often indefinite, characterized by certain events, processes, conditions, etc. 4 any of the portions of time into which an event of fixed duration, as a game, a school day, is divided 5 an occurrence of menstruation; menses; and many other applications of the word, as in Gram. period is a mark ending a sentence, etc.
periodic	περιοδικός, ή, ό (adj.)	occurring from time to time; intermittent
periodontal	περιοδοντικός, ή, ό (adj.)	1 around the tooth 2 affecting the gums, connective tissues, etc., surrounding the teeth
periodotics	περι-οδοντοτική	a branch of dentistry that deals with diseases of the supporting and investing structures of the teeth including the gums, cementum, periodontal ligaments, and alveolar bone; also called *periodondology*
periodontitis	περιοδοντίτις/ περιοδοντίτιδα	inflammation of the periodontal tissue
periodondium	πριδόντιον/ο	the supporting structures of the teeth including the cementum, the periodontal ligament, the bone of the alveolar process, and the gums
peri-odondo-clasia	περι-οδοντο-κλασία	any periodontal disease characterized by destruction of the periodontium
periodondologist	περι-οδοντο-λόγος	specialist in periodontics, also called *Periodontist*
periodontology	περι-οδοντολογία	the study of periodontal disease

periodondosis	περι-οδόντωσις /η	a severe degenerative disease of the periodontium
perionychia	περιονυχία	inflammation of the area around the nails
periost-	περιοστ- περιόστεο-	periosteum combining form [periostitis]
periosteum	περιόστεο(ν)	tissue around bone through which the bone is nourished
periostitis	περιοστίτις/ περιοστίτιδα	inflammation of the membrane surrounding a bone
periotic	περιωτικός, ή, ό (adj.)	surrounding the inner ear; specif. of the bone (periotic bone) enclosing the inner ear of mammals
peripancreatic	περι-πανκρεατικός, ή, ό (adj.)	of, relating to, occurring in, or being the tissue surrounding the pancreas
peripatetic	περιπατητικός, ή, ό (adj.) (περιπατείν – to walk)	1 referring to the philosophy or followers of Aristotle, who walked about in the Lyceum while teaching 2 a person walking from place to place
peripeteia	περιπέτεια	changing suddenly; a sudden change of fortune or reversal of circumstances as in a drama; adventure
peripheral	περιφερειακός, ή, ό (adj.)	lying at the outside or away of the central part; outer; external
peripheral nervous system	περιφεριακό νευρικό σύστημα	the part of the nervous system that is outside the nervous system and comprises the cranial nerves excepting the optic nerve, the spinal nerves, and the autonomic nervous system
peripheral vision	περιφερειακή όραση	area of vision lying just outside the line of direct sight
periphery	περιφέρεια	away from center or midline of body
periphrasis	περίφρασις/η	the use of many words where one or a few would do

periphrastic	περιφραστικός, ή, ό (adj.)	of, like, or expressed in periphrasis
perisarc	περισάρξ/περισάρκα	flesh, nonliving, outer skeleton layer of many hydroid colonies
periscope	περισκόπιο(ν)	an optical instrument consisting of a tube holding a system of lenses and mirrors or prisms so arranged that looking through the eyepiece at one end, one can see objects reflected at the other end
periscopic	περισκοπικός, ή, ό (adj.)	providing clear lateral or oblique range of view, as certain lenses
perisso-dactyl	περισσό + δάκτυλος/ more + finger/toe	having more than the usual number of fingers or toes
peristyle	περίστυλο(ν)	1 a row of columns forming an enclosure or supporting a roof, 2 any area or enclosure so formed, as a court
peritendinitis/ peritendonitis	περι-τεντονίτις / τεντονίτιδα περι τένοντας	inflammation of the tissues around the tendon
perithecium	περιθήκιον/ περιθήκη	case; box
peritoneum	περιτόναιον (περί + τείνειν/around + stretch)	transparent serous membrane lining the abdominal cavity and reflected inward at various places to cover the visceral organs
peritonitis	περιτονίτις/ περιτονίτιδα	inflammation of the peritoneum
petal	πέταλο(ν)	any of the component parts, or leaves of a corolla
petaloid	(ο, η) πεταλοειδής (το) πεταλοειδές (adj.)	resembling a petal
Peter	Πέτρος	rock, stone (believed that the name Petros was chosen by Jesus for St. Peter to build His church on it)

petra-	πέτρα	stone; rock
petrify	πετροποιείν/ πετροποιώ	1 to make rigid, inflexible, or inert; 2 to paralyze or make numb, as with fear; turn to stone
petroid	(ο, η) πετροειδής (το) πετροειδές (adj.)	rocky; resembling a rock; rocklike
petroleum	πετρέλαιο(ν)	an oily, flammable, liquid solution of hydrocarbons, yellowish, green or black in color, occurring naturally in the rock strata of certain geological formations
petrology	πετρολογία	the study of the classification, location and composition of rocks
petrophysics	πετροφυσική	the study of the physical properties of rocks
Ph	Φ, φι/Fi	the twenty-first letter of the Gr. alphabet
phaco-	φακός	lens, combining form (phacomatosis)
phacomatosis	φακομάτωσις/η	any of a group of hereditary or congenital diseases (as newροfibromatosis) affecting the central nervous system and characterized by the development of hamartomas
-phage	φάγε/φαγία /φαγεία	eating, feeding combining form (bacteriophage)
phago-	φάγος /φάγειν	one who eats or feeds on (as phytophage/eating plants)
phagocyte	φαγοκύτταρον/ο	a cell (as a macrophage or newtriphil) that engulfs and consumes foregn material (as microorganisms) and debris (as dead tissue cells) (phagocytic)
phagocytosis	φαγοκύτωσις /η	the engulfing and usually the destruction of particulate matter by phagocytes

-phagous	- φάγος	feeding, esp. in some specified kind of food, combining form [hematophagous]
-phagy	- φαγία/ φαγεία	eating, esp. of a specified type or substance, combining form [geophagy]
phalange	φάλανξ/φάλαγγος /φάλαγγα/ φάλαγγες (pl.)	military formation compining form [phalanx]
phalageal	φαλαγγιτικός, ή, ό (adj.)	of phalanx or, of phalanges
phalanx	φλαλανξ/φάλαγγος / φάλαγγα (Mod. Gr.)	1 an ancient military formation of infantry in close, deep ranks with shields overlapping and spears extended 2 a massed group of individuals; compact body; a group of people united for a common cause 3 Anat. any of the digital bones of the hand or foot, distal to metacarpus or metatarsus that in humans are three to each finger and toe, with the exception of the thumb and big toe which have two each
phallic	φαλλικός, ή, ό (adj.)	1 of, like, or relating to the phallus 2 of or relating to phallicism 3 of, relating to, or characterized by the stage of psychosexual development in psychoanalytic theory, during which a child becomes interested in his or her own sexual organs
phallicism	φαλλικισμός	(anc.) worship of the phallus as a symbol of the male generative power; also *phalism*
phallocentric	φαλλοκεντρικός, ή, ό (adj.)	based on or shaped by the attitude that men's concerns, needs, values, etc., are more important than women's and should be dominant in society

phalloplasty	φαλλοπλασία	plastic surgery of the penis or the scrotum
phallus	φαλλός	1 a representation of or image of the penis as in the Dionysiac festivals of ancient Greece 2 Anat. the undifferentiated embryonic tissue that develops into the penis or clitoris
-phane	φαίνειν / φάνια	to appear, combining form, a substance that specifies an appearance or semblance to something spesific [allophane; cymophane]
phanerogam	φανερόγαμος (φανερός + γάμος – visible + marriage)	early term for a seed plant or a flowering plant
phanerozoic	φανεροζωϊκός, ή, ό (adj.)	designating or of a geologic eon that includes the Paleozoic, Mesozoic, and Cenozoic eras
phantasm	φάντασμα	1 a perception of something that has no physical reality; figment of the mind, esp., a specter or ghost: also ***phantasma/phantasmata*** (pl.) 2 deceptive likeness 3 Philos. a mental impression of a real person or thing
phantasmagoria	φαντασμαγορία	1 an early type of magic-lantern show consisting of various optical illusions in which objects rapidly change size, blend into one another, etc. 2 a rapidly changing series of things seen or imagined, as the figures or events of a dream, also ***phantasmagory***
phantacy	φαντασία	see **Fantasy**

phantom	φάντασμα	1 something that seems to appear to the sight but has no physical existence; apparition; vision; specter 2 something faered or dreaded 3 something that exists only in the mind; illusion
Pharisaic	φαρισαϊκός, ή, ό (adj.)	1 of the Pharisees 2 [from the notion promulgated in the New Testament that Pharisees were so characterized] self-righteous; sanctimonious
Pharisaism	φαρισαϊσμός	1 the beliefs and practices of the Pharisees 2 Pharisaic behavior 3 pretending to be highly moral or virtuous without actually being so; hypocritical
Pharisee	Φαρισαίος	1 a member of an ancient Jewish party or fellowship that carefully observed the written law but also accepted the oral, or traditional law, advocated democratization of religious practices, etc. 2 a pharisaic person
pharmacist	φαρμακοποιός	druggist
pharmaceutical	φαρμακευτικός, ή, ό (adj.)	pertaining to drugs, medicine
pharmaco-	φάρμακο	medicine, drug, combining form
pharmacopoeia	φαρμακοποιία/ φαρμακοποιεία	the official listing of drugs and drug standards
pharmaco-dynamics	φαρμακο-δυναμική	the branch of pharmacology that deals with the effects and the reactions of drugs within the body
pharmaco-genetics	φαρμακο-γενετική	the study of the interrelation of hereditary constitution and response to the drugs
pharmaco-gnosist	φαρμακογνώστης	a specialist in pharmacognosy; one having knowledge of medicines

pharmaco-gnosy	φαρμακογνωσία	a branch of pharmacology dealing especially with the composition, use, and development of medicinal substances of biological origin
pharmaco-kinetics	φαρμακο-κινητική	1 the study of the bodily absorption, distribution, metabolism, and excretion
pharmacology	φαρμακολογία	1 the science dealing with the study of drugs in all their aspects, including their origin, composition, pharmacokinetics, therapeutic use, and toxicology 2 the properties and reactions of drugs, esp. with relation to their therapeutic value
pharmaco-therapeutic	φαρμακο-θεραπευτικός, ή, ό (adj.)	of or relating to pharmacotherapeutics or pharmacotherapy (a pharmacotherapeutic agent)
pharmacotherapeutics	φαρμακο-θεραπευτική	the study of the therapeutics uses and effects of drugs
pharmacotherapy	φαρμακοθεραπεία	the treatment of disease, and esp. mental disorder, with drugs
pharmacy	φαρμακείον/ο	1 the art, practice, or profession of preparing, preserving, compounding, and dispensing medical drugs 2 a) a place where medicines are compounded or dispensed b) drugstore 3 pharmacopoeia
pharyng- or pharyngo-	φάρυνξ/φάρυγγος (gen.) /φάρυγγας	pharynx, combining form (pharyngology) before a vowel; pharyng: (pharyngeal)
pharyngeal	φαρυγγικός, ή, ό (adj.)	of, or in the region of the pharynx
pharyngeal aponeurosis	φαρυγγική απονεύρωσις/η	the middle or fibrous coat of the walls of the pharynx
pharyghitis	φαρυγγίτις/ φαρυγγίτιδα	inflammation of the pharynx (as from bacteria infection)

pharyngo-	φαρυγγο-φάρυνξ/ φάρυγγας	the muscular and membranous cavity of the alimentary canal leading from the mouth and nasal passages to the larynx and esophagus
pharyngo-epiglottic	φαρυγγο- επιγλωττικός, ή, ό (adj.)	either of two folds of mucous membrane extending from the base of the tongue to the epiglottis with one on each side of the midline
pharyngo- esophageal	φαρυγγο- οισοφάγειος	of or relating to the pharynx and the esophagous
pharyngo- laryngectomy	φαρυγγο- λαρυγγεκτομή	surgical excision of the hypopharynx and the larynx
pharyngology	φαρυγγολογία	the branch of medicine dealing with the pharynx and its diseases
pharyngo-plasty	φαρυγγοπλασία	plastic surgery performed on the pharynx
pharyngoscope	φαρυγγοσκόπιο(ν)	instrument for examining the throat/pharynx
pharyngotomy	φαρυγγοτομή	**surgical incision into the pharynx**
pharynx	φάρυνξ/φάρυγγος (gen.)φάρυγγας	the muscular and membranous cavity of the alimentary canal leading from the mouth and nasal pessages to the larynx and esophagus; membranous tube

phase or phasis	φάσις /η	1 any of the recurrent stages of variation in the illumination and apparent shape of the moon or a planet 2 any of the changes or forms in any series or cycle of changes as in development 3 Chem. a solid, liquid, or gaseous homogeneous form existing as a distinct part in a heterogeneous system [ice is a phase of H2O] 4 Physics the fractional of a cycle through which an oscillation, as of light or sound waves, has advanced, measured from an arbitrary starting point 5 to put in phase; to move by phases 6 various phases, ways, aspects, or stages of a process
phasma	φάσμα (φαίνειν – to show)	Physics the total of the monochromatic rays that are produced by the analysis of the light [helios's phasma/ the phasma of the sun] 2 the different parts that together compose a multiformed and diversified to a compleat (ex: the total phasma of the political powers or of perceptions) 3 whatever is presented as a threat (ex: the phasma of war, etc.)
phasmid	φασματικός/ φασμικός, ή, ό (adj.) (akin to φαίνειν/ phainein- to show)	an apparition; any of various sticklike or leaflike insects (order of Phasmatoptera) including the walking sticks and leaf insects
phatic	φατικός, ή, ό/ φατός (adj.) (φημί –to speak)	of, constituting, or given to formulistic talk or meaningless sounds, used merely to establish social contact rather than to communicate ideas; also called phatic noises (ex: *how do you do ? nice weather today, etc.*)

pheasant	φασιανός	1 any of a number of large gallinaceous birds (family Phasianidae), usually with a long, sweeping tail and brilliant feathers: cf, *Partidge* 2 any of a number of birds resembling the pheasant, as the raffed grouse
Pheidippides	Φειδιππίδης	fifth cent. BC Athenian messenger who ran to Sparta to seek aid, and it is said (but many historians dispute it) after that long distance, he ran from Marathon to Athens to announce the defeat of the Persians by the Greeks, exhausted, after uttering "NENIKIKAMEN – WE HAVE WON' collapsed and died
phellem	φελλός	cork; the layer of dead, corky cells produced externally by the cork cambium in the bark of woody plants
phellogen	(ο, η) φελλογενής (το) φελλογενές/ φελλογόνον	cork cambium: Bot. a layer of formative cells between the cork and the cortex, from which the cork is formed
phelloderm	φελλόδερμα	phellos; cork; the layer of soft, living cells developed on the inner side by the phellogen
pheno-	φαίνειν - to show, shine	combining form (phenocryst)
phenocopy	φαίνειν τύπος –φαινότυπος – phenotype +copy	Genetics an environmentally induced change in an organism that is similar to a mutation but is nonhereditary
phenocryst	´φαίνειν + κρύσταλλο – to show + crystal	a relatively large and usually conspicuous crystal found in a fine-grained matrix in porphyritic igneous rock

phenomenal	φαινομενολογικός, ή, ό (adj.)	of or constituting a phenomenon or phenomena; extremely unusual; extraordinary; highly remarkable
phenomenalism	φαινομεναλισμός	the philosophic theory that knowledge is limited to phenomena, either because there is no reality beyond phenomena or because such knowledge is unknown
phenomenology	φαινομενολογία	1 the philosophical study of phenomena, as distinguished from ontology, the study of being, specif. such a study of perpetual experience in its purely subjective aspect 2 a descriptive or classificatory account of phenomena of a given body of knowledge without any further attempt at explanation
phenomenon	φαινόμενο(ν)/ φαινόμενα (pl.)	any event, circumstance or experience that is apparent to the senses and can be scientifically described or appraised, as an eclipse 2 in Kantian philosophy, a thing as it appears in perception as distinguished from the thing as it is in itself independent of sense experience: distinguished from NOUMENON 3 any extremely unusual or extraordinary thing or occurrence 4 {Coloq.} a person with an extraordinary quality, aptitude, etc., prodigy

phenotype	φαινότυπος	Biol. 1 the manifest characteristics of an organism collectively, including anatomical and psychological traits, that result from both its heredity and its environment 2 a) a group of organisms having a like phenotype b) an individual of such a group
pheromone	φέρειν/to bear	any of chemical substances secreted externally by certain animals
Phi Beta Kappa	Φι Βήτα Κάππα	initial letters of the Greek motto of the honorary society: Φιλοσοφία βίου κυβερνήτης / Philosophia biou kyvernetes/ Philosophy life's guide
Phidias	Φειδίας	the designer/ sculptor of the Parthenon
philanthropic	φιλανθρωπικός, ή, ό (adj.)	constituting a quality of being charitable; loving his/her fellowman
philanthropist	φιλάνθρωπος	one who practices philanthropy; humanitarian
philanthropy	φιλανθρωπία/ φίλος + ανθρωπος/ friend + man	love for your fellowman; benevolence; charity
philhellenic	φιλελληνικός, ή, ό (adj.)	friend of Greek/Hellenic language, history, culture
philhellene	φιλέλλην/ φιλέλληνας	friend of Hellenes; loving Greek people
philo/philos-	φίλος	friend, combining form
Philadelphia (brotherly love/ φίλος + αδέλφια/ friend/loving + brothers)	Φιλαδέλφια	(brotherly love)
philately	φίλος ατέλεια-τέλη/	**friend of no tax** tax exempt, collection of stamps and items related to the postal service

philharmonic	φιλαρμονική (φίλος + αρμονία/friend & harmony)	friend/lover of harmony
-philia	-φιλία	loving; friend + ship suffix forming nouns (hemophilia)
-philic	-φιλικός	friendly, loving prefix forming adjectives
philology	φιλολογία	1 love of learning; love of literature; the study of literary texts, in order to determine authenticity 2 the old term for liguistics
philosopher	φιλόσοφος	(φίλος/lover/friend-σοφία/ wisdom) lover of wisdom
philosophical	φιλοσοφικός, ή, ό (adj.)	pertaining to philosophy / philosophers
philosophy	φιλοσοφία	orig. love for search and wisdom; 2 theory or logical analysis of the principles underlying conduct, thought, knowledge, and the nature of the universe; philosophy includes ethics, aesthetics, logic, epistemology, metaphysics, etc.
philotimon / filotimo	φιλότιμον/ο (neuter of φιλότιμος) (φίλος + τιμή – lover/ friend + honor)	(this is a word that characterizes one who has intense sense of personal honor and dignity) honorable; trustworthy, etc. the greatest compliment to a person esp. a Greek is to say έχει φιλότιμο- he/she has philotimo) Note: The word PHILOTIMO was inducted to the Library of Congress (in 2014) for its uniqueness of its Greek definition and application
phlebitis	φλεβίτις/φλεβίτιδα	inflammation of the vein(s)
phlebo-	φλέβα	vein, prefix forming nouns (phlebotomy) before a vowel phleb- (phlebitis)

phlebogram	φλεβόγραμμα	1 a tracing made with sphygmograph that records the pulse in a vein 2 a radiograph of a vein after injection of a radiopaque medium
phlebograph	φλεβογράφημα	a sphygmograph adapted for recording the venous pulse
phlebography	φλεβογραφία	the process of making plebograms
phlebolith	φλεβόλιθος	a calculus in a vein usually resulting from the calcification of an old thrombus
phlebologist	φλεβολόγος	a specialist in phlebology
phlebology	φλεβολογία	a branch of medicine dealing with veins and their treatment
phlebo-thrombosis	φλεβο-θρόμβωσις /η	venous thrombosis accompanied by little or no inflammation
phlebotomist	φλεβοτόμος	one who practices phlebotomy
phlebotomy	φλεβοτομή	an incision of the vein(s); the old practice of blood letting as a therapeutic measure
phlegm	φλέγμα	thick mucus from the respiratory tract
phlegmatic	φλεγματικός, ή, ό (adj.)	1 sluggish, apathetic, dull 2 of, like, or producing the humor phlegm
phlegmasia	φλέγμα/ φλεγμονή	inflammation of the vein(s)
-phobe	φόβος	fear
phobia	φοβία	extreme fear
-phobia	-φοβία	suffix forming nouns indicating extreme or abnormal fear (nyctophobia/ extreme fear of the night/the dark)
phobic	φοβιστικός, ή, ό (adj.)/ φοβισμένος	one who exhibits a phobia
phonetics	φωνητική	science of vocal sounds

phonics	φώνησις/η —φωνητική	1 voice or speech production 2 a method of teaching beginners to read or enunciate by learning to associate certain letters or groups of letters with the sounds they commonly represent **(cf: Look-Say Method)** 3 the scientific study of sound; acoustics
phono-	φωνή	voice, sound, combining form (and phon before a vowel as in phonics)
phono-cardiogram	φωνο-καρδιόγραμμα	a graphic record of heart sounds made by means of a phonograph
phono-cardiograph	φωνογράφημα	a device for reproducing sound that has mechanically transcribed in a spiral groove on a circular disk
phonogram	φωνόγραμμα	a sign or symbol representing a word, syllable, or sound, as in shorthand
phonograph	φωνόγραφο(ν)	a device to reproduce sound that has been
phono-cardiography	φωνο-καρδιο-γραφία	the recording of heart sounds by means of a phonograph mechanically transcribed in a spiral groove on a circular disk or cylinder
phonology	φωνολογία	the study of speech sounds including phonetics and phonemics
-phoria	-φορία	combining form bearing: state: tendency [euphoria]
-phoric	φορικός, ή, ό (adj.)	suffix forming adjectives (euphoric)
phos-	φως -	light, combining form (phosgene)
phosgene	φωσγενές	a colorless, volatile, highly poisonous liquid

phospho-	φωσφορο-	a bronze having a very small amount of phosphorus in it, combining form
phosphoric	φωσφορικός, ή, ό (adj.)	of, like, or containg phosphorus
phosphorus	φώσφορος	bearer of light, to shine; a chemical element
photo-	φως/φωτός (gen.)	light, combining form
photoallergic	φωτ-αλλεργικός, ή, ό (adj.)	one having an allergic reaction to strong light
photoallergy	φωτο-αλλεργία	hypersensitivity to light
photobiology	φωτο-βιολογία	the branch of biology concerned with the effects of radiant energy (as light) on living things
photochemical	φωτο-χημικός, ή, ό(adj.)	relating to, or resulting from the chemical action of radiant energy and esp., light (as in photochemical smog)
photochemotherapy	φωτο-χημειο-θεραπεία	treatment esp., for psoriasis by applying a photosensitizing drug (as psoralen) which is followed with exposure to sunlight or ultraviolet radiation
photochromic	φωτο-χρωμικός, ή, ό (adj.)	changing color when exposed to radiant energy (as light) (eyeglasses with photochromic lenses)
photo-dermatitis	φωτο-δερματίτις / δερματίτιδα	any dermatitis caused by exposure to light
photo-dynamic	φωτο-δυναμικός, ή, ό (adj.)	relating to, or having the property of intensifying or inducing a toxic reaction to light (as to destroy cancer cells strained with a light-sensitive dye) in a living system (photodynamic thearapy)
photodynia	φωτοδύνη	pain in the eyes due to intense light

photogenic	(ο, η) φωτογενής (το) φωτογενές (adj.)	producing or giving off light that looks or is likely to look attractive in photographs, esp. a person
photograph	φωτογραφία (φωτο + γραφή- of light + imaging, writing),	picture, image
photography	φωτογραφική	the art or process of producing images of objects, persons, landscapes, etc.
photokeratitis	φωτο-κερατίτις / κερατίτιδα	keratitis of the cornea caused by exposure to ultraviolet radiation
photometry	φωτομετρία/ φωτομέτρηση	the measurement of the intensity of light; the branch of optics dealing with the intensity of light
photophobia	φωτοφοβία	extreme fear of light; painful sensitivity to strong light
phototherapy	φωτοθεραπεία	treatment by application of light for therapeutic purposes
phrase	φράσις/η	manner or style of speech, an incomplete sentence
phraseologist	φρασεολόγος	a person skilled in forming well-thought-out sentences
phraseology	φρασεολογία	choice and pattern of words, way of speaking or writing; diction
phratry	φρατρία	1 a subdivision of an ancient Greek phyle/tribe 2 any of the similar units, as a group of clans, of a primitive tribe
phrenetic	φρενετικός, ή, ό (adj.)	maniacal
phrenitis	φρενίτις/φρενίτιδα	delirium; frenzy
phreno -	φρένο	mind, mental capacity, combining form
phrenologist	φρενολόγος	expert in mental problems
phrenology	φρενολογία	study of the mind through the shape of the skull
phrenoplegia	φρενοπληγία	paralysis of the diaphragm

phthisic	φθισικός, ή, ό (adj.)	one suffering from phthisis/ tuberculosis
phthisio-	φθίσιο-	combining form (phthisiology)
phthisiology	φθισιολογία	the scientific study for the treatment and prevention of tuberculosis
phthisis	φθίσις/η	tuberculosis, brucellosis
phyceae	φύκος	seaweed, combining form used in forming scientific names of classes of algae
phylacist	φυλακιστής	jailer
phylactery	φυλακτήριον/ο	safeguard; guard
phylax	φύλαξ/φύλακας	watchman; guard
phylaxis	φύλαξις/η	safeguarding; bodily defense against infection
phyl-	φυλ-	race; tribe; ancestry combining form (phylogeny)
phyle	φυλή	race; tribe; the largest political subdivision in ancient Athenian state
phyletic	φυλετικός, ή, ό (adj.)	pertaining to race; tribe or ancestry
phyll	φύλλο	leaf, combining form
Phyllis	Φύλλις	feminine name
Phyllo/fillo	φύλλο	Mod. Gr. thin sheet (dough in very thin sheets used in desserts/appetizers)
phyllo-	φύλλο(ν)	leaf, combining form
phyllode/phylloid	(ο, η) φυλλοειδής/ (το)φυλλοειδές (adj.)	leaflike; a flat leafstalk functioning as a leaf
phyllophagous	φυλλοφάγος	feeding on leaves
pyllotaxis/ phyllotaxy	φυλλόταξις / φυλλοταξία	the arrangement of leaves on a stem; the study of such arrangement
physic	φύσις /η	physics, nature
physical	φυσικός, ή, ό (adj)	having to do with medicine, of nature, and of matter; of the body as opposed to the mind

physical anthropology	φυσικο/ φύσιο-ανθρωπολογία	the branch of anthropology dealing with the physical variation, characteristics, and evolution of humans physical geography φυσικο-γεωγραφία; the study of the features and nature of the earth's solid surface and oceans, atmosphere/climate, distribution of plant and animal life
physical therapy	φυσιοθεραπεία	the treatment of disease or injury by means other than drugs: exercise, massage, infrared or ultraviolet light,electrotherapy heat, etc.
physicist	φυσικός	expert; specialist in physics
physico-chemical	φυσικο-χημεία/ φυσικό-φύσιο-χημικός	of or pertaining to both physical and chemical properties, changes, and reactions
physics	φυσική	study of natural forces and phenomena
physio-	φύσις/η	nature, combining form
physiognomy	φυσιογνωμία	personality; face
physiology	φυσιολογία	science dealing with the functions of the body
-phyte	φυτό	a plant growing in a specified way, suffix (as in microphyte)
phyto-	φυτό(ν)	plant; shrub
phyto-chemistry	φυτο-χημεία	the branch of chemistry dealing with the chemical processes associated with the plant life and the chemical compounds produced by plants
phytology	φυτολογία	the study of plants; the early term for botany
phytotherapy	φυτοθεραπεία	using vegetables in medicine, drugs

Pi	Ππ (πι)	the sixteenth letter of the Gr. alphabet; a mathematical constant (approximately 3.14159) representing the ratio of the circumference of a circle to its diameter
piracy	πειρασία	1 robbery of ships in the high seas 2 the unauthorized publication, reproduction, or use of a copyrighted or patented work
pirate	πειρατής	a person who practices piracy; one who publishes, reproduces, or makes use of without authorization
pityriasis	πιτυρίασις/η	group of diseases in which the main symptom is scaly skin
plagio- prefix	πλάγιος, α, ο (adj.)	oblique; slanting
plagiotropic	πλάγιο-τροπικός	Bot. having the longer axes of roots or branches slanting from the vertical line
-plasia suffix	πλάσις/η/ πλάσσειν	a molding; to mold (as in cataplasia, dysplasia)
-plasm	πλάσμα	combining form, any of the components of protoplasm
plasma	πλάσμα	the fluid part of blood, lymph, milk, or intramuscular liquid; esp., the fluid part of blood, as distinguished from the corpuscles, used for transfusions; protoplasm
plasmacytoma/ plasmocytoma	πλάσμα-κύτωμα	a myeloma composed of plasma cells
plasmatic	πλασματικός, ή, ό (adj.)	relating to, or occurring in plasma esp., blood (plasmatic fibrils)
-plast suffix	πλαστός, ή, ό (adj.)	formed; molded (chromoplast)
Plato	Πλάτων	the great philosopher
platonic	πλατωνικός, ή, ό (adj.)	coming from Plato's teachings

platy-	πλατύ (πλατύς)	flat; broad (platypodus/ flat-footed)
platycrania	πλατυ-κρανία/ πλατύς & κρανίον	flattening of the skull
platypoda/platypus	πλατύπους/ πλατύποδας	flat-footed person
platypodia	πλατυποδία	flat feet
Pleiades	Πλειάδες	a cluster of stars in the constellation Taurus, six of which are readily visible and represent six daughters of Atlas, the seventh bright star (the Lost Pleiad) has apparently faded from sight since the original sightings
pleio-	πλέον/ πλείο(ν)/ πλείστον	more; most
pleiochroism	πλειοχρωϊσμός/ πλειο-χρωματισμός	more than usual colors, combination of many colors
pleionemia	πλειοναιμία	increased amount of blood in an area
pleomorphic	πλειομορφικός, ή, ό (adj.)	Biol. one having two or more forms in one life cycle
pleonasm	πλεονασμός (from πλεονάζειν- to be in excess)	the use of more words than necessary for the expression of an idea; redundancy
pleonexia	πλεονεξία	extreme greed
plethora	πληθώρα	extreme amount of something
plethoric	πληθωρικός, ή, ό (adj.)	characterized by excess or profusion; inflated (inflated speech)
pleothorhism	πληθωρισμός	inflation
pleur- or pleura-	πλευρόν/ ό	rib, combining word (pleuricy)
pleura	πλευρό(ν)/ πλευρά (pl.)	rib(s), side; thin tissue covering the lungs and lining the interior walls of the chest cavity
pleurectomy	πλευρό + εκτομή	surgical excision of part of the pleura
pleurisy	πλευρίτις/ πλευρίτιδα	inflammation of the pleura, the membrane that covers the lungs

pleuritis	πλευρίτις / πλευρίτιδα	inflammation of the pleura
pleurodynia	πλευρο -οδύνη	pain in the muscles between the ribs
pleuron	πλευρό(ν)/ πλευρά (pl.)	rib/ribs; either of the lateral plates on the thoracic and abdominal segments of an anthropod
pleuro-pneumonia	πλευρό-πνευμονία	pneumonia complicated by pleurisy
pluto-	πλούτος	wealth, combining form
plutocrat	πλουτοκράτης	a member of a wealthy ruling class
plutocracy	πλουτοκρατία	government by the wealthy
plutolatry	πλουτολατρεία	excessive love for wealth
pleurodynia	πλευρο -οδύνη	pain in the muscles between the ribs
pneoscope	πνευοσκόπιο(ν)	instrument that records breathing
pneum or pneumo -	πνεύμων/πνεύμονος	lung, combining form (pneumonia)
pneumococcus	πνευμονόκοκκος	germ which can attack the body, usually the lungs
pneumocystis	πνευμοκύστις/ κύστιδα	a form of pneumonia, often associated with AIDS, caused by a fungus (pneumocystis carinii pneumonia)
pneumon-	πνεύμων/πνεύμονας /πνευμόνι (Mod. Gr.)	lung
pneumon-ectomy	πνευμον-εκτομή	surgical removal of the lung(s)
pneumonia	πνευμονία	a general term for infection of he lungs
pneumonic	πνευμονικός, ή, ό (adj.)	pertaining to lungs; pulmonary
pneumonitis	πνευμονίτις/ πνευμονίτιδα	inflammation of the lungs
pneumono-centesis	πνευμονο-κέντησις/η	surgical puncture of a lung for aspiration
pneumonologist	πνευμονολόγος	lung specialist

pneumonology	πνευμολογία	the branch of medicine concerned with the lungs
pneumonolysis	πνευμονόλυσις/η	either of two surgical procedures to permit collapse of a lung
pneumonopathy	πνευμονοπάθεια	any lung disease
pneumorrhaia	πνευμονορραγία	lung hemorrhage
pneumono-sclerosis	πνευμονο-σκλήρωσις /η	a pathological condition of hardening of the lung
pneumono-thorax/ pneumothorax	πνευμονο-θώραξ/ πνευμονο-θώρακας	abnormal entrance of air or gas into lung sacs, causing difficult respiration
podiatrist	ποδίατρος	specialist in foot ailments
podiatry	ποδιατρική	the medical care and treatment of the feet
podo-dermatitis	ποδο'δερματίτις/ δερματ´τιδα	a condition characterized by inflammation of the dermal tissue underlying the horny layers of a hoof
podium	υπο-πόδιον/ο (πους/ποδός (gen.) πόδι (Mod. Gr.) υποπόδιον/ο	underfoot; footstool 1 a low wall serving as a pedestal or foundation 2 a low wall separating the seats from the arena in ancient amphitheaters 4 a small platform for a speaker or a conductor of an orchestra, etc., dais
-podium		suffix forming nouns indicating anything being under-foot; footlike or supporting part (monopodium, stylopodium, etc.)
podocarp/ podocarpus	ποδόκαρπος (πους/ ποδός – καρπός/ foot + fruit)	any of a genus (Corpocarpus) of tropical, evergreen trees and shrubs of the podocarp family with flattened needles, small cones, and fleshy seeds
-podous	-ποδός/ of foot	suffix forming adjectives having (a specified number or kind of) feet (gastropodous, decapodous/dekapodos, etc.)

poem	ποίημα (ποιείν –to make, create)	1 an arrangement of words written or spoken
poesy	ποίησις /η	1 old-fashioned variation of poetry; 2 (Obs.) a) a poem b) a motto 3 in Gr. poetry/ ποίησις /η
poet	ποιητής/ ποιήτρια (fem.)	1 a person who writes poems or verses 2 one who displays imaginative power and beauty of thought, language, character, etc.
poetaster	ποιητής + αστήρ/ αστέρος (gen.) / poet + star	a writer of mediocre verse; a rhymester; would-be poet
poetic	ποιητικός, ή, ό (adj.)	1 of, characteristic of, like, or fit for a poet and poetry 2 skilled in or fond of poetry 3 written in verse 4 displaying the beauty, imaginative qualities, etc., found in good poetry
poetics	ποιητική	1 a) the theory or structure of poetry b) the poetic theory or practice of a specific poet
pogonion	πώγων / πώγονος(anc. gen.)/ πιγούνι (mod. Gr.)	the most projecting median point on the anterior surface of the chin
poietic-	ποιητικός, η, ό (adj.)	combining form, making, producing, forming
polis	πόλις/η	city, in ancient Greece, a city-state
police	πόλις / πολίτης// πολιτεία (city, citizen, state)	the regulation within a community of morals, safety, sanitation, etc.; public order; law enforcement
political	πολιτικός, ή, ό (adj.)	of or concerned with government, the state or politics
politics	πολιτική	the science and art of political government; political science
poly-	πολύ/πολλά (pl.)	much, many
polyadelphous	πολυ-άδελφος	with many brothers, siblings

polyandry	πολυ-ανδρία	the state or practice of having two or more husbands at the same time
polyanthous	πολύανθος, η, ο (adj.)	any of many primroses with many flowers
poly-athralgia	πολύ + αρθραλγία	pain in one or more joints
polyarthritis	πολυαρθρίτις/ πολυαρθρίτιδα	inflammation of many joints
polycarpy	πολυκαρπία	flowering and fruiting a number of times
polycholia	πολύ-χολή	excessive bile secretion
poly-chromatic	πολυ-χρωματικός, ή, ό (adj.)	having various or changing colors
poly-chondritis	πολυ - χονδρίτις / χονδρίτιδα	inflammation of a cartilage at multiple site of the body
polychromy	πολυ-χρωμία	the art of combining many different colors
polycyesis	πολύ-κύησις/η	pregnancy with more than one fetus
polycytosis	πολυ-κύτταρη	excess of blood cells
polydactylism	πολύ-δακτυλισμός	having more than five fingers or toes
polydipsia	πολυ-δίψα	extreme thirst
polyemia	πολύ-αιμία	excessive blood in the body
polygamy	πολύ-γαμία	the practice of having two or more spouses at the same time
polygon	πολύγωνον/ο	a closed plane figure, esp., one with more than four sides and angles
polyglot	πολύγλωσσος, η, ο (adj.)	knowing many languages; multilingual
polygraph	πολύγραφος	instrument for simultaneously recording several different pulsations
polygyny	πολύ-γυνή (πολλές γυναίκες/ many women)	marriage to more than one woman at the same time
polymenorrhea	πολύ-εμηνορροή	unusual frequency of menstrual period

polymorph	πολύμορφος, η, ο (adj.)	1 Biol. A polymorphous organism 2 Chem., Minerology a) a substance that can crystallize in different forms b) one of these forms
polymorphism	πολυμορφισμός	the condition in which species have two or more very different morphological forms
polymorphous	πολύμορφος	having many forms, shapes
poly-myalgia	πολυ-μυαλγία	myalgia affecting several muscle groups
poly-melalgia rheumatic	πολύ –ρευματική μυαλγία	a disorder of the elderly characterized by muscular pain and stiffness in the neck, shoulders, and in the pelvic area
polymyositis	πολύ-μυοσίτις/ μυοσίτιδα	inflammation of many muscles
polyneuritis	πολυ-νευρίτις/ νευρίτιδα	inflammation of more than one group of nerves
polypathes	(ο, η) πολυπαθής (το) πολυπαθές (adj.)	one suffering from more than one disease at the same time
poly-neuropathy	πολυ-νευροπάθεια	an abnormal condition usually degenerative state of nervous system affecting many nerves
polyopia	πολύωπία	perception of more than one image of a single object, esp., with one eye
polyp	πολύ + πους/ ποδός(gen.) πολύπους- πολύποδας (Mod. Gr.)	a mucous membrane; a smooth projecting growth
polypathia	πολυπάθεια	having more than one disease at a time
polyp-ectomy	πολυ + εκτομή(πολλές εκτομές (pl.)	having many surgical procedures
polyphagia	πολυφαγεία	excessive eating

polyphasic	πολυφασικός, ή, ό (adj.)	of, having, generating, or using alternating currents differing in phase
Polyphemus	Πολύφημος	Homer's *Odyssey*: the Cyclop who confines Odysseus and his companions in a cave until Odysseus blinds him and all escape
polyphony	πολυφωνία	multiplicity of sounds, as in an echo; in Music, a number of independent but harmonizing melodies
polyplegia	πολυπληγία	paralysis of several muscles
polysyllable	πολυσύλλαβος	having many syllables
polysynaptic	πολυσυναπτικός, ή, ό (adj.) (σύναψις /η /συνάπτειν- connection/ to connect)	involving two or more synapses in the central nervous system
polytechnic	πολυτεχνικός, ή, ό (adj.)/πολύτεχνος	having many skills; providing instruction in technical and scientific subjects
polytheism	πολυθεϊσμός	the belief in or worship in many gods, or in more than one god: opposed to **Momotheism**
polytheist	πολυθεϊστής	one believing in many gods or idols
polytocous	πολύτοκος	1 having many offsprings; having many children 2 giving birth to more than one child
porno-	πορνο-	pertaining to prostitution, combining form
pornographer	πορνογράφος	one writing about, or promoting prostitution or pornography
pornographic	πορνογραφικός, ή, ό (adj.)	of or having to do with material of prostitution
pornography	πορνογραφία	the writings or production of pictures intended to arouse sexual desire

porphyrin	πορφυρίνη (πορφυρα + όψις – purple + appearance)	any of pyrrole derivatives, found in cytoplasm, that combine with iron and magnesium to form heme and chlorophyll, respectively
porphyry	πορφυρίτης (λίθος – porphyry rock/lithos)	any igneous rock with large, distinct crystals, esp., of alkali feldspar, embedded in a fine-grained matrix
Poseidon	Ποσειδών/ Ποσειδώνας	Gr. myth. the god of the sea and the horses: identified with the Roman Neptune
poso-	πόσος, η, ο (adj.)	how much; how many (pl.) combining form (posology) Med. the scientific study of drug-dosages
posology	ποσολογία	system/method of dosage
potamophobia	ποταμο-φοβία (ποταμός/ river +fear)	extreme fear of rivers or large bodies of water
pragmat-agnosia	πραγματο-αγνωσία	inability to recognize objects
pragmatic	πραγματικός, ή, ό (adj.)	real, genuine; dogmatic; opinionated; of, or having to do with philosophical pragmatism
pragmatism	πραγματισμός	the quality or condition of being pragmatic 2 a method or tendency in philosophy, which determines the meaning and truth of all concepts by their practical consequences
presb- or presbyo-	πρεσβ- πρεσβυο- (πρεσβύτερος – elder; a priest)	combining form
presby-acusia/ acusis	πρέσβυς + ακούειν- old + hearing	loss of hearing due to old age
presbyopia	πρεσβυωπία	loss of elasticity in eyes, occurring in old age
presbyter	πρεσβύτερος, α, ο (adj.)	elder, older; senior; also, title/rank of a priest

presymptomatic	πριν συμπτωματικός, ή, ό (adj.)	relating to, being, or occurring before symptoms appear **(presymptomatic diagnosis of a hereditary disease)**
presystolic	πριν συστολικός, ή, ό (adj.)	of, relating to, or occurring just before cardiac systole {a presystolic murmur}
pro-	προ	before, prior
probiotic	προβιωτικός, ή, ό (adj.)	a preparation (as a dietary supplement) containing live bacteria (as lactobacilli) that is taken orally to restore beneficial bacteria to the body; also, a bacterium in such a preparation
proboscis	προβοσκίς / προβοσκίδα (προ + βόσκειν – before +to feed; graze)	1 an elephant's trunk, or long, flexible snout, as of tapir 2 any tubular organ for sucking, food gathering, sensing, etc.
proct -	πρωκτ / πρωκτός	rectum, anus, combining form before a vowel
proctectomy	πρωκτεκτομή	surgical excision of the rectum
proctitis	πρωκτίτις/ πρωκτίτιδα	inflammation of the anus and rectum
procto-	πρωκτός	rectum, anus, combining form
proctocolitis	πρωκτο –κολίτις /κολίτιδα	inflammation of the rectum and colon
proctologist	πρωκτοκολόγος	a specialist in proctology
proctology	πρωκτολογία	the branch of medicine dealing with the rectum and anus and their diseases
proctoplasty	πρωκτο-πλαστική	plastic surgery of the rectum and anus
proctoscope	πρωκτοσκόπιο (ν)	an instrument for the direct examination of the interior of the rectum
proctotomy	πρωκτοτομή	surgical incision into the rectum

progeria	προ + γήρας **(before +old age)**	premature old age; a rare genetic disorder, esp. of early childhood: characterized by slowed physical growth, signs of baldness, wrinkled skin, and atherosclerosis exhibiting the rapid aging, with death usually occurring during puberty
prognathous	πρόγναθος	having the jaws projecting beyond the upper part of the face
prognosis	πρόγνωσις/η	forecasting a prediction of the probable course of a disease in an individual and the chances of recovery
prognostic	προγνωστικός, ή, ό (adj.)	a sign, indication, forecast for things to come; an omen
program	πρόγραμμα	1 proclamation; prospectus or syllabus; 2 a plan or procedure for dealing with some matter 3 scheduled activities, sports, entertainment, television, radio shows, etc.
programmer	προγραμματιστής	a specialist in programming esp. electronic devices
prokinetic	προκινητικός, ή, ό (adj.)	stimulating motility of the esophageal and gastrointestinal muscles
prologue	πρόλογος	an introduction to a book, play, poem, essay, etc.
pronephros	πρόνεφρος	either member of the first and most anterior pair of the three paired vertebrate renal organs present but nonfunctional in embryos of reptiles, birds, and mammals; compare *Mesonephros; Metanephros*
prophesy	προφητεία	to declare or predict (something) by or, as by the influence of divine guidance

prophet	προφήτης	a person who speaks for God or god(s), or as though of divine guidance
prophetic	προφητικός, ή, ό (adj.)	of, or having the power of predicting; pertaining to a prophet
prophylactic	προφυλακτικός, ή, ό (adj.)	preventing or protecting esp., against disease or pregnancy
prophylaxis	προφύλαξις/η	the prevention or protection against disease; prophylactic treatment
prosopo-	πρόσωπον/ο	person; also face, combining form
prosopodemic	πρόσωπο + επιδημία-pesron + epidemic	spread from one person to another
prosop-agnosia	πρόσωπο + αγνωσία	inability to recognize faces (persons)
prosopography	προσωπογραφία	the study of careers, esp. of individuals linked by family economic, political, or social relationships
prosopospasm	πρόσωπο + σπασμός –face + spasm	(in this instance, prosopo has a second meaning: face) facial spasm
prostate	προστάτης	1 of the bladder; the prostate gland 2 the word prostate/προστάτης, in Greek also means: **protector**
prostatectomy	εκτομή / εγχείρησις /η (του) προστάτη (surgical excision of the prostate)	the surgical removal of all or part of the prostate gland
prostatic urethra	ουρήθρα του προστάτη (urethra of the prostate)	the part of the male urethra from the base of the prostate gland, where the urethra begins as the outlet of the bladder, to the point where it emerges from the apex of the prostate gland

prostatism	προστατισμός	a chronic disorder of the prostate gland, esp., enlargement of the gland resulting in obstruction of the flow of urine
prostatitis	προστατίτις/ προστατίτιδα	inflammation of the prostate gland
prosthesis	πρόσθεσις/η	substitute for missing part of the body (in Gr. πρόσθεσις/η, it also means addition)
prosthetic	προσθετικός, ή, ό (adj.)	1 a prosthesis or prosthetics 2 Chem. designating or of any of a number of protein compounds when combined chemically with a protein molecule
prosthetics	προσθετική	the branch of surgery concerned with the replacement of missing parts, esp., limbs, by artificial substitutes
prosthetist	προσθετιστής	a specialist in prosthetics
prosth-odontics	οδοντο-προσθετική	the dental specialty dealing with the making of artificial replacements for missing parts of the mouth and jaw; also called *prosthetic dentistry*
prosth-odontist	οδοντο-προσθετής	an expert in prosthondontics
protagonist	πρωταγωνιστής/ πρωταγωνίστρια (fem.)	first/main character in a book, story, play, or movie
protein	πρωτεϊνη	the basic substance of every cell in the body
protein-uria	πρωτεϊνη + ουρία/ ούρα – protein + urine	excess presence of protein in the urine
proteo-glycan	γλυκο- πρωτεϊνη (sweet protein)	any of the class of glycoproteins of high molecular weight that are found in the extracellular matrix of connective tissue
proteo-lysis	προτεόλυσις	Biochem. The breaking down of proteins, as the gastric juices, to form simpler substances

proto-	πρώτος, η, ο (pron. adj.)	first in order, first in importance, etc.; first in time, original, primitive (protocol), combining form
protocol	πρωτόκολο(ν)	an original draft or record of a document, negotiation, etc.; a set of rules or a code for official events, etc.
proton	πρώτον	first (see; proto-) combining form (protoplasm)
protopathic	(ο, η) πρωτοπαθής (το) πρωτοπαθές) (adj.)	Physiol. designating or of certain sensory nerves having limited sensibility, that respond to heat and pain from a general area
protoplasm	πρωτόπλασμα	a semifluid, viscous, translucent colloid, the essential living matter in all animal and plant cells: it consists mainly of water, proteins, lipids, carbohydrates, and inorgamic salts, it is differentiated into nucleoplasm and cytoplasm
proto-porphyria	πρώτο + πορφυρία – first + porphyrin	the presence of porphyrin in the blood
prototheca	πρωτοθήκη	a genus of unicellular algae including two *(P. zopfii and P. wickerhamii)*
Protozoan	πρωτόζωα	any of a subkingdom (Protozoa) of microscopic animals made up of a single cell or a group of more or less identical cells, living in water or as parasites, including ciliates, flagellates, rhizopods, and sporozoans
proto-zoolology	πρωτο-ζωολογία	the branch of zoology concerned with the protozoan
prototype	πρωτότυπο(ν)	the first thing or being of its kind; original; model; archtype; pattern; a person or thing that serves as model for one of a later year

Ps; psi	Ψ, ψι	the twenty-third letter of the Gr. alphabet; (in Greek, *Ps* is pronounced as one letter Ψ,(as it is at the end of English words, such in tops, caps, pops, etc.; in English the letter *p* is silent, as in psychology)
psalm	ψαλμός (ψάλλειν – to sing praise, hymns)	1 sacred song or poem, hymn 2 any of the sacred songs in praise of God constituting the Book of Psalms in the Bible; to glorify in psalms
psellism	ψελλισμός;ψευδίζω/ to stutter	stuttering
pseud- or pseudo-	ψεύδος /(ο, η) ψευδής, (το) ψευδές (adj.)	false; lie; counterfeit; sham; spurious (pseudarthrosis), conbining form
Pseudarthrosis or pseudo-arthrosis	ψευδο-άρθρωσις	abnormal union formed by fibrous tissue between parts of a bone that has been fractured usually due to congenital weakness; false joint
pseudocrisis	ψευδο-κρίσις /η	false crisis; false alarm crisis
pseudocyesis	ψευδοκύησις /η	1 imaginary pregnancy with some physical symptoms 2 a psychosomatic state that occurs without conception and is marked by some of the physical symptoms (cessation of menses, enlargement of the abdomen, and apparent fetal movements) and changes in hormonal balance of pregnancy
pseudocyst	ψευδοκύστις /η	a cluster of toxoplasmas in a enucleate host cell
pseudo-hermaphrodite	ψευδο-ερμαφρόδιτος, η, ο (adj.)	a person or animal having gonads of one sex while the genital organs and secondary sex characteristics resemble in whole or in part those of the opposite sex

pseudo-hermaphroditism	ψευδο-ερμαφροδιτισμός	the condition of having the gonads of one sex and the external genitalia and other sex organs so variably developed that the sex of the individual is uncertain
pseudo-hypertrophic	ψευδο-υπερτροφικός, ή, ό (adj.)	falsely hypertrophic, specif. being a form of muscular dystrophy, in which the muscles swell due to deposits of fat and fibrous tissue
pseudo-membrane	ψευδο-μεμβράνη	it has the characteristics of formation of a false membrane *(as in pseudomembranous colitis)*
pseudo-neurotic	ψευδο-νευρωτικός, ή, ό (adj.)	characterized of, or, having neurotic symptoms which mask an underlying psychosis *[pseudoneurotic schizophrenia]*
pseudonym	ψευδώνυμο(ν)	fictitious name; pen name
pseudo-paralysis	ψευδο-παράλυσις/η	it appears as lack or loss of muscular power (as if produced by pain), but it is not accompanied by symptoms of true paralysis
pseudo-polyp	ψευδο-πολύπους/πολύποδας	a projecting mass of hypertrophied mucous membrane (as in the colon) the result of topical inflammation
psoriasis	ψωρίασις /η	chronic skin disease in which red scaly patches develop
psoriatic arthritis	ψωριάρικη αρθρίτις / αρθρίτιδα	a severe form of arthritis accompanied by inflammation, psoriasis of the skin or the nails, and a negative test for rheumatoid factor; also called *psoriatic arthropathy*
psych	ψυχή	soul; the intellect
psyche	ψυχή	mind, soul, intellect
psychiatrist	ψυχίατρος	specialist in psychiatry or mental disorders

psychic	ψυχικός, ή, ό (adj.)	pertaining to mind
psychedelia	ψυχεδέλεια	anything associated with drug-induced condition, escalated by technical lighting and psychedelic music to a frenzy
psychedelic	ψυχεδελικός, ή, ό (adj.)	one correlated to psychedelia
psycho -	ψυχο-ψυχή	soul, spirit, intellect (short for psychotic), combining form, the mind or mental processes [psychology]
psycho/psychos (pl.)	ψυχοπαθής/ ψυχοπαθείς (pl.)	short for psychotic; psychopathic
psycho-acoustics	ψυχο-ακουστική	the study of how sounds are heard subjectively and of the individual's response to sound stimuli
psychoanalysis	ψυχοανάλυσις/η	1 method of obtaining a patient's past emotional history 2 a method of analyzing psychic phenomena and treating mental and emptional disorders that is based on the concepts and theories of Sigmund Froyd, which emphasizes the importance of free association and dream analysis, involving treatment sessions when a person is encouraged to talk freely and express personal experiences, esp., of early childhood and dreams
psychoanalyst	ψυχοαναλυτής	specialist in psychoanalysis
psycho-biology	ψυχο-βιολογία	1 the branch of biology concerned with the interrelationship of the mental processes and the anatomy and physiology of the individual 2 psychology as being investigated by biological methods

psycho-diagnostics	ψυχο-διαγνωστική	the branch of psychology dealing with the use of tests in the evaluation of personality and the determination of factors underlying human behavior
psycho-drama	ψυχο-δράμα	an improvised dramatization designed to offer catharsis and social rehabilitation for one or more of the participants from whose life's history plot is abstracted
psycho- dynamics	ψυχο-δυναμική	1 the psychology of mental or emotional forces, or processes developing, esp., in early childhood and their effects on behavior and mental state 2 explanation or interpretation (as of behavior or mental state) in terms of mental or emotional forces or processes 3 motivational forces acting esp., at the unconscious level
psychogenesis	ψυχογένεσις /η	1 origination and development within the psyche or mind 2 development from mental as distinguished from physical origin
psycho-genetic	ψυχο-γενετικός, ή, ό (adj.)	originating in the mind or in mental or emotional conflict [psychogenic impotence] [a psychogenic disorder]
psycho-geriatrics	ψυχο-γηριατρική (ψυχή + γήρας – mind +old age)	a branch of psychiatry that studies the behavioral and emotional disorders among the elderly
psychognosis	ψυχόγνωσις /η	study of mental and emotional activity
psycho-kinesis	ψυχοκίνησις	movement of physical objects by the mind without use of physical means
psychological	ψυχολογικός, ή, ό (adj.)	of psychology, of the mind; mental; affecting or intended to affect the mind

psychologism	ψυχολογισμός	any attempt to discover psychological bases for historical events, philosophical concepts, etc.: usually a disparaging term
psychologist	ψυχολόγος	a specialist in psychology
psychologize	ψυχολογείν/ ψυχολογώ	to reason or theorize psychologically
psychology	ψυχολογία	the science of human behavior and mental functions
psycho-metric	ψυχο-μετρικός, ή, ό (adj.)	of or relating to psychometrics
psychometrics	ψυχομετρική	a branch of clinical or applied psychology concerned with the use and application of mental measurement 2 the technique of mental measurements: the use of quantitive devices for assessing psychological trends
psycometrist	ψυχομετριστής	a specialist (as a clinical psychologist) skilled in the administration and interpretation of objective psychological tests 2 a psychologist who devises, constructs, and standardizes psychometric tests; psychometrician
psychometry	ψυχομετρία	1 the supposed faculty of divining knowledge about an object or about a person connected with it, through contact with the object; psychometrics
psycho-neurosis	ψυχονεύρωσις /η	a neurosis based on emotional conflict in which an impulse that has been blocked seeks expression through a disguised response or symptom
psychoneurotic	ψυχονευρικός, ή, ό (adj.)	of, relating to, being, or affected with a psycho-neurosis (**a psychoneurotic disorder**)

psychopath	(ο, η) ψυχοπαθής (το) ψυχοπαθές (adj.)	a person suffering from a mental disorder
psychopathic	ψυχοπαθητικός, ή, ό (adj.)	characterized by psychopathy
psycho-pathology	ψυχοπαθολογία	1 the science concerned with the causes and development of mental disorders 2 psychological malfunctioning, as in a mental disorder
psychopathy	ψυχοπάθεια	mental disorder; antisocial personality
psycho-pharmaceutical	ψυχο-φαρμακευτικός, ή, ό (adj.)	a drug having an effect on the mental state of the user
psycho-pharmacology	ψυχο-φαρμακολογία	the scientific study of the effect of drugs on the mind and mental behavior
psycho-physics	ψυχοφυσική	the branch of psychology dealing with the effects of physical processes (as intensity of stimulation) on mental processes and esp. sensations of an organism
psycho-physiological	ψυχο-φυσιολογικός, ή, ό (adj.)	1 of, or relating to psychophysiology 2 combining or involving mental and bodily processes
psycho-physiology	ψυχο-φυσιολογία	a branch of psychology concerned with the effects of normal and pathological, physiological processes on mental functioning; also called *psysiological psychology*
psychosis	ψύχωσις /η	a major mental disorder in which the personality is seriously disorganized and contact with reality is usually impaired

psycho-somatic	ψυχο-σωματικός, ή, ό (adj.)	1 of, relating to, concerned with, or involving both mind and body 2 a) of, relating to, concerned or involving bodily symptoms, caused by mental or emotional disturbance b) exhibiting psychosomatic symptoms
psychosomatics	ψυχο-σωματική	the branch of medical science that concerns itself with interrelationships between the mind or emotions and the body; esp., with the relation of psychological conflict to somatic symptomatology
psycho-synthesis	ψυχο-σύνθεσις	a form of psychotherapy combining psychoanalytic techniques with meditation and exercise
psychotherapist	ψυχοθεραπευτής	specialist in psychotherapy
psychotherapy	ψυχοθεραπεία	treatment of mental or emotional disorders or maladjustment by psychological means involving verbal communication (as in psychoanalysis, nondirective psychotherapy, reeducation, or hypnosis)
psychotic	ψυχωτικός, ή, ό (adj.)	of, or having the nature of, a psychosis; a person having psychosis, or symptoms of psychosis
psychro-	ψυχρός, ή, ό (adj.)	cold, combining form (psychrophobia)
psychrometer	ψυχρόμετρο(ν)	an instrument with wet and dry thermometer, for measuring moisture in the air
psychrometrics	ψυχομετρική	the study of measuring various temperatures
psychrophile	ψυχροφιλικός, ή, ό (adj.)	a plant thriving in low temperatures

psychrophobia	ψυχροφοβία	excessive fear of low temperatures
pteridology	πτέρη/ φτέρη/fern -φτερόν/feather	**due to the similarity in shape** branch of botany dealing with ferns
ptero-	πτερό(ν)/φτερό(ν)	wing; feather, combining form (pterodactyl)
ptero-dactyl	πτερόν/ό/ φτερό- δάκτυλος	any of the extinct order of flying reptiles
pteropod	πτερόπους/ πτερόποδας	relating to certain orders of small, thin-shelled or shell-less gastropod mollusks
pteryg- or pterygo-	πτέρυγ- πτερυγο- (πτέρυξ /πτέρυγος (gen.) – having the form of a wing)	winglike, combining form (pterygium)
pterygium	πτερύγιον	an abnormal triangular mass of mucous membrane growing over the human cornea from the inner corner of the eye
pterygoid	(ο, η) πτερυγοειδής (το) πτερυγοειδές (adj.)	1 having the form of a wing; winglike; 2 designating, of, or near either of two winglike processes in the skull that descend from the sphenoid bone
pterygoid muscle	πτερυγοειδής μυς	either of two muscles extending from the sphenoid bone to the lower jaw
pterygoid nerve	πτερυγοειδές νεύρο	either of two branches of the mandibular nerve: a) one distributed to the lateral pterygoid muscle; also called *lateral pterygoid nerve* b) one that is distributed to the medial pterygoid muscle, tensor tympani, and tensor veli palatine—also called *medial pterygoid nerve*
ptosis	πτώσις /η	falling; drooping (as in the upper eyelid)/ due to the paralysis of the muscle

ptyal- or ptyalo-	πτυαλ- πτυαλο- (πτύειν –to spit)	saliva, combining form (ptyalism)
ptyalin	πτυαλίνη	an amylase in the saliva of humans and some other animals that converts starch into various dextrin sand maltose
ptyalism	πτυαλισμός	excess secretion of saliva
ptyalorrhea	πτυαλόρροια	extreme flow of saliva
-ptysis	-πτύσις /πτυσίσ	spewing: expectoration suffix forming nouns (hemoptysis/ αιμοπτυσία) spitting of blood
pycn- or pycno- or pykno-	πυκν- πυκνό- (πυκνός, ή, ό) (adj.)	thick; dense combining form (pycnosis)
pycnolepsy	πυκνολεψία	a condition marked by epileptiform attacks similar to those of petit mal epilepsy
pycnosis	πύκνωσις /η	thickening; 1 a process of thickening, esp., in the shrining nucleus of a degenerating cell; 2 a degenerative of a cell nucleus characterized by clumping of the chromosomes, hyperchromatism, and shrinking of the nucleus; also, **pyknosis**
pyarthrosis	πυάρθρωσις /η	pus in a joint cavity; the formation or presence of pus in a joint
pyel- or pyelo-	πυελ- πυελό (πύελος – pelvis)	renal pelvis, combining form (pyelography)
pyelitis	πυελίτις/πυελίτιδα	inflammation of the lining of the renal pelvis
pyelogram	πυελόγραμμα	a pyelograph taken by a pyelometer or a pyelography
pyelography	πυελογραφία	radiographic visualization of the renal pelvis after it has been injected with a radiopaque substance through the ureter or into a vein
pyelolithotomy	πυελολιθοτομή	surgical incision of the renal pelvis of a kidney for the removal of a kidney stone

pyel o*nephritis*	πυελονεφρίτις/ πυελονεφρίτιδα	inflammation on both the parenchyma of a kidney and the lining of its renal pelvis esp., due to bacterial infection; infection of one or both kidneys, usually involving both the pelvis and the functional tissue
pyeloplasty	πυελοπλαστική	plastic surgery of the renal pelvis of a kidney
pyemia	πυαιμία	form of blood poisoning (by the presence of pus-producing microorganisms)
pyo-	πύον	pus, combining form (pyogenesis)
pyocolpos	πύον-κόλπος	pus in the vagina
pyocyst	πυοκύστις/η	sac of pus in the body
pyoderma	πυοδερμία/ πύον/ο + δέρμα –pus + skin)	a bacterial skin inflammation characterized by pus- filled lesions; any skin inflammation that produces pus
pyogenic	(ο, η) πυογενής (το) πυογενές (adj.)	producing pus [**pyogenic bacteria**} also characterized by pus production [**pyogenic meningitis**]
pyogenesis	πυογέννησις/η	formation of pus; pyosis
pyometra	πυομήτρα	accumulation of pus in the uterine cavity
pyorrhea	πυόρροια	infection of the gums that causes the edges of the tooth sockets to bleed
pyosalpinx	πύο + σάλπιξ – pus + oviduct	collection of pus in an oviduct; discharge of pus
pyr- or pyro-	πυρ/ πυρός (gen.) πυρά/φωτιά	fire, combining form (pyrexia; pyromania)
pyra-	πυρά	fire, combining form

pyramid	πυραμίς / πυραμίδος(gen.)/ πυραμίδα (Mod. Gr.)	1 any huge structure with a square base and four sloping, triangular sides meeting at the top, as those built by the ancient Egyptians for royal tombs 2 an object formation, or structure shaped like or suggesting a pyramid 3 Geom. a solid figure having a polygonal base, the sides of which form the bases of triangular surfaces meeting at a common vertex 4 Biol. an anatomical structure resembling a pyramid: as a) Renal Pyramid b) either of two large bundles of motor fibers from the cerebral cortex that reach the medulla oblongata and are continuous with the corticospinal tracts of the spinal cord.
pyramidotomy	πυραμιδοτομή	a surgical procedure in which a corticospinal tract is severed) as for relief of parkinsonism
pyrene	πυρήν/πυρήνας	stone of a fruit, grain of wheat, 2 a colorless hydrocarbon obtained from coal tar
pyretic	πυρετικός, ή, ό (adj.)	pretaining to fever
pyretolysis	πυρετόλυσις /η (πυρετός/fever + λύσις/solution)	reducing the fever
pyrexia	πυρεξία	increased body temperature; high fever
pyro-	πυρ-πυρός (gen.)	fire; heat, combining form (pyromania)
pyrogen	πυρογενής / πυρογενές	Med. a substance that produces fever; fever producing subtance
pyrogenic	πυρογενικός, ή, ό (adj.)	producing, or produced by, heat or fever
pyrography	πυρογραφία	1 the art or process of burning designs on wooden or leather objects, by use of heated tools 2 a design made with that process

pyrolysis	πυρόλυσις	chemical decomposition of a substance by heat
pyromancy	πυρομαντεία	the practice some are claiming to fortell the future by examining and interpreting flames
pyromania	πυρομανία	obsessive compulsion to start fires; a persistent desire to start destructive fires
pyromaniac	(ο, η) πυρομανής (το) πυρομανές (adj.)	one who practices or is affected by pyromania
pyrometer	πυρόμετρον /ο	a device measuring high temperatures which are beyond he range of ordinary thermometers
pyromettry	πυρομετρία	the process or the scientific study of measuring very high temepatures
pyrophobia	πυροφοβία	excessive fear of fires
pyrophobic	πυροφοβικός, ή, ό (adj.)	one being extremely afraid of fires
pyrosis	πύρωσις /η	heartburn: a burning discomfort behing the lower part of the strernum usually, related to spasm of the lower end of the esophagus or of the upper part of the stomach
pyrotic	πυρωτικός, ή, ό (adj.)	burning; scorching; blistering
pyrotechnic	πυροτεχνικός, ή, ό (adj.)	of fireworks; designating or of devices or materials which activate propellants, safety systems, signals, etc., in a spacecraft, by igniting or exploding on command 2 brilliant; dazzling [pyrotechnic wit]
pyrotechnics	πυροτεχνική/ πυροτεχνικά	1 the art of making and using fireworks 2 a display of fireworks, also: *pyrotechny*

Pythagoras	Πυθαγόρας	sixth cen. BC, Gr. philosopher and mathematecian born on the island of Samos
Pythagoreian theorem	Πυθαγόρειον/ο θεώρημα	Geom. the theorem that in a right triangle the hypotenuse squared is equal to the sum of the squares of the other sides
Pythia	Πυθία	the high priestess of the famous oracle of Apollo at Delphi in ancient Greece
Pythian	πύθιος, α, ο (adj.) Πυθώ (ancient name of Delphi)	1 of Apollo as patron of Delphi and the oracle located there 2 designating of or the games which were held at Delphi every four years by the ancient Greeks in honor of Apollo
Python	πύθων /πύθωνος πύθωνας (mod. Gr.)	Gr. myth. the huge serpent that lived in a cave of Mt. Parnassus and which Apollo destroyed 1 any of the large nonpoisonous snakes of Asia, Africa, and Australia, which crush their prey to death (Python family Boidae)
pyuria	πυουρία	(πύον + ούρα + **urine**) pus in urine

Q

Quince	κυδώνιον/κυδώνι	1 a golden or greenish-yellow, hard, apple-shaped fruit of a small tree (Cidinia oblonga) of the rose family, makes delicious preserves 2 the quince tree
quinsy	κυνάγχη (κύων + άγχειν/ άγχη –dog + to choke)	lit. dog-chocking 1 Med. an abscess in the connective tissue around the tonsil, usually resulting from bacteria infection and often accompanied by fever, pain, and swelling, early term for tonsillitis 2 it is a fatal disease for dogs

R

Rachi-	ράχις	sp;ine combining form (rachitis)
rachialgia	ράχις/η + άλγος- spine + pain	pain in the spine
rachianalgesia	ραχιαναλγεσία	spinal anesthesia
rachicentesis	ραχικέντησις /η	puncture into the spinal canal
rachis	ράχις /η	1 spinal column; 2 Bot. the principal axis of an inflorescence or of a compound leaf 3 Zool. the shaft of a feather, esp., the partbearing the barbs
rachischisis	ράχις + σχίσις/ σκίσιμο,/ σχίζειν- to cut; cleave	a congenital abnormality **(as spina bifida) by a cleft** of the spinal column
rachitic	ραχιτικός, ή, ό (adj.)	of, relating to, or affected by rickets—**(rachitic lesions)**
rachitis	ραχίτις / ραχίτιδα	inflammation of the spine
raphe	ραφή/ράπτειν	seam; to stitch together 1 Anat. a seamlike joining of the two lateral halves of an organ, as of the tongue 2 Bot. a) a ridge of tissue along the side of an ovule, indicating the position of the vascular bundle which supplies the developing seed b) the line of union of the two carpels in the fruit of members of the umbel family c) a longitudinal fissure along the center of certain diatom shells
raphide	ραφίς/ραφίδος (gen.)ραφίδες (pl.)	needle 1 Bot. a needle-shaped crystal, usually of calcium oxalate, developed singly, or more often in bundles, in a plant cell
retin- retino-	ρετιν- ρέτινο-	retina, combining form (retinitis; retinoid)
retina	ρέτινα	part of the eye that receives the image and which is connected to the brain by the optic nerve

retinitis	ρετινίτις/ρετινίτιδα	inflammation of the retina
retino-blastoma	ρέτινα/ βλαστός / βλαστάνειν – to sprout / bud	a hereditary malignant tumor of the retina which develops during childhood; it is derived from retinal germ cells and is associated with a chromosomal abnormality
retinoid	(ο, η) ρετινοειδής (το) ρετινοειδές (adj.)	any of various synthetic or naturally occurring analogs of vitamin A
retinopathy	ρετινοπάθεια	any of noninflammatory disorders of the retina including some serious ones that cause blindness
retinoscopy	ρετινοσκόπησις /η	a method of determining the state of refraction of the eye by illuminating the retina with a mirror and observing the direction of movement of the retinal illumination and adjacent shadow when the mirror is turned
rhachis	ράχις/η	spinal column
rhachitis	ραχίτις /ραχίτιδα	see rachitis[2]
rhagades	ραγάδες	skin cracks
-rrhagia/ rrhage suffix	-(ρ)ραγια (αιμορραγία)	bleeding, combining form (hemorrhage)
rhaphe	ραφή	seam, ridge
rhapsode	ραψωδός	1 one who strings songs together 2 in ancient Gr. a person who recited epic poems; rhaphodies
rhapsody	ραψωδία	epic poetry; a part of any epic poem suitable for a single recitation (as in ancient Greece); great delight; ecstacy; a great musical composition
rheo-	ρέω-ρέειν	to flow current; stream, combining form
rheo-base	ρέω + βάσις – to flow + base	Physiol. the minimum electric current of unlimited duration needed to excite a nerve or muscle tissue

rheology	ρέω + λογία (λόγος)	the study of the change in form and the flow of matter, embracing elasticity, viscocity, and plasticity
rheometer	ρέω / μέτρο(ν)	an instrument for measuring verocity of fluid/ flow
rheophile	ρέω + φίλος	an animal or plant best adapted living in flowing water
rhetoric	ρητορική	the art of using words effectively in speaking and writing
rhetorical	ρητορικός, ή, ό (adj.)	having the nature of the rhetoric
rhetor	ρήτωρ/ ρήτορας	orator; in ancient Greece a master/teacher of rhetoric
rheumatalgia	ρευματαλγία	rheumatic pain
rheumatic	ρευματικός, ή, ό (adj.)	a person affected with rheumatism
rheumatism	ρευματισμός/ ρευματισμοί (pl.)	pain, swelling, and deformity of the joints
rheumatoid	(ο, η) ρευματώδης/ (το) ρεωματώδες (adj.)	pertaining to rheumatism
rheumatoid arthritis	ρευματώδης αρθρίτιδα	a chronic disease whosee cause is unkown, characterized by inflammation, pain, swelling of the joints and accompanied by spasms in adjacent muscles and often leads to deformity of the joints
rheumatoid spondylitis	ρευματώδης σπονδυλίτις/ σπονδυλίτιδα	it is the same as ankylosing spondylitis: stiffness or fixation of a joint by disease or surgery; rheumatoid spondylitis; also known as **Marie-Strumpell** disease
rheumatologist	ρευματολόγος	a specialist in rheumatology
rheumatology	ρευματολογία	a branch of medicine concerned with rheumatic diseases

rhin- or rhino-	ρίν- ρίνο- (ριν /ρινός (gen.) /ρίνα (acc.) μύτη (mod. Gr.)	nose combining form (rhinal)
rhinal	ρινικός, ή, ό (adj.)	of or relating to the nose; nasal
rhinalgia	ριναλγία	nasal pain
rhin-encephalon	ριν-εγκέφαλος	the part of the brain that receives sensory information from the olfactory nerves
rhinesthesia	ριναισθησία/ριν/ αίσθησις /η	the sense of smell
rhinitis	ρινίτις/ρινίτιδα	inflammation of the nasal, mucous membrane
rhino- prefix	ρις/ρινός (gen.) (ρίς-ρίνα (objective case) mod Gr. μύτη/	nose
rhinoceros	ρινόκερος	any heavy, thick-skinned mammals of tropical Africa and Asia with one or two upright horns on the snout
rhinocleisis	ρινόκλεισις /η	nasal obstruction
rhinology	ρινολογία	the branch of medicine dealing with the nose and its diseases
rhinopathy	ρινοπάθεια	any nasal disease
rhino-pharyngitis	ρινο-φαρυγγίτις	inflammation of the mucous membrane of the nose and pharynx, as in the common cold
rhinophonia	ρινοφωνία	nasal speaking tone
rhinoplasty	ρινοπλαστική	plastic surgery of the nose
rhino-pneumonitis	ρινο-πευμονίτις	an acute febrile respiratory disease of horses which is caused by two herpesviruses of the genus Varicellovirus (species Equid herpesvirus) (characterized esp., by rhinopharyngitis and tracheobronchitis)
rhinorrhagia	ρινορραγία	nosebleed; blood secretion from the nose
rhinorrhea or rinorroea	ρινόρροια	excessive mucous secretion from the nose

rhinoscope	ρινοσκόπιον/ o	an instrument (as an endoscope) for examining the cavities and passages of the nose
rhinoscopy	ρινοσκόπησις /η	examination of the nasal passages
rhinotomy	ρινοτομή	surgical incision of the nose
rhino-tracheitis	ρινοτραχείτις	inflammation of the nasal cavities and the trachea; esp., a disease of the upper respiratory system in cats and most esp., of young kittens with symptoms of sneezing, conjunctivitis with dishcharge, and nasal discharges
rhizo-	ριζο- (ρίζα- (ρίζα –root)	combining form, root (rhizogenic)
rhizobium	ριζόβιον	(ρίζα + βίος – root + life) any of a genus (Rhizobium) of rod-shaped, nitrogen-fixing bacteria found in nodules on the roots of certain leguminous plants, as the bean and clover
rhizocarpous	ριζόκαρπος	having perennial roots but annual stems and leaves
rhizocephalan	ριζο-κέφαλος	any of an order (Rhizocephala) of cirriped crustaceans that live as internal parasites on crabs
rhizogenic	ριζογενές	producing roots; also, rhizogenous
rhizoid	(ο, η) ριζογενής (το) ριζογενές (adj.)	rootlie; any of the rootlike filamens in a moss, fern, etc., which attach the the plant to the substratum
rhizome	ρίζωμα	a creeping stem lying, usually horizontally, at or under the surface at or under the surface of the soil and differing from a root in having scale leaves, bearing leaves or aerial shoots near the tips, and producing roots from its undersurface

rhizomorphous	ριζόμορφος	Bot. formed like a root; root-shaped
rhizopus	ριζόπους /ριζόποδας	any of a superclass (Rhizopoda) of fungi, including the the common bread mold and other species that cause various rots
rhizosphere	ριζόσφαιρα	Ecol. the part of the soil enclosing and influenced by the roots of a plant
rhizotomy	ριζοτομή	a surgical cutting of the spinal nerve roots, esp., of the posterior nerves, in order to relieve pain
rhod- or rhodo-	ροδ- ρόδο- (ρόδον- rose)	combining form, rose; rose-red (rhodolite)
rhodo prefix	ρόδον/ο	rose
rhododendron	ροδόδενδρο(ν) (ρόδο(ν)- τριαντάφυλλο (Mod. Gr.)/rose δένδρον/tree)	tree or shrub, mainly evergreen with beautiful flowers of pink, white, or purple
rhodolite	ροδολΐτης	a pink or rose-red variety of garnet, often used as a gem
rhodonite	ροδονίτης	a glassy, triclinic mineral
rhodoplast	ροδοπλάστης	a plastid found in red algae, containing red pigment as well as chlorophyll
rhodopsin	ροδοψίνη	a purplish protein pigment, contained in the rods of the retina that is transformed by the action of light which is necessary for vision in dim light
rhomb- or rhombo-	ρομβ- ρομβο- (ρόμβος –rhombus)	combining form (rhombic)
rhomb-encephalon	ρομβο- εγκέφαλον	the hindbrain, including the cerebellum, pons, and the medula oblongata
rhombic	ρομβικός, ή, ό (adj.)	of, or having the form of a rhombus

rhomboid	(ο, η) ρομβοειδής (το) ρομβοειδές	a parallelogram with oblique angles and only the opposite sides equal
rhombus	ρόμβος	an equilateral parallelogram, esp., one with oblique angles
rhonchos	ρόνχος	a whistling or snoring sound heard on auscultation of the chest when the air channels are partly obstructed— compare *rale; rattle*
Rho/ro	Ρ, ρ (ρω)	name of the seventeenth letter of the Greek alphabet
rhotacism	ρωτακισμός	to make wrong use of the letter rho, read it as *gh*; the change of a sound, esp. (s) or (z), to the sound (r)
rhyme	ρίμα	1 a piece of verse, or poem in which there is a regular recurrence of corresponding sounds, esp., at the end of lines 2 to compose in metrical form with rhymes
rhymester	ριμαδόρος	a maker of trivial or inferior rhyme or verse
rhyncho-	ρύγχος	snout, combining form (rhynchophoran)
rhynchocephalian	ρυγχοκεφαλικός, ή, ό (adj.) (ρύγχος + κεφαλή – snout + head)	designating or of a nearly extinct order (Rynchocephalia) of lizardlike beaked reptiles: the only existing species is the tuatara
rhynchophoran	ρυγχοφόρος (ρύγχος + φέρειν / -φόρος – snout + to bear/ bearer)	any of various beetles including the weevils, having the head extended to form a snout
rhyolite	ρεολίτης (ρυαξ/ ρέειν λίθος – stream / to flow + stone/rock)	a kind of volcanic rock, commoly occurring as a lava flow, containing much silica, granitelike in composition but with a fine-grained texture

rhypo-	ρύπος	filth, combining form (rhypophobia)
rhypophagy	ρυποφαγία	eating filth
rhypophobia	ρυποφοβία	extreme dislike of filth/dirt
rhythm	ρυθμός	measuring time or movement; also indicating the periods of fertility in females during the menstrual cycle
rhythm method	ρυθμική μέθοδος	a method of birth control involving abstinence during in which ovulation occurs
rhythmicity	ρυθμικότης / ρυθμικότητα	regularity in tempo, cyclic occurrence, etc.; rhythmic quality
rhythmic	ρυθμική	scientific study or system of rhythm and rhythmical forms
rhytid-	ρυτίς /ρυτίδος / ρυτίδα	wrinkle, combining form (rhytidosis)
rhytidectomy	ρυτιδεκτομή	the removal of wrinkles and skin folds from the face, by plastic surgery
rhytidosis	ρυτίδωσις/η	wrinkling of skin or cornea
rhyton	ρυτός, ή, ό (adj.) ρυτόν/ό (neu.) (ρητόν – flowing / ρέειν – to flow)	an ancient Greek cup shaped like a drinking horn, typically made in the form of an animal's head

S

Sac	σάκκος	pouch; sack
sacchar-	ζάχαρις / ζαχάρεως (gen.) / ζάχαρη (Mod.)	sugar, combining form
saccharine	ζαχαρίνη	1 of, having the nature of, containing, or producing sugar 2 too sweet or syrupy [a saccharine voice]
sccharo-	ζάχαρον	sugar, combining form (saccharometer)

saccharometer	ζαχαρόμετρον	an instrument like a hydrometer used for determining the amount of sugar in a solution
saccule	σακούλι	small sac
sadism	σαδισμός	perversion in which pain is inflicted by someone for sexual pleasure
sadist	σαδιστής	one who enjoys inflicting pain on others
salping- or salpingo-	σαλπίγκο – σάλπιγξ/ σάλπιγκος / σάλπιγκα	a trumpet; fallopian tube compining form
salping-ectomy	σαλπιγκ-εκτομή	1 surgical removal of the fallopian tube 2 the severing or excising of a fallopian tube, as in sterilizing a woman
salpingitis	σαλπιγκίτις/ σαλπιγκίτιδα	inflammation of the fallopian tubes, characterized by nodular thickening of the muscular coat
salpingography	σαλπιγκογραφία	visualization of a fallopian tube by radiography following injection of an opaque medium
salpingo-lysis	σαλπιγκόλυσις/ η	surgical correction of adhesions in the fallopian tube
salpinx	σάλπιγξ-σάλπιγγα	uterine tube that extends from the sides of the uterus to ovaries 2 Fallopian tube 3 Eustachian tube
sapphism	σαπφισμός / Σαπφώ (the first well-known lesbian, Sappho, the poet)	**from the island of Lesbos thus, the term:** lesbian and lesbianism
sarcasm	σαρκασμός	taunting, sneering, caustic remark
sarcastic	σαρκαστικός, ή, ό (adj.)	someone having the tendency to be using taunting, sneering, caustic remarks
sarc- or sarco-	σαρξ /σαρκός / σάρκα	flesh, combining for (sarcology)
sarcocyst	σαρκοκύστις / η	a genus of sporozoan protozoans of the family *Sarcocystis*

sarcoid	(ο, η) σαρκοειδής (το) σαρκοειδές (adj.)	fleshy; of, relating to, resembling, or being sarcoid or sarcoidosis [Sarcoid fibroblstic tissue]
sarcoma	σάρκωμα	one of the two main types of cancer, the other being carcinoma-καρκίνωμα; sarcomatosis
sarcophagus	σαρκοφάγος	any stone coffin, esp., one on display, as in a monumental tomb
sarcophagy	σαρκοφαγία	eating flesh
sarcoplasm	σαρκόπλασμα	the cytoplasm of a striated muscle fiber; compare *Myoplasm*
scatocratia	σκατοκράτια	fecal incontinence
scato-	σκατό	excrement, combining form
scatology	σκατολογία	study and analysis of body waste; of feces of fossil extrement; 2 obscenity or obsession with the obscene, esp., with excretion in literature
scelalgia	σκελαλγία (σκέλος + αλγία/ leg + pain)	pain in the leg
scene	σκηνή	tent, covered place, stage; the setting or locale of the action of a play, an opera, etc.
scenic	σκηνικός, ή, ό (adj.)	of the stage; dramatic, theatrical; stage effects; physical scenery, etc.
schema	σχήμα/σχήματα (pl.)	an outline, diagram, plan, a preliminary draft
schematic	σχηματικός, ή, ό (adj.)	of, or having the nature of a schema, plan, diagram, etc.; a schematic diagram as of electrical wiring in a circuit
schematism	σχηματισμός (σχηματίζειν –to form)	a set form for classification or exposition; arrangement of parts according to a scheme; design

schematize	σχηματίζειν / σχηματίζω	to form, form into, or arrange according to, a scheme or schemes
scheme	σχήμα/σχήματος (gen.)	a form, appearance; a carefully arranged a program of action or attaining some object or end; to plan in a deceitful way, to plot, to scheme
schism	σχισμός	a split or division in an organized group or society, esp., a church, as the result of opinion, of doctrine, etc.
schizo-	σκίζω/σχίζω/ σκίζειν	to cleave, to cut
schizoid	(ο, η) σχιζοειδής (το) σχιζοειδές (adj.)	characterized by, resulting from, tending toward, or suggestive of schizophrenia; schizoid a schizoid individual
schizophrenia	σκιζοφρένεια/ σχιζοφρένεια	psychiatric disorder
schizophrenic	σχιζοφρενικός, ή, ό (adj.)	one who suffers from schizophrenia
schizo-phreno-genic	(ο, η) σχιζο- φρενο-γενής (το) σκιζο-φρενο-γενές	reproduced by fusion
schizotypical	σχιζο-τυπικός, ή, ό (adj.)	characterized by, exhibiting, or being patterns of thought, perception, communication, and behavior suggestive of schizophrenia but not severe enough to be diagnosed as schizophrenia
sclera- or sclero-	σκληρός, ή, ό (adj.)	hard; tough, combining form (sclerosis)
sclera	σκληρά –pl. of σκληρό, neu.)	(hard; to dry out) the outer, tough, white, fibrous membrane covering all of the eyeball, except the area covered by the cornea

scleroderma	σκληρόδερμα	a slowly progressing disease characterized by the deposition of fibrous connective tissue in the skin and very often in internal organs and structures, by hand and foot pain upon exposure to cold, and by tightening and thickening of the skin
scleroma	σκληρύνω-σκλήρωσις/ σκλήρωση/ to harden/hardening	schlerosis (hardening of tissue)
scleraprotein	σκληρό πρωτεϊνη	any of various proteins (as collagen and keratin) occurrung usually in connective and skeletal tissues
sclerosis	σκλήρωσις/η	hardening of a tissue; a pathological condition in which a tissue is hardened and is produced by overgrowth of fibrous tissue and other changes (as in arteriosclerosis) or by increase in intersticial tissue and other changes (as in multiple sclerosis)
sclero-therapy	σκληροθεραπεία	an injection of a sclerosing agent (as saline) into a varicose vein in order to produce inflammation and scarring which closes the lumen and is followed by shrinkage
sclerotic	σκληρωτικός, ή, ό (adj.)	1 hard; sclerosed 2 of characterized by, or having sclerosis 3 of the sclera
sclerotomy	σκληροτομή	surgical incision into the sclera
scholastic	σχολαστικός, ή, ό (adj.)	a person devoted to logical subtleties and quibbling; pedant; a person who favors scholasticism

scholasticism	σχολαστικισμός	the system of logic, philosophy, and theology of medieval university scholars, from the tenth to the fifteenth century, based upon Aristotelian logic, the writings of the early Christian Fathers, and the authority of tradition and dogma
school	σχολή/σχολείο(ν)	a place of teaching and learing
scope	σκοπός,	goal; target; a mark; spy; watcher;
-scope	- σκόπιον /ο	used as suffix forming nouns (as in telescope)
scopophobia	σκοπός + φόβος –guard/ watcher + fear	extreme fear of being watched
-scopy	σκοπιά/σκόπησις /η	observation; examination, combining word, forming nouns (as in arthroscopy)
scotoma	σκότάδι/σκότος	darkness, dimness of vision
scotophobia	σκότος + φόβος –dark + fear	extreme fear of the dark
seismic	σεισμικός, ή, ό (adj.)	earthquake, moving
seismicity	σεισμικότητα	the state of an area of being seismic (being sensitive to earthquakes)
seismo-	σεισμός	combining form, earthquake
seismogram	σεισμογράφημα	the chart of an earthquake
seismograph	σεισμογφάφος σεισμός / γράφειν	instrument to record the intensity and duration of earthquakes
seismology	σεισμολογία	geophysical science dealing with earthquakes and related phenomena
seismometer	σεισμόμετρο(ν)	measuring the movements of the earth
selene	σελήνη	moon, light, gleam
selenium	σελήνιον/ο	a nonmetallic element that is an essential trace element found esp. in grains and meat

selenite	σεληνίτης	moonstone
seleno-	σελήνο-σελήνη	moon, combining form
selenosis	σελήνωσις /η	poisoning due to excessive intake of selenium; esp., poisoning of livestock by high levels of selenium consumed in plants grown in seleniferous soils; also called alkali disease
semantic	σημαντικός, ή, ό (adj.)	significant; relating to meaning esp. in linguistics and language
semantics	σημαντική/ σημασιολογία	the branch of linguistics dealing with the nature, structure, Development, and changes of meanings in speech forms, or with contextual meanings
semion /semeion	σημείο(ν)	mark, sign, point
semi-o-logy	σημειολογία	science or study of signs in general
semiotics	σημειωτική	general theory of signs and symbols
siderodromo-phobia	σιδηρόδρομος + φόβος/train + fear	extreme fear of travel by train
Sigma (Ss)	Σ, σ, ς, Σίγμα	eighteenth letter of the Greek alphabet
sigmoid	(ο, η) σιγμοειδής (το) σιγμοειδές (adj.)	having a double curve like a sigma (Σ/S)
sigmoid artery	σιγμοειδής αρτηρία	any of several branches of the inferior mesenteric that supply the sigmoid colon of the intestine
sigmoid colon	σιγμοειδές κόλον	the contracted and crooked part of the colon immediately above the rectum; also called *pelvic colon, sigmoid flexure*
sigmoid-ectomy	σιγμοειδής εκτομή	surgical excision of part of the sigmoid colon
sigmoidoscope	σιγμοειδο-σκόπιον	a device, as an endoscope that goes through the anus in order to inspect, diagnose, treat, and photograph mainly the sigmoid colon

sigmoidoscopy	σιγμοειδο-σκόπησις /η	the process of using a sigmdoidscope; also called *proctosigmatoidoscopy*
sinapism	σιναπισμός	mustard pluster
skelet- or skeleto-	σκελετός /σκελετο-	skeleton, combining form (skeletology)
skeletal	(ο, η) σκελετώδης (το) σκελετώδες (adj.)	of, relating to, forming, attached to, or resembling a skeleton [skeletal structures]
skeleton	σκελετός	usually a supportive or protective structure or framework of an organism; especially the bony more or less cartilaginous framework supporting the soft tissues and protecting the internal organs of vertebrates; scaffolding of the body
skeletology	σκελετολογία	the scientific study of skeletons
skeletophobia	σκελετοφοβία	excessive fear of skeletons
skeptic	σκεπτικός, ή, ό (adj.)	thoughtful; skeptical, used esp. in philosophy –a member of any of the ancient philosophical schools that denied the possibility of any certain knowledge
skepticism	σκεπτικισμός	1 the doctrines of the ancient Greek Skeptics 2 the philosophical doctrine that the truth of all knowledge must always be in question and that inquiry must be a process of doubting 3 skeptical or doubting attitude or state of mind 4 doubt about fundamental religious doctrines. Syn. *Uncertainty*
skepticist	σκεπτικιστής	a devotee of skepticism
skiagram	σκιάγαμμα	radiograph; skiagraph; tracing
skiagraph	σκιά / σκιαγραφία	radiograph
skiagraphy	σκιαγραφία / σκιαγράφησις /η	the scientific process of using and interpreting a skiagram or skiagraph

skiascope	σκιασκόπιον /o	an instrument as a retinoscope used for skianoscopy: *Retinoscope*
skiascopy	σκιασκόπησις /η	the scientific process of determining the results of the skianoscope examination; also called *Retinology*
soma-	σώμα/σώματος (gen.)	body, combining form (somatesthesia)
somalgia	σωματο-αλγία	bodily pain
somatesthesia	σωματ-αίσθησία	bodily sensation; also, *somataesthesia*
somatic	σωματικός, ή, ό (adj.)	1 pertaining to the body 2 of the body, as distinguished from the soul, mind, or psyche; corporal; physical 3 Biol. of the soma 4 Anat. Zool. of the outer walls of the body, as distinguished from the viscera
somatopause	σωματόπαυσις /η	a gradual and progressive decrease in growth hormone secretion that occurs normally with increasing age, during adult life, and is associated with an increase in adipose tissue and LDL levels and decrease in lean body mass
somatoplasm	σωματόπλασμα	protoplasm of somatic cells as distinguished from that of germ cells
somatopsychic	σωματο-ψυχικός, ή, ό (adj.)	of, or relating to the body and the mind
somatotherapy	σωματο-θεραπεία	therapy for psychological problems in which physiological intervention (as by drugs or surgery) is used
somatotype	σωματότυπος	a body type or physique esp. in a system or classification based on the relative development of ectomorphic, endomorphic, and mesomorphic components

sophisticated	σοφιστικέ (σοφία -	being urbane, wordly wise, or knowledgeable, refined, etc.
sophistry	σοφιστεία	unsound or misleading but clever, plausible and subtle argument or reasoning; sophism
spasm	σπασμός	contraction of any muscle that is sudden and involuntary: a **tonic spasm** is persistent and sustained, while a **chronic spasm** is one of a series of relative brief duration) contractions alternating with relaxations 2 any sudden, violent, temporary activity, feeling, etc.
spasmodic	σπασμωδικός, ή, ό (adj.)	incurring in spasms
spasmodic dysmenorrheal, σπασμωδική	δυσ- εμμηνορραγία /δυσ-εμμηνόρροια	dysmenorrheal associated with painful contractions of the uterus
spasmogenic	(ο, η) σπασμογενής (το) σπασμογενές	inducing spasms [spasmogenic drugs]
spasmophilia	σπασμοφιλία	tendency to spasms; an abnormal tendency to convulsions, tetany, or spasms from slight mechanical or electrical stimulation [spasmophilia associated with rickets]
spastic	σπαστικός, η, ό (adj.)	of, relating to, or characterized by spasms 2 affected or marked by spasticity or spastic paralysis [a spastic patient] [spastic hemiplegia]
spastic colon	σπαστικόν κόλον	irritable bowel syndrome: a chronic functional disorder of the colon that is of unknown etiology, usually associated with abnormal intestinal motility and increased sensitivity to visceral pain, marked by diarrhea or constipation, abdominal discomfort and, or bloating and passage of mucus in the stool

spasticity	σπαστικότητα	a spastic state or condition; esp., muscular hypertonicity with increased tendon reflexes
spastic paralysis	σπαστική παράλυσις /η	paralysis with tonic spasm of the affected muscles and with increased tendon reflexes
sperm- spermo- or spermi- spermat- or spermato-	σπέρμ- σπερμο- σπερματο- σπέρμα /σπέρματος (gen.)	sperm; seed, combining forms (spermatic, spermatogenic, etc.)
sperm	σπέρμα	male fertilizing cell
spermatic artery	σπερματική αρτηρία	internal spermatic artery: testicular artery: either of a pair of arteries which supply blood to the testes
spermato-genesis	σπερματο-γένεσις /η	1 the process of male gamete formation including formation of a primary spermatocyte 2 the production and development of spermatozoa
spermatogenic	(ο, η) σπερματογνής (το σπερματογενές (adj.)	of, or relating to, producing or developing permatozoa/ plural of spermatozoon
spermatorrea	σπερματόρροια	abnormally frequent or excessive emission of semen without orgasm
spermatozoon	σπερματόζωον /ο / σπερματόζωα (pl.)	a motile male gamete of an animal usually with rounded or elongated head along with a long posterior flagellum
sphene	σφην /σφηνός / σφήνα	a wedge 1 so named because of its crystal form; a silicate of calcium and titanium with varying amounts of other elements 2 a wedge like between the sphenoid bone and the superior nasal concha into which the sphenoid sinus opens, combining form (sphenoid)
spheno-	σφηνός (gen.)	of the sphenoid bone combining form (sphenogram)

sphenogram	σφηνόγραμμα	a cuneiform, or a wedge-shaped character
sphenoid	(ο, η)σφηνοειδής (το) σφηνοειδές (adj.)	1 resembling a wedge 2 Anat. designating or of the wedge-shaped compound bone at the base of the cranium
sphere	σφαίρα	any round body or figure having the surface equally distant from the center at all points; globe; ball 2 a star, planet, etc. 3 the physical heavens; sky
-sphere	- σφαίρα	suffix forming nouns 1 something resembling a sphere [oosphere] 2 any of the atmospheric layers surrounding a planet or a star [chromospheres]
spheroma	σφαίρα	a tumor in the shape of a sphere
sphygm- or sphygmo-	σφυγμ- σφυγμο- σφυγμός	pulse, combining forms (sphygmic; sphygmometer)
sphygmic	σφυγμικός, ή, ό (adj.)	pertaining to the pulse; of the pulse
sphygmogram	σφυγμόγραμμα	a tracing made by a sphygmograph, consisting of a series of curves that correspond to the heart's beats
sphygmograph	σφυγμογράφος	a device which graphically records the movements or character of the pulse
sphygmonometer	σφυγμονόμετρο(ν)	blood pressure gauge; an instrument for measuring blood pressure, esp., the arterial blood pressure
sphygmometry	σφυγμομέτρησις /η	the measuring and recording of the force and rate of the pulse
splanchlic	σπλαχνικός, ή, ό (adj.) (σπλάχνον/ο - gut)	pertaining to abdominal organs
splachno-	σπλαχνον/ο	gut; internal organ; the viscera, combining form, also splanch, before a vowel splanchic; splanchology)

splanchology	σπλαχνολογία	the scientific medical study concerned with the structure, functions, and diseases of the viscera
splen- or spleno-	σπλην- σπληνο-/ σπλήνα	organ situated in the left upper part of the abdomen combining forms (splenalgia; splenoma)
spleen	σπλήν/σπληνός (gen.) σπλήνα (Mod. Gr.)	1 a large, vascular, lymphatic organ in the upper left part of the abdominal cavity of vertebrates, near the stomach: one of its various functions is modifying the structure of the blood 1 it also used to be regarded as the seat of certain emotions 2 a) malice; spite; bad temper b) [Archaic] melancholy; low spirits c) [Obs] a caprice or whim.
splenalgia	σπληναλγία	pain in the spleen
splenectomy	σπληνεκτομή	surgical removal of the spleen
splenic artery	σπληνική αρτηρία	the branch of the celiac artery that carries blood to the spleen and sends also branches to the pancreas and the cardiac end of the stomach
splenitis	σπληνίτις/σπηνίτιδα	inflammation of the spleen
splenoma	σπλήνωμα	splenic tumor
splenomegaly	σπλην + μεγάλη	enlargement of the spleen
splenosis	σπλήνωσις /η	a rare condition in which fragments of tissue from a ruptured spleen are implanted throughout the peritoneal cavity and often undergo regeneration and vascularization
spondyl- or spondylo-	σπόνδυλος	vertebrae (spondylosis)
spondylitis	σπονδυλίτις / σπονδυλίτιδα	inflammation of the vertebrae [tuberculous spondylitis]
spondylo-arthritis	σπόνδυλο-αρθρίτις /αρθρίτιδα	arthritis of the spine

spondylo-arthropathy	σπονδυλο-αρθροπάθεια	any of several diseases (as ankylosing spondylitis) affecting the points of the spine
spondylolysis	σπονδυλόλυσις /η	any of various degenerative diseases of the spine
spondylopathy	σπονδυλοπάθεια	any disorder or disease of the vertebrae
spondylosis	σπονδύλωσις /η	any of various degenerative diseases of the spine
spondylo-sporadic	σπονδυλο - σποραδικός, ή, ό (adj.)	occurring at different times and places
spongi- or spongio	σπόγγι - σπόγγος	sponge, combining form (spongioblast; spongoid)
sponge	σπόγγος	1 any of a phylum (Porifera) of simple, aquatic, sessile animals having a porous structure and a tough, often siliceous or calcareous skeleton 2 a) a pad (as a folded gauze) used in surgery and medicine (as to remove discharge or apply medication) b) a porous dressing (as of fibrin or gelatin) applied in order to promote wound healing c) a plastic prosthesis used in chest cavities following lung surgery 3 an absorbent contraceptive device impregnated with spermicide which is inserted into the vagina prior to sexual intercource to cover the cervix and act as a barrier to sperm
spongioblast	σπογγοβλαστός	any of the ectodermal cells of the embryonic spinal cord or other nerve center that are at first columnar but become branched at one end and that give rise to the glial cells

spongio-cyte	σπογγο-κύτταρο	any of the cells of the adrenal cortex that have a spongy appearance due to lipid vacuoles the contents of which have been dissolved out
spongiosis	σπογγίωσις / η	swelling localized in the epidermis and often occurring in eczema
spongy or spongoid	(ο, η) σπογγοειδής (το) σπογγοειδές (adj.)	resembling a sponge; full of cavities
spor-, spori- or sporo-	σπόρι /σπόρος / σπόροι (pl.)	seed; sperm, combining form (sporadic; sporocyst)
Sporades	Σποράδες	1 all the Greek islands in the Aegean Sea except the Cyclades 2 the Greek islands along with the west coast of Turkey, esp., the Dodecanese also Southern Sporades
sporadic	σποραδικός, ή, ό (adj.)	1 happening once in awhile; not constant; irregular; occasional 2 widely separated from others, scattered, or isolated in occurrence
spore	σπορά/σπόρος (σπείρειν – to sow)	a sowing; seed; 1 Biol. any of various small reproductive bodies, usually consisting of a single cell, produced by bacteria, algae, mosses, ferns, certain protozoans, etc., either asexually (asexual spore) or by the union of gametes (sexual spore) 2 any small organism or cell that can develop into a new individual, seed, germ, etc.
sporoblast	σποροβλαστός	a cell of a sporozoan resulting from sexual reproduction and producing spores and sporozoites

sporocyst	σπορoκύστις /η	1 a cyst secreted by some sporozoans preliminary to sporogony 2 Zool. a) a saclike larval stage, of many tromatodes, which produces rediae by asexual development from germinal cells b) a protective cyst produced by some protozoans before sporulation, or a protozoan in such encystment
sporogenesis	σπορογένεσις /η	Biol. 1 reproduction by means of spores 2 the formation of spores
sporogony	σπορογόνος	reproduction by spores containing sporozoites which is characteristic of some sporozoans and that results from the encystment and subsequent division of a zygote
sporophore	σποροφόρος	Bot. an organ or structure in various fungi that bears spores
sporothrix	σπόρος τριξ _τριχός (gen)	1 a genus of imperfect fungi (family *Mmoniliaceae)* that includes causative agent *(S. schenckii)* of sporothichosis 2 any fungus of the genus *Sporotrix*
sporotrichosis	σποροτρίχωσις/η	infection with, or disease caused by a fungus of the genus
Sporothrix	(S. schenckii aka. Sporotrichum schenckii)	which is often characterized by ulcerating or suppurating nodules in the skin, subcutaneous tissues, and nearby lymph nodes, usually transmitted by entry of fungus through a skin abrasion or wound

sporozoan	σπορόζωον /ο	any of a class (Sporozoa) of strictly parasitic protozoans that have a complex life cycle, usually involving both asexual and sexual generations often in diferrent hosts including many serious pathogens (as malaria parasites and babesias)
stalactiform	στάλαξις /η / φόρμα/ σχήμα	having the form of stalactite
stalactite	σταλακτίτης (σταλάσσειν – to drop or drip)	an icicle-shaped secondary mineral deposit that hangs from the roof of a cave and formed by the evaporation of dripping water which is full of minerals
stalagmite	σταλαγμίτης	a cone-shaped secondary mineral deposit built up on the floor of a cave by dripping water, often from a slactite above
staph- or staphylo-	σταφ- σταφύλο- σταφυλή	a bunch of grapes, combining form 1 uvula staphylorrhaphy) 2 grapelike (staphylococcus)
staphylococcic	σταφυλο-κοκκικός, ή, ό (adj.)	any bacterium of the genus (Staphylococcus); broadly: *Micrococcus 2*
staphylococcosis	σταφυλοκοκκίασις /η	infection with or disease caused by staphilococci
staphylococcus	σταφυλόκοκκος	1 bacteria causing body infection 2 a genus of nonmotile grampositive spherical bacteria that is placed in either of two families (Staphyloccaceae) or (Micrococcaceae), the contained forms occur singly, in pairs or tetrads, or in irregular clusters, and includes causative agents of various diseases (as skin infections, food poisoning, and endocarditis)

staphylo-kinase	σταφυλοκίνησις /η	a protease from some pathogenic staphylococci that converts plasminogen to plasmin
staphyloma	σταφύλωμα	a protrusion of the cornea or sclera of the eye
staphyloplasty	σταφυλο-πλαστική	the use of plastic surgery to correct defects of the soft palate
staphylorrhaphy	σταφυλο-ραφή	the operation of uniting a cleft palate by plastic surgery
staphylotoxin	σταφυλοτοξίνη	a toxin produced by staphylococci
stasi- or staso-	στασι- στασο- (στάσις –ίσταναι / standing- to stand)	combining form (stasis)
stasis	στάσις /η	1 a) a stoppage of the flow of some fluid in the body, as of blood b) reduced peristalsis of the intestines resulting in the retention of feces 2 a state of equilibrium, balance, or stagnancy 3 **stasis/ στάσις/η** also in Greek means stop (as in bus stop); stoppage (as in work stoppage), posture (the manner one stands), attitude, etc.
stasophobia	στάσις + φόβος	extreme fear of stopping or standing up
static	στατικός, ή, ό (adj.)	causing to stand; 1 of bodies, masses, or forces at rest or in equilibrium: opposed to **Dynamic** 2 not moving or progressing; at rest; inactive; stationary
static electricity	στατικός ηλεκτρισμός	1 designating of producing stationary electrical charges, as those resulting from friction 2 a) electrical discharges in the atmosphere that interfere with radio or television reception, etc. b) interference or noises produced by such discharges

statics	στατική (fem) of στατικός	the branch of mechanics concerned with bodies, masses, or forces at rest or in equilibrium
steno-	στενός, ή, ό (adj.)	narrow; tight; thin; combining form (stenosis)
stenochoria	στενοχώρια	worry, concern, adverse psychological state of mind
stenograph	στενογράφημα	to write in shorthand; a keyboard machine that prints shorthand symbols
stenographer	στενογράφος	a person skilled in stenography
stenography	στενογραφία	shorthand writing; specif., the skill or work of writing down dictation, testimony, interviews, etc.; shorthand and later transcribing it, as in a typewriter or computer
stenosis	στένωσις/η/ στένωμα /στένεμα	narrowing/constriction of a passage, duct, opening, etc.
stenotic	στενωτικός, ή, ό (adj.)	of, relating to, characterized by, or causing stenosis: [stenotic lesions]
stenotype	στενότυπος	1 a symbol or symbols representing a sound, a word, or phrase in stenotypy 2 a keyboard machine that prints such symbols
stenotypy	στενοτυπία	shorthand in which symbols representing sounds, words, or phrases are typed on keyboard machine
stere- or stereo-	στερε- στερεο-	hard; firm; solid combining form (stereotomy)
stereo	στερεός, στερεά, στερεό (adj.)	hard; solid; firm; three-dimensional (stereoscope)
stereo-chemistry	στερεο-χημεία	the branch of chemistry concerned with the special arrangement of atoms or groups of atoms that make up molecules

stereognosy	στερεογνωσία	the ability to perceive or the perception of material qualities (as shape) of an object by handling or lifting it: tactile recognition
stereogram	στερεόγραμμα	1 a stereographic diagram or picture 2 stereogrph
stereograph	στερτεογράφημα	a picture or a pair of pictures prepared for use with a stereoscope
stereography	στερεογραφία	the art of representing the forms of solids on a plane surface; specif., the branch of solid geometry dealing with the construction of regularly defined solids
stereographic	στερεογραφικός, ή, ό (adj.)	pertaining to stereography
stereo-isomer	στερεο-ισομερής	any of two or more isomers containing the same number and kinds of atoms linked in an identical manner in the molecule and differing from each other only in the spatial arrangement of the atoms or groups of atoms
stereometry	στερομετρία / στερεο-μέτρησις /η	the art of determining the dimensions and volume of solids
stereophonic	στερεοφωνικός, ή, ό (adj.)	many dictionaries have it as sound reproduction, as in films, records, tapes, or broadcasting, using two or more channels to carry and reproduce through separate speakers a bland of sounds from separate sources
stereopsis	στερέοψις /η	stereoscopic vision
stereoscope	στερεοσκόπιον /o	an optical instrument with two eyepieces for helping the observer to combine the images of two pictures taken from points of view a little way apart; that way the effect of solidity and depth is achieved

stereoscopic	στερεοσκοπικός, ή, ό (adj.)	1 of or relating to the stereoscope or the production of three-dimensional images 2 characterized by the observing or the seeing of objects in three dimensions [stereoscopic vision]
stereoscopy	στερεοσκόπησις η	1 the scientific study of stereoscopic effects and tecniques 2 the viewing of objects as in three dimensions
stereotaxis	στερεό + τάξις /η – solid + order/ arrangement	Biol. the positive or negative response of a freely moving organism to cling to, or avoid a solid object after contact
stereotomy	στερεοτομή	the art or science of cutting solid bodies, esp., stone into desired shapes
stereotropism	στερεοτροπισμός	Biol. a tropism in which the directing stimulus in contact with a solid body
stereotype	στερεότυπος	1 something conforming to a fixed or general pattern (ex: an often oversimplified or biased mental picture one holds to characterize the typical individual of a group) 2 to repeat without variation [stereotyped behavior] 3 to develop a mental stereotype about someone or something
stereotypical	στερεοτυπικός, ή, ό (adj.)	1 of or produced by stereotypy 2 stereotyped; hackneyed
stereotypy	στερεοτυπία	1 process of making or printing from stereotype plates 2 abnormal repetition of an action, speech phrase, etc., or abnormal sustained maintenance of a position or posture, as seen in some phases of schizophrenia
stethalgia	στηθαλγία	(στήθος-αλγία/breast-pain) breast pain; chest pain

stetho-	στήθος	breast, combining form (stethoscopy)
stethoscope	στηθοσκόπιο(ν)	instrument used to listen to the sounds of the body and the chest area
stethoscopy	στηθοσκόπησις /η	the examination with a stethoscope
sthenic	σθεναρός, ή, ό (adj.) (σθένος – strength; vigor; bravery)	1 notably or excessively vigorous or active [sthenic fever] [sthenic emotions]
stich-	στιχ- στίχος	Prosody a line of prose or, esp., of verse
stichometry	στιχομετρία / στιχομέτρησις /η	the practice of expressing the successive ideas in a prose composition in single lines of lengths corresponding to natural cadences or sense divisions
stichomythia	στιχομυθία (στίχος + μύθος – line + speech/ myth)	dialogue in brief, alternate lines, as in ancient Greek drama
-stichous	-στίχος	line, suffix forming adjectives, having a specified number or kind of rows (octastichous /eight lines)
stigma	στίγμα	stain; mark of shame 1 something that detracts from the the character or reputation of a person, group, community, etc., mark of disgrace or reproach 2 a mark, sign, etc., indicating that something is not considered normal or standard 3 Med. an identifying mark or characteristic, esp., a specific diagnostic sign of a disease [stigmata of syphilis]
stigmatic	στιγματικός, ή, ό (adj.)	1 of, like, or having a stigma or stigmata (pl.) 2 of having stigmatism

stigmatism	στιγματισμός	1 the condition characterized by stigma or stigmata 2 the condition of a lens, and the normal condition of the eye, in which rays of light from a single point are focused upon a single point
stigmatize	στιγματίζω	mark with disgrace; to characterize as disgraceful
stoic	στωϊκός, ή, ό (adj.)	showing austere indifference to joy, grief, pleasure, or pain; calm and unflinching under suffering, misfortune, etc.
stoichiometry	στοιχείον/ο + μέτρησις /η – element + measurement	1 the determination of the proportions in which chemical elements combined or produced and the weight relation in any chemical reaction 2 the branch of chemistry concerned with the relationships of elements entering into and resulting from combination, esp., quantitative relationships
Stoicism	στωϊκισμός	1 the philosophical system of the stoics 2 indifference to pleasure or pain; stoical behavior; impassivity
stoma	στόμα	mouth 1 Bot. a microscopic opening in the epidermis of plants, surrounded by guard cells and serving for gaseous exchange 2 Zool. a mouth or mouthlike opening esp., an ingestive opening in lower invertebrates, also, combining form (stomatitis)

stomach	στομάχι	1 large pouch where food digestion begins 2 a) the large saclike organ of vertebrates into which food passes from the esophagus or gullet for storage, while undergoing the early processes of digestion b) any enlarged storage portion of the digestive cavity, as in the invertebrates 3 the abdomen or belly
stomachalgia	στομαχοαλγία	pain in the stomach or abdomen
stomachic	στομαχικός, ή, ό (adj.)	1 pertaining to the stomach 2 acting as a digestive tonic
stomatalgia	στοματαλγία	pain in the mouth
stomatitis	στοματίτις/ στοματίτιδα	inflammation of the mouth
stomato-	στοματο- στόμα/ στόματος (gen.)	of the mouth or relating to the mouth, combining form (stomatology)
stomatopathy	στοματοπάθεια	any mouth disorder
stomatologist	στματολόγος	a specialist of stomatology
stomatology	στοματολογία	a branch of medical science concerned with the mouth and mouth disorders
-stomy	-στομή (στόμιον)	surgery to make a permanent opening in a body part or Organ, combining form (enterostomy; colostomy)
strategic	στρατηγικός, ή, ό (adj.)	having to do with strategy; characterized by sound strategy
strategist	στρατηγιστής / στρατηγικός	one using strategy; one skilled in strategy
strategy	στρατηγική/ στρατηγία	the science of planning and directing large-scale military operations, esp. of maneuvering forces into the most advantageous position prior to actual engagement with the enemy

stratocracy	στρατοκρατία	government by the military; rule by chiefs of the army
strato-pause	στρατόπαυσις /η	an atmospheric transition zone or shell, located between the atmosphere and the mesosphere at an altitude of c. 50 to 55 km. (c.31 to 34 mi.), in which temperatures begin to drop with increasing altitude
stratosphere	στρατόσφαιρα	the atmospheric zone located above the tropopause at an altitude of c.20 to 50 km. (c. 12 to 35 mi.), and characterized by an increase in temperature with increasing altitude
strobile	στρόβιλος (στρέφειν –to twist)	anything twisted; a mass of air or water twisting cyclically with very fast speed
strongyle	στρογγύλη (στρογγυλός, ή, ό (adj.) – round; turned	a worm of the genus Strongylus or closely related genera that is parasitic, esp. in the intestines and tissues of the horse
strongyloid	(ο, η) στογγυλοειδής (το) στρογγυλοειδές (adj.) στρογγυλοειδή (neu. pl.)	any of a superfamily (Strongyloidea) of nematode worms including the hookworms, strongyles, and related forms
strongylosis	στρογγύλωσις /η / στρογγυλάδα	the condition being infested by strongyles
stroph-	στροφ- στροφή (στρέφειν – to turn)	a turning; twist, combining form (strophe)
strophanthin/ strophanthus	στροφ(η) + άνθος – twist/turn + flpwer	a glycoside or mixture of glycosides obtained from a tropical plant (Strophanthus combe) of the dogbane family, used as a heart stimulant; given in larger doses, however, a violent poison

strophe	στροφή	1 turning, twist; a stanza, esp. any of the irregular divisions of a poem 2 in the ancient Greek theater a) the movement of the chorus in turning from right to left or the stage **(cf. Antistrophe)** b) the part of the choric song performed during this
struthious	στρουθίον/ο/ στρουθί **(Mod. Gr.)**	sparrow, ostrich
strychnine	στρυχνίνη (στύφνος- a **poisonous plant)**	a highly poisonous colorless alkaloid, obtained from nux vomica, and other similar plants; poison
strychninism	στρυχνινισμός	a diseased condition the result of ingested with strychnine
Stygian	Στύγιος	of or characteristic of the river Styx and the infernal regions 2 (also s-) a) infernal or hellish b) dark or gloomy c) inviolable; completely binding, as an oath sworn by the river Styx
style - stylus	στύλος – στυλό / στυλός	pillar; pointed; 1 a sharp, slender pointed instrument used by the ancients in writing on wax tablets 2 any of several devices, etc., similar in shape or use as, a pen; an etching needle; a phonograph needle; an engraving tool, etc.; a stylus 2 a manner or mode of expression in language, as distinct of the ideas expressed; way of using thoughts, etc. 3 specific or characteristic manner of expression, execution, construction, or design in any art, period, profession, etc. as the Byzantine style or modern style. Syn. *Fashion*

stylite	στυλίτης (στύλος -pillar (dwelling on a pillar)	any of various Christian ascetics who lived on the tops of pillars
stylo- stylus	στυλό	a pen; a sharp, pointed instrument, combining form (stylograph)
stylobate	στυλοβάτης	1 Archit. a continuous base or coping for a row of columns 2 strong supporter; the foundation
stylograph	στυλογράφος	a fountain pen having a pierced conical point, rather than a nib, through which the ink flows
stylographic	στυλογραφικός, ή, ό (adj.)	1 of or like a stylograph 2 of or used in stylography
stylography	στυλογραφία	drawing, writing, or engraving done with a style or stylus
styloid stylet	(o, η) στυλοειδής (το) στυλοειδές (adj.)	1 resembling a style; styliform 2 Anat. designating or of any of various long, slender processes, esp., that at the base of the temporal bone
stylopharyngeus	στυλο-φαρύγγειος	a slender muscle that arises from the base of the styloid process of the temporal bone, inserts into the side of the pharynx, and acts with the contralateral muscle in swallowing to increase the transverse diameter of the pharynx, by drawing its sides upward and laterally
stylopodium	στυλοπόδιον /ο	a disk or swelling at the base of the style in plants of the umbel family
stypsis	στύψις /η (στύφειν- to contract, stop)	the action or the use of a syptic
styptic	στυπτικός, η, ό (adj.)	astringent; tending to halt bleeding by contracting the tissues or blood vessels
Styx	Στύξ lit. the Hateful	icy cold; Gr. myth. the river encircling Hades over Which Charon ferries the souls of the dead

sycamine	συκαμινιά	a tree mentioned in the Bible (Luke 17:6) believed to be a mulberry (Morus nigra) with dark fruit
sycamore	συκομουριά (σύκον – fig)	1 a fig tree (Ficus sycomorus) native to Egypt and Asia Minor, with edible fruit: the sycamore of the Bible 2 a tall maple tree (Acer pseudoplatanus) with yellow flowers, found in Europe and Asia 3 plane
sycophancy	συκοφαντία	servile flattery; the behavior or character or act of a sycophant; servile flattery
sycophant	συκοφάντης	informer; a person seeking favors by flattering people of wealth or influence; parasite; toady
sycophantic	συκοφαντικός, ή, ό (adj.)	pertaining to sycophancy and sycophant
sycosis	σύκωσις /η	a chronic disease of the hair follicles, esp., of the beard, caused by certain staphylococci and characterized by the formation of papules and pustules
syllabic	συλλαβικός, ή, ό (adj.)	1 of a syllable or syllables 2 forming a syllable or the nucleus of a syllable; specif., a) being the most prominent sound in a phonemic syllable (said of a vowel) b) constituting the more heavily stressed part of a diphthong, as the sound of o in boy c) standing by itself as the nucleus of a syllable without an accompanying vowel (said of consonant, as the sound of l in tattle (tat"l) 3 a syllabic sound; syllabic verse
syllabicate	συλλαβίζω	to form or divide into syllables; also: *syllabify*

syllabism	συλλαβισμός	1 the use of syllabic characters, rather than letters in writing 2 division into syllables
syllable	συλλαβή (συν + λαμβάνειν – together + to hold/receive)	1 a word or part of a word pronounced with a single uninterrupted sounding of the voice; unit of pronunciation, consisting of a single sound of great sonority (usually a vowel) and generally one or more sounds of lesser sonority (usually consonants) 2 any of the parts into which a written word is often divided
syllepsis	σύλληψις /η	a putting together; a grammatical construction in which a single word is used in a syntactical relationship with two or more words in the same sentence, although, it can agree only with one of them in gender, number, or case (ex: either they or I am wrong) **Notation: the word syllepsis/ σύλληψις/η (συν + λαμβάνειν –to hold (together,) also to conceive) a) arrest; b) for a woman the time she conceives**
syllogism	συλλογισμός	to reckon together; sum up; an argument or form of reasoning in which two statements or arguments are made and a logical conclusion is drawn from them
syllogistic	συλλογιστικός, ή, ό (adj.)	referring to syllogism: a reckoning together
syllogize	συλλογίζομαι	to reason or infer by the use of syllogisms
symbiont	σύμβιος (συνβιούντος - living in a state of symbiosis)	an organism living in a state of symbiosis /living together

symbiosis	συμβίωσις/η	a relationship between two organisms
symblepharon	συν + βλέφαρον - together + eyelid	adhesion between an eyelid and the eyeball
symbol	σύμβολο(ν)	token, pledge, or sign inferring to something abstract; the dove is the symbol of peace; emblem
symbolic	συμβολικός, ή, ό (adj.)	characterized by symbolism
symbolic logic	συμβολική λογική	a modern type of formal logic using special symbols for propositions, quantifiers, and relationships among propositions and concerned with the elucidation of permissible operations upon such symbols
symbolism	συμβολισμός	the use of symbols
symbolist	συμβολιστής	1 a person who uses symbols 2 a person who practices symbolism in representing ideas, etc., esp., in art, or literature 3 a person who studies or is a specialist in interpreting symbols or symbolism
symbolize	συμβολίζω	to be a symbol of, typify; stand for; to use symbols
symmetric	συμμετρικός, ή, ό (adj.)	having or showing symmetry
symmetrically	συμμετρικά (adv.)	something done according to symmetry
symmetry	συμμετρία	similarity of form or arrangement on either side of a dividing line or plane; correspondence of opposite parts in size, shape, or position
sympath- or sympatho-	σύμπαθ- συμπάθεια	sympathetic nerve combining form (sympathetic; sympatholytic)
sympathectomy	συμπαθ-εκτομή	the interruption by surgical means of part of the sympathetic nervous system

sympathetic	συμπαθητικός, ή, ό (adj.)	1 of expressing, resulting from, feeling, or showing sympathy; sympathizing 2 in agreement with one's tastes, mood, feelings, disposition, etc.; congenial 3 Physiol. designatingor of that part of the autonomic nervous system whose nerves originate in the lumbar and thoracic regions of the spinal cord and that is especially concerned with mediating the involuntary response to alarm, as by speeding the heart rate, raising the blood pressure, and dilating the pupils of the eyes: these nerves oppose the parasympathetic nerves in the regulation of many body processes
sympathetic nerve	συμπαθητικό νεύρο	a nerve of the sympathetic nervous system
sympathetic nervous system	συμπαθητικό νευρικό σύστημα	the part of the autonomic nervous system that contains chiefly adrenergic fibers and tends to depress secretion, decrease the tone and contractility of smooth muscle, increase heart rate, and that consists of preganglionic fibers arising in the thoracic and upper lumbar parts of the spinal cord: also called *sympathetic system*
sympathetic ophthalmia	συμπαθητική οφθαλμία	inflammation in an uninjured eye, resulting from an injury and inflammation of the other
sympathicolytic	συμπαθηκολυτικός, ή, ό (adj.)	having the effect of decreasing the activity of the sympathetic nervous system: said of certain drugs and chemicals, etc. also sympatholytic

sympathico-tonia	συμπαθητικο-τονία	a condition produced by relatively great activity or stimulation of the sympathetic nervous system, characterized by goose bumps, vascular spasm, and abnormally high blood pressure—also called *sympatheticotonia*
sympathin	συμπαθίνη	a substance (as norepripherine) that is secreted by sy sympathetic nerve endings and acts as a chemical mediator
sympathogonia	συμπαθογόνια	precursor cells of the sympathetic nervous system
sympatho-gonioma	συμπαθο-γονίωμα	a tumor derived from sympathogonia, also: *Nevroblastoma*
sympatholytic	συμπαθο-λυτικός	1 tending to oppose the physiological results of sympathetic nervous activity or of sympathomimetic drugs 2 having the effect of decreasing the activity of the sympathetic nervous system: said of certain drugs, chemicals, etc.
symphalagism	συμφαλαγγισμός	ankylosis of the joints of one or more digits
symphony	συμφωνική/ συμφωνία	harmony of sounds
symphysiotomy	συμφυσιοτομή	surgical procedure to divide the pubic symphysis
symphysis	σύμφυσις /η (φύειν – to grow)	a growing together or fusing, specif., a) Anat. the growing together of bones originally separate, as of two halves of the lower jaw, or the two pubic bones; b) Bot. the growing together of similar parts of a plant; coalescence
symposium	συμπόσιο(ν)	meeting where ideas are exchanged/drinking party

symptom	σύμπτωμα	perceptible change from normal function; Med. any condition accompanying or resulting from a disease or a physical disorder and serving as an aid to a diagnosis
symptomatic	συμπτωματικός, ή, ό (adj.)	accidental; of or having to do with symptoms
symptomatology	συμπτωματολογία	study of the symptoms of disease, collectively, or the symptoms of a given disease
symptomologic	συμπτωμολογικός, ή, ό (adj.)	pertaining to symptomatology
symptomless	ασύμπτωμος, η, ο (adj.)	without symptoms; exhibiting no symptoms
syn -	prefix, or sym (before a b or m)	συν - with, together, plus (syn-synopsis; sym- symbolism)
synagogue	συναγωγή	assembly, bringing together
synantrhropic	συνανθρωπικός, ή, ό (adj.)	ecologically associated with humans
synapse	σύναψη	the place at which a nervous impulse passes from one neuron to another; synapsis
synapsis	σύναψις /η	a junction; connection; the association of homologous chromosomes with chiasma formation characterized by the first meiotic prophase and it is held to be the mechanism for genetic crossing over
synaptic	συναπτικός, ή, ό (adj.)	1 of, relating to, or participating in synapsis [synaptic chromosomes] 2 of or relating to a synapse [synaptic transmission]
synaptogenesis	συναπτο-γένεσις /η	the formation of nerves synapses
synaptology	συναπτολογία	the scientific study of nerve synapses

synaptophysin	συναπτοφυσίνη	a transmembrane glycoprotein found mainly presynaptic vesicles of neurons and neurosecretory granules of neuro endocrine cells
synarthrosis	συνάρθρωσις /η	1 an immovable articulation in which the bones are united by intervening fibrous connective tissues 2 any of various immovable articulations, or joints
synchronial	σύγχρονος, η, ο (adj.) (συν + χρόνος – together + time–at the same time)	contemporary; 1 happening at the same time; occurring together; simultaneous 2 having the same period between movements, occurrences, etc.; having the same rate and phase, as vibrations
synchronicity	συγχρόνησις /η	the coincidental occurrence of events and esp., psychic events (as similar thoughts in widely separated persons) that seem related but are not explained by conventional mechanisms of causality—used esp., in the psychology of C. G. Jung
synchronize	συγχρονίζειν / συγχρονίζω	1 to cause to agree in time or rate of speed; regulate (clocks, a flash gun, and camera shutter, etc.) so as to make synchronous 2 to assign (events, appointments, etc.) to the same date or period 3 Film to align (picture and soundtrack)
syncope	συγκοπή	1 Med. loss of consciousness resulting from insufficient blood flow to the brain; fainting 2 Lingist. the dropping sounds from the middle of a word, as in (glas'ter) for Gloucester

syndactyl	συνδακτύλιος, α, ο (adj.) (συν + δάκτυλος – together + finger/toe)	1 having two or more digits united, as by webbing 2 a syndactyl mammal or bird
syndactylism	συνδακτυλισμός	a union of two or more digits that occurs in humans often as a hereditary disorder marked by the joining or webbing of two or more fingers ot toes; also, *Syndactyly*
syndesm- or syndesmo-	σύνδεσμος	ligament, combining form (syndesis; sindesmosis)
syndesis	σύνδεσις /η	binding; 1 the state of being bound, linked. or connected together 2 synapsis
syndesmosis	συνδέσμευσις /η (συνδέειν – to connect; to bind together)	the joining of adjacent bones as by ligaments
syndrome	σύνδρομον /ο	1 a number of symptoms occurring together, characterizing a specific disease or condition 2 any set of characteristics or symptoms regarded as an identifier of a certain type, condition, etc.
syndromic	συνδρομικός, ή, ό (adj.)	occurring as a syndrome or part of a syndrome as (**syndromic deafness**)
synechia	συνέχεια	an adhesion of parts and esp., one involving the iris to the cornea; also called *anterior syneschia* b) adhesion of the iris to the crystalline lens; also called *posterior synechia*, in Greek the word συνέχεια also means continuation
synergic	συνεργικός, ή, ό (adj.)	working together [synergic muscle contraction]

synergism	συνεργισμός	interaction of discreet agents (as drugs) such that the total effect is greater than the sum of the individual effects; also called *synergy*, compare **Antagonism**
synergist	συνεργός	1 an agent that increases the effectiveness of another agent when combined with it; esp., a drug that acts in synergism with another 2 an organ (as a muscle) that acts in concert with another to increase its effect; compare **Agonist**; **Antagonist**
synergy	συνεργία /συνεργείν – joint work/ to work together	combined or cooperative action or force; synergism
synesthesia	συναισθησία	1 Physiol. sensation felt in one part of the body when another part is stimulated 2 Psychol. a process in which one type of stimulus produces a secondary, subjective sensation, as when some color evokes a specific smell
syngamy	συνγαμία	sexual reproduction, union of gametes to form a fertilized ovum
syngeneic	συγγενικός, ή, ό (adj.)	genetically identical esp., with respect to antigens or immunological reaction [syngeneic tumor cell]; compare *Allogeneic/Allogenic and Xenogeneic/ Xenogenic*
synkaryon	συν + κάρυον – together + nut	the nucleus resulting from the fusion of male and female nuclei during fertilization
synkinesis	συγκίνησις /η (συν + κίνησις – together + motion	involuntary movement in one part when another part is moved: an associated movement; synkinesis/ συγκίνησις/η also in Gr.: emotion; sadness; dejection

synonym	συνώνυμον/ο – συνώνυμα (pl.)	1 a word having the same or close the name name opposed to antonym 2 Biol. an incorrect taxonomic name
synonymous	συνώνυμος, η, ο (adj.	relating to synomym; equal or similar in meaning
synonymy	συνωνυμία	1 the research or study of synonyms 2 the quality of being synonymous, the identity or close identity of meaning
synopsis	σύνοψις/η	brief review, summary
synoptic	συνοπτικός, ή, ό (adj.)	presenting a general view; summary
synostosis	συν + οστέωσις /η – together + bones	union of two or more separate bones to form a single bone; a union formed this way
syntactic	συντακτικός, ή, ό (adj.)	of, or in accordance with the rules of syntax
syntax	σύναταξις/η- συντακτικό	join or /put together; systematic arrangement
synthesis	σύνθεσις/η (syn /together + thesis/place)	the putting together of parts or elements as to form a whole
synthesize	συνθέτω	to put together separate parts; create
synthetic	συνθετικός, ή, ό (adj.)	of, or using synthesis; produced by chemical synthesis, rather than a natural origin
syphil- or syphilo-	σύφιλ- συφιλο-	syphilis, combining form (syphilis; syphilom)
syphilis	σύφιλις /η	a chronic contagious, usually venereal and often congenital, disease that is caused by a spirochete of the genus Treponema(T.pallidum) which produces chancres, and rashes if left untreated, along with systemic lesions in a clinical course with three stages continued over many years

syphilitic	συμφιλιτικός, ή, ό (adj.)	of, relating to, or infected with syphilis
syphiloma	συφίλωμα	a syphilitic tumor: *Gumma [a testicular syphiloma]*
syring- or syringo-	συριγγ- συριγγο-	syrinx; tube; fistula, combining form (syringue; **syringomyelia**)
syringe/syringa	σύριγξ/σύριγγα	tube, a reed; a device consisting of a narrow tube, designed to inject fluids into, or extract fluids from body cavities (as injections or cleansing wounds)
syringo-myelia	συριγκο-μυελία	a chronic progressive disease of the spinal cord associated with sensory disturbances, muscle atrophy, and spasticity
syrinx	σύρινξ/σύριγγος /σύριγγα	a pathological cavity in the brain or spinal cord, esp., in syringomyelia
system	σύστημα	1 α set of facts/principles or rules 2 a set or arrangement of things so related or connected as to form a unity or organic whole [a solar system, school system, company system, etc.] 3 a method or plan of classification or arrangement
systematic	συστηματικός, ή, ό (adj.)	1 forming a system, regular, orderly 2 made or arranged according to a system, method, or plan
systematics	συστηματική	the science or method of classification: taxonomy
systemic	συστημικός, ή, ό (adj.)	of, relating to, or common to a system

systems analysis	ανάλυσις συστημάτων – analysis of systems	1 an engineering technique that breaks down complex technical, social, etc., problems into basic elements whose interrelations are evaluated and programmed, with the aid of mathematics, into a complete and integrated system 2 the designing of an efficient computer system for a particular business, project, etc.
system analyst	αναλυτής συστημάτων	a specialist in systems analysis
systole	συστολή	the rhythmic contraction of the heart
systolic	συστολλικός, ή, ό (adj.)	as the action and dilation of the heart
syzygy	συζυγία (συν + ζυγός – together + yoke)	1 a pair of things, esp. a pair of opposites 2 Astron. either of two opposing points in the orbit of a celestial body, specif. of the moon, at which it is in conjunction with or in opposition to the sun 3 Gr. and Latin Prosody a measure of two feet, as a dipody

T

Tachisto-scope	ταχυτο-σκόπιον /ο (τάχιστος, η, ο (adj. Superlative of ταχύς – fast)	an apparatus that exposes words, pictures, etc., for a measured fraction of a second, used to increase reading speed or to test memory, perception, etc.
tachy- or tacho-	ταχύ- ταχο- (ταχύς, ταχεία, ταχύ – fast; quick; swift)	combining form (tachycardia)
tachometer	ταχύμετρον/ο	a device that measures or indicates the rate of rotation of a revolving shaft
tachometry	ταχυμετρία/ ταχυμέτρησις /η	the practice using a tachometer

tachy- prefix	ταχύς, ταχεία, ταχύ (adj.)	fast; rapid; quick (tachy –tachycardia; tacho- tachometry)
tachycardia	ταχυκαρδία (ταχύς /fast, rapid + καρδία/heart)	rapid beating of the heart, coming on in sudden attacks
tachygraph	ταχυγράφος	a specialist in tachygraphy
tachygraphy	ταχυγραφία	the art or use of rapid writing; esp., in anc. Greek and Roman shorthand, or the medieval cursive writing, with abbreviations, etc., in those languages
tachylalia	ταχυ-λαλιά	rapid speech
tachylyte	ταχυλύτης (ταχύς + λυτός/ λύειν- swift + soluble-to disolve)	a kind of basaltic volcanic glass
tachymeter	ταχύμετρον /ο	a surveying instrument for rapid determination of distances, elevations, etc.
tachyphagia	ταχυ-φαγεία	rapid eating
tachyphylaxis	ταχυφύλαξις /η	diminished response to later increments in a sequence of applications of a physiologically active substance
tachyphylactic	ταχυφυλακτικός, ή, ό (adj.)	pertaining to tachyphylaxis
tachypnoea	ταχυπνοϊα/ ταχυπνοή	unusually fast rate of breathing
tachyrhythmia	ταχυρρυθμία	rapid heart action; accelerated heartbeat
taenia	ταινία / τείνειν – tape, ribbon/ to stretch	1 in ancient Greek headband or filler 2 Anat. a ribbonlike part or structure, as of musc le or nerve tissue 3 Archit. a band between the frieze and the architrave of a Doric entablature 4 Zool. a tapeworm of the genus [Taenia]
taeniasis	ταινίασις /η	infestation with or disease caused by tapeworms

tarso-	ταρσο- ταρσός	flat of the foot, combining form (tarsus; tarsorrhaphy)
tarso-meta-tarsus	ταρσο-μετα-ταρσός	the large bone in the lower part of a bird's leg, connecting the tibia with the toes
tarsorrhaphy	ταρσοραφή	surgical procedure in suturing the eyelids together entirely or in part
tarsus	ταρσός	1 the part of the foot between the metatarsus and the leg; also, the small bones that support this part of the limb 2 *Tarsal Plate*
tauromachy	ταρσομαχεία (ταύρος + μάχη – bull + fight/battle)	literary term for "bullfighting," bullfight
taurus	ταύρος	bull; 1 a N constellation between Aries and Orion containing the Hyades and the Pleiades star clusters, the Crab nebula, and Aldebaran 2 the second sign of the zodiac, entered by the sun about the twenty-first of April; a person born under that sign
tauto-	το αυτό (ταυτό)	the same (tautology)
tautological	ταυτολογικός, ή, ό (adj.)	of, involving, or using tautology
tautology	ταυτολογία	1) needless repetition of an idea using a different word, phrase, or sentence; redundancy; pleonasm 2 Logic a proposition that is analytic
tautometer	ταυτόμετρον / ο	a substance exhibiting tautomerism
tautomerism	ταυτομερισμός (ταυτο + μέρος –same +part)	Chem. the property of some substances of being in a condition of equilibrium between two isomeric forms and of reacting readily to form either

tautonym	ταυτόνυμον	1 a scientific name consisting of two terms, in which the generic name and specific name are the same (ex: Vulpes vulpes, the red fox): this kind of name is no longer used in botany, but it is common in zoology 2 a scientific name consisting of three terms, in which the name of the typical subdivision of the species repeats the specific name (ex: Llama glama glama, a sophisticated llama)
tautonymy	ταυτονυμία	indicating that people or things are sharing the same name
taverna	ταβέρνα	small family restaurant in Greece
taxis	τάξις /η	order; arrangement; division; 1 in ancient Greece, a unit of troops of varying size 2 Biol. the movement of a free-moving cell or organism toward or away from some external stimulus 3 Surgery the replacement by hand of some displaced part without cutting any tissue
-taxis	-ταξις	order, arrangement, combining form (phyllotaxis/ the arrangement of leaves on a stem))
taxonomy	ταξινομία/ ταξινόμηση	order; the science of classification of laws and principles
techne -	τέχνη	art; science; skill (plus compound words)
technetronic	τεχνιτρονικός, ή, ό (adj.)	characterized by the application of technology and electronics to the solution of social, political, and economic problems [a technechronic society]
technic	τεχνικός, ή, ό (adj.)	pertaining to technique

technician	τεχνικός/ τεχνίτης	1 a person skilled in the technicalies of a subject 2 an artist, writer, musician, etc., with great knowledge and skill on the respective subject
technique	τεχνική	1 the study or principles of technology; an art or the arts 2 the degree of expertise 3 any method or manner of accomplishing a task
techno -	τέχνο- / τέχνη	skill, art, also short for technology combining form (technology)
technocracy	τεχνοκρατία	government by technicians; specif., the doctrine of a proposed system of government in which all economic resources, and hence the entire social system, would be controlled by scientists and engineers
technocrat	τεχνοκράτης	specialist in technocracy
technology	τεχνολογία	science or study of practical or industrial arts/applied sciences)
tele- prefix	τήλε-	ancient Greek adverb meaning far off, far away, combining form (telephone; telegraphy)
telegenic	(ο, η) τηλεγενής (το) τηλεγενές (adj.)	a person looking or likely to look attractive on television
telediagnosis	τηλεδιάγνωσις /η	medical diagnosis made from far by means of telemedicine
telegram	τηλέγραμμα	a message transmitten by telegraph
telegraph	τηλεγράφημα	1 originally any signaling apparatus 2 an apparatus or system that converts a coded message into electric impulses and sends it to a distant receiver 3 to send a message by telegraph
telegraphic	τηλεγραφικός, ή, ό (adj.)	of, or transmitted by telegraph 2 in the concise style of a telegram

telegraphy	τηλεγράφησις / η / τηλεγραφία	1 the operation of telegraph apparatus or the study of this 2 the transmission of messages by telegraph
telekinesis	τηλεκίνησις /η (τηλε + κίνησις / κινείν- far + motion / to move)	Parapsychology the causing of an object to move by means of psychic forces, as by a spiritualistic medium, and not by means of any physical force
Telemachus	Τηλέμαχος	Gr. legend, the son of Odysseus and Penelope who helped his father to slay his mother's suitors
telemeter	τηλέμετρον /ο	1 an instrument for determining the distance of a distant or remote object; range finder 2 any device for transmitting measurements of physical phenomena, as radiation, temperature, distance, etc., to a distant recorder or observer: used in satellites, spacecrafts, etc. and as a verb: to transmit via telemeter
telemetry	τηλεμετρία / τηλεμέτρησις /η	the technique, science, or process of determining the telemetering data 2 data transmitted by telemetry
tele-encephalon	τηλε- εγκέφαλον	the anterior subdivision of the embryonic forebrain or the corresponding part of the adult forebrain that includes the cerebral hemispheres and associated structures

teleology	τηλεολογία (τέλος + λογία- end +study)	1 the scientific study of final causes 2 the fact or quality of being directed toward a definite end, or of having an ultimate purpose; esp., as attributed to natural processes 3 a) a belief, as that of vitalism, that natural phenomena are determined not only by natural causes but by an overall design or purpose in nature b) the study of evidence for this belief 4 Ethics the evaluation of conduct, as in utilitarianism, in relation to the end or ends it serves
teleonomy	τηλεονομία	the concept of an organism's structures or functions must have given it an evolutionary advantage
teleost	τελ-οστεον – end + bone	any of many orders of bony fishes having a consolidated internal skeleton, swim bladder, thin cycloid scales, etc.
telepathy	τηλεπάθεια	Parapsychology communication between minds by some means other than the normal sensory channels; transference of thought
telephone	τηλέφωνο (τήλε/ far-φωνή/voice)	a system for transmitting speech of computerized information over distances
telephonist	τηλεφωνητής / τηλεφωνήτρια (fem)	a telephone switchboard operator
telephony	τηλεφωνία	1 the science of telephonic transmission 2 the making or operation of telephones

telephotography	τηλε-φωτογραφία / φωτογράφησις /η	the art or process of photographing distant objects by using a telephoto lens 2 the scientific study or process of transmitting photographs over distances by converting light rays into electric signals, which are sent over wire or light rays to which a photographic film is exposed
teleradiology	τηλε-ραδιο-λογία	radiology involved with transmitting digitized medical images over electronic networks along with the interpretation of the transmitted images for diagnostic purposes
telescope	τηλεσκόπιο(ν)	an optical instrument for making distant objects, as the stars, appear closer and consequently much larger
teletherapy	τηλεθεραπεία	the treatment of diseased tissue with high-intensity radiation (as gamma rays from radioactive cobalt)
telic	τελικός, ή, ό (adj.) (τέλος –end)	1 directed toward an end; purposeful 2 Linguis. perfective: tending to bring or to achieve perfection; the perfecting effect
telophase	τέλος + φασις/η- end + phase	Biol. the final stage of mitosis, in which the parent cell becomes completely divided into two cells, each having a reorganized nucleus
tendodynia	τένων + οδύνη	pain in the tendon
tendon	τένων/ τένοντος(gen.) τένοντας (Mod. Gr.)	fibrous tissue connecting muscles to other structures
tendonitis	τενοντίτις / τενοντίτιδα	inflammation of the tendon
tendon of Achilles	Αχίλειος τένων	Achilles's tendon

tendon organ	όργανον τένοντος	Golgi tendon organ: a spindle-shaped sensory end organ within a tendon that provides information about muscle tension; also called neuro-tendinous spindle
tendoplasty	τενοπλαστική	surgical repair of the tendon
teno-	τένο-	combining form (tenodesis)
tenodesis	τενόδεσις /η	the surgical procedure of suturing the end of a tendon to a bone
tenolysis	τενόλυσις /η	a surgical procedure to free a tendon from surrounding adhesions
tenomyotomy	τενομυοτομή	surgical excision of a portion of a tendon and muscle
tenotomy	τενοτομή	surgical division of a tendon
tephrosis	τέφρωσις /η	cremation
terat- or terato-	τρεατ- τέρατο- (τέρας/τέρατος (gen.)	monster also wonder, combining form (teratoid)
teras	τέρας	monster; fetal monster
terato-carcinoma	τερατο-καρκίνωμα	a malignant teratoma; esp., one involving germinal cells of the testis or ovary
teratogen	(ο, η) τερατο-γενής (το) τερατογενές (adj.)	an agent, as a chemical, disease, etc., that causes malformation of the fetus 2 Biol..resembling a monster; malformed
teratogenesis	τερατο-γένεσις /η	production of developmental malformations
teratoid	(ο, η) τερατώδης (το) τερατώδες (adj.)	pertaining to monster; abnormal or malformed
teratology	τερατολογία	the scientific study of biological monstrosities or malformations
teratoma	τεράτωμα	a tumor containing various kinds of embryonic tissue, as of hair and teeth

tetra-	base of τέσσαρις/ τέσσερα (Mod. Gr.)	four (as tetrapod)
tetrachord	τετράχορδον /ο /- four-stringed	Music a series of four tones contained in the interval of a perfect fourth
tetrad	τετράς/ τετράδος (gen.) /τετράδα (Mod. Gr.)	a group or set of four
tetralogy	τετραλογία	a series of four dramas, three tragic and one satiric, performed together at the ancient Athenian festival of Dionysos
tetraplegia	τετραπληγία	paralysis of all four extremities; quadriplegia
tetraplegic	τετραπληγικός, ή, ό (adj.)	quadriplegic; paralyzed involving four limbs
tetraploid	(ο, η) τετραπλειδής (το) τετραπλοειδές (adj.)	Biol. having four times the haploid number chromosomes; a tetraploid cell, or organism
tetrapod	τετράποδον	any vertebrate having four legs or limbs, including the mammals, birds, and reptiles
tetrarchy	τετραρχία	1 the rule or territory of a tetrarch 2 government by four persons; also: **tetrarchate**
tetrastich	τετράστιχος, η, ο (adj.) (τετράστιχον/ο, neu. of τετράστιχος)	a poem or stanza of four lines
tetrasyllable	τετρασύλλαβος	a word haing four syllables; also, **tetrasyllabic**
Th	Θθ (θήτα)	the eighth letter of the Gr. alphabet; theta (a soft th, as in theater/thesis)
thalam- or thalamo-	θάλαμ- θαλαμο- (θάλαμος – inner chamber)	combining form (thalamic; thalamotomy)
thalamic	θαλαμικός, ή, ό (adj.)	of, relating to, or involving the thalamus

thalamotomy	θαλαμοτομή	surgery involving electrocoagulation of areas of the thalamus to interrupt pathways of nervous transmission through the thalamus for relief of certain mental and psychomotor disorders
thalamus	θάλαμος	1 area in the brain dealing with many bodily functions 2 the largest subdivision of the diencephalon that consists mainly of an ovoid mass of nuclei in each lateral wall of the third ventricle and serves to relay impulses and esp. sensory impulses to and from the cerebral cortex
thalassemia or thalassaemia	θαλασσαιμία (θάλασσα + αίμα- sea + blood)	disease similar to sickle-cell anemia; an inherited chronic anemia, initially found in Mediterranean peoples, resulting from faulty hemoglobin production; also called *Mediterranean anemia* /*Μεσογειακή αναιμία*
thalassic	θαλάσσιος, α, ο (adj.)	1 of the sea or ocean; mar ine 2 of bays, gulfs, etc,. and island seas, as distinguished from the ocean
thalassemic	θαλασσαμικός, ή, ό (adj.)	of, related to, or affected with thalassemia
thalassophobia	θαλασσοφοβία	extreme fear of the sea
thalassotherapy	θαλασσοθεραπεία	exposure to seawater (as in a hot tub) or application of sea products (as seaweed or sea salt) to the body for health or beauty benefits
thanat- or thanato-	θάνατο- θάνατος	death, combining form (thanatophobia)
thanatobiology	θανατοβιολογία	pertaining to life and death

thanatoid	(ο, η) θανατώδης (το) θανατώδες (adj.)	resembling death
thanatology	θανατολογία	the scientific study of death, esp. of the medical, psychological, and social problems associated with dying
thanatomania	θανατομανία	suicidal obsession
thanato-phobia	θανατοφοβία	an abnormally great fear of death
thanatophoric	θανατοφόρος, α, ο (adj.	relating to, affected with, or being a severe form of congenital dwarfism resulting in early death
thanatopsis	θανατοψία	a view of, or musing upon death
thanatos and Thanatos	θάνατος	death; Gr. myth. death personified: identified with the Roman *Mors*
thelalgia	θηλαλγία (θηλή/ nipple −αλγία/pain)	pain in the nipple(s)
theleethism	θηλεερεθισμός	erection of the nipple
theater or theatre	θέατρον /ο	1 a place where plays, operas, concerts, films, etc., are performed, esp. a building or outdoor structure especially designed for such presentations 2 any place resembling a theater, as a lecture hall, surgical clinic, etc., having the floor of the seating space raked; 3 any place where events take place; scene of operations, etc.
theatrical	θεατρικός, ή, ό (adj.)	1 having to do with the theater, the play, drama,actors, stage, etc. 2 characteristic of the theater; dramatic, melodramatic, comedic, spectacular, etc.
theatrics	θεατρολογία	1 the art or study of the theater 2 something done or said for theatrical effect; histrionic actions, manners, devices, etc.

theca	θήκη	a case; 1 Bot. a spore, case, sac, or capsule 2 Zool. Anat. any sheath or sac enclosing an organ or a whole organism, as the covering of an insect pupa
theism	θεϊσμός	1 belief in a god or gods 2 belief in one God, *monotheism: opposed to pantheism, polytheism*
thematic	θεματικός, ή, ό (adj.)	1 of, or constituting a theme or themes 2 Linguis. of, or relating to the stem of a word, or to a vowel ending a stem that precedes an inflectional ending.
theme	θέμα	a topic or a subject as of a lecture, sermon, essay, etc.
Themis	Θέμις	Gr. myth. a goddess of law and justice, daughter of Uranus and Gaea: represented as holding a scale for weighing opposing issues or claims
th- or theo-	θε- θεο- (Θεός θεός –God, god)	combining form (theocracy)
Theo/ Theos/	Θεός –θεός	God or god
theocentric	θεοκεντρικός, ή, ό (adj.)	centering on or directed toward God
theocentric	θεοκρατικός, ή, ό (adj.)	pertaining to theocracy
theocracy	θεοκρατία	1 lit. the rule of a state by God or a god 2 government by a person or persons claiming to govern with divine authority 3 a country governed this way
theodicy	θεοδικία (θεος + δίκη- god + justice)	a system of natural theology aimed to seeking to vindicate divine justice in allowing evil to exist
Theodora	Θεοδώρα	meaning God's gift, feminine name
Theodore	Θεόδωρος	masculine name (gift of God)

Theodocius-Theodosia	Θεοδόσιος - Θεοδοσία	masculine and feminine names lit. given from God
theogony	Θεογονία	the origin or geneology of the gods as told in myths
theological	Θεολογικός, ή, ό (adj.)	religious scriptures, pertaining to theology
theologian	Θεολόγος	an expert or a student of theology
theology/ religion	Θεολογία	the study of religious doctrines and matters of divinity
theomachy	Θεομαχία	1 a battle against the gods 2 strife among gods
theomania	Θεομανία	delusion that one is a deity
theophany	Θεοφάνεια	1 manifestation of God 2 in many Christian churches and esp., in the Greek Orthodox Church January 6 Baptism of Jesus is celebrated; also called *Epiphany*
theorem	Θεώρημα	1 proposition to be proven 2 a proposition that is not self-evident but that can be proved from accepted premises and so is established as a law or principle 3 an expression of relations in an equation or formula 4 Math, physics a proposition embodying something that has to be proven
theoretical	Θεωρητικός, ή, ό (adj.)	limited to, or based on theory
theorize	Θεωρείν/Θεωρώ	form, evolve a theory; to put forth an opinion without prior substantiation
theoretician	Θεωρητικός	a person who theorizes, esp. someone who specializes in the theory of some art, science, etc.
theoretics	Θεωρητική	the theoretical part of a science or a field of knowledge
theory	Θεωρία	idea; principle; speculation

theosophy	Θεοσοφία	a religious or semireligious set of occult beliefs rejecting Judeo-Christian revelation and theology, often incorporating elements of Buddhism and Brahmanism
τherapeusis	Θεράπευσις /η (Θεραπεύειν – to cure / heal)	the treatment and healing of a disease
therapeutic	Θεραπευτικός, ή, ό (adj.)	pertaining to healing
therapeutics	Θεραπευτική	the branch of medicine dealing with the treatment of disease
therapist or therapeutist	Θεραπευτής/ Θεραπεύτρια (fem.)	one skilled in the treatment of a disease
therapy	Θεραπεία	treatment of disease
therm- or thermo-	θερμ- θερμο- θερμός/ θέρμη	hot; heat, combining form (thermanalgesia)
thermal	θερμός, ή, ό (adj.)	hot; pertaining to heat
thermanalgesia	θερμαν-αλγεσία	inability to react to heat
thermesthesia	θερμαισθησία	perception of heat or cold
thermaic	θερμαντικός, ή, ό (adj.)	pertaining to heat; producing heat
-thermia or -thermy	θέρμια- θερμη (θερμός, ή, ό adj.)	hot; warm, combining form (thermostat)
thermogenesis	θερμογένεσις /η	the production of heat, esp. by physiological action in an animal
thermogram	θερμόγραμμα	a record made by a thermograph
thermograph	θερμογράφος	a thermometer for recording variations in temperature automatically; specif. an infrared camera

thermography	θερμογραφία	I the recording of temperature variations by means of a thermograph 2 a process for imitating copperplate engraving, as on calling cards, by dusting the freshly printed surface with a resinous powder which, when heated, fuses with the ink to form a raised surface
thermolysis	θερμόλυσις /η	I Chem. dissociation of a compound by heat 2 Physiol. dispersion of heat from the body
thermometer	θερμόμετρο(ν)	instrument to measure heat/temperature
thermoplastic	θερμοπλαστικός, η, ό (adj.)	becoming or remaining soft and moldable when subjected to heat: said of certain plastics; a thermoplastic substance
thermoplegia	θερμοπληξία	heatstroke, sunstroke
thermostat	θερμοστάτης	device for controlling heat
thermotherapy	θερμοθεραπεία	treatment of disease by heat (as by hot air or hot baths)
therio-genologist	θηριο-γενολόγος	an expert in theriogeneology
therio-genology	θηριο-γενολογία	(θηρίον γένος –γέννα/ **wild beast + birth/obstetrics** a branch of veterinary medicine concerned with veterinary obstetrics and with the diseases of physiology of animal reproductive systems
thorac-thoraci- or thoraco-	θωραξ/ θώρακος (gen.)/θώρακας (Mod. Gr.)	thorax; chest, combining form (thoracentesis, thoracic, thoracocentesis)
thoracalgia	θωρακοαλγία / θερακαλγία	chest pain
thoracentesis	θωρακέντησις /η	aspiration of fluid from the chest (as in empysema) also called *thoracocentesis*
thoraces	θώρακες (pl.)	plural of thorax
thoracectomy	θωρακεκτομή	surgical removal of a rib(s)

thoracic	θωρακικός, ή, ό (adj.)	pertaining to chest
thoracic aorta	θωρακική αορτή	the part of the aorta that lies in the thorax and extends from the arch to the diaphragm
thoracic artery	θωρακική αρτηρία	either of two arteries that branch from the axillary artery or from one of its branches a) a small artery that supplies or sends branches to the two pectoralis muscles and the walls of the chest; also called *supreme thoracic artery* b) an artery that supplies both pectoralis muscles and the serratus anterior and sends branches to the lymph nodes of the axilla and to the subscapularis muscle; also called *lateral thoracic artery*; compare *Internal Thoracic Artery*
thoracic nerve	θωρακικό (ν) νεύρο (ν)	any of the spinal nerves of the thorasic region that consist of twelve pairs of which one pair emerges just below each thorasic vertebra
thoracodynia	θωρακο-οδύνη	pain in the thorax
thoraco-myodynia	θωρακο-μυοδύνη	pain in chest muscles
thoracoplasty	θωρακοπλαστική	the surgical procedure for removing or resecting one or more ribs in order to obliterate the pleura cavity and collapse a diseased lung
thoracoscope	θωρακοσκόπιον /o	an endoscope that is inserted through a puncture in the chest wall in an intercostal space (as for visual examination of the chest cavity)
thoracoscopic	θωρακοσκοπικός, ή, ό (adj.)	pertaining to thoracoscopy

thoracoscopy	θωρακοσκόπησις /η	examination of the chest, esp. the pleural cavity by means of a thoracoscope
thoracostomy	θωρακοστόμιον	surgical opening of the chest (as for drainage)
thoracotomy	θωρακοτομία/ θωρακοτομή	surgical opening of the chest
thorax	θώραξ/θώρακος (gen.) θώρακας (Mod. Gr.)	chest, breastplate
threpsology	θρεψολογία (θρέψη & λόγος)	study of nutrition
thromb- or thrombo-	θρομβ- θρόμβο- θρόμβος	blood clot, combining form (thrombosis)
thromb-asthenia	θρόμβο-ασθένεια	an inherited abnormality of the blood platelets characterized esp. by defective clot retraction and often prolonged bleeding time
thrombectomy	θρομβο-εκτομή	surgery to remove a clot from a blood vessel
thrombi (pl. of thombus)	θρόμβοι pl. of θρόμβος)	plural of thrombus
thrombin	θρομβίνη	a proteolytic enzyme formed from prothrobin that facilitates the clotting of blood by catalyzing conversion of fibrinogen to fibrin; also called **thrombase**
thrombo-angiits	θρομβτοκή- αγγειτίτις / αγγειτίτιδα	inflammation of the lining of a blood vessel with thrombus formation
thrombocyte	θρομβοκύτταρον/ο	platelet: 1 any of certain round or oval, nonnucleated disks, smaller than a red blood cell and containing no hemoglobin, found in the blood of mammals and associated with the process of blood clotting
thrombo-embolism	θρομβο-εμβολισμός	the obstruction of a blood vessel by an embolus that has broken away from a thrombus

thrombo-end-arterectomy	θρόμβος + αρτηρία + εκτομή	surgical excision of a thrombus and the adjacent arterial lining
thrombo-genesis	Θρομβογένεσις /η	the formation of a thrombus
thrombolytic	Θρομβο-λυτικός, ή, ό (adj.)	destroying or breaking up a thrombus (a thrombolytic agent) (a thrombolytic therapy) as a noun: clot-buster
thrombopathy	Θρομβοπάθεια	defective blot clotting
thrombophilia	Θρομβοφιλία	a hereditary or acquired predisposition to thrombosis
thrombo-phlebitis	Θρομβο-φλεβίτις/ Θρομβο-φλεδίτιδα	inflammation of the vein
thromboplastic	Θρομβο-πλαστικός, ή, ό (adj.)	initiating or accelerating the clotting of blood (a thromboplastic substance)
thrombosis	Θρόμβωσις/η	formation of a clot within a blood vessel
thrombus	Θρόμβος	blood clot
throne-	Θρόνος	a seat, a chair a king/cardinal/ bishop, etc., occupies on formal or ceremonial occasions, the power of a king; sovereignty
thym- or thymo-	θύμο- θύμος	orig. a warty excrescence; thymus, combining form
thyme	θυμάρι	1 any of the genus (Thymus esp., T, vulgaris) of shrubby plants or aromatic herbs of the mint family, with white, pink, or red flowers, along with fragrant leaves 2 the leaves are used as an herb for seasoning
thymic	θυμικός, ή, ό (adj.)	pertaining to thymus; of thymus
thymoma	θύμωμα	a tumor that arises from the tissue elements of the thymus

thymus	θύμος	1 a glandular structure of largely lymphoid tissue; 2 a gland in the upper thorax or neck of all vertebrates, involved in the production of lymphocytes: in humans, it is most prominent at puberty, after which it disappears or becomes vestigial; also, *thymus gland*
thyr- or thyro-	θυρ- θυρο- (θυροειδής- thyroid)	combining form (thyroadenitis)
thyroadenitis	θυρεο-αδενίτις/ θυρεο-αδενιτιδα	inflammation of the thyroid gland
thyrogenic	(ο, η) θυρεοειγενής (το) θυρεοειγενές (adj.)	originating in the thyroid
thyroid	θυρεοειδής	gland in the neck secreting thyroxin, a substance vital to life
thyroid artery	θυρεοειδής αρτηρία	either of two arteries supplying the thyroid glandand the nearby structures at the front of the neck a) one that branches from the external carotid artery or sometimes from the common carotid artery; also called *superior thyroid artery* b) one that branches from the thyro-cervical trunk; also called *inferior thyroid artery*
thyroid-ectomy	θυρεοειδ-εκτομή	surgical excision of thyroid gland tissue
thyroiditis	θυρεοειδίτις / θυρεοειδίτιδα	inflammation of the thyroid glad
thyroidology	θυρεοειδολογία	the study of medical science concerning the thyroid gland
thyrotomy	θυρεοτομή	surgical incision or division of the thyroid cartilage
thyrotoxic	θυρεοτοξικός, ή, ό (adj.)	of, relating to, or being the thyroid cartilage

thyrotropic	θυρεοτροπικός, ή, ό (adj.)	exerting or characterized by a direct influence on the secretory activity of the thyroid gland < *thyrotropic functions* >
tome	τόμος (τέμνειν – to cut)	(piece cut off, hence part of a book, volume;) 1 orig any volume of a book of several volume 2 a book, esp., a large, scholarly or ponderous one
-tome	-τόμος	suffix forming nouns 1 cutting instrumenet [microtome] 2 section, division [dermatome]
tomogram	τομόγραμμα/ τομογράφος	a radiograph made by tomography
tomography	τομογραφία	a method of producing a three-dimensional image of the internal structures of a solid object (as the human body) by the observation and recording of the differences in the effects on the passage of waves of energy impinging upon those structures
-tomy	τομή /τόμος (τέμνειν- to cut)	cutting, incision, combining form (as in lobotomy)

tone	τόνος (τείνειν –to stretch)	1 a) a vocal or musical sound b) its quality 2 an intonation, pitch, modulation, etc., of the voice that expresses a particular meaning or feeling of the speaker (as a tone of contempt) 3 Med. a) the state of a living body or of any of its organs or parts in which the functions are healthy and perform with due vigor b) normal tension or responsiveness 4 in Greek tone/ τόνος in Gram. means: accent; 5 Linguis. a) the relative height of pitch with which a syllable, word, etc., is pronounced b) the relative height of pitch that is a phoneme of a language and distinguishes meaning, as in the tones of languages 6 a manner of speaking or writing that indicates a certain attitude on the part of the speaker or writer, consisting in choice of words, phrasing, etc., [the pleasant tone of her speech, etc.]
-tonia	-τονία	suffix forming nouns, indicating a condition or degree of tonus (myotonia)
tonographic	τονογραφικός, ή, ό (adj.)	pertaining to tonography
tonography	τονογραφία	the procedure of recording measurements (as of intra-ocular pressure) with a tonometer
tonometer	τονόμετρον/ο	an instrument for measuring tension or pressure and esp. intraocular pressure

tonotopic	τονοτοπικός, ή, ό (adj.)	relating to, or being the anatomic organization by which specific sound frequencies are received by specific receptors in the inner ear with nerve impulses traveling along selected pathways to specific sites in the brain
-tony or –tonia	-τονια	suffix forming nouns (monotony)
-top or –topo	τόπο (τόπος)	area; local combining form (topectomy; topognosia)
topaz	τοπάζι (or τοπάζος)	1 a native solicate of aluminum and fluorine, usually containing hydroxyl and occurring in a white, yellow, pale-blue, or pale-green, orthrorhombic crystals; esp., a yellow variety of this, used as a gem 2) a) a yellow variety of sapphire b) a yellow variety of quartz 3 either of two brightly colored hummingbirds Topaza pyra or T. pella [of South America.]
topazolite	τοπαζολίνη	a yellow to greenish variety of andradite garnet
topectomy	τοπεκτομή	surgical excision of selected portions of the frontal cortex of the brain, esp., for the relief of medically intractable epilepsy
topic	τοπικός, ή, ό (adj.)	local; the subject of a paragraph, essay, speech, etc.
topognosia	τοπογνωσία	recognition of the location of a stimulus on the skin or elsewhere in the body
topographic or tropographical	τοπογραφικός, ή, ό (adj.)	1 of, relating to, or concerned with topography 2 of or relating to a mind made up of different strata and esp. of the conscious, preconscious, and unconscious

topograph	τοπογράφος	1 an expert or specialist in topography 2 a person who describes or maps the topography of a place or region
topography	τοπογραφία	1 orig. the accurate and detailed description of a place 2 the science concerned with the drawing on maps and charts or otherwise representing the surface features of a region, including its relief, rivers, lakes, etc., and such man-made features as canals, bridges, roads, etc. 3 topographic surveying 4 any similar study of an entity, as the mind, the atom, a particular discipline, etc.
topology	τοπολογία	a topographical study of a specific object, entity, place, etc., [the topology of the mind] 2 Math. the scientific study of those properties of geometric figures that remain unchanged even when under distortion, so long as no surfaces are torn, as of a Mobius strip 3 Med. a topographic anatomy of an area of the body
toponym	τοπόνυμον	1 a name of a place 2 a name that indicates origin, natural locale, etc., as in zoological nomenclature
toponymy	τοπονυμία	1 the place names of a country, district, etc., or the study of these 2 [Rare] Anat. the nomenclature of the regions of the body
topos	τόπος	place; 1 a common or recurring topic, theme, subject, etc. 2 a literary convention or formula

toxemia	τοξιαιμία	an abnormal condition associated with the presence of toxic substances in the blood a) as a generalized intoxication due to absorption and systemic dissemination of bacteria toxins from a focus of infection b) intoxication due to dissemination of toxic substances (as some byproducts of protein metabolism) that cause functional or organic disturbances (as in the kidneys)
toxic- or toxico-	τοξικό-	poison, combining form (toxic; toxicogenic)
toxicogenic	(ο, η) τοξικογενής (το) τοξικογενές (adj.)	producing toxic substances
toxicology	τοξικολογία	the science concerned with poisons and their effects, in addition, with antidotes to poisons, and all the problems involved (as clinical, industrial, or legal)
toxicosis	τοξίκωσις /η	1 a pathological condition caused by the action of a poison or toxin 2 any diseased condition caused by poisoning
toxin	τοξίνη	a poisonous substance that is a specific product of the metabolic activities of a living organism and is usually very unstable, notably toxic when introduced into the tissues, and typically capable of inducing antibody formation
toxoid	(ο, η) τοξοειδής (το) τοξοειδές (adj.)	a toxin of a pathogenic organism treated in such way so its toxicity is destroyed but left capable of inducing the formation of antibodies on injection (diphtheria toxoid)

toxo-philite	Τοξόφιλος/ Toxophilus (the title of a book)|τόξον/ο + φίλος- **arrow** + **friend, loving** |	one who loves. Archery; being fond of archery
toxoplasmosis	τοξοπλάσμωσις /η	a disease caused by a protozoan |**Toxoplasma gondii**|, affecting humans and animals, esp. in the tropics; in its congenital form, it damages the central nervous system, eyes, and viscera
trache- or tracheo-	τραχεία	trachea (tracheioscopy) 2 tracheal (tracheal-bronchial)
trachea artery	τραχεία αρτηρία	rough artery; windpipe; 1 the main trunk of the system of tubes by which air passes to and from the lungs that is about four inches (10 centimeres) long and somewhat less than an inch (2.5 centimeres) in diameter, extends down the front of the neck from the larynx, divides in two to form the bronchi; also called windpipe
tracheitis	τραχειίτις/ τραχειίτιδα	inflammation of the trachea
trachel- or trachelo-	τράχηλος	combining form 1 neck [trachelomastoid muscle] 2 uterine cervix [tracheloplasty]
trachelotomy	τραχηλοτομία or τραχηλοτομή	cervicectomy: surgical excision of the uterine cervix
trachelo-mastoid	τραχηλο-μαστοειδής	trachelomastoid muscle: longissimus capitis: a muscle that arises by tendons from the upper thoracic and lower cervical vertebrae, is inserted into the posterior margin of the mastoid process, and extends the head and bends rotating it to the side
tracheloplasty	τραχηλοπλαστική	a plastic operation on the neck of the uterus

tracheo-bronchial	τραχεο-βρογχικός, ή, ό (adj.)	of, relating to, affecting, or produced in the trachea and bronchi [tracheobronchial secretion] [tracheobronchial lesions]
tracheo-bronchitis	τραχεο-βρογχίτις / βρογχίτιδα	inflammation of the trachea and the bronchi
trancheo-esophageal	τραχεο-οισοφάγος	relating to, or connecting the trachea to the esophagus [a tracheoesophageal fisula]
tracheoplasty	τραχεο-πλαστική	plastic surgery on the trachea
tracheostoma	τραχειιόστομα/ τραχειοστόμιον	an opening into the trachea created by tracheostomy
tracheostomy	τραχειοστόμιον/ τραχειοστομή	1 the surgical formation of an opening into the trachea through the neck, esp. to allow passage of air 2 the opening itself
tracheotomy	τραχειοτομή	1 the surgical procedure of cutting into the trachea, esp. through the skin 2 the opening created by a tracheotomy
trachoma	τράχωμα	a chronic contagious conjunctivitis marked by inflammatory granulations on the conjunctival surfaces, caused by a bacterium of the genus **Clamydia (C. trachomatis)**, and commonly resulting in blindness if left untreated
trachyte	τραχύτης (τραχύς, τραχεία, τραχύ (adj.) rough)	a fine-grained, light-colored, extrusive, igneous rock, consisting mainly of alcalic feldspars and equivalent to syenite in composition
trachytic	τραχυτικός, ή, ό (adj.)	of or relating to the internal structure of some igneous rocks, as trachyte, in which hairlike feldspar crystals are in nearly parallel rows
tragedy	τραγωδία	**(lit. the song of a male goat/ τράγος + ωδή/song)**

tragic	τραγικός, ή, ό (adj.)	1 of, or having the nature of, tragedy 2 like or characteristic of tragedy; bringing misfortune, suffering, pain, etc.; disastrous, calamitous, fatal, etc.
tragi-comedy	τραγική κωμωδία/ κωμικο-τραγωδία	1 a play or other literary work combining tragic and comic elements 2 a situation or incident in life as the above
tragus	τράγος	lit. goat; the hairy part of the ear; the fleshy cartilaginous protrusion at the front of the external ear, partly extending over the opening of the ear
trapezium	τραπέζιον	lit. small table; 1 a plane figure with four sides, no two of which are parallel 2 Anat. a small bone of the wrist near the base of the thumb
trapezius	τραπεζοειδής	either of the large muscles on each side of the upper back
trapezoid	(ο, η) τραπεζοειδής (το) τραπεζοειδές (adj.)	1 a plane figure with four sides, only two of which are parallel 2 Anat. a small bone of th wrist near the base of the index finger 3 shaped as a trapezoid; trapezoidlike
trepan	τρύπανον /τρυπάνι	a carpenter's tool; 1 an early form of the trephine 2 a heavy boring tool for sinking shafts, quarrying, etc.; 3 to cut a disk out of (a metal plate, ingot, etc.)
treponema	τρεπόνημα (τρέπειν + νήμα– to turn + trhead)	any of the genus of (Treponema) of slender spirochetes parasitic in mammals and birds, including some which are pathogenic to humans, as the organisms causing syphilis and yaws

tri-	τρί- (τρεις/τρία)	three; prefix 1 having, combining, or involving three [triangle; triathlete] 2 triply, in three ways or directions [triphibian] 3 every three, every third [triweekly; Triennial] 4 Chem. having three atoms, groups, or equivalents of (something specified) [tribasic; triathlon]
triad	τριάς/τριάδα	1 a group of three people, ideas, or things 2 a musical chord of three tones
trialogue	τρίλογος	an interchange and discussion of ideas among three groups having diferrent origins, philosophies, principles, etc.
triangle	τρίγωνον /o (τρι + γωνία – three + angle)	1 a geometrical figure having three angles and three sides 2 any three-sided or three-cornered figure, area, object, part, etc. 3 a right-angled, flat, triangular instrument used in drawing geometrical figures 4 a situation involving three persons, esp., when a love affair involves three people 5 a musical instrument shaped as a trangle
triarchy	τριαρχία	a government by three people
Triassic	Τριάσσιος	designating or of the first period of the Mesozoic Era, following the Permian Period of the Paleozoic Era and characterized by the appearance of many reptiles, including the dinosaurs, and the dominance of cycads and ferns
triathlete	τριαθλητής	an athlete participating in a triathlon

triathlon	τρίαθλος	endurance race combining three consecutive events (swimming, bicycling, and running)
triatomic	τριατομικός, ή, ό (adj.)	1 designating or of a molecule consisting of three atoms 2 designating or of a molecule containing three replaceable atoms or groups
tribo-	τρίβειν – to rub	friction, combining form (triboelectricity)
tribo-electricity	τριβο-ηλεκτισμός	electric charge developed upon the surface of a material by friction, as by rubbing silk upon glass
triboelectricity	τρίβειν + ηλεκτρισμός – to rub + electricity	electric charge developed on the surface of a material by friction (ex: rubbing silk upon glass)
tribological	τριβολογικός, ή, ό (adj.)	pertaining to tribology
tribology	τριβολογία	the study of friction between interacting parts, such as gears, and ways of reducing it; or the study of interacting surfaces in relative motion and associated issues, such as friction, lubrication, or wear
tribrach	τρίβραχυς	Gr. and Lat. Prosody a metrical foot consisting of three short syllables
trichiasis	τριχίασις/η	an abnormal condition in which hairs, esp. the eyelashes growing inward, resulting often in irritation of the eyeball
trichina	τριχίνη (τρίχινος/ τριχωτός – hairy)	a very small nematode worm (Trichinella spiralis) that causes trichinosis

trichinosis	τριχίνωσις/η	infestation with or disease caused by trichinae contracted by eating raw or insufficiently cooked infested food, esp. pork and marked initially by abdominal pain, nausea, diarrhea, and later by muscular pain, dyspnea, fever, and edema; also called trichiniasis
trichite	τριχίτης	(τριξ /τριχός (gen.) – hair) a hairlike crystallite occurring in volcanic rocks in irregular or radiating groups
tricho-dectes	τριχοδέκτης	a genus of biting lice (family *Trichodectidae*) of domesticated mammals
tricho-epi-thelioma	τριχο-επιθηλίωμα	a bening epithelial tumor developing from the hair follicles, esp., on the face
tricho-	τρίχο-)τριξ / τριχός (gen.)	hair combining form (trichoid)
trichocyst	τριχοκύστις/η	any of the many tiny, rodlike, stinging and attachment organelles embedded in the ectoplasm of many ciliate protozoans
trichoid	(ο, η) τριχοειδής (το) τριχοειδές	resembling a hair; hairlike
trichology	τριχολογία	the scientic study concerned with the hair and its dieases
trichome	τρίχωμα	growth of hair; 1 any hairlike outgrowth from an epidermal cell of a plant, as a bristle, prickle, root hair, etc. 2 any of the threadlike structures, or filaments, of certain algae

tri-chromatic	τρίχρωμος, η, ο (adj.)	1 of having, or using three colors, as in three-color process in printing and photography 2 of, pertaining to, or having normal vision, in which the three primary colors are fully distinguished
tri-chromatism	τριχρωματισμός / τριχρωμία	color vision based on the perception of three primary colors, esp., red, green and blue; compare *Deuteranomaly; Protanomaly* – second and first anomaly
trichomonad	τριχο-μονάς/τριχο-μονάδος (gen.)	any of a genus (*Trichomonas*) of parasitic or commensal zooflagellates
tricho-moniasis	τριχο-μονίασις	infestation with trichomonads; esp., a) veginitis in women caused by a trichomonad (Trichomonas vaginalis) and characterized by a heavy discharge a) a disease of cows caused by a trichomonad (Trichomonas foetus) resulting in infertility or sometimes abortion
tricho-phyton	τριχόφυτον	1 a genus of dermotophytic fungi of the family (*Monilliaceae*) including several causing ringworm 2 any fungus of the genus (*Trichophyton*)
trichopteran	τριχόπτερα (τριχο πτερόν /πτερά (pl. – hair + wing)	caddis fly: any of the genus (*Trichoptera*) of small, mothlike insects with a soft body, long antennae and legs, along with two pairs of hairy, membranous wings
trichosis	τρίχωσις	any disease of the hair or caused by hair

tricho-sporon	τριχόσπορον	a genus of parasitic imperfect fungi (Monilliales) that includes the causative agent (*T. biegelii*) of white piedra
trichotomy	τριχοτομή	division into three parts, elements, groups, etc.
trichroism	τρ-χρωϊσμός/ τριχρωμία	the property that some crystals have of transmitting light of three different colors when looked at from three different directions
tricrotic	τρίκροτος, η, ο (adj.)	(rowed) with triple stroke (τρι + κροτείν- three + to strike) Physiol. designating or of a pulse having three separate rhythmic waves to each beat
tricycle	τρίκυκλον	a light three-wheeled vehicle, with one wheel in front and two in back, esp. one for children which is operated by pedals
tri-cyclic	τρίκυκλος, η, ο (adj.)	containing three fused rings of atoms in the molecule
tri-erarch	τριεράρχης/ τριέραρχος (τριήρης – trireme)	in ancient Greece, a) the commander of the trireme b) a person who built, outfitted, and maintained a trireme for the service of the state
tri-erarchy	τριεραρχία	1 the rank, authority, or duties of a trierarch 2 trierarchs collectively 3 the system of the trierarchs responsibilities
trigon	τρίγωνο(v)	triangle
trigonal	τριγωνικός, ή, ό (adj.)	triangular
trigonometry	τριγωνομετρία	the branch of mathematics that deals with the ratios between the sides of a right triangle with reference to either acute angle (trigonometric functions, etc.)
trigonous	τρίγωνος, η, ο (adj.)	of a triangle; having three angles or corners

tri-lingual or triglot	τρίγλωσσος, η, ο (adj.)	knowing ot speaking three languages
trilogy	τριλογία	a set of three related plays
trimerous	(ο, η) τριμερής (το) τριμερές (adj.)	1 having in sets of three: said of a flower; also written **3-merous** 2 having tarsi that are divided into three parts: said of some insects
trimetric	τριμετρικός, ή, ό (adj.)	1 having three metrical feet 2 orthrorhombic
trimetrogon	τριμετρόγωνον	a system of aerial photography in which three wide-angle cameras are used side by side to photograph the earth from horizon to horizon
tri-morphic	τρίμορφος, η, ο (adj.)	1 a substance that crystallizes in three distinct forms
tri-morphism	τρι-μορφισμός (τρι + μορφή –three + form/shape)	1 Crystallography the property of crystallizing in three distinct forms 2 Bot. the existence of three distinct forms of flowers, leaves, or other organs on the same plant or on different plants of the same species 3 Zool. the existence of three distinct forms of organs in the same species
trio	τρίο- τρία / τρεις	1 any group of three persons or things 2 Music a) a composition for three voices or three instruments b) the three performers of such composition c) the middle section of a minuet, scherzo, etc., orig. written in three voices or parts
trioecious	τρίο + οίκος – three + home /house – three + house	having male, female, and bisexual flowers on separate plants

triple	τριπλούς / τριπλούν	1 consisting of or including three; threefold 2 done, used, said, etc. three times. 3 Music containing three (or a multiple of three) beats to the measure [triple time]
triplo-blastic	τριπλούς βλαστός	Zool. of, or pertaining to the metazoan body structure, except that of cnidarians, with three basic cellular layers, the ectoderm, the endoderm, and the mesoderm
triploid	(ο, η) τριπλοειδής (το) τριπλοειδές	Biol. having three times the haploid number of chromosomes; a triploid cell or organism
triplets	τρίδυμα/τριπλά	birth of three babies of a single pregnancy
tripod	τρίποδο(ν)	having three parts, legs
triptych	τρίπτυχος, η, ο (adj.)	1 an ancient writing tablet of three leaves hung together 2 a set of three panels with pictures, designs, or carvings, often hinged so that the two side panels can be folded over the center
tris-kai-deka-phobia	δέκατριοφοβία (δέκα + τρία (τρις + δέκα) + φόβος – ten + three + fear)	extreme fear of the number 13 (thirteen)
triskelion	τρισκελές (τρία/τρις + σκέλος/ σκέλη (pl.) - leg/ legs)	three-legged; a design, usually symbolic, consisting of three curved branches, or three bent legs or arms radiating from the center; also; **triskele** (triskel)
tris-megistus	τριμέγιστος (lit. three times great)	see Hernes Trimegistus
trismus	τρισμός (τρίζειν – to gnash; chirp)	continuous contraction of the muscles of the jaw, specif. as a symptom of tetanus, or lockjaw; grinding or gnashing of the the teeth

tris-octa-hedron	τρεις/ τρις - οκτάεδρον	an isometric solid figure or crystal consisting of an octahedron that has each face divided into three faces
tristich	τρίστυχον (neuter of τρίστυχος)	a group or stanza consisting of three lines of verse; triplet
tristichous	τρίστυχος, η, ο (adj.)	1 arranged in three rows 2 Bot. arranged in three vertical rows, as leaves
trisyllable	τρισύλλαβος	a word of three syllables
tritoma	τρίτομος, η, ο (adj.) (τρίτομα, pl. of neuter)	cut three times; any of the genus [Kniphofia] of African plants of the lily family, with dense spikes of red to yellow tubular flowers in the autumn
triton	τρίτος, τρίτη, τριτον/ο)adj.)	(Gr. neuter of tritos/τρίτος) third; the nucleus of the tritium atom containing one proton and two neutrons, used as a projectile in nuclear reactions
triumph	θρίαμβος	victory, success, achievement
triumphalism	θριαμβολογία	a proud, often arrogant confidence in the validity and success of a set of beliefs, often, specifically religious beliefs
triumphant	θριαμβευτικός, ή, ό (adj.)	victorious; accomplished; successful
trochaic	τροχαϊκός, ή, ό (adj.) (τρέχειν/ τροχός - to run/ wheel)	of or made up of trochees; 1 a trocaic line of poetry
trochaism	τροχασμός	fast walking of a horse but not as fast as galloping
trochal	τροχός	Zool. resembling a wheel

trochee	τροχαίος, α, ο (adj.)	running; a metrical foot consisting in Greek and Latin verse, as of one long syllable following by one short one, or, as in English verse, one accented syllable followed by an unaccented one In Greek the word: trochee/τροχαίος, also is defined as: one dealing with moving vehicles
trochilus	τρόχιλος /τροχίλος	a runner; 1 any of various Old World birds, esp.., warblers 2 any of certain hummingbirds
trochlea	τροχαλία	Anat. a pulley-shaped part or structure, as the lower part of the humerous which articulates with a corresponding part of the ulna
trochoid	(ο, η) τροχοεϊδής (το) τροχοεϊδές (τροχός + είδος – wheel + type/kind)	round like a wheel; Geom. any cycloid, having a wheel-like rotary motion on an axis, as a joint
troche-phore	τροχοφόρος (τροχός + φέρειν or φορεύς – wheel + to bear/bearer)	a free-swimming ciliate larva or several invertebrate groups, including many marine annelid worms, mollucks, brachiopods and nemetreans
trochocardia	τροχο-καρδία	rotation of the heart on its axis
trochoid	(ο, η) τροχοειδής (το) τροχοειδές)	resembling a wheel
troglo-dyte	τρωγλοδύτης (τρώγλη + δύτης – cave, hole + dweller)	1 any of the prehistoric people who lived in caves; caveman 2 a person who chooses to live alone in seclusion 3 an anthropoid ape

Trojan horse/hippos	Δούρειος Ίππος	1 Gr. legend a giant wooden horse where Greek soldiers were hidden inside, that is left at the gates of Troy as a gift to the Trojans. When the Trojans brought it inside the city, the soldiers came out at night and opened the gates for the rest of the Greek army to get in and destroy the city 2 any person, group, or thing that seeks to subvert a nation, company, or organization, etc., from within
Trojan war	Τρωϊκός Πόλεμος	Gr. legend the ten-year war waged by the Greeks against Troy, in order to avenge the abduction of King Menelaus's wife Helen by the prince of Troy, Paris
-trophic	(τροφή-food; nutrition)	suffix forming adjectives relating to a specified kind of nutrition (phytotrophic / eating greens, plants)
trophic	τροφικός, ή, ό (adj.)	pertaining to nutrition
trophic nerves	τροφικά νεύρα	specialized nerves dealing with growth, nourishment, and repair of body tissue
tropho- or troph-	τροφή	food, nutrition; combining form (trophic; trophoblast)
trophoblast	τροφο-βλαστός	a layer of nutritive ectoderm outside of the blastoderm, by which the fertilized ovum is attached to the uterine wall and the developing embryo receives its nurishment
trophology	τροφολογία	science of body nutrition
trophonosis/ trophonosos	τροφονόσος (τροφή + νόσος- nutrition + disease)	any nutritional disease

trophy	τρόπαιον /o a token of an enemy's defeat	1 in ancient Greece and Rome, a memorial of victory erected on the battlefield or in some public place, orig. a display of captured arms or other spoils b) a representation of this on a medal 2) a lion's skin, deer's head, etc., displayed as evidence of hunting prowess 3 a) a prize, usually a silver cup, awarded in a sports contest or other competition b) anything serving as a reminder, as of a triumph
-trophy	-τροφία (τρέφειν –to nurish, feed)	suffix forming nouns indicating nutrition, nourishment, growth (hypertrophy/υπερτροφία – excessive development of an organ or part, specif.: increase in bulk, as by thinkening of muscle fibers) without multiplication of parts
tropic	τροπικός, ή, ό (adj.) (belonging to a turn (of the sun at the solstices)	1 Astron. either of two circles of the celestial sphere parallel to the celestial equator, one, the **Tropic of Cancer**, north, and the other the **Tropic of Capricorn,** south: they are limits of the apparent north-and-south journey of the sun determined by the obliquity of the ecliptic 2 Geog. Ither of two parallels of latitude (**Tropic of Cancer and Tropic of Capricorn**) situated on either side of the earth's equator that correspond to the astronomical tropics 3) (also T-) the region of the earth lying between these latitudes; **Torrid Zone**; also of the tropics; tropical

-tropic	- τροπή/ τρέπειν – turning/ to turn	suffix forming adjectives meaning: turning toward or from, changing because of, or otherwise responding to a (specified kind of) stimulus (phototropic)
tropical cyclone	τροπικός κυκλών κυκλώνος (gen.) /κυκλώνας (mod. Gr.)	Metereol. a cyclone, originating over tropical seas, ranging in diameter from c.96 to 1, 609 km(c. 60 to 1,000 mi.) and developing winds up to c. 321 km/hr. (c. 200 mi/hr.)
tropism	τροπισμός	1 Biol. involuntary orientation by an organism or one of its parts (as by differential growth) toward or away from a source of stimulation 2 the positive or negative, attraction of a plant or sessile animal toward, or away from, a stimulus, as in the turning of a sunflower toward the light
-tropism	τροπή/ τρέπειν	suffix forming nouns indicating a specified way of turning (heliotropism/ turning toward the sun)
tympanic	τυμπαικός, ή, ό (adj.)	1 of or like a drum or drumhead 2 Anat., Zool. of the tympanum, esp. the eardrum
tympanic membrane	τυμπανική μεμβράνη	a tightly stretched membrane separating the auditory canal from the middle ear
tympanites	τυμπανίτις/ τυμπανίτιδα	abdominal distention due to accumulation gas in the intestinal tract or peritoneal cavity
tympanitis	τυμπανίτις / τυμπανίτιδα	otitis: inflammation of the ear, esp. otitis media of the middle ear
tympanoplasty	τυμπανο-πλαστική	a reparative surgical operation performed on the middle ear

tympanostomy	τυμπανοστόμιον/ τυμπανοστομή	myringotomy: incision of the tympanic membrane; also called **tympanotomy**/τυμπανοτομή
tympanum	τύμπανο(v)	1 eardrum 2 the musical instrument
type	τύπος	(a figure; archetype; model) 1 a person, thing, or event that represents or symbolizes another, esp. another that is thought will appear later; symbol; token; sign 2 the general form, structure, plan, style, etc., characterizing the members of a class or group 3 a kind, class, or group having distinguishing characteristics in common [a new type of car, etc.] 4 a perfect example; model; pattern; archetype 5 Agric. The combination of characters of an animal or breed that make it most suitable for a particular use [beef type; dairy type; paultry type, etc.] 6 Biol. a) a single specimen designated as the one on which the original description and name of a taxon has been based b) Type Genus or Type Species 7 Math. the simplest of a set of equivalent forms 8 Printing a) a rectangular piece of metal, or (esp., formerly) wood, with a raised letter, figure, etc., in reverse on its upper end which when inked and pressed against a piece of paper or other material, leaves an ink impression of its face b) a character or characters formed electronically and produced by a computer printer c) photographic reproductions of print used in photocomposition

typhlitis	τυφλίτις/τυφλότητα (Anc. Gr.) /τύφλα (Mod. Gr.)	inflaμmation of the eye; / partial blindness
typhlo-	τυφλός, ή, ό (adj.)	blind
typhlosis	τύφλωσις/η	blindness
typhoid	(ο, η) τυφοειδής, (το) τυφοειδές (adj.)	any typhuslike disorder; an acute infectious disease caused by a bacillus (Salmonella typhi), it is acquired by ingesting food or water contaminated by excreta
typhomania	τυφομανία	delirium caused by typhoid fever
typhus	τύφος	any one of a group of diseases caused by a microorganism (rickettsiae)
typical	τυπικός, ή, ό (adj.)	serving as a type; symbolic
typo-	τύπο (ς)	combining form, also short for typographical error
typographer	τυπογράφος	one skilled in typography, printer, compositor, etc.
typographical	τυπογραφικός, ή, ό (adj.)	having to do with the setting of type, printing, typing, inputting, etc.
typography	τυπογραφία	1 the art or process of printing from type 2 the arrangement, style, or general appearance of the printed matter
typology	τυπολογία	the study of types, symbols, or symbolism
tyrannical	τυραννικός, ή, ό (adj.)	of or suited to a tyrant; despotic; arbitrary
tyranny	τυραννία	oppressive and unjust government; despotism
tyrant	τύραννος	an absolute ruler; an oppressive, cruel ruler

U

Ulcer	ελκος	abscess; 1 an open sore (other than a wound) on the skin or somemucous membrane, as the lining of the stomach (peptic ulcer), characterized by the disintegration of the tissue and, usually, the discharge of pus 2 corrupting or festering condition or influence
ulcerogenic	(ο, η) ελκογενής) το) ελκογενές (adj.)	tending to produce or develop ulcers or ulceration (an ulcerogenic drug)
ulitis	ουλίτις/ουλίτιδα	gum inflammation
ur- or uro-	ούρο- (ούρα (pl.)	urine combining form (uric; urology)
uracratia	ούρα-κρατείν/ to retain, hold	inability to retain urine
uraniscus	ουρανίσκος	palate
uremia or uraemia	ούρα αίμα/ουρεμία	poisoning from urinary substances in the blood
ureter	ουρητήρ/ ουρητήρας	the tube leading from the kidneys to the bladder
ureteritis	ουρηθρίτις / ουρηθρίτιδα	inflammation of the uterer
uretero-	ουρητήρ-ουρητήρος	ureter, combining form (uretography)
uterocele	ουρητήρ + κήλη/ ureter + hernia	cystic dilation of the lower part of a ureter into the bladder
ureterogram	ουρητηρό-γραμμα/ ουρητηρο-γράφημα	an x-ray photograph of the ureter after injection of a radiopaque substance
ureterolysis	ουρητηρόλυσις /η	a surgical procedure to free a ureter from abnormal adhesions or surrounding tissue (as in retroperitoneal fibrosis)
uteroplasty	ουρητηρο-πλαστική	plastic surgery performed on the ureter
ureterorrhaphy	ουρητηροραφή	the surgical procedure of suturing the ureter

ureteroscope	ουρητηροσκόπιον/ο	an endoscope for examining visually by passing an instrument into the interior of the ureter
ureterolith/ uretolith	ούρον-λίθος/ ουρόλιθος- urine-stone	stone in the ureter
urethra	ουρήθρα	tube carrying the urine from the bladder to the outside
urethritis	ουρηθρίτις/ ουρηθρίτιδα	inflammation of the urethra
urethroscope	ουρηθροσκόπιον /ο	an endoscope used for viewing the interior of the urethra
urethrotomy	ουρεθροτομή	surgical incision into the urethra in order to relieve a stricture
uretic	ουρητικός, ή, ό (adj.)	promoting urination
uric acid	ουρικό οξύ	organic substance of a solid waste product contained in urine
urinate	ουρείν/ουρώ	discharge urine
urine	ούρο(ν) /ούρα (pl.)	fluid end product of kidney activity
urinometer	ουρόμετρον/ο	a small hydrometer used to determine the specific gravity of urine
urodynamics	ουροδυναμική	the hydrodynamics of the urinary tract
uro-erythrin	ουρο-ερυθρίνη	a pink or reddish pigment found in many pathological urines and also frequently in normal urine in small quantity
urogastrone	ούρο + γάστρο(ν) −urine + abdomen	a polyptetide that has been isolated from urine and inhibits gastric secretion; compare Enteronegastrone
urogenital system	ουρογεννητικό σύστημα	genitourinary tract: the system of organs comprising those concerned with the production and excretion of urine and those concerned with reproduction

urography	ουρογραφία	radiography of a part of the urinary tract (as a kidney or ureter) after injection of a radiopaque substance
uro-gynecologist	ουρο-γυναικολόγος	a specialist in urogynecology
uro-gynecology	ουρο-γυναικολογία	the branch of medicine dealing with the urological problems (as urinary incontinence) of women
uro-lagnia	ουρολαγνεία/ ουρολαγνία	sexual excitement associated with urination
urolith	ουρόλιθος	urinary calculus: a calculus occurring in any portion of the urinary tract, and esp., in the pelvis of the kidney; also called urinary stone
urolithiasis	ουρολιθίασις/η	a condition distinguished by the formation or presence of calculi in the urinary tract
urologist	ουρολόγος	medical specialist dealing with the organs involved in the urinating system
urology	ουρολογία	branch of medicine dealing with the diseases of the urinary system
uro-patho-genic	(ο, η) ουρο-παθογενής (το) ουροπαθογενές (adj.)	of, relating to, or being a pathogen (as some strains of E. coli) of the urinary tract also **uropathogen**
uropathy	ουροπάθεια	a disease of the urinary or urogenital organs
uro-radiology	ουροραδιολογία	radiology of the urinary tract
uroscopy	ουροσκόπησις /η	radiology and examination of urine in order to determine disease
urosepsis	ουροσήψις / ουροσήψη	a toxic condition caused by the extravasation of urine into bodily tissues
urostomy	ουροστόμιον /ο	a surgical procedure to create a passage to eliminate urine from the body; an ostomy

V

The sound V in Greek is represted by the letter B
(βήτα) pronounced (vita) (see: letter Bb)

X

Xanthelasma	εξάνθημα- ξάνθωμα	a fatty irregular yellowish patch on the eyelid
xanthic	ξανθικός, ή, ό/ ξανθωπός, ή, ό (adj.)	yellow, blondish
Xanthippe	Ξανθίππη	fifth cen. BC wife of Socrates, the prototype of the quarrelsome, nagging wife
xantho-cyanopsia	ξανθό-κυανοψία	type of color blindness when a patient is unable to differentiate between green and red
xanth-/xantho-	ξανθό	yellow, blond
xantho-chromia	ξανθο-χρωμία	xanthochromic/ yellowish discoloration
xanthochromic	ξανθόχρωμος, η, ο (adj.)	yellowish discoloration
xanthoma	ξάνθωμα/(ε) ξάνθημα	a fatty irregular yellow patch or nodule on the skin that is associated esp. with disturbances of the cholesterol metabolism; a yellow tumor or growth
xantho-matosis	ξανθο-μάτωσις /η	a condition marked by the presence of multiple xanthomas
xantho-matous	ξάνθωμα / ξανθώματος (gen.)	of, relating to, marked by, the presence of multiple xanthomas/ yellow (often benign) tumors or growths
xathopsia	ξανθοψία	1 yellow vision, eyesight disease 2 a visual disturbance in which objects appear yellow

xanthosis	ξάνθισμα/ ξάνθωσις/η	jaundice; 1 a yellowish pigmentation of the skin, tissues, and certain body fluids caused by the deposition of bile pigments, which follows interference with normal production and discharge of bile (as in some liver diseases) or excessive breakdown of red blood cells (as after internal hemorrhage or in certain hemolytic states) 2 any abnormal condition (as hepatitis A or lepto-spirosis) that is characterized by jaundice
xanthophyl	ξανθό / φύλλο/ ξανθοφύλλη	a yellow, crystalline pigment found in plants
xanthous	ξανθός, ή (ειά), ό (adj.)	yellow, gold, blond/ blonde (fem.)
xen- or –xeno-	ξυνός, ή, ό (adj.)	foreign; stranger; ombining forms [xenophobia], also, before a vowel, xen- (xenia)
xenia	(φίλο-ξενία (φίλος + ξένος friend + stranger)	hospitality; xenia: Biol. the immediate influence of pollen from one strain of a plant upon the endosperm of another strain, resulting in hybrid characters in the form, color, etc., of the resulting growth, as in the colors of corn grains
xenobiotic	ξενο-βιωτικός, η, ό (adj)	designating or of a chemical substance that is foreign, and usually harmful, to living organisms
xeno-diagnosis	ξενο-διάγνωσις /η (foreign + diagnosis)	the detection of a parasite (as of humans) by feeding supposedly infected material (as blood) to a suitable intermediate host (as an insect) and later examining the intermediate host for the parasite

xeno-genesis	ξενογένεσις /η	Biol. 1 a) spontaneous generation b) alternation of generations 2 the supposed production of an individual completely different from either of its parents
xenomania	ξενομανία	excessive love for anything foreign
xenon	ξένον (ξένος, η, ο (ν) (adj.)	xenon/the neuter form of the adjective, meaning: foreigner; stranger
xenophobia	ξενοφοβία	extreme fear of anything foreign
xenophobic	ξενόφοβος, η, ο (adj.)	having extreme fear of strangers or foreigners
xenophthalmia	ξενοφθαλμία	inflammation of the eye due to a foreign body
xeno-trophic	ξενοτροπικός, η, ό (adj.)	replicating or reproducing only in cells other than those of the host species (xenotrophic viruses)
xer- or xero-	ξηρός/ξερός, ή, ό (adj.)	dry; arid, combining form (xeric; xerophthalmia)
xeransis	ξήρανσις/η	the process of drying
xerasia	ξηρασία	dryness
xeric	ξηρικός/ ξερικός, ή, ό (adj.)	1 of, pertaining to, or having dry or desertlike conditions 2 xerophytic
xero-derma	ξηρό + δέρμα	dry skin; a disease of the skin distinguished by dryness and roughness, a fine scaly desquamation; also called Ichthyosis
xerocheilia	ξηρο-χείλια/ ξηρά χείλη	dry lips
xerography	ξηρογραφία	1 a process for copying graphic matter by the action of light on an electrically charged surface in which the latent image is developed with a resinous powder 2 Xeroradiography

xero-mammography	ξηρο-μαοτογραφία (μαστός + γράφειν- breast + to write)	xeroradiography of the breast
xero-ophthalmia	ξηρό + οφθαλμός – dry + eye	a dry, thickened lusterless condition of the eyeball resulting esp. from a severe deficiency of vitamin A
xero-mammogram	ξηρομαστογράφημα	an image made by means of xeromammography
xero-philous	ξηρό & φίλος	capable of living in very dry climate; dry climate lover/friend
xerophobia	ξηροφοβία	excessive fear of very dry places, as deserts
xero-radiography	ξηρο-ραδιο-λογία	radiography used esp. in mammographic screening for breast cancer that produces an image using x-rays, the same way or a similar way to the way an image is produced by light in xerography
xerosis	ξήρωσις /η	abnormal dryness of a body part or tissue (as the skin)
xerostomia	ξηροστομία	dryness of the mouth
Xerrxes	Ξέρξης	c. 519–465 BC, Persia (486–465): son of Darius I; known as the Great
Xx (xi, ksi)	Ξξ (ξι)	fourteenth letter of the Greek alphabet
xiphias	ξιφίας	swordfish
xiphoid	(ο, η) ξιφοειδής, (το) ξιφοειδές (adj.)	sword-shaped cartilage
xylic	ξύλινος, η, ο (adj.)	wooden
xylo-	ξύλο-	wood, combining form
xyloid	(ο, η) ξυλοειδής (το) ξυλοειδές (adj.)	pertaining to wood; wooden
xylon	ξύλον/ο	wood; stick
xylophagous	ξυλοφάγος	eating or destroying wood
xylophone	ξυλόφωνον/ο	a musical instrument consisting of a series of wooden bars

xyster	ξύστρα	a surgical instrument for scraping bones. Also, in Gr. the word, ξύστρα, means: sharpener
xyston	ξυστός, ή, ό(ν) (adj.)	pertaining to scraping

Y

Yiayia	Γιαγιά /γιαγιά	grandmother in Greek (this word is dedicated to all Greek American grandchildren (including my own,) who fondly call their grandmothers "Yiayia")
yogurt	γιαούρτι	a thick, semisolid food made from milk fermented by a bacterium (**Lactobacillus bulgaricus**): it is now often prepared with various flavors: also: yo'ghurt/ yo'ghourt
Ypsilon	Υ,υ/ ύψιλον	the twentieth letter of the Gr. alphabet

Note: All Greek words starting with YU/ Yυ, were accented with the breathing sign daseia/δασεία (') which in English became an Hh. Look for them under the letter Hh (as hysreria; hysteron, hypo, originally; 'υστερία; 'υστερον, etc.)

-
Z

Zz	Ζζ (Ζήτα)	sixth letter of the Greek alphabet
zeal	ζήλος	ardor; intense enthusiasm
zealot	ζηλωτής	a zealous follower
zephyr	ζέφυρος	the west wind; a soft, gentle breeze
Zephyrus	Ζέφυρος	the west wind personified in myth. as a god
zither	κιθάρα	lute, any of the of a family of musical instruments with strings stretched across a flat soundboard, also, in Gr. kithara/ κιθάρα is guitar

zestocausis	ζεστόκαυσις /η (hot/burn)	to burn with steam
zodiac	ζώδιον/ ο- ζώδια (pl.)	1 circle of animals (zodiac circle/ ζωδιακός κύκλος 2 an imaginary belt in the heavens extending for about eight degrees on either side of the apparent path of the sun and including the paths of the moon and the major planets: it is divided into twelve equal parts or signs, each named for a different constellation 3 a figure or diagram representing the zodiac and its signs: used in astrology
zoa	ζώα (pl. of zoon)	animals
Zoe	Ζωή	life; also, a girl's name
zoic	(o, η) ζωώδης (το) ζωώδες/ ζωϊκός, ή, ό (adj.)	pertainingg to animals
zoanthropy	ζωανθρωπία	1 Psychol. one believing is an animal and adopts animal behavior 2 the belief that one is, or can become, a beast
zoetic	ζωτικός, ή, ό (adj.)	pertaining to life
zone	ζώνη	belt, also, any of the five latitudinal divisions of earth's surface
zonesthesia	ζώνη + αίσθησις – belt + sensation	sensation of tightness around the waist
zoon or zoo -	ζώο(ν) / ζώο-	animal, combining form (zoology)
zoo-geography	ζωο-γεωγραφία	science dealing with the geographical distribution of animals
zoo-graphy	ζωο-γραφία	branch of zoology dealing with description of animals, their characteristics, habits, etc.
zool-	ζώο + λόγος	combining form as in zoology, etc.

zoo-latry	ζωολατρεία	worship of animals
zoological	ζωολογικός, ή, ό (adj.)	a place where a collection of wild animals reside
zoologist	ζωολόγος	an expert in zoology
zoology	ζωολογία	science dealing with the life, structure, growth, classification of the animals
zoo-parasite	παρασιτικό-ζώο (παρασιτικός, ή, ό (adj.) parasite)	parasitic animal
zoo-phagous	ζωοφάγος	carnivorous; feeding on animals
zoo-philism	ζωοφιλισμός	extreme love for animals
zoophobia	ζωοφοβία	abnormal fear of animals
zoophyte	ζωόφυτος	any animal having the appearance as coral/sponge etc.
zoonoses	ζώο & νόσος ζωονόσος/ animal&illness	diseases of animals accidentally affect man
zoosis	ζώωσις/η	disease in man carried by animals
zygo-	ζυγό(ς)	yoke, combining form
zygoma	ζύγωμα	yoking two together, coupling
zyme-	ζύμη	leaven/ferment/enzyme; also, a combining form
zymic	ζυμικός, ή, ό (adj.)	relating to fermentation
zymo-	ζύμο-	fermentation, combining form
zymogenesis	ζυμογένεσις/η	the process when a zymogen becomes an enzyme
zymology	ζυμολογία	the science dealing with fermentation
zymoma	ζύμωμα	kneading and preparation of leaven
zymotic	ζυμωτικός, ή, ό (adj.)	causing to ferment
zymosis	ζύμωσις/η	kneading; fermenting
zymurgy	ζύμη + εργο/ εργασία	the branch of chemistry that deals with fermentation, as brewing

These and a noumerous additional words cover many pages of English dictionaries. The contribution of the total effect and influence of the Greek language, ethos, civilization, culture; scientific and mathematematical discoveries, etc.; and, most importantly, the constitutive cultural system of society, however, are incalculable.

People who have studied the Greek language and its history appreciate the foundation they had acquired which helped them in their future professions, being a doctor, a scientist, a teacher, a lawyer, an economist, or just acquiring the skills to understand and handle the English language much easier by using correct grammar, syntax, in short, developing incredible linguistic skills!

For those who do not read Greek, and wish to read the Greek vocabulary as well, they could study the Greek alphabet that follows. The ones who already know Greek and wish to have a refresher course, at the end, there is a bonus section, the text of my "Greek for Travelers."

GREEK ALPHABET

Key to Pronunciation

Corresponding Sound and Name

Αα	A ã	as in:	father	Άλφα - alpha
Β β	V v	as in:	vase, vote	Βήτα -vita
Γγ	Y y/gh	as in:	year, yet	Γάμμα - ghamma/yamma
Δδ	th (harsh)	as in:	this, that	Δέλτα - delta/thelta
Εε	ĕ	as in:	elephant, pet, red	Εψιλον - epsilon
Ζζ	Zz	as in:	zone, zoo	Ζήτα - zeta/zita
Ηη	ē	as in:	see, me, it	Ήτα - eta/ita
Θ θ	h(soft)	as in:	theater, theory, thesis	Θήτα - theta
Ι ι	ē	as in:	see, me, it	Γιώτα - iota/yiota
Κ κ	K k	as in:	king, kite, kind	Κάππα - kappa
Λ λ	L l	as in:	lake, light, love	Λάμδα - lamtha
Μ μ	M	as in:	mother, meat, me	Μι - me
Ν ν	N n	as in:	no, name, none	Νι - nee/ni
Ξ ξ	X(ks)	as in:	tax, accent, taxi	Ξι - ksi/xi
Ο ο	O o	as in:	over, oh, old	Όμικρον - omikron
Π π	P p	as in:	part, pear, poor	Πι - pi
Ρ ρ	R r	as in:	right, red, role	Ρω - rho
Σ σ ς	S s	as in:	sight, save, stop	Σίγμα - sigma
Ττ	T t	as in:	top, tough, ten	Ταφ - taf
Υυ	E ē	as in:	see, me, it	Ύψιλον - epsilon/ipsilon

Φ φ	F f	as in:	file, fry, foot	Φι - phi/fi
Χ χ	H h/ch	as in:	hero, hat, half	Χι - hi/chi
Ψ ψ	ps	as in:	tops, collapse, pepsi	Ψι - psi
Ω ω	O o	as in:	over, oh, Ωmega	Ωμέγα - omega

The following are a few comments from my lectures/articles and statements by others.

A FEW REMARKS AND STATEMENTS

I have taught for many years and have known students who loved to be fluent in Greek and others who would rather do something else than spend a few hours learning Greek.

That was of course true until they realized how much they were gaining from learning Greek, and how the language helped them with their own language. The understanding they were gaining of structure, mechanism, syntactical and linguistic elements was helping them comprehend English much better and apply those elements with confidence.

As we all know, Greek and Latin are the mothers of all languages. Especially, in some professions (medicine, mathematics, physics, science, economics, technology, etc.) most of the terms derive from those two aforementioned languages, with Greek playing the most prominent role. Besides the contribution of both languages to the enrichment of other tongues, the most significant contribution, to those who really study them, is the knowledge they gain of the aforementioned fundamental components.

As the German philosopher Goethe said, he had heard the Gospel in many languages; however, when he heard it in Greek, it seemed that the moon had appeared in the sky.

The famous French poet Claude Fauriel described the Greek language as the language that fits together the unified quality of German, the clarity of French, the beauty of Spanish, and the musicality of Italian.

Nikephoros Vrettakos, the "Poet of Peace, Brotherhood, and Solidarity," stated, "When I die and go to heaven, I will talk to the angels in Greek, because they only understand the language of music and brotherly love."

The writer Helen Keller compared the "preciseness and perfection of the human thought in the Greek language" to the " most perfect of the musical instruments, the violin."

Shiller, the great German philosopher, historian, poet, cursed the Greeks and said, "You have discovered everything: science, philosophy, democracy, politics, physics, geometry, theater, tragedy…you have left nothing for us to discover!"

Of course that is not true today. Many great things were discovered and invented in later centuries; however, the contribution of those discoveries have the inprints of the Greek language. As Bill Gates said in one of his lectures, modern technology borrowed principles and ideas of the ancient Greeks, and if we want to advance further, we should go back to those principles.

I could bring up many more statements of politicians, philosophers, historians, scientists, etc., who very eloquently lauded the contributions of the Greek language and profound thought! I will include very few of countless comments of former students who truly appreciated the benefits they received by learning the language!

One of my students, **a college professor**, once told me, "Greek is like acquiring a sixth sense, the only difference is **you appreciate it when you gain it and not when you lose it**." (The poor guy was losing his eyesight, so he spoke from experience.)

A Harvard professor taking Greek stated, "I'd rather be able to read and understand a page of the original *Odyssey and Iliad* than read the entire translation."

Another former student of mine, an English literature professor, has recently written to me the following. I summarize it since it was very lengthy!

I wanted to write to you for so long, however, I suspect was embarrassed to admit that in your class, I not only became fluent in Greek, but most importantly, understood what the English language was all about and that your class gave me confidence in the profession I had chosen.

I don't know if you remember me. In the mid-eighties, I was studying for my doctorate in English literature. I had taken ancient Greek previously, and when I saw, in the Hellenic Chronicle, that you were offering modern Greek at Hellenic College, I decided to take it. That was the best decision of my life. The benefits I derived were priceless. The simplified, methodical, and analytical way: the grammar; syntax; structure; mechanism and the relation/counterpart of English presented was not only easy to absorb but also motivated the student to master everything he/she learned in Greek and apply it it to English.

You were very polite not to embarrass by correcting a student of his/her mistakes in English. You were giving examples and letting the class point out the correct phrase/sentence. As an English major, I knew, most of the times, the correct way, the pronouns, adverbs, tenses, participles, gerunds, abstract nouns, etc., were used; I could not, however, for the life of me, explain with certainty or confidence why it was so. For example, when a student said "our futures," you asked him, "How many futures do we have? Future, past, or present are only one. The *our* makes it plural." I will remember that as long as I live! When I recently heard a politician saying "I will work hard for your children's futures," I had to laugh, remembering that statement you made! I truly say before that class I had to think when to use the correct pronoun and sometimes I suppose I was guessing, I did not have that foundation that the Greek language gave me to know how to distinguish the subject from the object, and that's why I am grateful for taking your class!

Evelyn Wells

I've decided to shorten Evelyn's very long letter, and although she insisted that the points she made would have helped others, I felt it was too lengthy for the dictionary. I feel gratification when I know that my dedication to teaching and my attempt to make the language a pleasure to learn found fertile soil!

Matina Psyhogeos
The Psyhogeos Program

IF YOU KNOW ENGLISH
THEN YOU KNOW GREEK

The article below was previously published in a British magazine. The words in red are exclusively English; the rest are Greek.

The genesis of classical drama was not symptomatic. An euphoria of charismatic and talented protagonists showed fantastic scenes of historic episodes. The prologue, the theme and the epilogue comprised the trilogy of drama, which synthesis, analysis and synopsis characterized the phraseology of the text.

The syntax and phraseology used by scholars, academicians, tragedians, and philosophers had many grammatical idioms and idiosyncracies.

The protagogonists paradoxically used pseudonyms. Anonymity was a syndrome that characterized the theatrical atmosphere.

The panoramic fantacy, the mystique, the melody, the aesthetics, the use of cosmetic epithets are characteristics of drama.

Many epistemologists of physics, aerodymamics, acoustics, electromagnetic, cannot analyze–explain the ideal and isometric acoustics, Hellenic theaters, even today.

There were many categories of drama: classical drama, melodrama, satiric, epic, comedy, etc.

The syndrome of xenophobia or dyslexia was overcome by the pathos of the actors, who practiced methodically and emphatically. Acrobatics were also euphoric.

There was a plethora of anecdotal themes, with which the acrobats would electrify the audience with scenes from mythical and hystorical episodes. Some theatric episodes were characterized as scandalous and blasthemous.

Pornography, bigamy, hemophilia, nymphomania, polyandry, polygamy and heterosexuality were dramatized in a pedagogical way, so the mysticism about them would not cause phobia or anathema, or taken as anomaly but through logic, dialogue and analysis, skepticism and the pathetic or cryptic mystery behind them would be dispelled.

It is historically and chronologically proven that theater emphasized pedagogy, idealism and harmony. Paradoxically, it also energized patriotism a phenomenon that symbolized ethnical character and phenomenal heroism!

Mike (the writer of the article)

As you can see, only very few verbs and of course conjuctions, prepositions, and articles were needed to write this syntactically correct article and make perfect sense. This was forwarded to me by my friend Vasilia Laskaris!

REFERENCES

Webster's New World College Dictionary (Third Edition, 1997)

Lexiko of the Modern Greek Language - Λεξικό Νέας Ελληνικής Γλώσσας

G. Babinioti *Γ. Μπαμπινιώτη* (1998)

Analytical Greek Lexicon Harold K Moulton (Revised Edition, 1978)

Oxford American Thesaurus of Current English Christine A. Lindberb (1999)

*Lexiko of Contemporary Greek Demotic Language/ Λεξικό της Σύγχρονης Ελληνικής Δημοτικής Γλώσσας Εμμ. Κριαρά-*Emmanuel Kriara

Medical Dictionary (Barnes and Noble books, a Division of Harper and Row Publishers, NY (1977)

The Story of Christianity David Bentley Hart (Metro Books, NY)

Black's Law Dictionary (Fifth Edition)

Encyclopedeia Brittanica

Merriam-Webster's Medical Dictionary Learner's Dictionary.com

Greek English Lexicon Abridged Edition Liddell and Scott

Web Sites

Wikipedia
Wikidictionary
AWAD
Lexicus

ADDITIONAL INFORMATION

As a bonus, for those who would like to review and also for anyone wishing to learn a little Greek, the text "Greek for Travelers" is included!

1. Introduction
    a. Preface.
    b. Brief history of the country you are about to visit.
    c. General information on Greece. (area; population; capital city; religion; currency; time; climate; electricity; helpful hints regarding shopping;sightseeing;and more).

2. Greek Language
    a. Alphabet; basic rules of grammar.
    b. Common expressions, vocabulary and everyday phrases.

3. Communicating in Greek
    a. Preparations for the trip
    b. At the airport/Departure
    c. At the airport/Arrival
    d. Passport Control
    e. Baggage

    f.   Customs

    g.   Information Desk/Currency Exchange

    h.   Transportation - general - means of transportation (e.g., bus, train, taxi, rent a car, plane, boat...)

4.   Accommodation/Hotel

5.   Restaurant/Taverna
    a.   General information
        –   foods (appetizers; Greek specialities; variety of meats; soups; vegetables; salads; cheeses; fruits)
        –   beverages; drinks; desserts.
    b.   Pastry/Coffee Shops
        –   Greek and international pastries
        –   Coffees; snacks; beverages; drinks

6.   Shopping
    a.   General information
    b.   Kiosks/newstands
    c.   Super Market
    d.   Green grocer's/butcher shop/bakery
    e.   Clothes; shoes; leather goods shops
    f.   Jewelery/watchmakers
    g.   Bookstore/stationery
    h.   Music shop
    i.   Souvenirs
    j.   Electrical appliances

7.   Services
    a.   Beauty salon/barber shop
    b.   Bank
    c.   Post office
    d.   Telephoning
    e.   Dry cleaning/laundry

8. Medical Services
    a. Emergency/hospital
    b. Visiting a Doctor/treatment
    c. Dentist
    d. Optician
    e. Problems/accidents/complaints/police

9. Entertainment/Recreation
    a. Theaters/movies
    b. Night clubs
    c. Festivals/concerts

10. Sports Events/Hobbies/Interests
    a. Golf/tennis/ski
    b. Indoor; outdoor sports
    c. Sports games
    d. On the beach
    e. Camping and walking

11. Social Life
    a. Meeting new people/friends
    b. Invitations/parties/dating

12. Sightseeing
    a. most interesting archeological places
    b. fascinating locales
    c. picturesque towns, enchanting islands and superb beaches

INTRODUCTION

General Information on Greece

Land Area: 54,949 sq. miles

Population: 10,264,156 (1991 Census)

Capital City: Athens

National Language: Modern Greek

Official Religion: Greek Orthodox (98% of the population)

Currency: Euro

Time: East European Time (when it's noon in Greece it is 11:00 a.m. in Rome, 10:00 a.m. in London, 5:00 a.m. in New York and Toronto, 2:00 a.m. in Los Angeles, 8:00 p.m. in Sydney, Australia).

Daylight-Savings time begins at 12:01 a.m. on the last Sunday of March, when clocks are set forward one hour and clocks are set back one hour at 12:01 a.m. on the last Sunday in September.

Electricity: 220 Volts. A transformer is needed for any electrical (120 volts) appliances

Climate: The climate in Greece will depend on the regional geography. The north of Greece (Northern Macedonia and Northern Epiros) has a more violent climate than the south. It is similar to the Balkan weather, with freezing stormy winters and very hot humid summers, while other regions like: the Attic Peninsula, the Cyclades, the Dodecanese, Crete, and the Central and Eastern Peloponnese have a more typically Mediterranean climate with very hot but dry summers and milder winters. Greece is best visited during early or late summer. July andAugust, if possible, should be avoided. Besides the brutal heat and the fact that it is known as the month of the strong northeasterly winds (meltemia)—equivalent to the mistrals—that blow over the entire country (with the exception of the western seaboard) and can make staying and swimming in the northern shores of the Aegean extremely difficult and hazardous, August is also the month that the majority of

Greeks take their vacation and every place except Athens is crowded. Avoid August if you possibly can.

You can also count on marvelous autumn weather. Spring can be very unreliable; anything can happen (weather-wise) then.

Flora and Fauna

The most spectacular varieties of wild flowers can be found in Greece. There are thousands of species, and a large number of various types of orchids adorn the Greek landscape. Due to the infertile ground, intensive agriculture is not pursued; thus, the land has escaped the ravages of destructive chemicals and spectacular flora has thrived. The mountains of Mani, in the Peloponnese and Crete, are the regions best known for their rare wild flower variety. Best time to admire the beautiful hillsides is spring when this natural wonder is in full bloom. There are not too many wild animals due to the long "open" hunting season, which opens August 20 and ends March 10. Hunting is very popular, and a very large number of animals and birds are killed both legally and illegally. Although, only thirty-five species of birds can be legally hunted, many more (out of the 400-odd bird species) are either killed or brought to the wildlife hospital (tel.: 0297-22 882) to be mended. Many migratory birds end up in Greece, building nests everywhere from church towers to electrical poles. The largest range of birds of prey in Europe can be found upstream the River Evros in Thrace, in the Dadia Forest Reserve.

Animals like birds are enthusiastically hunted in Greece, and many, although endangered (like the wolf), are not protected. Another endangered species is the brown bear, which roams, in small numbers, the mountains of Pindos. The dolphins can be enjoyed escorting your boat while island hopping.

There are few national parks in Greece: Parnitha National Park in Attica, Parnassos and Iti National Parks in Central Greece, Olympus National Park in Thessaly/Macedonia, and Samaria National Park in Crete.

Workforce/Economy

Prior WWII Greece was considered an agricultural country. Since then agriculture has declined drastically (due to the fact that the majority has moved to cities and especially the capital). The workforce now consists of people (50 percent) employed by state-run services, 22 percent in agriculture and 27 percent in industry and construction, contributing to the GNP—59 percent, 15 percent, and 26 percent respectively.

See more useful information in the reference section of the tour guide: "Make Your journey to Greece an Unforgettable Experience."

PART II
GREEK ALPHABET
Key to Pronunciation and Corresponding sounds

Α α (Ἀλφα/Alpha) — a as in car, father, are, apple
Β β (Βήτα/Vita/Beta) — v as in veal, village, vast
Γ γ (Γάμμα/yamma/ghamma) — y or w as in yet, year,week,work (a very soft gh sound)
Δ δ (Δέλτα/thelta/delta) — th (harsh) as in then, this, that
Ε ε (Ἐψιλον/epsilon) — e as in pet, red, get, end
Ζ ζ (Ζήτα/zeta) — z as in zone, zoo, zeal
Η η (Ἠτα/eta) — e/i as in me, see,sit,kit
Θ θ (Θήτα/theta) — th (soft) as in theater, thesis, theme
Ι ι (Ιώτα/γιώτα/yiota) — i/e as in me, see, sit, kit
Κ κ (Κάππα/kappa) — k as in kite, car, king
Λ λ (Λάμδα/lamtha/lamda) — l as in lake, love, light
Μ μ (Μι/mi) — m as in mother, me, comma
Ν ν (Νι/ni) — n as in no, not, next, vain
Ξ ξ (Ξι/ksi) — x (ks) as in taxes, extra, next
Ο ο (Ὀμικρον/omikron) — o as in over, oh, order
Π π (Πι/pi) — p as in pot, part, pet, top
Ρ ρ (Ρω/ro/rho) — r as in rear, red, read, stardom
Σ σ ς (Σίγμα/sighma) — s as in stop, save, store, bus
Τ t (Ταυ/ταφ/taf/taph — t as in ten, top, trip, part
Υ υ (Ὑψιλον/ipsilon) — u/i as in me, see, sit, kit
Φ φ (Φι/fi) — f/ph as in food, friend, photo, phase
Χ χ (Χι/hi/ch) — h/ch as in hero, hat, high
Ψ ψ (Ψι/psi) — ps as in pepsi, tops, lapse, eclipse
Ω ω (Ωμέγα/omegha) — o as in over, oh, order

Diphtongs (two vowels pronounced as one)

Ει(ει)=ι/e(i) as in see, me (είπα-`epa/ipa); είδα-`etha/itha)
Οι(οι)=ι/e (i) as in see, me (οι αδελφοί e/I athelfi)
Αι(αι)=ε/e as in pet, yet(αίμα-`ema,είμαι-`ime)
Ου(ου)=oo/ου as in book, foot (ουρανός-ooranos, πού-poo)
Αυ(αυ)=αβ/αφ/av,af as in avoid, after (αύριο-avrio, αυτός-aftos)
Ευ(ευ)=εβ/εφ/ ev, ef as in ever, effect (Ευρώπη-Evropi, ευχή-efhi)

Combination of consonants and their soundsf

Μπ (μπ)= b as in bear, but (μπαίνω-beno,μπήκα-bika) or (b) as in combination
Ντ (ντ) = d as in dress, drive (ντύνω-dino,ντύνομαι-dinome) or (nd) as in brandy
Τσ (τσ) = ch (ts) as in chair, lots (κορίτσι-koritsi, τσάντα-tsanta)
Γγ (γγ) = g (harsh) as in gang,goggle (αγγούρι-agouri)
Γκ(γκ) = g (harsh) as in tango, garage (γκαράζ-garaz,αγκινάρα-aginara)

Note: Throughout this book you will see the letters *gh* used instead of only the letter *g* (ex: Aghios instead of Agios). This is done purposely to draw your attention to the correct pronunciation: e.g., *gh* is pronounced as *y* at the beginning of a word, like year/yet or as a *w* (work/week and so forth). On the other hand the sound of the letter *g* is the compound sound of the two γγ or the γκ (like: αγγούρι-αγκινάρα). Emphasis should also be given to the *h* and *ch* (as in Hora instead of Chora), in order to avoid confusion in pronouncing the Greek χ as a ch(chair/chalk) the letter *h* (hot/here), the counterpart sound to the letter χ, is used.ff

Few remarks and suggestions regarding the Greek language will help you understand the fundamental differences between the two languages: English and Greek. The dialogues are designed to help you distinguish these grammatical and syntactical incongruities. In order to get the most out of them, study each dialogue individually, comprehend what you are saying, and try to use and apply the phrases. Read them phonetically if you must. You will be benefitted and gratified enormously, however, if you learn the alphabet and read everything in Greek. In order to avoid confusion, attention should be paid to the following:

- Genders/Γένη: There are three genders in the Greek language: the masculine(αρσενικό); the feminine(θηλυκό); and the neuter(ουδέτερο).
- Articles(definite and indefinite): masc. ο/ ένας (the/a,one); fem.η/μία (the/a,one); neu.το/ένα (the/a,one) Examples: ο πατέρας/ένας πατέρας (the father/a father); η μητέρα/μία μητέρα (the mother/a mother); το παιδί/ένα παιδί (the child/a child).

- Plural: οι πατέρες/πολλοί πατέρες (the fathers/many fathers); οι μητέρες/πολλές μητέρες (the mothers/many mothers); τα παιδιά/πολλά παιδιά (the children/many children).

- Accents and Punctuation marks: in demotic Greek, the accent circumflex(~) and the soft and rough breathing signs(''), are no longer in use. Only the(´) οξεία/acute, which is placed on the syllable stressed, is used on every word of two or more syllables.

(.) period-τελεία (,) comma-κόμμα
(;) question mark (?) /ερωτηματικό
(!) exclamation mark/θαυμαστικό
(·) semicolon(´;)/άνω τελεία
(:) colon/κόλον/διπλή στιγμή
(') apostrophe/απόστροφος

- Adjectives/επίθετα: the adjective has three genders masculine, feminine and neuter and always agrees with the noun in gender, case and number. If the noun is masculine the adjective will also be masculine, if it is plural, the adjective has to agree. The same rule applies for the other genders.

Examples: ο καλός πατέρας (the good father), οι καλοί πατέρες (the good fathers), η καλή μητέρα (the good mother), οι καλές μητέρες (the good mothers), το καλό παιδί (the good child), τα καλά παιδιά (the good children).

Most masculine adjectives end in –ος. If a consonant precedes the ending, the feminine changes to –η, (ex: ο μικρός-η μικρή (small), if a vowel or diphthong precedes the ending, then the feminine changes to –α (ex: ο ωραίος, η ωραία /beautiful, ο κρύος, η κρύα/cold). In order to form the neuter the –ος ending changes to –ο. (ex: ο μικρός, η μικρή, το μικρό. Ο κρύος, η κρύα, το κρύο).

- Adverbs/επιρρήματα: most adverbs of manner, which modify a verb by telling how something is done are usually formed by using the plural neuter of the adjective or remember to change the ending –ος to –α. Examples:adj. καλός, the neuter singular is -καλό plural: καλά, thus the adverb will also be καλά (well/good. I'm doiwell/είμαικαλά).

Ωραίος/ωραία(beautiful/beautifully);ακριβός/ακριβά (expensive/expensively); ευχάριστος/ευχάριστα (pleasant/ pleasantly) etc.

− Nouns/ουσιαστικά: masculine endings in:a).-ος/pl.-οι (ο αδελφός/οι αδελφοί,ο τοίχος/οι τοίχοι (the walls/,ο κήπος/ οι κήποι),b).-ας/pl.-ες(ο πατέρας/οι πατέρες,ο μήνας/οι μήνες),c.-ης/.-ες (ο μαθητής/οι μαθητές,ο αθλητής/οι αθλη-τές),d.–εας/pl.-εις(ο ιερέας/οι ιερείς,ο κουρέας/οι κουρείς), e.–ους/pl.- ούδες (ο παππούς/οι παππούδες), f. –ές/pl.-έδες (ο καναπές/οι καναπέδες, ο κεφτές/οι κεφτέδες). Feminine endings in: a. –α/pl.-ες(μητέρα/μητέρες), b. –η/pl.-ες (η αδελφή/ οι αδελφές), c. -η/pl.-εις (η λέξη/οι λέξεις,η πόλη/οι πόλεις), d. -ά(accented on the a)/pl. –άδες (η μαμά/οι μαμάδες,η για-γιά/οι γιαγιάδες).

Neuter endings in:a.-ι/pl.-α (το παιδί/τα παιδιά),b.-ο/pl.-α(το μήλο/τα μήλα), c.- μα/pl.-ματα(δέμα/δέματα) d.-ος/pl.-η(το δάσος/τα δάση, το λάθος/τα λάθη), and e.-ας/pl.-ατα(το τέρας/τα τέρατα, το κέρμα/τα κέρματα)

Another important point should be made regarding the objective/accusative case. Since the changes, in Greek, are very noticeable some exegesis/explanation is necessary. The article, adjective and noun change according to case. We are going to deal briefly with the nominative and objective cases only. The first is used when the noun is the subject (in other words, when it is doing something, e.g., ο πατέρας τρώγει-fa-ther is eating) and the latter when it receives the action (i.e., when it becomes the object, e.g., βλέπω τον πατέρα - I see father). The same applies for the feminine, e.g., η μητέρα πηγαίνει έξω - mother is going out. In this case mother is doing something. Αγαπώ τη μητέρα - I love mother. In this instance, I am doing something towards mother, therefore, the objective case is used, the article η changes to τη(ν). The neuter changes are not so obvious, since only the sequence of the sentence differs.(e. g., το παιδί παίζει-the child is playing/

Αγαπώ το παιδί-I love the child. Only syntactically the sentence changes, the ending and article remain intact.

- Pronouns/αντωνυμίες: personal pronouns(used as the subject): εγώ/I, εσύ/you, αυτός,αυτή, αυτό/he,she,it and plural: (ε)μείς/we, (ε)σείς/you, αυτοί, αυτές, αυτά/they, are usually omitted, unless they are used for emphasis or contrast.

- Verbs/ρήματα: verbs are one of the most important parts of speech and the backbone of the language. We cannot possibly deal extensively with all categories of verbs (and it is not necessary to do so) in this book. Some endings of the conjugations, and the use of them, however, are important in order to give you the chance to understand the various mutations. The active voice (showing an action of the subject) has two categories/conjugations of verbs: the first conjugation consists of verbs ending in –ω (without the accent on the –ω, as: δένω, ντύνω, μορφώνω).

The endings of the present for this conjugation are -ω, -εις,-ει, -ουμε,-ετε, -ουν (δένω/I tie,δένεις/you tie, δένει/ he,she,it ties, δένουμε/we tie, δένετε/you tie, δένουν/they tie). Apply these endings to any active verb ending in –ω, and you will be able to form many sentences, questions and answers. The second conjugation consists of verbs accended on the –ώ(contracted verbs and it has two groups), the endings of the first group in the present are: -(άω)ώ,-άς,-ά(άει),-άμε, άτε,-άνε(ούν) (αγαπάω(ώ)/I love,αγαπάς/ you love,αγαπάει(ά)he,she,it, loves, αγαπάμε/we love, αγαπάτε/ you love, αγαπάνε(ούν)/they love. The endings of the second group are:-ώ,-είς,-εί, ούμε,-είτε,-ούν (εξηγώ/I explain, εξηγείς/you explain, εξηγεί/he,she,it explains, εξηγούμε/we explain, εξηγείτε/you explain, εξηγούν/they explain).

Passive voice (indicates an action that the subject is acted upon). Verbs of the first conjugation ending in –ω (ντύνω/ I dress (someone else), form the passive voice by changing the –ω το –ομαι (ντύνομαι-I get dressed/ I dress myself). The endings are:-ομαι, -εσαι, -εται, -όμαστε, -όσαστε(εστε) -ονται,(ντύνομαι/I get dressed,ντύνεσαι/you get dressed, ντύνεται/he,she,it gets dressed, ντυνόμαστε/ we get dressedvτυνόσαστε/you get dressed, ντύνονται/they get dressed.

The second conjugation (first group) forms the passive voice by changing the accended –ώ το –ιέμαι(αγαπώ – αγαπιέμαι/I am loved), the endings are: -ιέμαι,-ιέσαι,-ιέται, ιόμαστε,-ιόσαστε, -ιούνται (αγαπιέμαι/I am(get) loved, αγαπιέσαι/ you are loved, αγαπιέται/he,she, it is loved, αγαπιόμαστε/we are loved(we love each other) αγαπιόσαστε/ you are loved, αγαπιούνται/they love each other.

The second group (of the second conjugation), forms its passive voice by changing the –ώ το ούμαι(εξηγώ/ I explain (something), εξηγούμαι/ I get explained/ I explain myself. The endings are -ούμαι,-είσαι,-είται,-ιόμαστε,-ιέστε,-ούνται (εξηγούμαι/ I am explained,εξηγείσαι/you are explained, εξηγείται/he,she,it is explained, εξηγιόμαστε/ we are explained, εξηγιέστε/ you are explained, εξηγούνται/ they are explained.

Some useful verbs follow, in order to give you the opportunity to apply whatever you have learned and expand your knowledge of the language (e.g., conjugate the present, form questions and answers, use them in the passive voice and so forth. You will be surprised at the skill you are acquiring and you will be motivated to study further. The numbers (1,2), next to the accented verbs indicate the group of conjugation they belong to, if both are included, either group used, is correct):Αγοράζω-I buy, ακούω-I hear/listen, ακολουθώ(2)-I follow, ανυπομονώ(2)-I am eager/anxious, ανησυχώ(2)-I worry, απαιτώ(2)-I demand, απεργώ(2)-I strike, απλοποιώ2)-I simplify, αποφασίζω-I decide, αρχίζω-I begin, αφήνω-I let/ abandon, βοηθώ(1,2)-I help/aid, βουρτσίζω-I brush, βρίζω-I swear/abuse, γεμίζω-I fill,γιορτάζω-I celebrate, γλεντάω(ώ) (1)-I have fun, γνωρίζω-I know/Get acquainted, γυρίζω-I return/turn, δανείζω-I lend, διαβάζω-I read, ενοικιάζω-I rent, ενοχλώ(2)-I annoy/bother, εξηγώ(1,2)-I explain,(ε) ρωτώ(1)-I ask, ετοιμάζω-I prepare, ευχαριστώ(2)-I thank/

please,ζητώ(1)-I ask for/seek, ζω(2)-I live, θαυμάζω-I admire, θυμώνω-I get angry, ιδρώνω-I sweat/perspire, ικανοποιώ(2)-I satisfy, καθαρίζω-I clean/clear, κλείνω-I close, κολυμπάω(ώ) (1)-I swim, κτυπάω/ώ/χτυπάω)(1)-I hit/beat, κυβερνώ(1)-I govern, λερώνω-I soil/dirty,λιποθυμώ(1)-I faint, μαλώνω-I fight/argue, μετράω/ώ(1)-I count/measure, μιλάω/ώ(1)-I speak/talk,νομίζω-I suppose/think, ξυπνάω/ώ-I wake up, οδηγώ(2)-I drive/guide, οργανώνω-I organize,σβήνω-I put out/extinguish, σιδερώνω-I iron/press,σκεπάζω-I cover/conseal, σκίζω-I tear/rip, σπάζω- I break, συζητάω/ώ(1,2)-I discuss/debate, συμφωνώ(2)-I agree, συναντώ(1)-I meet, ταχυδρομώ(2)-I mail/post, τελειώνω-I finish/complete, τηλεφωνώ(2)-I phone/call, φθάνω-I arrive/reach, φιλάω/ώ-I kiss, χαιρετώ(1)-I greet, χύνω-I spill/pour, χωρίζω-I separate/part, ψωνίζω-I purchase/shop.

Additional useful vocabulary follows the dialogues.

Preparations - Ετοιμασίες
Preparing for the Trip –Ετοιμασίες για το ταξίδι

Vocabulary

Passport Office - Γραφείο Διαβατηρίων (ghrafio thiavatirion)
Passport - το διαβατήριο (to thiavatirio)
Pictures/photos - φωτογραφίες (photoghrafies)
Travel Agency - το ταξιδιωτικό γραφείο (to taxidiotiko ghrafio)
Ticket - το εισιτήριο (to isitirio)
Air Line - αεροπορική εταιρεία (aeroporiki eteria)
I prepare - ετοιμάζω (etimazo)
I get prepared - ετοιμάζομαι (etimazome)
I go - πηγαίνω (pigheno)
I shop - ψωνίζω (psonizo)
Suitcases - βαλίτσες (valitses)

Questions and answers

When are you going on a trip?
Πότε θά πάτε (`ενα) ταξίδι;
(pote tha pate ena taxithi?)

We're leaving next month
Φεύγουμε τον `αλλο μήνα
(fevghoume ton alo mina)

Where are you going?
Πού θα πάτε;
(poo tha pate?)

We're going to Greece
Θα πάμε στην Ελλάδα.
(tha pame stin elatha)

Do you have a passport?
;Εχετε διαβατήριο;
(ehete thiavatirio?)

No, we're going tomorrow to the passport office.
`Οχι, θα πάμε αύριο στο γραφείο διαβατηρίων
(Ohi, tha pame avrio sto ghrafio diavatirion)

Do you have photos?
`Εχετε φωτογραφίες;
(ehete photografies?)

I do have photos, but my wife needs new ones.
Εγώ `εχω φωτογραφίες, αλλά η γυναίκα μου χρειάζεται καινούριες
(egho eho photografies ala i ghineka moo hriazete kenouries)

Do you have your tickets?
`Εχετε τα εισιτήριά σας;
(ehete ta isitiria sas?)

Yes, we called our travel agent. Everything is ready.
Ναι, τηλεφωνήσαμε στο πράκτορά μας όλα είναι έτοιμα
(Ne, tilephonisame sto taksithiotiko mas praktora, ola ine etima)
The airline had a great discount on tickets.
Η αεροπορική εταιρεία είχε μεγάλες εκπτώσεις στα εισιτήρια
(I aeroporiki eteria ihe meghales ekptosis sta isitiria

Did you do any shopping?
Ψωνίσατε;
psonisate?)

Yes, we bought whatever we need for the trip.
Ναι, αγοράσαμε ό,τι χρειαζόμαστε για το ταξίδι μας
(aghorasame o,ti hriazomaste ghia to taksithi)

We are soon going to pack our suitcases.
Σύντομα θα ετοιμάσουμε τις βαλίτσες μας
(sidoma tha etimasoume tis valitses mas)

b. At the airport/Departure – Στο αεροδρόμιο/αναχώρηση
(sto aerothromio/anahorisi)

Vocabulary

Airplane-το αεροπλάνο (to aeroplano)
Passengers-επιβάτες(epivates)
Crew-πλήρωμα (pliroma)
Airport employees-υπάλληλοι αεροδρομίου (ipalili aerothromiou)
Pilot-πιλότος (pilotos)
Stewardess-(η/ο)(f/m) συνοδός((ο/i) synothos)

Questions and answers

What time does the plane leave?
Τι ώρα φεύγει το αεροπλάνο;
(ti ora fevghi to aeroplano?)

The plane leaves at 10:00 a.m.
Το αεροπλάνο φεύγει στις δέκα το πρωί
(to aeroplano fevghi stis theka to proi)

Where are the passengers?
Πού είναι οι επιβάτες;
(pou ine i epivates?)

They're waiting to depart.
Περιμένουν ν'αναχωρήσουν
(perimenoun n´anahorisoun)

The airport employees are checking their passports, tickets, and
baggage.
Οι υπάλληλοι ελέγχουν τα διαβατήρια, εισιτήρια και αποσκευές
τους
(i ipalili eleghhoun ta thiavatiria, isitiria ke aposkeves tous)

Where is the crew?
Πού είναι το πλήρωμα;
(pou ine to pliroma?)

The crew is on the plane getting ready for the boarding of the
passangers.
Το πλήρωμα είναι στο αεροπλάνο και ετοιμάζεται για την
επιβίβαση Των
επιβατών (to pliroma ine sto aeroplano ke etimazete gha tin epivi-
vasi ton epivaton)

All is ready. The pilot gives his instructions and the plane takes off.
Όλα είναι έτοιμα. Ο πιλότος δίνει τις οδηγίες του και το αεροπλάνο
φεύγει
(ola ine etima. O pilotos thini tis othighies tou ke to aeroplano
apoghionete)

c. At the airport/Arrival –Στο αεροδρόμιο/Άφιξη
(sto aerothromio/afiksi)

Vocabulary

Landing – προσγείωση (prosghiosi)
Welcome – καλωσορίσατε (kalosorisate)
Passport control- έλεγχος διαβατηρίων (eleghos thiavatirion)
Baggage – αποσκευές (aposkeves)
Customs – τελωνείο (telonio)
Exchange bureau - γραφείο συναλλάγματος (ghrafio sinalaghmatos)
Information – πληροφορίες (plirofories)

Questions and answers

Welcome to Greece. Did you have a pleasant trip?
Καλωσορίσατε στην Ελλάδα. Είχατε ευχάριστο ταξίδι;
(kalosorisate stin Elatha. Ihate efharisto taksithi?)

Thank you. The trip was very pleasant and the landing very smooth.
Ευχαριστώ. Το ταξίδι ήταν πολύ ευχάριστο και η προσγείωση πολύ ομαλή
(Efharisto. To taksithi, itan poli efharisto ke i prosghiosi poli omali.)

Do you speak Greek?
Μιλάς/μιλάτε ελληνικά;
(milas/milate elinika?)

Do you understand Greek?
Καταλαβαίνεις/καταλαβαίνετε ελληνικά;
(katalavenis/katalavenete elinika)

I don't speak Greek.
Δεν μιλάω ελληνικά
(then milao elinika)

No, I don't understand but I am trying to learn some.
Όχι δεν καταλαβαίνω αλλά προσπαθώ να μάθω μερικά
(ohi, then katalaveno αla prospatho na matho merika)

d. Passport control-Έλεγχος Διαβατηρίων
(elenhos thiavatirion)

May I see your passport please?
Μπορώ να δω το διαβατήριό σου/σας, παρακαλώ;
(boro na tho to thiavatirio sou/sas parakalo?)

Here is my passport.
Ορίστε το διαβατήριό μου
(oriste to thiavatirio mou)

Are you travelling alone?
masc./fem.
Ταξιδεύετε μόνος/μόνη;
(taksithevete monos/moni?)

No, I'm traveling with my spouse/a friend
masc./fem.   masc./fem.
Όχι, ταξιδεύω με τον/την σύζυγο/φίλο/φίλη
(ohi, taksithevo me ton/tin sizigho (filo/fili)

Are you here on business or vacation?
Είστε εδώ για δουλειές ή διακοπές;
(iste etho ghia thoulies i thiakopes?)

We are spending our vacation here.
Θα κάνουμε τις διακοπές μας εδώ
(tha kanome tis thiakopes mas etho)

How long are you staying?
Πόσο καιρό θα μείνετε;
(poso kero tha minete?)

We're staying for two weeks/a month.
Θα μείνουμε για δύο εβδομάδες/ένα μήνα
(tha minoume ghia thio evthomades/ena mina)

e. Baggage-Αποσκευές
(aposkeves)

Where can I get a baggage trolley, please?
Που μπορώ να πάρω ένα καρότσι για τις αποσκευές παρακαλώ;
(pou boro na paro ena karotsi ghia tis aposkeves parakalo?)

Down the hall. Turn left/right.
Στο βάθος της αίθουσας αριστερά/δεξιά
(sto vathos tis ethousas aristera/thexia)

Pay the cashier.
   m./ f
Πληρώστε τον/την ταμία
(pliroste ton/tin tamia)

Porter can you please help me with my luggage?
Αχθοφόρε, παρακαλώ μπορείτε να με βοηθήσετε με τις βαλίτσες μου;
(achthofore, parakalo borite na me voithisete me tis valitses mou?)

How many suitcases do you have?
Πόσες βαλίτσες έχετε;
(poses valitses ehete?)

I have two/three suitcases.
Έχω δύο/τρεις βαλίτσες
(eho thio/tris valitses)

Are you taking the bus or a taxi?
Θα πάρετε το λεωφορείο ή ταξί;
(tha parete to leoforio i taxi?)

After I go through customs. I'd like you to call a taxi, please.
Μετά το τελωνείο θα ήθελα να καλέσετε ένα ταξί
(meta to telonio tha ithela na kalesete ena taxi, parakalo)

f. Customs-Τελωνείο
   (telonio)

How many suitcases do you have?
Πόσες βαλίτσες έχετε;
(poses valitses ehete)?

I have two suitcases.
Έχω δύο βαλίτσες
(eho thio valitses)

Do you have anything to declare?

Έχετε κάτι να δηλώσετε;

(ehete kati na thilosete?)

I have nothing to declare. I have only my personal things.

Δεν έχω τίποτα να δηλώσω. Έχω μόνο τα προσωπικά μου πράγματα

(then eho tipota na thiloso. Eho mono ta prosopika mou praghmata)

My spouse/friend has a camera, a carton of cigarettes, two bottles of wine, and one whiskey.

Ο/η σύζυγος/φίλος/φίλη έχει μια μηχανή, μια κούτα τσιγάρα, δύο μπουκάλια κρασί και ένα ουίσκι

(o/i sizighos/filos-fili ehi mia mihani, mia kouta tsighara, thio boukalia krasi ke ena ouiski)

Open this bag, please.

Ανοίξτε αυτή τη βαλίτσα, παρακαλώ

(anixste afti ti valitsa parakalo

Here it is. As I told you I have only my personal items.

Ορίστε, όπως σας είπα έχω μόνο τα προσωπικά μου αντικείμενα

(oriste, opos sas ipa, eho mono ta prosopika mou antikimena)

May I close my case now?

Μπορώ να κλείσω τη βαλίτσα μου τώρα;

(boro na kliso ti valitsa mou tora?)

You may, you don't have to pay duty on anything.

Μπορείτε, δεν έχετε να πληρώσετε φόρο για τίποτα

(borite, then ehete na plirosete foro ghia tipota)

You may go through. Have a nice stay in Greece.

Μπορείτε να περάσετε, καλή διαμονή στην Ελλάδα

(borite na perasete, kali thiamoni stin Elatha)

Thank you. Have a good day.
Ευχαριστώ. Καλή σας μέρα
(efharisto. Kali sas mera)

g. Information desk - Currency exchange-
Γραφείο Πληροφοριών Γραφείο Συναλλάγματος
(grafio Pliroforion-Grafio Sinalaghmatos)

I would like to cash a traveller's cheque.
Where is the Currency Exchange please?
Θα ήθελα να εξαργυρώσω μια ταξιδιωτική επιταγή; Πού είναι το
Γραφείο συναλλάγματος, παρακαλώ;
(tha ithela na exsarghiroso mia taksithiotiki epitaghi. Pou ine to
ghrafio sinalaghmatos parakalo?)

I'd like to change some American dollars money to euros please.
How much do I get for a dollar/pound?
Θα ήθελα να χαλάσω μερικά Αμερικανικά δολάρια. Πόσο έχει το
δολάριο/η Αγγλική λίρα;
(tha ithela na halaso merika Amerikanika/Aglika hrimata.
Poso ehi to thollario/e aggliki lira?)

May I see your passport, please?
Μπορώ να ιδώ το διαβατήριό σας, παρακαλώ;
(boro na itho to thiavatirio sas, parakalo?)

Here is your money/drachmas.
Ορίστε τα χρήματα/οι δραχμές σας
(oriste ta hrimata/i thrahmes sas)

May I have change, please?
Μπορώ να έχω ψιλά, παρακαλώ;
(boro na eho psila parakalo?)

Do you take a personal check?

Παίρνετε προσωπική επιταγή;

(pernete prosopiki epitaghi?)

No, I am sorry.

`Οχι, λυπάμαι.

(ohi, lipame)

h. Transportation-Συγκοινωνία
(sigkinonia)

Vocabulary

Means of transport - Μεταφορικά μέσα (metaphorika messa)

Airplane - (το) αεροπλάνο (aeroplano)

Helicopter - (το)ελικόπτερο (elicoptero)

Boat/ship - (το)πλοίο/βαπόρι/καράβι (plio/vapori/karavi)

Motor boat - (η)βενζινάκατος(venzinakatos)

Rowing boat - (η)βάρκα με κουπί (varka me coupi)

Sailing boat - (η)βάρκα με πανιά (varka me pania)

Yacht - (η)θαλαμηγός/(thalamighos/kotero)

Caique - (το) καϊκι (kaiki)

Bus - (το) λεωφορείο(leoforio)

Taxi - (το) ταξί (taksi)

Hitch – hiking - (το)ωτοστόπ (otostop)

I travel - ταξιδεύω (taksithevo)

Travel/trip - (το)ταξίδι (taksithi)

By/with - με(me)

Train - (το)τρένο/τραίνο (treno)

Underground (train/metro) - (ο) ηλεκτρικός/υπόγειος σιδηρόδρομος (ilektrikos/ipoghios sithirothromos)

Truck - (το)φορτηγό (fortigho)

Rented car - (το) νοικιασμένο αυτοκίνητο (nikiasmeno aftokinito)

Bicycle - (το)ποδήλατο (pothilato)

Motor bike/moped - (η) μηχανή/βέσπα (mihani/vespa)

a. Boat

I'd like to travel to the Aegean Islands. Do you have the timetable, please?

Θα ήθελα να ταξιδέψω στα νησιά του Αιγαίου, έχετε τα δρομολόγια;

(tha ithela na taksithepso sta nisia too Egheou, ehete ta thromologhia, parakalo?)

Are you going to travel by boat or plane?

Θα ταξιδέψετε με πλοίο ή με αεροπλάνο;

(tha taksithepsete me plio i aeroplano?)

These are the timetables for the whole country for plane, boat, or train.

Αυτά είναι τα δρομολόγια για όλη τη χώρα με αεροπλάνο, Πλοίο ή τρένο

(afta ine ta thromologhia ghia oli tin hora me aeroplano, plio i treno)

I want a ticket by boat for Paros/Mykonos/Santorini. How much does it cost?

Θέλω ένα εισιτήριο με πλοίο για την Πάρο/Μύκονο/Σαντορίνη, πόσο κοστίζει;

(thelo ena isitirio me plio ghia tin Paro/Mikono/Santorini, poso costizi?)

Here is your ticket. It costs eighteen euros.

Ορίστε το εισιτήριό σας, κοστίζει δέκα οκτώ ευρώ.

(oriste to isitirio sas, kostizi theka okto evro)

Could I rent a car on the island? Can I bring my car?

Θα μπορούσα να νοικιάσω ένα αυτοκίνητο στο νησί; Μπορώ να πάρω το αυτοκίνητό μου;

(tha borousa na nikiaso ena aftokinito sto nisi? Boro na fero to aftokinito moo?)

Yes, tell us what make you'd like and it will be waiting for you at
    the harbor. Or, if you wish, you may ferry your car.
Ναι, πείτε μας τι αυτοκίνητο θέλετε και θα σας περιμένει στο
    λιμάνι. Ή, αν θέλετε, μπορείτε να πάρετε το αυτοκίνητό σας
    στο φέρυ μπωτ.
(ne, pite mas ti aftokinito thelete ke tha sas perimeni sto limani.
    E, an thelete, borite na parete to aftokinito sas sto feriboat.)

Does the boat leave on time?
Φεύγει το πλοίο στην ώρα του;
(fevghi to plio stin ora too?)

Most of the times, sometimes there is a delay.
Τις περισσότερες φορές, μερικές φορές έχει καθυστέρηση
(tis perisoteres fores, merikes fores ehi kathisterisi)

.Are buses and taxis available on the island?
Υπάρχουν λεωφορεία και ταξί στο νησί;
(iparhoon leoforia ke taksi sto nisi?)

Plenty, you won't have any difficulty to find one
Αρκετά, δεν θα έχετε δυσκολία να βρείτε
(arketa, then tha ehete thiskolia na vrite)

What time does the boat leave?
Τι ώρα φεύγει το πλοίο;
(ti ora fevghi to plio?)

It leaves at 9:00 a.m.
Φεύγει στις εννέα η ώρα
(fevghi stis 9 to proi)

I thank you.
Σας ευχαριστώ
(sas efharisto)

b. Plane

Where is the airline office? I'd like to book two seats for Thessaloniki.
Πού είναι το γραφείο εισιτηρίων; Θέλω να κρατήσω δύο θέσεις για τη Θεσσαλονίκη
(poo ine to aeroporiko ghrafio, thelo na kratiso thio thesis ghiati thesaloniki)

What time does the next plane leave?
Τι ώρα φεύγει το επόμενο αεροπλάνο;
(ti ora fevghi to epomeno aeroplano?)

In an hour/two hours.
Σε μία ώρα/δύο ώρες
(se mia ora/thio ores)

What is the flight number and how much is the ticket?
Τι είναι ο αριθμός πτήσης και πόσο είναι το εισιτήριο;
(ti ine o arithmos ptisis ke poso ine to isitirio?)

The flight number is…and the ticket costs…euros.
Ο αριθμός πτήσης είναι…και το εισιτήριο κοστίζει…Ευρώ
(o arithmos ptisis ine…ke to isitirio costizi…evro)

Thank you very much.
Ευχαριστώ πολύ
(efharisto poli)

c. Bus and Train

Where is the bus/train station?
Πού είναι ο σταθμός λεωφορείων/τρένων;
(poo ine o stathmos leoforion/trenon?)

The bus station is at Omonia Square and the train station on
Deligianni St.

Ο σταθμός λεωφορείων είναι στην Ομόνοια και ο σταθμός τρένων
στην οδό Δεληγιάννη.

(o stathmos ton leoforion ine stin Omonia ke trenon stin
otho Thelighiani)

What is the easier way to get there?

Ποιός είναι ο ευκολότερος τρόπος να πάμε εκεί;

(pios ine o efkoloteros tropos na pame eki?)

By taxi

Με ταξί

(me taksi)

d. Taxi

Taxi, are you free?

Είστε ελεύθερος;

(iste eleftheros?)

Yes, where are you going?

Ναι, πού πηγαίνετε;

(ne, poo pighenete?)

Here is the address of the hotel. I'm in a hurry. Is there a lot of
traffic at this time?

Ορίστε η διεύθυνση του ξενοδοχείου, βιάζομαι, έχει μεγάλη
κίνηση Αυτή την ώρα;

(oriste i thiefthinsi too ksenothohioo, viazome, ehi meghali kinisi
afti tin ora?)

There is always traffic. It will take approximately half hour to get there.
Πάντα έχει μεγάλη κυκλοφορία, θα πάρει περίπου μισή ώρα να φτάσουμε
(panta ehi meghali kikloforia, tha pari peripou misi ora na fthasoome)

How much is it?
Πόσο κάνει;
(poso kani?)

Eight euros.
Οκτώ ευρώ
(okto evro)

Thank you, have a nice day.
Ευχαριστώ, καλή σας μέρα
(efharisto, kali sas mera)

e. Rent a Car

I'd like to rent a car, please.
Θα ήθελα να νοικιάσω ένα αυτοκίνητο, παρακαλώ
(tha ithela na nikiaso ena aftokinito, parakalo)

How long do you plan to have the car for?
Για πόσο καιρό σχεδιάζετε να έχετε το αυτοκίνητο;
(ghia poso kero schethiazete na ehete to aftokinito?)

One week/two weeks.
Μία εβδομάδα/δύο εβδομάδες
(mia evthomatha/thio evthomathes)

What size car would you like?
Τι μέγεθος αυτοκίνητο θέλετε;
(ti meghethos aftokinito thelete?)

I'd like a small car.
Θα ήθελα ένα μικρό αυτοκίνητο
(tha ithela ena mikro aftokinito)

What is the price and what does it include?
Ποιά είναι η τιμή και τι περιλαμβάνει;
(pia ine i timi ke ti perilamvani?)

The price is...euros a day and includes only the insurance, unlim-
ited mileage, the gas is yours.
Η τιμή είναι... ευρώ την ημέρα και περιλαμβάνει την Ασφάλεια
kai aperi;orista χιλιόμετρα, η βενζίνη είναι δική σας
(i timi ine...evro tin imera ke perilamvani tin asfalia, απεριοριστα
hiliometra, i venzini ine thikι sas)

You must leave a deposit and have an international driver's license.
Πρέπει ν'αφήσετε μια προκαταβολή και να έχετε διεθνή άδεια/
διεθνές δίπλωμα
(prepi n´afisete mia prokatavoli ke na ehete thiethni athia/diethnes
thiploma)

Thank you, when can I pick up the car?
Ευχαριστώ, πότε μπορώ να πάρω το αυτοκίνητο;
(efharisto, pote boro na paro to aftokinito?)

We're open twenty-four hours a day. You can pick it up anytime.
Είμαστε ανοικτοί είκοσι τέσσερες ώρες την ημέρα, μπορείτε να το
παραλάβετε οποιαδήποτε ώρα
(imaste anikti ikosi teseres ores tin imaera, borite na to paralavete
opiathipote ora)

4. Accomodation/Hotel-Κατάλυμα/Ξενοδοχείο
(katalima/ksenothohio)

Vocabulary

Hotel - (το) ξενοδοχείο (ksenothohio)
Inn - (το) πανδοχείο (panthohio)
Boarding house - (η) πανσιόν(pansion)
Youth hostel - (o)ξενώνας νεολαίας (ksenonas neoleas)
Bungalows - μπάγκαλόους (bagaloous)
Camping - (η) κατασκήνωση/κάμπιν(kataskinosi/kampin)
Rooms to let - ενοικιάζονται δωμάτια(enikiazonde thomatia)
Furnished apartments - επιπλωμένα διαμερίσματα
(epiplomena thiamerismata)
Room - (το) δωμάτιο(thomatio)
Suite - (η) σουίτα (sooita)
Ammenities/comforts -(h) άνεσις (i anesis)
Air condition - (o)κλημcατισμός (klimatismos)
Elevator - (το) ασσανσέρ (assanser)
Television - (η)τηλεόραση (tileorasi)
Bathroom - (το) μπάνιο/λουτρό (banio/lootro)
Room and board - δωμάτιο και φαγητό (thomatio ke faghito)
Room with breakfast - δωμάτιο με πρωινό (thomatio me proino)
Class/category - (η) τάξη/κατηγορία (taksi/katighoria)

I need a double room with a shower, do you have a good one?
Χρειάζομαι ένα διπλό δωμάτιο με ντους/μπάνιο, έχετε ένα καλό;
(hriazome ena thiplo thomatio me dous/banio, ehete ena kalo?)

Yes, we have a nice one overlooking the park/sea.
Ναι, έχουμε ένα ωραίο που κοιτάζει προς το πάρκο/τη θάλασσα
(ne, ehoume ena oreo poo kitazi pros to parko/ti thalassa)

Wonderful, can we see it? How much is it?
Θαυμάσια, μπορούμε να το δούμε;
(thavmasia, boroume na to thoume? Poso ehi?)

You may, this room is one hundred euros a day. Tomorrow there will be others available also.

Μπορείτε, αυτό το δωμάτιο είναι εκατό ευρώ την ημέρα, αύριο θα είναι κι άλλα διαθέσιμα

(borite, afto to thomatio ehi theka ekato evro tin imera, avrio tha ine ki ala thiathesima)

Will you have something cheaper/more expensive tomorrow?

Θα έχετε κάτι πιο φθηνό/πιο ακριβό αύριο;

(tha ehete kati pio fthino/pio akrivo avrio?)

Definitely so, come by the reception and you will see what vacancies we have.

Οπωσδήποτε, περάστε από τη ρεσεψιόν και θα δείτε ποιά είναι ελεύθερα

(oposthipote, peraste apo ti reseption ke tha thite pia ine eleftera)

Does the room offer the usual amenities (e.g., bath, air-conditioning, hot water, television, telephone)?

Παρέχει το δωμάτιο τις συνήθεις ανέσεις (δηλαδή:μπάνιο, κλιματισμό, ζεστό νερό, τηλεόραση, τηλέφωνο)

(parehi to thomatio tis sinithis anesis (thilathi: banio, klimatismo,zesto nero, tileorasi, tilephono)?

Yes, everything (except air conditioning).

Ναι, όλα (εκτός κλιματισμού)

(ne, ola (ektos klimatismou)

What else does the hotel offer?

Τι άλλο παρέχει το ξενοδοχείο;

(ti alo parehi to ksenothohio?)

There are the following services available: beauty salon, gym, gift shop, babysitters.

Οι ακόλουθες υπηρεσίες διαθέτονται:κομμωτήριο,γυμναστήριο, Κατάστημα δώρων, μπέιμπυ σιτερς/νταντάδες)

(i akolouthes ipiresies thiathetonte: komotirio, ghimnastirio, katastima thoron, baby sitters-dadathes)

Could you please reserve two rooms for our friends for next week? A double and a single? Thank you.

Μπορείτε σας παρακαλώ να κρατήστε δύο δωμάτια για τους φίλους μας, για την επόμενη εβδομάδα: ένα διπλό κι ένα μονό; Σας ευχαριστώ.

(borite sas parakalo na kratiste thio thomatia ghia tous filous mas ghia tin epomeni evthomatha: ena thiplo ki ena mono? Sas efharisto.)

5. Restaurant/Taverna-Εστιατόριο/Ταβέρνα
(estiatorio/taverna)

Vocabulary

Menu - (ο) κατάλογος (kataloghos)
Hors d'oeuvres/appetizers - (τα) ορεκτικά (orektika)
Salads - (οι) σαλάτες (salates)
Soups - (οι) σούπες (soupes)
Vegetables - (τα) λαχανικά(lahanika)
Cheeses - (τα) τυριά (tiria)

Sauces/dressings- (οι)σάλτσες (saltses)
Meats- (τα) κρέατα (kreata)
Poultry- (τα) πουλερικά (poulerika)
Seafood- (τα) θαλασσινά (thalassina)
Fruits- (τα) φρούτα (frouta)
Desserts- (το) επιδόρπιο/τα γλυκίσματα (epithorpia/ghlikismata)
Refreshments/beverages- (τα) αναψυκτικά (anapsiktika)
Wines- (τα) κρασιά (krasia)
Drinks/spirits- (τα) οινοπνευματώδη ποτά (inopnevmatothi pota)

a. Appetizers- (τα) ορεκτικά (orektika)

Tzatziki/yogurt sauce w/garlic- (το) τζατζίκι (tzatziki)
Fried juccini/courgettes- (τα) τηγανητά κολοκύθια
   (tighanita Kolokothia)
Stuffed grape vine leaves- (τα) ντολμαδάκια (dolmathakia)
Calamari (fried)/squid- (τα) καλαμάρια (kalamaria)
Sausage- (το) λουκάνικο (lookaniko)
Fried cheese- (το) σαγανάκι (saghanaki)
Olives- (οι) ελιές (elies)
Mushrooms- (τα) μανιτάρια (manitaria)
Chicken livers- (τα) σηκωτάκια (sikotakia)
Assorted appetizers- (η) ποικιλία ορεκτικών (pikilia orektikon)
Spinach pie- (η) σπανακόπιτα (spanakopita)
Cheese pie- (η) τυρόπιτα (tiropita)

b. Salads-σαλάτες (salates)

Tomato and cucumber- ντομάτα και αγγούρι (domata ke agouri)
Lettuce and tomatoes- μαρούλι και ντομάτες (marouli ke domates)
Horiatiki/greek salad (tomatoes, peppers, onions and feta)-
   χωριάτικη/ελληνική σαλάτα
Eggplant salad- (η) μελιτζανοσαλάτα (melitzanosalata)
Potato salad- (η) πατατοσαλάτα (patatosalata)
Cabbage salad- (η) λαχανο-σαλάτα (lahano-salata)
Shrimp salad- (η) γαριδο-σαλάτα (gharithosalata)

c. Soups - (οι) σούπες (soupes)

Soup of the day - (η) σούπα της ημέρας (soupa tis imeras)
Egg and lemon soup/with rice or orzo - (το)αυγολέμονο
   (avgholemono)
Fish chowder - (η) κακαβιά (kakavia)
Tomato soup - (η) τοματόσουπα (tomatosoupa)
Kidney bean soup - (η) φασολάδα (fasolada)
Vegetable soup - (η) χορτόσουπα (hortosoupa)

Fish soup - (η) ψαρόσουπα (psarosoupa)
Chicken soup - (η) κοτόσουπα (kotosoupa)

d. Wegetables - (τα) λαχανικά (lahanika)

Artichoke - (η) αγκινάρα (aginara)
Potato - (η) πατάτα (patata)
Carrot - (το) καρότο (karoto)
Lettuce - (το) μαρούλι (marouli)
Cabbage - (το) λάχανο (lahano)
Corn - (το) αραποσίτι (arapositi)
Mushrooms - (τα) μανιτάρια (manitaria)
Eggplant/aubergine - (η) μελιτζάνα (melidzana)
Tomato - (η) ντομάτα (domata)
Pepper - (η) πιπεριά (piperia)
Peas - (ο) αρακάς/(τα) μπιζέλια (arakas/bizelia)
Cucumber - (το) αγγούρι (agouri)
Celery - (το) σέλινο (selino)
Onion - (το) κρεμμύδι (kremithi)
Garlic - (το)σκόρδο (skortho)
String beans - (τα) φασολάκια (fasolakia)
Spinach - (το) σπανάκι (spanaki)
Okra - (οι) μπάμιες (bamies)
Squash - (το) κολοκύθι (kolokithi)
Chicory/endives- (τα) αντίδια (adithia)
(wild) chicory - (τα) ραδίκια (rathikia)
Brussel sprouts - (τα) λαχανάκια Βρυξελών (lahanakia vrikselon)
Beets - (τα) πατζάρια (padzaria)

e. Cheeses - (τα) τυριά (tiria)

Traditional cheece made from goat milk - (η) φέτα (feta) Graviera/
    similar to gruyere; (Mytilene, Crete, Corfu Varieties are the
    best) (η) γραβιέρα (ghraviera)
Kefalotyri:a stronger saltier kind of cheese - (to) κεφαλοτύρι
Soft cottage or cream cheese type - (to) μανούρι (manouri)

Saltier soft cheese made from ewe's milk - (η) μυζήθρα (mizithra)
Soft very light cheese (the least caloric) - (το) ανθότυρο (anthotiro)

f. Sauces/dressings - (οι) σάλτσες (saltses)

Sauce- (η) σάλτσα (saltsa)
Vinegrette - (το) λαδόξυδο (lathoksitho)
Oil and lemon dressing - (το) λαδολέμονο (latholemono)
Mayonnaise - (η) μαγιονέζα (maghionesa)
Egg and lemon sauce - (το) αυγολέμονο (avgholemono)
White sauce/bechame l- (η) άσπρη σάλτσα (aspri Saltsa/besamela)
Tomato/red sauce - (η) σάλτσα ντομάτα/κόκκινη σάλτσα
   (saltsadomata/kokini)

g. Meats - (τα) κρέατα (kreata)

Meat - (το) κρέας (kreas)
Lamb/mutton - (το) αρνί (arni)
Spring (baby) lamb - (το) αρνάκι (arnaki)
Beef - (το) βοδινό (vothino)
Veal - (το) μοσχάρι (moshari)
Pork - (το) χοιρινό (hirino)
Ham - (το) ζαμπόν (zabon)
Ground meat - (ο) κιμάς (kimas)
Sausage - (το) λουκάνικο (loukaniko)
Liver - (το) συκώτι (sikoti)
Poultry - (τα) πουλερικά (poulerika)
Chicken - (το) κοτόποθλο (kotopoulo)
Turkey - (η) γαλοπούλα (yalopoula)
Duck - (η) πάπια (papia)
Partridge - (η) πέρδικα (perthika)
Pheasant - (ο) φασιανός (fasianos)

h. Seafood - (τα) θαλασσινά (thalasina)

Fish- (το) ψάρι (psari)
Fresh (adj.-φρέσκος(m),φρέσκια(f),φρέσκο(n)
    (freskos/freskia/fresko)
Cured (adj.- παστός/παστή/παστό (pastos/pasti/pasto)
Frozen - κατεψυγμένος/η/ο (katepsighmenos/i/o)
Lobster- (ο) αστακός (astakos)
Shrimp/prawns - (οι) γαρίδες (gharithes)
Crab - (το) καβούρι (kavouri)
Cod - (ο) μπακαλιάρος (bakaliaros)
Squid/calamari - (τα) καλαμάρια (kalamaria)
Octopus - (το) χταπόδι(htapothi)
Red mullet - (το) μπαρμπούνι (barbouni)
Gray mullet - (το) λιθρίνι (lithrini)
Mussels - (τα) μύδια (mithia)
Oysters - (τα) στρείδια (strithia)
Trout - (η) πέστροφα (pestrofa)
Sardine - (η) σαρδέλα (sarthela)
Small fry/sparling(tiny smelts) - (η) μαρίδα (marida)
Tuna fish - (ο) τόνος (tonos)
Swordfish - (ο) ξιφίας(ksifias)

i. Fruits and Nuts- (τα) φρούτα και ξηροί (frouta ke xiri karpi)

Fruit - (το) φρούτο (frouto)
Apple - (το) μήλο (milo)
Pear - (το) αχλάδι (ahlathi)
Orange - (το) πορτοκάλι (portokali)
Melon/cantaloupe - (το) πεπόνι (peponi)
Peach - (το) ροδάκινο (rothakino)
Watermelon - (το) καρπούζι (karpouzi)
Cherries - (τα) κεράσια (kerasia)
Strawberries - (οι) φράουλες (fraoules)
Banana - (η) μπανάνα (banana)
Fig - (το) σύκο (siko)

Date - (ο) χουρμάς (hourmas)
Pineapple - (ο) ανανάς (ananas)
Coconut - (η) καρύδα (karitha)
Plum - (το) δαμάσκηνο (thamaskino)
Quince - (to) κυδώνι (kithoni)
Kiwi - (το) ακτινίδιο (aktinithio)
Walnut - (το) καρύδι (karithi)
Almond - (το) αμύγδαλο (amighthalo)
Raisins - (οι) σταφίδες (stafithes)
Chestnut - (το) κάστανο (kastano)
Peanut - (το) φυστίκι (fistiki)
Hazelnut - (το) φουντούκι (foudouki)
Pistaccios - (τα) φυστίκια Αιγίνης (fistikia Eginis)

j. Desserts/Sweets - (το) επιδόρπιο/τα γλυκίσματα (epithorpio/ghlikismata)

Sugar cookie - (ο) κουραμπιές (kourabies)
Custard type pastry (with fillo dough and syrup) -
    το γαλακτομπούρεκο (ghalaktoboureko)
Shredded dough filled with walnuts and dipped in syrup -
    (το) κοταΐφι (kataifi)
Almond cookie - (το) αμυγδαλωτό (amighthaloto)
Baklava - (ο) μπακλαβάς (baklavas)
Honey cookie - (το) μελομακάρονο (melomakarono)
Sponge cake with syrup - (το) ρεβανί (revani)
Turkish delight - (το) λουκούμι (loukoumi)
Honey and sesame bar - (το) παστέλι (pasteli)
Rice pudding - (το) ριζόγαλο (rizoghalo)
Ice cream - (το) παγωτό (paghoto)
Apple pie - (η) μηλόπιτα (milopita)
Walnut cake - (η) καρυδόπιτα (karithopita)
Almond gateau - (η) πάστα αμυγδάλου (pasta amighthalou)
Chocolate gateau - (η) πάστα σοκολάτας (pasta sokolatas)
Glazed fruit - φρουί γκλασέ (froui glasse)
Fruit salad - (η) φρουτοσαλάτα(froutosalata)

k. Refreshments/Beverages - (τα) αναψυκτικά (anapsiktika)

Mineral water - (το) μεταλλικό νερό (metalliko nero)
Fresh - φρέσκος,φρέσκια,φρέσκο (freskos/freskia/fresko)
Fresh juice - (ο) φρέσκος χυμός (freskos himos)
Orange - (το) πορτοκάλι (portokali)
Apple - (το) μήλο (milo)
Banana - (η) μπανάνα (banana)
Mixed - μικτός/μικτή/μικτό (miktos/mikti/mikto)
Lemonade - (η) λεμονάδα(lemonatha)
Carbonated/fizzy-με ανθρακικό (me anthrakiko)
Noncarbonated - χωρίς ανθρακικό (horis anthrakiko)
Soda water - (η) σόδα (sotha)
Milk - (το) γάλα (ghala)
Cream - (η) κρέμα/σαντιγύ (krema/santighi)
Tea - (το) τσάι (tsai)
Coffees- (οι) καφέδες (kafethes)
Turkish coffee - (ο) τούρκικος καφές (tourkikos kafes)
Without sugar (very bitter) - (ο) σκέτος (sketos)
Medium - μέτριος (metrios)
Very sweet - βαρύς γλυκός (vari ghlikos)

(The above mentioned ways are how the coffee is prepared and served in a demitasse cup.)

Other coffees - άλλοι καφέδες (ali kafethes)
Coffee with milk - καφές με γάλα (kafes me ghala)
French coffee (similarly brewed to the american coffee)-
(ο) γαλλικός καφές (ghalikos kafes)
Espresso - καφές εσπρέσσο (kafes espresso)
Capuccino - καπουτσίνο (kapoutsino)
Nescaffe frappe/iced coffee - νες φραπέ (nes frape)
Chocolate - (το) κακάο (kakao)

(You may order all other drinks by their brand name.)

l. Wines - (τα) κρασιά (krasia)

Wine - (το) κρασί (krasi)
Cheers/to your health - στην υγειά σας (stin ighia sas)
Bottle - (το) μπουκάλι (boukali)
Carafe - (η) καράφα (karafa)
Glass - (το) ποτήρι (potiri)
Chilled/cold - παγωμένος, η, ο (paghomenos,i,o)
Dry - ξηρός, η, ο (ksiros)
Sweet - γλυκός, ιά, ό (ghlikos,ιά,ό)
Old- παλιός, ά,ό (palios)
White - άσπρος, -η, -ο (aspros)
Rose - ροζέ/ροζ (roze/roz)
Red - κόκκινος,η,ο (k okinos)
Retsina - (η) ρετσίνα (retsina)
Unresinated - (το) αρετσίνωτο (aretsinoto)
Sparkling - αεριούχος,α,ο (aeriouhos,α,ο)
Champagne - (η) σαμπάνια (sampania)

m. Drinks/Spirits - (τα) ποτά/οινοπνευματώδη
(pota/inopnevmatothi)

Alcohol - (το) οινόπνευμα (inopnevma)
Aperitif - (το) απερετίφ (aperitif)
Cocktai l- (το) κοκτέιλ (kokteil)
Ouzo - (το) ούζο (ouzo)
Beer - (η) μπύρα α (bira)
Liqueur (various flavors) - (το) λικέρ (liker)

(Most cocktails and mixed drinks are named and served the same way as elsewhere (i.e., whiskey sour/ουίσκυ σάουερ, gin and tonic/τζιν ανδ τόνικ, etc.)

Rum - (το) ρούμι (roumi)
Vodka - (η) βότκα (votka)
Whiskey - (το) ουίσκυ (ouiski)

On the rocks - με πάγο/παγάκια (me pagho/paghakia)

Whiskey and soda - ουίσκι με σόδα (ouiski me sotha)

If you wish to have a highball specify with gingerale/Seven-up, cognac/brandy - (το) κονιάκ/ μπρέντυ (koniak/brandi)

n. Foods/Greek specialities - (τα) ελληνικά φαγητά
(elinika faghita)

Country lamb (specially spiced wrapped lamb) -
    (το) εξοχικό αρνάκι (eksohiko arnaki)

Baked/roast lamb - (το) ψητό αρνί (psito arni)

Roast lamb with potatoes - ψητό αρνί με πατάτες (psito arni me patates)

Lamb with:- αρνί με: (arni me):

String beans - φασολάκια (fasolakia)

Okra - μπάμιες (bamies)

Pasta/orzo - γιουβέτσι (ghiouvetsi)

Stuffed tomatoes/ peppers/ eggplants - γεμιστές ντομάτες/ πιπεριές/ μελιτζάνες (ghemistes doma tes/piperies/melitzanes)

Moussaka - (ο) μουσακάς (mousakas)

(eggplant/potato, ground meat and white sauce)

Pastitsio - (το) παστίτσιο (pastitsio) (pasta, ground meat and white sauce)

Meatballs - (οι) κεφτέδες (keftethes) (τα) κεφτεδάκια (keftethakia)

Stuffed grape - (οι) ντολμάδες (dolmathes)

Leaves - (τα) ντολμαδάκια (dolmathakia)

Shish-kebab - (τα) σουβλάκια (souvlakia)

Stew - (το) στυφάδο (stifatho)

Hamburger - (το) μπιφτέκι (bifteki)

Steak (chop) - (η) μπριζόλα (brizola)

Sirloin - (η)νεφραμιά (neframia)

Pork chop - (η) χοιρινή μπριζόλα (hirini brizola)

Veal chop - (η) μοσχαρίσια μπριζόλα (mosharisia brizola)

Lamb chop - (η) αρνίσια μπριζόλα/τα παϊδάκια (arnisia brizola/ ta piedakia)

Fillet - (το)φιλέτο(fileto)
Spit roasted chicken - (το) κοτόπουλο της σούβλας (kotopoulo tis souvlas)

Parts of the chicken:

Breast - (το) στήθος (stithos)
Leg - (το) μπούτι (bouti)
Wing - (η) φτερούγα(fterougha)

Ham and eggs - ζαμπόν με αυγά (zabon me avgha)
Boiled eggs - (τα) βραστά αυγά (vrasta avgha)
Fried eggs - (τα) τηγανιτά αυγά (tighanita avgha)
Scrambled eggs - (τα) κτυπητά αυγά (ktipita avgha)
Omelet - (η) ομελέτα (omeleta)

5b. Eating at the restaurant
Τρώγοντας στο εστιατόριο
(Troghontas sto estiatorio)

Waiter, may we see a menu, please?
Γκαρσόν, μπορούμε να δούμε έναν κατάλογο,παρακαλώ;
(garson, boroume na thoume enan katalogho parakalo?)

Do you have any specials today? What do you suggest?
Έχετε κάτι το ιδιαίτερο/σπέσιαλ σήμερα; Τι προτείνετε;
(ehete kati to ithietero/special simera? Ti protinete?)

We have fried cod with garlic sauce and braised chicken with mushrooms for today.
Έχουμε τηγανιτό μπακαλιάρο σκορδαλιά και κοτόπουλο με μανιτάρια σήμερα
(ehoume tighanito bakaliaro skorthalia ke kotopoulo me manitaria simera)

Wonderful, we will start with ouzo and some appetizers. My spouse/friend will have the chicken with mushrooms and I will have the traditional moussaka.

Θαυμάσια, θα αρχίσουμε με ούζο και μερικά ορεκτικά ο(m.)/ η(f.) σύζυγος/φίλος/φίλη μου θα έχει το κοτόπουλο με τα μανιτάρια κι εγώ Θα έχω τον παραδοσιακό μουσακά

(thavmasia, tha archisoume me ouzo ke merika orektika. O(m.)/i (f.) sizighos/filos(m.)/i(f.) tha pari to kotopoulo me manitaria ki egho to parathosiako moussaka)

We will also have butter for our bread and a lettuce and tomato salad.

Επίσης θα έχουμε βούτυρο για το ψωμί μας και μια σαλάτα μαρούλι και ντομάτα

(episis tha ehoume voutiro ghia to psomi mas ke mia salata marouli ke domata)

What are you going to drink with your meal?

Τι θα πιείτε με το φαγητό σας;

(ti tha piite me to faghito sas?)

We will have a carafe of the house wine, if it's unresinated.

Θα έχουμε μια καράφα από το κρασί σας, αν είναι αρετσίνοτο

(tha ehoume mia karafa apo to krasi sas, an ine aretsinoto)

Everything was very tasty and the wine superb. May we have the check, please?

Όλα ήταν πολύ νόστιμα και το κρασί υπέροχο. Μπορούμε να έχουμε το λογαριασμό, παρακαλώ

(ola itan poli nostima ke to krasi iperoho. Boroume na ehoume to logharias-mo, parakalo?)

Thank you sir/madam, here is the check. Have a good night.

Σας ευχαριστούμε κύριε/κυρία, ορίστε ο λογαριασμός. Καλή σας νύχτα

(sas efharistoume kirie/kiria, oriste o loghariasmos. Kali sas nichta)

6. Shopping-Ψώνια (psonia)

General Vocabulary

Store/shop - κατάστημα/μαγαζί (katastima/ma/maghazi)
Bakery shop- (το) αρτοποιείο/(ο) φούρνος (artopiio/fournos)
Grocery- (το) παντοπωλείο, (το) μπακάλικο (pantopolio/bakaliko)
Butcher shop- (το) κρεοπωλείο (kreopolio)
Green grocer's- (το) μανάβικο (manaviko)
Fish market- (το) ιχθυοπωλείο (το) ψαράδικο (ihhiopolio/
     psarathiko)
Supermarket- (το) σουπερ μάρκετ(sooper market)
Patisserie/pastry shop- (το) ζαχαροπλαστείο (zaharoplastio)
Cafe- (το) καφενείο (kafenio)
Florist's shop- (το) ανθοπωλείο (anthopolio)
Drugstore/pharmacy/chemist's- (το) φαρμακείο (farmakio)
Department store- (το) πολυκατάστημα (polikatastima)
Shopping center/mall-εμπορικό κέντρο(emboriko kentro)
Clothing store- (το) κατάστηνα ρούχων (katastima rouhon)
Shoe store- (το) κατάστημα υποδημάτων (katastima ipothimaton)
Leather goods- (τα) δερμάτινα είδη (thermatina ithi)
Jewelry shop- (το) κοσμηματοπωλείο/ χρυσοχοείο
     (kosmimatopolio/hrisohoio)
Bookstore/stationery- (το) βιβλιοπωλείο/χαρτοπωλείο
     (vivliopolio/har-topolio)
Photo/camera shop- (το) φωτογραφείο (photografio)
Souvenir/gift shop- (το) κατάστημα σουβενίρ/δώρων (katastima
     souvenir/horon)
Toy shop/store- (το) κατάστημα παιχνιδιών (katastima pehnithion)
Sporting goods- (τα) αθλητικά είδη (athlitika ithi)
Art gallery- (η) γκαλερύ τέχνης (galeri technis)
Arts and crafts- (τα) είδη λαικής τέχνης (ithi la•kis technis)
Antique shop- (το) κατάστημα για αντίκες (katastima ghia antikes)

1. Where are you going?
Πού πηγαίνετε;
(pou pighenete?)

We are going shopping. Where is the nearest shopping center, please?

Πηγαίνουμε να ψωνίσουμε/πάμε για ψώνια. Πού είναι το πλησιέστερο εμπορικό κέντρο, παρακαλώ;

(pighenoume na psonisoume. Poo ine to plisiestero eboriko kedro parakalo?)

The nearest shopping center is in Kifissia. What are you interested in?

Το πλησιέστερο εμπορικό κέντρο είναι στη Κηφισσιά.
Για τι ενδιαφέρεστε;

(to plisiestero eboriko kedro ine sti Kifissia. Ghia ti enthiafereste;)

We want to buy a pair of shoes, a leather pocketbook, jewelry and other items.

Θέλουμε ν'αγοράσουμε ένα ζευγάρι παπούτσια, μία δερμάτινη τσάντα, Κοσμήματα κι άλλα αντικείμενα

(theloume n'aghorasoume ena zevghari papoutsia, mia thermatini tsanta, kosmimata ki ala antikimena)

Beautiful! You will be able to find there whatever you want. There is a variety of stores.

Ωραία! θα βρείτε εκεί ό,τι θέλετε. Υπάρχει μεγάλη ποικιλία καταστημάτων

(orea! tha vrite ekei oti thelete. Iparhi pikilia katastimaton)

3. Are the sale clerks helpful? We need help with sizes and prices.

Είναι οι πωλητές/πωλήτριες ευγενικοί/ευγενικές; Χρειαζόμαστε βοήθεια με τα μεγέθη και τις τιμές

(ine i polites/politries eksipiretiki/es? Hriazomaste vo•thia me ta meghethi ke tis times)

Yes, they will help you a lot. Tell them your size and they will give you the corresponding European/Greek size.

Ναι, θα σας βοηθήσουν πολύ. Πείτε τους το μέγεθός σας και θα σας δώσουν το αντίστοιχο ευρωπαικό/ελληνικό μέγεθος

(ne, tha sas voithisoon poli. Pite tous to meghethos sas ke tha sas thosoon to andistiho evropaiko meghethos)

4. Could you please show me those shoes in the window? I'm size 8.

Μπορείτε να μου δείξετε αυτά τα παπούτσια στη βιτρίνα; Φορώ νούμερο οχτώ

(borite na moo thiksete afta ta papoutsia sti vitrina? Foro noumero ohto)

With pleasure! The same color?

Ευχαρίστως! Το ίδιο χρώμα;

(efharistos! To ithio hroma?)

Yes, thank you. How much are they?

Ναι, ευχαριστώ. Πόσο κάνουν;

(ne, efharisto. Poso kanoun?)

18,000 drachmas.

Δεκαοκτώ χιλιάδες δραχμές.

(theka okto hiliathes thrahmes)

5. What else would you like?

Τι άλλο θα θέλατε;

(ti alo tha thelate?)

We will look around to see what else we need.

Θα κοιτάξουμε να δούμε τι άλλο χρειαζόμαστε.

(tha kitaksoume na thoume ti alo hriazomaste)

Go ahead, browse as long as you want.

Κοιτάξτε με την ησυχία σας, όσο θέλετε.

(kitakste me tin isihia sas, oso thelete)

Where is the men's department please?

Πού είναι τα ανδρικά ρούχα, παρακαλώ;

(poo ine ta anthrika rooha parakalo?)

Men's clothes are on the second floor.
Τα ανδρικά ρούχα είναι στο δεύτερο όροφο
(ta anthrika rooha ine sto theftero orofo)

May I help you, please?
Μπορώ να σας βοηθήσω, παρακαλώ;
(boro na sas voithiso parakalo?)

Yes, I'd like to buy a shirt please.
Ναι, θα ήθελα ν'αγοράσω ένα πουκάμισο,παρακαλώ.
(ne, tha ithela n'aghoraso ena pookamiso,parakalo)

What color and what size, please?
Τι χρώμα και τι νούμερο παρακαλώ;
(ti hroma ke ti noomero parakalo?)

I think this is the one I want. How much does it cost?
Νομίζω ότι αυτό θέλω, πόσο κοστίζει;
(nomizo oti afto thelo, poso costizi?)

Thirty euros.
τριάντα ευρώ
Trianta evro

Thank you very much. I'll take that and I will continue my shop-
    ping at the bookstore to get the books I'm interested in.
Ευχαριστώ πολύ. Θα το πάρω αυτό και θα συνεχίσω τα ψώνια μου
    στο βιβλιοπωλείο για να πάρω τα βιβλία που ενδιαφέρομαι.
(efharisto poli, tha to paro afto ke tha sinehiso ta psonia moo sto
    vivliopolio ghia na paro ta vivlia poo m'enthiaferoon)

What books are you interested in?
Τι βιβλία σας ενδιαφέρουν;
(ti vivlia sas enthiaferoon?)

History, art, and language books. Also English magazines and
  newspapers.
Βιβλία ιστορίας και γλώσσας. Επίσης περιοδικά και εφημερίδες
  στην αγγλική.
(vlvlia istorias, technis ke ghlossas. Episis periothika ke efimerithes
  stin agliki)

You will find the books you need at the bookstore and the rest at
  a kiosk.
Θα βρείτε τα βιβλία που χρειάζεστε στο βιβλιοπωλείο και τα
  υπόλοιπα στο περίπτερο.
(tha vrite ta vivlia poo hriazeste sto vivliopolio ke ta ipolipa s' ena
  periptero)

7. Services-Υπηρεσίες (ipiresies)

a. Beauty salon/Barber shop
Κομμωτήριο/κουρείο
(Komotirio/Koorio)

Vocabulary

Beautician- (η)κομμώτρια (f.), (ο) κομμωτής (m.) (komotria/komotis)
Color- (το) χρώμα (hroma)
Haircut- (το) κούρεμα/κόψιμο (koorema/kopsimo malion)
Permanent- περμανάντ (permanant)
Shampoo- (το) σαμπουαν/λούσιμο (sampouan/loosimo)
Touch-up- (το) χρωμο-σαμπουάν (hromo-sampouan)
Manicure- (το) μανικιούρ (manikiour)
Pedicure- (το) πεντικιούρ (pendikiour)
Barber- (ο) κουρέας (kooreas)
Shaving- (το) ξύρισμα (ksirisma)

1. Where is a good beauty salon, please?
Πού είναι ένα καλό κομμωτήριο, παρακαλώ;
(poo ine ena kalo komotirio, parakalo?)

Your hotel has a good beauty salon.

Το ξενοδοχείο σας έχει καλό κομμωτήριο.

(to ksenothohio sas ehi kalo komotirio)

2. I'd like to make an appointment for tomorrow morning at 9:30.

Θέλω να κάνω ένα ραντεβού για αύριο το πρωϊ, στις εννεα και μιση.

(thelo na kano ena rantevoo ghia avrio to proi stis enea ke misi)

Sorry, but we have nothing in the morning. You may have one in the afternoon at four o'clock, if you wish.

Λυπάμαι, αλλά δεν έχουμε τίποτε για το πρωϊ. Μπορείτε να έχετε το απόγευμα στις τέσσερες η ώρα, εάν θέλετε.

(lipame ala then ehoume tipote ghia to proi. Borite na ehete to apoghevma stis tesseres i ora, ean thelete)

3. What would you like done?

Τι θα θέλατε;

(ti tha thelate?)

I'd like to have my hair shampooed, cut, and blow-dried.

Θέλω λούσιμο, κόψιμο και φορμάρισμα.

(thelo loosimo, kopsimo ke pistolaki/formarisma)

I would also like to have my nails done.

Επίσης θα ήθελα ένα μανικιούρ.

(episis tha ithela ena manikiour)

b. Bank- Τράπεζα (trapeza)

Vocabulary

Work hours- (οι) ώρες εργασίας (ores erghasias)
Banker- (ο) τραπεζίτης (trapezitis)
Bank employee- (ο, η) τραπεζιτικός υπάλληλος (trapezitikos ipalilos)
Teller/cashier- (ο) ταμίας (tamias)

Bank window- (η) θυρίδα (thiritha)

Exchange- (το) συνάλλαγμα (sinalaghma)

Passbook- (το) βιβλιάριο (vivliario)

Account- (ο) λογαριασμός (loghariasmos)

Check/draft- (η) επιταγή (epitaghi)

Foreign currency- (το) ξένο νόμισμα (kseno nomisma)

Greek currency- (το) ελληνικό νόμισμα (eliniko nomisma)

Money- (τα) χρήματα (hrimata)

Coin(s)- (το/τα) κέρμα/κέρματα (kerma/ta)

Drachma/drachmas- (η/οι) δραχμή/δραχμές (thrahmi/thrahmes)

5 drs- (το) τάληρο/πέντε (taliro/pende thrahmes)

10 drs- (το) δεκάρικο/δέκα δραχμές (thekariko/theka thrahmes)

20 drs- (το) εικοσάρικο/είκοσι δραχμές (ikosariko/ikosi thrahmes)

50 drs- (το) πενηντάρικο/πενήντα δραχμές (penintariko/peninda thrahmes)

100 drs- (το) κατοστάρικο/ εκατό δραχμές (katostariko/ekato thrahmes)

500 drs- (το) πεντακοσάρικο/πεντακόσιες δραχμές (pendakosariko/pendakosies thrahmes)

1.000 drs- (το) χιλιάρικο/χίλιες δραχμές (hiliariko/hilies thrahmes)

5.000 drs- (το) πεντοχίλιαρο/πέντε χιλιάδες (pendohiliaro/pende Hiliathes thrahmes)

10.000 drs- (το) δεκαχίλιαρο/δέκα χιλιάδες (thekahiliaro/theka Hiliathes thrahmes)

Million- (το) εκατομμύριο (ekatomirio)

1. Where is the nearest bank? I need to have some dollars/Br. pounds changed.

Πού είναι η πλησιέστερη τράπεζα; Χρειάζομαι ν'αλλάξω μερικά δολλάρια/στερλίνες

(poo ine i plisiesteri trapeza? Hriazome n'alakso merika tholaria/ sterlines)

The National Bank of Greece is on this street.

Η Εθνική Τράπεζα της Ελλάδας είναι σ'αυτή την οδό.

(i Ethniki Trapeza Elathas ine s'afti tin otho)

2. What is the exchange rate for US dollar today?
Ποιά είναι η ισοτιμία για το αμερικανικό δολλάριο σήμερα;
(pia ine i isotimia ghia to amerikaniko tholario simera?)

The price of the dollar today is 1,120 euro.
Η τιμή του δολλαρίου σήμερα είναι ένα ευρώ και 12 λεπτά.
(i timi too tholarioo simera ine ena evro kai dodeka lepta)

Thank you. I'd like to change $500.
Ευχαριστώ. Θέλω να αλλάξω/χαλάσω πεντακόσια δολλάρια
(efharisto. Thelo na alakso/halaso pendakosia tholaria)

May I have your passport, please?
Μπορώ να έχω το διαβατήριό σας, παρακαλώ;
(boro na eho to thiavatirio sas, parakalo?)

c. Post office-Ταχυδρομείο Tahidromio

Vocabulary

Postman- (ο) ταχυδρόμος (tahithromos)
Letter- (το) γράμμα(η) επιστολή (ghrama/epistoli)
Parcel/package- (το) δέμα/πακέτο (thema/paketo)
Stamp(s)- (το/τα) γραμματόσημο/α (ghramatosimo/a)
Air mail-αεροπορικώς (aeroporikos)
Registered- συστημένος,η,ο (sistimenos/i/o)
Address- (η) διεύθυνση (thiefthinsi)
Postal order- (η) ταχυδρομική επιταγή (tahithromiki epitaghi)
Amount- (το) ποσό(ν)(poso(n))

1. Where is the post office, please?
Πού είναι το ταχυδρομείο, παρακαλώ;
(poo ine to tahithromio parakalo?)

2. What time does the post office open/close?
Τι ώρα ανοίγει/κλείνει το ταχυδρομείο;
(ti ora anighi/klini to tahithromio?)

Most post offices open at eight o' clock in the morning and close at two in the afternoon.

Τα περισσότερα ταχυδρομεία ανοίγουν στις οκτώ η ώρα το πφωί και κλείνουν στις δύο το απόγευμα.

(ta perisotera tahithromia anighoon stis okto i ora to proi ke klinoon stis thio to apoghevma)

3. I'd like to send a letter by express mail to New York and a package in England.

Θέλω να στείλω ένα επείγον γράμμα στην Νέα Υόρκη και ένα πακέτο στην Αγγλία.

(thelo na stilo ena epighon ghrama stin Nea Iorki ke ena thema stin Aglia)

4. Please put the zip code. It's very important.

Παρακαλώ βάλτε τον κωδικό αριθμό, είναι σημαντικό.

(parakalo, valte ton kothiko arithmo, ine simantiko)

Fill in this form and sign it.

Συμπληρώστε αυτό το έντυπο και υπογράψτε το.

(simpliroste afto to entipo ke ipoghrapste to)

Pay at that window, please.

Πληρώστε σ'αυτή τη θυρίδα, παρακαλώ.

(pliroste s'afti ti thiritha, parakalo)

Note: The Greek Post Office (ELTA) is not involved with telegrams or telephones. It deals exclusively with correspondence, money orders, stamps, and parcels. Also, phone cards can be purchased there. In addition, anything that has to do with UNICEF and other philanthropic organizations. OTE, the Greek Telecommunications Organization, controls telephones, telegrams, and cables. Many mobile phone companies are established constantly, and the competition is evident via the attractive offers that each company tenders to new customers. The most convenient and economical way to call is at phone booths using a previously purchased telecard (τηλεκάρτα/tilekarta). Phone cards are sold at most kiosks. Metered phones are also provided in most kiosks for easy phoning. The nearest OTE office, hopefully, will accommodate you in sending telegrams/cables/faxes or e-mail.

d. Telephones/telegrams-Τηλέφωνα/τηλεγραφήματα Tilefona/tileghrafimata

Vocabulary

Phone booth- (ο) τηλεφωνικός θάλαμος (tilefonikos thalamos)
Public/pay phone- (το) τηλέφωνο για το κοινό (tilefono ghia to kino)
Meter- (ο) μετρητής (metritis)
Area code- (ο) κωδικός περιοχής/πόλης (kothikos periohis/polis)
Answering machine- (ο) τηλεφωνητής (tilephonitis)
Message- (το) μήνυμα (minima)
Wrong number- λάθος αριθμός (lathos arithmos)
Out of order- δεν λειτουργεί/ έχει βλάβη (then litoorghi/ ehi vlavi)
Telephone number- (ο) αριθμός τηλεφώνου (arithmos tilephonou)
Cable office- (το) τηλεγραφείο (tileghrafio)
Cable/telegram- (το) τηλεγράφημα (tileghrafima)

1. I'd like to make a phone call but I have to reverse the charges, is it possible?
Θέλω να κάνω ένα τηλεφώνημα, αλλά πρέπει να χρεωθεί ο παραλήπτης, είναι δυνατόν;
(thelo na kano ena tilephonima ala prepi na hreothi o paraliptis, ine thina-ton?)

Yes, it is. What is the number and what is your name?
Μάλιστα, είναι. Ποιός είναι ο αριθμός και πώς λέγεστε;
(malista, ine. Pios ine o arithmos ke pos legheste?)

2. Sorry, no one is there. There is an answering machine. Would you like to leave a message?
Λυπάμαι, δεν απαντά κανείς, έχουν τηλεφωνητή θέλετε ν'αφήσετε μήνυμα;
(lipame,then apanda kanis,ehoun tilefoniti thelete n'afisete minima?

No, thank you. I will call later.
Οχι, ευχαριστώ. Θα τηλεφωνήσω αργότερα.
(ohi, efharisto. Tha tilephoniso arghotera)

3. I want to send a cable to Boston, where is the nearest OTE office, please?
Θέλω να στείλω ένα τηλεγράφημα στη Βοστώνη, πού είναι το πλησιέστερο γραφείο του ΟΤΕ, παρακαλώ;
(thelo na stilo ena tileghrafima sti Vostoni, poo ine to plisiestero ghrafio too OTE, parakalo?)

4. May I have a form?
Μπορώ να έχω ένα έντυπο;
(boro na eho ena entipo?)

How much will it cost? It will be about eighteen words.
Πόσο θα στοιχίσει; Θα είναι περίπου δεκαοκτώ λέξεις.
(poso tha stihisi? tha ine peripoo theka okto leksis)

It's approximately 80 drs per word.
Είναι περίπου ογδόντα δραχμές η λέξη.
(ine peripou oghthonda thrahmes i leksi)

5. When will they receive it?
Πότε θα το λάβουν;
(pote tha to lavoon?)

It should get there tomorrow noon (Boston time).
Θα πρέπει να φθάσει αύριο το μεσημέρι(ώρα Βοστώνης).
(tha prepi na fthasi avrio to mesimeri (ora Vostonis))

That's fine, thank you.

Εντάξει, σας ευχαριστώ.

(entaksi, sas efharisto)

e. Dry cleaning/Laundromat-Στεγνωκαθαριστήριο/Πλυντήριο (steghnokatharistirio/Plintirio)

Vocabulary

Cleaner's- (το) καθαριστήριο (katharistirio)
Cleaning- (το) καθάρισμα (katharisma)
Dry-cleaning- (το) στεγνό καθάρισμα (steghno katharisma)
Washing- (το) πλύσιμο (plisimo)
Ironing- (το) σιδέρωμα (sitheroma)
Stain- (ο) λεκές(lekes)

1. I need to have some clothes cleaned. Does the hotel provide dry cleaner's?

Πρέπεινακαθαρίσωμερικάρούχα,έχειτοξενοδοχείοκαθαριστήριο;

(prepi na kathariso merika rooha, ehi to ksenothohio katharistirio?)

No, unfortunately, there is one near by, though.

Όχι, δυστυχως, αλλά είναι ένα πολύ κοντά όμως.

(ohi, thistihos, ala ine ena poli konda)

2. These pants need to be pressed. Could you also remove a stain from a silk blouse/shirt?

Αυτά τα παντελόνια πρέπει να σιδερωθούν. Μπορείτε επίσης να βγάλετε ένα λεκέ από μία μεταξωτή μπλούζα/ένα πουκάμισο;

(afta ta pandelonia prepi na sitherothoon. Borite episis na vghalete ena leke apo mia metaksoti blouza/ena pookamiso?)

3. How much does it cost to have a suit cleaned?

Πόσο κοστίίζει να καθαριστεί ένα κουστούνι;

(poso kostizi na katharisti ena koostoomi,?)

It depends on the material. It's about 2.000 to 3.000 drs.
Εξαρτάται από το ύφασμα, είναι περίπου δύο με τρεις χιλιάδες
δραχμές.
(eksartate apo to ifasma, ine peripoo thio me tris hiliathes thrahmes)

4. Is there a laudromat nearby? I have to do my laundry.
Υπάρχει κανένα πλυντήριο εδώ κοντά; Πρέπει να πλύνω τα ρούχα
μου.
(iparhi kanena plintirio etho konda? Prepi na plino ta rooha moo)

There is one next to the cleaner's.
Υπάρχει ένα δίπλα στο καθαριστήριο.
(ine ena thipla sto katharistirio)

Thank you.
Ευχαριστώ.
(efharisto)

8. Medical services-Ιατρικές Υπηρεσίες
(iatrikes ipiresies)

General Vocabulary

Mmedical care- (η) ιατρική περίθαλψη (iatriki perithalpsi)
Doctor- (ο, η) ιατρός/γιατρός (yiatros)
Emergency- (η) έκτακτη ανάγκη (ektakti anagi)
Illness- (η) αρρώστια/ασθένεια (arostia/asthenia)
Ill/sick/patient- (ο, η) ασθενής/άρρωστος,η.ο (asthenis/arostos,i,o)
Abscess- (το) απόστημα/οίδημα (apostima/ithima)
Ache/pain- (ο) πόνος (ponos)
Acute pain- (ο) δυνατός πόνος (thinatos/entonos ponos)
It aches/hurts- πονάει (ponai)
I am ill/sick- είμαι άρρωστος (m)/η (f) (ime arostos/i)
I'm feverish- έχω πυρετό(eho pireto)
Cold- (το)κρύο/κρυολόγημα (krio/kriologhima)
I'm cold- κρυώνω (kriono)

I have chills-έχω ρίγη/κρυάδες (eho righi/κρυάδες)
Antibiotic- (το) αντιβιωτικό (antiviotiko)
Asthma- (το) άσθμα (asthma)
Allergy-(η) αλλεργία (alerghia)
Appendicitis- (η) σκωληκοειδίτιδα (skolikoithititha)
Appetite- (η) όρεξη (oreksi)
Bleeding- (η) αιμορραγία (emoraghia)
Bckache- (ο) πόνος στη πλάτη (ponos sti plati)
Bruise- (ο) μόλωπας (molopas/melania)
Blister- (η) φουσκάλα (fouskala)
Burn- (το) έγκαυμα (egavma)
Bite- (το) τσίμπημα (tsimpima)
Cancer- (ο) καρκίνος (karkinos)
Concussion- (η) διάσηση (thiasisi)
Constipation- (θ) δυσκοιλιότητατα (thiskiliotita)
Convulsion(s)- (ο) σπασμός/οί (spasmos/i)
Cough- (ο) βήχας (vihas)
I'm choking- πνίγομαι (pnighome)
Cramp- (ο) σπασμός/(η) κράμπα (spasmos/kraba)
I cut –κόβω/έκοψα (kovo/ekopsa)
Dehydration- (η) αφιδάτωση (afithatosi)
Diabetes- (ο) διαβήτης/(το) ζάχαρο (thiavitis/zaharo)
Diabetic- (adj.) διαβητικός,η,ο (thavitikos,i,o)
Diarrhoea- (η) διάρροια (thiaria)
Dizziness- (η) ζάλη/ζαλάδα (zali/zalatha)
Ear ache- (ο) πόνος στο αυτί (ponos sto afti)
Fainting- (η) λιποθυμία (lipothimia)
Fatigue- (η) κόποση/έντονη κούραση (koposi/entoni kourasi)
Food poisoning- (η) τροφική δηλητηρίαση (trofiki thilitiriasi)
Fracture- (το) κάταγμα (kataghma)
Heart attack- (η) καρδιακή προσβολή/(το) έμφραγμα
(karthiaki prosvoli/emfraghma)
Headache- (ο) πονοκέφαλος (ponokefalos)
Hay fever- (το) αλλεργικό συνάχι (alerghiko sinahi)
Indigestion- (η) δυσπεψία (thispepsia)
Infection- (η) μόλυνση (molinsi)

Inflammation- (η) ανάφλεξη/φλεγμονή (anafleksi/fleghmoni)
Infuenza/flu- (η) γρίπη/(ο)ιός (ghripi))
Insomnia- (η) αυπνία (aipnia)
Itch- (η) φαγούρα (faghoura)
Lump- (ο) όγκος/(η) μάζα (ogos/maza)
Mausea/sea-sickness- (η) ναυτία (naftia)
Palpitations- (ο) παλμός/(η) ταχυκαρδία (palmos/tahikarthia)
Rash- (το) εξάνθημα (eksanthima)
Arthritis/rheumatism- (η) αρθρίτιδα/(οι) ρευματισμοί
　　(arthrititha/revmatismi)
Sore throat- (ο) πονόλαιμος (ponolemos)
Sting- (το) κέντρισμα (kentrisma)
Sprain- (το) διάστρεμα (thiastrema)
Stomachache- (ο) στομαχόπονος (stomahoponos)
Sunburn- (το) έγκαυμα/ηλίαση (egavma/iliako)
Stroke- (η) αποπληξία/(το) εγκεφαλικό (apopliskia/egefaliko)
Sunstroke- (η) ηλίαση (iliasi)
Swelling- (το) πρήξιμο (priksimo)
Symptom- (το) σύμπτωμα (simptoma)
Tonsillitis- (η) αμυγδαλίτιδα (amighthalititha)
Ulcer- (το) έλκος (elkos)

a. At the hospital-το νοσοκομείο- (nosokomio)

Visiting a doctor-Επίσκεψη σε γιατρό-(episkepsi se ghiatro

1. I must go to a hospital. I'm not feeling well. I have to see a
　　doctor.
Πρέπει να πάω στο νοσοκομείο, δεν αισθάνομαι καλά, πρέπει να
　　ιδώ ένα γιατρό
(prepi na pao sto nosokomio, then esthanome kala, prepi na itho
　　ena ghiatro)

What is the matter? Are you in pain? Do you have a temperature?
Τι συμβαίνει; Πονάτε; Έχετε πυρετό;
(ti simveni? ponate? ehete pireto?)

2. I can't exactly describe my symptoms but I feel ill. I haven't taken my temperature yet.

Δεν μπορώ να σας περιγράψω τα συμπτώματά μου ακριβώς, αλλά Νοιώθω άρρωστος (m) άρρωστη (f). Δεν έχω πάρει την θερμοκρασία μου/Δεν έβαλα θερμόμετρο.

(then boro na sas perighrapso ta simptomata mou akrivos, ala niotho arostos/i. Then eho pari ti thermokrasia moo/then evala thermometro)

3. Your temperature is normal and your blood pressure is fine. Are you taking any medication?

Η θερμοκρασία σας είναι φυσιολογική και η πίεσή σας εντάξει. Παίρνετε κανένα φάρμακο;

(i thermokrasia sas ine phisiologhiki ke i piesi sas entaksi. Pernete kanena farmako?)

I dont see anything disturbing, just to make sure, however, we'll have some tests done.

Δεν βλέπω τίποτε το ανησυχιστικό, για να βεβαιωθούμε όμως θα κάνουμε μερικές εξετάσεις.

(then vlepo tipote to anisihitiko, ghia na veveothoume omos tha kanoume merikes eksetasis)

4. What kind of tests? Do I have to stay in the hospital?

Τι είδους εξετάσεις; Πρέπει να μείνω στο νοσοκομείο;

(ti ithous eksetasis? Prepi na mino sto nosokomio?)

We'll have a cardiogram, blood and urine tests. The whole thing willtake approximately two hours.

Θα κάνουμε ένα καρδιογράφημα και εξέταση αίματος και ούρων. Η όλη υπόθεση θα πάρει περίπου δύο ώρες.

(tha kanoume ena karthioghrafima ke eksetasi ematos ke ouron. I oli ipothesi tha pari peripou thio ores)

5. I think that you're suffering from exhaustion. Rest for a couple
   of days and you will feel much better.
   Νομίζω ότι υποφέρετε από υπερκόπωση, ξεκουραστείτε λίγο και
   θα αισθανθείτε καλύτερα.
   (nomizo oti ipoferete apo iperkoposi, ksekoorastite ligho ke tha
   esthanthite kalitera)

Thank you, Doctor. Should I take any medication? What do I owe
   you? I will call you for the test results.
   Σας ευχαριστώ γιατρέ. Θα πάρω κανένα φάρμακο; Τι σας οφείλω;
   Θα σας τηλεφωνήσω για τ'αποτελέσματα.
   (sas efharisto ghiatre. Tha paro kanena farmako? Ti sas ofilo? Tha
   sas tilephoniso ghia t'apotelesmata)

b. Symptoms and complaints

I'm wounded- είμαι πληγωμένος/η/ο (ime plighomenos,i,o)
My arm is broken- ο βραχίονας είναι σπασμένος/ραγισμένος (ο
   vrahionas moo ine spasmenos/raghismenos)
I need an x-ray- χρειάζομαι ακτινογραφία (hriazome aktinoghrafia)
My head hurts, I need a pain killer- το κεφάλι μου πονάει, χρειάζομαι
   παυσίπονο. (to kefali moo ponai, hriazome pafsipono)
I have a heart condition, I must see a doctor- Έχω πρόβλημα καρδιάς,
   πρέπει να δω γιατρό. (eho provlima karthias, prepi na tho ghiatro)
I'm diabetic, I need insulin- είμαι διαβητικός/η, πρέπει να έχω
   ινσουλίνη. (ime thiavitikos,i prepi na eho insoulini)
I have some burns. I'd like an antiseptic- Έχω εγκαύματα, θέλω
   αντισηπτικό.(eho egavmata, thelo antisiptiko)
Please call an ambulance- παρακαλώ καλέστε ένα ασθενοφόρο
   (parakalo kaleste ena asthenoforo)

c. Denstist- (ο, η) οδοντίατρος/οδοντογιατρός (othodiatros/othodoghiatros)

1. Could you recommend a dentist? I have a terrible toothache.
Μπορείτε να συστήσετε έναν οδοντογιατρό; `Εχω φοβερό πονόδοντο.
(borite na mas sistisete enan othodoghiatro? eho fovero ponothodo)

There is a good dentist in my neighborhood. He will help you.
Είναι ένας καλός οδοντογιατρός στη γειτονιά μου, θα σας βοηθήσει.
(ine enas kalos othondoghiatros sti ghitonia moo, tha sas voithisi)

2. Your tooth is abscessed. It must be extracted.
`Εχετε ένα απόστημα, το δόντι σας πρέπει να βγει.
(ehete ena apostima, to thonti sas prepi na vghi)

Could you do something temporarily?
Μπορείτε να κάνετε κάτι προσωρινά ;
(borite na kanete kati prosorina?)

I'm afraid not, but if you insist, I'll give a prescription to relieve the pain.
Φοβάμαι πως όχι, αλλά εάν επιμένετε θα σας δώσω μια συνταγή να πάρετε κάτι για τον πόνο.
(fovame pos ohi, ala ean epimenete tha sas thoso mia syntaghi na parete kati ghia ton pono)

Thank you. I also need something for my gums. They're irritated.
Ευχαριστώ, επίσης χρειάζομαι κάτι για τα ούλα μου, είναι ερεθισμένα.
(efharisto, episis hriazome kati ghia ta oola moo, ine erethismena)

d. Optician- Οπτικός (optikos)

1. I need a pair of glasses immediately.
Χρειάζομαι ένα ζευγάρι γιαλιά επειγόντως.
(hriazome ena zevghari ghialia epighontos)

Do you have your prescription or you need an examination?
Έχετε την συνταγή σας ή χρειάζεστε εξέταση;
(ehete tin sintaghi sas i hriazeste eksetasi?)

I always carry my prescription with me. Here it is.
Πάντα έχω τη συνταγή μαζί μου, ορίστε.
(panda eho ti sintaghi mazi moo, oriste)

2. The lenses have to be tinted.
Οι φακοί πρέπει να είναι φιμέ.
(i faki prepi na ine fime)

Are they more expensive?
Είναι πιο ακριβοί; (ine pio akrivi?)

Certainly. Βεβαίως (veveos)

3. My friend lost his/her contact lenses. Do you carry any?
(Ο/η) φίλος/φίλη μου έχασε τους φακούς επαφής, έχετε;
((o,i) filos/i moo ehase toos fakous epafis, ehete?)

Yes, we carry a great variety.
Ναι, έχουμε μεγάλη ποικιλία.
(ne, ehoume meghali pikilia)

e. Problems/accidents/complaints/police
Προβλήματα/ατυχήματα/παράπονα/αστυνομία
(provlimata/atihimata/parapona/astinomia)

Vocabulary

Problem- (το) πρόβλημα (provlima)
Trouble/disturbance- (η) φασαρία)
(traffic) accident- (το) (τροχαίο) ατύχημα ((troheo) atihima)
Help- (η) βοήθεια (voithia)
Police- (η) αστυνομία (astinomia)

Policeman- (ο) αστυφύλακας/αστυνομικός (astifilakas/astinomikos)
Injury/injured- (το) τραύμα/τραυματισμένος,η,ο
    (travma/travmatismenos,i,o)
Driver- (ο, η) οδηγός (othighos)
Passenger- (ο) επιβάτης (epivatis)
Thief/burglar- (ο) κλέφτης (kleftis)
Patrol wagon- (η) κλούβα (kloova)
Prison/jail- (η) φυλακή (filaki)
Violation- (η) παράβαση (paravasi)
Summons- (η) κλήση (klisi)
Speed limit- (το) όριο ταχύτητας (orio tahititas)
Witness- (ο, η) μάρτυρας (martiras)

1. Help, someone is drowning- βοήθεια, κάποιος πνίγεται
(voithia, kapios pnighete)

May I have your name and address, please?
Μπορώ να έχω το όνομα ΄και διεύθυνσή σας, παρακαλώ;
(boro na eho to onoma ke thiefthinsi, sas parakalo?)

2. Does anyone speak English? We need help.
Μιλάει κανείς αγγλικά; Χρειαζόμαστε βοήθεια.
(milai kanis aglika? Hriazomaste voithia)

Yes, what's wrong? How can we help?
Ναι, τι συμβαίνει; Πώς μπορούμε να βοηθήσουμε;
(ne, ti simveni? Pos boroume na voithisoume?)

Call the police, please. We have been in an accident.
Καλέστε την αστυνομία, παρακαλώ. Είχαμε ένα δυστύχημα.
(kaleste tin astinomia parakalo. Ihame ena thistihima)

Is anyone hurt? Do you need an ambulance?
Χτύπησε κανείς; Χρειάζεστε ασθενοφόρο;
(htipise kanis? Hriazeste asthenoforo?)

9. Entertainment/Recreation-Διασκέδαση/Ψυχαγωγία
(thiaskethasi/psihaghoghia)

Vocabulary

Theater- (το) θέατρο (theatro)
Movie theater/cinema- (ο) κινηματογράφος /(το) σινεμά
   (kinimatoghrafos/sinema)
Play- (το) θεατρικό έργο (theatriko ergho)
Movie- (το) κινηματογραφικό έργο (kinimatografiko ergho)
Director- (ο, η) σκηνοθέτης (skinothetis)
Producer- (ο, η) παραγωγός (paraghoghos)
Drama- (το) δράμα (drama)
Musical- (το) μουσικό (moosiko)
Comedy- (η) κωμωδία (komothia)
Thriller- (το) αστυνομικό/ (astinomiko)
Ticket- (το) εισιτήριο (isitirio)
Usher/usherette- (ο) ταξιθέτης/(η) ταξιθέτρια
   (taksithetis/taksithetria)
Entertainment guide- (ο) οδηγός ψυχαγωγίας
   (othighos psihaghoghias)
Nightclub- (το) νυκτερινό κέντρο (nikterino kedro)
Musical show/floorshow/review- (η) επιθεώρηση/
   (η) επιθεώρηση/(το) μουσικό πρόγραμμα
   (epitheorisi/moosiko proghrama)
I dance-χορεύω (horevo)
Dancing/dance- (ο) χορός (horos)
Dancer- (ο) χορευτής/(η) χορεύτρια (horeftis/horeftria)
Type of music- (το) είδος μουσικής (ithos moosikis)
Musician- (ο, η) μουσικός (moosikos)
Singer- (ο) τραγουδιστής/(η) τραγουδίστρια
   (traghouthistis/traghouthistria)
Song- (το) τραγούδι (traghouthi)
Concert- (η) συναυλία (sinavlia)
Festival- (το) φεστιβάλ/πανηγύρι (festival/panighiri)

Cultural activities- (οι) πολιτιστικές εκδηλώσεις
(politistikes ekthilosis)
Greek tragedy- (η) ελληνική τραγωδία (eliniki traghothia)

1. Is a theater nearby? What is it playing? Is the play good? Are the actors well-known?
Είναι ένα θέατρο εδώ κοντά; Τι παίζει; Είναι το έργο καλό; Είναι οι ηθοποιοί διάσημοι/γνωστοί;
(ine ena theatro etho plision? Ti pezi? Ine to ergho kalo? Ine i ithopii thiasimi/ghnosti?)

The National Theater is nearby and the plays are always well selected. The acting is excellent.
Το Εθνικό Θέατρο είναι κοντά και τα έργα είναι πάντα καλοδιαλεγμένα, η εκτέλεση είναι υπέροχη.
(to ethniko theatro ine konta ke ta ergha ine panta kalothialeghmena, i ektelesi ine iperohi)

2. Is there a Greek tragedy playing around Athens?
Παίζεται καμιά ελληνική τραγωδία γύρω στην Αθήνα;
(pezete kamia eliniki traghothia ghiro stin Athina?)

Yes, on Mt. Lycavettos at that theater Euripides' Medea is playing.
Ναι, στο Λυκαβηττό, σ'αυτό το θέατρο παίζεται η Μήδεια του Ευριπίδη.
(ne, sto Likavito, s'afto to theatro pezete i Mithia too Evripithi)

3. Where can I attend a concert tonight?
Πού μπορώ να παρακολουθήσω μία συναυλία απόψε;
(poo boro na parakolouthiso mia sinavlia apopse?)

There is a concert tonight at a very nice Music Hall, called Megharo Mousikis. I hope you can find tickets.
Είναι μία συναυλία απόψε σε μια θαυμάσια αίθουσα μουσικής, που ονομάζεται Μέγαρο Μουσικής. Ελπίζω να βρείτε εισιτήρια.

(ine mia sinavlia apopse se mia thavmasia ethousa mousikis poo onomazete Megharo Mousikis. Elpizo na vrite isitiria)

10. Sports Events/Hobbies/Interests-
Αθλητικές Εκδηλώσεις/ Χόμππις/Ενδιαφέροντα
(athlitikes ekdhlosis/hobis/enthiaferonta)

Vocabulary

Athletics- (ο) αθλητιισμός (τα) σπορ (athlitismos/spor)
Soccer- (το) ποδόσφαιρο (pothosfero)
Ball- (η) μπάλα (bala)
Stadium/field/park/court- (το) στάδιο/γήπεδο (stathio/ghipetho)
Coach/manager- (ο) προπονητής (proponitis)
Referee- (ο) διαιτητής (thietitis)
Player- (ο) παίκτης/παίχτης(οι) παίκτες/παίχτες
    (pektis/pextis)/pextes
Team- (η) ομάδα (omatha)
Championship- (το) πρωτάθλημα (protathlima)
Gym/athletic club- (το) αθλητικό κέντρο/γυμναστήριο
    (athlitiko kedro/ghimnastirio)
Activities- (οι) δραστηριότητες/εκδηλώσεις
    (thrastiriotites/ekthilosis)
Tennis/golf/volley ball- (το) τέννις/γκολφ/βόλεϋ,
    (tennis/golf/volei)
Swimming- (το) κολύμπι (kolimbi)
Pool- (η) πισίνα (pisina)
Beach- (η) ακρογιαλιά/πλαζ (akroghialia/plaz)
Sailing- (η) ιστιοπλοΐα (istioploia)
Water ski- (το) θαλάσσιο σκι (thalasio ski)
Surfing- (το) σερφ (serf)
Diving board- (η) εξέδρα (eksethra)
Skin-diving- (το) υποβρύχιο κολύμπι (ipovrihio kolimbi)
Fishing- (το) ψάρεμα (psarema)
Fisherman- (ο) ψαράς (psaras)
Bait- (το) δόλωμα (tholoma)

Net- (το) δίχτυ (thihti)
Fishing rod- (το) καλάμι ψαρέματος (kalami psarematos)
Fishing hook- (το) αγκίστρι (agistri)
Bicycling- (η) ποδηλασία (pothilasia)
Bicycle- (το) ποδήλατο (pothilato)
Horse riding- (η) ιππασία (ipasia)

1. Do you like sports? What kind?
Σας αρέσουν τα σπόρ; Τι είδους;
(sas aresoon ta spor? ti ithous?)

I like all kinds of sports, especially outdoor sports: hiking, biking, jogging, running, walking, tennis, swimming and other water sports.
Μου αρέσουν όλα τα είδη σπορ, ιδιαίτερα τα σπορ εξοχής: πεζοπορεία, ποδηλασία, τζόγκιν, τρέξιμο, βάδισμα, περπάτημα, τέννις, κολύμπι και άλλα θαλάσσια σπορ.
(moo aresoon ola ta ithi spor, ithietera ta spor eksohis: pezoporia, pothilasia, jogging, treksimo, vathisma, permatima, tennis, kolimbi ke la thalasia spor)

2. Do you watch soccer/football and basketball games on TV?
Παρακολουθείτε αγώνες ποδοσφαίρου και
    μπάσκετ στη τηλεόραση;
(parakoloothite aghones pothosferou ke basket sti tileorasi?)

Certainly, I enjoy them very much.
Βέβαια, τους απολαμβάνω πολύ.
(vevea, toos apolamvano poli)

I also like to watch boxing and wrestling sometimes.
Επίσης μου αρέσει μερικές φορές να βλέπω πυγμαχία και πάλη.
(epis, merikes fores, moo aresi na vlepo pighmahia ke pali)

3. Do you swim a lot?
Κολυμμάτε πολύ;
(kolimbate poli?)

Swimming is my favorite sport.
Το κολύμπι είναι το αγαπημένο μου σπορ.
(to kolimbi ine to aghapimeno moo spor)

4. Do you prefer swimming at a beach, lake, or pool?
Προτιμάτε το κολύμπι στη θάλασσα, λίμνη ή πισίνα.
(protimate to kolimbi sti thalasa, limni i pisina?)

I prefer the beach.- προτιμώ τη θάλασσα. (protimo ti thalasa)

5. Do you go camping? Do you have a trailer/camper?
Κατασκηνώνετε; Έχετε ένα τροχόσπιτο;
(kataskinonete? ehete ena trohospito?)

We do camp, we don't have a trailer, but we have a tent and oth-
erequipment for the camping grounds.
Κατασκηνώνουμε, δεν έχουμε τροχόσπιτο, αλλά έχουμε μια
σκηνή, άλλον εφοδιασμό για περιοχή κατασκήνωσης/κάμπιν.
(kataskinonoume, then ehoume trohospito ala ehoume mia skini ki
alo efothiasmo ghia periohi kataskinosis/kampin)

Beautiful! There are some wonderful camping sites. You will be
very pleased.
Ωραία! Υπάρχουν θαυμάσιες κατασκηνώσεις/κάμπινς, θα
ευχαριστηθείτε πολύ.
(orea! iparhoon thavmasies kataskinosis/kampings, tha efharis-
tithite poli)

Have a good stay! Καλή διαμονή. (kali thiamoni)

11. Social life/Κοινωνική/κοσμική ζωή (kinoniki/kosmiki zoi)

Vocabulary/phrases

Hello, hi- γεια σας (ghia sas)
Visitor- (ο) επισκέπτης/(η) επισκέπτρια (episkeptis/episkeptria)

I'm American/Canadian/British/Australian- Είμαι Αμερικανός/ Αμερικανίδα, Καναδός/Καναδέζα, Άγγλος/Αγγλίδα, Αυστραλός/Αυστραλέζα (ime Americanos/Americanitha, Kanathos/Kanatheza, Aglos/Aglitha, Afstralos/-Afstraleza)

I'm very pleased to meet you- χαίρω πολύ (hero poli).

How long are you staying?- πόσο καιρό θα μείνετε; (poso kero tha minete?)

I'm staying for two weeks- θα μείνω δύο εβδομάδες (tha mino thio evthomathes)

Are you married?- είστε(pl.)/είσαι(sing.) παντρεμένος/η; (iste/ise (pantremenos/i?)

I'm single- είμαι ανύπαντρος,η,ο/ελεύθερος,η,ο (adj.) (ime anipantros,i,o/eleftheros,i,o)

Friend- (ο) φίλος (m), (η) φίλη (f) (filos/fili)
Companion- (ο, η) σύντροφος (sintrofos)
Spouse- (ο, η) σύζυγος (sizighos)
Husband/man- (ο) άνδρας (anthras)
Wife/woman- (η) γυναίκα (ghineka)
Meeting- (η) συνάντηση (sinantisi)

1. Id like to invite you to my house. Some friends are coming over tomorrow night, and I would like you to meet them.

Θέλω να σας προσκαλέσω στο σπίτι μου. Μερικοί φίλοι θάρθουν αύριο το βράδυ και θα ήθελα να τους συναντήσετε.

(thelo na sas proskaleso sto spiti moo. Meriki fili tharthoon avrio to vrathi ke tha ithela na toos sinantisete)

I would like that very much. May I have your address please? What time should I come?

Θα το ήθελα πολύ. Μπορώ να έχω τη διεύθυνσή σας; Τι ώρα να ρθω;

(tha to ithela poli. Boro na eho ti thiefthinsi sas? Ti ora prepi na rtho?)

2. I'd like to introduce to you my friend Paul/Mary.

Paul/Mary this is John/Ann, he/she is an American. He/she is visiting Greece for the first time.

Θέλω να σου συστήσω τον φίλο μου Παύλο/την φίλη μου Μαίρη. Παύλο/Μαίρη απο δω ο Γιάννης/ η Μαίρη, είναι Αμερικανός/ Αμερικανίδα, επισκέπτεται την Ελλάδα για πρώτη φορά.
(thelo na soo sistiso ton filo moo Pavlo/tin fili moo Meri. Pavlo/ Meri apo tho o Ghianis/i Ana. Ine Americanos/Americanitha. Episkeptete tin Elatha ghia proti fora)

Hi, John/Mary. Welcome to Greece. I'm pleased to meet you. Would you like to dance?

Γεια σου Γιάννη/Μαίρη, καλωσόρισες στην Ελλάδα. Χαίρω πολύ για τη γνωριμία, θα ήθελες να χορέψουμε;
(ghia soo Ghiani/Meri. Kalosorises stin Elatha. Hero poli ghia ti ghnorimia,tha itheles na horepsoume?) With pleasure-Ευχαρίστως (efharistos)

Some words and phrases of high frequency, useful expressions and idioms are included in this section. If you have learned the alphabet, you should be able to read them with ease.

Αλλά-but, αμέσως-immediately, από-from, αργά-late, αργότερα-later, γιατί-why/because, (ε)αν-if, εδώ-here, εκεί-there, εμπρός (μπροστά) -in front/front, (ε)νωρίς-early, έξω-outside, (ε) πάνω-up/upstairs, επίσης-also/too, καλά-good/well,κοντά-near, λίγο-little, λιγότερο-less, λοιπόν-consequently/therfore, μέσα-in/ inside, μόνο-only, όμως-however, όταν-when, όχι-no, πάντα-always, ποτέ-never, πότε-when(interrogative), πού-where(when accented), που-that(no accent),πριν-before/ago, πώς-how(accented),πως-that, συγνώμη(ν)-excuse me/pardon,σχεδόν-almost, τι-what, τίποτε/α-nothing, τέλος-end.

Περαστικά-get well, έχω δίκηο-I am right, είναι αλήθεια-it is true, εκτός αν-unless, πέρασα ωραία-I had a good time, καλά να περάστε-have a good time, δεν με νοιάζει-I don't care, μη σε νοιάζει-don't worry, βλάπτει-it's harmful, χθες το βράδυ-last night, τη περασμένη εβδομάδα-last week, την άλλη εβδομάδα-next week, χάνω καιρό-I'm wasting time, δεν έχω καιρό-I don't have time, χάνεις τον καιρό σου-you're waisting your time, ανάβω το φως-I turn the light on, σβήνω το φως-I turn the light off, καλωσορίσατε/καλώς ήρθατε-welcome, κάνω παζά ρια/παζαρεύω-I bargain, δεν έχω διάθεση-I 'm not in the mood, προς το παρόν-for the time being, μέχρι την ώρα-so far, εν τάξει-all right/okay, αν και-although.

Αριθμοί/νούμερα: numbers, ένα-one, δύο-two, τρία-three, τέσσερα-four, πέντε-five, έξι-six, επτά-seven, οκτώ-eight, εννέα-nine, δέκα-ten, έντεκα-eleven, δώδεκα-twelve, δεκατρία-thirteen, δεκατέσσερα-fourteen, δεκαπέντε-fifteen, δεκαέξι-sixteen, δεκαεπτά-seventeen, δεκαοκτώ-eighteen, δεκαεννέα-nineteen, είκοσι-twenty.

Χρόνος-year/time, εποχή-season, μήνας-month, εβδομάδα-week, ημέρα-day, νύκτα-night, πρωί-morning, μεσημέρι-noon,βράδυ-evening, μεσάνυχτα-midnight, ώρα-time, λεπτό-minute, δευτερόλεπτο-second, χθες-yesterday, σήμερα-today, αύριο-tomorrow, πέρυσι-last year, (ε)φέτος-this year,του χρόνου-next year, εποχές-seasons, άνοιξη-spring, καλοκαίρι-summer, φθινόπωρο-fall/autumn, χειμώνας-winter.

Μήνες-months, ΙανουάριοςΓενάρης-January, Φεβρουάριος/Φλεβάρης-February, Μάρτιος/Μάρτης-March, Απρίλιος/Απρίλης-April, Μάιος/Μάης-May, Ιούνιος-June, Ιούλιος-July,Αύγουστος-August, Σεπτέμβριος-September, Οκτώβριος-October, Νοέμβριος-November, Δεκέμβριος-December.

Ημέρες-,Κυριακή-Sunday, Δευτέρα-Monday, Τρίτη-Tuesday, Τετάρτη-Wednesday, Πέμπτη-Thursday, Παρασκευή-Friday, Σάββατο-Saturday.

Χαιρετισμοί-greetings/cordialities, γειά σου/σας-hello/hi, καλημέρα-good morning, χαίρετε-good afternoon, αντίο-goodbye, καλησπέρα-good evening, καληνύχτα-good night, τι κάνεις;(informal)/κάνετε;(formal)-how are you/how do you do? Or- πώς είσαι; /είστε;-how are you? είμαι καλά, ευχαριστώ-I'm fine/well, thank you. Συγνώμη που άργησα-sorry I'm late.

Τέλος — End

ABOUT THE AUTHOR

Matina K. Psyhogeos, the well-known educator/author, was born and educated in Greece where she majored in education and linguistics-. At a young age, she moved to the U.S., continued her studies and raised her family! She taught Modern Greek in many schools in the greater Boston area, her longest tenure being at Hellenic College/Holy Cross, Brookline, MA, where she had the opportunity to instill her love, dedication, and enthusiasm for the perpetuation of the Greek language and culture, to future teachers and priests.

Psyhogeos developed her own comprehensive program (The Psyhogeos Program) for the teaching of foreign languages and especially the Greek language. She has written thirteen books, eight of which are based on her program!

Psyhogeos returned to Greece for a few years where she authored and published:

"Make Your Journey to Greece an Unforgettable Experience"
"Olympic Games, Past, Present & Future: Passing the Torch to a New Millenium"
"Greek for Travelers"
"Reaching for the Sky: Childhood Recollections of War and Peace"
"History of Greece in a Nutshell" Personalities that illuminated mankind throughout the ages

More information on her websites: Matina Psyhogeos or The Psyhogeos Program.

CPSIA information can be obtained
at www.ICGtesting.com
Printed in the USA
FFOW04n0555051017
40572FF